S0-ARO-232

Developmental Therapy–
Developmental Teaching

Developmental Therapy–Developmental Teaching:
Fostering Social-Emotional Competence in Troubled Children and Youth

Third Edition

Mary M. Wood
with
Karen R. Davis, Faye L. Swindle, and Constance Quirk

pro·ed
8700 Shoal Creek Boulevard
Austin, Texas 78757

pro·ed

© 1996 by PRO-ED, Inc.
8700 Shoal Creek Boulevard
Austin, Texas 78757-6897

All rights reserved. No part of the material protected by this copyright notice may be reproduced or utilized in any form or by any means, electronic or mechanical, including photocopying, recording, or by an information storage and retrieval system, without the prior written permission of the copyright owner.

Production Manager: Alan Grimes
Production Coordinator: Karen Swain
Art Director: Lori Kopp
Reprints Buyer: Alicia Woods
Editor: Helen Hyams
Editorial Assistant: Claudette Landry

Printed in the United States of America

1 2 3 4 5 6 7 8 9 10 00 99 98 97 96 95

This work is dedicated to

dearly loved grandchildren, whose lives authenticate
the stages of social-emotional development
and the joys of infancy, childhood, and adolescence:

Britt
Margaret
Alexandria
Elizabeth
Creagh
Elizabeth
Sarah
Alan

and also to their mothers and fathers—
loving and responsible parents.

Contents

APPENDIXES

INDEXES

Developmental Therapy–Developmental Teaching
... *in Brief*

The *Developmental Therapy–Developmental Teaching* curriculum provides a framework for guiding social-emotional development and responsible behavior in children and teens. It matches a child's current social, emotional, and behavioral status with specific goals, objectives, behavior management strategies, curriculum materials, activities, and evaluation procedures. It also defines specific roles for adults to facilitate a child's development. The curriculum sequentially spans social, emotional, and behavioral development for children and youth from birth to 16 years.

The curriculum has four areas: *Behavior, Communication, Socialization,* and *(Pre)Academics/Cognition,* for *doing, saying, caring,* and *thinking.* Within each of these four areas specific teaching objectives follow developmental sequences for social-emotional competence and responsible behavior. These sequences suggest five distinct stages in the psychosocial development of all children and youth and define both the long- and short-term program goals for each student. Detailed curriculum activities, environments, and intervention strategies are provided with specific adaptations for early childhood, school-age children, preadolescents, and adolescents. The curriculum also describes the types of strategies used by adults and the necessary adult role models needed by children and youth at these various stages of development.

Three measurement instruments provide additional elements in this curriculum approach. The *Developmental Teaching Objectives Rating Form–Revised* (DTORF–R) is used to obtain a profile of a child's social-emotional growth through the stages. It also identifies objectives for social-emotional competence in a student's Individualized Education Program (IEP), Individualized Family Service Plan (IFSP), or Individual Transition Plan (ITP), and is used to evaluate progress. The *Developmental Therapy Rating Inventory of Teacher Skills* (DT/RITS) provides a measure of adults' acquisition of needed skills. Finally, an *Administrative Support Checklist* assesses the quality of administrative support necessary for maintaining high levels of program quality.

Preface

It has been 8 years since the last edition of this book, *Developmental Therapy in the Classroom.* As a curriculum for fostering social-emotional competence, Developmental Therapy continues to be used in a broad range of environments where people are concerned about the social behavior and emotional stability of children and youth. As in the past, we continue to see that it is not so much the type of service delivery model but the skills and attitudes of adults and what they believe that make the difference between a successful or failed intervention. Again and again, we have seen the positive effect on students when the important adults in their lives believe in them. These adults are able to communicate their belief in students' potential to improve and become responsible individuals. In short, they set a course to help their students master increasingly complex skills for social, emotional, and behavioral competence. This same attitude is the central message in *Developmental Therapy–Developmental Teaching.*

In this latest edition, we have not changed the fundamentals of our previous work. The priority is to offer a program in which the developmental needs of students and the role of the adult team in the socialization process remain the central focus. We believe that an effective program must be highly positive in tone and sequentially organized in its delivery. The environment of a truly effective program should be a microcosm of the very best that we can provide young people—where both individual and group learning occur around objectives for acquiring social skills, mastering social problem solving, managing feelings, and behaving responsibly.

What we have learned in the 8 years since the previous edition is that these practices have extensive applications beyond treating students with emotional or behavioral disabilities. We find them being used in a wide variety of settings and with children of many ages and with various disabilities. Many parents of young children with special needs have worked with us to make adaptations they can use at home to guide their children's development. Early childhood specialists have made many exciting uses of the curriculum in typical child care settings. And teachers at every grade level have shown us how to put these ideas to work with typical students who are struggling with the stresses of contemporary life. Psychologists, psychiatrists, court workers, and case workers also have used adaptations of Developmental Therapy. These expanding applications prompted us to extend our focus and to call this new edition *Developmental Therapy–Developmental Teaching.*

Our concern is not only those young people who have been selected for special education programs, but also all students who deserve a "special" education—and a special adult to believe in them. The increasing number of troubled families and troubled children is the most compelling reason for this new edition. Students of every age have been pushed aside by our contemporary social system, which talks about responsible behavior but fails to set an example or teach personal responsibility to its young. Some parents have such heavy burdens themselves that they are unable to be active in raising their own children. Others seem to have abdicated their responsibility. It is doubtful whether children who have experienced little genuine caring can learn to care for others, or even to simulate caring behavior. These are the many, many children and youth often referred to as "at risk" or "abused." It is a tragic commentary on life today that almost every young person is vulnerable. And it is this potential that makes it so necessary for Developmental Therapy–Developmental Teaching to be a part of the general curriculum available in every young person's program, from preschool through high school. We hope that it will also be helpful to parents who are seeking to expand their own skills in raising responsible children.

If you are already using Developmental Therapy, we believe you will find additional information in this new edition that will be helpful in designing strategies to solve the difficult situations that arise from time to time, wherever you are working with children or youth. We also believe that this new edition will be of assistance in communicating to others—parents, teachers, administrators, other professionals, and paraprofessionals—exactly what it is that Developmental Therapy–Developmental Teaching offers. If you are new to this approach, perhaps the material can convince you that a developmental foundation has merit because it recognizes the interchange between sequential, maturational processes and cultural expectations as a powerful force in every child's development. If you find the model compatible with your strategies, we believe you will also find direction for integrating this approach into your present program.

The pursuit of *self-esteem, identity,* and *personal responsibility* (a defined self within a social reality) is at the heart of Developmental Therapy–Developmental Teaching. The curriculum recognizes that personal success must precede group success. This is not an easy approach. It requires understanding what is in the heart and head of a child. It requires knowing what that child has experienced in the past, what is happening now, and what lies ahead in expectations and needed skills to meet the future successfully. This approach requires a broad, inclusive approach to intervention. To illustrate the complexity of the constructs and the theoretical scope, here are several major elements of the expanded Developmental Therapy–Developmental Teaching approach.

Understanding a Child's Heart and Head

- Developmental expectations for social-emotional competence
- *Doing, saying, caring,* and *thinking* with success at every age
- Emotional memory—a child's private reality
- Developmental anxieties
- Defense mechanisms
- Values that motivate and regulate behavior
- Social roles and social power
- Social knowledge—understanding others
- Moral development and responsible behavior

For the Adult

- Developmental teaching objectives
- Skills for listening and responding with empathy
- Skills for decoding a child's behavior
- Developmentally appropriate discipline and behavior management
- Psychological importance of schedules, materials, and activities
- Creative arts for communicating with children
- Adult behaviors for each stage of a child's development
- Adults as a team with defined roles that change as children mature

This new edition is organized sequentially to provide sufficient instruction to put these ideas to work. The chapters in Part 1 describe the theoretical and practical foundations of the model. Chapter 1, "Addressing Social Competence in Today's Children," looks at the way Developmental Therapy–Developmental Teaching responds to the psychosocial stresses and crises in the lives of children and youth of all ages, from birth to 16 years. The chapter introduces the basics of how a developmental orientation can be helpful to adults—professionals, paraprofessionals, and parents. It includes a revised section on evaluation that reports on three separate validations of the Developmental Therapy–Developmental Teaching model by independent-panel review. It also summarizes two studies that have researched the question, "Is this model effective?" Finally, this first chapter reviews how the model evolved over three decades and summarizes the new direction for the future.

Chapter 2, "Social Competence, Emotions, and Responsible Behavior," defines and translates the theoretical foundations for social competence into the four curriculum areas of *doing, saying, caring,* and *thinking.* It traces the key concepts for fostering responsible behavior and illustrates how all children experience developmental anxieties and defense mechanisms as a natural part of growing up. This chapter includes a review of emotions and the importance of emotional memory in the learning process. There is also a section on how adults who work with troubled children and youth are often cast in the role of stand-in, or surrogate, adults by students who have had difficult experiences with other adults in the past.

Part 2, "Putting the Curriculum into Practice," features the fundamentals that are applicable for using the curriculum with children and youth of all ages and stages. Chapter 3, "Getting Started . . . ," contains the assumptions that shape the curriculum. There is a summary of the most frequently asked questions and answers about putting Developmental Therapy–Developmental Teaching to work in preschools and elementary, middle, and high schools. Included are questions about how the curriculum is used with students who are at risk in inclusive settings as well as with those who have severe disabilities; how it has been adapted to home programs and mentor programs; and what type of administrative support promotes higher performance levels for classroom teachers using the curriculum. This chapter also describes how the social-emotional status of students is assessed to establish IEP, IFSP, or ITP objectives for social-emotional competence, and how the evaluation system for documenting student progress is an integral part of the model. The chapter ends with a review of schedule variations that illustrates several ways to implement the curriculum into ongoing programs, offering suggestions for both process- and outcome-oriented evaluation procedures.

Chapter 4, "Keeping It Going . . . Successfully," is a pedagogical overview of the curriculum. It contains details of a successful program in a step-by-step outline for general planning that is applicable for all ages and settings. The benefits of using social-emotional goals and objectives for grouping students are discussed, and guidelines are provided for selecting developmentally appropriate materials and activities that are also age-suitable and designed to meet individual needs. The language arts curriculum, especially creative writing, is used to illustrate in some detail the importance of selecting content that activates a student's emotional memory and contributes to positive changes in how the student thinks and feels. This chapter ends with a review of the core requirements for effective instruction at every stage, with explanations of how the core procedures are modified to the students' stages of social-emotional development.

In Chapter 5, "When Behavior Is the Issue," we discuss the importance of using strategies that are individually and culturally relevant, are developmentally appropriate, and have developmental continuity, leading to the acquisition of increasingly advanced social skills and personal responsibility. There is a brief explanation of how we initially identified the most frequently used management strategies in Developmental Therapy–Developmental Teaching and how the strategies represent widely used practices of kindergarten, elementary, and high school teachers. The chapter also contains an outline of six general steps we use when designing an individual student's behavior management plan. This chapter ends with a discussion of specific management of some of the most challenging behaviors of students: physical violence, passive aggression, and thought disorders.

Chapter 6, "Management Strategies To Foster Development," begins with a discussion of the importance of participation, use of selective ignoring, and strategies for offering alternatives, depersonalizing, and recalling previous success as ways to prevent discipline problems and misbehavior. The remainder of the chapter reviews the most frequently used management strategies, including positive feedback and praise, motivating with materials, structure, redirection, reflection, interpretation, verbal interactions between adults, rules, Life Space Intervention, control of materials by adults, and physical proximity. Each strategy is defined and illustrated with modifications needed for the five stages. Four additional strategies are included that are used less frequently, and primarily with students who have severe behavioral problems: confrontation, physical intervention, removal from the room, and removal from the group while remaining in the room. We explain how these strategies are used and give developmental reasons why they do or do not have particular applications at each stage of development.

Chapter 7, "Adults as Agents for Change," puts emphasis on the skills of adults. Working with children who have challenging behaviors is a demanding job, and competencies are not always easy to develop. We have found that adults can develop proficiency in using Developmental Therapy–Developmental Teaching through self-monitoring and with individual observations and feedback about their performance. We use the *Developmental Therapy Rating Inventory of Teacher Skills* (DT/RITS) to help both professionals and paraprofessionals monitor their own skill acquisition. There is a separate form of this instrument for working with children at each of the first four stages of development that can be used from preschool through high school. In this chapter, we also provide a summary of current research that has identified skills that adults acquire quickly and those that appear too difficult to master during a single year of staff development.

The last five chapters are the "stage chapters." Here we describe in detail how to use Developmental Therapy–Developmental Teaching with children at each of the five stages of social-emotional development. These chapters are intended to aid adults in focusing each child's individual program to his or her unique characteristics, in whatever setting the child's program is provided. Each chapter is devoted to a single stage and illustrates specific applications of the principles from the earlier chapters for the purpose of accomplishing the social-emotional goals for each stage. Sequentially, these are

Stage 1: responding to the environment with pleasure;

Stage 2: responding to the environment with success;

Stage 3: learning skills for successful group participation;

Stage 4: investing in group processes; and

Stage 5: applying individual and group skills in new situations.

The key social and emotional characteristics of the stages are reviewed. Specific unit themes, time blocks, activities, and materials are described. There is a review of the stage-appropriate roles for the adults and strategies are described to convey the roles effectively. At the end of each of these chapters, we summarize the curriculum and provide a typical situation as practice in applying the key concepts about each developmental stage.

The appendixes contain materials that are too lengthy to insert into the body of a chapter but are essential for those planning to use Developmental Therapy–Developmental Teaching in their own programs. Appendix 1 contains a comprehensive list of publications documenting the Developmental Therapy–Developmental Teaching movement through three decades. The entries are organized by topic and chronologically within each topic area. Appendix 2 contains the four forms of the instrument professionals and paraprofessionals can use to rate their own performance (the DT/RITS). Appendix 3 provides the *Developmental Therapy Administrative Checklist* of program components that have been shown to support high levels of performance by adults in programs using Developmental Therapy. Appendix 4 includes the theoretical content analyses that were done to establish the original content validity. These charts outline the key processes that comprise each of the four major developmental systems included in *Developmental Therapy–Developmental Teaching* as well as the trajectories of social-emotional development. Appendix 5 is an index of theories of motivation applied to the five curriculum stages, and Appendix 6 contains data tables from two studies evaluating the progress of students in Developmental Therapy–Developmental Teaching programs. Data tables from research into the acquisition of skills by adults participating in a Developmental Therapy–Developmental Teaching staff development program are also included.

A comment is needed here about the terms used in this edition. We refer interchangeably to *students* and *children,* meaning those of all ages who need assistance in learning skills for social and emotional competence and responsible behavior. We recognize also that sometimes adults are involved in nonstudent situations where Developmental Therapy–Developmental Teaching has applications. Throughout, we use the generic term *adults* to include parents, teachers, aides, clinicians, coaches, case workers, mentors, and all who work with children and youth in one way or another.

We often find ourselves referring to this approach as a *curriculum.* We do so because the term implies a course of learning, and we believe that social-emotional development and responsible behavior have distinct pathways of learning. When we use the term *Developmental Therapy* by itself, it is our abbreviated way of conveying a specific application of this curriculum to students with special needs because of severe social, emotional, or behavioral disabilities. Implicit in this approach is the belief that Developmental Therapy becomes *Developmental Teaching* as students require less intensive interventions. Both terms are based on the idea that a curriculum designed to foster social-emotional competence and responsible behavior in children and youth requires a foundation in *doing, saying, caring,* and *thinking.*

An effort of this scope to expand theory and research findings into contemporary practices to foster the well-being of infants, children, and teens cannot be accomplished by a single individual. This latest revision is no exception. It has required a sustained, focused, day-to-day effort by many working directly with children and youth. Sustained contributions in teacher preparation have been made through the leadership of Diane Weller and Carolyn Combs at the Rutland Psychoeducational Program in Athens, Georgia, and Barbara Reid and Mary Bross Weinlein at the University of Wisconsin–Whitewater. The gifted demonstration teaching by Betty Martin in Maryland; Anna Leigh Kubbe in Michigan; Phyllis Busch in Kennewick, Washington; and Vicky Grove in Minnesota, who work with young children in Stages One and Two, has continued for over a decade to give the effort depth and new insights. Outstanding demonstrations by Bonnie McCarty and Andrea Gillen have expanded our understanding of applications for school-age children and teens in Stages Three, Four, and Five. The fieldwork and thoughtful evaluations by these gifted individuals have assisted us in reshaping Developmental Therapy–Developmental Teaching into broad new applications.

There are several psychoeducational programs in Georgia that continue their close associations with the Developmental Therapy Institute in Athens, Georgia, even though many of the original staff have changed. We particularly thank program directors George Andros, Dan Burns, Robert Gordon, Robert Jacob, Juanda Ponsell, and Larry Weiner for their collegiality and for opportunities for professional exchanges through staff training. In the Virgin Islands, Wanda Hamilton, state coordinator for early childhood special education, has continued over the years with us in mutual exchanges that focus on cultural diversity. In Germany, we have exciting new applications concerning cross-cultural uses of Developmental Therapy–Developmental Teaching with Marita Bergsson and the staff at her special school.

Closer to home, the staff at the Developmental Therapy Institute in Athens continues to sustain our research and training efforts, nationally and internationally. Julie Hendrick and Esin Esendal have creatively focused on home programs in which parents of very young children can use this curriculum. They also have adapted the model to provide early childhood special education in inclusive settings. Carrie Rowland has assisted in designing and producing many of the new visual aids used in our training. This manuscript would never have been completed without the careful reading, insights, and encouragement provided by Betty DeLorme, in Athens, who has read many, many drafts and has found applications in after-school programs for children of all ages. The school photography for the back cover was done by Dan McClure of McClure Studios, Athens. The charming sketches that enhance the manuscript are the creative work of Elizabeth Hancock who, at age 10, understood how to convey the essence of children and teens at each stage of their development. The invaluable editorial skills of Helen Hyams in Austin, Texas, and the cooperation of the editors and staff of PRO-ED have truly brought the book to fruition.

At the end of the book, we include the original acknowledgments from both the first and second editions. We do this because *Developmental Therapy–Developmental Teaching* represents the efforts of several hundred people over many, many years. Whether the contribution was great or small, each was essential. It would be thoughtless to fail to acknowledge their contributions again. We extend our deepest respect and appreciation to each. Their efforts and those of countless teachers, parents, and students who have worked with us for over 25 years have enriched our own efforts beyond measure.

PART I

Theoretical Foundations for Developmental Therapy–Developmental Teaching

CHAPTER 1

Addressing Social Competence in Today's Children

Without belonging, mastery, independence and generosity there can be no courage but only discouragement. DISCOURAGEMENT IS COURAGE DENIED. *When the circle of courage is broken, the lives of children are no longer in harmony and balance.*

—*L. K. BRENDTRO, M. BROKENLEG, AND S. VAN BOCKERN, 1990, P. 46*

PSYCHOSOCIAL STRESS: A NATIONAL EPIDEMIC

Profound changes are occurring in the fabric of this nation's social and family life. We are a society with one of the highest infant mortality rates among the industrialized nations of the world, the highest murder rate, and a steadily increasing rate of newborns damaged from alcohol, cocaine addiction, and HIV infection. Children are bringing guns to school for protection. Reports of child abuse, child violence, adolescent suicide, child and teen pregnancy, child substance abuse, and child murders are daily fare in the news. Community violence has become a way of life. Consider just a few statistics (Children's Defense Fund, 1994):

- Every night, 100,000 children have no place to call home.
- About 2,901,000 children were reported abused or neglected in 1992.
- Approximately 3 million children are emotionally disturbed.
- Over 1 million children are living with relatives apart from parents.
- Approximately 25 children are killed by guns every two days.
- The average preschooler has watched thousands of TV murders.

The Children's Defense Fund (p. xvi) cogently describes this war against children in America as "a total breakdown in American values, common sense, and parent and community responsibility to protect and nurture children." We are a nation of troubled families and children in crisis. Most child development authorities believe that today's children are at great risk for serious delays or distortions in social-emotional-behavioral development. Environments dominated by violence and alienation provide negative but powerful models for children and youth. Further, the majority of our nation's children are living at or near the poverty level, being raised in single-parent homes with working mothers. Poverty has an impact on the quality of their lives both physically and psychologically, and drug abuse compounds its effect on their already fragile capabilities.

The high birth rate for teen parents means that children are having children who will be at serious risk. Young parents have their own developmental needs and typically

The War Against Children

"Never before has our country seen or permitted the epidemic of gun death and violence that is turning our communities into fearful armed camps and sapping the lives and hopes of our children.

"Never has America permitted children to rely on guns and gangs rather than parents and neighbors for protection and love or pushed so many onto the tumultuous sea of life without the life vests of nurturing families and communities, challenged mind, job prospects, and hope.

"Never have we exposed children so early and relentlessly to cultural messages glamorizing violence, sex, possessions, alcohol, and tobacco with so few mediating influences from responsible adults. Never have we let children grow up listening to violent rap instead of nursery rhymes, worrying about guns and drugs rather than grades and dates, and dodging bullets rather than balls.

"And never have we experienced such a numbing and reckless reliance on violence to resolve problems, feel powerful, or be entertained."

Source: From "Introduction," by M. Wright Edelman, 1994, *The State of America's Children Yearbook*, pp. xvi, xvii, Children's Defense Fund, Washington, DC: Author. Reprinted with permission.

need support

are not able to provide essential parenting care. A young adolescent parent often is unable to provide what an infant or toddler needs for healthy psychological development. And abused or abandoned children become abusing parents. Further, in attempting to find their place in society, many teens and young adults are using television as the source for role models and behavioral guides. With television violence at its highest, the result is an inundation of psychologically destructive messages about who to become, how to behave, what sort of personal relationships to seek, how to solve personal problems, and how to cope with stress. Problems can begin small, but without assistance, they can become serious. The development of problem behaviors is shown in Figure 1.1.

What Are We Doing . . . and Where Are We Going?

As adults we have failed to provide psychological and social conditions where our young can develop in security. Our anxious adult society has unrestrainedly poured out its own preoccupations without attempting to protect, limit, or shield our children and youth. We bombard them with alienation, violence and grief—in popular music, tele-

Figure 1.1. Levels of problem behaviors along developmental lines.

Developmental Lines: from ⇨	*Mild Problems* ... *to* ... ⇨	*Severe Problems*
Thinking ⇨	Does not understand, makes mistakes, and will not try	Becomes so disorganized that no learning occurs
Participating ⇨	Wants to watch rather than play or contribute	Withdraws and refuses to participate, or engages in destructive or disorganized activities
Communicating ⇨	Does not have much to say	Will not or cannot talk; words do not make sense or are used for aggression
Making Friends ⇨	Plays alone	Is isolated or a victim
Relating to Adults ⇨	Reserved with adults	Ignores, avoids, or defies adults
Controlling Impulses ⇨	Has temper tantrums	Rages, physically attacks others, or destroys things
Meeting Expectations ⇨	Disobeys	Acts like a baby

vision, advertising, news, movies, books, fashions, entertainment, pornography, and art. We are too preoccupied to provide emotional support to our children. And we seldom stop to consider that our children and youth may not be equipped mentally or emotionally to deal with society's barrage of adult experiences. The result is a stressed and anxious generation of young people living in a psychologically complex, unpredictable, generally nonsupportive, adult-oriented society. It is a problem so widespread that it has reached epidemic proportions. It touches every child and family in America, every race, income level, personality, and intellectual level (Rogers & Ginzberg, 1992).

It is hard to imagine that educated people are not aware that children's fundamental personalities are shaped during infancy and early childhood, or that daily experiences with adults and peers contribute to the expanding behavioral repertoire of a developing young person (Parke, Burks, Carson, Neville, & Boyum, 1994). We tend to take for granted the findings of researchers who have studied extensively the development of interpersonal skills—taking responsibility for oneself and others. We say that we know conscience develops early, as do moral judgment, social knowledge, empathy, and altruism. We recognize that these are essential attributes of a civilized and decent human being. Yet there is an outpouring of concern by television, the press, educators, politicians, law enforcement officials, and parents lamenting the failure of one group or another to raise responsible children. The knowledge is there, but as a society we have failed to put this knowledge into widespread practice.

While many suggestions have been proposed for solving the nation's social and psychological ills, adults who have the day-to-day responsibility for rearing America's children require immediate and focused priorities. A child's successes in school, in relationships with others, and in the future workplace depend upon the quality of the adults encountered along the way. To ensure children's progress in developing social competence and emotional stability, adults must understand how to provide experiences and relationships in which prosocial behavior, responsibility, and social competence emerge. What happens to a child is the bridge to what the child becomes. Every response to every event contributes to the shaping of a child's social, emotional, and motivational characteristics. In turn, these attributes contribute to general social competence, personal responsibility, and the ability to learn. In short, how children behave, speak, feel, relate, and think directly shapes their future.

If children are to mature socially and emotionally, they must have experiences that cultivate these essential dimensions of human development and deleterious experiences must be diminished. In his 1994 State of the Union address, President of the United States Bill Clinton offered an eloquent plea for society to come to the aid of its children, especially those "who have no future . . . they must have a chance to walk into a better tomorrow!" The Children's Defense Fund (1994, p. xviii) added its efforts by providing steps to ensure that we "leave no child behind." Following this lead, the U.S. Congress enacted the Goals 2000: Educate America Act (1994). The 1995 *Head Start Program Performance Standards* (p. 1) also responded to the challenge by reiterating that the program's priority for "a greater degree of social competence in children of low-income families . . . is based on the premise that all children share certain needs, and that children of low-income families, in particular, can benefit from a comprehensive developmental program to meet these needs." There is little doubt that America is beginning to awaken to its responsibility to its children. However, as parents, teachers, and other helping adults, we must see that this happens. Adults are the significant role models and the major sources of children's emotional support. We must be buffers for children against the destructive effects of stress. We must be skilled in strengthening a child's capacity to cope successfully with daily pressures and adversity. We must be able to clarify the meaning of daily events in ways that are understandable and reassuring to a child. These efforts require a great deal from adults: sensitivity, awareness of needs, understanding of developmental processes, and skill to respond, teach, and problem-solve constructively. Ideally, the outcome of our efforts should be a responsible child fortified with trust of others and confidence in self. Recognizing that the

Adults Must Accept Responsibility

"It is adults who have engaged in epidemic neglect and abuse of children and of each other in our homes. It is adults who have taught children to kill and disrespect human life. It is adults who manufacture, market, and profit from the guns that have turned many neighborhoods and schools into war zones. It is adults who have preached moral values we have not practiced. It is adults who have financed, produced, directed, and performed in the movies, television shows, and music that have made graphic violence ubiquitous in our culture. It is adults who have taught our children that hate, racial and gender intolerance, violence, greed, and selfishness are family values. It is adults who have borne children and then left them to raise themselves."

Source: From "Introduction," by M. Wright Edelman, 1994, *The State of America's Children Yearbook*, p. xxv, Children's Defense Fund, 1994, Washington, DC: Author. Reprinted with permission.

responsibility for guiding our children and youth as they mature is no longer limited to families but belongs also to teachers, child care workers, and caring communities, this book focuses on the skills and knowledge adults need to facilitate the development of social and emotional competence in children and youth.

Adults' Responsibility to Foster the Social-Emotional Development of Children with Severe Behavioral Problems

What do you see as your mission with children and youth who have social, emotional, or behavioral problems? The answer seems both clear and complex: The mission is to help them get along successfully with others as social beings. This simple statement summarizes our mission; to accomplish it, we must systematically and sequentially teach successful social, communication, and behavioral skills. Troubled children and youth need to learn to understand the social behavior of others, and they must learn to communicate their intentions and needs in ways that bring positive social results. As significant adults in their lives, we are a part of this social learning equation (Greenspan, 1992; Holland, 1991). Children need adults who can communicate values with clarity and stand as constructive role models. Our own characteristics can facilitate their growth or impede their progress. The task is not an easy one. Consider working with children who seem to "have no future" (Figure 1.2).

These children need to increase their social competence. Their behaviors violate social standards and the expectations of those who care for them. Some have withdrawn from interactions with people; others are rejected or excluded from normal social contact. Some find acceptance by serving as receptacles for others' aberrant needs. In other instances, their social behavior is overtly destructive and disturbing to those close to them, unfulfilling to themselves, or self-destructive. Whatever form children's ineffective efforts take, it is first and most significantly a need to learn how to live and communicate successfully with others.

Their behaviors are attempts to cope with themselves, their feelings, and the world around them. They represent different ages, cultures, and stages of social, emotional, and behavioral development. They have developmental differences that increase in complexity with age. Each child, at his or her own stage of development, is trying to cope through verbal and nonverbal attempts to communicate. Each attempt is symbolic of deep feelings and is infinitely complex, and the adults who care for them and teach them are central players in these scenes. In short, these children are trying to express, in the best way they can, their thoughts and feelings about their social environments—the people, expectations, and experiences that have significance in their lives.

Certainly no students have more difficulty adjusting to the regular school environment than those with social, emotional, or behavioral problems. Their unusual behaviors, appearance, or coping strategies often perplex the adults with whom they come in contact. Frequently, their

Figure 1.2. What is their future?

Student	*Age*	*Observation*
Ann	3	Forty-six biting episodes in a 2-hour period: no speech.
Edward	5	Piercing screams and body rigidity each time he is asked to change his activity; no speech.
Arthur	7	Elective mute; drags a small chair behind him (protection from real or imagined sexual assault).
Philip	9	To teacher in a private conversation, "I control the Junior Army. You can't pass the pain test."
Cathy	10	To teacher about another student, "I'll kill him if you don't get him away from me!"
Tony	11	A high-IQ student to his teacher, "I put chemicals in this jar. If you shake it, it'll explode and blow you up."
Estelle	15	To teacher, "How would you feel if you knew no one would ever love you?"
Daniel	17	When finishing his autobiography, "Looking at your life is like picking up a dead dog out of a ditch . . . that's been hit by a car."

lack of responsiveness, failure to participate, and general disregard for educational activities cause enormous frustration in their teachers and parents. We hear descriptions such as *strange, bizarre, weird, lazy, wild, off the wall, crazy,* and *mean.* With labels like these, the positive attributes of the students often go unnoticed. Adults may overlook aspects of their behavior that are constructive and acceptable because of the dramatic effect of their deviant behaviors. Attitudes of others contribute to a student's self-perception as *one who cannot do.* On the other hand, experiences that involve success with others reinforce a student's identity as *one who can succeed.*

The frustration most often voiced today by their parents and teachers is one of conflicting objectives. Some parents and school administrators want teachers to emphasize academics "so the kids won't be as far behind" or "because we don't want them to feel ashamed that they can't do what others can do." Taking just the opposite position, other parents and administrators will urge the teacher to "shape up that behavior so they won't be disruptive to the other students." Yet the experienced educator knows that these students have serious, complex disabilities in getting along with others. Teachers also know that these students have powerful emotions just below their surface behaviors that impede their capacity to learn and behave in acceptable ways. Emotions seem to fuel students' behavior, smothering academic progress and distorting their relationships with others. As educators and parents, we cannot turn our backs on these dynamic social and emotional forces. They are central in the learning process, and they do not go away when they are ignored. We believe that these students have potential and that they will become socialized to the extent that they are taught to think, regulate their own feelings and behavior, communicate effectively, and mediate their own needs with the expectations of others. We know that if these students are to achieve personal responsibility and social-emotional competence they must have appropriate interpersonal and group models as well as successful relationships with significant adults and peers.

THE BASICS OF DEVELOPMENTAL THERAPY–DEVELOPMENTAL TEACHING

This edition of *Developmental Therapy–Developmental Teaching* is directed toward contemporary concerns for all children. We respond to the challenge to expand and enhance the knowledge and skills of adults who shape the lives of infants, children, and teens. To this end, the book focuses on providing sufficient detail about the Developmental Therapy–Developmental Teaching curriculum to put it into practice in many different settings and with any child who needs assistance in developing social-emotional competence.

To expand your background understanding of Developmental Therapy–Development Teaching before going further into the book, we selected several questions most frequently asked by adults when they are first introduced to this approach.

What is Developmental Therapy–Developmental Teaching?

This is a curriculum for students of any age who need to acquire skills for social-emotional competence. *Developmental Therapy* is the structured application for students with severe social, emotional, or behavioral disabilities that require systematic, therapeutic intervention. Developmental Therapy becomes *Developmental Teaching* as students require less intensive and less structured interventions. Developmental Teaching has emerged as a response to adults working with students without disabilities who voice concerns about the need for fostering social-emotional competence and responsible behavior in all children and youth.

For both applications of the curriculum, instructional goals and objectives are sequenced in the order in which key social competencies occur in typical human development (see Figure 1.3). The approach draws from theory and research about social, emotional, cognitive, communicative, and behavioral development and integrates this knowledge for practical use. At the risk of oversimplifying the complexity and voluminous amount of knowledge about human personality and how it develops, we suggest two basic points that have shaped this curriculum: First, children and youth progress through fairly predictable hierarchical sequences in personality development, and second, the environment profoundly affects the form individual development takes. Our society has misinterpreted or ignored the powerful impact of these two fundamental truths. Case after case describes children who have been denied environments that foster their development—physical, mental, social, and emotional. If our schools are to achieve the level of effectiveness needed by today's children, we must provide experiences and environments known to have beneficial effects on the orderly development of personality and learning. We believe that a developmental orientation adds an essential dimension for providing these experiences to all children and youth. It represents a blueprint for acquisition of the processes that produce social-emotional competence and responsible behavior.

The Developmental Therapy–Developmental Teaching approach to social-emotional competence emphasizes selecting curriculum content and instructional strategies from knowledge about the sequences in which most students, of all ages, with or without disabilities, learn increasingly complex social behaviors. This knowledge

Figure 1.3. The sequence of instructional goals for key social-emotional competencies. Stages One–Five are from *Developmental Therapy in the Classroom: Methods for Teaching Students with Social, Emotional, or Behavioral Handicaps*, 2nd ed., by M. M. Wood, 1986, Austin, TX: PRO-ED. Applications for young adults are from *Developmental Therapy: Theory into Practice*, by A. E. Ivey, 1986, San Francisco: Jossey-Bass.

Erikson's Stages of Psychosocial Development	Piaget's Stages of Cognitive Development			Age Continuum	Associated Developmental Anxieties
Intimacy versus isolation	Dialectic reasoning	Deconstructing and reinterpreting self-knowledge and behavior			
Identity versus role diffusion	Late formal operations	Knowing personal reality in relation to others		About age 18	Personal identity in relation to others
	Formal operations (abstract thinking)	Applying individual and group skills in new situations	Stage Five	About age 12	Search for identity as an independent person
Industry versus inferiority	Transition between late concrete operations and early formal operations	Investing in group processes	Stage Four	About age 9	Conflict between independence and need for others' approval
Initiative versus guilt	Concrete operations	Learning skills for successful group participation	Stage Three	About age 6	Guilt for failing others
Autonomy versus shame and doubt	Preoperational	Responding to the environment with success	Stage Two	About age 2	Personal inadequacy and punishment by other powerful forces
Basic trust versus mistrust	Sensorimotor	Responding to the environment with pleasure	Stage One	Birth	Abandonment and deprivation by others

GROWTH:

describes the changing nature of human needs and how to promote development across the age span. Rather than focusing on problem behaviors, the emphasis is on fostering the sequence of skills needed for increasing social competence and emotional maturity. The curriculum and teaching objectives offer a properly sequenced guide for selecting developmentally appropriate practices in an age-appropriate context. By adjusting activities, materials, and behavior management strategies to each student's age and individual profile of skills and deficits, adults are able to provide a program to match students' skill levels with a greater likelihood of motivating them to success.

The curriculum contains these skills, sequenced into five distinct stages. Each stage has a clustering of characteristics defined by a general description summarized in Figure 1.4. Each stage also defines the unique types of experiences, activities, materials, and behavior management typically needed by students at that stage. Progress through these stages is guided by a series of instructional objectives that reflect the sequence of social-emotional development that all children and youth experience. These steps are the goals and objectives of Developmental Therapy–Developmental Teaching, providing a social-emotional competence dimension for a student's IEP, IFSP, or ITP (U.S. Department of Education, 1990). As you consider these stages and goals, notice that the characteristics of adults (teachers, parents, and others) change with each stage. Such changes in roles are essential if adults wish to influence the social and emotional development of students.

How do a student's culture, age, and school placement relate to Developmental Therapy–Developmental Teaching?

The relevance of Developmental Therapy for troubled children in other cultures has been a matter of continuing interest and study. Comparing cultural similarities and differences among troubled children has been the subject of several professional international conferences and much informal exchange. Educators from Canada, India, Germany, Holland, Italy, New Zealand, Peru, Puerto Rico, Scotland, the Virgin Islands, and Quebec have studied Developmental Therapy at the demonstration site. We find that we hold generally similar views about social-emotional development and the necessity for establishing standards for culturally relevant behavior. Those who have studied the curriculum and then used it in other countries report that it allows freedom for cultural differences in assessing how a student demonstrates mastery of the specified major milestones of development. They also report that it allows for the inclusion of the expectations and values that are unique to individuals, families, schools, and communities while maintaining a direction that fosters increasing social-emotional maturation.[1]

Sections of Developmental Therapy have been translated into German as *Entwicklungstherapie im klassenzimmer* by Bergsson (1993) and Benkmann and Bergsson (1994); into Chinese by Wu Jiajin (1988) at Anhui Normal University of Wuhu, China; into French as *Recherché en musecotherapie de development* by Marsé at the Universite Laval, Quebec; and into several versions of Spanish, including *Terapia de desarrollo* by Cudich, González, and Stinga (1981) in Buenos Aires, Argentina, and *Terapia evolutiva* by Alegría-Martín (1975) in Trujillo, Peru. In Puerto Rico, sections of the curriculum have been translated for use by the Departamanto de Instrucción Pública, Programa de Educación Especial (1976).[2] The curriculum also has been used with fidelity in the Virgin Islands and in 135 replications in 27 U.S. states (Davis, 1994a). These replications include children of all races, ethnic backgrounds, personalities, socioeconomic levels, disabilities, and geographic areas, both urban and rural.

The typical age and school placements for children and youth with corresponding stages in the Developmental Therapy–Developmental Teaching curriculum are portrayed in Figure 1.5. An infant or toddler without disabilities generally accomplishes Stage One goals during the first 18 months of life. As the child continues to develop, Stage Two goals emerge and are typically mastered by the time the preschool years are completed, usually between ages 5 and 6. About age 6, the beginning of first grade, most children are acquiring the social and emotional goals needed for Stage Three, ending in mastery of the stage by the time they have completed third grade—about age 9. Stage Four includes the developmental goals of students in the upper elementary school grades, ending at about age 12. Adolescent development is the focus of goals in Stage Five, mastered between the ages of 12 and 16.

All children progress through these stages of social-emotional maturation as they master sequences of developmental milestones. They make this growth in a fairly predictable order if they have had a reasonable childhood, without deleterious experiences (Pianta & Nimetz, 1992). Developmental Therapy provides a way to assess each student's accomplishments through this developmental progression by using the *Developmental Teaching Objectives Rating Form–Revised* (DTORF–R) to identify instructional objectives for each stage. For example, a typically developing 4-year-old would be accomplishing DTORF–R objectives somewhere about mid–Stage Two and usually would not have mastered the objectives in Stages Three, Four, or

[1]Chapter 4 contains a discussion of the importance of establishing behavioral expectations that are culturally and developmentally appropriate for individual students. See also Bowman and Stott (1994) and the *Journal of Emotional and Behavioral Problems* (1994).

[2]See Appendix 1 for references to these international publications and others documenting the Developmental Therapy–Developmental Teaching movement through 3 decades. Information about these materials can be provided through the Developmental Therapy Institute, Athens, Georgia.

Figure 1.4. Summary of the stages in the Developmental Therapy–Developmental Teaching curriculum.

Stage One: Responding to the Environment with Pleasure

General Description:	*Responding and trusting*
Adult's Role:	Arouser and satisfier of basic needs
Techniques:	Body contact and touch; physical intervention; classroom structure and consistent routine; control of materials by teacher; limited language (vocabulary, sequence, amount)
Intervention:	Constant physical contact; caring, arousing
Environment and Experiences:	Routine consistent, luring rather than demanding; stimulating, arousing sensory activities

Stage Two: Responding to the Environment with Success

General Description:	*Learning individual skills*
Adult's Role:	Motivator; redirector of old coping behavior to successful outcomes; reflector of success; predictable point of reference
Techniques:	Classroom structure; consistent routine; positive verbal interaction between lead and support teachers; physical and verbal redirection; holding limits; reflection of action, feelings, and success
Intervention:	Frequent, both physical and verbal; supportive
Environment and Experiences:	Structured, successful exploration; activities leading to self-confidence and organization; communication activities; beginning cooperative activities; simple group experiences

Stage Three: Learning Skills for Successful Group Participation

General Description:	*Applying individual skills to group procedures*
Adult's Role:	Model for group participation; stimulator and encourager of appropriate group interaction; upholder of limits and group expectations; reflector and interpreter of behavior, feelings, and progress
Techniques:	Redirection; reflection; verbal interaction between lead and support teachers; individual Life Space Intervention; predictable structure and expectations; reflection of feelings; frequent verbal intervention; consistency
Intervention:	Frequent, primarily verbal, group focus
Environment and Experiences:	Group activities that stimulate cooperation, sharing, and beginning friendships; focus on group procedures and expectations; approximation of real-life situations and conditions as much as group can resolve successfully

Stage Four: Investing in Group Processes

General Description:	*Valuing one's group*
Adult's Role:	Group leader; counselor; reflector of reality
Techniques:	Interpretation of feelings and behavior; individual and group Life Space Intervention; reality reflection
Intervention:	Intermittent; approximating real life
Environment and Experiences:	Reality-oriented environment; activities, procedures, and expectations determined by the group; emphasis on group academic learning experiences, role play, field trips, elements of normal competition

Stage Five: Applying Individual and Group Skills in New Situations

General Description:	*Generalizing and valuing*
Adult's Role:	Counselor; teacher; friend
Techniques:	Normal expectations; relationships between feelings, behaviors, and consequences
Intervention:	Infrequent
Environment and Experiences:	Normal settings; conversations about real-life experiences; support in solving problem situations; independent skill building

Figure 1.5. Typical age and school placements with corresponding curriculum stages.

Curriculum Stage	*Developmental Phase*	*Age Range, Years*	*School Level*
One	Infant/toddler	0–2	Infant/toddler program
Two	Toddler/preschooler	2–5	Preschool/kindergarten
Three	Middle childhood	6–9	Primary grade school
Four	Middle childhood	10–12	Upper elementary and middle school
Five	Adolescence	13–16	High school

Five. Similarly, a typically developing 8-year-old will have mastered all of the Stage One and Stage Two objectives and many of the objectives for Stage Three. By age 10, a student typically will have mastered all of the objectives in the first three stages and be well into mastery of Stage Four objectives. By age 12, a student should have mastered almost all of the objectives in the first four stages and should be beginning Stage Five. By age 13, the student should have mastered about 25% of the objectives in this last stage and by age 15 or 16, about 70% to 80% of the Stage Five objectives.

When social, emotional, or behavioral problems are present, these age-stage relationships may be delayed. A disability can affect development, producing increasingly significant lags with age or increased severity. Figure 1.6 illustrates this cumulative effect.

The top line on the graph is the predicted line for typical social-emotional development. Most children follow this general progression. The middle line shows the general pattern of delay for students who have moderately severe social or emotional disabilities. By age 3, a child with moderately severe social, emotional, or behavioral problems may be near mastery of Stage One (not too far behind typical development) and by age 6 may have mastered all of the goals and objectives for Stage One and about half for Stage Two. When the student reaches age 12, the program goals probably will be Stage Three—learning skills to be successful in a group—quite a bit behind the typical development of peers who would have mastered almost all of the Stage Four goals and objectives. This gap increases during adolescence, when a student with moderate delays in social-emotional development will be working toward Stage Four goals, while age peers are focusing on goals for Stage Five.

The most dramatic lags are evident in the lower line of Figure 1.5. Students with severe autism, those who are deaf and blind, or those who have psychotic disorders, significant mental delay, or major neurological dysfunctions often experience severe social, emotional, or behavioral

Figure 1.6. The cumulative effect of disability on development.

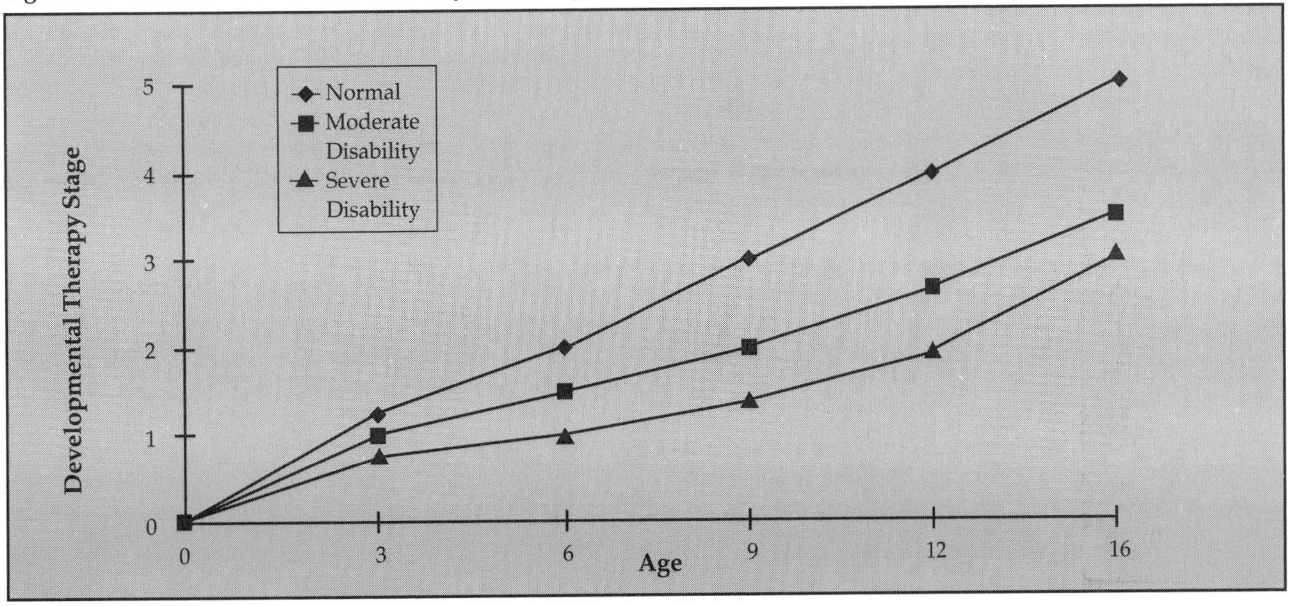

lags in addition to their primary disability (Bailey & Wolery, 1992; Guralnick, 1990; Odom, McConnell, & McEvoy, 1992a). A 3-year-old with such a severe disability may not yet have accomplished half of the Stage One objectives but by age 6 should be mastering the last of the Stage One goals and objectives, while age peers without disabilities will be completing Stage Two. By age 12, the student will be advancing into the last half of Stage Two—learning individual skills—and making slow but incremental progress while age peers are well into Stage Four. The value of Developmental Therapy–Developmental Teaching in such situations is that it keeps adults focused on program interventions that foster steady, incremental learning of the skills for social competence that all children and youth are learning, with or without disabilities.

Can this curriculum help adults select culturally and developmentally appropriate practices?

In a properly sequenced curriculum, the skills and knowledge required of students are introduced sequentially and with increasingly complex content. Such sequences are hierarchical, with mastery of advanced tasks clearly dependent upon mastery of prerequisite tasks. If complex expectations are set before fundamental skills are in place, a student will not have the preparation to achieve success, and frustration is inevitable. We have observed that teachers have little difficulty recognizing this problem in academic areas and are able to plan an academic program to ensure incremental learning in sequential steps. Yet in the social, emotional, and behavioral arena, teachers generally seem less comfortable with the task of sequencing the content and skills to be mastered. There are many examples of adults' successes and failures as they select instructional and management practices for their students. Usually, the failures can be traced directly to a mismatch between a student's stage of social-emotional development and the strategy used by the adult. Here are several mismatched practices (i.e., practices that are acceptable but are used in developmentally inappropriate ways) that can be avoided with a working knowledge of Developmental Therapy–Developmental Teaching:

Examples of Mismatched Practices
That Can Be Avoided with Developmental Therapy–Developmental Teaching

- allowing natural consequences to befall a student who has not yet developed skills for understanding the sequence of events
- placing an expectation for time-on-task behavior that is too high or too low for a student's level of development and attention span
- isolating a student when heightened visual or interpersonal stimulation is needed for motivation to participate
- attempting to use peer pressure with a student who does not value peers
- using individual study carrels to separate students when their developmental need is to learn group social skills
- rewarding a student's acceptable behavior with tangible prizes or treats when interpersonal forms of recognition by adults or peers are of greater value

A developmental approach to intervention uses culturally and individually appropriate interventions while following a sequential, age-appropriate pattern. This approach helps make sense of the uneven patterns of development that are often evident in many students. A young child with a distinctly uneven profile may want to do everything and get into everything, yet cannot succeed, and so communicates the resulting frustration by whining, crying, or having a temper tantrum. Eagerness to explore seems to get ahead of ability to manage frustration, anxiety, or needs. In older students, these uneven patterns of development are usually more subtle. While their speech and mannerisms reflect those of their age peers or television role models, their levels of understanding, control, and feelings may be more like those of younger students. Adults who work with older students know that they must respond to the students' higher-level surface behaviors. Yet they must also adjust their instructional practices to the students' uneven developmental patterns, to ensure solid mastery of tasks. Without such adjustments, instruction and behavior management strategies may be inappropriate for a student's actual developmental needs, and interventions that are designed to help may only increase the fragility of the student in coping with stress. Without solidly established coping skills, such students tend to easily lose control or fall apart emotionally. Unfortunately, this is all too common in today's children and youth.

To illustrate this, here is the example of Mario, whose teacher uses her knowledge of Developmental Therapy–Developmental Teaching goals and objectives to make a developmentally appropriate choice in response to his unacceptable behavior. Mario's teacher recognizes that he does not see benefits in participating with the group. Perhaps he is protecting himself from possible failure in front of his peers. Perhaps he senses their rejection and wants to avoid the truth that others do not like him. Perhaps the activity does not catch his interest. Perhaps he resents adult authority. Any or all of these explanations may be true. The more his teacher knows about Mario and his previous experiences, the more likely it is that she will know which explanation applies.

Why is change an essential part of an effective curriculum?

A curriculum is a guide for growth through the acquisition of increasingly complex skills. It monitors where a

Mario

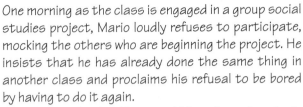

One morning as the class is engaged in a group social studies project, Mario loudly refuses to participate, mocking the others who are beginning the project. He insists that he has already done the same thing in another class and proclaims his refusal to be bored by having to do it again.

Mario is a bright, 10-year-old fourth grader who is very anxious. He is distractible, impulsive, and disorganized. His mother calls him "hyper." He also has great difficulty participating with a group cooperatively. He cannot stand for another student to have the group's attention or lead an activity. He constantly criticizes others while suggesting that his ideas are better. He expects the others to follow the rules but denies that there is a rule that he has violated. He has a good vocabulary and sequences his ideas well in one-to-one situations.

Using the curriculum goals as a guide, the teacher realizes that Mario has not mastered the overall goal of Stage Three, learning skills for successful group participation. Students typically master this stage as they make the transition from third to fourth grade in school. However, Mario's teacher knows that his intellectual ability has enabled him to master academic objectives beyond his social-emotional level of development. This uneven, cross-stage pattern of development will continue to cause difficulties until Mario masters the behavioral, communication, and socialization goals and objectives in Stage Three. Mario's teacher uses his intellectual ability to motivate him. She directly addresses a Stage Three objective—participate in group discussions in ways not disruptive to the group.

To focus on this objective, the teacher restructures the activity for Mario: "Mario, this project needs someone to keep track of the jobs. I want you to take notes of the group's discussion. After everyone chooses a job and tells about it, write it down. Then we'll review each job with the students to see if they are clear about exactly what to do." By altering Mario's task, emphasizing his academic skills, the teacher assures Mario that he can achieve the task with success and look good in the eyes of his peers. The task is genuinely important. At the same time, the teacher is simplifying Mario's task socially, where he is developmentally far behind his peers. She carefully restructures his responsibility to the group project by making his social contacts primarily one-to-one, even though they are in a group setting. This activity becomes another success for Mario and begins the gradual shift of his views of himself to *one who can do* within the group.

student is in the progression through the learning sequences. When program strategies have been developmentally on-target, the students will be acquiring new skills. This very success often is an indication that it is time to change strategies. Changing strategies that have produced successful results is frequently difficult for adults because they have worked hard to match their practices with the needs of their students. If a strategy works, why not continue to use it?

It may be essential to change strategies because mastery has occurred and some students may now be at a new stage of development. The practices that worked wonders in accomplishing the goals and objectives of the previous stage may be obsolete now. We know this to be true in everyday life. Consider how you respond to a toddler, then think of your behavior when you interact with a 6-year-old or a teenager. Each has uniquely different skills that require different strategies and a different sort of adult. This applies in the Developmental Therapy–Developmental Teaching curriculum, too. If we do not change our practices as students change, we may actually be holding them back, keeping them at a plateau in development rather than stimulating them to continue their progression in development as rapidly as possible. Both changing adults' strategies to adjust to students' new skills and changing adults' roles are central for promoting maximum positive change in students through the Developmental Therapy–Developmental Teaching approach.

There are times, however, when strategies should not be changed. If a student has demonstrated solid mastery of skills and then unexpectedly behaves like a much younger child, or seems to lose previously mastered skills, it may be a form of *regression*—reverting to more primitive behavior. We know that some regression is normal for all people under some circumstances. We also know that regressive behavior is a temporary and healthy defense; unless it continues for extended periods, it will end with a return to the previous level of functioning. Unfortunately, a student who is regressing often causes adults to react negatively or to question the efficacy of the program.

While such a questioning attitude is generally a good way to self-monitor, it may result in unnecessary changes in strategy. Or, if an adult blames the student, viewing the student as intentionally causing trouble or wanting excessive attention, the relationship between them may become adversarial.

When a student seems to be backsliding, the decision about whether or not to change program strategies rests with how fully the student has mastered the goals and objectives of the preceding stages of development. When adults respond too quickly to regression by shifting to strategies associated with a lower stage of development, less acceptable behavior may be unintentionally reinforced. On the other hand, ignoring the regressive behavior may reinforce it when adults fail to use strategies from a previous stage of development that are needed to keep the student participating successfully.

If a student has shown mastery of previous goals and objectives and then uses less acceptable behaviors because of a transient stress, it probably is best to maintain the present strategies while conveying understanding and support. In contrast, if regression continues, it may be necessary to shift to strategies associated with the previous stage. The point to emphasize is that adults' strategies do not necessarily have to change as soon as regression occurs, nor do we need to blame a student for intentionally obstructing our plans for a successful intervention. The guideline is to know the extent to which a student has mastered effective coping skills that can be recalled and remobilized.

How is the curriculum used to enhance a behavior management plan?

There are four major schools of thought about behavior management, each generating specific recommendations for intervention strategies, with some similarities between them (Kauffman, 1993). Each approach makes a unique contribution to an educator's total arsenal of skills and strategies. In managing students' behavior, learn about all of the approaches, and then match strategies with your students' developmental needs. Developmental Therapy and Developmental Teaching provide a way to do this so that a behavior management plan has internal consistency with a student's current social-emotional status and profile of skills and deficits.[3] Here is an example, illustrating management strategies from several different theoretical orientations. Can you imagine what would be missing if an individualized program for Joe included only one of these approaches?

[3]See Chapter 5 for details of how we prepare a behavior management plan for a student's individual needs and stage of development. See also Chapter 6 for descriptions of the most frequently used management strategies and how they change form and frequency of use at each stage of development. Neel and Cessna (1993) also provide a helpful discussion of ways to identify behavioral intent and use curriculum to promote social competence.

Joe: A Typical Classroom Incident

Your students are working on arithmetic assignments. You are helping three students work with fractions. Another student, Joe, with an individual arithmetic assignment, is frantically waving his arms and calling for you. He says he needs you *now.* How do you respond?

A *psychoeducational* approach to Joe may emphasize social relationships and feelings that enhance his insight into himself and expand his prosocial behavior toward others. By helping students recognize such forces within themselves, adults can help them learn behaviors that bring better responses from those around them. The result is better feelings inside the students and more productive adjustment to the demands of life. If you use a psychoeducational orientation, you may interpret Joe's urgent hand-waving as a need for reassurance and respond by reflecting confidence back to him, saying,

> *"It's hard to wait for the teacher, but you did it yesterday. I know you can do it now."*

A *behavioral* approach may target specific behaviors to change, using highly specified objectives that can be observed and quantified to document Joe's responses. With careful control of antecedent conditions, the intervention, and the consequences influencing the targeted behaviors, an adult can shape students' behaviors to achieve the specified objectives. If you choose a behavioral approach, you might identify Joe's behavior as off-task and respond by reminding him of the consequences:

> *"When you finish your work, you will be able to go on our field trip today."*

An *ecological* approach may emphasize intervening in the environment with changes in key factors that influence Joe's behavior. By identifying important influences on a student's behavior, an adult can either modify the detrimental circumstances, change the student's behaviors to adjust to the circumstances, or combine the efforts so that there is some amount of enhanced synchrony between the student and the surrounding realities. If you use an ecological approach, you may recognize something in the situation itself that is causing Joe's problem behavior and needs changing. If the problem seems to be anxiety about not being able to finish, or lack of motivation, you might respond,

"Joe, I'll be there in a minute to look at what you have done. I want to be sure you will finish when the others do."

A *developmental* approach advocates simultaneously using the sequence of social, psychological, and physical skills leading up to a student's current status. By intervening at the student's current developmental level, an adult using a developmental orientation can begin at the point where the student has sufficient mastery of prerequisite skills to be successful in the task at hand. The adult then gradually adjusts the task to move the student successfully through an increasingly complex hierarchy for skill attainment. If you respond to Joe using the Developmental Therapy–Developmental Teaching approach, you will recognize that he has not completely mastered the Stage Two goals and objectives for social, emotional, and behavioral development. His most important motivation is still the adult, not the other students in his group. You will suspect that field trips are anxiety-provoking and not rewarding to him because he does not have the developmental skills necessary to feel success in such situations. You also may have observed that Joe has difficulty with sustained waiting, a skill requiring a conception of time and impulse control that he has not yet developed. And because you recognize that Joe, like most Stage Two students, is more interested in action, attention, and response from adults than from other students, you may choose to use adult praise as the reinforcement and respond,

"It's hard to wait, Joe, but while you wait I want you to find that excellent arithmetic paper in your notebook from yesterday. Put a check by the problems that you did correctly, especially if they were very hard. I want to see how they compare with today's problems."

As you may have observed, this response includes elements from the psychoeducational, behavioral, and ecological perspectives. What is added is a developmental frame of reference to answer the question: "How can I use my knowledge of Joe's individual level of social-emotional development to select the particular strategies that are best for him?" Let's review the response of the teacher to Joe's behavior, using the Developmental Therapy–Developmental Teaching approach. Joe is an intellectually average 8-year-old who should typically be completing the goals and objectives associated with Stage Three in Developmental Therapy: learning to be a successful group member. But Joe's behavior is more like the behavior of a 5-year-old. A typical 8-year-old can wait for a period of time, while an 8-year-old with the distractibility, low frustration tolerance, and impulsivity of a 5-year-old cannot. In the Developmental Therapy–Developmental Teaching curriculum, this behavior would be typical for Stage Two, where the overall goal is to respond to the environment with individual success.

We can draw a number of conclusions from this knowledge. Clearly, Joe needs more movement activities than a typical 8-year-old, yet it would be counterproductive to allow him to wander around the classroom or play games during this academic time. He needs to participate in the expected activities. For this reason, the teacher does not tell Joe to wait until she finishes working with the other students but instead gives him a substitute fine motor activity that emphasizes success until she can help him individually. The teacher has engaged in ecological intervention by restructuring the activity to Joe's developmental level.

Did you notice in this example that the teacher reflects Joe's feelings before she uses any other intervention strategy? By putting words to Joe's feelings, his teacher is helping him to eventually use words rather than impulsive actions to express himself. Developmentally, one of Joe's strengths is in communication, his most advanced skill, and she is building on this strength. Additionally, her response helps to ally her with Joe as someone he can count on. This is important not only from a developmental perspective but from a psychoeducational point of view as well. The alliance implicit in his teacher's statement meets Joe's need for primary relationships with adults. The teacher's positive response to Joe recognizes his feelings yet continues to focus on the arithmetic activity while restructuring the task. From a behavioral perspective, Joe's reinforcement for continuing to comply with the teacher's new direction is adult contact and approval—still a fundamental motivation for him at his stage of social-emotional development. Her response is also preferable to the common practice of asking a more able student to give assistance to a student having difficulty. Another student would provide insufficient reinforcement in this situation because Joe is not yet at the point in his social-emotional development where peers become a satisfactory substitute for a needed adult.

How is the curriculum used for successful inclusion of troubled children in general education programs?

In every Developmental Therapy–Developmental Teaching program, inclusion is an essential ingredient. Inclusion provides the opportunity for children to have appropriate peer models and to practice new skills in open settings. David Rostetter describes inclusion as it should be viewed by those using the Developmental Therapy–Developmental Teaching curriculum: "The goal of inclusion is that all students are going to school together, learning together, playing together, and growing up together" (Rostetter, 1994, p. 3).

For preschool children in Stages One and Two, inclusion is a natural part of participation in their neighborhood Head Start, preschool, or kindergarten programs. This inclusion is essential because of the extent to which young children learn by socializing, playing, and exploring together. As they master new success-producing behaviors, they also need the opportunity to practice these newly learned skills spontaneously and in less structured ways than may be needed as part of an early childhood special education intervention.

For children with severe social, emotional, and behavioral disabilities—in elementary, middle, or high school—inclusion is equally important. For these older children, who are usually in Stages Three or Four, successful inclusion means being accepted by friends in a neighborhood peer group. Inclusion that fails to bring peer acceptance can be a psychological and developmental disaster. Unfortunately, acceptance by peers is difficult for these children to achieve because they are frequently primitive in their impulse control and poorly socialized. In every instance, however, it is necessary to provide successful experiences and activities with age peers. A part of their inclusion must also provide ways to generalize new learning in open settings, free from highly controlled interventions, if these experiences are to be successful. An IEP identifies specific goals, the milestones needed, and the settings in which these needs can be met successfully. The amount of inclusion should also be precisely planned as a part of a child's IEP.

We use the following account of Marty to illustrate some of the problems and strategies of successful inclusion and the importance of persistent teamwork.

This example illustrates many typical difficulties encountered in attempting to provide a successful inclusive program for students who have severe emotional and behavioral problems. Peers fear such students and try to avoid associating with them, often making the student's

Marty

Marty is insecure and highly anxious. At age 8, he has lived in three different foster homes, none of which met the normal needs of a growing child. Marty describes his present home as a "scary place." He feels inadequate about his own abilities and harbors much hostility caused by the neglect and abuse he has experienced. His anxiety is evident in school, where he demands constant attention—banging on tables, provoking other children, cursing, crawling under desks, refusing to complete tasks, and sulking. He is a highly disruptive influence, which his third-grade teachers find frustrating and intolerable to the other children.

When he is first enrolled in a Stage Three Developmental Therapy–Developmental Teaching group, the same disruptive conduct occurs. He presents a strange combination of behaviors. He appears to be a child who has superficially adopted the very proper codes of behavior set by his present foster parents. But underneath is a torrent of primitive anger and fury that is uncontrollable when unleashed. He tries to please with the proper words: "Please," "Thank you," "Yes, Ma'am," "May I help you?" But when his insecurity and anxiety overwhelm him, rage results. He is feared by his foster parents, is avoided by his peers, and has to be physically restrained by his teachers.

Although he is participating in a Stage Three program for 2 hours daily, Marty continues to be included in his regular third-grade class for the remainder of each day. There, his teachers also use Developmental Teaching strategies. He responds to adults who provide firm, consistent limits and clearly communicate what is expected of him. Because he has different third-grade teachers for each subject area, it is essential that they work together to maintain consistency, so team meetings are held several times each week with the third-grade teachers and the Developmental Therapy–Developmental Teaching team. Whenever possible, the principal joins these team meetings.

Helping Marty maintain himself in school demands intensive communication between all of his teachers and parents. They must convey the same expectations. They also focus on his behavior and responses to the activities, materials, and management strategies. His home management and his special education program must be coordinated with his regular education programs.

When the adults meet together at the end of the school day, Marty's third-grade teachers describe what happened throughout the school day. Often these experiences give the Stage Three team clues as to why he seems particularly upset or out of control on certain days. Similarly, as the team develops new insights and strategies that prove to be successful, they share this information with the third-grade teachers.

(continues)

The principal's role, as the adult authority for enforcing the building rules,[4] is clearly developed so that Marty will be aware of the behavioral expectations anywhere on the school grounds. In addition, the third-grade teachers use Developmental Teaching practices in managing Marty in their classrooms.

Together, they design a system to cover his out-of-control episodes. The third-grade teachers immediately call for backup when he cannot be managed in the classroom. At these times, Marty is removed from the room to the hall, where an attempt is made to redirect him so that he can return to the room very quickly and continue to participate. At other times, he is so disruptive and out of control that he is taken to the Developmental Therapy classroom for crisis intervention. An example of such an intervention follows.

This particular morning, Marty has fought repeatedly with children in his third-grade class during recess and during the restroom breaks. He has been sent to the principal's office several times. After each episode, he returns to class and continues to provoke other students. After numerous attempts to handle Marty, the teacher calls the Developmental Therapy–Developmental Teaching team. The lead teacher meets Marty at the principal's office. She attempts to convey understanding and at the same time to communicate that the situation is quite serious. Her conversation with the principal centers around letting Marty know that she is highly concerned for Marty. She asks questions about his morning that are directed toward getting any background information that might be helpful in choosing the intervention strategies she will use. Because it is lunchtime, she asks the principal if something could be provided for Marty's lunch, since he will miss his lunchtime in the cafeteria while they talk. The principal agrees to provide something for him. Then, Marty and the teacher go to the room used by the Developmental Therapy team. (The other students have gone to lunch.) Here is how the teacher handles the situation.

She begins by reflecting Marty's feelings: "Sounds like it was a really hard day. You seem to be feeling bad." This, along with supportive statements such as "It's good you're here so I can help you" and "I can see you're really in control of yourself now," sets the tone for the session, and Marty relaxes somewhat. But he remains unresponsive and reluctant to talk.

The teacher decides that Marty needs still more time to settle down emotionally before the events can be discussed logically. They make sandwiches together, allowing time for Marty to get his feelings under control and to feel sufficiently trusting of the teacher to respond. After eating, Marty seems more relaxed but refuses to discuss the incidents. He restlessly leaves the table. Because of their previous relationship, the teacher knows that Marty will seek contact with her. She interprets his feelings in a supportive way: "Sometimes it's really hard to talk about things like this" and "Sometimes a boy just needs to think things over for himself."

Knowing that Marty is burdened with much guilt about his own inadequacy, she adds, "Marty, I'm going to get materials ready for the students who come in the afternoon, while you think." She begins to straighten up a shelf, ignoring Marty but believing that he will eventually make a spontaneous move toward helping her. In less than 2 minutes, Marty is hard at work straightening the shelf with her. She remarks how nice it is to have such good help and generally reinforces Marty for his helpful behavior. Marty's attitude changes from sullen, ashamed withdrawal to reserved cooperation and pleasure in helping. After cleaning up, he suggests that he and the teacher read a story together.

The teacher knows that the good feelings Marty has about helping her with the materials are not enough to enable him to discuss his morning, nor to prepare him to return to the third-grade classroom in control of himself. "Take the time needed," the teacher reminds herself. "Make him more confident about walking into the classroom. Be sure he feels better about himself before you push for discussion of the incident."

Reading, fortunately, is a good activity for doing this. She knows that Marty can be praised for his reading skills and given much nurturance at the same time. They decide to read the story on the floor, side by side. As soon as the story is finished, the teacher moves around in front of Marty. Sitting facing him, she reviews his behavior from the time he walked into the room until the present moment. She emphasizes the appropriate behavior that Marty has exhibited—particularly the behavior that will enable him to function more successfully in school. She reflects several specific examples for him: walking in the door, greeting the teacher politely, walking

[4] A discussion of levels of rules is given in Chapter 6.

(*continues*)

straight to his own chair, helping the teacher organize the materials for the afternoon group, cooperating in a reading activity, listening and talking in a friendly way.

Marty smiles broadly as he listens. He feels better about himself than he did when he walked in the door 30 minutes earlier. He seems ready to forget that there had been trouble earlier in the day. This is symptomatic of his behavior; he rarely learns from his experiences. The teacher knows that now is the time to go back to the original problem and say, "Marty, I know you're ready to go back to class now, but before you go, we need to talk about what happened in school this morning."

Marty protests briefly, testing the teacher's determination to have the talk. He eventually describes the events and the rules for conduct in the classroom. The teacher does not ask him to explain his behavior, because she knows that he is not yet developmentally able to do this or to discuss alternative behaviors himself. She helps him by suggesting other ways he can behave that will let his other teachers and the students know that he has some fine qualities. To end the session, Marty and the teacher role-play to practice alternative behaviors he might use.

The support teacher on the Stage Three team accompanies Marty back to the third grade, and for the remainder of the day his behavior is consistently appropriate and successful.

After school, a conference is held with his third-grade teachers. They describe Marty's behavior during the morning, and the Stage Three teacher shares what occurred during the crisis intervention. This results in greater insight and understanding for all about how Marty is attempting to cope with stress and anxiety. It also results in refinements in the teachers' strategies for spotting small indications of spiraling stress and intervening sooner with praise and redirection. Consistency among all teachers in managing Marty's behavior is emphasized.

In time Marty begins to demonstrate greater self-control and more self-confidence in participating in the group's activities. Through the school year, he becomes increasingly successful in small ways. He makes strides in his ability to express feelings, refrain from aggressive behavior, and convey self-confidence. During the summer he participates fairly successfully in a relatively unstructured recreation program. He begins to demonstrate a degree of behavioral control that was not evident before, showing an increasing ability to get along with other students his age. Because of the progress shown in these new situations, the Stage Three team, the principal, and the fourth-grade teachers investigate the possibility of a new school situation where Marty can begin the next school year free from the negative reputation he has established among the other teachers and students in his elementary school. His foster parents continue in their attempts to be more consistent and fair with their discipline at home. They begin to show understanding of the milestones the program is helping him to reach and more acceptance of him as he continues to improve. They provide new opportunities for inclusion by attending the Boy's Club and other recreation programs, something they had not permitted in the past.

sense of alienation, inadequacy, and guilt even greater. The principal may be forced to become the disciplinarian. The general education teachers spend considerable time with discipline instead of instruction. There must be someone skilled in crisis intervention and some appropriate place available to protect the other students and to ensure that disruptive behavior is dealt with in ways that eventually result in social-emotional growth and responsible behavior.

The program is effective for Marty because of the shared information and close collaboration between everyone involved. The principal appropriately represents authority and order, maintaining the expectation that Marty will conduct himself as he should in the school and in his third-grade classes. At the same time, Marty sees the principal and teachers working together to help him when he loses control. This gives him the message that he can change his situation for the better. The third-grade teachers use Developmental Teaching strategies in the inclusive program, while the foster parents use the same management strategies at home. The schedule of the Developmental Therapy teacher allows her to be free during the lunch hour and she is also available for crisis intervention. She has an experienced and skilled support teacher, an aide, who can conduct the afternoon program until the teacher completes the session with Marty. This support person is able to return to the regular classroom with Marty and is available for backup if she is needed. Without all of these program elements present, Marty's successful integration into an inclusive third-grade program would flounder and progress would be jeopardized.

IS DEVELOPMENTAL THERAPY–DEVELOPMENTAL TEACHING EFFECTIVE?

Over the three decades of model development and expansions, repeated studies have been made to evaluate the effect of Developmental Therapy–Developmental Teaching with children of different ages, with varying disabilities, and in many service settings. Because documentation of progress at regular intervals is essential when using this curriculum, adults are consistently able to provide data about children's progress. Similarly, all staff development programs for using the curriculum include periodic assessment of adults' performance while working with children, so that the adults' skill acquisition and performance levels can be documented. Two instruments are the core of the evaluation system: the DTORF–R, which measures a child's progress, and the DT/RITS, which measures the proficiency with which adults are able to implement the curriculum (Developmental Therapy Institute, 1992).[5]

Although claims that attribute an effect to an intervention have long been a problem for research design, there are several methods by which these concerns can be addressed in service-oriented programs. Various studies investigating the effect of Developmental Therapy–Developmental Teaching have made a concerted effort to introduce such controls using research procedures that provide reasonable justifications for claims of effectiveness in field-based settings. Three national reviews of performance data have been made by independent panels. We summarize their findings here and then review two other controlled studies of effectiveness. The first investigation documents the effectiveness of Developmental Therapy on students' achievement of the social-emotional goals and objectives. The second study examines parents' ratings of their children's problem behaviors before and after receiving Developmental Therapy. Studies documenting the acquisition of skills by teachers and paraprofessionals participating in staff development programs for Developmental Therapy–Developmental Teaching are reviewed in Chapter 7.

Validation by Outside Panel Review

In 1993, the model received the Significant Achievement Award from the American Psychiatric Association, Hospital and Community Psychiatry Service (American Psychiatric Association, 1993). The plaque said, "In recognition of an innovative and well-researched program that applies the Developmental Therapy Model in the treatment of emotionally disturbed children, resulting in outstanding clinical care and professional development." After reviewing the model components, curriculum, evaluation system, and outcome data for children participating in Developmental Therapy programs, the professional review panel made this competitive award for "outstanding contributions to the mental health field, that provide a model for other programs, and that have met the challenges presented by limited financial or staff resources or other significant obstacles. . . . At a time when the emotional health of the nation's children has become a major focus of leaders and policy makers, the Rutland's Developmental Therapy Program offers a successful model of treatment for children and training for adults" (pp. 994–996).

In earlier studies of model effectiveness, the Developmental Therapy model has been twice validated for national dissemination by the Joint Dissemination Review Panel (JDRP) of the U.S. Office of Education and the National Institute of Education. The first validation (U.S. Department of Education, 1975, JDRP No. 75-63) resulted in its designation as an effective and replicable program for young children with severe emotional and behavioral disabilities in need of increasing social, emotional, and behavioral skills (Hoyt, 1978; Wood & Swan, 1978). In this submission, performance data for 49 children ages 2–6 years (the average age was 4 years 11 months, at the time of enrollment) showed gains in all four curriculum areas of Developmental Therapy during one school year.[6]

In 1981, the model received a second validation from the U.S. Office of Education when data were submitted showing the effectiveness of the staff development component of the model (U.S. Department of Education, 1981, JDRP No. 81-19; Wood & Combs, 1981). Evidence of effectiveness was obtained for 45 teachers and aides participating in a year-long in-service project while teaching school-age children with severe emotional and behavioral disabilities in 13 public elementary schools in four states and at the original demonstration site, the Rutland Psychoeducational Services Program. Statistically significant evidence supported the model's claim that personnel participating in the staff development program became proficient in using Developmental Therapy with fidelity in their classrooms and achieved accuracy in assessing the social-emotional status of their students. Results also indicated that personnel can reach a passing level of proficiency or better within 30 hours of seminar instruction accompanied by individual in-class consultation and feedback.

Students' Gains in Mastery of Social-Emotional Objectives

We recently completed a field-based study to compare gains made by 112 students aged 2–12 years with varying

[5] The evaluation system and instruments, including the DTORF–R, are described in Chapter 3. The DT/RITS is reviewed in Chapter 5 and is included as Appendix 2.

[6] As a result of this first validation, the model was included in the National Diffusion Network publication, *Educational Programs That Work*, for dissemination and replication on a national scale. It continues to be cited annually in that publication (Davis, 1994b).

disabilities who participated in Developmental Therapy programs during a 3-year period in six different schools in four states. The sample included all students in these programs whose teachers had staff development training in Developmental Therapy–Developmental Teaching. From an initial pool of 135 students, 23 students were excluded from the study because their data were incomplete or judged to be improperly recorded; data were therefore analyzed for 112 students. The sample was 71% male and 29% female. The racial distribution consisted of 63% Caucasians and 37% African Americans. The students had a range of disabilities: 51% had severe emotional or behavioral disabilities, whereas 49% had other disabilities, including a fairly even distribution of cognitive delays, speech or language problems, autism, and other physical or health impairments. Half of the students (56) were between the ages of 6 and 9, whereas slightly more than a third (44) were aged 2 through 5 and 12 (11%) were aged 10 through 12. The students' average age at the initiation of the study was 6 years 2 months. During the time of this study, the median length of intervention was one school year.

Classroom teachers and others working with the students as a team completed a consensus rating for each student at the beginning of the study (or at the time the student entered if it was after the study began). Ratings were repeated at the end of the school year to determine gains and to calculate rates of change during the intervention. Pre- and postprogram scores were analyzed to allow comparisons that included students with differing disabilities and levels of severity, stages of development, ages, and lengths of intervention. In the first analysis, students' individual rates of development prior to the intervention were calculated to provide predicted scores for comparison to actual scores achieved by the end of the intervention period.[7]

Results showed statistically significant gains in social-emotional development by the students from preprogram to postprogram. Similar results occurred in each performance area: Behavior, Communication, Socialization, and (Pre)Academics/Cognition and at all of the locations, as evidenced by greater actual gains than those predicted without intervention and higher rates of development during intervention than prior to intervention. An additional statistical analysis was done to compare the program's effect on students within each of the three age groups: up to age 6, ages 6 through 9, and ages 10 through 12. The results showed similar gains among young preschool children, primary-age students, and those in upper elementary or middle school, to age 12. Finally, a statistical comparison was made of gains in social-emotional development from pre- to postprogram by students with various disabilities and ages at all six locations. From these results, it appears that Developmental Therapy is effective in producing gains in social competence and that these gains are not influenced by a student's age, type of disability, or geographic location.

Parents' Ratings of Changes in Their Children's Behavior

In an earlier study using parents' ratings of their children's problem behaviors, Kaufman, Paget, and Wood (1981) found encouraging evidence that Developmental Therapy is effective in reducing the severe problem behaviors of students participating in a Developmental Therapy program at the original demonstration site, the Rutland Psychoeducational Services Program. Although problems associated with securing good control groups necessarily limit interpretation, the results contributed to a growing body of similar findings. The authors identified all children in the program whose behavior had been rated twice by one of their parents. Each child had been identified as having severe emotional and behavioral disabilities and had been rated by a parent at the time of referral. However, the time of completion of the second rating by a parent varied. For some children, the exit rating was done at the time the child was reassigned to a less intensive program. For others, a designated follow-up rating was obtained approximately 2 years afterward, as a part of a routine follow-up after the child had exited the program. These differences in times for the postratings were used to establish two samples. One group, the *exit group*, was used to evaluate changes during the intervention period. This group contained 37 children who were rated at the time they were referred and again at the time they exited the program for a different educational placement. The *tracking group* was used to study the stability of the effect over time. This group was composed of 36 children who were rated at the time of referral and again 2 years after they exited the program. Analysis of data from these groups permitted evaluation of the immediate and long-term benefits of Developmental Therapy in reducing severe problem behaviors.

The exit group ranged in age from 3 years 2 months to 11 years 5 months (mean age = 7 years 4 months; *SD* = 2 years 2 months); 65% were male and 35% female; 62% were Caucasian, 35% African American, and 3% of unrecorded race. The mean length of intervention was 11.5 months (the range was from 2 months to 27 months). The tracking group ranged in age from 3 years 8 months to 12 years 2 months (mean age = 8 years 3 months; *SD* = 2 years 6 months); 63% were male and 33% female; 50% were Caucasian, 47% African American, and 3% of unrecorded race. The mean length of intervention for this group was 10.0 months (*SD* = 5.8 months). The mean length of time between a student's exiting the program

[7] We include a description of the analysis and the students' performance data in Tables 1.1 through 1.4 in Appendix 6. A similar design is described by Clark (1989).

and the follow-up rating by the parent was 2 years 2 months (*SD* = 9.2 months). Because of the 10 months these children spent receiving Developmental Therapy and the interval of more than 2 years between their exit and the follow-up rating, on average 3 years elapsed between the referral rating and the follow-up rating for this sample.

Parents rated their children at the time of referral on the *Referral Form Checklist* (RFCL), which contains the 54 problem behaviors most often mentioned by parents and teachers when referring children for special help. The exit group had a mean of 14.9 severe problem behaviors at the time of referral, and the tracking group had a mean of 13.4 problem behaviors, corroborating that the referred children had severe emotional disabilities.

Results showed an 89% reduction in the number of severe problem behaviors for the exit group and an 81% reduction for the tracking group (from referral until 2 years after they had exited the program); statistically significant reductions in severe problem behaviors occurred in three of the curriculum areas and for all three factor scores. No reduction occurred in the Academics/Cognition area, which is not surprising because Developmental Therapy is designed for social-emotional rather than academic intervention. In a sense, the lack of reduction in severe academic problems served as a control for the significant reductions in the social-emotional areas. This finding also emphasizes the importance of using Developmental Therapy in conjunction with clearly defined academic therapies when a student has severe academic disabilities.[8]

Results were strikingly similar for the tracking group, showing statistically significant reductions in severe problem behaviors, as perceived by the parents from referral to follow-up ratings, 2 years after exiting the program. Again, the Academics/Cognition area was the only one that failed to produce a statistically significant reduction in severe problems. The results led Kaufman et al. (1981) to conclude that the substantial reduction in severe problem behaviors that was evident at the end of the children's programs was maintained after the intervention.

HOW THE DEVELOPMENTAL THERAPY–DEVELOPMENTAL TEACHING MODEL EVOLVED

The Developmental Therapy–Developmental Teaching movement has been an effort extending over 3 decades to translate theory and research about the social and emotional development of children and youth into classroom practices. Figure 1.7 illustrates this evolution, with each decade bringing its own particular emphasis to the model.[9]

The Original Model Development

The first work in forming Developmental Therapy began in the decade of the 1970s when we created a guide for teachers, clinicians, and parents of children identified as having severe emotional and behavioral disabilities. The popular label at that time was *severely emotionally disturbed.* We spoke of them as *troubled children* and addressed the urgent need for services.[10] Very few mental health services and even fewer special education services were available for such children. It was almost impossible, outside the largest urban areas, to find clinical psychologists who specialized in children's mental health services; most special education services were limited to students with cognitive disabilities or developmental delay. Consequently, a large portion of the instruments developed for assessment at that time reflected concerns about intellectual, not emotional, status.

Recognizing that being effective in helping troubled children and youth was a vastly complex undertaking, we embarked on a large-scale psychoeducational project with Rutland Psychoeducational Services in the public schools in Athens, Georgia. We selected the term *psychoeducational* to describe our efforts to integrate knowledge from psychology and education in defining the parameters for effective intervention. The result was an extensive analysis of theories from clinical psychology, educational psychology, learning theory, and child development about the social, emotional, cognitive, and language skills needed for the successful social and emotional adjustment of children aged 3–8 years. From this, we identified key findings that had implications for practice and developed the first set of developmentally oriented goals and objectives for therapeutic intervention. Within a year, the age range was expanded upward to include 14-year-olds. We called the resulting approach *Developmental Therapy.* The term *developmental* conveys a foundation built on findings about the changing, developmental nature of the social and emotional characteristics of children as they mature, and the term *therapy* (rather than *education*) conveys the rehabilitative nature of the approach (Wood, 1975, 1986).

The need to have a reliable and valid instrument to assess a child's social and emotional status was an early and urgent priority, leading to construction of the *Developmental Therapy Objectives Rating Form* (DTORF) (Wood, 1979). Field tests and revisions of the instructional objectives continued for 5 years, in concert with extensive

[8]Tables 1.5 and 1.6 in Appendix 6 contain the parents' rating data from this earlier study.

[9]A list of publications documenting the Developmental Therapy–Developmental Teaching movement through 3 decades, from 1970 to 1994, is contained in Appendix 1.

[10]Terms have changed frequently over the past decades. The most recent label to appear in professional journals is *behaviorally challenged.* We continue to prefer *troubled children* as being a more cogent description.

Figure 1.7. Expansion of the Developmental Therapy–Developmental Teaching model over 3 decades.

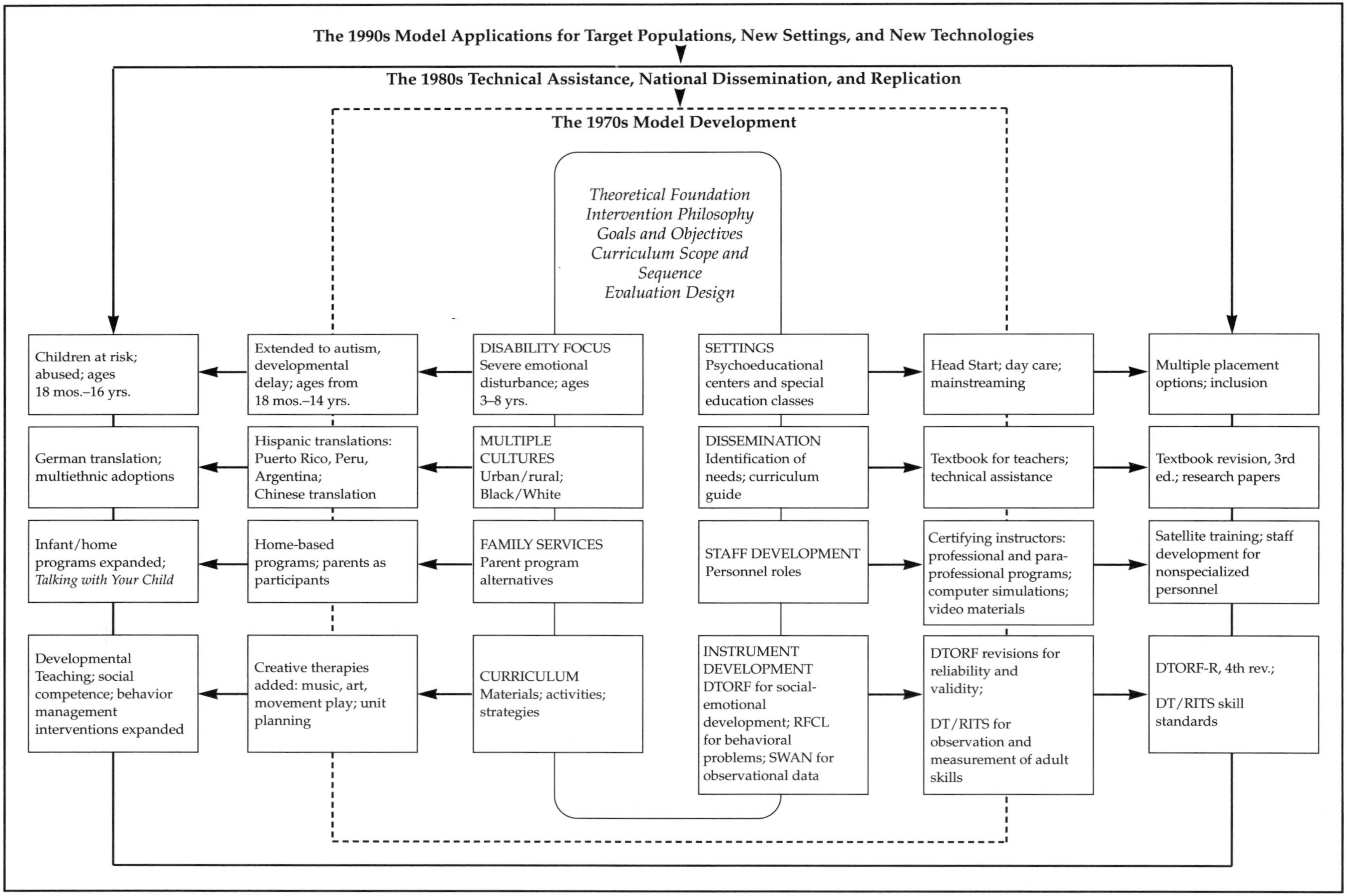

Note. In 1975 and 1981, the model was validated for dissemination by the U.S. Office of Education Joint Dissemination Review Panel; in 1993, it received the Significant Achievement Award from the American Psychiatric Association, Hospital and Community Psychiatry Service. DTORF = *Developmental Teaching Objectives Rating Form;* RFCL = *Referral Form Checklist;* SWAN = *Systematic Who to Whom Notation;* DT/RITS = *Developmental Therapy Rating Inventory of Teacher Skills;* DTORF-R = *Developmental Teaching Objectives Rating Form–Revised.*

studies identifying interventions that were developmentally suited to achieve these objectives. The DTORF items were criterion-referenced to the Developmental Therapy instructional objectives. Reliability studies reported item-by-item interrater agreement of 95% to 98%, following a standard training program (Gunn, 1983). Construct validity was established during the initial model development from theory and research in social-emotional development. In 1991–1992, the instrument was again revised after extensive statistical analysis of the item hierarchies using the Rasch statistical procedure (Weller, 1991). With this latest revision of the instrument (the DTORF–R) (Developmental Therapy Institute, 1992), teachers, clinicians, and case workers can (a) identify students with social, emotional, or behavioral problems in need of referral for special help; (b) make placement decisions for grouping a student in environments and with other students where optimal growth can occur; (c) identify instructional and therapeutic objectives in the social-emotional domain; (d) select curriculum activities to foster social and emotional competence; and (e) document student progress in social-emotional maturation (Wood, 1992a, 1992b).[11]

Expansion in the 1980s

Because we view the skills of adults as essential elements in an effective program, we followed the first phases of model development with an intensive project in the 1980s to expand the staff development component. During this period, 63 instructional modules, computer simulations for practicing classroom management strategies, and video materials were developed to assist teachers learning to use the model (Wood & Combs, 1981; Wood, Combs, & Swan, 1985; Wood, Combs, & Walters, 1986; Wood, Skaar, Mayfield, Morrison, & Gillespie, 1984). Simultaneously, a leadership development program was established, with an emphasis on certifying skilled master teachers for exemplary demonstrations of Developmental Therapy in their classrooms and for supervision, consultation, and teaching other teachers (Wood & Gunn, 1985).

As part of this staff development effort, a 212-item observational instrument was designed, field-tested, and refined to measure the classroom performance of adults working in the classroom, both professionals and paraprofessionals.[12] The result was the *Developmental Therapy Rating Inventory of Teacher Skills* (DT/RITS), shown to be a reliable, valid, and practical instrument when used by trained supervisors (Robinson, 1982; Robinson, Wood, & Combs, 1982). To establish content validity, each item in the instrument was cross-referenced to the Developmental Therapy curriculum. A panel of expert Developmental Therapy instructors and supervisors then rated each item on a scale to determine if it was essential to Developmental Therapy. Raters also judged the appropriateness of item classifications within each section of the instrument. The sections of the instrument were Materials, Activities and Schedules, and Techniques. Items judged by the panel to be ambiguous or less than essential were either eliminated or rewritten for panel consensus. Interrater reliability studies resulted in an r of .89, and the mean item-by-item agreement between trained rater pairs was 75%. There are four forms of the DT/RITS, applicable to adults who are teaching students at different developmental stages—early childhood through secondary programs. The DT/RITS has been used continuously since that time for in-service staff development and research about adults' acquisition of skills in using the curriculum (Quirk, 1993).[13]

Gradually, the model was extended to other types of students, with and without disabilities, covering a broad age range, from 18 months to 16 years. Early age extensions of the model expanded curriculum applications for the very young, and Developmental Therapy became widely accepted as an early childhood curriculum (Knoblock, 1982; Wood & Hurley, 1977; Zabel, 1991).[14] At the same time, Developmental Therapy received attention as a curriculum with applications for older students and those in secondary programs (Braaten, 1982a, 1982b; Rich, 1982; Rizzo & Zabel, 1988; Shea & Bauer, 1987). The usefulness of Developmental Therapy–Developmental Teaching for students with varied disabilities also became apparent during this decade. For example, in collaboration with parents, we found many applications of the curriculum for children with autism and published a guidebook for adapting Developmental Therapy in schools and home programs serving young students with autism (Bachrach, Mosley, Swindle, & Wood, 1978; Gunn, 1985; Wood, Hendrick, & Gunn, 1983; Wood, Swan, & Newman, 1981).

During the 1980s there were also numerous urban and rural applications and replications of the model in many different service delivery settings: psychoeducational programs, special classes, mental health clinics, day care, Head Start, regular school classes, and home, community, and residential programs (Wood et al., 1981). When it appeared that the model had considerable potential for transportability and replication, a technical assistance and outreach office was established to provide consultation

[11] Chapter 3 describes the results of the latest research on this instrument.

[12] Parents often are members of the DTORF–R rating team. We intend that our references to professionals and paraprofessionals always include parents.

[13] Chapter 4 describes the staff development program and the development of the DT/RITS in greater detail. The four forms of the DT/RITS for teachers of students in Stages One through Four are included in Appendix 2.

[14] In 1992, Geter conducted a longitudinal study to investigate 10 years of educational placements for children with severe emotional and behavioral disabilities who received Developmental Therapy in preschool programs. Her findings showed that one-third required no further special education when they reached school age.

and staff training to any program seeking to introduce a social-emotional dimension into its curriculum and services (Davis, 1983, 1985). Because of its documented effectiveness, the model became the prototype for the statewide Georgia Psychoeducational Services Network, which currently provides mental health and special education services to about 8,500 children and youth, from birth to age 21, each year in Georgia through 24 similar networking programs. This network, replicating the original Rutland Developmental Therapy Program, includes both mental health and special education services and requires each program to use an evaluation system to document student progress. The network also specifies necessary mental health and education personnel, an array of family services, essential administrative support, and multiple placement options for obtaining a psychologically healthy educational environment in which a student can obtain the experiences essential for social and emotional maturation (Swan & Brown, 1992; Swan, Wood, & Jordan, 1991).[15]

Focus for the 1990s

The Developmental Therapy–Developmental Teaching movement continues to expand in the 1990s in response to increasing concerns about the social and emotional competence of children and youth and the underutilized power of adults to shape the direction of this development (Davis, 1994a). It is our belief that, in the context of today's social realities, adults must expand their skills and assume greater responsibility than ever before in directing the formation of social competence among our young. This is particularly true for educators and those who work in child care, in the juvenile justice system, and in social services. The current revised Developmental Therapy–Developmental Teaching curriculum and DTORF–R respond to this need.[16] Together, the curriculum and objectives comprise a model providing young people with protection against feelings of alienation, unworthiness, or an inability to control what happens to them. It also builds on universal human needs for gratification, relationships, success, attainment, and mastery as antidotes to anxiety. It responds to the plea, "Help me believe in myself." Developmental Therapy–Developmental Teaching offers adults a way to help children and youth accomplish this as they grow and develop.

For the 1990s, we believe that there must be a social-emotional-behavioral dimension to every program for children and youth. This mission challenges us to expand the applications and clarify the ways in which Developmental Therapy–Developmental Teaching is used in many different environments, with many cultural differences, and for a variety of conditions. While the model continues to be effective for children and youth who have serious emotional, social, and behavioral disabilities, we have found that those who have used Developmental Therapy in the past now are making adaptations for its use in inclusive settings for many types of children with and without disabilities. We have refocused our terms for them, calling these new applications *developmental teaching for social-emotional competence.*[17] Figure 1.8 illustrates the principal components. Developmental Teaching begins with the adult's knowledge of typical developmental milestones for social-emotional growth. This knowledge in turn guides the choices for developmentally appropriate materials and activities. Decoding behavior in order to understand students' emotional needs and feelings provides additional information for selecting growth-producing behavior management strategies. Together these elements enable adults to guide children and youth through every age and stage of development toward social-emotional competence.

This expansion has been a natural evolution of the model because this approach to teaching social-emotional competence and responsible behavior has its historical foundation in widely accepted theories about personality, behavior, and the social and emotional needs of infants, children, and youth. Recent findings about the formation of values, responsibility, social perspective-taking, social knowledge, interpersonal understanding, and moral behavior enhance the fundamental theories underlying the original model.[18] Even with this new emphasis, the expanded model should be quite familiar and comfortable to those who have used aspects of Developmental Therapy in the past, while those who are new to this curriculum should find the new edition, with its expanded emphasis on Developmental Teaching, a helpful guide for facilitating students' growth in social-emotional competence and responsible behavior through every age and stage of development.

[15]Current concerns about inclusion for students with disabilities are not new to Developmental Therapy–Developmental Teaching with its emphasis on multiple placement options. This curriculum can add a focus on social-emotional competence to educational programs for infants, children, or youth in any setting.

[16]This latest edition describes the curriculum revised since the 1986 edition of *Developmental Therapy in the Classroom.* The most recent revision of the teaching objectives is the DTORF–R, described in Chapter 3 (Wood, 1992a, 1992b).

[17]Because social competence is a latent trait, we operationalize it as a composite of four interdependent developmental domains—*doing, saying, caring,* and *thinking*—that interact to produce a social-emotional status through which social competence is inferred.

[18]The theoretical foundations for Developmental Therapy–Developmental Teaching are summarized in Chapter 2.

Figure 1.8. The principal components of Developmental Teaching.

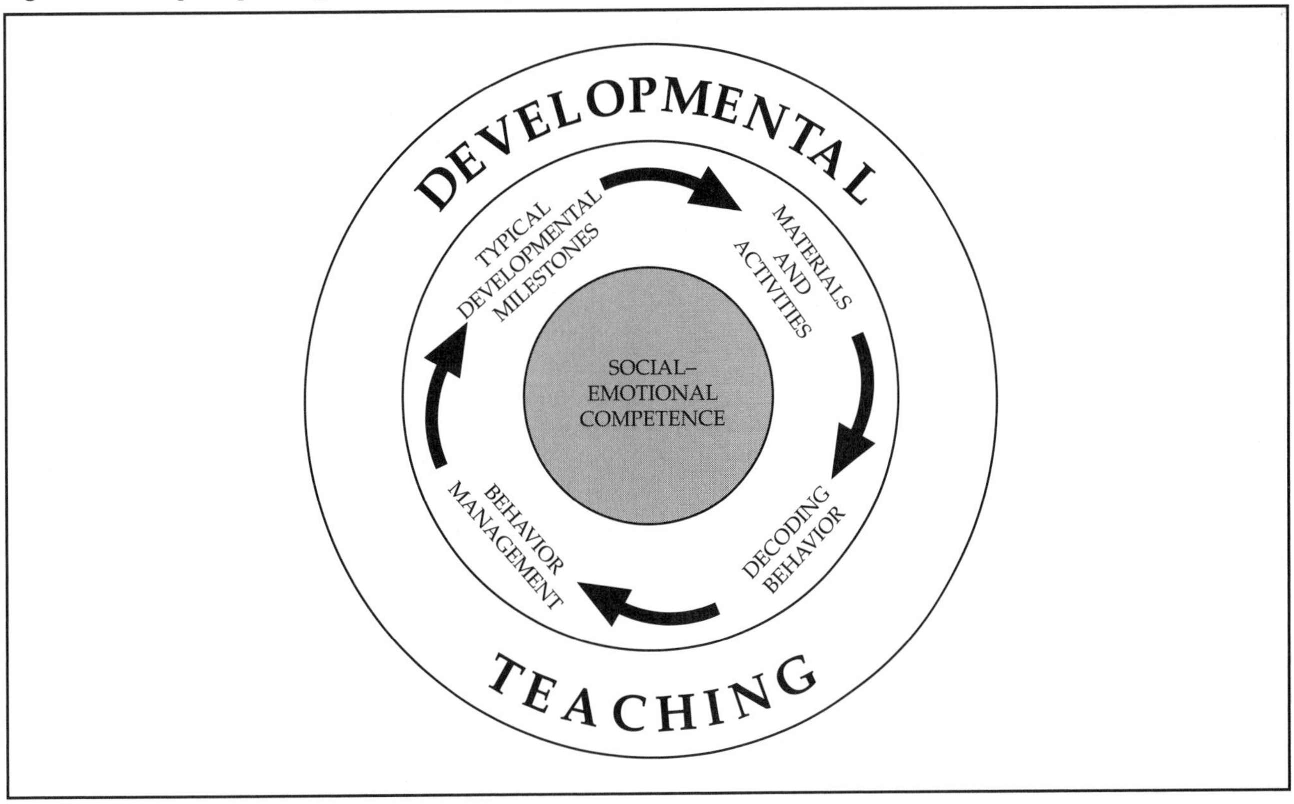

SUMMARY

The notion that all children can be rated at certain developmental levels is certainly not new. Most adults make some type of developmental assessment, formally or informally, as they plan their students' programs. What is new is the Developmental Therapy–Developmental Teaching translation of knowledge about students' social and emotional needs into effective practices—a curriculum that enhances students' social, emotional, and behavioral development. Developmental Therapy–Developmental Teaching provides a systematic way for adults to do this and to adjust their strategies to the changing characteristics of students as they progress. This approach provides a way to plan the most effective program and environments to facilitate continuing development. By understanding the complex connection between a student's social and emotional development, culture, age, prior experience, and environment, adults can provide programs that are directly relevant to the individual student's needs.

After 25 years of development, demonstration, evaluation, revisions, refinements, and replications, the following observations can be made:

- Developmental Therapy–Developmental Teaching focuses on improving the social competence of students for whom traditional programs have been limited in effectiveness or incomplete in scope.
- The model is used with infants, children, and youth from birth to 16 years of age, with and without disabilities.
- It has been shown to be effective with students with disabilities, especially those with social, emotional, and behavioral problems or autism, and with those who have special needs or who are at risk.
- The model has been successfully applied in many settings, from typical and inclusive programs in elementary and secondary schools, day care, preschools, kindergartens, children's homes, and Head Start programs to specialized services in clinics, special education programs, residential schools, and mental health clinics.

- There is a philosophy and theory that professionals, paraprofessionals, volunteers, case workers, clinicians, and parents find easy to understand and implement.
- The curriculum is used in conjunction with other academic and social skills curricula, expanding options for simultaneously enchancing the academic achievement and personal development of students.
- The Developmental Teaching Objectives are used in the IEP, the ITP, or the IFSP for social-emotional goals and objectives as required by U.S. Public Laws 94-142, 99-457, and 102-119.
- There is built-in evaluation to document student progress.
- A reliable and valid instrument (the DTORF–R) is used to assess a student's social-emotional status, select teaching objectives, and document students' progress.
- The model has a detailed staff development plan and a reliable instrument (the DT/RITS) to assess acquisition of skills by staff.
- The model advocates multioption educational placements, seeking the environments that are best able to provide for a student's social-emotional growth.
- There are multicultural applications and translations of Developmental Therapy in Argentina, Canada, China, Germany, Peru, Puerto Rico, Quebec, Scotland, and the Virgin Islands, as well as 135 quality replications in 27 U.S. states.

We hope this introduction to *Developmental Therapy–Developmental Teaching* has led you to consider your own beliefs and practices concerning the social and emotional needs of students. We hope you have seen the widespread application of the curriculum for all children and youth who are in need of help in developing social and emotional competence and responsible behavior. We also hope you have seen how Developmental Therapy can help in the process of educating students with special needs, especially those with severe social, emotional, and behavioral problems. We believe that this approach will be helpful to adults who seek ways to stay focused and relevant to individual students. We think often of the comment made by an experienced teacher of students with learning disabilities and severe social, emotional, and behavioral problems:

> *"Once you learn to think developmentally, you think that way for life!"*

PRACTICE

Using the key points in this chapter

Here are minivignettes of several students recently referred for special education by their regular classroom teachers. To give you practice thinking with a Developmental Therapy–Developmental Teaching frame of reference, answer the questions below for each child. You may find it frustrating to try to answer these questions with such limited information. However, this practice should help you think about the relationship of the students' ages to the impact of their problems on their social-emotional competence. This exercise should help you learn to identify the stages and goals of the Developmental Therapy–Developmental Teaching curriculum and to accommodate an individual student's social-emotional stage into an effective educational program.

1. What typical stage of social-emotional development would you expect for this student's age?
2. Based on this limited description, which developmental stage describes the student's level of social-emotional functioning, and what is the goal for that stage?
3. Is the student just beginning the stage, well into it, or about to finish it?
4. What adult role would enhance the student's social-emotional development in this stage?
5. As a teacher, what could you do to convey this role to the student?
6. What activities might catch this student's interest and help promote social-emotional development at the same time?
7. What other information would you need before planning this student's educational program?

Alice

Five-year-old Alice is in a Head Start program. She is in constant motion and frequently talks to herself. She seems unable to concentrate on anything. She will not participate with other children and avoids adults. When she is pressured to join in or participate, her face twitches and she mutters unintelligible jargon under her breath. When she is disciplined or required to do something, she seems to lose all control, screaming, crying, kicking, cursing, and occasionally hitting her parents.

Bob

Bob is a gifted, creative, and violent 9-year-old with an IQ of 134. He is highly verbal, cruel, and hostile to adults and peers. His academic profile shows fifth- to seventh-grade achievement.

Clark

A physically large and awkward 10-year-old, Clark was referred to a special education program because of marked swings in mood. He is sullen, noncompliant, and given to violent rages. Presently achieving at the first-grade level, Clark has a lifelong history of street experience, antisocial behavior, and extreme psychological and socioeconomic deprivation. He says he is a member of a gang, but others say he only hangs around them.

Ellen

Ellen is an 11-year-old girl who centers her energies on peer relationships and modeling seductive adult behaviors. She is verbally and socially interactive with peers and adults. However, her skills are only evident when she is in charge, selecting an activity, or directing others. When crossed, she stops participating or becomes physically abusive, attacking teachers or peers. Her academic achievement is generally at the fifth-grade level.

Drew

Almost 13 years old, Drew has no friends and seeks none. He has a long history of negative behaviors, verbal abuse, and acting out toward his family, teachers, neighbors, and peers. Lately, his antisocial behavior outside of school has increased. His parents reported him to the juvenile justice authorities for stealing from neighbors' homes and mailboxes. In class he loses control if teachers attempt to direct him.

CHAPTER 2

Social Competence, Emotions, and Responsible Behavior

Self-esteem grows to be a conviction that one is learning effective steps toward a tangible future, and is developing into a defined self within a social reality.

—ERIC H. ERIKSON, 1950/1963, P. 235

SOCIAL-EMOTIONAL COMPETENCE: FROM THEORY TO PERSONAL RESPONSIBILITY

Personal conduct, day by day, shapes the person. As educators and parents, in acknowledging the importance of preparing our young people to be competent, we are saying that they must learn personal responsibility. Responsibility requires regulating one's own conduct—being accountable and answering for one's own deeds. Unfortunately, the idea of personal responsibility seems to have fallen into some disfavor. In its place, we frequently hear that it is someone else's fault. Whatever the mistake, incident, or crisis, someone else is to blame. Too often we hear our students say, "It's his fault," "That's not my problem," "I didn't do it!" "Why should I?" "You can blame her," "That's their problem." These comments are simply everyday indicators of a lack of responsibility.

Responsible behavior does not come easily in the process of growing up. We know many adults who have failed. Responsible behavior comes with the gradual expansion of a child's capacity to behave in ways that are responsive both to inner needs and to the expectations of others. In guiding this development, teachers and parents must have the big picture about how young people characteristically *behave, speak, relate,* and *think* at every age and stage of development. This knowledge provides the principles and guidelines that direct the day-to-day choices we make in our interactions with all children.

In every stage of life, the goals and objectives change as the demands and expectations made upon children change. The extent to which they can successfully fulfill the demands at one stage and adapt to the expectations of the next is an indicator of their general adjustment and social-emotional competence. We set a course using this knowledge and continually remind ourselves of the developmental goals and objectives as we interact with our children in each situation and in every stage of life. It is a greater challenge to assist children with social, emotional, and behavioral disabilities. We must understand the events that have shaped their development. Then we must plan their educational programs to minimize the destructive impact of these problems on their present and future ability to succeed.

In this chapter, we draw together the major translations we have made from theory and research about the nature of social-emotional development, with implications for providing therapeutic assistance in the schools. To organize the material, we refer you again to the focus we have chosen for the last decade of this century—*Developmental Teaching for social-emotional competence.* We believe that an effective curriculum must maintain the focus on adults as the essential influence in shaping the social-emotional development of children and youth. We explore the theoretical foundations for this approach using developmental stages and developmental characteristics of children and youth when designing educational practices. We review the current definitions and theories about what constitutes social-emotional competence. Then we trace the trajectories of typical development through each age and stage, from birth to age 16. We end the chapter with a summary of theories about how emotions, anxiety, and values shape social competence and responsible behavior. These theories are the foundation for the Developmental Therapy–Developmental Teaching curriculum.

How are theories about developmental stages useful?

Developmental stages are simply descriptions of clusters of characteristics that can typically be found occurring together in normal patterns of development. Stages provide guidelines for grouping children with similar characteristics, thereby allowing adults to focus their selection of activities, materials, and instructional techniques to meet specific developmental needs. Stages also define changes that are needed in the roles of the adult to facilitate the social-emotional growth of children.

By keeping a general stage focus in teaching a specific group of children, you can avoid programming that is too *advanced* for their current level of development. And by using developmental knowledge about them, you also can avoid holding them back with programs that are *below* their current level of development. This latter problem occurs frequently in the best of situations. It may happen because you find a highly successful activity or teaching strategy. It works so you use it, and with repeated use of a successful technique a child will progress. Progress means change. But when change occurs in a child, your teaching strategy generally must also change. The principle is quite clear: When a teaching strategy works, it is usually time to change. The sequence of stages and the developmental milestones within stages provide a guide for the changes you must continually make in your own strategies as you respond to changes in the development of children.

Surprisingly, teachers who use stage concepts in grouping students report that this procedure also simplifies the task of individualizing instruction within a group. Is this a contradiction—providing for individual needs in a group? Not when you consider the theoretical structure of a stage and apply it to a group of students at a particular stage. Figure 2.1 illustrates this.

Think of a stage as a bell-shaped curve representing the *overall stage*. The stage is organized and bound together by a set of structures, each possessing an organized pattern of characteristics and relationships to each other. Any stage is characterized by the sum of these relationships, and an overall stage name is used to describe it. This description provides the adult with a global description for the entire group.

The structures within the stage each have their own purposes and goals that contribute to social-emotional development. The sensorimotor-behavioral system, cognitive system, social-affective system, and social-communication system are examples of structures. Each system can serve as a *curriculum area*. Thus, the teacher working with students at a particular stage will have not only a general goal for the stage but also a set of goals reflecting what is to be accomplished within each curriculum area at that stage.

Further analysis of each system reveals a series of very specific operations. This is where individual differences are identified by the actual individual behaviors of each student during any given activity. When specified, they become the individual program *objectives* used by the adult to guide the activities of each individual within the group.

Finally, moment by moment during the instructional process, there is a sequence of small *learning units*. Identified through task analysis, these small steps combine to produce specific task mastery, which in turn links to mastery of the objectives. Learning theorists call this process "chaining." Cognitive developmentalists call this "transformation of structures" (Loevinger, 1987).

This schematic way of looking at a stage also gives us a way to conceptualize the process of development. The process probably occurs like this: First, a child is generally recognized to be at a particular stage of development. This stage is described in a broad way, but by analyzing the parts of the stage, you see a number of structures operating. You select objectives for changing the operation of these structures by further analysis of each student's individual profile of current developmental functioning. When you break down each objective into small steps, you individualize your plan for teaching the objectives. As you teach and the child participates, changes in the operating structures are set in motion. When these changes become assimilated into a child's structures, we say that objectives have been mastered. Mastery occurs in two forms: (a) incremental changes in the structures and (b) qualitative changes through acquisition of new elements and directions in the structures.

When both types of changes result in satisfying outcomes, they become assimilated into the core of a child's response system. Thus, a spiraling expansion of capacities can occur. Over time such a process produces social and emotional growth. For example, consider impulse control. On a continuum, a child develops from no control of impulses at birth to possession of a highly sophisticated control system as an adult. The common characteristic is impulsivity,

Figure 2.1. Theoretical structure of a group of students at the same stage of development with educational referents.

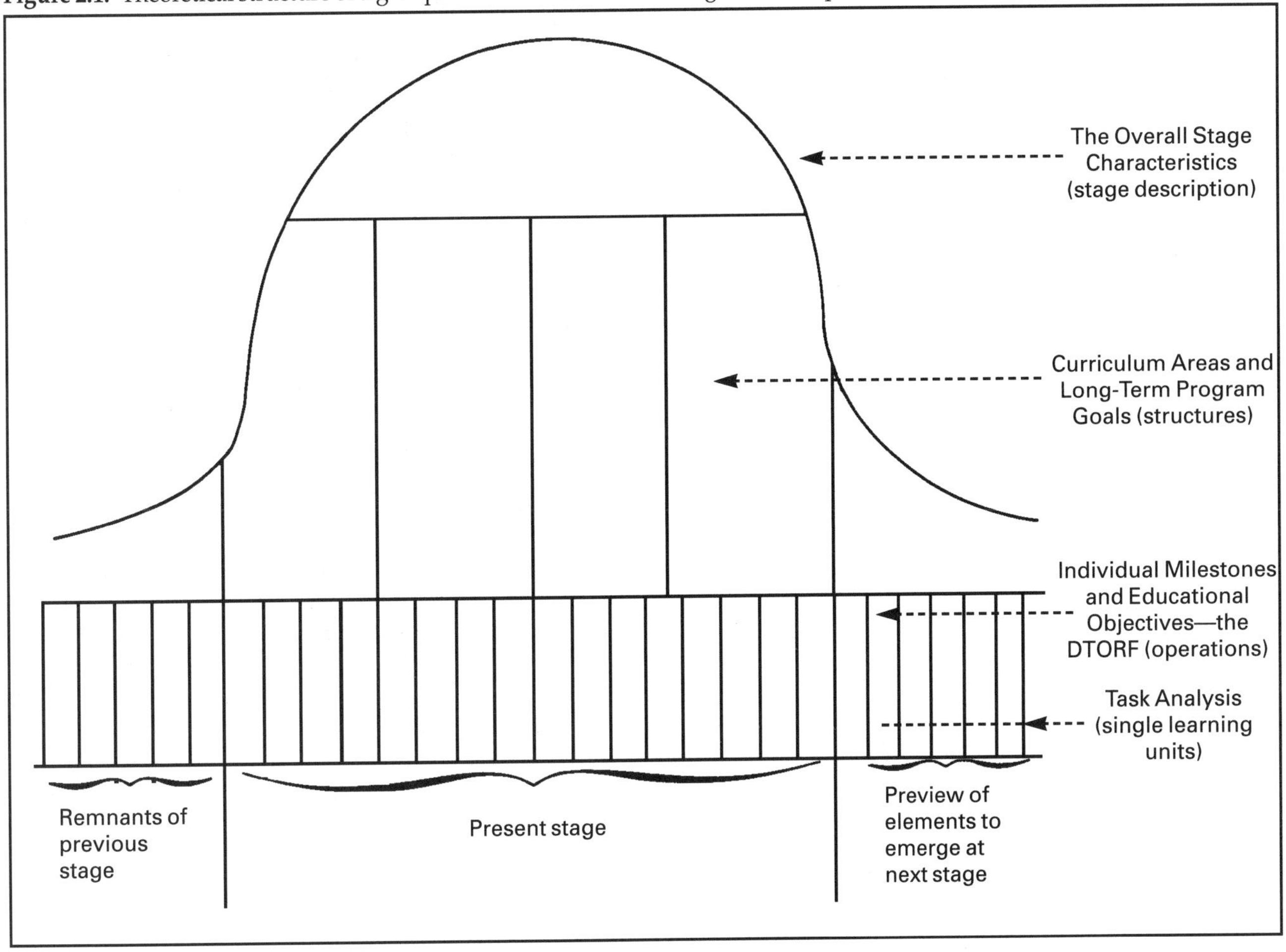

occurring at all phases of life. The incremental aspect of this developmental line is the amount of control exercised. More and more control develops with age. However, the strategies used by an individual for impulse control at various stages of development are qualitatively different.

One caution about stages. They have complex and unique characteristics that both differentiate them from past stages and connect them to the stage that follows. A child in a particular stage may exhibit remnants of the previous stage while showing characteristics of the present stage and also manifesting a preview of behavior that will emerge more fully at the next stage. Piaget (1972, p. 21) identifies this phenomenon as *décalage*, and Turiel (1983, p. 19) explains further that these developmental transitions from stage to stage are gradual and occur within domains rather than abruptly across all domains at the same time. Bandura (1986, p. 81) describes this process, calling it a *mixed index of developmental level.* In a critique of current findings about social learning theories and cognitive developmentalism, Loevinger (1987, pp. 191–193) also describes this view that diversity of skills at a given stage should be called "horizontal décalage." For the adult, it is helpful to keep this phenomenon in mind when regression occurs in a child's behavior. Remember, it may be only a remnant of past behavior that will not be difficult to restructure. It is also important to watch for unexpected new behaviors. These tell you that development is occurring, an indication that it is time to begin changing instructional strategies.

Stages, then, are clusters of characteristics. They have a connection to the stage occurring before and the one that will develop next. Consideration of developmental stages and sequences permits you to identify both individual, qualitative differences within a stage and incremental progress on a number of specific, continuous stage dimensions. From individual differences you can obtain information about the unique coping strategies of a child at any point in time. These short-term fluctuations are important because they represent day-to-day expressions of the individual. From the study of the incremental trends over time, you can obtain information about where an individual is on a continuum of tasks when a program begins, the time it takes to accomplish several developmental sequences, patterns of mastery, and sequences for the future. Such information is extremely useful in the context of preparing, implementing, and evaluating an IEP, IFSP, or ITP.

How can developmental characteristics of children be used to shape educational practices?

Although there continues to be debate about what constitute the most significant developmental characteristics of children and youth to address in a program, we believe that in Developmental Therapy–Developmental Teaching significant characteristics have been identified for social and emotional development. We also believe that these are among the developmental characteristics with universal relevance when they are applied in the context of an individual's unique life space. We have seen children of all ages, with and without disabilities and with diverse cultural values, who have common developmental skills that appear to transcend cultural differences. Among the skills that appear to be universally recognized are those described by Bowman and Stott (1994, p. 120): "establishing mutually satisfying social relationships, organizing and integrating perceptions, learning language, developing category systems, thinking, imagining, and creating." At particular ages, these skills are expressed in unique sets of characteristics called *stage characteristics*. These are not narrow and restrictive attributes but, rather, are broad and relevant to individual uniqueness. When adults use these stage characteristics as a guide in planning individualized programs for children, they are able to match strategies to the unique needs of each student. This approach holds great promise for increasingly responsive forms of interaction and intervention. By incorporating a transactional perspective into a developmental framework, a program "places development and learning squarely within its social context, with careful examination of the role of the social partner in supporting a child's role within the situation being examined" (McCollum & Blair, 1994, p. 95). It seems evident that when developmentally appropriate practices are individually relevant, they provide a way to create a sense of comfort and confidence in children of every age and can lead to increased social-emotional competence and personal responsibility.

Among some early childhood educators, debate continues about the efficacy of the "developmentally appropriate practices" (DAP) published as guidelines by the National Association for the Education of Young Children (Bredekamp, 1987). Although many have acclaimed the guidelines as an important contribution to increasing basic standards for early childhood education, others have mobilized arguments against theoretical limitations and didactic constraints of DAP (Carta, Schwartz, Atwater, & McConnell, 1991). The resulting discourse has opened new inquiry into old views of child development. Traditional interpretations of theory have been challenged, voicing many of the same concerns that prompted the formulation of the practices we now call Developmental Therapy–Developmental Teaching. New and Mallory (1994, p. 9) summarize the common themes in this debate: "(a) agreement that the DAP guidelines were necessary at the time they were produced but represent an insufficient framework when they are limited to theory that is *ethnocentrically narrow*; (b) a need for congruence between values, beliefs, and goals . . . in early childhood programs and those of the children and families for whom the programs are designed; and (c) finding new means of assessment, instruction, and program design that are responsive to the most significant characteristics of young children."

What is social-emotional competence?

To have social-emotional competence is to get along with others in life as a social being while fulfilling one's own needs. The process is also called *socialization*. The *Head Start Program Performance Standards* (1995, pp. 1–2, Sec. 1304.1–3) describe social competence as "the child's everyday effectiveness in dealing with both present environment and later responsibilities in school and life. Social competence takes into account the interrelatedness of cognitive and intellectual development, physical and mental health, nutritional needs, and other factors that enable a developmental approach to helping children achieve social competence." Theorists agree that socialization simultaneously involves experiences with others and forces within an individual. There is also agreement that many interacting processes within an individual combine to produce social competence: thoughts (cognition), social knowledge, language, feelings (emotions), values, interests, and motivations. An individual's *experience* provides the mix for these processes and is the catalyst for change and development. Elliot Turiel (1983) describes social development as "a process by which individuals generate understandings of the social world, by making inferences and forming theories about experienced social events." Eric Erikson (1977, p. 139) provides an action-oriented expansion of this view, describing development as "an expanding arena of interplay" between self and society—a lifelong process. This definition of social development suggests two powerful and demanding forces—the self and others—which cannot be one-sided or adversarial and still be productive. It implies that social development is characteristically different at each stage of an individual's life, gaining in complexity and breadth as the individual develops. It also suggests that these competing forces somehow involve an individual's striving for satisfaction and gratifying associations with others. Robert Selman's model of interpersonal understanding (1980, pp. 22–23) provides a systematic way of looking at this developmental process of gaining social knowledge. Sometimes called social cognition, social perspective taking, or interpersonal perspective taking, social knowledge is an essential part of acquiring social competence—understanding others and interacting effectively.

Most theorists acknowledge that cognition and emotions interact in significant ways for social development. When an experience evokes an emotion, the mind recognizes some familiar aspect of the experience that has particular meaning. A feeling is attached to this recognition and an unsolicited physical alteration in behavior occurs. The behavioral reaction is not a deliberate response to the symbols or feelings but is activated somehow by that memory. The exact nature of this remembering-feeling-thinking-behaving relationship is not clearly understood. Questions have been raised about whether cognition leads to an emotional state or whether the reverse is true—that is, a feeling triggers a cognitive sequence. Lewis and Rosenblum (1978, pp. 4–5) introduce the idea that feelings (negative and positive) involve an alteration in a person's physical state, a thinking response, an observable behavior, and an actual awareness of each of these conditions by the individual, who then adds further meaning to the condition in an evaluative-interpretive process. The implication is that feelings are ever expanding with each experience. The authors also emphasize the point that any single process cannot fully explain emotions and their development: "Affect and its development may best be viewed as embedded in the child's total social, psychological, and physical maturation. In our view, study of neither the child's biology nor his experiences, neither his social network nor his intraindividual dynamics can afford us the body of information we seek for an understanding of affect, its expression, its development, and its meaning" (p. 10).

It seems evident that emotions (affect) influence behavior, cognition, motivation, attitudes, and values. And all of these processes are directly influenced by experiences with people—the social environment. Michael Guralnick (1992, p. 41) proposes a theoretical model to illustrate how these many components result in social competence. His model emphasizes the integration of language, cognition, affect, and motor skills on social and communication skills needed to effectively carry out a social task. In his model, Guralnick bridges from theory to implications for practice through his emphasis on "strategies within a social task." He hypothesizes that there are certain trajectories or pathways by which several processes develop, interact, and emerge as social competencies, which he calls "strategies" for specific social tasks.

These fundamental processes provide the theoretical foundations for defining social-emotional development and building a curriculum for social-emotional competence. We believe it is necessary to integrate all of these processes if the knowledge is to be applied successfully. It is also necessary to adjust a curriculum to children's individual responses to others and their life experiences at different ages and stages of development. Yet the developmental trajectories for acquiring social-emotional competence are fairly predictable, and most individuals follow the same major milestones in developing social-emotional competence.

Figure 2.2 illustrates the way the Developmental Therapy–Developmental Teaching curriculum integrates these same complex processes. The idea is that social-emotional competence is the integration of several basic systems: the sensorimotor-behavioral system, the social-communication system, the social-affective system, and the cognitive system. These systems begin developing before birth and increase in complexity as the child becomes an adult. The Developmental Therapy–Developmental Teaching curriculum operationalizes this framework with a particular emphasis on *doing, saying, caring*, and *thinking*. These four systems interact to produce social-emotional growth progressively through each stage. Neither social-emotional competence nor responsible behavior can develop without involvement of all four of these processes.[1]

Notice that the sequence of growth in this illustration combines the four basic developmental processes into a general statement about the primary focus for each stage and identifies a typical age when the goals and objectives for the stage should be accomplished under optimal conditions.[2] Adults use these goals in sequential steps with the Developmental Teaching Objectives to guide the process and the DTORF–R to track each other's progress.

Doing: The Sensorimotor-Behavioral System

The sensorimotor-behavioral system, with its reflexes, senses, and neuromuscular functions, is the means by which a child interacts with each person and every event in the environment. This system is the enabler through which the other systems find expression. At its beginning, *doing* involves simply being aware. With awareness, other processes begin to grow: attending to a stimulus, simple motor responses, body control, coordination, recognizing essentials and nonessentials in the environment, and participating in routine activities. More advanced processes include impulse control, attention span, organizing responses into systems, and involvement with rules as a basis for regulating individual behavior. These processes must be acquired before more complex behavioral skills can develop. As behavior comes under increasing verbal and cognitive control, skills are sufficiently well developed to expect acceptable group behavior, which in turn fosters success in games, sports, and teamwork. Rules, fairness, and justice become powerful behavioral regulators. Group social skills increase. Friendships emerge as

[1] Appendix 4 contains summary charts detailing the processes that make up the four systems for doing, saying, caring, and thinking, and shows where these processes occur in the sequences of the curriculum stages. We use these charts to describe the content validity of the curriculum.

[2] The unique focus and characteristics of each curriculum stage are summarized in Figure 1.4. The specific instructional goals for each process at each stage are outlined in Figure 3.2.

Figure 2.2. The elements of social-emotional development and the stages of the Developmental Therapy–Developmental Teaching curriculum.

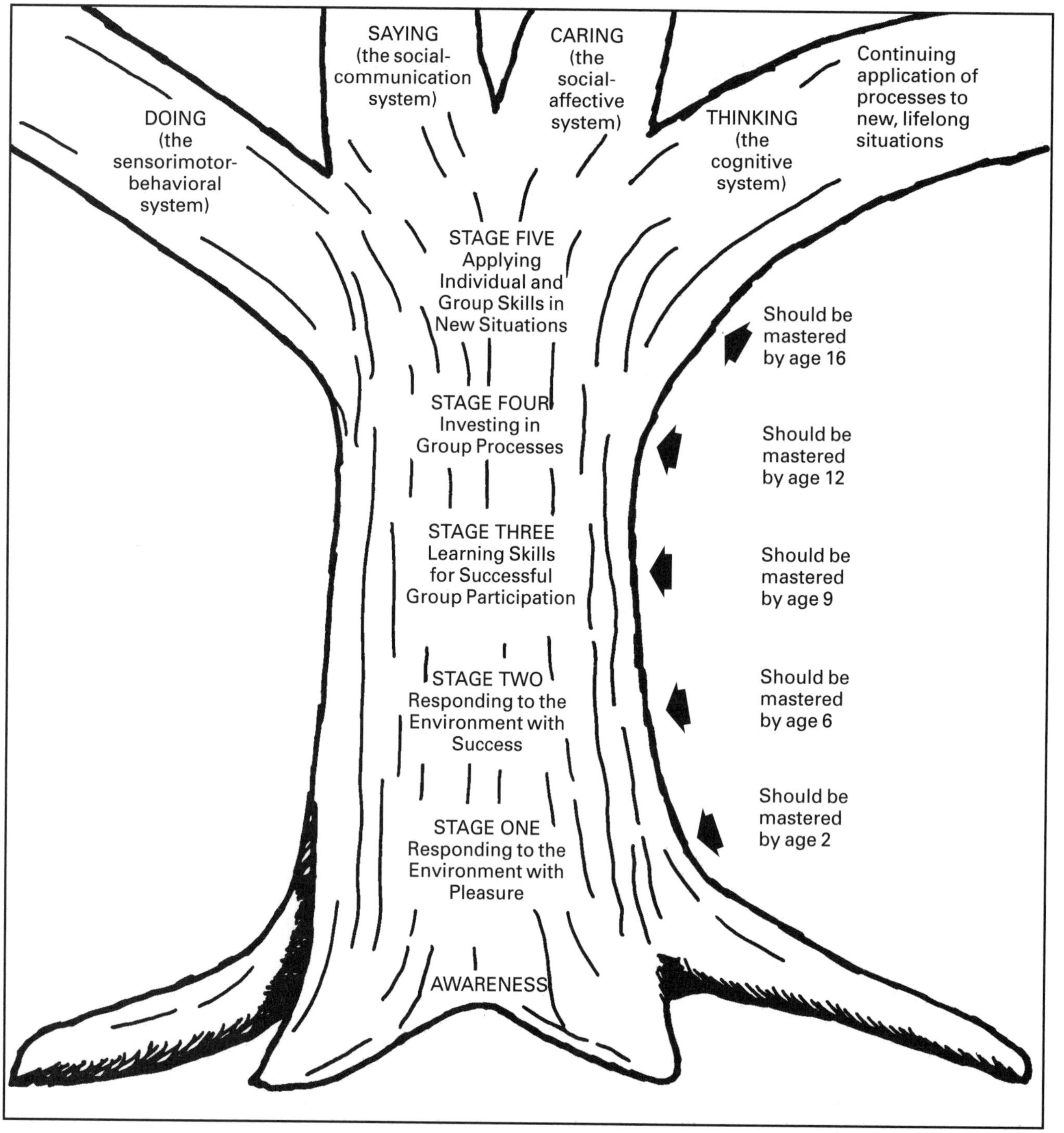

significant influences on behavior, and, increasingly, values regulate personal behavior.

From the viewpoint of this curriculum, observed behavior at any point on this continuum of skills is the outward evidence of previously learned behavior activated by memories—thoughts and feelings—in response to a specific person or event in the present. Adults observe the behavior of children to determine if they are studying, learning, participating, and progressing as planned. We also observe behavior that may indicate if things are not going smoothly for a child. The most important caution to use when observing behavior is to avoid evaluating a behavior in isolation. Behavior should not be considered apart from its meaning to the child and the context where it occurs. To apply a developmental orientation to observed behavior is to use knowledge about a child's previous behaviors (historical as well as immediately preceding events). It also means considering expectations about the child's future behavior.

Doing: The Sensorimotor-Behavioral System

Attending with awareness
Responding
Playing
Participating
Understanding rules and expectations
Regulating one's own behavior
Imitating behavioral role models
Accepting responsibility for one's actions
Seeking new skills and new experiences
Participating in group governance
Regulating personal behavior by values

Social learning theorists continue to address the question of how behavior is acquired, maintained, and changed. Although their findings are not usually expressed in a developmental context, they provide important explanations about the origins of responsible behavior (Bandura, 1986). Bandura's studies of the subprocesses involved in observational learning—specifically attentional, retentional, production, and motivational processes—provide a valuable synthesis of decades of research into social learning and the phenomenon of acquisition of behavior by modeling the behavior of others (pp. 47–105). In Developmental Therapy–Developmental Teaching, we find that this social learning theory guides our understanding that children's behavior develops in many different ways. We use these strategies from social learning theory, applying them to behavioral learning in a developmental sequence (Bandura & Walters, 1963, pp. 47–60):

- direct experience that has a successful outcome
- attention to the modeled behavior of others
- social meaning communicated through TV, stories, pictures, drama, and role play
- examples set by others
- memory and thinking processes
- vicarious experiences of others' successes and failures
- social status in the peer group
- self-reinforcement, self-reward, self-censure, and self-disengagement

In summary, a developmentalist looking at the sensorimotor-behavioral system sees a gradual expansion of a child's capacity to use behavior to mediate between a personal need to express oneself and the forces in the environment impinging on that personal need. With increasingly sophisticated ways to monitor and modify personal behavior, a child gradually changes behavioral style so that behavior becomes a way to expand the social self, rather than an end in itself.

Saying: The Social-Communication System

This curriculum area emphasizes the social purpose in communication and includes both verbal and nonverbal forms of conveying meaning. The social-communication system expands gradually in semantic and linguistic skills in interaction with cognition and social knowledge. An individual's path of development moves from vocal utterances to communal language and inner thought, and in doing so it becomes an essential aspect of an individual's quest for identity and a sense of self. The most basic acts of communication are social in nature: smiling, crying, gesturing, watching, imitating others, producing speech sounds, and using simple word sequences in experiences with others. As language skills, cognition, and social knowledge increase, a child is able to listen, describe feelings and characteristics of self and others, convey information, and express feelings through words. Clearly a child must have these basic language skills to progress in social-emotional development. For older children, communication skills are essential to the development of more elaborate forms of language and inner thought and take on an increasingly complex social dimension. Coping with the complexities in their lives demands effective communication skills. Many children with social, emotional, and behavioral problems have failed to develop the basic communication skills and social knowledge needed for successful interaction with others. At the juncture of verbal exchanges between adults and children or between children, failure to understand is often exacerbated into crisis proportions.

A conversational or natural teaching approach to social communication is used in Developmental Therapy–Developmental Teaching because of our concern for learning and generalizing language in everyday social conversations. In

Saying: The Social-Communication System

Conveying needs with preverbal speech
Listening with receptive language
Responding with spontaneous language
Thinking aloud
Conveying intentions and information
Describing experiences
Describing characteristics of oneself and others
Exchanging in social groups
Elaborating on experiences
Expressing feelings of oneself and others
Conveying abstract thoughts and ideas

the program, we emphasize language skills in a social context and provide opportunities for children to influence others directly through their language. Arwood (1991) provides a series of fundamental suggestions that we have found useful in adjusting instruction to a child's developmental level concerned with the social aspects of language development (pp. 20–22):

- Teach simple semantic structures before more elaborate speech forms are taught.
- Provide many varied experiences in using language to expand knowledge of people and understanding of experiences.
- Keep semantic tasks at children's levels of individual development.
- Provide variations in materials and activities that promote expanding and enriching concepts.
- Promote abundant verbal productions from children.
- Encourage spontaneous productions instead of structured responses or direct imitation of adults' language.

Our basic guideline for social communication in Developmental Therapy–Developmental Teaching is to systematically include abundant opportunities for speech acts in the daily program for students at all stages of development. A classroom that is focused this way is a room where student conversation is dynamic and evident. Requests for objects, materials, and information are frequent, with much conversation about actions and exchange of information. Language preferably flows between students. And adults redirect language interactions from themselves to promote increased peer exchanges from student to student.

Caring: The Social-Affective System

Positive relationships with others are the centerpiece of the social-affective part of this curriculum—caring for oneself and caring for others. Effective relationships require social knowledge, conscience, interpersonal perspective-taking, empathy, friendship, altruism, and moral values. In turn, these processes combine to govern social behavior. Feelings and emotions are the affective dimension of this complex system and are present in every social experience. At every age and stage of development, inner needs, feelings, and emotions shape children's interactions with others, influencing how they view themselves and others. The process is called *identity formation* by psychologists (Erikson, 1959/1980, p. 122). A sense of identity and self-esteem is fundamental for healthy personality development. In this process, social knowledge, self-esteem, and moral values are formed from personal experiences, friendships, and relationships with others, both peers and adults. Relationships with a potential for physical or psychological harm, matters of reward and punishment, and observations about violence, life, and death all contribute to children's capacity to care about themselves or others (Kohlberg, 1981). The two necessary ingredients in successful relationships between child and adult are care and respect (Selman, 1989). Successful relationships influence a young person's values and conscience development—choices about right and wrong, justice and injustice.

In the curriculum, *caring* begins with teaching children to be aware of adults—to look to them for stimulation, interaction, and pleasure. By receiving nurture and care from adults, a child responds with positive feelings. The earliest goal is to create in a child the feeling that the environment is a good place to be and adults really care. This early nurture and care meet fundamental dependency needs and are the essential foundations for successful interpersonal relationships later—caring for others, love relationships, attitudes, feelings, and values. Socialization becomes an organized system when a child has learned interpersonal skills for successful interactions with a number of different people—peers and adults (Howes, Droege, & Phillipsein, 1992). To do this, a positive sense of self and self-confidence, growing from successful experiences with others must be developed

Caring: The Social-Affective System

Recognizing and trusting adults
Forming attachment and dependency
Achieving autonomy and mastery
Asserting oneself
Valuing oneself
Cooperating with others
Forming friendships and a social self
Learning to be a group member
Forming personal convictions
Regulating relationships with moral values

(Kegan, 1982). More advanced socialization processes then can include expanding social awareness, taking turns, suggesting activities, sharing, participating in what others suggest, recognizing characteristics of others, developing preferences for friends, supporting others, and eventually participating as an invested member of a group (Parke, Cassidy, Burks, Carson, & Boyum, 1992).

During these sequential stages of social-affective development, a child seeks and finds people, ideas, and behaviors to imitate and value. This process demands top priority in planning successful interventions; this is why we put such an emphasis on the roles played by adults in a program. They are surrogates for all adults the students have experienced in the past—the stand-in for authority, kindness, brutality, or any other image created by their experiences with other adults. Children bring these feelings to the program each day. Their private realities are full of attitudes and beliefs about adults, setting the stage for their behavior in each interaction with adults.[3]

Thinking: The Cognitive System

Cognition is an essential dimension of social-emotional competence. In a broad sense, cognition is the mental act of knowing and the process by which knowledge is acquired. However, this definition is insufficient for an understanding of the role of cognition in social-emotional development. Flavell, Miller, and Miller (1993, p. 2) speak to the difficulty in determining what is to be included and left out of a definition of cognition: "Mental processes habitually intrude themselves into virtually *all* human psychological processes and activities, and consequently there is no really principled, nonarbitrary place to stop." However, there is general agreement among theorists that cognition is a dynamic, simultaneous exchange between a person and the environment in which learning is generated from direct experience, feelings, ideas, and actions with people, materials, and events. This constantly changing process is a social-cognitive model of learning and it blends easily into a developmental perspective that emphasizes the ever-changing organization and reorganization of mental structures. According to Piaget (1967, 1977), the preeminent developmental theorist, cognitive structures either permit or impede a student's capacity to use an experience constructively.

At beginning levels, the *thinking* part of the curriculum involves kinesthetic sensations, sensorimotor learning, attention, eye-hand coordination, perceptual processing, memory, discriminating similarities and differences, classifying, concept building, receptive language, use of objects, recognizing details in pictures, and concepts of number and conservation. With increased development, these basic processes lead to more complex ones—recognizing signs and symbols, producing ideas, evaluating, and using principles to solve problems. Cognition is necessary for understanding cause-and-effect relationships, reality consequences, right and wrong, values, and social knowledge. Such advanced processes also are essential for academic achievement, personal enrichment, management of feelings and anxieties, effective social behavior, and creative interpersonal problem solving.

Just as the other systems in the curriculum depend upon each other, *thinking* depends upon behavior and language for expression—and change is the dynamic force in its development. The curriculum uses change as a fundamental principle for planning learning experiences and choosing management strategies that support learning. The entire curriculum is built on the premise that change is the process through which goals are achieved. The process of change in a child's cognitive structure may occur something like this: First, the child's existing mental structure has a homeostatic quality, suggesting balance and stability. This is the time when adults usually relax and continue their proven strategies. Then, changes in mental structures are put in motion when inner or environmental demands disrupt the balance, causing mental or emotional disequilibrium in the child.

[3]Later in this chapter, we discuss the role of adults in greater detail and explain how it should be varied according to a child's stage of social-emotional development. See also Chapter 7 for a detailed exploration of adults' skills.

Thinking: The Cognitive System

Forming sensorimotor responses
Imitating
Forming object permanence and memory
Coordinating body movements
Playing
Processing visual perceptions
Sequencing
Forming concepts
Understanding relational concepts
Using symbol systems
Recognizing cause-and-effect relationships
Using rules for problem solving
Evaluating ideas
Communicating through writing
Generalizing
Using decision making and logic
Distinguishing process and outcome

This is when adults face the child's disruption, behavioral problems, and crises, which usually require a response. How the adult responds will influence, in turn, how the child responds. Depending on the results, selective mental assimilation and accommodation of the child's new responses and understanding occur. In this way, old cognitive structures become new structures. The change takes two forms: incremental changes in the previous structures and acquisition of new ones.[4]

Play deserves a special comment here. Teachers often ask why play is included in the cognitive system for Developmental Therapy–Developmental Teaching. Play belongs in the social-affective system, as well as in the behavioral- and social-communication systems. Some basic ideas from Piaget and Erikson have guided the way play is included in the curriculum and the reasons we address it here, in the *thinking* part of the curriculum. Erikson suggests that play is a major way for children to develop social understanding (cognition). He believes that play changes form as social, interpersonal, and cognitive learning occurs from stage to stage and from experience to experience. He says, "The play of the human child, however, must orient him within the possibilities and the boundaries first of what is imaginable and possible, and then to what is most effective and most permissible in a cultural setting. . . . what he gradually learns is his society's version of reality and to become himself within the roles and techniques at his disposal" (Erikson, 1972, p. 152).

The earliest forms of play are repetitive sensorimotor activities that are learned by exploration and imitation. Then simple forms of symbolic representation emerge in which play objects are used to represent concepts in make-believe. When concepts are well developed and language becomes an essential part of play, experience is no longer bound by place, time, or object. Piaget calls this phase of play *interiorized imitations* through which a child understands something by experiencing it in play (Piaget, 1951, 1962, p. 5). Repetition in play is the way children reconstruct ideas and then, through reflexive abstractions, create new ideas. Erikson describes this phase of play as the socialization of thought. The importance of play in the development of social competence is so irrefutable that we have often suggested that almost every developmental milestone could be achieved through play activities if they were carefully designed with particular objectives in mind.

Who should be responsible for regulating children's conduct?

There is no argument among adults that children must develop responsible behavior to have social competence. Yet many adults simply take the process for granted, hoping that, somehow, children will grow into responsible behavior. Or they make great demands for responsible behavior without quite understanding how it develops. Unfortunately, personal responsibility in children and youth does not happen without careful, daily involvement of adults in the process. And because responsible behavior is redefined with each stage of maturation and every new expectation set by society, it requires continuing attention by all parents and teachers.

Responsible behavior by children does not occur when adults maintain external control at all times. These children, expecting authority and control from others, fail to

[4] Piaget (1967, p. 113) calls the process of equilibration "compensation for external intrusion."

see personal responsibility as something they must take on for themselves at some point in their lives. As they get older, such individuals, who feel that others are responsible, simply test and defy the standards for behavior set by others. Nor does responsible behavior usually happen when we turn children loose to figure it out for themselves in the "school of hard knocks." These children typically find it very difficult to accept authority or allow others to direct them. They often seek recognition and approval from adults while lashing out at them in defiance and anger.

Many psychologists believe that this hidden anger grows from disappointment. In young children, insecurity and anger come when adults fail to give them care, security, and dependability. In older children and youth, disenchantment with adults comes from a paradox in their needs—independence versus dependence. This paradox becomes increasingly important when children are in upper elementary school; if it is unresolved, it will explode during adolescence. There is a balance between these two extremes that can be regulated by the age and developmental stage of a child. For those who do mature into personal responsibility for behavior, the shift comes when there are daily opportunities for self-authority and self-regulation. Much of this growth happens in the process of making choices. A successful choice promotes greater independence and self-regulation. Each failure expands a child's defensiveness toward the people and event that brought about the failure.

In this curriculum, we gradually shift the source of authority from adults (external controls) to the child (controls from within). During the first two stages of a young child's social-emotional development, it is the adult's responsibility to convey expectations for behavior and to see that the child successfully achieves the adult's expectations. Then, during the last three stages of a child's development, the responsibility for regulating behavior is gradually shifted from adult to child.

We use the concept of the *existential crisis* to indicate whether the adult or the child should bear the primary responsibility for regulating the child's behavior at any particular point in time. The existential crisis is a developmental phenomenon that describes a shift in a child's view away from an absolute belief in the authority and omnipotence of adults. For most young children, the person with authority is the source of responsibility for behavior regulation. Their emotional need is for a caring, expert, and all-powerful adult who directs behavior, can handle all problems, provides protection, and guarantees that the world is a good place in which to be. We call this the *preexistential* phase of development, in which the adult is the benevolent authority who solves problems and dictates the required behavior that produces satisfying results. First-grade teachers know this phase of development well. Every first-grade student seeks to tell the teacher about infractions of the rules by others: "Teacher! Teacher! He's doing . . ." Such behavior is typical for this age. It indicates allegiance to adult authority. It tells us that the students are relying on adults for the regulation of behavior, still looking to adults for security, and not yet viewing themselves as able to intercede independently of adults when crisis is at hand.

Somewhere between 6 and 9 years of age for most children, an emerging self-reliance and independence indicates a shift in their view about who has absolute authority and who should be responsible for what happens. The change occurs as they begin to view themselves as individuals who can do things well and do not always have to listen to adults to be successful. As this change occurs, children begin to change their perspectives of adults and to see themselves as independent. This is the beginning of the existential crisis, when children become aware that important adults cannot solve all their serious problems. They are uncertain about how to behave. The dilemma is whether to continue to look compliantly to adults for direction or to act independently. When they are confronted with stress and crisis, they often assume that they are responsible, as either the cause of a problem or the person who must correct it. And if they are also confronted with incidents that reveal how inept adults are in handling life's problems, the existential crisis is under way!

Death and divorce are two common examples of situations that adults are not always able to handle successfully. Crime, alcoholism, and violence in families also produce the existential crisis, often earlier than is typical. Awareness of adult impotence greatly increases anxiety and raises specters: "Who's going to handle this?" "Who's in charge?" "Who will protect me?" A child who has self-confidence and some independent skills before this time will gradually come through the existential crisis using logical problem-solving skills and continuing to trust adults, but in a new way. Those without these resources experience increased insecurity and anxiety. They act out their concerns, make abortive attempts to control and test

A Preexistential Student Views Adults

"Adults are all-powerful. They solve problems, make rules to control behavior, judge violators, and punish those who are guilty. When students conform, adults like them and will reward them. Solving problems is up to the adult. What's comfortable is a teacher in charge who makes everyone mind the rules. What's good is adults who let you know they like you. Rewards are good too."

A Student in the Existential Crisis Views Adults

"You don't know about adults. Sometimes they act like they know it all. They're always telling you to do this and do that. They have dumb rules. I just pretend I don't know. Sometimes I don't hear it. Anyway, it's not my problem. I just mind my own business. They don't understand, anyway. I want to help out but they never give me a chance."

adults, and, when their defenses fail to protect them, often show marked regression into highly unacceptable behaviors. This volatility and lack of stability in student-adult relationships make this phase particularly taxing for many teachers. At one moment they will need to use preexistential strategies; they then must switch to postexistential strategies when a student begins to show control and responsible self-management.

The existential crisis is evident in almost all children who are beginning Stage Three. Adults who are effective in working with children during Stage Three use abundant positive feedback and praise to encourage good decisions and self-regulated behavior. To develop self-esteem during this phase, adults reflect back to the children their successes and their words and actions that indicate increasing maturity. Adults also find it productive to expand children's insight and understanding by decoding behavior—connecting their own feelings and behavior to the responses of others.[5] Throughout the existential crisis, adults must maintain sufficient structure to enforce the rules of conduct and the consequences of rule violations. In short, they must maintain authority and control until the children demonstrate success in responsible self-regulated behavior.

In the typical *postexistential* phase, there is increased detachment from psychological dependency on adults, as children turn to peers for behavioral models and affirmation about themselves. This change becomes fairly evident in most children about age 9. The role for adults now is to provide mirrors for children to see themselves as others see them and to encourage them to choose acceptable self-regulated behavior. Respect and recognition from adults are essential if children are to continue to develop responsible personal behavior. Adults are needed as new role models and as backstops to help when challenges become overwhelming.

Although new skills are not always sufficient for successful navigation through a crisis, postexistential children are on a course toward independence. Effective parents and teachers in upper elementary grades and high school know how to guide this growth. They have interpersonal styles that promote independence while providing sufficient direction for children to achieve success in personal and educational endeavors. They serve as role models for effective relationships and teach independence in problem solving. These are also the characteristics of an effective teacher using Developmental Therapy–Developmental Teaching with children who have passed through the existential crisis, usually having completed Stage Three and beginning to move into Stage Four. Examples of management strategies used in Developmental Therapy–Developmental Teaching with postexistential children include group Life Space Intervention (LSI) and other counseling strategies, reality therapy, affirmation of positive qualities, confrontation, evaluative feedback with peers and teachers, interpretation of behavior and feelings, group planning and rule making, and use of peers as appropriate social role models. Group planning sessions with individual input are essential when helping postexistential students develop responsible behavior. Choices are provided for how activities will be conducted, what rules will be used, how activities can be changed, and how individual group members can achieve respect from each other. Every successful choice puts development one step forward toward self-governance and regulation of personal behavior. Every failed choice halts the process and leaves authority and control external to the student.

Should we be concerned about young children who have gone through the existential crisis too soon because of life experiences that have thrown them on their own at an early age? What about older children who have failed to resolve the existential crisis satisfactorily and continue to pit themselves against adults? Will such deviations in the normal sequence of development affect their behavior and the way they are managed in their programs? The answer is clearly yes. These will be controlling, untrusting, and manipulative children who do not take adult direction yet avoid responsibility for their own behavior. They cannot accept authority and cannot allow adults to direct them. They seek reassurance and nurturance while lashing out at the very adults from whom they seek approval and support. They will continue to be immobilized developmentally in Stage Three. Their teachers and other adults will find them unlikely to change, regardless of their age, until their Developmental Therapy–Developmental Teaching programs focus intensely on achieving mastery of Stage Three goals and objectives, moving them into Stage Four and resolution of the existential crisis.

To summarize, the closer an adult's management strategies match a developing child's view of authority and belief about who is responsible for controlling behav-

[5]Chapter 5 includes a review of how we decode behavior.

A Postexistential Student Views Adults

"Adults should let you alone. They should let you be yourself. When I mess up, I'm the one who pays for it. Some teachers know how to give you confidence. Maybe its because they show you respect. I know what I have to do and I can handle it myself. Sometimes I get in over my head. I have a teacher that's great about that. I don't mind talking it out with her. She's got her head on straight and her ideas usually work out. At least she's fair and she listens to both sides of an argument. When she sees I'm heading for trouble she lets me know what's ahead but doesn't try to make me over. She even lets me tell her things about the way I'd run things if I was in charge. And it's not always her way. She's the kind of person I want to be like."

ior, the more receptive the child will be to gradually assuming responsibility for personal actions. When we plan a child's program, we use all available information to determine the child's view of adults and belief about who solves problems. If children are *preexistential*, they view adults as authorities and hold them responsible for keeping them under control. If the children are going through the *existential crisis*, they convey ambiguity and vacillation about adult authority and test it frequently to see how much control the adults really have. Children who have resolved the existential crisis comfortably are in the *postexistential* phase and are ready to work with adults to handle crises and accept responsibility for their own behavior. This basic information tells a great deal about how they will respond to adults and how much personal responsibility they are able to assume for their own conduct.

What part do values play in motivating responsible behavior?

Values are the internal rules we live by, fixed points of reference for daily behavior—the glue that holds together the structure we know as personality and character. We draw on our personal values as we direct our own activities, solve social problems, and regulate our own behavior. Children are much the same, choosing to behave in ways that satisfy their current, developing value systems and avoiding behavior that produces unsatisfying results. If a child's development of values is arrested or delayed, the result at any age is primitive behavior. Such children are angry, volatile, self-serving, and highly anxious. As they grow older, their lack of values makes them vulnerable to drug and alcohol addictions, sexual promiscuity, vandalism, violence, truancy, delinquency, decreases in achievement, and lack of empathy, compassion, and altruism. When so many problems arise from a lack of values to guide responsible behavior, it is imperative that adults give greater attention to how values develop and what they can do to foster their steady growth in all children and youth.

There is a large body of psychological literature that describes many theories about the values that motivate behavior.[6] The forces that motivate children to modify their behavior in constructive or destructive ways—to cooperate or not, interact or retreat, learn or fail—involve complex and highly personal values that grow gradually as a child matures. The origins of a child's values are in experiences with people and are shaped by knowledge, feelings, attitudes, pleasures, fears, and anxieties. Frequently the values that motivate behavior are hidden beneath protective cover-ups. It is difficult for parents and teachers to identify the "turn-on" behind a behavior they observe in a child. But to manage a child's behavior to successful outcomes, adults must understand the specific feelings, emotions, and meanings that shape the child's values and directly motivate behavior. We consider knowledge of motivational forces and the values that regulate behavior central to successful use of the Developmental Therapy–Developmental Teaching curriculum and specific classroom practices.

There is a typical sequence of stages in the development of values that motivate children's social problem solving and self-regulation of behavior (see Figure 2.3). The sequence begins with an orientation that one's own needs are paramount. Any behavior that meets these needs is satisfactory. Gradually, children move from that orientation to a belief that adults' standards are the ones that bring personal benefits, and therefore behavior should conform in order to please adults and avoid their punishment. A child's development then broadens into the view that justice and fairness are values that shape the behavior of others toward oneself and so are acceptable. Finally, values emerge that reflect an individual's embrace of society's standard of responsible behavior and care of others with empathy and altruism, added to justice and fairness as values that regulate behavior (Kohlberg & Hersh, 1977).

When planning a child's program, we use the following simple outline of the sequence of developing values to initially identify what the child really values:

[6] Madsen (1968) has a thoughtful and comprehensive review of 20 different theories of motivation. He concludes that (a) motivation works in concert with cognition to shape behavior and (b) every force that influences behavior is a part of the motivational field. Although few theorists or researchers have attempted to put the many master motivators into a developmental hierarchy, each has a logical place in the sequence of development. In Appendix 5 we reference motivational systems according to the stage of the Developmental Therapy–Developmental Teaching curriculum in which a particular system is developmentally feasible.

Figure 2.3. The developmental sequence of values used to determine "satisfactory" results. From *Life Space Intervention: Talking with Children and Youth in Crisis* (p. 89), by Mary M. Wood and Nicholas J. Long, 1991, Austin, TX: PRO-ED. Copyright 1991 by PRO-ED. Reprinted with permission.

Types of Values	*Examples of "Satisfactory" Solutions*	*Challenge Student to a Higher-Level Value*	
Own Needs	"What I want." "What feels good." "Look after yourself first." →	Adult approves of student. Rules to follow. Leave it to adults.	Pre-existential Phase
Adult Approval	"I do what I'm told so adults will approve of me." "Good people obey; bad people deserve to be punished." "If you break rules, you get punished." →	Reasons for rules. Right versus wrong. Respect others' feelings. Adults model fairness and value what's right and fair.	Pre-existential Phase
Fairness	"Fairness is right for me." "Kids have rights." "Doing things with others brings rewards to me." "Do to them what they do to you." →	Expand values to "kindness," "leadership," and "friendship." Live up to others' expectations. Consider others' feelings.	Existential Crisis
Responsibility for Self	"What do others think of me?" "Everybody does it." "I don't want to be left out." "People who like you will help you." "You can have friends by being a friend." "It's important for people to like you." →	Expand personal goals. Emphasize personal goals. Personal responsibility. Social responsibility. Fairness and justice for everyone.	Post-existential Phase
Responsibility for Others	"How does my behavior affect others?" "The system should protect everyone." "Be a responsible person for society." "Live by a creed." "Fulfill obligations." →	Respect yourself as a moral person. Actions based on principles. Think for yourself about others' needs. Follow others who act on moral principles.	Post-existential Phase

My needs	"What I want is what's important."
Please adults	"I do what I'm told so adults will like me and not punish me."
Be fair	"I do things for others so they will treat me right."
Be responsible	"Be a nice person so people will like you."
Care for others	"Others have feelings and deserve respect."

Children's ideas about what is satisfactory are somewhat age-related, and this gives us a beginning point. We want children's "ownership" of the idea that the program will help, goals will be accomplished, and effort on their part will pay off in ways that they value. If a behavior management plan is designed with consequences and contingencies that are beyond their ability to achieve or if it fails to produce outcomes that they really value, the plan will fail. The program will have no value for the children or the expectations will be too great a leap forward for them to accomplish.[7]

We are often asked if the curriculum's emphasis on values includes *moral values*. The answer is yes; we see them as part of the same developing continuum. We are inclined to the viewpoints of Erikson and Bennett on the importance of focusing on virtues as a way to develop responsible behavior. Erikson (1964, p. 115) speaks of "*basic virtues*, with which human beings steer themselves and others through life," naming "*Hope, Will, Purpose*, and *Competence* as the rudiments of virtue developed in childhood; of *Fidelity* as the adolescent virtue; and of *Love, Care*, and *Wisdom* as the central virtues of adulthood." Bennett (1993) suggests 10 similar virtues that he believes shape the personality and behavior of moral people: self-discipline, compassion, responsibility, friendship, work, courage, perseverance, honesty, loyalty, and faith.[8] By the time most children and youth begin school, they can recognize some of these values as issues in social situations, yet frequently they do not know how to deal with them. They understand ideas of right and wrong, fairness and unfairness, justice and injustice, life and death, and truth and untruth. These values are included in Developmental Therapy–Developmental Teaching, through the stages, because they are essential to the gradual development of a child's personal responsibility and social-emotional competence.

EMOTIONS: THE FUEL FOR SOCIAL-EMOTIONAL COMPETENCE

Many children worry excessively or go to extremes to deny any worry at all. They are caught up in hurried lifestyles that are unpredictable and stressful. Relationships and personal, emotional needs often are ignored in the push for things, action, and achievement. Then, when clashes between unmet emotional needs and the expectations set by others occur and are unresolved, there are fears or chronic emotional pain that demand relief. Without relief, anxiety results, which is a chronic reaction to worry, fear, insecurity, or stress. Oppositional behaviors, behavioral problems in the classroom, and failure to learn are frequently defensive maneuvers to protect against being overwhelmed by these feelings. Children go to great lengths to protect themselves from this inner discomfort just as adults do. Fears and emotions have a pervasive effect on the development of social competence, influencing the way children learn and how they respond to adults, peers, and daily events (Lewis, 1990, 1993; Lewis & Rosenblum, 1978).

In the course of normal social and emotional development, from birth through adolescence, fears and anxieties occur as the result of interplay between a child's emotional needs and the demands made on the child by the environment. Fears may take several forms:

Realistic fears	"It could happen."
Remote fears	"It might happen."
Mystical, symbolic fears	"Wouldn't it be awful if this happened?"

The form fear takes usually depends upon experiences and relationships with adults. Most characteristic fears of children are those expressed through nightmares, or through symbolic play and other creative art forms. Typically, fears concern abandonment, death, failing to measure up, and punishment. Obsessions and compulsions are extreme forms of these basic fears (A. Freud, 1965; Ausubel, Sullivan, & Ives, 1980).

Children's emotions are often difficult for adults. Perhaps adults have little training or experience in using children's emotional episodes as positive forces for helping. In this section, we review how four major emotional forces—*the attachment-separation conflict, emotional memory, developmental anxieties*, and *defense mechanisms*—are used in the Developmental Therapy–Developmental Teaching curriculum.

The Attachment-Separation Conflict: Teachers as Stand-Ins

Attachment describes the essential human need to be connected and cared for. It provides us with unshaken confidence that we are valued by others. We are free to venture beyond the attachment. Like a turtle's shell, the emotional sustenance we gain from attachments goes with us everywhere and serves as our protective shield. When we have a satisfying emotional attachment, we do not have to

[7]Chapter 5 describes ways to adjust behavior management plans to students' values and stages of social-emotional development.

[8]Bennett provides an anthology of children's literature to teach virtues.

struggle to retain it. The natural developmental counterforce to attachment is *separation*. Willingness to give up attachment, to separate, occurs as a developing child matures (Ainsworth, 1973; Bowlby, 1973, 1980, 1982, 1988; Mahler, 1968/1987; Mahler, Pine, & Bergman, 1975). Separation provides freedom to seek increasing independence. This interplay between attachment and separation centers on significant adults who provide security and comfort while gradually allowing independence to emerge as newly discovered independence brings successful results. This is a daily occurrence between children and adults, teachers and students.

The roles of adults in this developmental process are well known. Babies need a particular type of nurture and care, consisting of particular adult behaviors that convey security and attachment. We also know that we must manage a 2-year-old toddler in quite a different way—still providing security and care but allowing the first steps toward independence by teaching skills for success and mastery in the world beyond attachment. We lead 6-year-olds into new learning that expands mental and physical achievements, introducing them to independence. Teaching and guiding students through the elementary school years requires adults to shift their focus from external direction to encouraging students to choose responsible behavior independent of adult regulation or the influence of peers who are providing a new form of emotional attachment. During adolescence, adults are used as models for values and mirrors for newly emerging identity. Adults guide and teach in a framework that recognizes the adolescent as a person who is completing the last phase of the attachment-separation cycle. The conclusion of adolescence is the beginning of the young adult life stage, with attachments diminished and separation at a peak of intensity.

If attachments fail, or never develop, a child has to put a major effort into seeking a substitute. This fundamental need to be cared for may supersede all other behavioral motivators. Failed attachment is a major part of the first developmental anxiety, *abandonment*, discussed in this next section. If it is unresolved, it eats away at all subsequent interpersonal exchanges and severely modifies the course of an individual's personality development as an adult. Similarly, if the separation process fails to produce successful alternatives, psychological independence may not be achieved. Fears of failure and inadequacy, and of not measuring up to the expectations of others, spiral and a restricted personality develops.

When either the attachment process or the separation process breaks down, a child's relationship to significant adults is the critical issue, and anger is a major emotional element. There is anger toward adults in the family who have failed to provide nurturance and protection, or who have ridiculed failures and restricted a child's attempts at independence. These failed relationships from home permeate a child's view of adults at school. Children bring this emotional baggage with them. And their teachers, in innocence, become the substitute adults—the unsolicited recipients of the anger a child holds toward other adults outside of school.

The first point is to be aware that much of the anger and disruptive behavior teachers receive from students in a classroom usually is not caused by something the teacher has done. Yet it requires considerably understanding and skill on a teacher's part to rechannel the anger and break through the cycle in which students cast and recast the teacher as a stand-in for every feeling they have toward adults. These are students who are struggling with anger toward other adults over unmet emotional needs.

Remembering that the essence of the problem often is failed attachment (caring) or unsuccessful separation (freedom), a teacher can introduce these elements into a Developmental Therapy–Developmental Teaching program. We identify ways to provide attachment needs vicariously through secondary sources: an abundance of food, curricular content that portrays nurturing and caring by people and animals, a predictable and structured classroom environment with low stress levels and high satisfaction levels, and relationships with adults that are rich with respect and affirmations. Even in high school, legitimate forms of this content exist in cooking classes, vocational training for child care, job training in food service, and veterinary lab training. Such courses of study offer emotional satisfaction to meet students' unfulfilled need for caring relationships.

Prior unsuccessful separation experiences for a young child require carefully orchestrated, limited choices. Making choices represents independence and should be introduced gradually. Initially, choices offered to young children should be limited and should always result in success. When children are allowed to gradually regulate their own conduct through successful choices and decision making, they begin to see themselves as competent. As their view of themselves expands, choices widen and the results of the choices become important. Both negative and positive results then must be faced. With the Developmental Teaching Objectives as the guide, we systematically use choice and decision making, in gradually expanding forms, in every young child's program on a daily basis.

Unmet separation needs of older students require similar plans for gradually expanding choices and participating in self-governance. Additionally, a curriculum rich in vicarious experiences of adventure, challenge, and victory over adversity fulfills an older student's natural emotional need for separation from dependency. Although residual fears of failure or abandonment may remain, the drive for freedom and conquest often arouses a young person to move beyond a symbiotic or self-protective stage toward responsible behavior and social competence.

When we know what a child has experienced in attachment or separation, we will know where that child is in the

The Changing Roles of Teachers as Stand-In Adults

Satisfier of basic needs
Teacher of basic social and learning skills
Motivator and director of behavior and group processes
Upholder of law and order
Teacher
Group facilitator
Individual advocate
Social role model
Counselor, adviser, and confidant

continuum from dependence to independence. This also tells us where the child is in relation to the existential crisis described earlier in this section. For Developmental Therapy–Developmental Teaching, this information characterizes the adult-student relationship and defines the behavior of adults needed to facilitate a particular phase of development. In this curriculum, each stage of a child's social-emotional development requires a particular type of adult behavior to promote the goals and objectives of that stage.[9] When adults convey these roles with clarity, they are in harmony with the developmental needs of each student. Adult-child relationships are built on this solid foundation—neither restricting children by unhealthy attachments nor abandoning them to fail on their own. As children change with mastery of each sequential stage, the characteristic behavior of their teachers also changes, adjusting to the maturation of the child. When this happens, the tendency diminishes for a child to displace anger onto the teacher as a stand-in for other adults who represent failed relationships in the past.

Emotional Memory: A Priority for This Curriculum

Education has always respected the role of memory in the learning process. But seldom do we hear educators talk about *emotional memory* and a student's *private reality* as necessary ingredients for learning and a legitimate concern for instruction. There is also little discussion about the need to mobilize *mental energy* for successful educational intervention. Mental energy is the fuel for doing, saying, caring, and thinking. Produced by neurons, synapses, and gray cells, this energy attaches to what is most important to a student. When mental energy is activated, it is the drive that makes learning possible. It enables a student to accrue information by storing and expanding networks of knowledge. It also stores and arouses emotional memories and the situations associated with these emotions. It is close to impossible to keep emotional memories bottled up inside when they are aroused. Anger is particularly devastating, often generating aggression and violence. Without reduction, repressed or disguised emotions are expressed in destructive ways and divert mental energy away from learning.

Behind their public words and actions all children carry a powerful and elaborate memory bank of private thoughts and feelings. Yet they seldom express these thoughts and feelings openly. In this private storehouse, memories of previous experiences are filed away with attached emotional notations. This is their private reality—real to them but unknown to others. Emotions and feelings attached to memory are powerful forces, waiting for expression and triggered by even the most insignificant event. For example, consider rage, believed by some people to be an open, primitive, and direct expression of emotion. But as you examine the circumstances surrounding an outburst of rage by a child, you can see it as an expression of other complex feelings and ideas that cannot find expression in another form.

Refocusing Mental Energy. Every person who has been involved in the life of a healthy, happy child or adolescent has seen mental energy released for spontaneous participation in life and learning. In contrast, when mental energy is deflected or impoverished, a child's "get up and go" is gone. Worry, anxiety, concerns, or preoccupations seem to deplete mental energy, making it unavailable for learning. When there is a crisis in the emotional storehouse, it receives first attention. A child's mental energy flows to cope with the problem of managing emotions. When a child has severe emotional, behavioral, or social problems, the mental energy available for participating and learning is greatly reduced. Such students are sometimes labeled *depressed, unmotivated, distractible,* or *hyperactive.* Teachers observe how little mental energy these students have in comparison with their peers. No ordinary effort on a teacher's part can compete when attention is drawn away from the task at hand.

In Developmental Therapy–Developmental Teaching, we consider how much mental energy a student has each

[9] Chapter 6 provides details of ways to adjust adults' strategies to the developmental stages of students.

day and where it is being expended. We also seek information about the storehouse of emotional memories, for these are the truly dynamic forces that fuel each child's behavior. One way to mobilize and redirect mental energy is through curriculum materials and activities. We select specific materials and activities specially designed with each student's emotional needs and anxieties in mind. The competition for their attention is tough. They see more intense drama and violence every day on television and in their communities than ordinary curriculum materials can compete against. When students are also struggling with emotional, social, or behavioral disabilities, the challenge to channel their mental energy for learning is formidable.

Effective materials must provide content that includes admired people as role models struggling with similar problems and feelings. The content must attract and hold that mental energy, vicariously provide emotional outlets, offer hopes and dreams, and portray very human dilemmas confronted and resolved. Words that evoke vivid mental images can attract this energy; so can content that taps a child's real-life concerns. Action-based activities connected to deeper concerns attract displaced energy, especially when they are focused on ways to resolve the children's problems.[10]

The Energy Force Field. Another source for activating mental energy on behalf of learning is the energy force field that can exist between individuals. Anyone in love can vouch for its existence. Young people and musicians call it "vibes." They use it spontaneously and often without conscious effort. People who work extensively with animals use it to communicate; so do actors who want to reach an audience with their "presence." Some successful teachers recognize that this nonverbal communication mode may be more powerful than all of the oral language used between adults and students. They use this nonverbal force with dynamic results. We all have known adults who can walk into a room and have an immediate effect on the children who are there even though they have said little. They are generating nonverbal messages that the children read. Try it yourself in a public place where children are free to respond spontaneously, or join a group of teens in a nonauthoritarian role. You will probably learn something about your own ability to communicate in the powerful nonverbal world. When you can use this type of communication with deliberation, you can convey all sorts of messages that will be "heard" by children who are otherwise tuning out adults' words and ideas. It is a tool for unobtrusively conveying support, affirming a child, and building a relationship. If you fail to put it to work, you may be inadvertently sending out all sorts of messages about frustration, dislike, and despair to the child. Such messages are received, whether they are intended or not.[11]

Changing the Private Reality. If there is to be lasting change and carryover in a program, the negative contents and anger of a child's private reality must eventually change to positive memories of success, pleasure, self-confidence, security, and trust. We should not leave such changes to chance. Each day, each adult, with every troubled child, should ensure that there has been some replacement of negative and destructive memories with positive memories of pleasure and confidence. End every activity with a close-down procedure to teach appraisal of positive aspects of the just-completed activity. This simple strategy is designed to change children's emotional memory banks by teaching them to use a basic process of review and critical thinking.[12] Effective teachers already use this procedure for academic growth, yet few deliberately use it to modify students' emotional memory banks. Simple recall and appraisal of a positive aspect of each student's participation teach students to search their memories for the best moments in an activity. When this positive evaluation procedure becomes a routine ending to every activity, students rapidly begin to do it themselves, and new, positive emotional memories are added to their private reality. We see dramatic changes in their faces when this happens. They smile spontaneously.[13] There is a climate of buoyancy. The message is that real experiences are producing positive feelings—and students are aware of those feelings. The memory bank is taking on positive charges!

Developmental Anxieties: Influencing Behavior in Powerful Ways

Anxiety, sometimes called distress, is an active reaction of uneasiness, worry, or apprehension, with a physiological component, to a situation recalling past emotional discomfort or helplessness (Brody & Axelrad, 1970, pp. 36–39; Lewis & Rosenblum, 1978, p. 4). Ordinary life is full of anxiety-producing situations for people of all ages, and there is a predictable sequence in which anxiety takes unique forms at specific stages of development. Because these anxieties are believed to be the product of a particu-

[10] Chapters 3 and 4 provide general guidelines for adapting materials and activities to every stage of development and emotional need. For detailed descriptions of the program for each developmental stage, see Chapters 8 through 12.

[11] Skills adults need to build constructive relationships with children are discussed in greater detail in Chapter 6.

[12] Chapter 4 reviews the steps in introducing, conducting, and evaluating activities and adjusting them to children's developmental stages. Chapters 5 and 6 consider ways to manage behavior that foster social-emotional maturation. For a practical guide for helping adolescents change their own private reality, see also Eggert (1994).

[13] Research about students' smiling in the classroom would provide extremely useful information for educators. Until it is available, we must rely on the information from infant research indicating that the smiling reflex quickly becomes a sign of social learning.

lar phase of development and are recognized as occurring in most people, we call them *developmental anxieties*:

Abandonment	"No one cares."
Inadequacy	"I can't do anything right."
Guilt	"I'm so bad I should be punished."
Conflict	"They're making me, and I don't want to" or "I want to and they won't let me."
Identity	"Who am I?" or "What am I to become?"

Developmental anxieties influence children's behavior in subtle but powerful ways.

In typical development, each stage produces a unique set of concerns and fears, resulting in a *developmental anxiety*. Each developmental anxiety must be addressed and overcome to free the child to cope successfully with a new set of challenges brought about by the progression of age and experience. Every person passes through the same predictable sequence of anxieties in the course of personality development. For some it is a normal progression through each developmental crisis to resolution and maturation. For others, particularly those who are disturbed or have experienced destructive childhoods, each developmental crisis compounds the scope of the anxieties. Unresolved, each anxiety makes it more difficult to cope successfully with the emerging anxiety of the next stage. Figure 2.4 shows schematically the way developmental anxieties emerge in different forms, depending upon the phase of development and the conditions that provoke it. Two themes represent the primary motivational forces that cause anxieties to occur: *inner needs* and *drives* and *sociocultural expectations.*

According to Anna Freud's model of developmental lines (1973), *instinctual anxieties* are formed first, arising from fears of being overwhelmed by forces within oneself (impulses out of control) or by self-threatening external forces (the unfamiliar, separation, abandonment, emotional deprivation). These earliest anxieties are identified as developmental change 1 in Figure 2.4; they result in a sense of abandonment and aloneness. *Objective anxieties* result during developmental change 2, when a child develops an increasing awareness of reality and personal inadequacy. Fantasy runs rampant, and the child perceives

Figure 2.4. How typical developmental anxieties emerge.

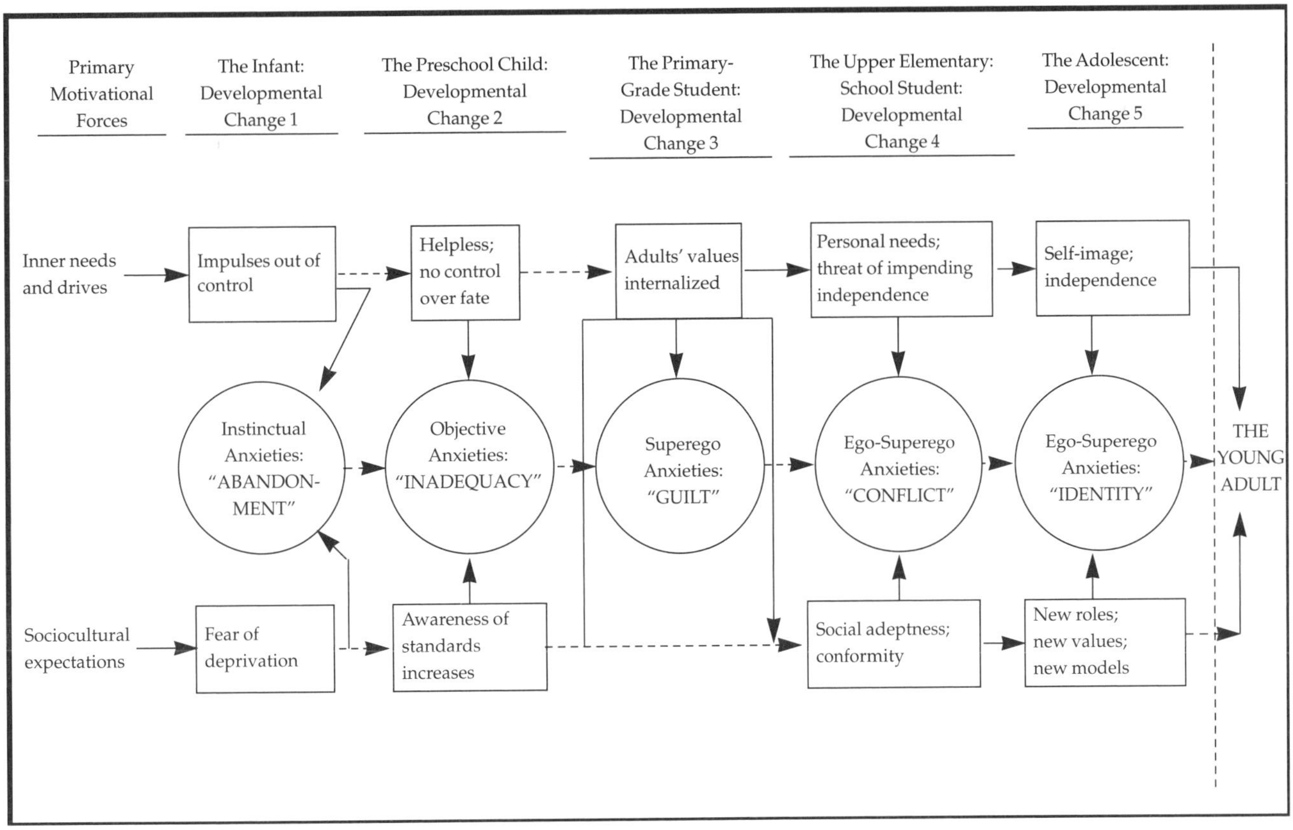

Note: Solid lines denote major influences; dotted lines, contributing influences. Adapted from *Childhood and Society* (2nd ed., pp. 247–263, 406–407) by E. H. Erikson, 1950/1963, New York: W. W. Norton; and *Identity, Youth and Crisis* (pp. 93–96) by E. H. Erikson, 1968, New York: W. W. Norton.

imminent punishment from powerful external sources over which there is no control or escape (magical forces, parents, teachers). Later, developmental change 3 results in *superego anxieties* when a child has internalized the values of significant adults, conscience has developed, and guilt over personal inadequacies results. In this latter form of anxiety, the child's own simple value system operates to self-judge and self-punish, whereas in the previous stage of development the child sees judgment and punishment as coming down from outside forces. With increasing self-confidence and social adeptness, a child's strong need to identify and conform to group values comes in conflict with personal needs and a sense of insecurity about independence. This is developmental stage 4. These opposing forces create the dynamic tensions of change 4, which often result in heightened conflict. The resolution of this conflict does not usually occur until late adolescence, during developmental change 5, as the problems of *self-image* and *identity* emerge as the greatest sources of anxiety.

In the Developmental Therapy–Developmental Teaching curriculum, knowledge about developmental anxieties aids in understanding the forces driving a child's behavior and the type of adult needed. We try to identify the predominating anxieties at the time a child begins the program. When we know where each child is in this developmental progression and understand the natural developmental anxiety associated with the child's stage of development, we can counter an anxiety with specific curriculum content and intervention strategies that reduce or reshape the power of the anxiety that dominates the child's life.

A language arts curriculum is a particularly effective vehicle for dealing with developmental anxieties.[14] Think of the potential to embody specific feelings and problems of students in reading, storytelling, literature, creative dramatics, role play, creative writing, and experience stories. Television and videotapes also are dynamic resources. Many adults already use these resources but sometimes they do not analyze the emotional content as a way to select an antidote for a specific anxiety. Fictional and imaginary people serve as role models and provide easy identification. When a student "accesses" a character, there is abundant opportunity to learn new ways to behave, to handle unbearable problems, and to gain greater understanding of emotions. Stories should always have endings with reassuring resolutions that address children's specific anxieties. Here are several examples: For older students who still carry anxiety about abandonment and being unloved, the *Star Wars* series holds the ultimate resolution when the evil Darth Vader finally sacrifices his own life for that of his noble son, Luke Skywalker. In an entirely different style, Bambi and Barney catch the sense of care and nurture needed by younger children struggling with the same developmental anxiety of abandonment. "The Cosby Show" was a good example of material that dealt with several developmental anxieties, most often conflict and identity. Each episode included conflict between dependency (the need to be a loved and valued member of a family) and the need for independence and personal identity. The developmental anxieties were resolved in each script with reassurance about care and connection while sanctioning independence and personal identity.

Real life is often far from reassuring and many real problems have ugly endings. Imagination and make-believe are healthy ways to resolve anxiety vicariously and reconstruct reality so that it will be bearable. This is not as easy as it may seem. You may recall Michael Jackson's popular video, *Thriller*, viewed by thousands of children. As the story line progressed to the climax and ending, the message was convincingly clear: You cannot (and should not) trust anyone, even those who say they love you. This is not a reassuring message for troubled children.

When the curriculum provides content that helps troubled children deal with anxieties satisfactorily and an environment that avoids adding unnecessary stress to emotional vulnerability, they begin to participate with a new spontaneity. Gradually they respond with fewer defenses and lessened anxiety. There is a new freedom to learn and a confidence that the classroom will not exacerbate their problems.

Defense Mechanisms: Protection Against Anxiety

Defense mechanisms are complex behavioral responses that protect the self from anxiety. They are used by individuals at all stages of development, although the form will change with age and increasing social sophistication. In the previous discussion of developmental anxieties, we illustrated how anxieties are a natural product of the changing emotional needs of a developing child. Each stage has its unique developmental crisis followed by attempts on the child's part to resolve the crisis by balancing the demands of others against one's own inner demands. Defense mechanisms are the means by which they typically accomplish this balancing act and eventually resolve the developmental crisis. As children try to protect themselves from the stress of increased social demands, defense mechanisms come into action. We see this every day, in every social situation. Following are examples of frequently used defense mechanisms:

- *Denial:* A child who has been promised a new bike as a reward for doing well in school fails two subjects. When confronted with his lack of success, he responds, "I didn't want a bike anyway."
- *Repression:* A 5-year-old who witnessed the death of her brother in a bicycle accident has no memory or recollection of the incident.

[14] In Chapter 4 we outline resources in language arts that address the developmental anxieties. In Chapters 8–12, we review each of these anxieties in greater detail.

- *Rationalization:* The overprotective mother of a teenager justifies her overbearing mothering by recalling his frequent bouts with illness during infancy and reminding others of his frailty.
- *Projection:* A student who is making failing grades in social studies blames his failure on his teacher, whom he describes as a "terrible" instructor.
- *Reaction formation* (defense through the opposite): An 8-year-old who is extremely jealous of her 3-year-old sister has become excessively protective and mothering toward her.
- *Withdrawal:* On the playground, a second grader who has difficulty forming relationships with peers sits under a tree by herself, bundled in her coat.
- *Intellectualization:* The teenage daughter of a businessman who died unexpectedly of a heart attack comforts herself with the conviction that since he died suddenly, he didn't suffer.
- *Regression:* A 9-year-old boy deals with frustration in school by sucking his thumb.
- *Displacement:* A teacher who is angry at a student picks up a book and hurls it across the room.
- *Compensation:* A high school freshman who is not doing well in the school's athletic program becomes a valuable member of the debating team.
- *Sublimation:* A young unmarried woman with no children develops an extremely intense attachment to her cats, whom she refers to as "my babies."
- *Identification:* A college student joins a fraternity, adopting the dress styles, interests, and activities of its members.

It is not always evident why an individual chooses to use one particular defense mechanism instead of another. However, when an adult recognizes a defense mechanism in a child's behavior, it signals stress on the child's part. We use these signals to alert us that the child is in need of emotional relief one way or another.[15] If the defense mechanism is successful in relieving the child's anxiety, it is an indication that the child has found a satisfactory way to accommodate inner needs to outer realities. If the defense mechanism fails, greater anxiety results. The child becomes increasingly uncomfortable and finds more defenses. When defense mechanisms are used excessively, perceptions become distorted and functioning is impaired. In a sense, these defensive behaviors do a good job of providing an emotional shield, keeping distance between a child and psychological discomfort or pain. However, extended periods with sustained use of defense mechanisms may result in a number of clinically identifiable problems such as depression, attention deficit disorders, phobias, conduct disorders, severe withdrawal, and the like.

Several classic defense mechanisms are essential to the developmental process all children experience as they cope with the developmental anxieties. Five frequently used defense mechanisms serve to illustrate the developmental changes in the choices of defense mechanisms used by children in this process of balancing social expectations and interpersonal needs (Cramer, 1990; A. Freud, 1942, 1973):[16]

1. *Introjection:* The very young child incorporates parental demands and values.
2. *Projection:* The preschool child transposes own views outward to others.
3. *Identification:* The primary school–age child begins assimilating the values, behaviors, and ideas of others. A "satellite" attachment of self to parents' qualities occurs with dependence and temporary devaluation of self in favor of parents.
4. *Ego formation:* The preadolescent becomes aware of individuality with increasing recognition from others, resulting in detaching self from parents and exercising moral prerogatives.
5. *Identity ideal:* The adolescent searches for an ideal—the "best" self.

Close parallels are evident between the use of defense mechanisms in typical development and resolution of each developmental crisis with its associated developmental anxiety. In both, a first phase in development exists in which there is no differentiated sense of self from others. The resulting anxiety is fear of abandonment, and the mechanism of defense is to be "as one with another" (*introjection*). Then as the self takes shape, new anxiety of inadequacy appears, with its comfortable defense that there is a single viewpoint and that the entire world can be seen from the perspective of that viewpoint (*projection*). This is followed by the difficult phase when the differentiated self must be subjugated to others. The anxiety is guilt over failure to "measure up." The defense in resolving this crisis is to embrace others' views as one's own (*identification*). With that crisis resolved, the developing child struggles with conflict between emerging independence and continuing dependence on others. The defense is detachment of the self from dependency on others (*ego identity formation*). This is a difficult and gradual transformation, extending into adolescence. As a young person searches for values and ideals to replace those rejected in the previous stage, the anxiety is now the search for a new identity. The defense is in forming a redefined self (*ego ideal*) (Erikson, 1959/1980, pp. 121–122).

When these typical anxieties and crises of development are unresolved, defense mechanisms continue to be used for psychological comfort to combat anxiety. Extensive

[15]Guidelines for approaching the problems relating to crisis are discussed in Chapter 4. We also recommend Chapter 1 in *Life Space Intervention: Talking with Children and Youth in Crisis* (Wood & Long, 1991).

[16]Cramer (1990) has a comprehensive review of theory, research, and assessment in the development of defense mechanisms.

reliance on certain defensive behaviors, repeatedly or uncharacteristically for a child's age, usually results in severe problem behaviors. For example, children in the first stages of development typically are impulsive, demanding, and self-centered. We understand this behavior as a part of the adjustment and growth process and it is generally tolerated as acceptable for children under 2 years of age. However, if a 9-year-old exhibits this behavior, we would be concerned, and if the behavior persists at age 13, there would be serious concern. It is important to recognize that the behaviors are not typical or acceptable for the child's age. We view these unacceptable behaviors as poor choices for older children's defenses against anxieties. We see a task of Developmental Therapy-Developmental Teaching as helping children learn new and more effective defenses to use in navigating through life.

SUMMARY

Over many years, knowledge from theorists, researchers and classroom teachers has expanded our understanding of the social and emotional development of infants, children, and youth. Their findings are important foundations for successful work with children and youth of all ages. They describe intricate interrelationships among the developmental processes that produce social-emotional competence. They give us explanations about how relationships are formed and responsible behavior is acquired. Theories also explain the role of emotions, emotional memory, and mental energy in learning. They expand our understanding of anxiety and its pervasive role in all human personality development. Theories show how values become a motivating force in behavioral choices. This knowledge applies to children of all ages but is particularly relevant for those who have social, emotional, and behavioral disabilities.

We have chosen these constructs to highlight in this chapter because they are essential to helping children develop social-emotional competence and responsible behavior. They are also the less well known and obvious aspects of personality and learning. This knowledge directs us toward combining transactional, sociological, and clinical orientations to understanding the social-emotional development of children and youth. We believe that theory broadens our view of each child as a person whose most significant experiences are occurring outside of the program. As adults who are playing a significant role in the lives of children and youth, we must expand our practices to embrace a view that learning and personality development are inseparable. We hope that this brief review also strengthens adults' commitment to include a social-emotional dimension in every program for children and youth of every age.

PRACTICE

Using the key points in this chapter

Hannah is an 8-year-old student in the second grade. On a standardized achievement test, she has a grade equivalent of 2.6 in reading comprehension, 1.9 in math, and 2.1 in spelling. Her IQ is reported to be in the average ability range. Hannah is a cooperative and compliant child who can usually deal with her problems constructively.

On the previous night, Hannah had an argument with her older brother over what to watch on TV. Hannah hit him on the head with a block, causing a wound that required stitches in the emergency room at the hospital. The following incident takes place during a math lesson the next day.

HANNAH: *(a)* (Throws a pencil down on the floor)
(b) "I can't do this stupid work!"

TEACHER: "Hannah, you can do it. You did several problems yesterday just like those."

HANNAH: *(c)* "No, I didn't! You made these harder!"
(d) "Besides, the lunch was terrible and it gave me a stomachache."

TEACHER: "Hannah, bring me your paper and I'll see if I can help you."

HANNAH: *(e)* (sulking) (Puts her head on the desk)
(f) "You don't care about me, and everybody hates me! But I don't care. I hate you all!"
(g) "I only love my mother and my brother."
(h) "Besides, you never teach me anything. You always teach the other kids, but you never teach me."

TEACHER: "Hannah, I know you're upset. Let's go out in the hall where we can talk privately."

HANNAH: *(i)* "I don't need to talk! I'm okay. Besides, it's baby work and I don't need to do it." (Hannah walks to the door as she talks)

TEACHER: (outside the door, in the hall) "Hannah, the work is really hard."

HANNAH: *(j)* "Yeah." (Sucks her thumb)
(k) "But I do okay in reading."

TEACHER: "Yes, you do! My job is to help you with hard work. Sometimes when things are tough at home it's difficult for a student to concentrate at school. Sometimes talking helps."

HANNAH: *(l)* "Yeah, but I was having trouble with math. Everything's fine at home."

TEACHER: "Did anything happen last night?"

HANNAH: *(m)* (acting surprised) "No, we had supper, played outside, and then I went to bed."

This incident illustrates how intensely a child will protect herself against feeling psychological pain. While it may be tempting to respond by concluding that Hannah is lying to her teacher, use the incident to practice your own skills in identifying defense mechanisms and developmental anxieties. Match Hannah's statements (identified with the letters *a–m*) with the corresponding defense mechanisms listed below. Then think through the information provided to identify which developmental anxiety Hannah may be protecting herself against.

Compensation: _____
Denial: _____
Displacement: _____
Identification: _____
Projection: _____
Rationalization: _____
Regression: _____
Reaction formation (defense through the opposite): _____
Repression: _____
Withdrawal: _____

Hannah's developmental anxiety: ____

PART II

Putting the Curriculum into Practice from Birth Through the Teen Years

CHAPTER 3

Getting Started . . .

This curriculum is a growth model instead of a deficit model. It emphasizes the healthy processes in children and youth and works systematically to build upon them. Because behavior, personality, and intellect evolve through the sum of small, daily experiences, a curriculum that ensures a positive outcome to each experience with others can expedite the emergence of social-emotional competence. New, more responsible behaviors and attitudes will emerge as old, maladaptive responses fade. This is how social and emotional growth occurs.

—*FROM INTRODUCTION TO* DEVELOPMENTAL THERAPY, *FIRST EDITION, 1975*

DEVELOPMENTAL THERAPY–DEVELOPMENTAL TEACHING

As adults plan educational programs to effectively promote the academic achievement of children and youth, they are equally concerned about the students' personal characteristics as they relate to learning and participating as contributing members of a group. Experienced parents and professionals know that the social, emotional, and behavioral characteristics of a child ultimately shape the future. In any group of children or youth, many will have social, emotional, and behavioral problems, lacking needed skills for successfully negotiating the challenges they face every day. Each child has abilities, problems, and a particular family situation and lifestyle. Our task is to build an effective program around each individual's unique characteristics.

The programs we design should mobilize a child step by step through a series of learning experiences that will produce social, emotional, and behavioral growth. The very young may need a home program conducted by their own parents. For those ready for group experiences, early childhood programs may provide for their special needs by including them in a general educational setting. For others, a more intensive special education intervention may be needed. And as a student grows older, the need to acquire social-emotional competence and behavioral responsibility intensifies. The Developmental Therapy–Developmental Teaching curriculum has distinct applications for each of these age groups—early childhood, elementary, middle, or high school. It also has a unifying approach, providing continuity across programs and settings. It can be used as a part of any program for a student, with or without disabilities, who needs help in learning social-emotional competence and responsible behavior.

For those in need of special education, the referral process includes psychological, educational, observational, clinical, and developmental assessments. Parents and professionals work together to identify the goals and expectations for each child. They identify the child's strengths and vulnerabilities, uniquely different profiles of achievement, cultural experiences, developmental trajectories, anxieties, interests, values, and concerns. The resulting plan will be an IEP, IFSP, or ITP, which most often will be carried out in a group setting, sometimes in a special place, but often in an inclusive setting with age peers.

We offer this chapter as an overview of how to begin to use this curriculum with typical children and youth, as well as with those in special education. Although the chapter focuses directly on implementing the program in educational settings, the applications for home and community programs are implicit. We hope parents will find the material useful in working with their children's teachers and in monitoring how effectively their children's needs are being met. The chapter content includes the essential ingredients that apply to every age group, organized around these topics:

- beliefs about child development underlying this curriculum
- frequently asked questions about using this curriculum
- assessing children's social-emotional development to establish teaching objectives
- evaluating students' progress
- schedules for various educational settings

BELIEFS ABOUT CHILDREN'S DEVELOPMENT UNDERLYING THIS CURRICULUM

The pursuit of social-emotional competence and responsible behavior implies a priority on living successfully in a social world with others, while finding personal satisfaction in the process. This statement could be a working definition of emotional adjustment. It suggests that self-esteem and personal identity must develop within a social reality. This is at the heart of the curriculum. In the previous chapter we reviewed theories that provide the conceptual base for Development Therapy–Developmental Teaching, focusing on ways to promote typical social, emotional, and behavioral development across the age span. In this chapter we describe how these theories shaped four fundamental ideas about children and youth that we believe are essential for successful educational programming. If they fit with your beliefs about educating students with social, emotional, and behavioral problems, you should be comfortable using Developmental Therapy–Developmental Teaching. If not, perhaps the material in the following chapters can convince you that this approach has merit because it recognizes the powerful interchange between sequential maturation, individual and cultural values, and educational effort.

Belief 1: Deviant Versus Typical Behavior. *Deviant, unacceptable behavior is always interwoven with typical, acceptable behavior.*

Program Implication. Adults often generalize about a child as being a "discipline problem" or a "bad kid," viewing most of the child's behavior as being atypical or totally deviant, and overlooking age-appropriate behavior. The child becomes labeled, and positive aspects of behavior go unnoticed. This type of bias from others fosters a child's view of self as "one who is unable to do"—restricting self-esteem and limiting potential ability.

An intervention program must put a priority on promoting acceptable behaviors to discourage unacceptable conduct. If a program focuses only on reducing unacceptable behavior, it runs the risk of failing to respond to age-typical characteristics in students and will probably not result in responsible, self-controlled conduct. On the other hand, focusing interventions on a child's acceptable, typical characteristics and teaching new behaviors that bring satisfying responses from others will usually bring about social-emotional competence and an increasingly responsible individual. Experiences with adults and peers that bring satisfaction and success strengthen a child's identity as "one who can succeed" and promote a healthy association with all that is considered acceptable rather than encouraging identification as a "bad kid."

Belief 2: Sequential Development. *The normal process of social, emotional, and behavioral development follows an orderly and predictable sequence, yet it also is uniquely individual because of biological predispositions and the foundations laid in prior experiences with people.*

Program Implication. This belief implies that adults need to be aware of the course of development for children and youth of all ages. Rates of development and individual developmental patterns will differ from child to child, but the general sequence of development will be similar. A program can be truly effective in promoting positive growth by being sensitive to the uniqueness of each child within the pattern of typical development.

Growth and change should be systematically included in a program with two basic standards in mind: (a) the general course of development for all individuals and (b) the unique patterns of an individual's development—strengths and weaknesses—revealed through the presence or absence of typical developmental milestones. When we respond to individual profiles of development, we allow each individual's uniqueness to be recognized. And when we guide individuals within the general stream of development, we assist them in responding successfully to the expectations of others. This not only reinforces existing skills but also stimulates development of new skills.

It is not always easy to sequence programs to meet individual needs. Children and youth of any age who are instructed inappropriately for their stage of development may find themselves at either end of a mismatch, expected to do too little or too much. Repeated failures create a history of failure. Children with this history become debilitated and increasingly unable to meet the demands placed upon them. Equally ineffective is a program that continues to maintain a child at a plateau. This can happen when the program does not change after the child responds successfully to a particular program and demonstrates mastery of a skill. Allowing a young child who has learned to stack blocks to continue this activity each day, rather than to explore new play materials, illustrates an educational practice that maintains a student at the present level but does not produce growth. Similarly, an adult who allows a withdrawn student to play a solitaire card game every day instead of structuring social interactions with peers is failing to stimulate the student's growth. If a program fails to refocus on new skills and use new strategies, a student will continue at the old level of performance, and continuing progress is not likely.

Belief 3: Pleasure and Success.
Productive changes occur when behavior brings successful and satisfying results.

Program Implication. Positive, success-producing behavior is the key to lasting change and development. A child's willingness to try a new behavior results from significant, pleasurable past experiences. The program must provide a way for every child to have these kinds of experiences in order to feel successful. If experiences tend to be pleasurable and successful, a child will participate and assimilate the learning. If experiences are frightening, confusing, complicated, meaningless, or failure-producing, a child may tend to avoid further involvement. As a result, no learning (or negative learning) may occur.

This belief seems so obvious that explanation should be unnecessary, until we look at the number of negative experiences children have in their schools, homes, and neighborhoods. Consider little Lisa, a 4-year-old who was regularly asked by her day care teacher to put together puzzles with many pieces. When the puzzles were brought out, Lisa actively resisted them—trying to get other students' play materials or running out of the room. When puzzles with fewer, larger pieces were provided, Lisa responded positively and a cycle of success began. There was a sense of inner pride in her independent accomplishment of the new puzzle that was reinforced by the approval and recognition she received from the adults.

Lucille gives us a good example of what happens when older students with disabilities have negative experiences in a classroom. The feeling of having done something of value serves to consolidate and focus Lucille's psychological resources for learning even more skills. By recognizing every possible avenue for success, adults provide children all possible opportunities for experiencing the rewards of success. The more often children feel this flush of accomplishment, the more likely it is that they will focus on the part of themselves that others see as acceptable or desirable. And they will begin to see themselves as valued members of society.

Belief 4: Relevant Experiences.
A student learns and grows by culturally and personally meaningful experiences.

Program Implication. A program must relate to a child's personal world so that skills learned in the program produce satisfying results in real-life situations. A child's self-esteem depends upon experiences that have personal significance and social value. When significant experiences are absorbed, they become sources of continued growth and development. If a child's actions are viewed positively, then society and the child are in synchrony. A cycle of success begins: The child's development is nurtured by an encouraging environment, and the individual feels acclaimed and comfortable in the environment (Figure 3.1).

Culturally relevant skills open the door to future potential as an active and confident individual. Consider the cultural relevance of teaching young children to tie shoes or work a zipper. In mastering these tasks, they can feel the accomplishment of getting dressed in the morning with a growing sense of independence and competence. An example of a task that might have cultural relevance for older students is assembling a bicycle. If a student is given the opportunity to learn gainful employment as a bicycle assembler, then well and good. Or if the student has a bicycle, he can have a feeling of accomplishment in replacing a part when needed. If the student can ride the bicycle, this provides the experience of freedom of independent travel. These skills also enable the student to be acclaimed by others as a productive, useful individual. The bicycle repair skills lead to the development of other life skills, accompanied by an expanding confidence in becoming more and more capable. In contrast, if subsequent opportunities are not provided for using these skills, then the student has learned a skill that leads nowhere.

In summary, these four beliefs are the guiding principles in the design of the Developmental Therapy–Developmental Teaching curriculum. They lead us to an understanding of the imperative need to respond with programs that are positive and personally relevant to each child. They keep us focused on the potential for healthy, acceptable behavior in every student and emphasize the importance of successful, emotionally satisfying experiences in bringing about change and growth. Such results can occur only when a program reflects the values of the individual and the expectations of those who are important in the individual's life.

Lucille

Lucille, at age 14, has many unusual behaviors, one of which is her refusal to stay at her desk for any length of time. In a general education high school, this behavior accentuates her differences. But Lucille uses acceptable behavior in many other situations. One of her most normal and healthy desires, and one that is quite typical of her peers in regular classroom settings, is a desire to be like other girls her age. She seems to yearn for peer acceptance and inclusion in their groups.

Lucille has two teachers during her school day. One of these teachers focuses on eliminating Lucille's inappropriate behaviors. Lucille's refusal to stay at her desk is the primary program concern for this teacher because it seems to interfere with Lucille's ability to concentrate on her academic work.

The other teacher takes an entirely different approach and focuses on acceptable behavior that is a part of Lucille's age-appropriate behavioral repertoire—peer modeling. This teacher encourages Lucille to model the language of others in class discussions. She structures many activities for Lucille that do not involve sitting down, and she is quick to reflect to Lucille when her acceptable behavior is like that of the other students whom Lucille admires.

Lucille's behavior in the two classes is markedly different. She spends much of her time in the first class in either physical or verbal confrontation with her teacher—a contest of wills. In the second classroom, a great proportion of Lucille's time is spent participating in acceptable ways and interacting with peers in appropriate social exchanges.

What makes the difference?

Since the first class, during which Lucille was bodily forced to sit in her chair, she has begun resisting going to class. When she is forced into the room, she refuses to participate. Observational data show marked acceleration of unacceptable behavior, including negative statements, cursing, tantrums, and perseverative, ritualistic movements with her hands during the period immediately preceding the class. In contrast, when developmentally appropriate behaviors are encouraged, Lucille responds positively, and a cycle of success begins. There is a sense of inner pride in her personal success reinforced by the spoken and unspoken accolades from teachers and others who witness her success.

Figure 3.1. A cycle of success.

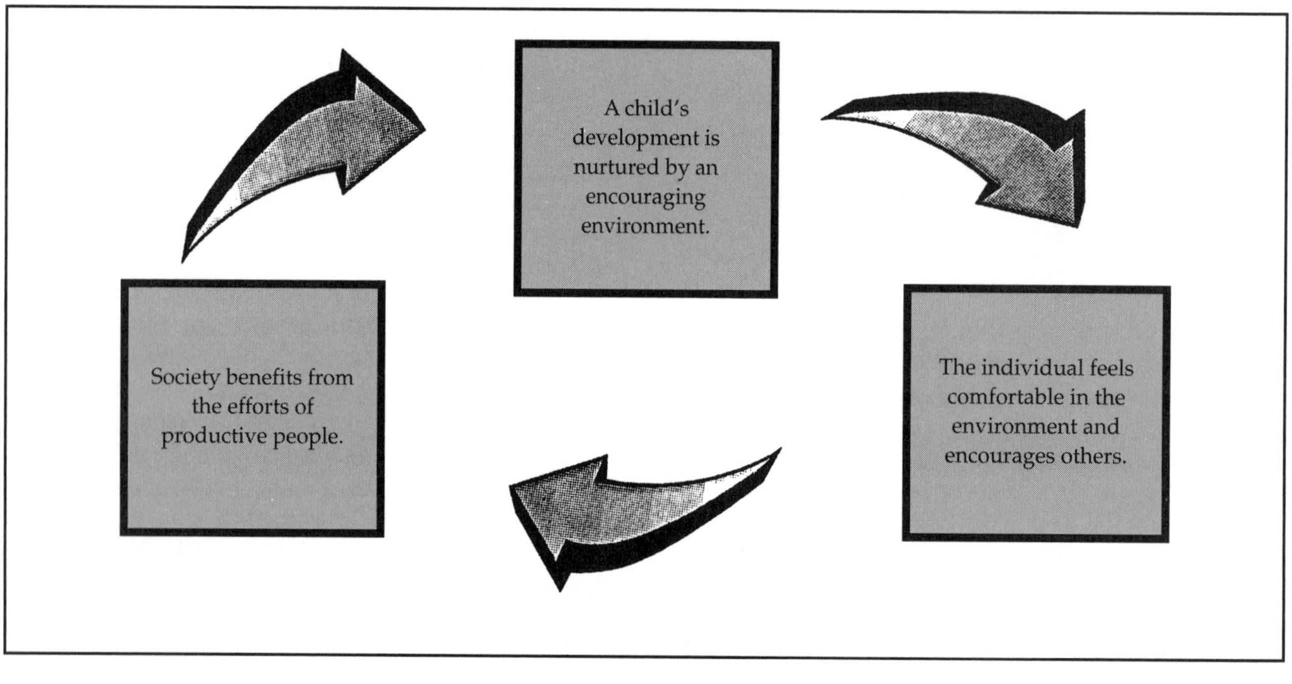

Young people can learn the basics of new behaviors and culturally valued conduct in many different program settings. But if they are to develop beyond a controlled practice level and learn more than superficial responses, their programs also must provide the richness and subtle nuances of genuine social relevance. All children should be given the chance to use newly learned skills in real situations. The implication is clear that, at some point, every child must be assisted into success in the mainstream of the school and community.

FREQUENTLY ASKED QUESTIONS ABOUT USING THIS CURRICULUM

Has the curriculum been used with students who are at risk but have no identified disabilities?

In early childhood programs and in primary grades of elementary school, teachers have applied Developmental Therapy–Developmental Teaching practices informally with entire classes. The strength of this approach is that education for social-emotional competence goes on within an inclusive general education curriculum.[1] It also offers adults a way to provide preventive programs, assisting students who are at risk for social and emotional problems. Within these programs, adults respond to students' varying social-emotional needs using developmental teaching strategies in the context of the regular, ongoing curriculum—whether it be creative activity centers, language arts, science, or math. They assess their students' social-emotional competence with the DTORF–R and use the management practices recommended for their students' stages of development. They learn to recognize the messages conveyed by students' behavior, responding verbally and nonverbally to validate and encourage them. They also conduct developmental teaching activities designed for the corresponding developmental stages. The applications have been so successful that we refer to them as *Developmental Teaching.*

This approach to prevention has prompted several school principals to provide in-service training for all teachers in their schools. In one instance, Developmental Teaching strategies were used system-wide in combination with a vigorous home-parent program component. The result was significant reductions in numbers of young children referred for special education when they entered school.

Can Developmental Therapy be used with students who have severe disabilities?

Well over 2 decades ago, Developmental Therapy had its origins in efforts to develop an effective psychoeducational program for students with severe social, emotional, and behavioral disabilities. The underlying assumption was that they needed to develop, to the extent possible, the skills that are expected of all children and youth as they mature. We also assumed that gains can be made more rapidly when these students have opportunities to learn from students who have already mastered the needed skills, usually in general education settings. Today the process is called *inclusion,* and it remains a major option of this curriculum, finding the optimal environment where adults can foster a student's achievement of needed social-emotional goals and objectives.

Developmental Therapy continues to be used with students of all ages whose disabilities take many different forms. There seems to be a nearly universal need among students for greater social-emotional competence (Guralnick, 1990, 1992). The curriculum's goals, objectives, activities, materials, and adult strategies recommended for use at a particular stage of development are applicable to students with many different and often challenging disabilities, including autism (Bachrach, Mosley, Swindle, & Wood, 1978). We have used the curriculum effectively with students of all ages and in many different educational environments: inclusive special education programs, day care and preschool programs, and programs in elementary, middle, and high schools, in both general and special education. It has been used with students in therapeutic recreation and camping programs, in psychiatric hospitals, and in residential schools for children and youth with profound hearing disabilities.

There are three forms of severely deviant behavior that most teachers face at one time or another: *physical violence, passive aggression,* and *thought disorders.* This curriculum approach is effective with students who have these disabilities. It guides us in the selection of program objectives by targeting developmental stages, emotional needs, and developmental anxieties. It contributes needed organization and structure to students' programs, and it assists adults in selecting management strategies that are effective in fostering their social-emotional growth.[2]

Has Developmental Therapy been used in special education programs when the IEP does not specify opportunities to include the student in a regular classroom?

Examples of effective applications exist in all-day programs, especially in special education classes for students with severe developmental disabilities. However, all-day, self-contained classes are less likely to be successful than

[1] The current debate over the efficacy of full inclusion for children with disabilities is reviewed extensively in Kauffman and Hallahan (1995). The *Journal of Emotional and Behavioral Problems* (1994) also has an entire issue on this topic. Inclusion loses its divisiveness when the Developmental Therapy–Developmental Teaching curriculum is used in both general education and special education settings. Each student should receive what is uniquely needed in whatever setting fosters the maximum opportunity for development.

[2] Management of severe behaviors is discussed in detail in Chapter 5.

those incorporating daily opportunities for peer modeling in inclusive general education settings or with students who have less debilitating disabilities. We have seen students cycle downward if left too long in completely segregated classes or in groups where their peers have not achieved the same levels of social, emotional, and behavioral skills. In such groups, higher developmental skills are not stimulated or reinforced by peers, so lower-level skills are modeled instead. When inclusive opportunities are not provided, in time, students may show loss of skills that were previously mastered.

Can this approach be used by one adult when there is no team?

In school, preschool, and after-school programs, we have seen successful Developmental Therapy–Developmental Teaching programs conducted by one highly experienced teacher with no other adult to assist. Several rather different program designs are used in these demonstrations. One is a typical early childhood program in which the activities are loosely organized around blocks of time, with areas of the room designated as activity centers. The teacher moves from area to area, interacting with the children in ways that promote their individual acquisition of DTORF–R objectives. In another, a small preschool program, the teacher designed a schedule and conducted activities with her entire group, using Stage Two Developmental Teaching practices. A third variation is one in which the teacher rated all first-grade students on the DTORF–R at the beginning of the school year and then instructed them in small groups composed of students working on similar objectives. In all of these program variations, the number of students in the groups, and the extent of their special needs, will influence the degree of success—as does the skill of the teacher.[3]

Although these arrangements can be successful if only a few students in a group have special needs, we do not recommend a solo attempt when several children have severe disabilities. Adults must be available to provide individual assistance to a student in need. When no adult is available, a student often does not continue to benefit from an activity, and gains are slow or nonexistent. This need for adults to be available is particularly important for students with severe emotional and behavioral disabilities. We have seldom seen severely disturbed students who can be left alone without adult supervision. Without an adult in charge, a group remains highly vulnerable to violence or other disruptions. When someone who is unknown to the students or not trained to provide skilled crisis intervention is used as backup, the probability of therapeutic management is greatly reduced.

Actual transfer of a student in crisis to another person also may be interpreted by the student as an inability by the adult to handle the crisis. This is seriously detrimental to the future effectiveness of the adult in charge. In many schools, no one is available for crisis management except the principal or assistant principal. Involvement of school administrators moves a crisis from the domain of therapeutic management to the area of school discipline. Sometimes administrative authority is appropriate in crisis resolution, but not always. With students who have severe, chronic emotional and behavioral problems, it is probably more therapeutic if the crisis is managed by an adult with whom the student has an ongoing relationship.

Can the curriculum be used by parents in home-based programs or by volunteers in mentoring programs?

Perhaps parents provide the best illustration of the use of this curriculum without a team. Informally, parents who learn the key milestones of development needed by the child, and who can identify the child's stage of social-emotional development, begin to "think developmentally." This orientation helps parents choose management strategies that will assist their children in acquiring needed skills. Then the process is completely informal and portable! The process can be carried out wherever a parent and child may be. Adult-child interactions and relationships are meaningful, and activities are focused in developmentally and personally relevant ways.

We also have used the model in more formal ways to provide home programs for young children when a parent seeks assistance in conducting home routines or structured activities for home teaching. The value of home programs is that the parent or primary caretaker incorporates developmental tasks for the child in daily life at home and in the community. When we begin a home program at a parent's request, we have a home intervention specialist work with the parent, and the extended family if available, to start the program. This person establishes a working relationship with the parent. Together, they define the activities that will be provided by the staff person. Most frequently, the "visitor" and the parent teach the child together. During this initial phase, the visitor (sometimes called the child's teacher) models developmentally appropriate management strategies and the style of interacting with the child that reflects the child's unique needs. The parent continues the management strategies, tasks, and routines independently until the next visit of the staff person. The child's success with the selected tasks and a positive relationship with the parent are the goals of the home program. However, an added benefit is the growth of parents in their parenting skills and their confidence in themselves as successful parents.

[3] More extensive discussion of schedule variations is provided in the last part of this chapter.

Effective variations of a home program have been provided by volunteer mentors. Mentoring is a highly successful way to reach children in need of a relationship and guidance from a significant adult. Mentors provide wonderful role models and opportunities for relationships with accepting adults. However, the mentors should have an understanding of the students' needs and of the way they can most effectively use their limited volunteer time to meet these needs. Mentors are able to foster noticeable growth in their students when a few specific objectives from the student's DTORF–R are identified for them. The mentor then understands the student's needs, the strategies required to increase social-emotional competence, and the type of adult needed by the student.

Does Developmental Therapy–Developmental Teaching need special administrative support?

A critical variable in the successful performance of special education teachers using the curriculum in elementary and middle school classrooms is the level of administrative support provided. To determine the level of administrative support available in a particular school, we use the *Developmental Therapy Administrative Checklist*, containing 41 program elements or administrative procedures considered necessary for the successful support of a special education program using this curriculum.[4] The items are rated as either "present" or "absent" and no attempt is made to judge the quality of the support. A simple count of the items rated "present" provides an administrative support score for the school. This score can then be compared to the administrative support scores of other schools with successful special education programs in Developmental Therapy–Developmental Teaching.

In a study involving 13 schools and 45 special education teachers and aides, we found a statistically significant correlation between a school's level of administrative support and the levels of classroom proficiency of teachers and aides using Developmental Therapy (Wood & Combs, 1981).[5] On the basis of these findings, we recommend an administrative support score of 32 or higher for maximum success in using the curriculum in special education programs. To plan for this level of support, administrators use the checklist to identify the current level of support in a school. If the total score (the sum of the procedures and resources in the school) is less than 32, it indicates that additional resources are needed to provide an adequate support system. These resources and procedures should be put into priority order. As additional resources become available, the needed program support elements can be added.

[4] The *Developmental Therapy Administrative Checklist* is contained in Appendix 3.

[5] This study is reviewed in greater detail in the section on model effectiveness in Chapter 1.

ASSESSING CHILDREN'S SOCIAL-EMOTIONAL DEVELOPMENT TO ESTABLISH TEACHING OBJECTIVES

We base our assessment practices on theories of social competence and beliefs about how it develops. We recognize that all children and youth progress through developmental sequences in acquiring social-emotional competence at varying rates and in different styles. To identify where a child is in this progression, we need a broad range of information, which we obtain from many sources: talking with parents, individual psychological and educational assessments, school and agency records, and observations of the student in school, in the neighborhood, and at home.

From this broad information base we are able to complete a *Preliminary Profile*. The Preliminary Profile identifies the extent to which the child has already accomplished each of the sequential goals for social-emotional competence in each curriculum area and stage. Figure 3.2 contains these general goals, which we use with parents during an IEP, IFSP, or ITP meeting.

Each student will have mastered some of these goals, be ready to work on others, and not yet be prepared to take on others. The consensus of those present at the IEP, IFSP, or ITP meeting shapes the selection of the goals. This step in assessment, identifying a student's Preliminary Profile, gives us general goal statements for the student in each of the four curriculum areas—four general goals that the student needs to begin working toward. The student's overall stage of social-emotional development is the predominant stage where the majority of these four goals occur. When the overall stage of development is identified, it provides us with the general indicator for placement and program planning—the foundation for subsequent assessment; IEP, IFSP, and ITP objectives; grouping for instruction; and evaluation procedures.

We have summarized case material on Roger to illustrate how we use the outline to systematically gather and interpret information.

The importance of obtaining and interpreting all of this information cannot be overemphasized. We recognize that a well-organized classroom with a mentally healthy climate can be conducted effectively for less severely troubled students without such depth of information. However, more seriously disturbed students will not make the hoped-for gains without a program that responds to deep concerns and anxieties. Awareness of underlying anxieties and knowledge of what such students value are essential. Materials and activities, especially those involving the creative arts, are excellent ways to reach such students and eventually produce genuine change and growth.

Because the curriculum is designed as a road map for social-emotional development, it is necessary to follow the Preliminary Profile with a more detailed assessment of

Figure 3.2. The Preliminary Profile: General goals for social-emotional development in Developmental Therapy–Developmental Teaching.

Stage	*Behavior*	*Communication*	*Socialization*	*(Pre)Academics/Cognition*
One	Trust own body skills	Use words to gain needs	Trust an adult sufficiently to respond	Respond to the environment with intentional body movements and basic mental processes of memory, classification, and receptive vocabulary
Two	Participate in routines and activities with success	Use words to affect others in constructive ways	Participate successfully in activities	Participate in activities with self-help, motor coordination, language, and mental processes of discrimination, sequencing, and numeration
Three	Apply skills to individual success as a group member	Use words to express self constructively in groups	Find satisfaction in group activities	Participate in an academic group successfully, using primary academic skills, language concepts, and symbolic representation of experiences
Four	Contribute individual effort to group success	Use words to convey understanding of feelings and behavior in self and others	Participate spontaneously and successfully as a group member	Use academic skills for successful social group experiences
Five	Respond to life experiences with constructive behavior	Use words to establish and enrich relationships	Initiate and maintain effective interpersonal relationships independently	Use academic skills successfully for personal enrichment

Helpful Background Information
for Assessment of Social-Emotional Development

Interests

Characteristic socialization style with adults
Characteristic socialization style with peers
Concerns and preoccupations
How needs and feelings are communicated
Defense mechanisms
Developmental anxieties
Role in peer group
Forms of social power
Values

Sources

Family information: Forms of discipline, concerns, relationships, friendships, family values, prior successes and failures, early development, notable events, significant adults, TV habits, sleep patterns, and eating habits

School history: Promotions, attendance, suspensions, grades, and prior successes and failures

Medical history: Prenatal care; birth events; psychiatric interviews; medications; hospitalizations; vision, hearing, language, and speech assessment; and health history

Standardized tests: Intellectual, behavioral, developmental, achievement, adaptive, and creative

Clinical assessments: Personality and projective

Nonstandardized assessments: Observations, developmental ratings, interest inventories, drawings and other creative products

Roger

Name: Roger

Age: 11 years 4 months **Grade:** 5th

Special Help: Resource room for help with a learning disability (LD)

Referral Notes: (from the principal)
Roger is constantly getting into power struggles with his 5th-grade teacher. The teacher is somewhat stern with Roger, but this does not seem to be working. The teacher is very frustrated as Roger is a constant troublemaker. When the teacher has conferences with Roger's mother, she accuses the school of being "out to get" Roger. He recently has been suspended several times for physically abusing students on the bus and in the halls. The LD teacher has not had problems with Roger's behavior, but she reports that he has made no academic gains in the year she has been working with him. Uneven attendance seems to be a contributing factor.

Special problem behaviors: Poor impulse control; easily enraged; passive disobedience to adults; states that others are against him; frequent verbal and physical encounters with peers and adults.

Classroom Observation: (by the school psychologist)
Roger was observed on two sequential days, and his behavior was similar on both days. With individual math assignments, Roger spent very little time on task. He wandered around the room but interacted with no one. During a geography lesson, the teacher was instructing the group. Roger listened but spent brief intervals (approximately 1 minute each) looking at the text and his written assignment sheet. For the remainder of the class period (35 minutes), Roger did the following: played with a Chapstick, looked at papers from a shelf behind his desk, pulled papers down off the shelf, looked at papers in file baskets by the door, examined another student's work sheet, and talked briefly to another student.

Information from Records:

I. *Intellectual Testing: Wechsler Intelligence Scale for Children–Revised (WISC–R)*
Verbal score—106
Performance score—106
Full scale—106

Verbal subtests		*Performance subtests*	
Information	11	Picture Completion	14
Similarities	9	Picture Arrangement	11
Arithmetic	13	Block Design	12
Vocabulary	9	Object Assembly	10
Comprehension	13	Coding	8
Digit Span	8		

Comments:
Roger scored in the 65th percentile rank, indicating that he is above average in ability compared with the WISC–R norming sample. These results may not be an optimal estimate of his ability, as he appeared to have trouble attending to several of the tasks. Some difficulties are noted in short-term memory and auditory memory tasks. Strongest area is ability to interpret social situations.

On the *Bender Visual-Motor Gestalt Test* Roger made only one error. This suggests that he does not have a visual-motor problem.

II. *Achievement testing: Wide Range Achievement Test*
Reading 2.7
Math 3.9

III. *Behavioral screening:* (by classroom teacher)
Significant problem behaviors
Acting Out and Distractibility

Bristol Social Adjustment Guide: Scored in severe range in areas of overreaction, hostility, peer maladaptiveness, and impulsivity.

IV. *Developmental Assessments:* None given.

V. *Adaptive Assessments:* None given.

VI. *Creativity:* None given.

Clinical Assessments: (given by clinical psychologist)

Personality and Projective Testing: Thematic Apperception Test; Bloom Sentence Completion Survey
Roger is highly egocentric. He has difficulty seeing things from the point of view of others. This makes it difficult for him to accept limits and discipline from adults. He is preoccupied with his physical appearance and sees himself as unattractive. He recognizes that he does not get along with other children

(continues)

and would like to be "like the other kids." His major area of expressed concern is difficulty interacting positively with peers. He reports "playing with some kids" to be the hardest thing in school.

Roger may have feelings of inadequacy and guilt that tend to cause him to be hostile and aggressive as a defense. Unmet drives, uninhibited personality, and traumatic events also were suggested in Roger's responses. In his stories, the need for aggression and achievement appeared to be very important to his heroes. Signs of affection and concern between parental figures followed acts of violence between these figures. Ego integration appears inadequate, with the severity of punishment often exceeding the "crimes" in his plots.

Roger has significantly negative feelings toward people in general and teachers in particular. He exhibits indecisiveness and tends to overstate a positive view of physical and psychological self as a defense against low self-esteem.

Other Nonstandardized Assessments:
The Developmental Therapy Objectives Rating Form–Revised (DTORF–R) (consensus rating by referring teacher, parent, and Developmental Therapy teacher)

Roger needs to work on the following goals for social-emotional competence (see Figure 3.2):

Behavior: To apply skills to individual success as a group member and to contribute individual effort to group success (transition from Stage Three to Stage Four)

Communication: To use words to express oneself constructively in groups (Stage Three)

Socialization: To find satisfaction in group activities (Stage Three)

Academics/Cognition: To use academic skills for successful social group experiences (Stage Four)

Overall, Roger is in Stage Three of social-emotional development. He is ready to develop skills to be a successful participant in a peer group. For Stage Three, he has mastered 57% of the Behavior milestones, 44% of the Communication milestones, 13% of the Socialization milestones, and 94% of the Academic/Cognition milestones.

Family drawings indicate that Roger has developed an age-appropriate schematic style (Stage Four—"Dawning realism"). He produces realistic interpretations and elaborations of human figures; there is attention to detail and links between visual and verbal communication modes. (See Figure 3.3.) While producing this drawing, Roger had some difficulty starting. A large male-type figure was begun and partially erased, and then the "son" and "mother" were drawn over the erasure.

Family History: (taken by a school social worker)
Roger is an only child. His mother reported that she changed jobs several times during her pregnancy and was anemic, emotionally upset, and depressed. She reported no problems with Roger's birth or early development. She expressed concern about him and some guilt over his troublesome school experiences.

(*continues*)

Figure 3.3. Drawing by Roger, an 11-year-old, severely disturbed Stage Three student, reflecting an age-appropriate schematic style (Stage Four) with realistic interpretation, elaboration of human figures, and attention to detail.

She lived with Roger's father until Roger was 2. She then married a violent and alcoholic man who beat her in front of Roger many times. She never saw him beat Roger but expressed fear that Roger might have been beaten when she was not at home. Subsequently she divorced her second husband but continued seeing him until he was killed recently in a fight. Roger seemed very upset about his death.

To discipline Roger, his mother reports that she keeps a list of "bad things" he has done. When the list has five items, she wakes him up after he has gone to sleep and whips him with a belt. She reports that this is not particularly successful.

School History: (from the school files)
Roger has attended two schools, and he has not repeated any grades. Suspensions were first recorded during the fourth grade. Attendance has always been erratic.

In December of his first year in school, Roger's *Wide Range Achievement Test* (WRAT) scores were: Reading, K.1; Spelling, 1.4; Math, 1.7. The *Peabody Individual Achievement Test* (PIAT) scores were: Reading Recognition, 1.3; Spelling, .97; Math, 1.4; General Information, 3.7. He was then 6 years 11 months old. A WISC–R was done at that time and was reported to have resulted in a full-scale score of 112 (verbal, 114; performance, 108). He passed both vision and hearing screenings. Evaluation by a speech and language pathologist revealed abilities above the mean in auditory comprehension, antonyms, and analogies. He was reported to have excellent receptive and expressive language but some difficulty with word retrieval.

He was provided assistance in an LD resource room following this testing to improve reading skills and on-task behavior. Specific IEP objectives focused on (a) learning the alphabet, (b) increasing sight vocabulary, (c) learning initial and final consonant sounds, (d) improving reading comprehension, and (e) increasing the amount of work accomplished. At the end of first grade, 5 months later, his achievement scores on the WRAT were: Reading, 2.2; Math, 2.6. At the end of second grade, 1 year later, WRAT scores were: Reading, 2.4; Spelling, 2.8; Math, 2.9. At the end of third grade, WRAT scores were Reading, 2.7; Math, 3.9.

Medical History: (by a psychiatrist)
No history of illness or hospitalization. Observations suggest hyperactivity and severe learning disability secondary to severe problems of adjustment and aggression. It was noted that the stepfather was an aggressive role model and possibly abused Roger. Abandonment by his natural father and the death of his stepfather seem to be critical in Roger's current adjustment problems. Observe for possible use of Ritalin to reduce hyperactivity (tried temporarily and discontinued by parent).

Interpretation of Records for Classroom Planning:

Chronological age interests: Horror films with realistic violence, food, adventure, karate.

Characteristic socialization style: Roger is in Stage Three—concerned with self-esteem and social recognition. He is very self-protective in responses to others. This will make him unresponsive to the needs of other students in a group but motivated to look good to others. He will seek recognition in any form.

Characteristic cognitive style: Roger seems to handle academic tasks and social problems at a semiconcrete level. He does not seem able to generalize processes or events from one experience to benefit himself in subsequent experiences. He is using wishful thinking and imaginary ideas to deny or compensate for overwhelming anxiety. His reasoning skills are organized, and he is beginning to sequence events but does not see cause and effect yet. This will limit the LSI procedure to the beginning steps only.

Defense mechanisms: Roger is using many defense mechanisms, but none seems to be working to give relief he needs from anxiety.[6] For example, he was observed to almost continually use compensation, denial, rationalization, intellectualization, displacement, withdrawal, and regression. Here are several observations: When situations are extremely difficult for him, he will put his coat over his head or will curl up on the floor in the corner of the room; at other times he refuses to discuss an issue. He may respond by saying, "It doesn't matter if I get suspended. I like staying away." He explains that his mother can't come in to talk with the principal because she is tired after work and works hard. When events build up to crisis proportions, he will attack a bus driver or other students.

---

[6]See also Chapter 2 for a review of defense mechanisms and developmental anxieties.

These defenses create a volatile classroom climate where neither students nor teachers can predict how Roger will react or what will set him off.

Developmental anxieties: There is evidence to suggest Roger is protecting himself from four major anxieties: *abandonment, inadequacy, guilt* and *conflict.* He may feel abandoned by his natural father and his stepfather, and he is uncertain about trusting his mother as she threatens to send him away and seems unable to help him with his problems at school. Because he is a bright student, Roger also realizes that he has somehow failed his mother by being such a problem to her and perhaps played a role in his mother and stepfather's separating (guilt). The daily problems with his teachers reinforce his sense of failure (inadequacy). And the failure of all adults (parents, teachers, and authorities) to help him promotes a level of resentment and anger that is the antithesis of his need to be assisted, cared for, and acclaimed as a worthy person by significant adults.

Stage of ego development: Roger's behavior suggests that he is functioning in the self-protective stage (Stage Three), where he often reconstructs reality with defense mechanisms such as rationalization and intellectualization in order to hide and control his feelings. This will make it difficult for his teachers to discuss and confront him with problems involving other students or adults.

Roles in group and social power: (For more information on this topic, see Chapter 10, which describes the steps we use in determining students' roles in the group, social power, and group dynamics.[7]) Roger's role in the classroom has varied, as might be expected. He has been the bully, clown, instigator, isolate, and occasionally the leader. The roles seem to be generated by the type of social power Roger elects to use when trying to get the attention of his peers or the teacher. When using *coercion,* he becomes violent toward the students who are less able to retaliate (the bully). From time to time he uses *likeability,* trying to attract the other students through jokes or silly behavior (the clown). Because he is bright and verbal, he frequently uses *expertness* to impress or influence other students (the leader). Yet his insensitivity to the needs of the other students usually leads to rejection by them (the isolate). When he is feeling particularly anxious and angry toward the teacher, Roger also uses *manipulation* to test the teacher or to set up other students to get into trouble (the instigator). The end result of these apparently unpredictable swings in role and social power is a classroom where the group dynamics cannot form into a productive effort. This will become a major poblem for the teacher.

Summary: Roger is in need of a Stage Three program. Normally he should be in Stage Four. One of Roger's basic problems has been the lack of consistency from adults. He has learned not to trust them. The Developmental Therapy–Developmental Teaching team will need to plan a Stage Three program for Roger that enhances his successes and provides a strong, predictable adult. The teacher will need to recognize Roger's need to be self-protective. She also should provide nurturing in the curriculum through food and symbolic events where adults care for other adults and children alike. The teacher should avoid confrontation and power struggles, yet be able to guarantee his psychological protection as well as the protection of the others from him. It is essential to build a relationship with Roger and recognize him as a desirable person. The prediction is that change will be slow and stormy. He should progress through Stage Three in about a year and probably will need another year in Stage Four. If Roger's mother obtains counseling for herself and training in positive parenting practices, the long-term outlook for Roger is favorable. He is a student with many assets and has the desire to achieve and be admired as a worthy person.

[7]See also Chapter 5 for a description of the social roles children have in groups.

skills mastered, current status, and future direction. Because most students begin to feel comfortable in a new classroom setting and show typical behavior after the first week, we make a detailed assessment of social-emotional competence after a student has been in the program for 8–10 class days. This generally allows for an accurate baseline assessment of a student's current level of functioning. At that time, we use the DTORF–R to obtain this information and to identify specific instructional objectives for social-emotional competence for the IEP or ITP. The DTORF–R contains 171 items in developmental sequences criterion-referenced to the four curriculum areas—Behavior, Communication, Socialization, and (Pre)Academics/Cognition. Within each area, items range from very basic low-level behaviors at the awareness level to very complex behaviors reflecting high levels of social and cognitive development. The items are sequenced into the five distinct stages of development, with Stage One being the lowest level and Stage Five the highest. These stages correspond with the age range in the curriculum—from birth to 16 years.[8]

The DTORF–R as an Assessment Instrument

The DTORF–R is the curriculum's road map. It was developed as a practical tool for teachers to use in planning classroom programs in social-emotional development and in evaluating student progress. Because of this emphasis, the DTORF–R is unlike other developmental assessment instruments such as those developed by Bayley, Catell, Gesell, Frankenburg, Kaufman, and McCarthy (Barnett, Macmann, & Carey, 1991). These instruments provide a standardized developmental score (a developmental age quotient) derived by comparing a child's responses in standard testing situations to the responses of a normative group. Because the resulting scores are designed to indicate a developmental status relative to a norm group, the resulting score serves a diagnostic function, indicating the extent to which a child's performance matches the performance of age peers. Neither the scores nor the items are intended to provide a framework for instruction. In contrast, the DTORF–R is not administered with a strictly standardized testing procedure, nor does it produce scores for comparison with a norm group. Rather, it emphasizes the sequential mastery of each item and its direct application to instruction.[9]

The DTORF–R uses an ordinal scale to assess whether a student has mastered an item (marked "✓"), is ready to work on an item (marked "X"), or is not yet ready to begin work on an item (marked "NR").[10] Subjective and observational data are used in rating a student's behavior in the home, neighborhood, and school. The rating clearly indicates what a student has already mastered, the current instructional focus, and what the student is not developmentally prepared to work on (Wood, 1992b).[11] The items selected for current work become the teaching objectives. Because the items are sequenced in order of difficulty, teaching objectives are selected in the order in which the items appear on the rating form.

The rating is done by consensus of a three-person team, usually consisting of the teacher or other adult who will provide the Developmental Therapy–Developmental Teaching program, the regular classroom teacher, and a parent. If a parent is not available, the primary caregiver, a family program specialist, or a case manager should provide input concerning how the student functions at home and in the neighborhood. It also is helpful to include the observations and opinions of others who may be working with the student. These may include aides, psychologists, psychiatrists, and recreation, music, art, reading, and language therapists. We have also involved older students in rating themselves on the DTORF–R. Although it is time-consuming, this procedure has been very effective in teaching students how to set goals. Older students like to participate in identifying their program objectives and in monitoring their own daily progress toward achieving the objectives. Those who are nearing the end of Stage Three or beginning Stage Four are particularly responsive to doing this and learn personal goal-setting skills in the process. We include an example of a completed DTORF–R for a preschool child (Figure 3.4).[11]

DTORF–R Instrument Reliability and Validity

The DTORF–R has a user's manual (Wood, 1992b) with specific instructions for learning to administer the instrument and score the results with reliability. A technical report (Wood, 1992a) also is available that describes the instrument's psychometric properties and provides procedures for reporting gains as percentages mastered or converting ratings to standardized *T* scores using goal attainment scaling.[12] With the use of standard training materials included in the user's guide, overall item-by-item interrater agreement has increased from .76 to .95. Interrater agreement within subscales reflects excellent reliability: Behavior = .93, Communication = .94, Socialization = .94, and (Pre)Academics/Cognition = .96 (Gunn, 1985). As a part of a statistical analysis of item difficulty, Kuder-Richardson–type reliability estimates of internal consistency among items were greater than .99 for each subscale, using 300 DTORF–R ratings (Weller, 1991).

Construct validity for the DTORF–R was established during the first phase of the model's development when the psychological processes believed to underlie the construct of social-emotional competence were identified from theory and research. As a latent trait, the construct needed to be defined in operational terms. To do this, four major developmental domains were analyzed to identify the specific processes that contributed to each. Following

---

[8] See Figure 1.5 for an outline of the ages, stages, and grades in school relationships.

[9] The complete DTORF–R instrument, user's manual (Wood, 1992b), technical report (Wood, 1992a), and computer program for IEP record keeping are available from the Developmental Therapy Institute, P.O. Box 5153, Athens, Georgia 30604.

[10] Although the DTORF–R is fundamentally an ordinal scale, when ratings are converted to *T* scores it also has the psychometric characteristics of an interval scale. See Cardillo and Smith (1994), pp. 181–187, for a discussion of concerns about interval-level measurement. For purposes of data analysis, conversion of DTORF–R ratings to *T* scores or developmental age scores is recommended.

[11] A blank DTORF–R form is included as Appendix 7.

[12] See Chapter 1 for a review of the development and expansion of the DTORF–R over three decades.

Figure 3.4. *Developmental Teaching Objectives Rating Form–Revised.* Completed for a preschool child.

Stage		Behavior		Communication		Socialization
Stage I	☑	1. Indicates Awareness	☑	1. Produces Sounds	☑	1. Indicates Awareness/Others
		___ Tactile ___ Aud. ___ Motor	☑	2. Attends to Speaker	☑	2. Attends/Other's Behavior
		___ Taste ___ Visual ___ Smell	☑	3. Responds/Verbal Stim./Motor Behav.	☑	3. Responds to Name
	☑	2. Reacts by Attending	☑	4. Responds/Cues/Word Approx.	☑	4. Engages/Solitary Play
	☑	3. Responds by Sustained Attending	☑	5. ▲Use Word Approx. Spon.	☑	5. Interacts Non-Verbally/Adult
	☑	4. Responds to Simple Stim./Motor Behav.	☑	6. Uses Word/To Adult	☑	6. Responds/Request/Come
	☑	5. Responds to Complex Stim.	☒	7. Uses Word/To Peer	☑	7. Dems. Underst./Request
	☑	6. Assists in Self-Help	☒	8. ▲Uses Word Sequence/No Model	☑	8. Same as C-6
	☑	7. ▲Responds Independently/Play Materials			☑	9. Begins Emergence/Self
	☑	8. ▲Indicates Recall of Routine			☑	10. ▲Participates/Parallel Play
					☒	11. Same as C-7
					☑	12. ▲Seeks Contact/Familiar Adults
Stage II	☒	9. Uses Play Material Appropriately	☑	9. Answers with Recog. Words	☑	13. ▲Demonstrates Imaginative Play
	☒	10. Waits/No Intervention	☑	10. Exhibits Receptive Vocabulary	☒	14. Same as B-10
	☒	11. Participates/Sitting/No Intervention	☒	11. ▲Commands, Questions/Word Sequence	☒	15. ▲Initiates Social Movement/Peer
	☒	12. Participates/Movement/No Intervention	☒	12. ▲Shares Minimal Information/Adult	☒	16. Participates/Directed Sharing Activity
	NR	13. ▲Participates Spontaneously	NR	13. Describes Characteristics/Self, Others	NR	17. Participates/Interactive Play
	☐	14. ▲Accepts Praise, Success with Control	☐	14. ▲Shares Minimal Information/Peer	☐	18. ▲Cooperates/Peer/Organ. Times
Stage III	☐	15. ▲Completes Individual Tasks Independently	☐	15. ▲Describes Personal Experiences	☐	19. ▲Shares Material, Takes Turns
	☐	16. Conveys Awareness/Expected Conduct	☐	16. Shows Feeling Responses Approp.	☐	20. ▲Imitates Approp. Behavior
	☐	17. Gives Reasons for Expectations	☐	17. Participates Approp./Group Discussion	☐	21. Labels Situation/Values
	☐	18. Tells Other Appropriate Behavior	☐	18. ▲Indicates Pride in Self	☐	22. Leads, Demonstrates for Group
	☐	19. ▲Responds Approp./Leader Choice	☐	19. Describes Attributes/Self	☐	23. Participates/Activity Suggested by Peer
	☐	20. ▲Refrains Behavior/Others Lose Control	☐	20. Describes Attributes/Others	☐	24. Sequences Own Experiences
	☐	21. ▲Maintains Acceptable Behavior in Group	☐	21. Recognizes Others' Feelings	☐	25. Indicates Developing Friendship
			☐	22. Verbalizes Pride/Group Achievement	☐	26. ▲Seeks Assistance, Praise/Peer
					☐	27. ▲Assists Others/Conforming
Stage IV	☐	22. Indicates Begin. Awareness/Own Progress	☐	23. Channels Feelings/Creative Media	☐	28. Identifies with Adult Heroes
	☐	23. Indicates Flexibility/Procedures	☐	24. Same as B-22	☐	29. Sequences Group Experience
	☐	24. Participates/New Experience With Control	☐	25. Explains/Behavior Influences Others'	☐	30. ▲Suggest Activ./Peer Group
	☐	25. Implements Alternative Behaviors	☐	26. ▲Verbalizes Feelings Approp. in Group	☐	31. Expresses Aware./Others' Different Actions
	☐	26. ▲Responds/Provocation With Control	☐	27. ▲Initiates Positive Relationship Verbally	☐	32. Listens to Others' Opinions
	☐	27. Accepts Responsibility/Actions, Attitudes	☐	28. ▲Praises, Supports Others Verbally	☐	33. Expr. Inter./Peer Opinion of Self
	☐	28. ▲Suggests Interpersonal & Group Solutions	☐	29. ▲Expresses Cause-Effect/Feelings, Behavior	☐	34. Suggests Solutions to Problems
					☐	35. Discrims. Opposite Social Values
					☐	36. Draws Infer. from Social Situations
Stage V	☐	29. ▲Seeks New Work Skills	☐	30. Uses Complex, Figurative Statements	☐	37. ▲Understands, Respects Others
	☐	30. ▲Seeks Desired Group Role	☐	31. ▲Uses Conciliatory Verbal Responses	☐	38. ▲Interacts Successfully/Multiple Roles
	☐	31. Understands, Accepts Law & Order	☐	32. ▲Recognizes, Includes Others' Contribu.	☐	39. ▲Makes Personal Choices/Values
	☐	32. Participates/Group Self-Governance	☐	33. Describes Multiple Motives, Values	☐	40. Indicates Self Understanding/Goals
	☐	33. Solves Personal Problems	☐	34. ▲Expresses Values, Ideals	☐	41. ▲Sustains Relationships
			☐	35. Sustains Interpersonal, Group Relations		

▲ = Student must do this spontaneously for item mastery, without direct adult cues or control to elicit the behavior.

Figure 3.4. continued

Academics/Cognition

Stage I

- ☑ 1. Same as B-2
- ☑ 2. Same as B-3
- ☑ 3. ▲Shows Short Term Memory
- ☑ 4. Same as B-5
- ☑ 5. ▲Imitates Acts of Adults
- ☑ 6. Shows Fine, Gross Motor/18 months
- ☑ 7. Knows Names/Objects
- ☑ 8. Same as C-4
- ☑ 9. ▲Same as C-5
- ☑ 10. Matches Shapes, Objects with Spaces
- ☑ 11. Identifies Body Parts (4)
- ☒ 12. Recognizes Detail/Pictures
- ☑ 13. Sorts Objects
- ☑ 14. Labels Pictures

Stage II

- ☑ 15. Recognizes Use of Objects
- ☑ 16. Performs Body Coord./3 year
- ☑ 17. Matches Identical Pictures (of 3)
- ☑ 18. Performs Fine Motor Coord./3 year
- ☑ 19. Recognizes Different Object (of 3)
- ☒ 20. Understands 3 Opposites
- ☒ 21. Categorizes Diff. Pictures/Similar Assoc.
- ☑ 22. Counts to 4 (1 to 1)
- ☑ 23. Identifies 4 colors, 3 shapes
- ☒ 24. Alternates Same, Different Pict. or Object
- ☑ 25. Counts to 10 (1 to 1)
- NR 26. Performs Eye-Hand Coord./5 year
- ☐ 27. Discrims. Num., Designs, Upr. Case Letters
- ☐ 28. Performs Body Coord./5 year
- ☐ 29. Recognizes Groups to 5
- ☐ 30. Dem. Rote Memory/5 year
- ☐ 31. Sequences 3 Pictures

Stage III

- ☐ 32. Performs Eye-Hand Coord./6 year
- ☐ 33. Performs Body Coord./6 year
- ☐ 34. Reads 50 Primary Words
- ☐ 35. Recogs., Writes Numerals/Groups 1–10
- ☐ 36. Writes 50 Primary Words/Mem., Dictation
- ☐ 37. Listens/Story/Comprehension
- ☐ 38. Explains Others' Behavior
- ☐ 39. Reads Sentences/Comprehension
- ☐ 40. Adds, Subtracts/1–9
- ☐ 41. Identifies Illogical Elements
- ☐ 42. Writes Sentences About Story
- ☐ 43. Performs Physical Skills, Games/Elem.
- ☐ 44. Writes Simple Sentences
- ☐ 45. Adds, Subtracts/Time/Money
- ☐ 46. Reads, Explains Meas. Words
- ☐ 47. Reads, Tells About Stories
- ☐ 48. Uses Place Value, Regroup, Mult. Seriation

Stage IV

- ☐ 49. Writes to Communicate
- ☐ 50. Multiplies, Divides to 100
- ☐ 51. ▲Reads for Pleasure, Information
- ☐ 52. Computes Money to $10.00
- ☐ 53. Explains Fiction Characters
- ☐ 54. Uses Grammatical Rules/Writing
- ☐ 55. Same as S-35
- ☐ 56. Solves Measurement, Logic Problems

Stage V

- ☐ 57. Seeks Others' Opinions/Current Issues
- ☐ 58. Discriminates Fact/Opinion
- ☐ 59. Recognizes, Explains Illogical Behavior
- ☐ 60. Solves Word Problems/Fractions, Decimals
- ☐ 61. Same as B-33
- ☐ 62. ▲Uses Academic Tools/Citizen, Worker

Notes

____
Parent's Signature

____
Family/Services Coordinator Signature

____
Teacher's Signature—General Education

____
Teacher's Signature—Special Education

DTORF–R SUMMARY (sum ✓s = items mastered)

Behavior items mastered:	8
Communication items mastered:	8
Socialization items mastered:	12
Academics/Cognition items mastered:	21
Total DTORF–R items mastered:	49
Developmental stage:	Two
Chronological age at rating:	4 yrs–4 mos

that phase of analysis, we again reviewed theory and research to determine how each process was expressed in its developmental evolution from birth onward. Each item in the DTORF–R is referenced to this domain analysis; because of its importance to the theoretical foundation of the curriculum, we include the orginal content analyses of the four developmental domains as Appendix 4.

The content validity of these particular items for the population of students, from birth to 16 years of age, with emotional, social, and behavioral disabilities was established by field-testing the instrument with several thousand students over a 5-year period, resulting in the first and second revisions of the instrument. Over the following 10-year period, evaluation of demonstrations of the model and replications with several thousand students in 27 states and internationally have documented the validity of this approach with students having a range of disabilities including autism, intellectual delay, and language, hearing, and vision disabilities; those who have multiple disabilities; those who have no disabilities; and those who are gifted.[13]

Two studies have been conducted to examine the hierarchical sequences of item difficulty for the instrument. The first was a Guttman-type scalogram using ratings of 87 students with severe emotional and behavioral disabilities, obtained at repeated intervals over 9 months. Results indicated that the sequence of items on the original instrument was essentially in the correct order of difficulty. The second study analyzed 300 entry profiles of students with serious social, emotional, and behavioral disabilities between the ages of 2 and 14 years. In this study, the Rasch dichotomous model was used for the statistical recalibration of order of item difficulty for the DTORF–R. The Rasch method frees the estimations of item difficulty from the usual statistical procedure requiring a randomly selected sample from a normal distribution of the trait being measured. When the trait is social-emotional growth, a latent trait, and the population is students with problems in this area of development, traditional statistical procedures may not be as precise as the Rasch model, which eliminates sample effects. As a result of this analysis, several items on the DTORF–R were reordered to improve the order of item difficulty (Rasch, 1960; Snyder & Sheehan, 1992; Weller, 1991).

The latest revision, resulting in the 1992 DTORF–R, expanded the content validity with an analysis of item correspondence to other current developmental inventories and early childhood curricula. A panel of six expert professional teachers and teacher educators did an item-by-item comparison of DTORF–R items in the (Pre)Academics/Cognition subscale with the *Bayley Scales of Infant Development* (Bayley, 1969); the *Battelle Developmental Inventory Screening Test* (Newborg, Stock, Wnek, Guidabaldi, & Svinicki, 1984); the *Brigance Diagnostic Inventory of Early Development, Revised* (Brigance, 1991); *Developmental Diagnosis, third edition* (Gesell & Amatruda, 1975); the *Developmental Profile II* (Alpern, Boll, & Shearer, 1986); and the *Learning Accomplishment Profile–Revised* (Sanford & Zelman, 1981). Each DTORF–R item was compared for wording, level of difficulty, and place in the developmental sequence. Where indicated, DTORF–R items were reworded for greater clarity and a few items were reordered to correspond with prevailing judgments about hierarchical sequence.

Experience with many school districts has shown the DTORF–R to be a highly practical and reliable way of identifying instructional objectives for social-emotional competence. A computer program that contains the complete set of 171 teaching objectives assists teachers, parents, and administrators in preparation of the IEP, IFSP, and ITP. This permits ease in documenting student progress over specified intervals during a school year. Because of the age span covered (birth to 16 years), it also permits longitudinal record keeping and provides program continuity across school grades.

[13]See Chapter 1 and Appendix 6 for documentation of the effectiveness of this curriculum model.

EVALUATING STUDENTS' PROGRESS

Careful attention to each student's rate of progress in mastering IEP, IFSP, or ITP objectives is an essential part of this curriculum model. Ideally, the evaluation process should permeate an educational program, providing information for continuing adjustment and refinements on an ongoing basis (formative evaluation) as well as for documenting program outcomes and student progress (summative evaluation). When used correctly, the DTORF–R can satisfy requirements for both ongoing and outcome evaluation.

Ongoing (Formative) Evaluation

The first step in establishing an evaluation system for a Developmental Therapy–Developmental Teaching program is to learn to use the DTORF–R with accuracy. This instrument can provide a profile of social-emotional competence for every student in the program. These baseline ratings should verify the appropriateness of the social-emotional objectives selected for each student's program. The next step is to establish an evaluation schedule for the school year. Most teachers and administrators prefer to follow the regularly scheduled grading periods used by the school system (typically about every 3 months). Plan to include parents and other adults involved in working with each student to make these periodic ratings.

We repeat the rating at scheduled grading or testing intervals throughout the school year. This tends to be about 12-week intervals in most schools. Each rating offers an opportunity for refocusing the student's program on new objectives as soon as the chosen ones have been mastered. In this way we avoid the problem of continuing an objective that is obsolete once a student has achieved mastery. We also use these periodic ratings to regroup students, so that those who are progressing can be moved to a group with comparable peers.[14] For summer programs, we use the end-of-the-school-year DTORF–R rating as the summer baseline and rate only once, at the end of the summer program. This last rating is used again in the fall as the initial rating for the next school year.

By rating students at repeated intervals using the DTORF–R, parents and teachers stay in communication about the students' progress and changes in their developmental status. These ratings also alert parents and teachers to times when program adjustments are necessary. If a student is not progressing as rapidly as expected, or perhaps is not progressing at all, a number of explanations must be reviewed. Clearly, the type of instructional activities and materials used, the role of adults, and management strategies must be considered. All sorts of events outside of school impinge on students' progress. It is essential to take these events into account when reviewing a student's program. We also consider the developmental profiles of the others in the group. Sometimes particular students make significant negative contributions to the developmental progress of the others. Regrouping one student with a different group may benefit the others significantly and should be considered. Occasionally we also find an unhappy chemistry between student and adult. This requires thoughtful review of the student's social and emotional needs and a review of the available adults who can be most effective in meeting these needs.[15]

Analysis of a student's DTORF–R profile is most helpful in understanding what has happened since the last rating and what to expect during the next grading period. Consider first the actual time span between grading periods. For example, if only 12 weeks have passed since the baseline rating, developmental gains would be expected to be small in some areas and may not be evident at all in other, more difficult areas for a particular student. On the other hand, if an entire school year has passed, gains should be evident on every subscale, reflecting progress in every curriculum area, unless some extraordinary circumstance has occurred in the student's life to produce regression with a negative effect on learning.

Patterns of gains and lack of gains across the four subscales also indicate what to expect during the next rating period. Typically, a large gain on one subscale will be followed by a plateau period where the student makes negligible gains or remains at the same level in that particular area of development. This lack of gain should not necessarily be considered program ineffectiveness. Rather, we interpret this to be the practice phase of mastery, reminding ourselves that no student can sustain dramatic increments in learning indefinitely without periodic plateaus for "rest"—practice and assimilation. Such periods of rest seem essential to the developmental process. However, during the rest phase for one curriculum area, expect gains in other areas. We have observed that with good planning, a student can often make large gains in an area where there has been little previous progress. This information gives clear direction for a shift in emphasis during the next program period.

If a student is just beginning a stage, with about 20% of the DTORF–R items mastered in that stage and curriculum area, it is likely that the program should continue with previously successful, stage-related activities. However, when a student is nearing the end of a stage, as shown by mastery of at least 80% of the DTORF–R items in that stage, regrouping the student with others in the next highest developmental group may be needed. Students who have made solid gains and gone through the plateau period need to move forward. For them, regrouping with higher-functioning students may accelerate development. As noted previously, without this regrouping, we have seen regression and "down-cycling," where students actually lose skills they have recently acquired. On the other hand, being placed with students too far advanced may keep success out of reach.

Outcome (Summative) Evaluation

Most intervention programs must provide summative data documenting students' progress in achieving IEP, IFSP, or ITP goals and objectives. There are many ways to approach this problem of establishing solid data to evaluate outcomes in a service-based program. The basic evaluation system used with this curriculum model is one designed a number of years ago by William Swan, Carl Huberty, and Alan Kaufman (Swan & Wood, 1975). It remains the primary evaluation system and has been shown to be efficient and effective in collecting dependable evidence to answer the basic evaluation question, Have the students acquired the specified goals and objectives while participating in the program? We continue to use this criterion-referenced approach for in-house summative program evaluations by teachers and school administrators to report student progress (Figure 3.5).

When outcome data need to be summarized for an individual or group, we recommend a simple and straightforward procedure to calculate the percentage of DTORF–R objectives mastered between two specified time periods.

[14] At every stage, it appears that students who make rapid gains need to be moved forward to benefit from higher-functioning peer role models. We have observed that troubled students left together for an entire year tend to cycle downward in their behavior after making gains.

[15] Chapter 2 contains a discussion of the psychological impact of adults on a student's ability to learn. Chapters 5 and 6 provide management strategies to avoid or overcome many of the potential difficulties between students and teachers.

Figure 3.5. The criterion-referenced evaluation system. Adapted from Swan and Wood, 1975, p. 40.

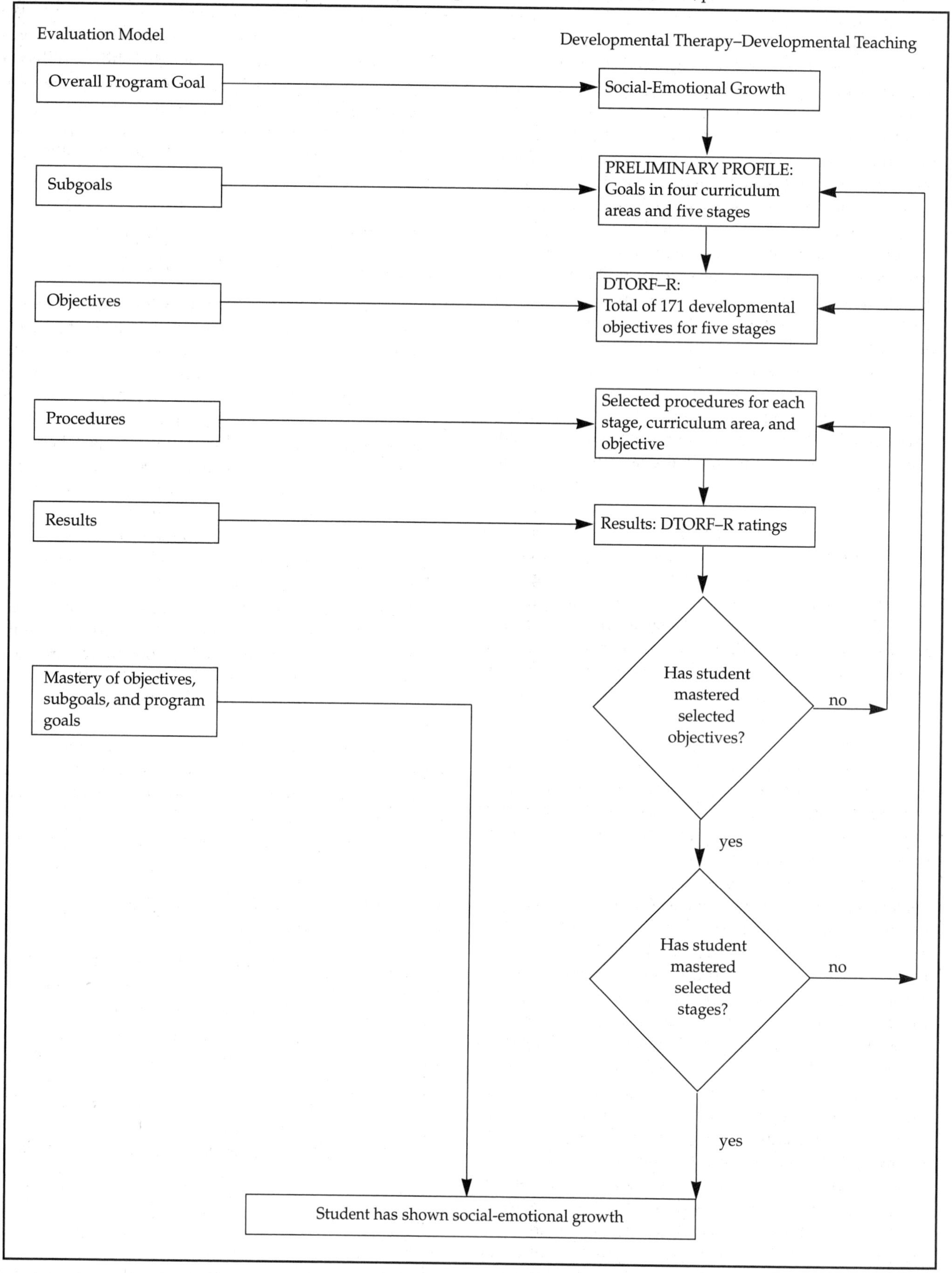

Percentages provide basic outcome data documenting that an individual or group made gains (or no gains) during a specified time in the program. These percentages can be calculated separately for each stage and the four curriculum areas or aggregated into a single percentage of the whole. By comparing the actual number of objectives mastered to the total that can be mastered, it is possible to see the proportional and cumulative progress in achieving objectives through the stages and the comparative areas of strengths and weaknesses. With the DTORF–R computer program now available, these calculations are not time-consuming, and they provide ongoing documentation of progress for each student, for several groups in a school, and for a system-wide evaluation of student gains. Computerized data also make it easy for a school system to build up its own local normative tables for comparisons between groups of students served by ages, groupings, classes, stages, teachers, or content areas.

Several more complicated, but less direct, procedures have been developed recently in response to special educators' concerns about individual goals, individual rates of change, and the confounding influence of the type and severity of a disability on documentation of a student's progress. A proportional change index (PCI) has been used by Wolery to measure the relationship between an individual student's rate of development during intervention and a preintervention rate of development. The PCI is the ratio of developmental age to chronological age at these two different times. By comparing the rate of development over the years before intervention to the rate of development during the intervention, some claim for control for maturation without intervention can be made (Wolery, 1983). To use this approach in summative evaluations for groups of students, DTORF–R gains can be converted to developmental age scores, assuming that gains with age are stable and equal in incremental values over months and years. It is not recommended for conversion of an individual student's scores.

Goal attainment scaling (GAS) is another procedure for solving summative evaluation problems associated with documenting individual differences in response to program intervention (Kiresuk, Smith, & Cardillo, 1994). GAS is a mathematical procedure for "assessing the amount of relevant change brought about by participation in a treatment program, educational experience, or other intervention" (Smith, 1994, p. 5). GAS scores allow comparisons of relative success of individuals in achieving their unique program objectives. By converting an individual's goal achievement to a *T* score, numerical comparisons can be made between individuals or groups following intervention, even though the goals and objectives may differ among the individuals. This procedure has been developed and refined over the past 30 years for applications in the mental health and clinical fields. GAS also has been used for evaluation of populations of young children with disabilities (Maloney, Mirrett, Brooke, & Johannes, 1978; Simeonsson, Bailey, Huntington, & Brandon, 1991; Simeonsson, Huntington, & Short, 1982). We have found GAS to be a useful procedure when comparing DTORF–R gains data between students at different stages, with different program objectives, in varying locations, and with different disabling conditions and degrees of severity. It can be calculated with a computer program, providing a standard *T* score for both formative and summative evaluation.[16]

SCHEDULES FOR VARIOUS EDUCATIONAL SETTINGS

Developmental Therapy–Developmental Teaching can be used within any program concerned with fostering social-emotional development and responsible behavior. The range of applications extends from informal programs at home to totally inclusive educational settings, from clinics and residential programs to intensive, concentrated intervention programs provided by school systems. It has been used in community programs and in special education all-day or half-day sessions, resource rooms, special classes, and vocational or transition programs. Variations in settings and schedules reflect individual students' needs and developmental continuity (Barbour & Seefeldt, 1993).

The amount of time scheduled in these various settings and the number of students in a group depend upon their ages, their developmental stages, and the degree of severity of their needs. The students' program objectives from their IEPs, IFSPs, and ITPs determine the schedule, group assignments, and amount of time provided. The most frequently used variations in schedules and settings are summarized in this section. We organize this review around four major categories of education: early childhood, elementary school, middle school, and high school. (The last part of the book provides the chapters that detail the program variations for students at each stage of development.)

In Early Childhood, Preschool, or Day Care Settings

Children with and without disabilities in early childhood, preschool, or day care programs are developmentally in either Stage One or Stage Two, depending upon their age and life experiences.[17] In the pattern of social-emotional development, they must first learn to respond to the environment with trust. Then they must acquire skills that help them to respond to the environment with success. During these early years of childhood, they are vulnerable to two developmental anxieties: abandonment

[16] Procedures for converting DTORF–R data to *T* scores or developmental age scores and for calculating PCIs and goal attainment scaling are described in the DTORF–R *Technical Report* (Wood, 1992a).

[17] Chapters 8 and 9 provide details for using the curriculum with young children.

and inadequacy. Programs that meet their social-emotional needs must address both of these goals and fortify them against these developmental anxieties.

It is fairly easy to blend a Developmental Therapy–Developmental Teaching curriculum into home programs or into totally inclusive early childhood education programs. When young children are at risk or have a disability that impedes their progress socially, emotionally, or behaviorally, they seem to benefit from an inclusive, integrated approach to learning skills for social-emotional competence. However, in all settings, considerable care must be given to ensure that each child receives the necessary individual attention from the adults providing the programs.

As young children begin to acquire fundamental skills for social and emotional competence, they need to gain functional language and some ability to participate, follow directions, and use preschool materials appropriately. They need carefully planned experiences in order to learn social interaction, social communication, appropriate behavior, and play skills. To assist in the successful participation of these young children in an inclusive early childhood program using Developmental Therapy–Developmental Teaching, at least two skilled adults are usually necessary. The number of children in each group who require high levels of adult attention should be carefully monitored. A group of five young children with disabilities in Stage One is the maximum number for experienced adults and parents. About six young children with disabilities should be the maximum number in Stage Two.

In large, inclusive early childhood programs, if adults are not able to provide the necessary experiences for the children who need to learn fundamental social-emotional skills, consideration should be given to providing intensive, concentrated assistance for brief periods daily. Sometimes very young children and those with the most severe disabilities are in enormous need of adult attention and guidance. These children often show gains with as little as 1 hour daily of additional, concentrated Developmental Therapy–Developmental Teaching. In these programs, the adults work on specific DTORF–R objectives also in the inclusive setting during the entire day using Developmental Teaching strategies.[18]

In Elementary Schools

Typically, in most elementary schools at the beginning of a school year, social-emotional development among all students will range from Stage Two with children in kindergarten and Stage Three in the primary grades through the middle of Stage Four with students beyond the fourth grade.[19] The general social-emotional accomplishment for primary-grade students typically is to learn skills for successful group participation. Students in the upper elementary grades are learning to invest in group processes. This latter goal carries over into the middle school years, as it is a difficult stage of development—learning to take the viewpoint of others and to recognize that individual priorities must sometimes give way for participation in the well-being of the group. During these stages of development, primary-grade students are vulnerable to the developmental anxiety of guilt—over failure to live up to the standards of others—while upper elementary students are coping with the developmental anxiety of conflict—between the need for independence from reliance on adults and the continuing need for dependence on adults. Students who are progressing in typical patterns will need little special intervention as they move from grade to grade in school unless they experience crisis in their lives.

However, students at risk and those referred for special education because of emotional or behavioral disabilities need carefully planned daily programs in Developmental Therapy–Developmental Teaching. Their programs can be provided in inclusive settings or in special education areas, depending upon their needs and the specifications of their IEPs and IFSPs. These students usually are in Stages Two and Three.[20] Because of this two-stage distribution, we recommend multiple groupings, using the student's IEP or IFSP goals and objectives. At the beginning of a school year there will be some students who are still in Stage Two and others making the transition from Stage Two to Stage Three. However, it is not unusual for some students to be solidly into Stage Three.

These groups of students have quite different social-emotional needs and require different programs. To accommodate this range of program needs, at least two groups are essential, but three groups offer more precision in programming. By having three groups available, flexibility is provided for grouping and regrouping students as they make progress. Some students achieve developmental gains at faster rates than others and should be regrouped with students who are also working to acquire more advanced skills. Before the end of a school year, an effective program will have moved some of these students into Stage Four, making a third group essential.

When older elementary school students progress into Stage Four, they should be in general education programs for most of the day, and 1 hour of an intensive Developmental Therapy program each day should be sufficient. Many of these students should be ready to exit the pro-

[18] There is an extensive body of literature on the importance of social competence in the lives of preschool children with disabilities. It is estimated that 10% of all children lack sufficient social competence, and for those with disabilities the estimate is even higher. For a comprehensive review, see Odom, McConnell, & McEvoy (1992b).

[19] Chapter 10 contains details of using the curriculum in the primary grades and Chapter 11 focuses on the curriculum's applications for students in upper elementary grades and middle school.

[20] It is unusual to find an elementary school–age student in Stage One unless the student has other severe disabilities. When such students are also in need of social, emotional, or behavioral assistance, they need an intensive Developmental Therapy program in addition to other special education.

gram at the end of the school year. In some elementary schools, resource room programs provide students with intensive Developmental Therapy–Developmental Teaching for 45 minutes to an hour a day. This limited amount of assistance seems to be sufficient for (a) students with mild social or behavioral problems; (b) those who are experiencing a severe transient crisis in their lives such as death, divorce, illness, or abuse; (c) those who are participating in a special education program in an inclusive setting and are in need of short, daily periods of intensive special help; and (d) those who have made the desired gains and are in the process of exiting a special education program in Developmental Therapy.

If students are in need of intensive intervention in special education, we recommend providing a minimum of two teachers and two aides, in a typical elementary school. We illustrate a schedule for them in Figure 3.6. This schedule provides an intensive, individualized program, using groupings by instructional goals and objectives to meet the specific social-emotional needs of up to 28 students daily.

In this schedule, one teacher and aide provide Developmental Therapy–Developmental Teaching programs to two groups of Stage Two students daily, and the second teacher and aide work with two groups of Stage Three students daily. The schedule provides the flexibility to have separate groups for beginning and advanced Stage Three students. The schedule also provides time for the teachers and aides to follow up their students' progress and assist as needed in inclusion programs in the general education classrooms. When the students are not participating in the Developmental Therapy programs, they are in typical classrooms where their teachers also use Developmental Teaching. The students are scheduled for classes in the grades and academic areas in which they are the strongest. Daily inclusion in a regular education program is essential for successful progress. This is where generalization of learning happens, with peer modeling and practice of new social and communication skills.

The schedule in Figure 3.6 has a drawback to consider: There is no time for teachers to collaborate with parents in home management programs. Therefore, it may be necessary to have a clinically experienced case manager assigned to the Developmental Therapy–Developmental Teaching team to work with parents whose children have special needs. In some school districts where case managers are not available, the teachers' schedules are modified to 4 days per week for the afternoon classes so that the teachers can use one afternoon each week to meet with parents.

In Middle Schools

Typical middle school students without disabilities are progressing developmentally through Stage Four.[21] For these students, the overall goal for social-emotional development is to invest in group processes. The typical developmental anxiety during this stage is conflict between the need for

[21] Chapter 11 provides details for using the curriculum with students in middle schools. When middle school students are severely troubled, they may require a Stage Three program, described in Chapter 10.

Figure 3.6. A sample schedule for elementary school.

	Teacher and Aide (14 students in Stage Two)	*Teacher and Aide* (14 students in Stage Three)
Morning:	Two-hour block for group of six Stage Two students	One hour for backup with students in inclusive placements
	One hour for backup with students in inclusive placements	Two-hour block for group of six Stage Three students
Lunch:	Teacher eats with group not able to handle lunch independently in cafeteria; aide assists students in inclusive placements	Teacher and aide assist as needed in cafeteria
Afternoon:	Two-hour block for group of eight students making transition from Stage Two to Stage Three	One hour for backup with students in inclusive placements
	One hour for backup with students in inclusive placements	Two-hour block for eight students making transition from Stage Three to Stage Four
	One hour debriefing and planning	One hour debriefing and planning

independence and the need for dependence. There also will be a number of troubled students, some with additional disabilities, who will be experiencing such difficulties with social-emotional development that they will still be in Stage Two or Three and may be struggling with all of the previous, unresolved developmental anxieties. This three-stage spread reflects the range of severity of students' problems frequently found in middle schools. For example, middle school students who have only progressed to Stage Two usually have severe disabilities such as psychosis, thought disorders, autism, severe passive aggression, or severe depression. They are frequently violent and often far behind their peers in academic skills. Providing an effective program for them requires meeting their individual developmental and emotional needs while providing programs in settings that fully support their need for associations with their age peers.

Middle school students whose social-emotional development is in Stage Three exhibit the full range of moderate to severe problems, whereas those in Stage Four usually are less severely troubled and have greater potential for participating successfully as a member of a typical group in an inclusive setting. In middle schools, Stage Three and Stage Four students who are receiving Developmental Therapy–Developmental Teaching programs, either through special education or regular education programs, have regular homeroom teachers and usually spend at least half of each day in inclusive settings. The Developmental Therapy–Developmental Teaching team assists in the inclusive program to the extent specified in each student's IEP. The team is also on call as needed for crisis intervention.

Because of the wide range of program needs for students in middle school, we recommend two teachers and one aide to provide Developmental Therapy–Developmental Teaching for students in need of special assistance. Some of their work is done in inclusive settings and some is done in small-group settings, depending upon students' IEPs. The teachers' schedules are flexible and often change after each grading and DTORF–R rating period, when some students are regrouped with students who share common instructional goals and objectives. Figure 3.7 illustrates the way the team is scheduled in a middle school operating on a 7-hour school day with two teachers and one aide working with about 26 students daily.

One teacher and aide provide middle school programs for groups of students in Stage Three and the few Stage Two students. These programs vary in length from 1 to 2 hours, depending upon the IEPs and the severity of the students' social, emotional, and behavioral disabilities. At this stage of development, about 10 students with severe problems is the optimum number a team can work with effectively in 1 day, particularly if successful inclusive opportunities are attempted in the general education program for these students. The teacher and aide schedule a 2-hour block of time in the morning for a group of about six severely troubled students making the transition from Stage Two into Stage Three. In the afternoon, the team schedules another 2-hour block for four more students in Stage Two who are severely disabled. When the students are not participating in the Developmental Therapy program, Developmental Teaching strategies are continued in their inclusive programs with the on-call backup from the Developmental Therapy team.

The second teacher provides a Stage Four program for students in regularly scheduled class periods, following the schedule for the school. Students are assigned to the classroom as they would be scheduled into any other teacher's class—by IEP instructional goals and objectives. The teacher has two 1-hour classes in the morning, which can be expanded into double periods if students' IEPs indicate the need. About 16 students in Stage Three or Four with moderately severe problems are an optimum number for one teacher to work with effectively during the course of a day. Additionally, the teacher is on call for crisis work for students trying to maintain themselves in the inclusive programs. This flexibility also allows other students in crisis to receive assistance, counseling, and support in social-emotional development as a part of their regular education program.

In High Schools

Typical high schools tend to have students predominantly in Stage Five of social-emotional development.[22] The typical developmental anxiety experienced by most teens aged 12 to 16 years is the search for a new identity, and they are learning to apply individual and group skills in new situations. Many typical Stage Five students are at risk because of the tumultuous environments they live in. They need backup, support, assistance, and counseling on a scheduled basis; many others need crisis intervention. The Developmental Therapy–Developmental Teaching curriculum provides a guide to these students and to those who provide this assistance, who may be a guidance counselor, assistant principal, school psychologist, school nurse, or coach. Often an admired teacher is informally chosen by a student to be a mentor.

Unfortunately, a sizable number of teens have not developed social-emotional competence and are not functioning in Stage Five. In addition to the problems of the past, they are coping unsuccessfully with the added stress of the teen years. High schools have many students at Stages Three and Four and an occasional student in Stage Two with such severe disabilities that there is need for additional community and school resources for part of each day, such as day treatment, vocational or technical preparation, or other special education classes.

[22]Chapters 11 and 12 provide details for using the curriculum with teens in high school.

Figure 3.7. A sample schedule for middle school.

	Teacher and Aide (10 students in Stages Two and Three)	*Teacher and Aide* (16 students in Stages Three and Four)
Morning:	Two-hour block for group of six students in Stage Two making transition to Stage Three	Two-hour block for eight students in Stage Four
	One hour for backup with students in inclusive programs	One hour for backup with students in inclusive programs
Lunch:	Students in inclusive programs; teacher and aide assist as needed in cafeteria	Students in inclusive programs; teacher assists in crisis intervention
Afternoon:	Two-hour block for four students in Stage Two	One hour for backup with students in inclusive placements
	One hour for backup with students in inclusive placements	Two-hour block for eight students making transition from Stage Three to Stage Four
	One hour debriefing and planning	One hour debriefing and planning

Developmental Therapy–Developmental Teaching can be used informally by adults working with teens in any capacity. Yet the curriculum also can be offered as an elective course, with such titles as "Personal Growth," "Planning Ahead," or "Developmental Studies," scheduled during the same time periods as other courses. It is particularly important for high school teachers who provide this curriculum to be a part of the general faculty and to be available to work with all of the students in extracurricular activities. We have observed that when students with and without disabilities are a part of groups in Developmental Therapy–Developmental Teaching programs on a scheduled basis, the program also provides a dynamic mental health function for the school.

Figure 3.8 illustrates a sample schedule for two teachers and one aide working with about 40 students daily in a secondary school with 1-hour class periods and a 7-hour school day. Most of these students have been referred for

Figure 3.8. A sample schedule for high school.

	Teacher and Aide (14 students in Stages Two and Three)	*Teacher* (26 students in Stages Three and Four)
Morning:	Students participate in regular homerooms	Students participate in regular homerooms and inclusive programs
	One hour for backup with students in inclusive placements	Three 1-hour periods for 18 students
	Three-hour block for group of six Stage Two students making transition to Stage Three	Teacher provides individual counseling, crisis intervention, and backup as needed
Lunch:	Students in inclusive programs; teacher and aide assist as needed in cafeteria	Students in inclusive programs; teacher assists in crisis intervention
Afternoon:	Two-hour block for group of eight Stage Three students	Two 1-hour classes for eight students in Stages Three and Four
	Students participate in homerooms and extracurricular activities	Students participate in homerooms and extracurricular activities
	One hour debriefing and planning	One hour debriefing and planning

special education and have specified social-emotional IEP goals and objectives from their DTORF–R profiles. A few older students also may have an ITP that includes specific DTORF–R objectives for increasing social-emotional competence as they prepare to make the transition into post-secondary, leisure activities, and work-related programs.

The schedule in Figure 3.8 includes a three-period time block in the morning with a teacher and aide for six students in Stage Three with severe emotional and behavioral problems. These students will likely be finishing Stage Two and beginning Stage Three.[23] Recognizing their need for appropriate peer models, the students participate in some general education classes during this time block. They are assigned to regular homerooms and have lunch with their homeroom peers to the extent possible. They participate in transitional, prevocational, or additional day treatment programs outside of school. In the afternoon, the teacher and aide have a double period for eight advanced Stage Three students who are included in general education programs in the morning.

Another teacher, without an aide, conducts three 1-hour periods in the morning for about 18 Stage Four students, scheduled in groups of six. In the afternoon, eight students with serious emotional problems, in Stages Three and Four, are scheduled for an hour period each, in two groups of four students each period. A variation of this might be an intensive two-period program in the afternoon. This arrangement typically would be for students just entering the program in Stages Three and Four.

The importance of having the teacher of Stage Four students available to students for drop-in consultation before school, during the morning homeroom period, and at lunchtime cannot be overemphasized. These students are attempting to manage their own lives in the general school setting, and crisis assistance with support from a skilled adult is an essential ingredient for success.

SUMMARY

Curriculum is understood to be a course of study and, as such, the Developmental Therapy–Developmental Teaching curriculum translates theory concerning social and emotional competence into programs and practices that produce increased social-emotional competence and responsible behavior in students. The curriculum is based on four fundamental beliefs about how children and youth develop social-emotional competence. These beliefs emphasize every student's capability to acquire acceptable, success-producing behavior. They direct us toward an orderly approach to guiding students in acquiring social-emotional competence. They commit us to ensuring positive and valued outcomes with the interventions we plan. And they require an approach that results in harmony between a student's personal needs, cultural values, and the expectations of daily life.

The first step in getting started with this curriculum is to assess each student's social-emotional competence. Working with parents and other professionals, we use the curriculum goals to prepare an individual Preliminary Profile and the DTORF–R to do a detailed assessment of a student's social-emotional development. The instrument is also used to evaluate program outcomes in the four areas of development that contribute to social-emotional competence: Behavior, Communication, Socialization, and (Pre)Academics/Cognition. A student's IEP, IFSP, or ITP objectives are identified from the sequences of learning that comprise progress in these four areas.

Because development is continuous throughout a life span, effective intervention for social-emotional competence must have developmental continuity. The curriculum provides the structure for this continuity in the selected content, teaching strategies, physical environment, relationships with adults, associations with other children, and emotional experiences. When adults identify a student's stage of development and know the specific goals and objectives that need attention, the curriculum becomes highly portable and independent of any particular program model, organizational structure, or service setting. Many successful applications have been demonstrated. Developmental Therapy–Developmental Teaching has been used informally and in planned home teaching programs by parents, with volunteer mentors, and in a wide range of educational programs in early childhood, elementary, middle, and high school programs for students with and without disabilities.

[23] There is a discussion in Chapter 1 of the compounding impact of disability on the development of older students.

PRACTICE

Using the key points in this chapter

At the end of Chapter 1, short vignettes about Alice, Bob, Clark, Ellen, and Drew gave you practice in thinking about students in a developmental context. Now, for each of these students, apply the procedure described in this chapter for identifying a Preliminary Profile from Figure 3.2 when the student is first referred for special help. As you do this exercise, think also about the four beliefs that are the foundation of this curriculum. Select one of these students and describe, in brief, the program implications for that student, based on these four beliefs.

CHAPTER 4

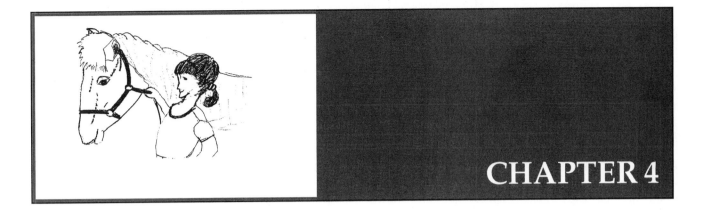

Keeping It Going . . . Successfully

If learning is inherently social and co-constructed, then teacher and child play equally active roles, and motivation to learn resides neither in the child nor the adult, but rather is tied to the relationship.

—BARBARA BOWMAN AND FRANCES STOTT, 1994, P. 126

INGREDIENTS FOR A SUCCESSFUL PROGRAM

The success of a student and a program can usually be traced to careful anticipation and planning by the adults responsible for providing the program. The more troubled the students, the more complex successful program planning will be. We try not to leave anything to chance, using the old saying, "Hope for the best and prepare for the worst." To introduce this chapter, we summarize the basic steps we use in preparing to put the program into action for students of all ages and stages of development:

Steps in Planning

1. Review program records, the IEP, IFSP, ITP, and home, neighborhood, and clinical evaluation information, making an initial developmental analysis about the program needs of each student.
2. Prepare a baseline DTORF–R for each student in collaboration with the regular classroom teacher, parents, and other members of the evaluation and placement team.
3. Identify specific objectives for each student and then compile a group profile to identify the objectives unique to each student and those shared in common by everyone in the group.
4. Organize daily time periods to group students together for work on similar objectives.
5. Select themes and activities that touch students' interests and deep concerns, and plan week-long units around these themes for maximum opportunities to work on objectives.
6. Choose materials with particular attention to symbolic content, motivational potential, and students' chronological age, interests, and intellectual abilities.
7. Prepare areas of the room with a posted schedule, furniture, and equipment to facilitate work on the selected objectives, ease in teaching objectives, and positive behavior management.
8. Anticipate how to manage severe behavioral problems by locating a quiet area to use for crises, and plan a strategy with other adults to provide for the group when an individual student is in crisis.
9. Organize evaluation procedures to monitor students' progress daily and at intervals to coincide with school grading periods.
10. Consider the minimum number of classroom rules (expectations) you plan to use and state them in positive terms to increase opportunities to reinforce positive behavior.

We use students' IEP, IFSP, and ITP objectives as we design schedules, materials, and activities to implement their programs. Some activities lend themselves to fostering social-emotional growth more readily than others. For this reason, there are several core activities that are always included in a program—with proper adaptation to a student's age and stage of development. When planning, we also find it essential to consider carefully a student's current group associations and available options for alternative groups that could foster each student's development. Then, as we put this careful planning into action, our focus shifts to how each activity is conducted for maximum benefit to every student in the group.

This chapter is a follow-up for getting started with Developmental Therapy–Developmental Teaching. It contains the basic core ingredients for a successful program for students of all ages and at all stages of the curriculum. The material describes these program fundamentals, organized around five major topics:

- grouping by instructional goals and objectives
- selecting effective activities and materials
- curriculum content for communicating between the heart, the head, and the emotional memory bank
- the essentials for effective instruction
- making responsible choices

GROUPING BY INSTRUCTIONAL GOALS AND OBJECTIVES

Every adult who works with children and youth and every parent who has more than one child uses *grouping*. Grouping is the way to provide for associations between individuals. Some grouping is done with students who have shared characteristics, experiences, or interests. Other forms of grouping involve students of diverse characteristics. In both approaches, the idea in grouping is that students learn from each other. Traditionally, the most commonly used criteria in grouping students for instruction have been age, academic achievement, intelligence, and special abilities. The criticism of these approaches is the limitation on diversity resulting from using any of these grouping criteria. A criticism of grouping across a broad range of diverse characteristics is that differences can become so great that individuals lacking the prerequisite skills cannot make the connections for learning a particular task that others are ready to achieve.

While the debate over grouping continues, it is an urgent concern for adults working with students who have social, emotional, and behavioral disabilities. In 1994 an entire issue of the *Journal of Emotional and Behavioral Problems* was concerned with inclusion. Some advocates argue for placing these students in inclusive settings so that they have the benefit of acceptable behavioral models and the stimulation of academic priorities. Others caution that inclusion can be of benefit only when it offers genuine opportunity to be a participating member. According to New and Mallory (1994, p. 11), *"To be included is not merely to be present, but to participate, to influence, and to be influenced by the communities [groups] in which one lives, works, and learns."*

Although views about the efficacy of inclusion are supported by theories of learning, the same theories are used to argue that inclusion can also result in reinforcement of a student's low self-esteem because of a lack of prerequisite skills for participation. There is little argument about the need to be a participating part of a group. Putting a student in a group in which the others have more advanced or complex skills leaves the student feeling that it is impossible to participate successfully and be a part of the group.

Others argue that students who are violent or seriously delayed in social-emotional development are poor behavior models for other students who may be at risk for problems themselves. Problems invariably arise in classrooms when disruptive students are grouped according to age or grade because many of them are so far behind their peers in social-emotional competence that successful participation in group activities with their peers is highly unlikely. For them, the peer group often produces further social isolation, or a student may develop more negative coping behaviors as an attempt at psychological defense. When this happens, the student's behavior creates a climate of insecurity and distrust among the group members and the student is increasingly rejected or isolated by the group. This is illustrated by Victor and Rocky, two troubled students in the same school grade with vastly different social-emotional needs that drive their behavior to catastrophic interactions with others.

Victor and Rocky exhibit two different stages of social-emotional development; different developmental anxieties driving their behavior; different behavioral styles; different levels of cognition, communication, and socialization skills; and two very different ways of expressing their lack of social competence and responsible behavior. Victor is clearly a boy who lacks fundamental Stage Two skills, whereas Rocky typifies the problems facing a student who has developed into Stage Three. Each boy is in urgent need of assistance and should benefit from a group in which success with activities and peers is forthcoming. For them, intensive, focused programs in Developmental Therapy, along with their regular classroom academic curriculum and Developmental Teaching, should move them forward in accomplishing their IEP goals and objectives.

Instead of using traditional grouping criteria, we recommend a multidimensional grouping procedure based on a student's general developmental goals for social-emotional development.[1] Grouping students with similar goals provides individual diversity for age, sex, ethnicity, type of behavior, intelligence, prior experiences with adults, and emotional needs. The common criterion for a grouping is that all of the group members have similar

[1] Table 3.1 summarizes these general goals, which also provide a student's preliminary profile.

Victor

Victor's third-grade teacher describes him this way: "In school, 8-year-old Victor uses two-word sentences, if he talks at all. He is seldom spontaneous. He can answer questions from the other children or from teachers but does so very, very quietly and not often. He will not share materials or supplies. He participates in each activity, but always passively. He seems to have difficulty understanding directions if no visual demonstration is provided along with the verbal direction. When he fails at a task, or anticipates that he may have difficulty, he withdraws and refuses all offers of help. Usually he runs out of the room or destroys the materials; sometimes he attacks other children. When others behave inappropriately, Victor usually gets involved and imitates them. Afterward, he refuses to talk about the incident or his own role in it.

"When Victor is praised for something he has done, he quickly destroys it. This same sensitivity is displayed when he recognizes that he has accomplished something and promptly behaves in as unacceptable a way as possible."

Rocky

Rocky is 9 1/2 years old. His third-grade teacher describes him this way: "Rocky's foster mother has told me that she is concerned about him but doesn't know how to help him. She says he steals from her at home, never does what he is told to do, fights with the few friends he has in the neighborhood, and still has lingering episodes of enuresis and encopresis at night. Nothing she does seems to help. When she disciplines him, he curses her and threatens to get even with her. When confronted, he lies about what happened and usually blames others.

"Rocky easily does third-grade work, but cannot be left unsupervised in the restroom or the playground. He tries to get the other children to do something outrageous and then loses control and beats up those who won't go along with him. When we talk about it, he says they hit him first, so he has to hit back.

"He was suspended from Boy's Club for a week at a time on several occasions for 'dunking' other children in the pool and then holding them under water. He tells everyone that he can swim but he is afraid of the water. When I asked him about Boy's Club, he said he doesn't go anymore because his mother won't let him."

IEP, IFSP, or ITP goals and objectives for acquiring increased social-emotional competence. By using their individually specified objectives as a basis for grouping, students respond to the program in somewhat similar ways. They have many shared interests, social skills, and life experiences, and their styles of interacting with adults are somewhat similar. There is a paradox in this approach to grouping by social-emotional goals and objectives: It levels the playing field to ensure that an individual's needs can be successfully addressed while diversity is maintained in the characteristics of the group's members.

There are a number of advantages to grouping by social-emotional goals and objectives. Chief among them is the opportunity to provide experiences, materials, and management strategies that are highly motivating and relevant for the entire group as well as for the individual student in the group. This increases the probability of meeting most of a student's needs in group settings and provides reinforcement that the student is a fully participating, successful group member. Also, perhaps most important, the adult is able to consistently provide the needed adult role model that will promote the social-emotional development of all members of the group.

Effective grouping requires careful planning and a full understanding of the needs and abilities of each student. In programs where few students need special help in increasing their social-emotional competence, it may not be possible to have groups composed of students with similar goals. In such situations, the principle we use is to individualize, or form a subgroup for each activity, using a student's individual social-emotional profile and specific goals and objectives as a guide to group assignments.

Whatever group activity is planned, a small, manageable number is essential. It is better to keep groups small enough to maintain an individual focus on goals and objectives. Whether students are grouped for going to the restroom, working on an art project, reading together, playing a game, participating on a sports team, or learning teamwork skills, small groups offer opportunities for each student to participate as a full, contributing member. We prefer groups of 4–10 students for an intensive program in Developmental Therapy–Developmental Teaching. Having fewer than four students in a group seriously reduces the opportunities to foster socialization and communication skills, and the adult's role as a significant person for a student becomes disproportionately important in the psychological climate. In contrast, more than 8–10 students in a group, depending on their age, can dilute the quality of adults' interventions and communication with individual students. Small signals of impending problems often are missed, and unnecessary crises may arise.

SELECTING EFFECTIVE ACTIVITIES AND MATERIALS

Nowhere is the interaction between behavior, cognition, motivation, and emotions more evident than in students' responses to activities and materials. The cartoons in Figure 4.1 illustrate this point. A student's willingness to participate in a particular task is a product of expectations and confidence built from past experiences. The content of an activity, its materials, and the way it is introduced will set the tone. Keeping in mind the message from these cartoons, an alert adult will know the potential responses to expect from each student.

Many behavioral problems are triggered by a problem with a student's attitude toward the content of a material or the structure of an activity. But all students, even those with the most severe disabilities, usually do not display behavioral problems while engaged in tasks that they have confidence they can handle successfully. The basic guidelines we use for planning activities and selecting materials to minimize behavioral problems are these:

- The students understand the sequence of steps to be followed in the task.
- They have confidence that they can handle the task successfully.
- The content is valued by the students so that they are eager to try.

These are dependable predictors as to whether or not an activity and its materials will be successful. These are also essential conditions for maintaining a mentally healthy classroom where even the most severely troubled students make developmental gains.

The task is to help each student acquire particular goals and objectives. This requires careful and systematic planning. Activities and materials play a big part in how successful a student will be. Although effective planning is time-consuming and requires considerable effort, the dividends are well worth the effort and time. Figure 4.2 illustrates the way we think through this process of selecting activities and materials to accomplish a particular objective for each individual in a group.

Begin by identifying the specific objectives and the needed prerequisite skills. A task analysis is helpful in doing this. Outline the sequence of steps involved in mastery of the objective and anticipate the responses each step should evoke from individual students. Next, consider which activities, materials, and special conditions will make mastery of the steps easy, rapid, and pleasurable for each student. Look for ways to include a number of objectives within the same activity. Inform students about where they are in the process of achieving an objective. Immediate, positive feedback is an effective strategy to use, for example,

> *"Remember when you didn't think you could do this? Today, you tried really hard not to lose control. You did so well with the music lesson, you are ready to make a recording of it tomorrow."*

Planning should also include ways to obtain ongoing, daily evaluation of program strategies and students' reactions. Process evaluation, using the students' individual program objectives as reference points, should set the standard for each day and shape the activities for the following day. While an activity is going on, continually estimate each student's investment and attention span, the cognitive and emotional processes involved, and whether or not progress has been made toward mastery of the selected objectives. Follow closely the mental processes each student is using in the activity to identify what the next step should be. It may be necessary to repeat a lesson with a variation, to drop back to a less difficult step, or to move forward to the next, more complex step.

If an activity flounders or a student drifts away from participation, be prepared to redirect or restructure the task. Always plan to have alternative activities and materials as backup. Because troubled students tend to fluctuate in their investment in participating, continual readjustments in activities and materials may be necessary. Consider whether the activity is so easy that there is no new challenge or is too difficult for the students to achieve success. Be sensitive to the possibility that the activity was unfamiliar or that there were too many new materials, diluting the learning process.

Then, when any one of the student's several objectives is mastered, go back to the individual DTORF–R profile and select the next objective in the sequence of development to

Figure 4.1. Same material . . . four meanings . . . four behaviors.

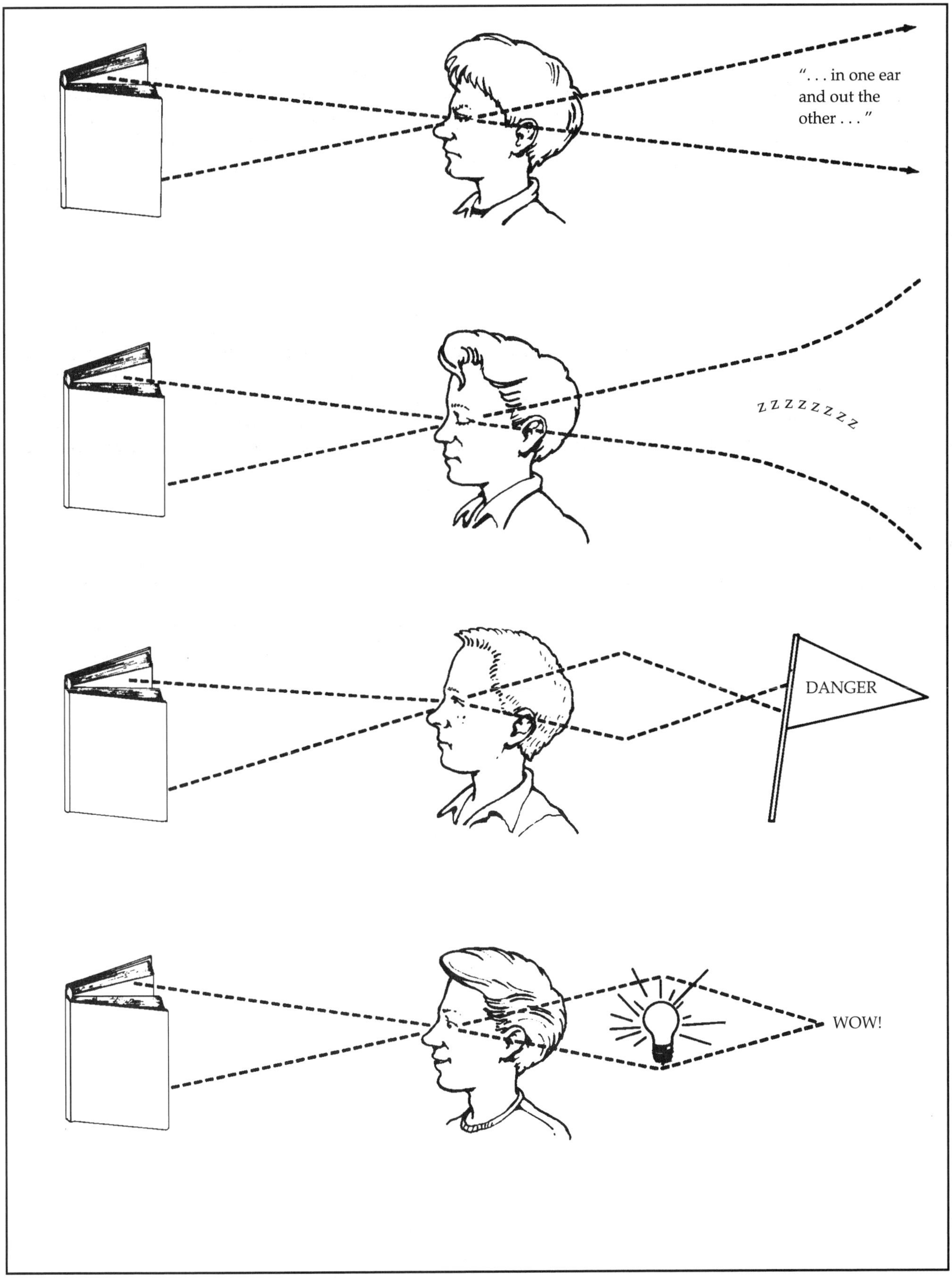

Figure 4.2. A schematic way to look at planning for a specific objective.

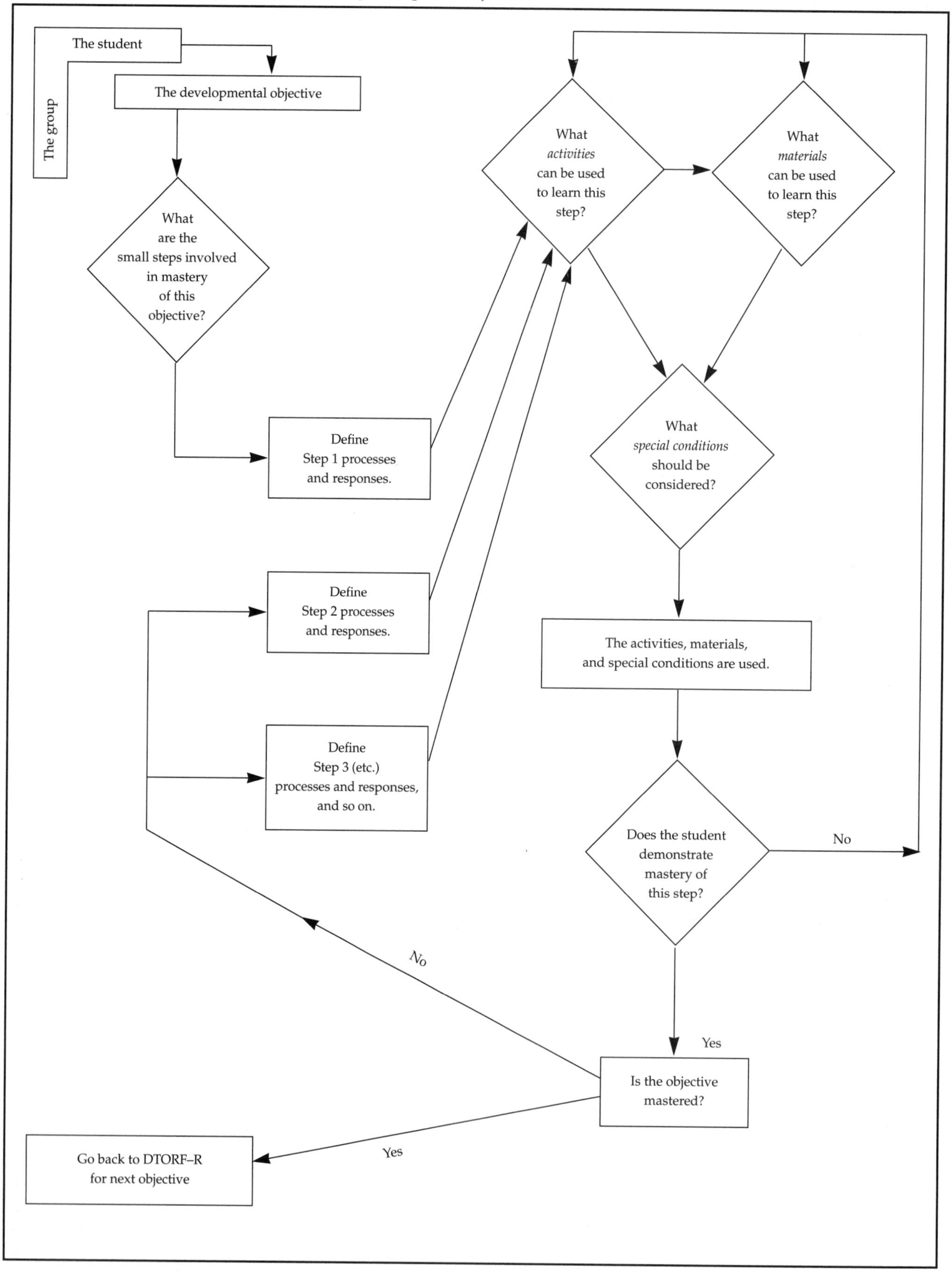

add to the objectives currently being worked on. This process keeps anywhere from 4 to 16 objectives as a current focus at any given time for an individual student's program. This change may require a new task analysis of the steps and processes involved in mastering the new objective. It may also require new activities, new materials, and new strategies. In fact, program changes should be distinctly obvious with every change in a student's program objectives.

The Schedule of Activities

Four basic activities are always included in every Developmental Therapy–Developmental Teaching program: *(pre)-academic/cognitive time, group time* or *play, language time,* and *snack time.* The activities do not necessarily occur in this order. However, they are the minimum daily core activities needed to provide opportunities for students at all stages to work on goals and objectives in all four curriculum areas—Behavior, Communication, Socialization, and (Pre)-Academics/Cognition. Because these activities are generic, they allow great flexibility. For example, for younger children, group time can be play; preacademic/cognitive time incorporated into activity centers; a "table time," when several youngsters gather at the table for a collaborative activity; or individual interest centers. With older students, group time or academic time might be designed around civic projects, field trips, or fund-raisers for the class, and snack time might involve cooking classes or prevocational training. We also prefer that each group have a group beginning together and a group ending time. These gatherings are very important means of teaching social interchange, goal setting, interpersonal understanding, and evaluative appraisal of self and others.

We begin program planning by dividing the allotted time into smaller time units for each activity. The length of any one activity is generally influenced by the students' stage of development.[2] A decrease in the number of activities at each successive stage indicates that students can sustain themselves in one activity through longer periods of time and are capable of involvement in increasingly complex activities. Within these periods of time, the same general sequence of activities is maintained each day, whereas specific activities and materials may change from day to day.[3] To maintain continuity and predictability, the name of the activity, its location in the room, and the general concepts remain the same, whereas the specific materials and activities may vary from day to day or week to week as the students' skills and interests change. Figure 4.3 illustrates examples of activity schedules at each stage that provide daily continuity while remaining sufficiently general to permit daily changes and variety for motivating and maintaining students' interest and positive attitudes. (If the curriculum is used in the home or in recreational or after-school programs, the schedule is relaxed and allows for private time if student's choose.)

The average number of activities scheduled for any 2-hour time block directly reflects the length of time the students in a group can be expected to attend to a single activity. These general estimates are summarized below:

Average Time for an Activity
To Maintain Maximum Attention

Stage One	5–10 minutes
Stage Two	10–15 minutes
Beginning Stage Three	12–18 minutes
Advanced Stage Three	15–25 minutes
Stage Four	20–30 minutes
Stage Five	45–60 minutes

If there is doubt about whether an activity is too short or too long, we prefer to err on the side of brevity—stopping an activity while motivation is at a peak, rather than dragging it on until the students, one by one, lose interest and the activity degenerates into restlessness and boredom.

A carefully prepared schedule of activities balances time to work on individual tasks and time to participate in group endeavors. Even at Stage One, where students are scarcely aware of each other, individual programs are designed to be conducted within a group setting. Include many activities for verbal and nonverbal communication and intersperse activities requiring physical activity with those requiring quite times. Alternate activities between those requiring high energy and those with low energy requirements. Vary the types of responses required of the students (motor, verbal, nonverbal, and eye-hand). Follow a structured activity with a less structured activity that gives students the chance to use newly learned responses on their own.

At all stages, students need to know what is going to happen and when to expect it. A chart of the daily schedule of activities, displayed where students can see it, provides them with the security of a predictable routine. For students who lack internal organization and for those who test boundaries or have difficulties with reality, the visible daily program provides security and some amount of external organization. Try to include each scheduled activity every day. If a particular activity continues beyond the allotted time, making it impossible to include other scheduled activities, let the students know about the change and why it is necessary. However, within the same daily routine, the schedule should be sufficiently flexible to allow you to introduce new activities to motivate the

[2]When an adult is having difficulties managing a group of students, we often find that the basic problem is simply one of dragging out an activity too long to hold the attention and enthusiasm of the students. We call this problem one of *pacing* and *timing*.

[3]Examples of general time schedules are included in Chapter 3. Illustrations of activity schedules for each stage are included in Part 3 of this book.

Figure 4.3. Examples of activity schedules for typical and special classes.

	Stage Two		*Stage Three*		
Stage One	***Special Class***	***Typical Class***	***Special Class***	***Typical Class***	***Stage Four***
Play[a]	Hello	Hello	Discussion	Discussion[a]	Discussion
Hello	Work[a]	Circle	Academics[a]	Math[a]	Academics[a]
Work[a]	Play[a]	Talk Time	Project[a]	Project[a]	Group[a]
Wiggle	Story[a]	Story[a]	(Story)	Reading[a]	Outside
Story[a]	Art	Centers	Art or Music	Hands On	Snack[a]
Art	Music	Work[a]	Outside	Music	Group review[a]
Bathroom	Outside	Art[a]	Snack[a]	Snack[a]	
Snack[a]	Snack[a]	Play[a]	Group review[a]	Art	
Outside	Special	Outside		Outside	
Surprise	Group good-bye[a]	Music		Science[a]	
Table		Snack		Cleanup	
Music		Special		Lunch[a]	
Good-bye[a]		Group good-bye[a]		Recess	
				Story or Language[a]	
				Social Studies[a]	
				Group review[a]	

[a] These activities should always be included at this stage, but not necessarily in this order.

group members and to make on-the-spot changes when a crisis develops.

To help students organize themselves, designate certain physical areas for specific activities. Students should have a change in the physical space when an activity changes. Many options are available for changing to a different physical space: table, floor, outside, corner of the room, playground, cafeteria, hall, library, or media center. This allows physical movement between activities, with clear distinctions for the beginning and ending of each activity. This procedure is an essential part of providing the psychological security in a classroom that we call structure. By structuring the schedule, the location for each activity, and the beginning and ending point of the activity, you teach students what kind of behavior is expected and acceptable for each activity. For example, with younger students, say, "We sit for juice and cookies at the table" or "We play over there." With older students, the area designations might be "Let's discuss current events here and then go over to the table to do written reports."

Selecting Effective Materials

Well-chosen materials can be the catalyst for catching students' attention and sustaining their involvement at every stage of social-emotional development. Materials should have motivational elements and intrinsic qualities that do not need much salesmanship to interest the students. Generally, materials that hold the interest of all students in a group are more useful than those that interest only a few. Materials also should be selected for their potential to elicit active, not passive, participation. For example, merely listening to a story is not as effective as being asked to respond, role-play an event, create a new ending, describe characters, or design a new sequence of events.

Materials should have the explicit purpose of enhancing the success of a planned activity in achieving specific IEP, IFSP, or ITP objectives in the least possible time. Therefore, materials that allow the students to work on several objectives simultaneously are preferred. When they are used in a group activity, materials also should be suited to the developmental skills of each student in the group, so that everyone can participate and be personally successful. An effective material is one that encourages participation and involvement. The result should be a gratifying outcome for each student. Success should not depend upon the teacher's providing a reward but should have an intrinsic value—the student should be able to say, "There's something in it for me!"[4] When a material also allows for individual exploration, it encourages students to experiment with variations in ways to use it creatively. Following is a quick checklist that summarizes these guidelines. Ideally, the materials selected for students at every stage should be rated "yes" on each of these nine questions:[5]

1. Does the material have qualities that attract your particular students?
2. Do the students have the prerequisite skills needed to have a satisfactory outcome?
3. Can the students achieve a sense of accomplishment without your feedback?
4. Will the outcome be something a student can value?
5. Does the material encourage socialization among students?
6. Will the material evoke language and social communication skills?
7. Does the material contribute to a process that culminates in mastery of a particular developmental objective?
8. Does the material provide opportunities to work on several objectives simultaneously?
9. Can the material be used by all members of the group?

Some materials are effective only for a particular stage or with a specific age group. If they are used with older or younger students at a preceding or following stage, they may be ineffective or detrimental. Other materials can be used at all stages if they are modified to meet the developmental characteristics of a stage. Figure 4.4 provides general guidelines for how we differentiate between materials across the stages of Developmental Therapy–Developmental Teaching.

The purpose in using a specific material and the type of materials used at each stage change as the skills of students increase. At the lower stages, basic skills are being learned that require many simple, manipulative, concrete materials. These individual skills become the building blocks for higher, more abstract, and more expressive skills at later stages, which require materials with fewer manipulative elements but more complex content.

The source of management of materials also changes through the stages. At Stage One, an adult must manage every material, control its introduction into the activity, teach students acceptable ways to use it, help the students find pleasure in using it, and assist the students in returning it to the proper place at the end of an activity. At subsequent stages, adults gradually shift management and control from themselves to students as the students' skills increase. By Stage Four, we like to see the students themselves selecting the materials needed, planning the way they will be used, regulating their use, planning ahead to obtain or replace the materials needed to complete an activity in the future, evaluating the process, and storing the materials properly at the end of the activity. The content and materials used in Stage Five reflect the belief of

[4]Chapter 5 contains a discussion of the place of success and rewards in the curriculum.

[5]For further ideas on using materials by stages, see Part 3 of this book.

Figure 4.4. How materials change across stages of the curriculum.

	Stage One	*Stage Two*	*Stage Three*	*Stage Four*	*Stage Five*
Purpose of Materials	Used for individual mobilization	Used to stimulate individual skills	Used to increase individual effectiveness in group	Used as vehicle for social understanding	Used to explore human issues
Type of Material	Special materials with sense-arousing properties	Exploratory adaptations of regular (pre)school materials	Regular school materials, adapted as needed	Regular school materials, adapted as needed	Materials from culture, the high school curriculum, and the world beyond; adapted as needed
Content	Concrete: with references to nurture and pleasure	Semiconcrete: exploratory; with references to individual process	Semiabstract: with references to group collaboration	Abstract: with references to understanding others	Symbolic and complex: with references to human values and principles
Source of Control[a]	Teacher provides control of materials	Teacher assists individuals in control of materials	Teacher assists group in controlling materials	Group develops, uses, and controls materials	Group directs as a part of social interchange

[a]See Chapter 6 for a discussion of teacher's control of materials as a management strategy.

Myers (1993, p. 200), who proposes that adolescent learning "is embedded in valued enterprises in which knowledge is constructed by participation."

CURRICULUM CONTENT FOR COMMUNICATING BETWEEN THE HEART, THE HEAD, AND THE EMOTIONAL MEMORY BANK

Studies show that there are distinct trends by age group in the concerns, interests, preoccupations, and types of emotional memories of children and youth. These forces also take very unique and personal forms as a result of the experiences of each individual. We refer to them as the *emotional memory bank*—the place where an individual's feelings and emotions concerning experiences, as well as thoughts and ideas, are stored. Real events (such as those involving people, classroom materials, or activities) activate stored feelings, emotions, thoughts, and ideas. When something triggers stored feelings and emotions, they become conscious, and mental images are activated by connecting feelings and emotions to thoughts and ideas. These memories are not usually consciously recalled experiences or feelings. Through the filter of these stored past experiences, with their personal and cultural meanings, each child responds to an event in a very personal way, using both cognitive and affective memory resources. Stored memory is transmitted to an active status through mental images (symbols) that represent thoughts and ideas, feelings and emotions. These symbols give personal meaning to an event for each individual, enabling a child to know, to feel, and to respond. (See Figure 4.5.)

Emotional memory banks provide the content for effective curriculum themes in Developmental Therapy–Developmental Teaching.[6] They are also targets for change. If students are to change their beliefs about themselves, their attitudes, and their emotional reactions to others (from negative to positive), any destructive, defeating thoughts, ideas, feelings, and emotions that are stored unconsciously in their memory banks must change. Content themes contribute to this positive process. As a theme reconstructs the personal realities that engulf each student, we find that the curriculum must be increasingly responsive to developmental differences and to the unique needs of each member in a group. When materials and activities engage a student actively, they have tapped into the mental images stored in each individual's personal memory bank. Further, if a program seeks to change the emotional memory of a student who has a history of abuse, neglect, failure, or betrayal by others, it must not only tap into the memory bank—it must *change the memories*, from negative to positive. We do this through the content we select for each activity.

[6]The significance of emotional memory and private reality for students' social-emotional competence and learning is discussed in Chapter 2.

Figure 4.5. How the emotional memory bank is activated.

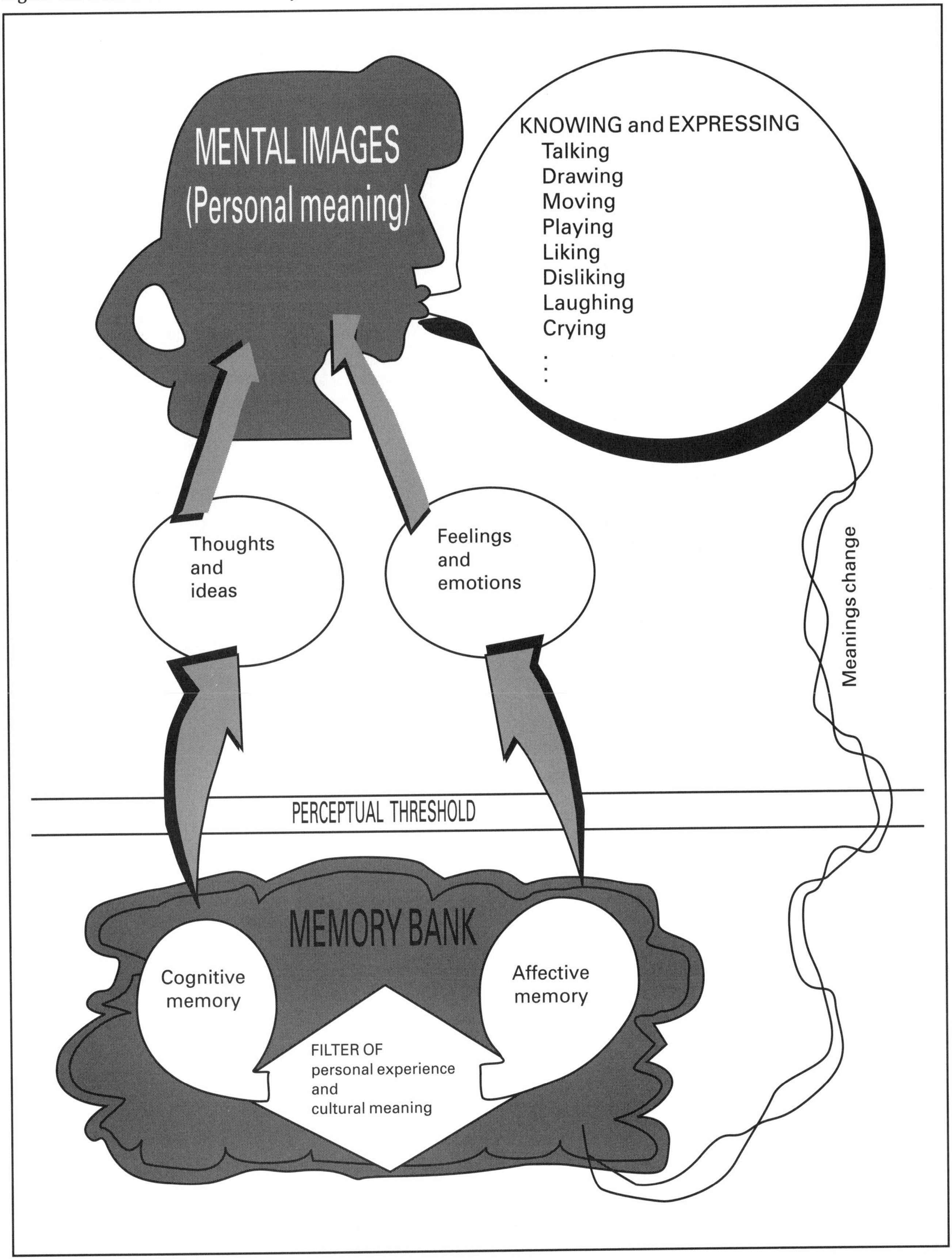

The mental images of children and youth take many forms. Young children most often express them through the fantasy of imaginative play, make-believe, role play, storytelling, and dramatic play. Older children turn to wishing, reading, watching television and movies, listening to music, sharing "secrets" with friends, and daydreaming. Adolescents and young adults also use these forms of fantasy, along with more sophisticated versions provided by theater, television, creative arts, dance, fashions, music, verse, "causes," and writing. All of these activities are important tools in the struggle to come to terms with self and society (Erikson, 1977). The important point is that the fantasy content selected by an individual is an attempt to bring about a comfortable accommodation with reality. We see fantasy and creative activities as powerful tools for fostering crisis resolution, adjustment, and social-emotional growth. They also are major resources for increasing positive emotional memories and reducing the negative parts of a child's emotional memory bank.

In choosing a content theme for curriculum activities, we consider first the general developmental differences in how children and youth of different age groups use fantasy and make-believe in their play. These developmental characteristics help us address typical concerns and anxieties through the content themes chosen for a group:

To Age 6

Little awareness of conflict, minimal expression

Little projection or transference

Absence of authority figures

Roles not defined

Personal and make-believe subjects

Responses directed toward concrete, external cues

To Age 8

Magical solutions and wishful thinking

Power is outside of child

Absence of connection between actions and consequences

Food and independence

Desires and impulses projected on others

Adults seen in categories

Little recognition of group functions

To Age 10

Adults and others solve problems

Concern over nonconformists

Recognition that adults can be manipulated

Uncomfortable in independence

Need adult approval

Personal possessions important even in group context

Modification of inner feelings

To Age 12

Predicts consequences

Participation in group without losing individuality

Mutual giving and receiving

Interest in roles of others

Unacceptable drives curbed by expression of guilt

Aware of adult feelings

Anxious about responsibility for own independence

If children do not learn to play or use make-believe and fantasy, they lack a significant tool for coping constructively with the stresses they face in contemporary society. However, these skills can be taught. According to Piaget, the foundations for play and fantasy lie in imitation (Piaget, 1951/1962). As young children refine their skills for imitating reality (the people around them), they begin to "interiorize" these imitations, that is, to recall the images when the actual model is not present. Thus, a child who completes the goals and objectives for social-emotional competence for Stage One has acquired the basic developmental milestones for future skills in play, make-believe, and storytelling. These skills lead to the formation of advanced forms of symbolic play and fantasy—the cognitive representation of events and feelings that extend beyond an individual's immediate perceptual and motor field of activity.

Armed with words, movements, and visual imagery, a child is equipped to confront new, complex realities during the elementary school years. The intensity of this developmental period is heightened by a student's confrontation with increasingly complex, intense reality. Gradually, the use of make-believe and fantasy declines during the primary grades or before the completion of the goals and objectives of Stage Three. In its place, new forms of symbolic representation are available through a language arts curriculum that includes activities such as reading, story dramatization, storytelling, role play, creative writing, sociodrama, and dance improvisations. These new forms of symbolic representation for older students have one characteristic that separates them from the make-believe and dramatic play of students in Stages Two and Three—a rational problem-solving approach to an explicitly defined problem or concern, used consciously and deliberately. In short, the spontaneous, unconscious use of fantasy and make-believe for conflict resolution by children at earlier developmental periods finally emerges as a comfortable and effective tool for rational problem solving by students at advanced developmental stages.

Albert Bandura recognized the essential link between mental symbols, communications, and human development, when he wrote, "The extraordinary capacity of humans to use symbols enables them to represent events, to analyze their conscious experience, to communicate with others at any distance in time and space, to plan, to create, to imagine, and to engage in foresightful action" (Bandura, 1977, p. vii). It is true that the symbols of the communication processes provide the only bridge between a student's inner self and the reality of others. It is essential, therefore, that teachers, parents, and therapists provide many alternative ways of communicating. When such opportunities are planned, they must be adjusted to each student's current level of performance. But most important, expectations in a communication activity should be directly in line with the student's social-emotional needs. In this way, activities are linked to communicate about what is in the student's heart and head.

When they are struggling with emotions or stressful interpersonal experiences, students may use communication tools in four forms: *body communication, nonverbal media, spoken communication,* or *written communication* (Wood, 1981). They seldom are able to express their feelings and thoughts accurately or satisfactorily. Yet within themselves, they may be thinking and feeling at levels of complexity that are far beyond visible behavioral and verbal performance.

The closer students' experiences come to touching emotional wounds, the greater the gulf between how they perform and their real capabilities. Some may communicate eloquently in written form but will not utter a word. Others will keep a continual verbal barrage going in order to hide from confusion, to avoid acknowledging issues, or to dodge emotional pain. Some may turn to drawing, music, and dance. For others, difficulties may be developmental in nature—that is, a particular communication skill has not emerged because prerequisite skills have not yet been mastered. In other instances, the difficulty in communicating rests entirely in a student's reticence to express personal ideas and feelings. In any case, an effective curriculum for social-emotional growth must provide students with increasingly effective opportunities to bridge the gap between their private emotional memory banks and the realities they face daily.

Unifying Activities with a Content Theme

At every stage, activities should be connected by a content theme that unifies the activities during an entire day or week, allowing students to expand and generalize what they have learned in one activity into the next.[7] Selection of effective content themes comes from understanding students as individuals, including their developmental anxieties and cultural uniqueness. Figure 4.6 lists some of the emotional problems, fears, and anxieties common to almost all children in the course of growing up, and it provides suggestions for content themes and symbols that can be used to address these problems.

Listen to students as they play or talk with friends during their free-time discussions about after-school and weekend activities. How they choose to play and their preferences for toys, books, and games provide sources for understanding their interests and concerns. Another source is what they watch on television and what they say about what they see. Favorite group activities, movies, musicians, film stars, and sport heroes are yet other sources of theme material. We also seek such information from parents. With older children and teens, we have discussion sessions during the first week of a school year to identify their interests, especially what they like to watch on television. Once a general theme topic is selected, it is adapted to the developmental stage of the group and the specific objectives for each student in the group. Then we add dramatic tone to ensure that the topic holds the students' interest and will touch their emotional memory banks in helpful and positive ways. We have sometimes seen school-wide themes, but most often the themes are targeted to the specific interests and developmental characteristics of the students in a particular group and stage. The following are qualities of effective content themes:

- A theme should stimulate all students in the group by touching the real experiences, interests, or feelings of every student.
- A theme should translate into all of the daily scheduled activities and apply to all the selected objectives.
- A theme should build upon students' previous knowledge and skills to ensure individual and group success.
- A theme should offer the opportunity for independent, student-directed exploration, resulting in purposeful effort.

In Developmental Therapy–Developmental Teaching, these qualities are woven into unit themes that address the unique characteristics, interests, and concerns of the participating children. The following examples of unit themes illustrate how content can reflect developmental characteristics, address developmental anxieties, and unify activities. While these themes and activities are uniquely suited to the particular development stages of the children in these groups, the examples also show how the unit weaves specific curriculum goals and teaching objectives for social-emotional competence into the daily program.

[7] Examples of meaningful content themes for each stage of development are included in Chapters 8–12.

Figure 4.6. Examples of emotional problems, anxieties, and content themes.

Emotional Problems and Fears	*Developmental Anxieties*	*Examples of Content and Symbolic Themes*
Feelings of anger and desertion	Abandonment	The spirit in the bottle
Fear of evil forces	Abandonment	Ferocious animals
Sibling rivalry	Abandonment	*Cinderella*
A need to be nurtured	Abandonment	Food
The world as a vast and lonely place	Abandonment	Sky; outer space
Fear of forbidding, unknown places	Abandonment	Dark caves; locked rooms; dark forests
An angry, rejecting mother	Abandonment	The cruel stepmother
Feelings of unworthiness	Inadequacy	Frogs and toads; rags
"The stupid child"	Inadequacy	A simpleton or fool
Fear of demanding standards set by others	Inadequacy	The witch
Fear of overwhelming adults	Inadequacy	Giants
Questioning one's own abilities	Inadequacy	*The Three Little Pigs*
The burden of resolving a bad situation	Inadequacy	Magical objects
Being undesirable to others	Inadequacy	*Beauty and the Beast*
The need to be punished	Guilt	The poisoned apple
Doing something wrong	Guilt	Thieves; stealing
Disappointing parents	Guilt	Turning into an ugly creature
Overwhelming remorse	Guilt	Swallowed by a whale; dying
Bad behavior	Guilt	Locked away
Having evil thoughts	Guilt	Monsters
Striving for independence	Conflict	Flying; running away; taking a trip
Seeking recognition	Conflict	The golden ring; jewels
The need to do right	Conflict	Mythical heroes; virtuous deeds
Knowing, but keeping silent	Conflict	Stones
Receiving rewards for doing right	Conflict	Treasure
Freedom from demands	Conflict	Birds; magic carpet
Feelings of control or security	Conflict	The king or queen

Note: For additional resources, see Bettelheim (1977).

Example of a Stage Two Unit Theme. Here is an example of how a teacher of Head Start children integrated creative activities into a daily morning schedule.[a] The unifying theme is "Bears."

8:30	Arrival and Restroom	
8:40–8:50	Hello Time	"Panda Bear Puppets"—At Hello Time each child has a turn holding the Panda Bear puppet to say "Hello" to the group. The teacher draws each child into the conversation by using the puppet to ask the children questions about who is present, what they are wearing, and what changes they have observed in the room today. The Panda Bear also becomes the vehicle for structuring the next activity before the transition to the play area begins. The props are introduced, the bear sounds are practiced, and the need for a cave is discussed.
8:50–9:15	Play Centers a pretend cave blocks art materials	"Pretend Bears"—Two children build a "cave" from cardboard blocks. The other bears are foraging for make-believe berries in the deep forest. When the cave is finished, the two children invite the others to come into the bear cave for a party. All the bears join in and share the make-believe feast.

[a] This unit was designed by Muncie Cooper.

9:15–9:40	Work	"The Bears Go to School"—The Panda Bear rings a small hand bell and the bears leave the cave in the deep, dark woods to go to the schoolhouse. On the table, each finds his own "bear folder" with a picture of a bear cutout pasted on the front. The folder contains individualized readiness activities. For those who finish first, the teacher has a new selection of picture books, storybooks, and *National Geographic* magazines with "bear" themes.
9:40–9:55	Outside Time—group game Child-initiated free time	"Bear Wants a Cave"—The teacher puts hula hoops in a circle. They are the make-believe caves for the bears. Each bear has a cave and stands inside his hula hoop. The teacher starts the game in the middle of the circle, saying, "Bear wants a cave. May I have your cave?" Everyone responds by saying, "No!" The teacher then says, "Change caves!" Everyone changes to a different cave. Jungle gym for bears going over a mountain; sandbox for caves.
9:55–10:00	Restroom and Water Fountain	
10:00–10:15	Snack Time	"Honey and Crackers"—The children and teacher discuss why honey is a bear's favorite food. This leads to several spontaneous contributions about the children's favorite foods. As Snack Time ends, the teacher sets the structure and motivation for the next three activities, which involve making simple props and dramatizing "Goldilocks and the Bears."
10:15–10:30	Art Time	"Making Porridge"—Each child selects a favorite color of construction paper for a placemat. Using a circle template and Magic Marker, each child draws a bowl on a placemat. Then, using scraps of various colors, the children glue paper pieces into the bowls for porridge. The teacher encourages the use of color and design.
10:30–10:45	Story Time	"Goldilocks and the Bears"—The children leave their completed placemats and go to the story corner. Here the teacher and the children tell the familiar story together. Considerable discussion ensues about the porridge and the bears' wanting to be friends with Goldilocks. At the end of the story, the teacher chooses one child to play Goldilocks, one to be the Baby Bear, and others to be Father Bear, Mother Bear, Grandmother Bear, and so on. Each child has a specific role.
10:45–10:55	Special Time	"Dramatizing 'Goldilocks and the Bears'"—Beginning in the story corner, the teacher narrates the story again. She moves the bears to their favorite dinner table to find their very own bowls of porridge. After make-believe eating, all the bears go to the play area to find their make-believe beds. There they pretend to fall asleep. Goldilocks arrives, hungry. Nothing is left on the table. She goes to find the bears asleep and is so frightened that she runs away into the deep, dark woods. However, Baby Bear wants a friend and goes after her to return. She does, and they all become good friends.
10:55–11:00	Group Good-bye	"How Bears Make Friends"—The teacher reviews the "making friends" part of the dramatization and highlights the various feelings of Goldilocks and the bears. The teacher concludes the discussion by asking the children what sort of adventure the bears might have tomorrow.

Example of a Stage Three Unit Theme. Here is an example of how a highly motivating theme, "Super Heroes," is used to help students make the transition to Stage Three in a special education group.[b]

Group Meeting

"What Is a Hero?"—This activity introduces the unit theme on the first day. The discussion is structured to obtain each student's ideas, which are written down on a chart by the teacher as they are presented. The students respond enthusiastically and more vocally than in previous discussions. Each student contributes to the topic.

Then, the day's schedule is outlined by the teacher. She introduces the idea that they will be making "Superman masks" during Art Time and using the masks at a special time.[c] This leads to a discussion of all the superheroes who could be included. The students volunteer comments about Superman and Wonder Woman. Spontaneously, several describe how Superman and Wonderwoman help others to follow rules by solving crimes. The unit is launched with enthusiasm.

Academic Time

"Superman's Adventures"—Superhero comic books are used for the reading groups and parallel seatwork assignments. Parts of stories are selected to control the vocabulary and reading level for each student. Comprehension never seems to present a problem with Superman!

Outside Time

"Superhero Volleyball"—Students form a single line facing the teacher, who is Superman. She tosses to each student a "high-powered" ball that the students return with their "secret powers." This simple make-believe channels the enthusiasm of the group. All participate and the behavioral problems usually associated with this activity are seldom evident.

"Ring of Power"—On a rainy day, an alternative inside game involves keeping the "bomb" (the ball) from destroying the "city." The students make the "Ring of Power" by sitting in a circle with their legs apart but not touching the next person's foot. They keep the ball in motion on the floor with their hands. As long as the ball does not go outside the "Ring of Power" more than 10 times, the city will not be destroyed. This make-believe is exactly in line with the developmental and emotional needs of students making the transition to Stage Three.

Art Time

"Superman Masks"—This is a highly motivating activity in which each child draws on his own prior knowledge. The students participate with the confidence that comes from knowing about the subject and feeling certain that they can handle the task successfully. The mask shapes are predrawn and the students decorate them with crayons and glitter. The strings to tie the masks on are measured to fit each student's head. An important element in this activity is a discussion about using these masks during Special Time.

Special Time

"Superman to the Rescue"—Using the masks made during Art Time, the students practice being Superman on a dangerous adventure. The teacher begins the story: "One dark and windy night Superman was trying to catch up on his sleep . . ." The students begin the drama lying on the floor in the story corner. "The secret telephone rings and Superman takes off. (The students all pantomime the action at the same time.) "And away he goes . . ." The teacher uses body motions to signal the turns as they race around the room. To keep the activity from getting out of control the teacher states: "Superheroes lose their powers when they touch other superheroes." This will prevent the children from allowing their excitement to spill over into body contact. To close the activity the students return Superman "into his secret cave at the North Pole where the forces of evil cannot enter."

"Superpowers"—On another day for Special Time, each student selects and becomes a superhero character. The students sit in a circle on the floor. The

[b] This unit was designed by Muncie Cooper.
[c] Making T-shirts can be substituted on another day.

teacher tells them to use their "superhero imaginations and power" as she starts a small block of wood around the circle. On the first go-around they pass the wooden block as if it is a building stone weighing 1,000 pounds. Then the block starts around again, this time as a wounded bird. The make-believe continues with helping a crippled man and defusing a bomb, all with that one block. This imaginative make-believe stimulates the students to use their own ideas and provides abundant opportunities for impulse control, taking turns, and social interactions. The make-believe holds their attention and meets their developmental needs.

Example of a Stage Four Unit Theme. Here is an example of a highly successful Stage Four unit, "Flashlight."[d] Because Stage Four requires less structure and has longer time periods for each activity, a unit in Stage Four has fewer activities. There are four activities in this unit.

Group Time

Illustration 1

"Flashlight"—This is the first activity of the day. The students arrive on different buses at varying times, so the activity is informal. Group planning for this unit occurred on the previous day. The tape of "Flashlight" is played while the students complete a large poster on the wall. The 4′ × 4′ poster has a previously outlined drawing of a burst of light (see Illustration 1). The students talk and interact freely as they color in the flashlight with red and yellow Magic Markers. They know from the previous day's planning that this poster will be part of a backdrop for their "Flashlight Disco" and photo album, which will culminate the unit.

Academic Time

"An Essay: Why 'Flashlight' Is a Success"—A language arts lesson is built around this theme using an "essay" developed with contributions from each student. The students' ideas are written on chart paper by the teacher and posted for reference. Each student's individual seatwork, spelling, composition, and reading lessons are drawn from the chart as reference. In this way a wide range of academic needs can be met within a group context.

Music and Movement Time

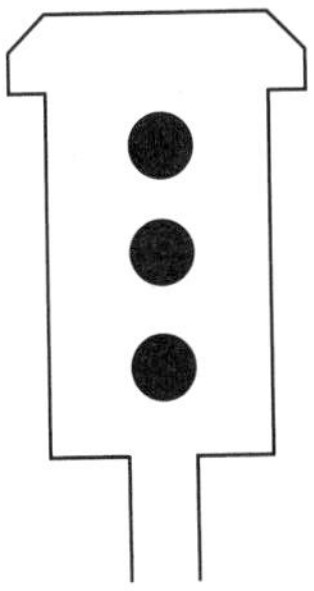

Illustration 2

"Flashlight Disco"—Each student receives a small pocket flashlight. The idea in this activity is to keep the beams of light moving in rhythm to the music. This activity is especially effective with students who are self-conscious about their bodies or movement activities; the emphasis is on the moving light beams in a darkened room. The flashlights are incredible motivators; even a negative student cannot resist. To provide some structure to the activity, the teacher uses a large poster with a traffic light painted on it (see Illustration 2). She beams her flashlight on the green light to indicate "keep dancing"; on the yellow light, to "slow down"; and on the red light to "stop." When the red light comes on, one of the students stops the music and they discuss the effects they are getting from the flashlight movements.

Over this week-long unit, the students and teacher also use this activity to pantomime parts of the lyrics.

Special Time

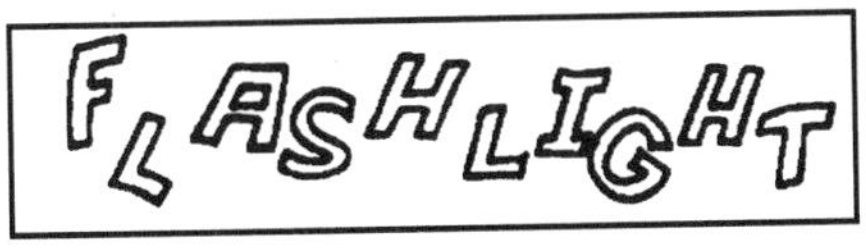

Illustration 3

"Flashlight Photos"—Several days of planning and work have preceded this final activity. There are two ideas in this activity. One is to take a flash photo of each student in front of a sign, "Flashlight," carefully lettered by the group members during previous group times (see Illustration 3). The second idea is to take photos that show the group pantomiming the song. The first photos meet the students' need for individual recognition and their desire to look good. The second photos enhance the success of the group effort.

[d] This unit was designed by Bonnie McCarty and Dan Hurt.

Expressing Social-Emotional Concerns Through Language Arts and Creative Writing

When selecting content that addresses students' concerns, anxieties, and personal realities, we find language arts particularly inclusive, offering opportunities for all forms of communication. Following is a sequence of language arts activities involving many means for symbolic communication. It shows a developmental progression and the stages at which each activity is of optimal usefulness for fostering social-emotional growth:

Developmental Sequence for Language Arts

Stage One	Imitation and play, movement and rhythm
Stage Two	Storytelling, dramatic play, puppets, storybooks, role play, and pretend
Stage Three	Story dramatization, storytelling, creative writing, role play, and pantomime
Stage Four	Reading and writing fiction, creative dramatics, sociodrama, dance improvisations, critical analysis, and creative writing
Stage Five	Writing, producing, and acting in plays; reading and writing fiction and poetry; sociodrama; critical analysis; character improvisations

This summary of language arts is not intended to limit the applications; rather, it illustrates the sequence in which activities blend from simple to complex. When used in connection with the chart illustrating the developmental processes in the Socialization and (Pre)Academics/Cognition domains contained in Appendix 4, this outline provides a general guide for selecting curriculum activities for language arts that can be used to foster the social-emotional growth of students at any stage of development.

Although all of the Language Arts activities outlined in the above list should be included in Developmental Therapy–Developmental Teaching, we use creative writing here to illustrate one particular academic (and preacademic) area with broad applications for fostering social-emotional growth. We choose creative writing because it can be a satisfying yet safe way to express the self. In the process of writing creatively, something new is produced. For each child, it is the recombination of *what is* into *what could be*. Each transformation can be a step in development. Sometimes the process enhances development simply by bringing pleasure: "Look what I can do!" Sometimes it brings new insights for the student: "I never thought about it that way before." Most often, the process provides children with immense satisfaction in themselves: "I didn't know my ideas were that good." In each instance, the opportunity to write creatively is a chance to make a visible, outward statement of self. It is essential for all children to have this opportunity to make a visible mark on the world beyond themselves. Without it, a child's emotional growth is restricted by private fantasy and is isolated from exchanges in understanding with others.

There is a place for some form of creative writing, or a related readiness skill, in every stage of the curriculum except for Stage One. Figure 4.7 illustrates the changing goals, skill emphasis, and types of creative writing activities used through the stages.[8]

Readiness for creative writing begins in early childhood programs for students in Stage Two with an emphasis on spoken communication—learning self-expression by connecting words to experiences, ideas, events, and people. Without careful, systematic opportunities for prewriting communication experiences during the preschool years, a student is less likely to have the tools for effective creative written expression during the elementary school grades. When preparing students in Stage Two for creative writing, the single most important task is to teach them to put thoughts into words. Whether this is done with written words, spoken words, drawings, pictures, or experiences depends upon the individual skills of the student. All of these types of expression have an important place in the Stage Two curriculum, but experiences that help students acquire habits of verbal spontaneity are the most important. The point is to help students in Stage Two organize their own ideas and sequence events with words.

With basic verbal skills acquired, students in Stage Three learn to be successful using written symbols to express their own experiences. For a student to be successful in independent creative writing, about a third-grade academic level is helpful. Short essays, captions for pictures, experience stories, letters and notes to friends, riddles, jokes, and open-ended adventure stories (often "written for TV") are a few of the forms creative writing can take with students in Stage Three. By the end of this stage, students should be able to write sentences and spell basic words with some degree of accuracy. They also have improved considerably in their ability to comprehend, remember, communicate experiences, and express personal feelings about those experiences.

Writing is a natural way for students in Stage Four to express themselves and their new attempts at psychological independence. Writing formats and assignments continue to be similar to those for students in Stage Three; however, the content changes. Students in Stage Four are able to use writing to explore the meaning of experiences,

[8]Examples of creative writing lessons designed for different stages of development are included in Chapters 9–12. See also Reinhart (1991) for additional resources in the management of creative instruction.

Figure 4.7. Creative writing activities.

	Stage Two	*Stage Three*	*Stage Four*	*Stage Five*
Creative Writing Goal	To develop readiness skills for self-expression	To be successful using written symbols to express oneself	To use written forms to explore experiences, feelings, and problems of self and others	To use written forms to communicate "Who am I?" and "Where do I fit?"
Skill Emphasis	Spoken words and sentences Describing pictures, experiences, ideas	Written sentences Spelling All of the previous stage skills	Rules of grammar Punctuation Organizing ideas in outline form All of the previous stage skills	Various forms of written expression Proofreading All of the previous stage skills
Examples of Activities and Materials	Drawing pictures without stereotyped subject matter Making up oral word games Making up oral experience stories: individual and group Storytelling Reading teacher-made picture storybooks Writing picture books Writing experience stories Rhyming Playing listening games	Writing messages about school or teacher Writing notes to other children Writing letters to teacher or family Writing mini-essays Writing captions for pictures and artwork Writing experience stories: individual and group Making up riddles and jokes Constructing lists	Writing poems and lyrics Writing essays Writing opinion statements Writing diaries Writing "A book about me" Writing news reports about people and problems Writing journalistic columns Making up cartoons Writing letters to the editors of local newspapers Writing to pen pals Writing letters of advice Writing position statements Writing scientific reports	Writing autobiography Writing poetry Writing plays Performing creativity tasks Writing TV scripts Writing short stories Writing biographies Writing letters to the editor and political leaders Writing critiques of others' works Writing historical fiction Writing science fiction

feelings, and problems within themselves and with others. They are learning to use rules of grammar and are working on style and structure in organizing ideas into cohesive units of thought. They are encouraged to use a wide range of creative writing forms, such as original poetry, cartoons, letters, news reports, essays, and diaries.

By Stage Five, students can use creative writing as a major tool for self-understanding and conflict resolution. The Stage Five adolescent needs many opportunities to explore the questions "Who am I?" and "Where do I fit in?" Written forms of communication should be used every day to explore the increasingly complex nature of self, others, and the global community. Ideas, values, attitudes, experiences, and logic are all ingredients to be woven into creative writing assignments. For teens in this developmental stage, creative writing serves the same purposes that puppets, storytelling, role play, and dramatic play do for younger children. It provides a safe means for self-understanding and expansion of the self.

Concern is sometimes expressed by adults about the wide range of academic skills in any group of students. This is seen by many as a major deterrent to using creative writing. There are several ways to handle these individual differences in writing and communicating skills. First, select content themes based on the most representative socialization stage for the entire group. Choose a form and length of writing according to the predominant academic skills of the group. This gives considerable leeway for individual modifications of the writing assignment to each student's individual skill level. Then structure the content, in the introduction to the lesson, according to the communication skills of each student. This last strategy is the one that gives adults the greatest flexibility for completely individualizing the writing assignment without focusing negatively on the limitations a particular student may have. As the lesson begins, individualize further or restructure the tasks as needed for success. Following is a summary of the steps in structuring a creative writing lesson for Stages Two through Four—short and simple:

1. Select a theme.
2. Provide the title as a focus for the students as a group.
3. Stimulate thinking about the theme with group discussion before individual writing begins.
4. List key words on the chalkboard to make spelling easy.
5. Limit the length of the assignment (two sentences, one paragraph, one page).
6. Circulate among the students as they are doing their individual work to be available at their request for help with spelling, to talk over a point, or to remotivate a student who runs out of ideas.
7. Respond to the content of each student's work in an individual way.
8. Provide an individual folder for saving each student's writings.

Another concern expressed by adults is how to respond to students' creative writing efforts. Often the work lacks content or is technically of poor quality for the expectations of the students as a group. Following is a summary of the guidelines we use:

- Ensure that writing has a positive outcome, either after the task is completed or during the process.
- Respond to the content and leave the mechanics for another time and activity.
- Protect the personal privacy of a student from others.
- Use neither evaluation, suggestions for improvement, nor praise. It is the content that requires adults' interest and response.
- Emphasize the value in an idea, and deemphasize the way the writing looks.
- Preserve all creative writing attempts, regardless of quality.
- Review written products individually to help students expand their own insights and self-confidence.

In keeping with our philosophy of success, even though every member of the group is writing about the same general theme, each individual has an assignment that is unique and designed for that student's skill and motivational level. And, in responding to the efforts, we keep a focus on content rather than mechanics. We want each writing assignment to be a real "turn-on" for every student. Without a burning need to write, an assignment becomes drudgery and creative writing no longer exists.

THE ESSENTIALS FOR EFFECTIVE INSTRUCTION

A chapter that reviews the essential ingredients for a successful program with a child of any age would be lacking if it did not include an emphasis on the actual process of teaching a lesson effectively. In the previous sections we described the way children can be grouped for instruction to enhance learning. We also described the way activities, materials, and curriculum content are selected with themes to reflect the characteristics of the children and to respond to their needs for communicating about their social-emotional concerns. In this section we focus on the structure inherent in every successful instructional activity and the psychological tone of trust and respect that must be present to ensure that the instruction will be received. Without this climate, it is likely that even the most brilliantly designed instruction will be ineffective.

The Structure for Each Activity

Think of conducting every activity in four distinct phases: (a) the *introduction*, (b) the *step-by-step procedure*, (c) the *ending*, and (d) the *transition* to the next activity. By adhering to this structure for every activity, adults find themselves increasingly sensitive to the places in a daily program that are most successful in obtaining high levels of participation by students, as well as the parts of the program where participation drops off and behavioral problems begin.

The Introduction. A highly motivating introduction to a lesson or an activity is essential. It should catch students' attention and convey the purpose for doing the lesson. Begin with a simple statement, demonstration, or material that heightens each student's desire to participate. An effective introduction has age- and stage-appropriate content that builds on the students' interests and experiences. There is an implicit lead into something of value to each student, and the adult conveys that the anticipated activity has some definite boundaries. An easy way to check the motivational quality of an introduction is to ask yourself, "If I were a student performing this activity, how would I answer the question, 'What's in it for me?'"

An introduction should also convey basic information (an overview) about what is to happen, the steps to follow, and the materials to be used. It also is helpful to convey some expectation about the time required for the activity and the place or spaces involved. A good way to end the introduction is to describe a tangible signal that the students will recognize as the cue to the approaching end of the activity. We always include this in the introduction.

When an introduction contains these motivational and organizational elements, initial participation by students is almost always ensured. There is a climate of trust and confidence that the activity will have a legitimate purpose, be personally pleasing, and produce satisfactory results. These are the ingredients for social-emotional development.

The Step-by-Step Procedure. A task-analysis format for conducting a lesson or activity provides an organization,

Examples of Introductions to Activities
Adjusted to Developmental Stage

Stage One: The teacher extends a brightly painted box and rattles the contents, saying, "Look! Box! What is in the box?"

Stage Two: The teacher holds up a storybook, saying, "Remember the 'wild things' in the story yesterday? What color were their eyes? What did they do? After we read the story today, we will pretend to be Max, who knows how to control the 'wild things.'"

Stage Three: The teacher, introducing a creative writing lesson, displays a news photo and says, "Did you see this picture in the newspaper last night? This is the boy who found a bag with a million dollars in it. The picture would make a great story."

The resulting discussion precedes individual writing tasks.

Stage Four: The teacher, introducing math, says, "What would you do with $100,000?" With the resulting discussion, the teacher introduces budget planning and computations.

Stage Five: For a literature class, the teacher begins a new unit by saying, "The person we'll be studying this week wrote the story of his own life. In this autobiography, what do you consider his lowest moment? How did he resolve it?"

structure, and sequence that generally lead to students' success. By knowing what they are to do first and wanting to do it, most students move into a task with considerable spontaneity. With an accurate task analysis, each student can move from step to step with confidence. Observe student behavior for signs that one step has been completed and the student is beginning the next step. By being nearby, you may be able to provide reassurance to the student to continue into the next step. Or it may be necessary to intervene unobtrusively at this point to redirect or remotivate the student for the next step. Sometimes restructuring the step or providing praise and positive comments about the step just completed gives a boost to the student to begin the next step.

During the step-by-step part of an activity, it is important for adults to monitor the extent to which they are involved. At all stages, permit the maximum possible self-direction by students; that is, minimize adult interventions unless they are needed to sustain students' participation. Also, at several points during the step-by-step portion of every activity, provide positive feedback to each individual, but pick the opportunity carefully so that the adult feedback does not interrupt a student's attention to the task. Intermittently, each student in a group needs some brief psychological contact from the adults. Although interruption of a student involved in a task is counterproductive, typically adults are not as careful as they might be about conveying interest in each student.[9]

The Ending. It sometimes startles adults to hear the importance we put on endings. Successful endings do not just happen. An effective ending is an evaluative activity that should be part of every activity. It is the way we transform doing into knowing. The ending should be an analysis of what happened and of the value of the activity, rather than a focus solely on praise for performance.

Usually, students participate without thinking about what they are actually doing while they are doing it. Yet this is what they need—to understand what they have experienced and learned. A good ending transforms the actions and accomplishments of the students into rational appraisal of what occurred. It provides closure to the activity and a synthesis of what has happened. An effective ending reviews the content or the process of the activity by recalling the sequence of steps. It links each student to the past event by remembering, sequencing, and then generalizing about the student's involvement. When an ending provides such a summary, students at every stage seem to be better organized, more confident, and increasingly willing to participate.

For transitions from activity to activity with students in all stages, adults summarize the central theme of the activity with a summary discussion, describing, reflecting, or questioning the students about the activity just completed. The talk generally centers around the positive and tangible aspects of the activity: "Who did that?" "How?" "What was done first? next? last?" The ending may be connected to past activities that reemerged in the recently completed activity, or it may be linked to the next activity. In either case, an effective ending relates the completed activity to real situations that the students face and their own inner needs and feelings. As students' own skills develop, they can assume a large role in the ending, providing synthesis and adding expressions of attitudes, feelings, values, and new insights they have as a result of the activity.

The Transition. As the organizational and motivational bridge between activities, a transition is an essential part of each activity. Many adults do not seem to recognize that endings and transitions have distinctly different functions, each with a unique contribution to the structure and

[9] We use *every 5 minutes* as a general guideline for teachers to self-monitor the frequency of their contacts with each student. Younger students with special needs may require more frequent contact.

Examples of Endings to Activities

Adjusted to Developmental Stage

Stage One: The teacher reopens the brightly painted box and repeats, "It goes in the box . . ." as each student returns the object to the box. When each student has completed the task, the teacher asks, "What did we do?" and models a unison response, "We put it in the box."

Stage Two: The teacher ends the role play by saying, "Max knows how to control the 'wild things.' When we were Max today, how did we control those 'wild things'?"

Stage Three: The teacher collects the writing papers from each student and says, "There were some very imaginative ideas from this group today. Some of you wrote about the person who lost the money. And others wrote about what the boy did with the money. Tomorrow, for writing, we will see if we can put these ideas all together into one story to go with the picture on the bulletin board."

Stage Four: The teacher ends the math period with a group meeting where each student reports the "big ticket" item from individual budget planning. The ensuing discussion includes estimations of how long it would take people in different income brackets to earn the items.

Stage Five: The literature reports are shared among group members, with the teacher facilitating discussion and insight by asking questions such as "How often do people we know have that same experience? Have you ever had to face that? How did you handle it? How did they handle it?"

success of an activity (Ostrosky, Skellenger, Odom, McConnell, & Peterson, 1994). Whereas an ending serves to wrap up an activity and give closure to students, a transition takes advantage of students' investment and success in the closing activity and carries over some of the enthusiasm and learning to motivate them for the next activity.

We find it essential to plan transitions as carefully as if they were structured tasks, for in fact they are. It is during transitions that students without emotional or behavioral problems take responsibility for their own conduct, moving into the next assignment by themselves with little structure or guidance from adults. When students have social, emotional, or behavioral problems, they seem to be unable to manage the level of self-control needed to shift from one task to another without considerable structure. This is the task of the transition.

Like every other phase in conducting an activity or teaching a lesson, a successful transition to the next activity is so smooth that it is not noticed. It is a sign of an experienced and skilled adult. In contrast, lack of a well-executed transition is obvious to everyone—the students mill around, wander off, or begin to display their insecurity or anxiety about what is to come next. Effective transitions reflect the developmental characteristics of the students. At the lower stages, the transitions are very specific and the physical movement of the students to the next activity is

Examples of Transitions Between Activities

Adjusted to Developmental Stage

Stage One: The box of materials disappears as the activity comes to an end. The students clap to the rhythm of the teacher's simple chant, "We're going to the playground," as she begins the movement of the group toward the door.

Stage Two: Students are sitting on the floor as role play ends. The teacher says, "Now that we know Max can control those 'wild things,' we are going over to the art table to make a wild thing. Think about the color you want for the eyes of your wild thing while we walk to the table."

Stage Three: The teacher ends a writing lesson and prepares the students for math by saying, "Money is always interesting to people. I've put a money problem in your folder for math today. As soon as you have your folder, we'll talk about these money problems."

Stage Four: As the math period ends, the teacher says, "Let's take a short break and then discuss how we can use some of these good ideas to do our video project next."

Stage Five: The class period is over. The teacher says, "Tonight, give some thought to this person's life. Why did he take the trouble to write his autobiography?"

carefully directed. Teachers often use chants, imitative movements, or make-believe actions to propel the students from one place to the next, while providing some mental expectation of what is to come next. At higher stages, transitions are a bridge between activities, with ideas and motivating challenges for the next task, expanding the notion that each activity is of value.

Trust and Respect

When adults are competent and self-controlled, and when students have a secure belief that the adults will not put them on the spot, betray feelings, reveal private confidences, or allow them to fail, an atmosphere of trust and respect permeates the effective learning environment. These conditions can prevail when adults have empathy; competence in structuring each activity in a series of small, manageable steps; an inner strength for the students to draw upon; and an ability to clearly convey reasonable and fair expectations for performance. In addition, these adults have skill in projecting enthusiasm, interest, and a positive feeling for the students and the activity.

Trust does not happen quickly. It is built gradually, through consistency, incident by incident. During the period of building a positive psychological climate, do not expect high levels of investment or eager participation. This is a time when students usually take a wait-and-see attitude. It also may be a time for testing the adults; students may think "Is she really as good as I want her to be?" "He really must be like all the rest, and I'll prove it!" "She doesn't mean what she says," or "I'm not going to get involved; someone else can answer that question."

Here are 12 general dos and don'ts for overcoming such initial attitudes. They are guides for building trust and conducting successful activities for the social-emotional growth of students.

Do . . .

Create a personal bond with each student; show the student that he is important in a very unique way.

Create an atmosphere where *doing* (using the materials) is the important thing and will bring good feelings.

Create an atmosphere where there is no right or wrong. Everyone is creative.

Be a model students can imitate, including voice, behavior, reactions to crisis, and interpersonal relationships.

Restructure, redefine, and improvise as each activity goes along.

Look for tangible themes that are relevant for all the students.

Select themes and materials that are significant to each student.

Plan activities that elaborate on a central theme. Use variations of the central theme to develop units.

Encourage students to think about the theme in each activity and relate it to other activities.

Be ready for some new elaborations or creative applications of the theme by a student.

Select activities that attract every student in your group.

Ensure every student's participation and don't allow any students to extract themselves from participation.

Don't . . .

Use activities as a reward or punishment.

Be perfunctory in your responses to the students and their work.

Imply that the end result is more important than the student.

Foster an "anything goes" attitude, because without structure an activity becomes counterproductive.

Be so perfect that the students feel that their efforts are inferior to yours.

Make an activity turn out just as you planned it.

Permit one student to express her uniqueness if it may cause her to be rejected by the others in your group.

Select themes that reflect your own interests.

Plan themes and units that have emotional overload or cognitive complexity or that lack emotional elements.

Fail to recognize a connection a student is trying to make between particular activities.

Fail to build on each new suggestion or idea from the students, however remote or unusual.

Select activities only because they are supported by the majority.

MAKING RESPONSIBLE CHOICES

Contemporary child-rearing practices have many parents and early childhood teachers convinced that they should let children decide things for themselves. Unfortunately for the children, parents, and society, the classic question "What do you want?" is both helpful and destructive. Encouraging choices is an effective strategy for empowerment and fostering independent thinking, decision making, and self-assertion. But encouraging choices may also produce a "willful," undisciplined, demanding, inconsiderate, self-centered child when those choices are offered too early in a child's development.

Parents who begin using this strategy, allowing a child open-ended choices around age 2 (or earlier), often wonder why their child subsequently becomes difficult to manage, refusing to go to bed at night, refusing to eat what has been prepared, ignoring adults' requests, and having a tantrum when disappointed or frustrated about what is happening or fails to happen. They seldom realize that these undesirable characteristics may come from a simple strategy they have used in good faith—*giving their child opportunities to choose*.

How can a strategy that is supposed to produce desirable characteristics in children produce such undesirable behavior? Offering choices is simply a matter of timing; the strategy is fundamentally effective, but unbounded choices must not be used until a child has sufficient understanding of daily living to grasp the scope of the choices available. When asked, "What do you want to do? to eat? to wear? to play?" a child must be able to understand what will happen as a result of the choice. Making intelligent choices in response to such questions requires judgment and decision-making skills that are not characteristic of children until about age 6 or 7. Before that, children typically rely on impulse, sensory stimulation, or habit in making choices.

Although open-ended encouragement in choices is easy for adults, it gives no guidance to children and fails to teach them how to make good choices. Good choices are those that result in satisfying and successful outcomes for a child. Keep in mind that the fundamental satisfactions of children during Stage One are pleasure and comfort; during Stage Two, satisfaction comes from adult approval. If a child in Stage One or Two makes a choice that results in stress, failure, frustration, or adult disapproval, the choice was not a good one—neither satisfying nor successful.

Why do parents and teachers offer choices as extensively as they do? There are many reasons, for example:

- They have not given it much thought, but they hear their friends using this approach with their children.
- They want the best for the child and mistakenly believe that allowing free choice communicates their abundant love and respect.
- They want the child to know that they are totally supportive.
- They want to encourage independence and good judgment in the child.
- Personal stresses of parents or teachers make it easier to let a child be self-directed than to provide the firmness, time, and guidance the child needs in order to learn to make good choices.

If encouraging children to make choices is a strategy to use at some point in a child's development, how does an adult know when to apply it? We follow a three-step guide in Developmental Therapy–Developmental Teaching to help us adjust the choices we provide children:

Guide to Making Choices

Stage One	Simple choices between two toys
Stage Two	Decisions between two, and then three, choices for materials, activities, and toys, with talk about the pleasant results of each
Stage Three	Open-ended decisions about choices for activities or behavior, with discussion of consequences for each

We begin offering choices—usually between two toys—as a child nears the end of Stage One in social-emotional development. Children in this first stage are struggling to learn the fundamentals of touch, sight, sound, and taste. Learning to discriminate between the characteristics of two different objects is a major (Pre)Academics/Cognition milestone for children in Stage One, and making choices is a part of this process. However, sensory systems must be sufficiently developed and connected with meaning before open-ended choices are helpful to Stage One children. The choices must be between two equally desirable alternatives, and the decision must have a satisfactory ending. This begins the lifelong sequence of learning to make good choices.

When choices are first used in Stage Two, a child is asked to make a decision between two or three materials, activities, or toys, with talk about the benefits resulting from each. Gradually, toward the end of the stage, typically about age 4, children are able to make good decisions between three or more choices—if adults have spent time talking with them about the choices and the benefits of each. Making comparisons between alternatives is essential for making good choices. If this has not been taught by adults, a child is not ready to make good choices. This capacity is seen in preschool children who are able to use activity centers independently and purposefully in an early childhood program. They have learned to make choices between learning centers, and know how to use the centers to their own satisfaction. However, this ability is not always developed in preschool children. Celia is an example.

If successful results do not happen from the choices made, the child's behavior becomes a problem. Or, for a child like Celia who is unable to make a decision, nothing positive happens. Then it is the adults' responsibility to limit the number of choices and guide a child in making a satisfying decision.

As children enter Stage Three, typically around age 6 or 7, they are given increasingly more choices for activities and behavior. With this expanded opportunity for independent choices comes the need to know the positive and negative consequences of each alternative. If children have previously learned to make good decisions between two or three choices, their alternatives are well chosen and result in feelings of success in their relationships with other people—both peers and adults. When offering children in Stage Three choices, consider the relative value of the alternatives by asking, "How much does this child really value one choice over another?" One alternative may be to avoid painful consequences, which indicates that the child is using rational problem solving to self-regulate behavioral choices. As children learn about how their behavior affects others, and as they learn to participate as successful members of groups, they can make behavioral choices between an open-ended array of alternatives. That is, they have developed the ability to respond in almost any fashion they choose. It is then that previous learning about making good choices—those that result in satisfaction, success, and approval—becomes worthwhile for the child, parents, and teachers.

Celia—Too Many Choices

Four-year-old Celia stands in the middle of the room in her new preschool, watching the teacher hang little pictures on a chart. She hears the teacher say, ". . . and we have the block area open, the housekeeping area, the art tables, the sand table, the book corner, the science area, and the dress-up square."

Such a lot of things to remember! What did she mean?

Then Celia hears the teacher saying, "Now choose your activity and put your badge on the right chart. Celia, what would you like to do this morning?" The teacher is smiling. She seems to be saying, "You need to do something now."

Celia looks down at the floor, feeling very uncomfortable and confused about what to do. Maybe the teacher will leave her alone if she keeps looking at the floor. Then Celia hears the teacher saying, "Celia, you need to make a choice. The other girls and boys are already playing."

Shortly afterward, Celia wanders around the room, picks up a paintbrush loaded with paint, and drips it across the floor. The teacher is upset with Celia and sends her to the time-out chair.

How could Celia have been helped to make good choices that bring success?

SUMMARY

Careful and systematic planning should be done for students of all ages and developmental stages. By using the Developmental Therapy–Developmental Teaching curriculum to group and schedule students, and by selecting curriculum materials and activities matched to their developmental profile of needs, anxieties, and motivations, adults have opportunities to break into the negative cycle of failures with its resulting problem behaviors and often devastating attitudes.

The curriculum seeks to provide children with new ways to respond that bring success and pleasure. Materials and activities should provide that opportunity—stimulating and motivating them to participate—and should touch on children's concerns in ways that provide hope and increase optimism. Perhaps most important of all, the materials and activities should provide content that is developmentally suitable and that has emotional and cognitive meaning to each individual child. Without these qualities in the materials and activities, negative emotional memory may continue to fuel their responses, resulting in increased defensiveness and unacceptable behavior.

True progress occurs when a child develops an increasing ability to use rational approaches to cope with feelings and make constructive choices for personal conduct. With increased social-emotional competence, children will have more satisfying and appropriate experiences with others. In short, the Developmental Therapy–Developmental Teaching curriculum can provide a high degree of success in tasks requiring a child to *do, say, care* and *think* in ways that bring satisfying results.

In this chapter we focused on general strategies for keeping an effective program going successfully. To summarize, here are the fundamentals of a successful program for any setting. By following these guidelines, adults can provide a program designed to foster social-emotional development and responsible behavior, while fortifying children against developmental anxieties:

General Program Guidelines for Children of All Ages and Stages

- Choose materials and activities to accomplish specific goals and objectives.
- Design activities that provide success and promote pleasure-producing responses for every child.
- Provide time every day for activities that focus on cognitive and communicative processes to foster rational problem solving.
- Include a daily snack time and use it to stimulate social communication and socialization skills.
- Design creative activities that include art, music, and play to allow children's own values and concerns to be expressed while they work on specific objectives and goals.
- Alternate tasks and activities requiring physical movement with those requiring less physical action and more quiet attention.
- Provide opportunities for children to initiate choices and practice new skills independently.
- Select materials that capture the specific interests and objectives of the children.
- Communicate the plan for each day to the children.
- Convey the steps and expected behavior needed to carry out the activity successfully.
- Keep an alternative activity available to use as a substitute if a planned activity proves unsatisfactory or unworkable.
- Conduct all activities in a way that encourages the participation of each individual in the group.
- Never allow an activity to extend beyond its peak of motivation for a group or individual.
- End each activity with a closing that focuses on the positive aspects of what has happened.

PRACTICE

Using the key points in this chapter

Return once more to the short vignettes about Alice, Bob, Clark, Ellen, and Drew in Chapter 1 and the Preliminary Profiles you prepared for each student after reading Chapter 3. With the brief amount of information and understanding you now have about these students, design a preliminary daily schedule of activities that applies the standards for schedules described in this chapter. Select a day-long content theme that can be applied in every activity and that can touch the interests and concerns of all five of these students. Using the guidelines for effective materials and activities, choose from among those with which you are already familiar, to hold these students' interests, meet their developmental needs, and carry out a content theme.

For each activity, write a brief introduction and ending, reflecting the standards described in this chapter. Anticipate how you will individualize the ending of each activity for the students, then briefly structure the transition to motivate the students into the next activity.

CHAPTER 5

When Behavior Is the Issue

Whatever we learn to do, we learn by actually doing it: men come to be builders, for instance, by building, and harp players, by playing the harp. In the same way, by doing just acts we come to be just; by doing self-controlled acts, we come to be self-controlled; and by doing brave acts, we become brave.

—*WILLIAM J. BENNETT, 1993, P. 101*

SOCIAL COMPETENCE AND RESPONSIBLE BEHAVIOR ARE INSEPARABLE

Behavior management in Developmental Therapy–Developmental Teaching involves a decision-making process for choosing strategies that foster students' social-emotional competence and responsible behavior. We define *behavior* from a social interaction perspective: outward evidence of previously learned responses, activated by memories of past experience—thoughts and feelings—and aroused by a specific person, object, or event in the present. This definition refers to all behavior, recognizing that there is no universal standard for what is acceptable and unacceptable. We share the views expressed by Bowman and Stott (1994, p. 120) that most children and youth "learn to balance their needs and wishes with the constraints and freedoms of the social world in which they live, to express their developmental predispositions in ways that are consistent with their family's and culture's practices."

Thus, in Developmental Therapy–Developmental Teaching, each student's behavior is viewed as an exchange with others, affected by many feelings, needs, and current cultural forces unique to that student. Patterns of cultural life and developmental accomplishments provide the organizational guides, while awareness of students' emotional memories provides the understanding. With acceptable behavior, a student can continue to develop socially and emotionally. With unacceptable behavior, developmental trajectories are distorted, taking directions that eventually lead to failure in what is considered culturally adequate behavior.

The long-term purpose in a behavior management plan is achievement of a student's IEP, IFSP, or ITP goals and objectives for social-emotional growth, resulting in increasingly responsible behavior. The short-term purpose is to systematically foster the continued use of students' acceptable behaviors and to redirect nonacceptable behaviors to more acceptable alternatives that produce satisfying outcomes for the student. The strategies selected for implementing the plan should always be based on full background information to be certain that the selected strategies are individually and culturally relevant, are developmentally appropriate, and have developmental continuity leading to expanding personal responsibility on a student's part.

When a student uses behavior that is interfering with developmental progress and cultural maturation, it generally indicates that (a) better alternatives are unknown to the student, (b) the behavior is a habit that repeats earlier learned responses, or (c) the situation has evoked such anxiety that emotions are driving the behavioral choices. Because inadequate behavior from any source is seldom self-correcting, adults must intervene. This view of intervention for the management of misbehavior and discipline problems is clearly a teaching-learning paradigm. That is, adults design individual learning experiences based upon a student's previously learned behaviors (both adequate and inadequate) that generate new, more acceptable alternatives for the student, resulting in more satisfying outcomes and increased insight into feelings and behavior.

In this approach, a carefully planned behavior management program provides an individualized system with which adults can select strategies for intervening in both the physical and psychological environments of a student. Intervention in the physical environment includes some fairly straightforward ways to guide behavior, such as instituting rules with associated rewards and consequences, as well as more subtle procedures, such as structuring choices, organizing activities and procedures, selecting materials, controlling, time, designing schedules, and planning space. Intervention in the psychological environment is much more subtle and is often difficult for adults to learn. It involves using strategies that activate students' motivation to participate in constructive ways, building from a student's private reality of emotions, attitudes, and values.

Intervention in a student's physical and psychological environments requires integration of information from every dimension of the student's world—school, home, and community. It requires knowing about the student's cultural heritage, academic strengths and weaknesses, learning style, significant prior experiences, social roles in peer groups, attitudes, values, concerns, and behavioral defenses. It takes into account a student's age, developmental anxieties, anger, and need for dependence or independence in relationships with adults. When all of this information is synthesized, it reveals the student's profile of social-emotional competence, including specific strengths, needs, goals, and instructional objectives.

Consider Karen, a preschool child with enormous capabilities—and serious problems adjusting to life with other people. Her strategies are self-defeating and hold no promise for the future. Similarly, Tony, a middle school student with well-fortified defenses against people and the feelings they evoke in him, is a student whose behavior is leading him to a point where development is arrested. Both students present serious management problems in school. Without effective management plans individually designed for their unique circumstances, the school year will be a total loss for both these students.

To carry out a behavior management plan effectively, it is essential to understand the environmental and psychological conditions that generate each student's behavior and to understand the meaning the situation holds for each of the involved students. It is essential to make careful observations of the physical and psychological events occurring before, during, and after a critical incident or crisis event. This combined information about individual students and the group can help in making behavior management decisions that are personally relevant to the student and helpful to the group. This understanding should greatly enhance the therapeutic quality of a behavior management plan and guide decisions to make changes as students progress.

Effective behavior management requires adults to clearly convey their expectations to the students. The behavior of an individual student converges at a single point in time around a particular situation with a corresponding set of expectations in the minds of the adults. The student reacts to a situation, and the adults are required to do something or to do nothing. The resulting adult behavior in turn evokes a wide range of reactions from the student—behaviors and feelings expressed in words and actions. Sometimes adults' expectations are clearly conveyed to a student, but with some students, adults have failed to communicate their expectations, or they hold expectations for a student that are developmentally inappropriate. To complicate matters more, student behavior is vulnerable to emotional forces that can change rapidly. In a matter of moments, adults must be able to "decode" a behavior and the situation surrounding it to determine whether or not to change a management strategy. Keeping objectives and outcomes in mind is necessary when making the decision to change strategies.[1]

It is important to remember that a student's mastery of new behavior is an ongoing process requiring much practice, encouragement, and success. It requires adults to modify their own strategies to meet the changing needs and growth of students. Continuing observations and evaluation of the outcome of each intervention is essential. The long-range effectiveness of each behavior management plan can be judged by the extent to which students achieve mastery of their IEP, IFSP, or ITP objectives for social-emotional competence and take personal responsibility for regulating their own behavior.

In this chapter, we offer an overview of behavior management in the context of Developmental Therapy–Developmental Teaching, in which the mission is increased social competence and responsible behavior. In the next chapter, we provide detailed descriptions of the most frequently used intervention strategies and how they are applied in different ways for each stage in a student's development. The topics in this overview of behavior management are divided into three broad sections:

- the search for the most effective management strategies

[1]The first two chapters provide the theoretical framework for this approach to behavior management. In Chapter 1 we discussed the importance of change in fostering social-emotional growth. In Chapter 2 we discussed the forces involved in producing social competence and responsible behavior, including the role of adults, the existential crisis, emotions, developmental anxieties, and values as forces for motivating behavior.

Karen

Karen is 5 years old. Her teachers and parents are concerned about her. She refuses to comply with requests until her demands are met. Whenever she cannot have her way, she has a temper tantrum. She screams at the top of her lungs and slaps or bites anyone who gets near her (including parents and teachers).

Karen is extremely bright. Her parents and teachers describe her ability to read words and recognize number groups. She has an excellent vocabulary and speaks at a linguistic level much above that of the other children in her kindergarten. She is awkward in coordination and unable to bounce or catch a ball. She rarely speaks in normal tones, choosing to scream or shout her demands or her answers to questions. At other times, she refuses to speak at all.

Her parents have noticed that she will not play with other children, preferring imaginary, solitary play instead. In her play, she whispers to her "friends" (unseen by anyone else). It was this behavior that finally persuaded her parents that Karen needs some special help. She seems to be retreating from reality more and more each day. At school, she isolates herself, talking to her "friends" exclusively rather than participating in classroom activities. At home, she prefers to stay in a corner of her own room and screams at any family member who intrudes.

Tony

Tony is a gifted 11-year-old. He has a consuming anger toward people and contains it in a tight defense system built around intellectual activity devoid of feelings or people. He claims to "like no one, need no one, and care about nothing." He has learned to out-talk and out-manipulate adults. In his classes, the teachers say that the single biggest challenge is to get Tony to do anything at all. His disdainful refusal to participate in any classroom activity, along with reports from neighbors that he spends his afternoons going through their garbage cans, has alarmed his family, who put great pride in his intellectual ability. His parents and grandparents do not understand why he does this when they provide him with everything he asks for.

- steps in designing a behavior management plan
- managing severe problem behaviors, including physical violence, passive aggression, and thought disorders

THE SEARCH FOR THE MOST EFFECTIVE MANAGEMENT STRATEGIES

The management strategies for Developmental Therapy–Developmental Teaching were selected from an extensive review of many theories and research about the characteristic needs of children and youth as they develop social-emotional competence from birth to age 16. The strategies appear in most behavior management literature, including one of the largest studies concerning classroom behavior problems, conducted by Martens, Peterson, Witt, and Cirone (1986). They surveyed over 2,000 teachers from general and special education who were teaching in regular classrooms, special education resource rooms, and programs for students with behavioral disorders. The teachers had varying philosophies and training in behavior management. They were asked to rate the *extent* to which they used 65 strategies identified from numerous current approaches. The teachers were also asked to rate the *ease* in using each strategy and their perception of its *effectiveness*. The list contained a wide array of strategies from both psychological and educational orientations. All but 10 of the strategies are recommended for use at one stage or another in Developmental Therapy–Developmental Teaching. The researchers concluded that there were few differences in the way regular and special educators viewed the ease and effectiveness of the strategies, although special educators reported more frequent use over a year's time.

In a follow-up study, Wood, Peterson, Combs, and Quirk (1987) examined the strategies reported to be most effective by the 946 general education teachers in the previous study. Their ratings on these strategies were compared with the developmental appropriateness of the strategies for the age groups of the students they taught. The questions concerned the extent to which teachers and theory agree on "best" and "appropriate" practices. A second question was whether teachers' judgments about strategies may be related to their students' ages and stage of development. For example, it was possible that teachers of younger students would rate strategies such as physical touch as more effective than would teachers of high school students. The following lists summarize the strategies where kindergarten, elementary, and high school teachers agree with developmental theory about what constitutes "best" and "appropriate" behavior management practices:

Elementary School Teachers, K–6

"Best" Developmental Strategies

Reflecting student's behavior—words, actions, and feelings

Signaling student

Providing positive feedback and praise

Modeling desired behavior for student

Redirecting or restructuring the task

Verbally encouraging—giving a "pep" talk

Establishing rules and expectations for behavior

LSI and counseling

Motivating with materials

"Adequate" Strategies

Classroom structure

Confrontation

High School Teachers, Grades 9–12

"Best" Developmental Strategies

Counseling with LSI

Providing positive feedback and praise

Using interpretation

"Adequate" Strategies

Motivating with materials

Verbally encouraging—giving a "pep talk"

Establishing rules and expectations for behavior

Signaling student

Confronting student about behavior

Using classroom structure

Redirecting student to the task

Reflecting student's behavior—words, actions, and feelings

Changing the task

The findings suggest that elementary school teachers appear to have a higher level of agreement with developmental theory than high school teachers on what constitute the "best" strategies. However, their ratings of "adequate" strategies differ somewhat. The difference may be that teachers of high school students generally tend to focus on academic tasks rather than on enhancing the social competence or interpersonal skills of their students. It may also be that high school teachers have too little time with their students (one class period daily), or too many students. Or high school teachers might have been prepared in subject matter areas but have not received as much child development theory as have kindergarten and elementary school teachers.

Research continues into the effectiveness of various behavior management strategies. Tobin and Sugai (1993, p. 113) surveyed general and special educators for their perceptions of least aversive management techniques—those that are proactive in support of students while attempting to change their behavior. The strategies they report as least aversive and proactive are

- talking about rules
- reflecting on a student's emotional state
- changing the seating arrangement
- making changes in the physical environment
- signaling to stop
- verbally warning a student

These strategies are included among the management strategies recommended for Developmental Therapy–Developmental Teaching. Similarly, Shores, Gunner, and Jack (1993, p. 99) reported on management techniques that appeared to promote positive rather than coercive interactions. They concluded that to reduce detrimental interactions between students and teachers, the following management strategies should be considered:

- positive rules clearly stated with positive consequences
- classroom arrangements that increase adults' close proximity and responsiveness to students and that facilitate teacher-student interaction
- movement patterns of adults in the room to maintain control

- tangible reinforcement systems with positive social responses from teachers

These conclusions also are in agreement with management practices used in Developmental Therapy–Developmental Teaching. Another current line of inquiry into management strategies is reported by Hyman (in press) in a survey of strategies needed by adults to communicate effectively with troubled children and youth. Among the strategies he selected for study that are also included in Developmental Therapy–Developmental Teaching are the following:

- accepting feelings
- reflecting feelings, ideas, and behavior
- giving feedback to students about desirable and undesirable behavior
- conveying high regard, encouragement, and praise
- using dialogue and facial expressions to help students identify feelings
- modifying classroom and school ecology

In the last strategy Hyman includes cooperative learning, classroom problem solving, class meetings, rules of conduct and safety, violence prevention, and crisis intervention strategies that prevent serious breakdowns in behavior. Such strategies are increasingly necessary and effective when used with students in Stage Three or beyond and may include loss of privileges, suspension, detention, and expulsion as options.

These studies lead us to conclude that there is considerable agreement between theory and those who are working directly with children and youth regarding the effectiveness of certain management practices. The important point is to know which strategy to use with each student. Even the best strategy will not produce results if it is used with a student who is culturally, emotionally, or developmentally unable to respond to it successfully. On the other hand, any number of strategies can produce social-emotional growth if they are individually relevant and used at the appropriate time in a student's development. When knowledge of a student's individual social-emotional status, cultural values, and current developmental profile are understood, strategies can be adjusted to be responsive to the student's unique needs.

STEPS IN DESIGNING A BEHAVIOR MANAGEMENT PLAN

A good behavior management plan must be oriented to a specific outcome; that is, specific goals and objectives must be kept clearly in mind. When using Developmental Therapy–Developmental Teaching, intervention strategies are selected for achieving participation in activities that lead to eventual mastery of goals and objectives to increase social-emotional competence. The first planning task is to determine (a) what behaviors are interfering with the student's ability to achieve the specified objectives, (b) the extent to which present events are exacerbating the problems, (c) the defense mechanisms being used by the student for protection against psychological discomfort, (d) which developmental anxiety is being touched by the situation, and (e) the values, interests, and concerns that motivate the student. In addition to direct observation, we use all available information about the student's social-emotional development, clinical assessments, and social history, as well as information about current family, school, and community circumstances. This information is essential to answering questions about the meaning of the student's behavior. It is also essential for developing an effective behavior management program. We use the following six steps:

1. Identify the student's stage of social–emotional development for goals and objectives.
2. Observe the context in which a behavioral problem occurs.
3. Decode the behavior for defense mechanisms, developmental anxieties, social roles in groups, motivators, and values.
4. Select specific behavior management strategies that are developmentally appropriate to the student's needs.
5. Observe and evaluate results to determine which strategies will be continued and which will be changed.
6. Make changes to higher-stage or lower-stage strategies when indicated.

Step 1: Identify the Student's Stage of Social-Emotional Development

Specific management strategies are determined by goals and objectives. Because we use the DTORF–R to identify these goals and objectives, we automatically know the stage of development. It also can be estimated with a fair amount of accuracy by using the chart of specific goals in each domain outlined in Figure 3.2. By following those procedures, you can construct a Preliminary Profile of social-emotional development. This is a sufficient base to begin planning a behavior management program for a new student, recognizing that it will have to be adjusted and reformulated as you learn more about the student.

This profile indicates areas where a student is achieving and lagging behind. You can anticipate behavioral problems with the lagging skills. The student's successful skills should be used as the foundation for the behavior management plan. It is essential to build this plan on the areas of ability (mastered DTORF–R objectives) to ensure success in learning new behaviors as alternatives to behaviors that generate problems. Students will be responsive to trying new alternatives if they have confidence that they can be successful and the outcome will bring greater satisfaction.

Step 2: Observe the Context in Which a Behavioral Problem Occurs

When a problem behavior arises, we analyze the event to isolate the elements that might have provoked that particular behavior. We look for the meaning of the situation to the student and the observable antecedents. We specifically ask ourselves whether the behavior is *situation-specific* or *diffused* (nonspecific). When a direct connection can be made between an event and a student's behavior, it is situation-specific. This means that the behavior is a direct response to the specific situation. Because the adult is present and has seen the event, the relevant aspects of the issue can be drawn from the situation and addressed directly. This makes selection of an appropriate management strategy fairly clear, focusing on the student's specific IEP, IFSP, or ITP objectives and responding with a management strategy that suits the situation, the objectives, and the student's stage of development.

When a behavioral problem erupts for no apparent reason and appears to have no logical antecedent, we call it diffused (or nonspecific). It does not seem clear why the student responded in a particular way, and it does not seem that the situation generated the behavioral problem. Frequently, these nonspecific, diffused behaviors may be a response to anxiety generated by distant events. In Chapter 2 we referred to this as the *private reality*, with its storehouse of emotional memories. This type of problem behavior is difficult to understand. It often requires the adult to develop a considerable relationship with the student. Management strategies for these types of behavioral problems should be directed toward alleviating the anxiety and assisting the student in gaining greater insight and learning effective alternative coping behaviors.

Step 3: Decode the Behavior

This step focuses specifically on gaining more understanding of the student's private reality. We call this *decoding behavior*.[2] To decode behavior is to make specific connections between observed behavior and the underlying psychological forces that produce the behavior. Students behave in certain ways for psychological protection, or from habit. Both types of behavior are the product of prior learning. When we decode behavior, we consider first the student's actual age and stage of social-emotional development. Then we review what we already understand about the student's defense mechanisms, development anxieties, progress through the existential crises, social role in the group, type of social power, behavioral motivators, and values. These theoretical constructs are discussed in Chapter 2, but we review them here to illustrate how they are considered as a part of decoding a student's behavior and to actually put them into practice.

Defense Mechanisms. When decoding a student's unacceptable, regressive, or counterproductive behavior, we first consider the possibility that it is defensive—in other words, that the behavior is a defense against stress and anxiety and is a signal that the student is making an attempt at self-protection. A behavior generated for psychological protection is called a *defense mechanism*.[3]

Because defense mechanisms can take many different forms, we find it helpful to consider the direction of a student's defensive behavior: Some behaviors provide retreat and withdrawal from the stress, another group of defensive behaviors mobilizes the individual to attack the source of the stress, and a third group simply protects through denial that there is any stress at all. The actual form the defense takes does not tell us the nature of the stress or anxiety—only that anxiety is present.

The presence of defense mechanisms alerts us that a student is attempting to protect against anxiety-producing conditions, even though the anxiety may not be apparent. When many different defense mechanisms are observed or used frequently, it is reasonable to assume that the student is highly stressed and the behaviors are not providing psychological relief.

Development Anxieties. As we continue to decode a student's behavior, we put it in the context of what we know about developmental anxieties. In reviewing our previous knowledge about a student's life and observations of defense mechanisms, we begin to understand the developmental anxieties and what that student is protecting against. We find it easy to recall the five major developmental anxieties by these representative statements:

1. "No one cares." (*Abandonment*)
2. "I can't do anything right." (*Inadequacy*)
3. "I'm so bad I should be punished." (*Guilt*)
4. "They're making me, and I don't want to" or "I want to and they won't let me." (*Conflict*)
5. "Who am I?" or "What am I to become?" (*Identity crisis*)

We keep in mind that actual age plays an important role in forming typical developmental anxieties. Society and life experiences make certain demands upon youngsters at various ages, and these expectations form the

[2]For an extended discussion of this process of decoding behavior, see Wood and Long (1991); Morgan (1991); Ivey (1994).

[3]Defense mechanisms and developmental anxieties are discussed in Chapter 2. See also A. Freud (1942, 1965, 1973).

Roles of Individuals in Groups

Instigator	Acts behind the scenes and gets other people moving
Leader	Overtly organizes and directs group action
Follower	Can be counted on to take part as the group moves toward some particular goal that the leader or instigator has chosen
Group conscience	Reminds the members of their responsibilities
Bully (aggressor)	Influences individuals by force or threat
Group clown	Gets attention through humor or comic action
Isolate	Is ignored by all
Scapegoat	Absorbs the brunt of bad feelings members have toward themselves and each other
Baby	Is cared for by others, by giving others passive permission to take care of things and solve problems

foundation for normal developmental anxieties. A student's age provides the first check point for understanding the typical anxieties of that age group and how a particular situation may be interpreted. If the student is delayed in social-emotional development, the situation is complicated further by the inclusion of other, unresolved anxieties from previous stages of development. In most crisis situations, students use age-appropriate and developmentally inappropriate behaviors, depending on the nature of the event and its meaning to the student. Both types of behaviors must be considered as self-protection against anxiety when selecting management strategies.

Social Roles in Groups. Before we complete the decoding process, we consider what is known about a student's role in relations with others. Each individual typically is a member of many groups—family groups, community groups, church memberships, play groups, gangs, school classes, sports teams, work teams, and friendships. In each group, the individual has a characteristic role. Sometimes the *social roles* are given to a student by group consensus about how to interact with that individual. Often, the role is assigned by an influential member of the group, whereas in other situations, an individual may seek a particular role in a group. The roles a student plays in the various groups may not always foster social-emotional development or responsible behavior. Problem behavior often is generated from roles that meet the psychological needs of the student or others and may not serve the best interests of the student.

When planning a behavior management program for an individual, at any age or stage, it is essential to know what groups the student interacts with and what roles the student plays in each group. When we know the position an individual has in a group we can judge the positive or negative effects on that role on the student's progress. If the role is clearly impeding further development of more responsible behavior, it may be necessary to help the student learn behaviors that will produce a different role within the group, or it may be necessary to provide a new group for the student and begin the new associations with new behaviors for a new role.

Changing groups and roles is more applicable in programs for older students and those who are into Stage Three or beyond. At Stages Four and Five, students are able to work through the ideas of roles themselves and participate in planning the new roles and new behaviors required to be successful.[4] If a change in a student's role in the family is indicated, it is necessary to collaborate with the parents; child-rearing styles, discipline, and family expectations are involved. For younger children, especially those in early childhood education programs, planning with parents about ways to create a new role for a child at home can be quite productive in changing the direction of potential problem behaviors.

Motivations and Values. Finally, to complete the decoding process, we must understand what motivations and values typically shape children's behavior. Every child can be motivated. The task in planning a behavior management program is to know what motivates that particular student—to understand what is valued by the student. As a quick guide to a student's values, we use the simple sequence described in Figure 2.3, in Chapter 2:

Sequence of Values

Stage One	"My needs."
Stage Two	"Please adults."
Stage Three	"Be fair."
Stage Four	"Be responsible."
Stage Five	"Care for others."

We try to identify all of the interests, pleasures, concerns, and preoccupations that are foremost with each student. We obtain this sort of information by observing and

[4]Because Stage Three has a major focus on group participation, we expand on group dynamics, social power, and roles in groups in Chapter 10.

listening closely to students during less structured, creative times, such as free play, dramatic play, discussion groups, lunch, recess, and spontaneous conversations during group activities. Drawings, music, and television viewing also reveal student's interests and preoccupations. When students are involved with materials and activities representing a potential for pleasure or deep interest, inappropriate behaviors usually are reduced. We seldom find unacceptable behavior during times when a student is participating in a valued activity. We have also observed that students will participate in activities that may be less than valued if they have seen a connection to something they value.[5]

Step 4: Select Specific Behavior Management Strategies

When selecting specific behavior management strategies to use with an individual student, we refer to the charts in Figures 6.1 and 6.2. These charts contain the strategies most frequently used at each stage of development. Because the management of behavior requires adult responses to a vast number of behaviors from students—which cannot always be predicted beforehand—adults need a clear idea about the management of each student. A student's overall stage of social-emotional development provides the organization for clarifying a general approach, allowing adults to respond consistently and appropriately to very insignificant incidents or enormously important ones. It is a problem-solving task to determine which behavior of students needs a response and which should be ignored. Choices also must be made about whether to seek short-term results from one set of strategies or concentrate on long-term changes with a different set of strategies. These decisions are made from the student's IEP, IFSP, or ITP objectives and all that is known about the student's public and private realities.

Effective strategies should also provide experiences for the student that alter old feelings and attitudes as well as changing outward behaviors. This is a sensitive process in which an adult's personal qualities and relationship with the student provide a foundation for mutual trust. Such a climate promotes constructive change—new behaviors, increased personal responsibility, independent use of new behaviors in new settings, and achievement of developmental objectives.[6]

Step 5: Observe and Evaluate Results

Evaluation is an essential process in every behavior management plan. Process (formative) evaluation should be a continuing event. Keep in mind that evaluative feedback is essential for fine-tuning a behavior management program. It is not a static program that continues unchanged once it has been designed. Quite the contrary. Dynamic change should be an ongoing part of behavior management, and process evaluation is necessary if this is to happen effectively.

After beginning a behavior management program, make ongoing observations of the resulting behavior. The following standards are used for judging the quality of an intervention:

- The intervention is positive and constructive.
- The student responds in a constructive manner.
- The student's sense of self-esteem is enhanced.
- Adult-student (or student-student) relationships are enhanced.

Judge the effectiveness of a specific intervention by the extent to which the resulting behavior meets the standards and expectations that have been set. Exaggerated, defensive, or catastrophic responses by a student to a strategy may indicate that the strategy has touched an underlying anxiety but violates the student's psychological space. The student may not be ready to allow the adult access to the anxiety, or there may be insufficient trust between student and adult. Continuing defensive behavior from the student conveys that the plan is off-target, either in analysis of the underlying anxiety or in the choice of intervention strategies. In either case, the plan fails to provide the student with a means to cope with the anxiety or to alleviate it. In contrast, compliant behavior generally indicates acceptance of the intervention. It suggests that the plan provides a sense of psychological comfort and makes the student willing to allow the adult further access to the private reality.

In addition to daily process evaluation (debriefing), it is important to schedule periodic data collection procedures that can provide data about each student's progress. We use the DTORF–R at repeated intervals for this purpose, making changes in management plans and group placements based on the results.

Step 6: Make Changes in the Strategies

The basic skills needed for an effective behavior management program are precise observation, careful attention to what students say, and accurate analysis of the meaning of the behavior to the student. When we understand what students' behavior means and put it into a developmental and cultural context, we are able to respond to their behavior in ways that are constructive for them and those around them. Although it is not productive to change strategies with every negative reaction from a student to a

[5]Appendix 5 lists major behavioral motivators from 20 different systems and the stage of development in which each seems to be most applicable.

[6]Chapter 4 describes procedures for effectively ending every activity to help students change their emotional memories and, in doing so, to make changes in behavior more permanent.

strategy, precise observation and analysis will enable us to know when to maintain a strategy and when to change.

Daily debriefings among adults working with a student are essential to maintaining precision in making changes in management strategies. Brief daily meetings to review the events of the day help adults stay alert to developmental changes in the students, either growth or regression, that require distinct changes in management strategies. Also, continued self-monitoring by adults about their own reactions and responses to the students is as necessary as monitoring the students' behavior. We discuss debriefing and self-monitoring in greater detail in Chapter 7, where we focus on adults as the agents for change.

SEVERE BEHAVIORAL PROBLEMS

At least three forms of severe behavioral problems are faced at one time or another by all teachers of students with social, emotional, or behavioral disabilities: *physical violence, debilitating passive aggression,* and *thought disorders*. We use the same six steps and strategies in designing a behavior management program for students with severe emotional and behavioral problems described in the previous section. We find that knowing the student's stage of social-emotional development is essential. The Preliminary Profile, outlined in Chapter 3, provides the goals and objectives that these students need in order to increase their social-emotional competence. Knowledge of their development anxieties, private realities, roles in groups, and relations with adults and peers are all essential in designing a successful management program. Equally important is confidence that the adults have the skills to deal effectively with the problem. Keep in mind that the presence of a severe behavioral problem is not usually a deliberate action on the student's part, nor does it indicate a lack of skill on the adult's part.

Well over 2 decades ago, the curriculum had its origins in our efforts to develop an effective psychoeducational program for severely troubled students. At that time they were receiving educational services in mental health settings. Our underlying assumptions concerned the belief that they need to develop, to the greatest extent possible, normal skills in behavior, communication, socialization, and cognition. We also assumed that gains could be made more rapidly when such students had opportunities to model students with more appropriate and constructive coping strategies in general education settings. Over the years these assumptions have been supported. We continue to use Developmental Therapy with severely disturbed students. Their DTORF–R profiles provide the IEP, IFSP, and ITP objectives, which focus on the skills they need to function successfully. We find that Developmental Therapy procedures, objectives, behavior management strategies, materials, activities, and adult roles for each developmental stage are applicable guidelines for fostering the social-emotional competence of students with severe problem behaviors.

These students tend to show considerable progress on the DTORF–R fairly quickly at first. Then they often level off and experience a plateau phase, followed by slow but steady progress in uneven increments. Many of these students, including those with autism and schizophrenia, participate in regular education programs after receiving Developmental Therapy for several years.[7] The following material contains observations we have made about the nature of the specific problems teachers face with such students. Because these problems present some unique management problems, we focus here on students who use physical violence, express passive aggression, and have thought disorders.

Physical Violence and Aggression

When a student hurls a chair, attacks another student, or strikes out at an adult, panic, overwhelming anxiety, or

[7] Representative case studies are reported in Wood (1981); Williams and Wood (1977); and Wood, Hendrick, and Gunn (1983).

> **Messages to Convey to Students Who Use Severely Deviant Behavior**
>
> - The student's behavior has been noticed.
> - The behavior will not produce satisfying results.
> - Nothing bad will happen to the student.
> - Nothing harmful will be allowed to happen to others.
> - When behavior changes, better things will happen.
> - You can help the student change the situation.

anger can very well be the adult's response, as well as that of the student. But adults must mobilize themselves to appear calm and protect students from physically or psychologically harming themselves or others. The first responsibility of adults is to provide protection so that no one is harmed—the student, other students, or adults. It is never acceptable to allow a student to hurt anyone else. This is psychologically destructive to the student and completely unacceptable. The message must always be

"No one is hurt here!"

Usually a few experiences with physical aggression are needed to convince a beginning teacher that he or she is psychologically stronger than most students and can successfully cope with violence. In cases where a student is bigger and physically stronger, adults must develop verbal skills to provide a sense of social power required to control situations successfully.[8] It is equally important to learn when a physically violent student is really out of control and cannot exercise self-control without help from adults. In these situations, careful planning is absolutely essential before an outburst of violence happens. There must be a "safe place" where a student in an extreme rage can be protected until the rage is under control. Backup adults must always be available to assist a teacher if a student goes completely out of control. When an adult endures such a crisis with a student, protecting the student from himself and others, and responds in a strong but supportive manner, a bond of trust is established. The student learns that adults are in control and have the expertise to manage the situation. The adults learn that they have nothing to fear, even though such experiences are physically and emotionally draining for both adults and the student.

A backup person is always necessary when a student has a potential for violence. When dealing with a violent student, it is essential to separate the student and the group, and a second adult is necessary to do this smoothly and safely. However, there are times when a student is too violent to move. Then have the others in the group go to another place to continue the activity with the second adult, while one trusted adult stays with the student who is out of control. Never leave a violent, out-of-control student without adult supervision. Although there is considerable resistance to isolation as a means of controlling violent students, during a school year there can be outbursts of such intensity that some form of isolation is essential for safety until the student is under some degree of rational control.

We do not use isolation as a form of behavior management, preferring instead to use it only for safety and as a means of assisting the student to gain sufficient control to participate in a rational exploration of the crisis. We use Life Space Intervention (LSI) as the preferred strategy, to rationally explore the crisis, feelings, behaviors, consequences, and alternative solutions. However, a violent student who is out of control is not yet ready for LSI. Most students who are out of control go through several emotional phases—aggression, regression, and compliance—before they are ready to participate in rational discussion and problem solving. Look for these phases in a student who has lost control. The indicators of each phase are clear and will signal the opportunity for adults to change their strategies and move the student toward control and problem solving.

The Aggressive Phase. In the first phase, aggression may be physical or verbal and may be directed toward the adult. Initially, verbally aggressive outbursts often are handled best by ignoring the content and redirecting the student's attention toward participation in the ongoing activity. Attempting to stop a student from verbal aggression will only serve to take the focus away from the precipitating crisis and cause the student to take a longer period to calm down.

During physically aggressive outbursts, students may need help controlling themselves and may have to be restrained physically. This should be done only in the most extreme circumstances—when they may hurt themselves or you. Never attempt this if you are not absolutely confident that you can maintain control and do so in a nonpunitive manner. Restraining a student with firmness while conveying support takes practice. Grabbing a student's arms is never advisable, as it will only provoke increased resistance or combat. We prefer the term *holding* instead of *restraining*, as it implies support and adult assistance rather than a confrontational exchange. *A student's aggression should never deteriorate into combat between adult and student.*[9]

If you have to hold a student, move in quickly and use restraint only until there is some indication of self-control. Be matter-of-fact about holding. Holding a student should be a supportive technique. Never hold a student in a rough, demeaning, or provocative way. For some students physical touch can be sexually arousing; for others, intolerable. Remember, you want the student to walk away from a crisis feeling good about himself and you. Watch for signs that the crisis is passing: relaxed muscles, decreased body rigidity, or a more regulated breathing pattern. As soon as possible, end your holding. You may want to ease your hold gradually. Limit your talk. Verbalizations used during this phase could include:

---

[8]Chapter 7 contains a discussion of types of social power helpful to adults in building relationships with students. For a detailed approach to understanding and preventing violence, see also Arllen, Gable, and Hendrickson (1994); Myles and Simpson (1994); and Rutter and Rutter (1993, pp. 176–177).

[9]Holding, as a form of physical intervention, is discussed further in the following chapter, in the section on physical intervention.

"I won't let you hurt yourself [or others]."

"We protect children here so that no one gets hurt."

"No one hits here. Hitting hurts."

"I'll have to help you now, but you'll be able to control yourself soon."

If you have to restrain a student, give emotions time to subside. Always be positive. Help the student gain control by firm but supportive restraint, if needed. Never let a student hurt you, and never get into a fight with a student. To end any type of physical holding, give verbal cues as to what is expected, such as

"When you seem ready to control yourself, I can let you go."

Avoid the question, "Are you ready to control yourself?" Sometimes a student is not able to tell you or will say she is when she is not. When the physical or verbal aggression subsides, the student usually will move into the next phase—regression.

The Regressive Phase. In this second phase, a student reverts to earlier, regressive patterns of response, sometimes exhibiting the behavior of a much younger student looking for nurturance—whining, crying, thumb sucking, rocking, or curling up to withdraw physically. The student may reach out to the adult physically for support (moving close) or make an initial overture verbally such as "You don't like me." The siege is over. The student has gestured toward the adult, and the adult must respond. Create a nonverbal bond of support. Sometimes silent acceptance is the best way to support a student at this point; occasionally, a student will need a reassuring touch. But remember, too much touching or talking can set things off again at this phase. Watch for the time when the student indicates an ability to talk about what happened. This is a signal that the regression is diminishing and the final phase is beginning.

The Compliant Phase. In this last phase, a student will be receptive to some amount of rational problem solving. At this point begin LSI, described in greater detail in Chapter 6.[10] Young students who have mastered the communication goals and objectives of Stage Two may be able to respond to a modified LSI. If a student does not have the prerequisite skills, use reflection to provide simple, nonjudgmental statements about the events and the central issue. Then restructure the situation by establishing a few basic responses that the student must make in order to return to the classroom.

Students who are developmentally at Stage Three, but who are essentially nonverbal, can be helped to use words to solve problems when they enter the compliant phase. Talk about the event with sensitivity and understanding. By supplying simple phrases to describe the basic aspects of the crisis in a noncritical manner, adults can help a student learn to describe what happened, even if it is only in a few phrases. Without fear of judgment from adults, a student's capacity and willingness to talk will increase rapidly.

The important goal to keep in mind in dealing with a student's violent or aggressive behavior is to foster a more rational approach to stress and crisis. This goal cannot be achieved in one or two encounters. But over a series of exchanges that communicate your understanding and unwillingness to have students suffer needlessly from their own actions, you can help them gain greater insight into their own needs and substitute constructive behaviors that bring them greater comfort. Eventually, the goal is to use words to solve problems in rational, responsible ways, rather than to react physically to stress and crisis.

Passive Aggression

Passive aggression is anger and aggression disguised. It is also described as "oppositional," "a power struggle," "manipulation," or "setting up someone else"—teachers, other students, or parents (Anthony, 1976). Passive aggression is expressed as learned helplessness, deliberate failure, the "innocent bystander," declared disinterest, and a host of other ways to appear to be uninvolved in events that result in others' discomfort or failure. The most typical social role of a passive-aggressive student in a group is that of instigator. The student manipulates situations and other people in order to control them or have them act out aggression without the instigator's apparent involvement.

It is important to understand that the conflict between a student's need to hide feelings of anger and the need to express the anger is the central issue in passive aggression. Resolution of the conflict is brought about by manipulating people or events so that others act out the aggression, bringing relief to the instigator's anger without any apparent involvement. This conflict is quite typical of the normal developmental anxiety experienced by some students in upper elementary school and many young adolescents in middle school. The factors that seem to determine when passive aggression is a severe problem are the amount or intensity of the hidden anger and the extent to which a student feels threatened, abandoned, or betrayed by trusted adults.

If adults fail to identify a student's oppositional actions as passive-aggressive behavior, it is easy to become increasingly negative toward the student and the group being manipulated. The control of the classroom seems to be slipping away. As this happens, adults often increase their demands for strict adherence to classroom rules and

[10] See also Wood and Long (1991) and Wood and Weller (1981).

Examples of Passive Aggression in the Classroom

"That's not the way my teacher last year taught me to do it."

"I was only cleaning up. How was I to know the lid wasn't on the paint?"

"He doesn't like to be leader, so I took his place."

"You've gotten it all wrong, I was just trying to break up the fight."

"My mother says we're going to move away, so I don't have to do this work."

employ punitive measures to enforce adherence to these rules. Removal of students' privileges or removal from the group usually results. Punishing the manipulated students for infractions of the rules brings outcries of "Unfair!" and produces increased anger on the part of the members of the group, which in turn may generate more anger and rigidity in the adults. A senseless cycle is created. This type of problem calls for rather radical changes in management strategies to help the adults and students redefine limits and plan new expectations for group conduct.

An even more challenging situation occurs when a student is passive aggressive in interactions with adults—usually parents and teachers. This can catch a teacher unawares. The student tries to be "helpful" and rapidly begins assuming the teacher's role and authority. Or the student verbally controls the classroom instruction, frequently telling the adults that they are mistaken, inadequate, or not up to the standard of a previous teacher. A natural reaction is to dislike the student intensely and to try to smooth things over to avoid a confrontation. This approach seldom solves the conflict raging within a passive-aggressive student. Address the problem by understanding the underlying conflict and building a relationship based on this understanding. Select behavior management strategies to convey that you are in control, can be trusted, can help the student, and will not allow the student to manipulate you or others, even in the smallest ways. Carefully monitor the student's manipulative behavior, then, end the manipulation with firm control and structure so that the student cannot be in control. At the same time, promote legitimate success and positive feedback to the student during times when passive-aggressive behavior is not exhibited.

With Stage One students, it is difficult, if not impossible, to identify passive aggression as such. If you suspect its presence, the techniques that produce pleasurable results from participation are those that seem to work the best (for example, *physical intervention* to ensure participation and *motivation with materials*). For students in Stages Two and Three, structure, highly motivating materials, reflection, redirection, and positive feedback seem to be effective. For students in Stages Four and Five, when a relationship has been firmly established with the adults, interpretation and confrontation usually are helpful. The purpose in using these strategies is to create awareness of the underlying anger (through interpretation) and discomfort with the reality of the results (through confrontation), so that the student has both understanding and motivation to change behavior. Historically, this strategy has also been called "symptom estrangement" (Wood & Long, 1991).

For students with passive-aggressive characteristics, at all stages, creative activities provide excellent vehicles for reaching hidden anger. Symbolic material in a creative activity often results in redirection and reduction in the intensity of the anger. However, creative activities must always have a positive resolution if the underlying anxiety is to be reduced.

Questions remain about whether or not passive anger must be expressed openly at some point for mental health. Some authorities believe that reduction in anger can occur spontaneously and that the anger can simply drain away as more positive events occur. Others believe that overt expression of anger is a necessary step for a passive-aggressive person to experience in order to be free from the constraints of hiding it for psychological safety. We are inclined to believe that a child's stage of development should influence the choice. Overt expression of anger can be productive if a child has developed sufficiently to gain insight into the responses that may occur from others as a result. Children seldom have these skills until Stage Four. If you have a severely passive-aggressive student, it is wise to discuss this issue with your consulting clinician and carefully plan together the strategies you will and will not use.

Thought Disorders

Students with thought disorders can pose formidable challenges to adults because of their very unusual behavior. These students perceive, process, and express information in ways that deviate significantly from individuals with typical patterns of thought. Their thoughts, which are most accessible through their language, are characterized by loose association of ideas, illogical statements, perseveration, delusions, hallucinations, disorganization, and incoherence. Excitability and emotional lability are some-

General Guidelines for Working with Students in All Stages Who Have Severe Thought Disorders

- **Maintain a well-organized environment.** Order and predictability aid in developing internal organization. Store materials in a designated place and in an orderly manner. Use particular areas of the room for specific activities. Follow a consistent schedule to help the student recall *when* and *where* activities occur.
- **Keep instructions clear and succinct.** Instructions aid students in beginning a new task. Simple, clear instructions assist in overcoming a student's difficulties with logical sequencing and dealing with large amounts of information and their tendency to form loose associations that may result in irrelevant behavior.
- **Sequence activities into short segments.** Simplify an activity into a series of short, simple steps to help the student keep track of the progression through an activity. Convey the beginning, the step-by-step process, and the ending with clarity. These steps can be listed on large cards or on the chalkboard for visual as well as auditory processing. Older students can help in this process by tracking their own progress through the segments of an activity. Younger students can be helped by verbal reflection of where they are in the process.
- **Regulate the amount of structure.** Highly structured tasks are important during the initial stages of learning, but as a student becomes more organized, it is equally important to loosen the structure so that she learns to operate in a more typical environment. If this does not occur, the student will only be able to function in an artificial environment, and efforts toward normalization will be thwarted.
- **Use verbal cues.** Verbal cues from an adult that have particular meaning to a student help the student maintain more organized behavior and thought patterns. Even with medication, the mental activity of these students can be so different, so lacking in organization, and so unbounded by reality that they are highly dependent on external cues for organized, socially acceptable behavior. Verbal cues offered with clarity and simplicity may be their organizing point. They quickly recognize the value in this form of assistance and accept it when they have trust in the adult.

times evident as well. They often engage in behaviors (motoric, social, or language) that are nonproductive, irrelevant, bizarre, or inappropriate. There is a wide range of severity in the behavior of these students, with some exhibiting only a few of the symptoms to a limited degree, whereas others display all of the symptoms in their most extreme forms. Because thought and language influence all forms of behavior, these students' disabilities cut across all domains of functioning, resulting in impairments in cognition, language, psychomotor skills, and socialization. Additionally, their stage of development affects the ways in which these students manifest their disability. For example, students whose cognitive skills are limited probably will have limited language. Their idiosyncratic thought patterns can only be deduced by observing perseverative motor patterns, motoric rituals, disorganized approaches to tasks, or a tendency to retreat into their own world and resist intrusion. In contrast, a student with higher cognitive skills might discuss elaborate fantasies with no distinction made between the real and the unreal, talk excessively and tangentially about topics that may have little apparent association with the topic under discussion, insist on specific speech rituals at the beginning or end of an activity, or use inner language as a way to avoid or retreat from interaction.

Guiding such students into participation in acceptable ways is quite a challenge. With Stage One and Stage Two students, physical and verbal *redirection* can be used to guide them to more productive participation. Here is a simple illustration of both physical and verbal redirection used with a Stage Two student, Rob, who is absorbed in hallucinations while gazing at the palm of his hand during Art Time. His teacher takes the paintbrush, puts it in Rob's palm, and moves his hand toward the paint, saying, "Let's finish this house you were painting." For a Stage Three student, the same strategy is applied with an emphasis on more complex verbal content to redirect the student's thought to the topic under discussion.

Selecting materials and activities that are motivating to these students is also a difficult task. Sometimes they are so withdrawn that it is hard to discern their interests. At other times their interests seem so bizarre or obscure that it is difficult, if not impossible, to connect their interests to classroom activities. With students who seem to show no interest, watch carefully for those times when they do engage in spontaneous activity even if it is nonproductive. What element in the activity engages them? How could this motivating element be used in a more productive task? Here is an example: A young teenage girl with a long-standing thought disorder realized that her behaviors made her different from her peers and she was very concerned about this "difference." When she was feeling anxious and insecure, especially when faced with a new task, she engaged in obsessive and perseverative discussions regarding herself and her differences. Her teacher recognized that she also had a normal, adolescent yearning for peer acceptance. They had a series of LSI conversations together about ways to participate successfully in group activities, in which the teacher guided her to monitor and change her behavior by building on her desire to be a participating and successful group member.

Students with bizarre interests or preoccupations present a different sort of problem. We first attempt to redirect them to a new interest, and if this does not work, we enter into their private world, using the bizarre interest as a medium for communicating. Then we use this communication link to redirect and expand their preoccupation into something more closely approximating reality. Both strategies can work, depending on how heavily invested the students are in maintaining the preoccupation. The key is to ally yourself with the student, building trust and communication.

Matt and Selene illustrate the difficulties in working with students who have severe thought disorders. With Matt, his teacher applies the strategy of first using his preoccupation with being an air conditioner to reach him. When he seems to "let her in," psychological contact is made and he allows her to redirect him back to reality. Selene and her teacher illustrate a more advanced step in this process, where they have agreed upon key words to help Selene help herself. In both examples, the adult is able to reengage the student in participating in the group activity.

In all programs for students with thought disorders, the possibility of medical and psychiatric intervention should be reviewed periodically. It has been suggested that these students may have much more access to their conscious and unconscious thought processes than do typical students, making it difficult for them to selectively

Matt

Matt is highly interested in home appliances and at times insists that he is an air conditioner. When he is highly anxious, he blows air rapidly in and out of his mouth. The teacher enters into Matt's fantasy, reflecting that the air condition is, indeed, on. She tells him that it is quite comfortable in the room, and to conserve energy the air conditioner should be turned off. Matt ceases his blowing, but the teacher knows it will return with the next stress.

After several discussions with Matt about the air conditioner, the teacher begins interpreting to him, "Sometimes when things are rough, it is a lot easier to pretend to be an air conditioner."

Matt listens and appears to grasp the idea. When he starts to blow again, the teacher reflects the behavior and redirects it by saying, "Matt, things are a little rough right now. Let me help you with this math problem."

As the year progresses, Matt is increasingly able to redirect himself with only the cue, "Rough?" from the teacher.

Selene

Several Stage Three teens are discussing a TV show they saw about environmental pollution. Selene, who has a severe thought disorder, has been able to participate in the discussion about the different ways the environment can be polluted. However, when the name Love Canal is mentioned, she beings a monologue: "Love . . . Love is a many-splendored thing . . . Give love and you shall receive it . . . Love, love, love and love little ducks . . . For God so loved the world . . ."

The teacher touches Selene and uses a cognitive restructuring approach, saying in a firm voice, "Selene, we are talking about pollution. You are talking *off the subject!*" (a signal phrase used with her).

The teacher gets Selene's attention and then continues, "Off-the-subject talk makes it hard for our class to continue. You were saying that industrial chemicals are a source of pollution. When you watched the show on TV, was there anything that made you think chemicals caused that problem in New Jersey?"

respond or ignore their thoughts. Others suggest that neural activity in the brain is erratic. In either event, these disorders create thought and behavior unbounded by typical concepts of time, spatial relationships, or logic. These difficulties in mental activity can sometimes be ameliorated with prescriptive drugs shown to be effective in reducing the symptoms of thought disorders. In younger children, these drugs have been of some use in reducing other symptoms such as hyperactivity, aggressiveness, attention deficits, or anxiety. Caution must be exercised in the prescription, administration, and monitoring of these drugs, as they can produce unwanted side effects that may be debilitating or dangerous. Drug therapy must be carefully monitored by a consulting psychiatrist to ensure that side effects do not occur and outweigh the advantages produced by the medications.

SUMMARY

A developmentalist looking at behavior sees the gradual expansion of an individual's capacity to make constructive behavioral choices independently. Transactional psychologists and social learning theorists acknowledge that the force behind change and growth is the universal human need to mediate between personal needs and the demands of society. Adults responsible for fostering social-emotional competence and responsible behavior in children and youth need to know how this process occurs in a cultural context, and how it changes from age to age and stage to stage. With this knowledge, adults can make informed decisions in selecting the strategies they use in guiding students' behavior constructively.

The strategies most frequently used in Developmental Therapy–Developmental Teaching are not unique to this particular curriculum. They have been used effectively for years by parents, teachers, and clinicians working with children and youth. What this curriculum has done is to organize the strategies to make it easier for adults to understand each student's unique needs and to target needed strategies more precisely. The result is an approach to guiding behavior that is culturally and developmentally appropriate for each individual student. Emphasis is placed on information gathering—understanding a student's unique private reality and the meanings that have been attached to the life experiences that have produced the behaviors. Equally important is to identify clearly the next behaviors that must be acquired, in the sequence of maturation, for a student to continue to grow in social-emotional competence. In short, an effective behavior management plan operationalizes specific IEP, IFSP, or ITP goals and objectives, responding to changes in the student with corresponding changes in objectives and management strategies.

A successful program requires careful and systematic planning about how behavioral problems will be managed as an integrated part of the overall program. The managment strategies used by adults create and convey the adult roles needed to foster maximum development of students at each of the stages. When a student has severe problem behaviors, adults working with the student must plan together how the strategies will be used. They must be consistent; all the adults on the team must convey the same messages, the same expectations, and the same management strategies. To do this, daily debriefings are essential for a team working with students who have severe problems. Preparation of suitable space and provision of adequate staff are also essential. Quiet areas are needed to assist students who lose control and to conduct LSI and counseling. Reasonable expectations for conduct should be established by the adult team, conveyed clearly, and followed consistently. From these expectations, a few fundamental rules should be established to provide psychological and physical security to both students and adults. Finally, and most important, at the heart of an effective behavior management program are attitudes of respect and fairness. Adults must model these values if they hope to see them demonstrated by the students.

Clark and Ellen

It is the first day of class. As Ellen and Clark arrive, you tell them your name and then ask them their names. Clark simply stares at you and says nothing. Ellen says, "I hope you know more than that stupid teacher we had last year."

Clark keeps his eyes on the floor. He slowly sits down and bites his fingernails.

Ellen stalks out of the room, saying, "I've got to comb my hair! I'll bet you aren't even a teacher."

PRACTICE

Using the key points in this chapter

At the end of Chapter 1, we included vignettes about Alice, Bob, Clark, Ellen, and Drew. We asked you to think about them from a developmental perspective. In Chapter 3 we asked you to identify program goals for these students in each curriculum area, using Figure 3.2 to prepare their Preliminary Profiles for social-emotional competence. The "Practice" section in Chapter 4 focused on designing a daily schedule and selecting themes, materials, and activities for them. Now, using that information, outline a preliminary behavior management program for each student. Follow the six steps outlined in this chapter.

After you complete the management plans, apply your plans with Clark and Ellen. Here is an incident—imagine that you are their teacher!

1. Is this problem behavior likely to have been generated by the classroom situation (*situation-specific* or *diffused*)?
2. What defense mechanism or mechanisms could be operating here?
3. What possible developmental anxiety or anxieties could these two students be defending against?
4. What motivations and values do the students have that might be helpful in handling the situation therapeutically?
5. What characteristics make these students vulnerable to continuing the problem behaviors?
6. What are these students probably feeling?
7. What type of social power and adult role should you maintain to assist them, from the perspective of developmental needs?
8. What response or responses are needed from you, as the teacher, to alleviate their anxieties?

NOTES

CHAPTER 6

Management Strategies To Foster Development

Management begins with us! A student "reads" us to sense if we are going to respond with compassion or cruelty . . . with help or hostility. The message is in our attitudes, values, voice, and body language.

—NICHOLAS J. LONG, DIRECTOR, INSTITUTE OF PSYCHOEDUCATIONAL TRAINING, HAGERSTOWN, MARYLAND

PARTICIPATION IS A "MUST" IF RESPONSIBLE BEHAVIOR IS THE GOAL

For Rita and David, the world is not a happy place. There are countless Ritas and Davids, of all ages, in every grade, in every school and neighborhood, throughout the world. Each day, the adults who work with them respond as best they can. They acutely recognize the difficulties these students face. They see the daily failures, frustrations, lack of progress, and dismal future. The students' behavior is extremely difficult to manage—at times, almost impossible! Yet most of these adults hold a strong belief that such students have inner resources that *can* be mobilized—that there *must* be a way to provide genuine assistance. Wherever they work with students like these—at school, in after-school programs, in churches, in clinics, or as mentors for Girls' and Boys' Clubs—adults care and want to help. The question is how?

In previous chapters we reviewed key concepts that shape our strategies about how to encourage social-emotional competence and responsible behavior in students of all ages. In this chapter, we continue the topic, describing in greater detail each of the most frequently used strategies in Developmental Therapy–Developmental Teaching for managing students' behavior in ways that foster development. We approach this task by defining each strategy and describing how it is adjusted and changed to meet the needs of individual students at each developmental stage.

The essential task in implementing an effective behavior management plan is to know precisely which objectives for increased social-emotional competence the plan should address.[1] These objectives define the behavioral, communication, and socialization responses expected of a student. We use the DTORF–R profile to do this—identifying previous skills a student has acquired that can be used to teach new, more advanced behaviors. Next, we look at the student's age-related characteristics, motivations, developmental anxieties, and personal history for information that will help us select management strategies to catch and hold the student's motivation to participate in acceptable ways with successful outcomes.

Because the curriculum is built on several fundamental assumptions about the nature of learning and positive

[1]Previous chapters describe the process of identifying the necessary background information for planning an effective program, including use of the Preliminary Profile, shown in Figure 3.2.

Rita

Four-year-old Rita has a severe developmental disability. Her teacher describes her this way:

"Rita's sensory systems do not seem to be fully functioning. She seems to respond with pleasure to food, visual stimuli, and body movement, but no responses are evident when objects are put in her hands or when sounds are made. When her attention is obtained, she often reacts with a startled, jerking movement, but the reaction is fleeting and she pays little attention to the source of the stimulation.

"Rita's only interest in people is associated with being rocked or fed. She appears to be aware of her mother and the adults in the program who care for her. However, she does not respond when her name is called if she cannot see the speaker. She will not come when her mother or teacher gestures for her. Her preferred activity is aimlessly running in a small area, flapping her arms or twisting her fingers in front of her eyes. She periodically shrieks, using two patterns—one when she wants something, another when she seems to be comfortable. Other sounds occur at random."

David

David's mother is frantic about him. When she talks with his second-grade teacher, she describes the characteristics of David's that are highly disturbing to her:

- Pleads sickness to avoid coming to school
- Demands her attention all the time
- Fights with other children
- Makes bad remarks about her, himself, and others
- Tears up his toys or loses them
- Makes unreasonable demands on her
- Can't seem to pay attention
- Doesn't seem to understand when she tells him something
- Gets frustrated easily
- Won't tell her what is worrying him
- Complains about feeling bad
- Won't join the family in activities
- Won't try anything new
- Won't eat the meals she prepares but sneaks snacks

David's teacher describes him as a child with "inappropriate school behavior and difficulty in relating to peers." She sees many of the same problems reported by his mother. She also expresses concern about his distractibility, restlessness, resistance to discipline, aggression toward property, silliness, temper tantrums, immature behavior, and irresponsibility. She sees no problems in basic academic skills yet, but predicts that David will begin to fall behind in achievement if his behavioral problems persist.

outcomes, participation and the need for positive results are the essential elements of these behavior management strategies. We put this idea into operation by requiring participation of all students in all activities, in every stage of development. Even if an activity is unstructured and "free," it is expected that each student will participate. If a student cannot—or will not—participate, it is the adults' responsibility to ensure that participation is achieved and the result is positive. We recognize that it is the power of the student-adult relationship and the skill of the adult that are at the heart of the success of this approach.

Selectively Ignoring Misbehavior

When adults orchestrate a group activity with the idea that all must participate, some members of the group will always resist participating. Many management strategies can be used to respond; however, the best strategy may sometimes be to preempt confrontation, crisis, or the need for disciplinary action by *selectively ignoring* a student's actions, thereby avoiding unnecessary interventions. Perhaps a discussion of ways to do this and still foster responsible behavior would be useful before we review the behavior management strategies most frequently used in Developmental Therapy–Developmental Teaching.

In determining whether or not to ignore a student's actions, an adult must be aware of (a) how secure the student's internal controls are, (b) the extent to which the student trusts or respects the adult, and (c) the degree of motivation the student has for the activity. The more these qualities are present, the more likely it is that ignoring a minor conduct problem will be effective. Conversely, the fewer of these qualities that are present, the more likely it is that ignoring a student's actions or words will fuel negative behavior until some adult stops it. A general guideline we find helpful is to consider whether the student will continue participating in the expected activity with a high probability of a successful outcome. If the answer is yes, then ignoring a negative behavior usually is a good alternative for the adult. If the answer is no, a behavior management strategy is probably necessary.

By ignoring disturbing behavior, an adult takes away a student's audience. The adult also is communicating to the student, "I know you can stop that by yourself, and you don't need me to stop you." For example, one student in a Stage Four group climbed out on a window ledge during an art lesson and threatened to jump down. The teacher commented, "You can come join the group" and proceeded with the art lesson, ignoring the student. He soon joined the group in productive activity. This teacher knew the student well; had a good relationship with him; knew that he had reached Stage Four in social-emotional development, indicating considerable self-control and some insight; and knew that he had a record of success in art classes. Without this information, the teacher would not have chosen to ignore the student's behavior. Had the student continued to stay on the ledge, the gamble would have been lost and the teacher would have had to backtrack to the point of possible physical intervention. But each time an adult's gamble to ignore behavior is taken and won, the student's inner controls are strengthened and another step has been made toward responsible behavior.

Although a student who is misbehaving to control or test an adult may sometimes benefit from ignoring by the adult, there are many more situations in which ignoring may be counterproductive. Ignoring students who are out of control is dangerous, and ignoring students in crisis is seldom helpful to the students. Ignoring students who are misbehaving for adult attention may result in intensified behavioral problems. Or students may interpret an adult's failure to respond as lack of power, or ineptness, on the adult's part. The students may believe that the adult is someone who lets things go by or is not swift enough to keep up with them. Such interpretations (true or not) inevitably produce a series of confrontations as the students attempt to test adults' limits to find out what sort of person these adults really are. For these reasons, it is important for the adult to ignore behavior selectively.

Offering Alternatives

Another way of avoiding an unnecessary confrontation is by giving a student alternatives instead of commands. This allows students to choose their own course of action and have some control in the situation rather than buckling under to adult authority ("Where would be the best place for your comb, in your pocket or on the shelf?"). Alternatives provide a structure, setting limits while providing for choice.

There are times when students will request things or opportunities they know belong to others. A confrontation may be avoided by reminding the student, through a question, about the established expectations. For example, if a student says, "I want the volleyball," the adult responds, "I know you do; what day are you in charge of equipment?" In this way the adult communicates understanding of the student's wishes and concern about them and reminds the student that everyone will have a turn again.

Depersonalizing

Another technique that helps students conform to limits and learn new behavior without unnecessary confrontation consists of depersonalizing the limits by referring to the universal condition or using the editorial "we." If a student hits another student, the adult might intervene with the statement: "The rule here is, 'People don't hit because hitting hurts.'" By invoking a group rule, "Everyone participates," an adult communicates that all students are expected to do an assignment, instead of focusing on an individual by saying, "You have to stay at your desk until you do it."

Recalling Previous Successes

Previous success experiences can be used to challenge the best in a student or a group ("I remember how you stayed in control that day when everybody had such a hard time, and I bet you can do it today, even though you are upset"). This technique uses the relationship between the adult and student. The student trusts the adult to require of him only what he can do. Challenge to a group based upon a previous success is particularly effective at Stage Three ("This group stayed in control all day yesterday; I bet you can do it again by helping each other today").

In short, effective behavior management requires conveying expectations to each student about what is expected. Adults save considerable time and energy if they convey expectations so clearly and respond so consistently that students have no need to test them to find out how they will respond. Expectations must also provide a way for students to participate and manage stress successfully. An expectation for behavior that is embarrassing, unnecessary, or too difficult to achieve sets a student up for a crisis, requiring further intervention by the adult. The adult's responsibility is to guide the resolution and provide a sense of security by communicating what achievable actions will be expected from the student. Also, when a student has committed a wrong, there must be an opportunity to make it right. For example, if a student breaks a window, part of the ensuing discussion must resolve how the situation will be corrected and how retribution can be made by the student.

THE MOST FREQUENTLY USED BEHAVIOR MANAGEMENT STRATEGIES

Figure 6.1 summarizes the 11 management strategies most frequently used in Developmental Therapy–Developmental Teaching. All except the last two are essentially verbal forms of intervention. We have found that these strategies foster students' social-emotional growth at all ages and stages of development. When they are used with skill and sensitivity, they provide ways to minimize students' disruptive, destructive behavior and teach acceptable, productive alternatives. They are the foundation for a mentally healthy learning environment that is positive in approach and emphasizes students' participation in the program.

Figure 6.2 summarizes four additional strategies that are less frequently used but that are necessary from time to time when working with students who have severe behavioral problems. These strategies involve essentially physical forms of management and generally are used *after* a behavioral incident has occurred. Although they are used frequently or occasionally at the first stages of development, use of these four strategies decreases at higher stages as students' personal responsibility increases.

The strategies are listed according to frequency of use, in descending order. The series of bar graphs indicates the extent to which a strategy is used in each stage and how the strategies change in use and form at each stage. By reading across a row you can follow the changes an adult must make in using a strategy with students at different stages of development. By reading down a column, for any particular stage, you can find the pattern of management strategies most frequently used for a particular stage. Strategies with weights of 3 are major strategies for a stage; those weighted 2 are used frequently; and a weight of 1 or 0 indicates that a strategy is used only occasionally or not at all. A progression from physical to verbal strategies is characteristic of behavior management strategies in Developmental Therapy–Developmental Teaching, with students in the first stages of development frequently needing physical forms of intervention while they are learning to respond to verbal interventions. However, at all stages, we prefer to use verbal strategies in preference to physical forms of intervention whenever possible.

A comment is needed here about punishment and rewards. We have deliberately removed these two terms from the list of most frequently used strategies to convey our strong belief that they are among the least effective strategies over the long run. In fact, they may contribute to retarding a student's development of higher-order thinking, self-regulated behavior, and values.

Punishment is generally defined as producing pain or loss. Although it may be a natural consequence of misbehaving or making poor choices in responding to others, it can be a powerful negative force in a relationship between an adult and student or a parent and child. It should not be a major strategy used by adults in behavior management. For punishment to be effective in changing a student's behavior, it must not result in a breakdown of the relationship between the student and the adult. We prefer to refocus the concept of punishment as natural consequences that result when students make poor choices or rules are violated. In the following section we discuss how this idea is implemented through a wide range of strategies that do not focus on punishment per se but, instead, focus on fostering social-emotional growth and responsible behavior.

Rewards present many of the same potential pitfalls to development as punishment. We have seen tangible

Four Keys to Successful Behavior Management

1. Convey expectations clearly.
2. Always follow through.
3. Show concern for the student.
4. Understand the forces that drive the student's behavior.

Figure 6.1. Most frequently used management strategies in Developmental Therapy–Developmental Teaching. Key: 3 = used as a major technique; 2 = used frequently; 1 = used occasionally; 0 = used seldom or not used.

Strategy	*Stage One*	*Stage Two*	*Stage Three*	*Stage Four*	*Stage Five*
Postitive Feedback and Praise	3 From sensory experiences and nurturing adults	3 From adults about individual activity	3 From adults about group activity	3 From peers and adults	2 From peers, adults, and self
Motivate with Materials	3	3	3	2	0
Structure	3	3	2	1	1
Redirection	2 Usually physical	3 Changes to verbal	3	1	1
Reflection	2 Actions	3 Words and actions	3 Words, actions, and feelings	1 Usually feelings	1
Interpretation	0	1	3 Adult interprets	3 Adult helps student interpret	3
Verbal Interaction Between Adults	1	3 Response model	3 Group process model	1 Interpersonal model	1
Rules	0	2	3 Adult is rule authority	2 Group develops rules	1 Individual selects values
Life Space Intervention	0	0	3 Individual	3 Group and individual	2 Individual
Control of Materials by Adults	3	2	1	0	0
Physical Proximity	3 Body contact	2 Touch	1 Physical closeness	0	0

Figure 6.2. Less frequently used management strategies necessary for managing severely disruptive behavior. Key: 3 = used as a major technique; 2 = used frequently; 1 = used occasionally; 0 = used seldom or not used.

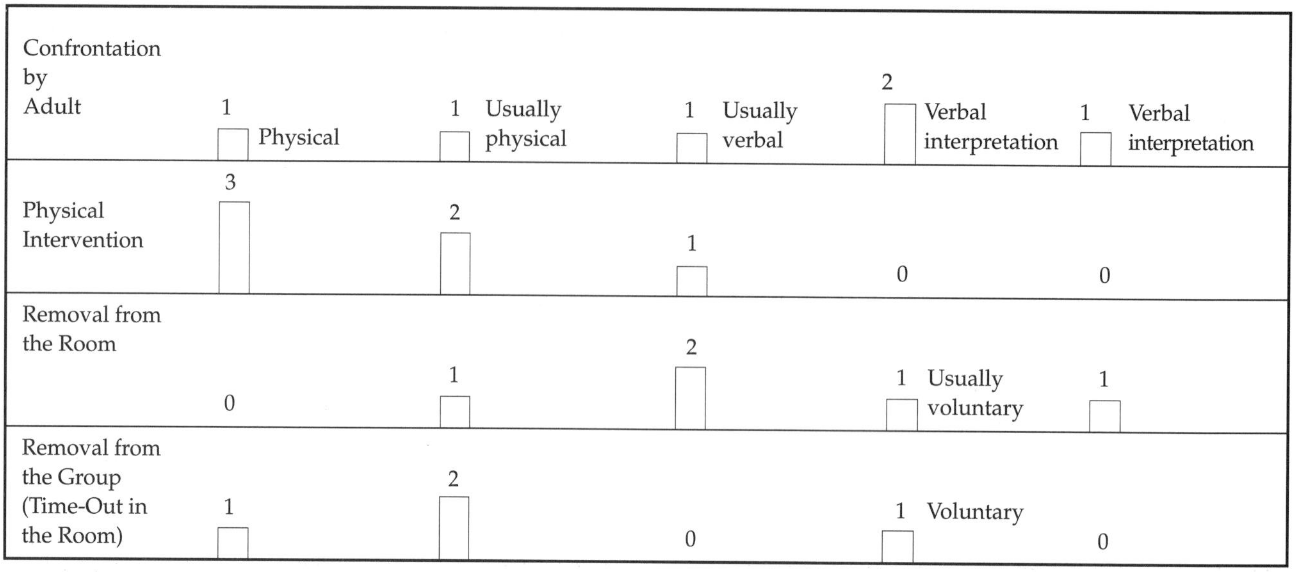

rewards such as food, candy, treats, trips, stars, TV viewing, and toys frequently and extensively used in American schools and families as a substitute for rewards such as successful interpersonal relationships with adults and peers. This gives us great concern. Although it is clear that some children and teens may need such rewards when they have developed no other value system, rewards are not generally justified by the time students begin to think abstractly and develop values. If it appears necessary to include a reward system in a behavior management plan, it is equally necessary to include a systematic plan for gradually reducing the reward system and substituting more intrinsic forms of motivation. As long as students work only for material rewards, we doubt that responsible social behavior will develop.

We have also been asked why *point systems* are not included in these lists of strategies. These methods are widely taught in teacher preparation programs and are used extensively in programs for students with emotional or behavioral disabilities. We have not found them necessary for the successful management of behavior, however severely disturbed or disturbing a student's behavior may be. In our original model development, we explored these strategies as alternatives and found several negative aspects that dissuaded us from using them further. First, we were concerned with the lack of evidence that behaviors practiced under a point system can generalize for the student in everyday living. Second, elaborate sets of rewards and punishments or detailed record-keeping systems can communicate a priority for the system instead of for the student. With too much focus on keeping count of successes and failures, the broader meanings of personal participation can be lost on a student, leading to the materialistic view that every behavior has an associated point value. Third, we see point systems misused by well-intentioned teachers who become reinforcers of a student's image of self as "one who cannot do," as the teacher reviews and evaluates the student's failures-of-the-day. Finally, we are concerned that externally managed systems of control may contribute to restricting a student's acceptance of personal responsibility for behavior. However, if a point system takes these concerns into account, there is no reason why it cannot be used in conjunction with the other management strategies recommended for Developmental Therapy–Developmental Teaching.

We have some of the same concerns over strategies that use *levels* and *contracts*. The essential idea in students' working for increasing privileges by moving from level to level as they progress is theoretically supportable. Designated levels of accomplishment can provide students with incentives to regulate their own behavior. We have found these strategies to be effective as students begin to master goals and objectives in Stage Three and beyond. Students who participate in self-ratings with the DTORF–R learn that they are progressing from stage to stage. This strategy allows IEP or ITP objectives to be selected by the students and their families, giving them a sense of where they are heading and how they are progressing day by day. They see their own actions resulting in progress, and they experience success in achieving valued results, which are usually related to peer acclaim, respect, and recognition. If rewards for achieving developmental objectives or fulfilling a contract are age-relevant as well as culturally and developmentally appropriate, both contracts and levels can be effective and can be easily included in the Developmental Therapy–Developmental Teaching approach.

Positive Feedback and Praise

Positive feedback and praise encourage students by verbally and nonverbally reflecting the positive aspects of their participation. This is a major strategy in Developmental Therapy–Developmental Teaching, used with students at all stages of development. By letting students know that they are doing a good job, adults convey respect, recognition, and relationship. Because these qualities are essential to the continuing development of social competence and personal responsibility, they are essential ingredients for every program. Students seldom see their own successes and often have a history of experiences with adults that has negated opportunities to build trust and self-confidence. Positive feedback and praise from adults are essential if the adults hope to foster a student's participation in positive ways. When students see themselves as being able to do, they are willing to participate and try new ways of behaving.

The type of positive feedback and praise used varies with students' individual profiles and stages of development. With some students, a successful outcome—a sense of mastery and accomplishment—is the motivation to continue to participate in acceptable ways. For others, recognition by significant adults or peers provides the motivation. A student in Stage One receives much positive feedback through body contact, hugging, touching, and other pleasurable sensations provided by adults, activities, and materials. Used initially to arouse and elicit responses, these forms of positive contact soon become interpersonal encouragement, praise, and reward for spontaneous responses and participation.

By Stage Two, students are mobilized and are responding to highly motivating, individualized materials and activities for the pleasure of participating. The pleasure of doing is the reward. Adults verbally reflect this pleasure and encourage the positive aspects of students' participation while assisting them in the fundamental skills needed for successful accomplishment of the activity. Abundant and frequent verbal praise must be used, often accompanied by physical contact and touch. Even the smallest accomplishments must be recognized, as there are very few things that a student beginning Stage Two can accomplish successfully without adult support and guidance.

During Stage Three, students have progressed to a level where verbal praise from adults is usually sufficient to communicate recognition of their accomplishments and good feelings about an activity. This praise is often difficult for a student beginning Stage Three to accept. There is a developmental milestone that marks the transition from Stage Two to Stage Three: *"to accept praise or success without inappropriate behavior or loss of control."* This objective must be achieved before a student can master an important communication objective in Stage Three: *"to use words or nonverbal gestures spontaneously to show pride in own work and activity, or to make positive statements about self."*

Because successful participation in group activities is a major social-emotional goal for students in Stage Three, adults frequently use positive feedback and praise in combination with verbal reflection of success and redirection to encourage students' positive outcomes, making praise legitimate. Adults' own credibility with students in Stage Three increases and the students begin to internalize feelings of being successful. At this point, the students begin to depend much less on adults for praise and to focus on recognition from peers, indicating that they are moving into Stage Four.

For students in Stage Four, peer recognition is a major motivating force. Adults confirm peer judgments about individual successes and accomplishments. Positive feedback and praise should come from group interaction and have an authentic, real-life meaning. A group of Stage Four students can establish their own rewards by learning what options bring the results they seek. A major challenge for adults with students at this stage is to avoid superimposing a preconceived reward system on the group. To be truly effective, the motivation for responsible behavior and participation as an acceptable group member must be defined and monitored by the individuals in the group itself.

In Stage Five, students recognize their own accomplishments and those of others. It often takes very little modeling on an adult's part to establish a pattern of making positive statements about others and acknowledging the successes and desirable characteristics of others. In short, Stage Five offers students opportunities to use positive feedback and praise as a strategy for themselves in their relationships with others.

Motivate with Materials

Motivating with toys, materials, activities, supplies, equipment, and media is a major behavior management strategy for use with students in Stages One through Three. Tangible objects with great appeal are the catalysts for successful participation of students in these stages. To be effective, material must evoke participating behavior from the students. However, adults usually must introduce the material in ways that motivate and establish meaning (value) for the students. By Stage Three, students are generally able to attach meaning to selected materials themselves, but the meaning may be negative or nonconstructive. It is the adults' responsibility to select materials with such powerful and positive motivational qualities that participation in an activity will be successful.[2] Here are examples of the use of motivating

[2] Chapter 4 contains a section on the use of materials and activities for students at all stages of development. Appendix 5 contains a summary of motivational systems with reference to typical stages of development. This summary can be helpful in selecting developmentally appropriate and motivating materials and activities.

materials to promote mastery of specific IEP or IFSP objectives for Stages One through Three.

Motivating with Materials in Stage One. Several students with severe disabilities are working on a behavioral objective, *"to respond spontaneously to a simple environmental stimulus with a motor behavior."* The adult gives each student a small basin of warm water with a small washable baby doll and washcloth. She says, "The doll needs a bath. Let's wash the doll." The motivating material is the warm water that has previously proved to be highly motivating to these students. The sensory elements in the material ensure sustained attention. The doll in the water presents a new task in a familiar setting. The students watch as the adult provides a simple demonstration, putting the washcloth on the doll. The children respond by attempting to imitate the movement or to create their own movement. When a student does not respond, the adult remotivates him by moving his hands through the water, picking up the cloth, and laying it across the doll.

Motivating with Materials in Stage Two. A group of students in Stage Two is working on a behavioral objective, *"to wait without physical intervention by an adult."* The use of motivating materials in a big box is essential to counteract the distractibility and impulsivity of these students. The teacher presents the box and says, "There is a surprise inside our box today. To get this surprise, we have to do something we have never done before." She pulls a string from the box with an attached "secret message." She reads the rhyming message to the students: "Pull me. Pull me. Pull me slow. Then I'll show what you need to know." She pulls another string with a message that says, "Everyone will have a chance. Pull now, it's your turn, Lance." The teacher gives the string to Lance and he pulls until another message appears. Each message is written using either words, pictures, or symbols so that each student is able to "read" a message. Each message directs the reader to pass it on to another student in the group until every student has had a turn. The last message directs the reader to tell everyone to pull on the string together until the surprise comes out of the box.

In this activity the motivation is the element of surprise and the aura created by the adult in discovering the hidden object. To allay any anxiety about being able to participate, each student is assured that everyone will have a turn. The messages are written individually at each student's ability level so that they all will experience success. The students who are the most impulsive find their names being called early in the activity so that waiting time is reduced for them. To ensure that no student feels slighted, the "grand finale" involves all of them in the most motivating part of the activity—the final tug that reveals the surprise.

Motivating with Materials in Stage Three. Several students in Stage Three are having difficulty mastering a behavioral objective, *"to tell other, more appropriate ways to behave in a given situation."* The teacher uses a motivating role play involving reverse practice to work on this objective. She sets the scenario for the group by describing a pretend classroom where students are involved in arithmetic when another student walks into the classroom. The teacher says, "What's the most rude way to enter a classroom?" She encourages descriptions of a rude entry from members of the group, and a few examples are selected by the students for role play by the entire group. A discussion follows each role play concerning the effect of the behavior on others in the group, the rude student's feelings, reasons for the behavior, and so forth. To end the activity, the students role-play a more acceptable way to enter a classroom.

This activity uses no tangible material but motivates because excitement and humor are connected with the prospect of being allowed the freedom to act in unacceptable ways, but within the safe boundaries of role play and pretend. The drama allows the students to feel the repercussions of unacceptable behavior without actually having to experience it. These feelings bring an "aliveness" to discussions that is not present as a motivating factor when these ideas are simply discussed.

Motivating with Materials in Stages Four and Five. Students in Stage Four and Five respond to materials that closely relate to their real-life interests—people and peers. The meanings evoked by materials should be individually and culturally relevant and, if accurately chosen, can trigger instant involvement. Particularly during Stage Five, students draw their major motivation from people. For this reason, attempts to motivate with materials are not particularly effective as a behavior management strategy unless they contain content reflecting personal and social concerns. Television, music, movies, and print media are major sources for motivating content. Students respond to well-chosen materials with heightened responsiveness and sustained involvement in the tasks or activity.

Finally, presentation of materials must cause students at all stages of development to want to become involved and to participate. When you are introducing materials, provide clear information about how they will be used in an activity and what the expected outcome will be. Each student must be able to use the materials successfully. If a student reacts enthusiastically to a material and then flounders, the situation will invariably result in a behavioral problem, usually requiring further adult intervention. In contrast, if a student reacts to a material with confidence and enthusiasm and knows exactly how to go about using it successfully, further adult involvement is not needed until the conclusion of the activity. This climate is one in which involvement with the material and activity is promoting acceptable, self-regulated behavior and social-emotional growth through participation.

Structure

Structure is organization. It is a major management strategy for use with students in Stages One and Two and is used frequently in Stage Three. By Stages Four and Five, structure is generally within the students themselves, and it is no longer necessary to provide extensive structure in the program. Structure provides order, consistency, predictability, and psychological security. In a carefully structured program, students know what to expect, when it will occur, and what behavior is expected of them. Almost paradoxically, structure leads to individual freedom and initiative. When students learn that they can cope with what is planned, they participate with increasing willingness. And when their efforts are successful, they become increasingly spontaneous in their participation. Through structure, adults foster social-emotional maturity in students.

Structure is made up of many small details of organization involving schedules, activities, space, routines, pacing, timing, and amount of adult control (or lack of control). When a program is going smoothly, structure is at work. In a well-structured program, adult control does not predominate, and authoritarian management is not evident. It is the actual flow of the activities in the program that appears to generate participation and involvement.

Through the stages of Developmental Therapy–Developmental Teaching, external structure decreases as students' internal structure increases. Structure follows a pattern that changes from chiefly physical elements, clearly evident in Stages One and Two, to verbal, implicit structure by Stage Three. For example, in Stage One, the adult may use chanting and rhythmic marching to assist students in making a successful transition from the story corner to an art activity area. In Stage Two, the adult might structure a transition by moving to the table before the students, bringing out a "treasure box," and inviting the students to come to the table for a treasure hunt. In Stage Three, the adult might structure a transition by recalling the successful activity accomplished by the students yesterday and describing how the next activity will be used as a part of the school's open house for parents. With Stage Four students, structure is readjusted to suit the needs expressed by the group members, such as growing agitation over the attempts of one individual to control the group activity.

Several forms of structure are a part of every Developmental Therapy–Developmental Teaching program for students of all ages and stages of development: routines and schedules, use of space, the expectation of participating, and the amount of adult control. These program elements were discussed in the previous chapters but are summarized again here because of their importance in behavior management.

Routines and Schedules Are the Foundation for Structure. Psychological security comes with consistency and predictable events. Each program in Developmental Therapy–Developmental Teaching, at home or school, maintains a consistent routine for daily activity. This routine provides the external organization for the students and builds security. The positive effect on students is particularly noticeable for those who lack internal organization themselves, such as students who are hyperactive; those with attention deficit disorders; those who have neurological impairments, including drug- or alcohol-induced damage; and those with thought or communication disorders such as schizophrenia or autism.

For students in Stage One, adults focus on making the routine a remembered sequence, reviewing an illustrated schedule that is clearly in view. Each student understands the symbols used and then learns to recall the event when the adult points to the illustration on the schedule of activities and asks, "What comes next?" Often, students in Stage One will have to hear the adults answer the question until the routine is learned. In Stage Two, students anticipate the routine and can use the posted schedule of activities to practice beginning word or symbol recognition. For them, the daily schedule of events is a form of success—they know the routine without having to be told! By Stage Three, students are reviewing the schedule of daily activities themselves and most can recognize the written form. They also begin to learn that variations for special events can be included in the daily routine without disruption to the psychological security in the order of things. In Stage Four, students develop the schedule themselves and participate as a group in changing it to meet the group's needs. Students in Stage Five follow the routines and schedules of the regular program or activity in which they are participating. For those in high school, the daily routine is planned around the same class periods designed for all students.

Space and Activity Areas Are Intrinsic to Structure. Another major element in structure is the use of designated spaces for each activity. Specific areas of the room (or home, if it is a family's program) are reserved for certain activities. It should be clear to students that there are expected behaviors for each activity, and the consistent use of a designated space helps to remind them of these expectations. It is, therefore, not necessary for adults to do the reminding after the students have learned the expectation for a particular area. Space designations give students cues about the expected behavior for an activity. There are spaces for exuberant, free movement, and other spaces and activities that require constrained, careful movements. Some activities require the use of large muscles, whereas others require well-controlled fine-muscle movements. Designated spaces and activity areas convey these natural requirements.

Activity areas encourage students to begin the process of learning self-regulated behavior. If materials in an activity area are well chosen and students are motivated by them, the intrinsic drive for *doing* carries a student forward into participating. Exploratory and spontaneous behavior becomes the added benefit as students have opportunities to try out newly acquired skills in independent ways.

Structure Includes the Expectation of Participation. Every student is expected to participate in each activity. Yet expectations are different at each stage and are individualized for each student. Here are examples of how adults individualize the structure when students show signs of stress, without modifying the general expectation about participation. When a young girl in Stage One becomes extremely excited and begins flapping her hands, the adult takes her hand and moves her through the expected movement ("motoring"). With an agitated boy in Stage Two, the adult redefines the task by saying, "You've done so well with making your go-cart, it is almost finished now. Just put the wheels on and it is done!" With a small group of angry Stage Three boys, the adult says, "Sometimes guys are too upset over something else to finish their work. Let's go talk about what's really on your mind before you try to finish this." And with students in Stage Four who are showing signs of stress, the adult involves the entire group in a discussion of what is generating the stress and the problems it is presenting to the group members. In each of these situations, the adult has restructured the behavioral expectations in order to meet the most important developmental need at the moment, while returning to closure on the activity and emphasizing the importance of participating.

Too Much Adult Control Can Destroy Structure. The amount of adult control is the most delicate force to consider when planning and implementing the structure to be used in an individual behavior management plan.[3] Adult control is absolutely essential for psychological safety; that is, students must know that the adults will protect them. No one should be hurt. Students also must trust that the adults can handle the crisis competently and without losing control of themselves or other students. In general, we prefer that the adults responsible for a student's program in Developmental Therapy–Developmental Teaching handle a crisis themselves, conveying competence and control of the situation. When an outsider is called in, it may be interpreted by students as an inability by the adults to handle the situation. This usually causes a breakdown in the psychological security needed in a program.

Another form of adult control is the extent to which adults attempt to regulate and control students' behavior as they participate in an activity. We find that the stage of development is our best guide to the proper amount of adult control. We know that young children need adults to guide them into satisfying participation. This often requires the adults to control the experience, teach the expected behaviors, structure the elements in an activity, and intervene from time to time to ensure that it has a successful outcome for every student regardless of skill level. An adult who is reluctant to use control to ensure satisfying outcomes for the students is contributing to the failure of the program and to the students' lack of progress. On the other hand, as students begin to acquire skills that can be used independently for satisfying and successful outcomes, adults must pull back in their control and permit the students the freedom to participate in the activity in a way that can become uniquely their own. These experiences lead to responsible behavior.

Redirection

Redirection is the process of guiding a student back to a task or activity by remotivating the student, modifying the task, or redefining the expected behaviors. Redirection can be used to help a student choose a more acceptable behavior. When students make a choice that brings satisfying results, social-emotional growth occurs because it is a step toward responsible behavior. Redirection can also refocus a student's attention to the activity while avoiding unnecessary confrontation. Verbal redirection is a major management strategy for use with students in Stages Two and Three, where sustained participation in an activity is a major focus. It also is used frequently in Stage One, where redirection is chiefly physical. For example, physical touch is used to obtain a student's attention for a task in Stage One, and motoring a student through a movement is used to teach the student how to participate.

Students in Stage Two learn to respond to verbal cues to guide their behavior. For example, during Play Time, a young student who has difficulty controlling aggression becomes quite stressed while playing with a toy truck and crashes the truck into structures other students have built with blocks. The adult takes several blocks and quickly builds a road for the student, saying, "This is the superhighway for your emergency vehicle. Your truck has the right to speed on this road to get to the next town." (The block road leads in a direction away from the other students' buildings.) Further restructuring may be needed by involving a second student in building a new town of blocks or in a play adventure where the truck can deliver the supplies at the end of the superhighway.

With a student in Stage Three, an adult might use redirection by saying, "Here's the wastebasket," pushing it toward a student who is about to throw a ball of paper across the room. Or an adult might respond to a student's

[3] In the next chapter we discuss in greater detail the characteristics adults need to foster the social-emotional development of students. A discussion concerning adults as psychological stand-ins for past relationships students have had with other adults is found in Chapter 2.

question with another question in order to redirect the focus of a conversation. An example of this in an academic task is when a student asks, "Is this right?" The teacher answers, "Let's see, will 9 and 9 make 17?" An example of redirection in the area of social communication is when a student asks, "Why do you comb your hair that way?" The adult says, "Have you noticed how many people wear their hair in different ways? Let's look around at the others." This redirection turns the exchange toward a specific communication objective, "to describe characteristic attributes of others." This strategy also avoids burdening the student with personal information about the adult that is not in itself important or useful to the student's progress in acquiring needed skills for social-emotional growth.

By the time students enter Stage Four, a simple, direct verbal reminder usually is sufficient for redirection. For example, redirections such as "The wastebasket is over there," "Check your addition on that one," or "Is there anything more you could add to that picture?" should be sufficient to redirect a student to using expected behavior or to remotivate a student to complete a task correctly. One of the most powerful strategies involving redirection with students in Stage Four involves work on a behavioral objective, *"to indicate awareness of one's own behavioral progress."* When a student is working on this objective and begins to show signs of loss of control, redirection to his past record of progress or success often is sufficient to maintain him on the task.

Adults working with students in Stage Five seldom use redirection except in the form of purposeful questions or reflections. These comments should cue a student to reconsider the direction in which a situation is going, or provoke thought regarding the potential effectiveness of the student's choice between alternatives. The adult must assist the student in concentrating on the socialization goals and objectives for this stage, emphasizing interpersonal skills through the use of this cognitive form of redirection.

Reflection

Reflection is nonjudgmental feedback mirroring verbally what a student is doing, saying, or feeling. It also may be a statement describing an event. With reflection, an adult provides a mirror for students to see their own attributes:

Positive characteristics	"Others look to you for leadership."
Successes	"You made it down the length of the walking board."
Pleasures	"It's great fun to have a field trip together."
Activities	"This group has produced an interesting script for the TV show."

A reflection tells a student that the adult is noticing what is being done (or said), yet no judgments, demands, or interpretations are made. We generally do not reflect students' negative actions or feelings because that would reinforce their negative beliefs about themselves. Reflection requires no response from students but serves to sensitize them to what they are doing, saying, or feeling. This is a particularly effective strategy with students who have few verbal skills—the adult provides the verbal models from the students' actions.

Reflection is one of the most useful strategies an adult has.[4] Although it can be used with students at any stage of development, it is a major strategy to use with students in Stages Two and Three as they struggle to convert from physical to verbal ways of interacting with their environment. It is also used frequently with students in Stage One to connect actions to words. Because reflection sensitizes students to what is happening around them, it can provide a verbal dimension to every experience, stimulating their mental language and cognition. This is especially important for students in Stage One, who are learning to associate words with actions; for example:

"Alanda has the truck. She makes it go."

"You have a cookie."

"Sally throws the ball to you."

With students in Stage Two, reflection offers a verbal model for putting simple experiences into words:

"We all played that game together."

"Roger wants to tell us about his trip."

Reflection for students in Stage Three provides a language model for using words in nonjudgmental ways for social communication objectives, such as describing characteristic attributes in themselves and others and recognizing the feelings of others:

"Joanne is not feeling good about her part in the project."

"This is Neil's special day. He wants to make it a good one."

"You were chosen by the others because they know you are a good leader."

Reflection by an adult helps put into words how students in Stage Three feel, when they may not be able to express those feelings. It communicates that adults care and understand feelings. Reflection helps students look good in front of their peers. It also may verbally link students in a group by encouraging cooperative interaction, teaching them to value the group members. For example,

[4] "When in doubt, reflect" is a guideline that should be recommended to all parents, teachers, and others who are beginning to use Developmental Therapy–Developmental Teaching.

when several students in Stage Three work together to clean up after a project, the adult reflects, "This is a great group!"

During Stages Four and Five, reflection further expands a student's capacity to share feelings. It provides models for social communication skills and helps students convey feelings appropriately to a group. Reflection with teens in Stage Five is a nondirective strategy for helping them to examine their own feelings, values, and ideas, thereby enhancing their communication, socialization, and interpersonal skills with peers and other adults. It is particularly useful when working with teens on objectives from their ITPs in preparation for job skills.

By using *reflection* rather than questions, adults avoid conveying the impression that a student is being interrogated or challenged. Consider this question asked by a teacher: "Are you finished yet?" The student answers, "No. And I'm not going to do this dumb work." Using reflection, the teacher would be more likely to motivate the student to return to the task. He might say, "I see you are almost finished with your work and ready for a break." If this reflection is not sufficient to remotivate the student, the teacher might add *redirection* by saying, "I'll bet you can use those last three words all in one sentence."

Reflection combined with redirection is an effective way to handle minor conduct problems without excessive emphasis or confrontation. By reflecting what has happened, an adult can let a student know that the behavior has been noticed and the adult is aware of the situation; by redirecting the focus, the adult redefines what is important and provides a way for the student to get back on task in a face-saving way. This same double strategy is also effective with manipulative students and those who continually try to test adult authority. By reflecting what was observed, an adult can convey in a matter-of-fact way that an unacceptable behavior was observed and the adult has chosen to ignore it. Then, by reflecting in a concerned way that the behavior might result in misfortune to the student, the adult conveys understanding and acceptance while reminding the student of the consequences of continuing. Finally, the adult uses redirection to an alternative that allows the student to continue to participate in a way that is acceptable, thereby defusing the potential confrontation.

For example, a student walks into a classroom after recess, knocks books off his desk, grabs another student's pencil, and begins cursing. The teacher reflects in a matter-of-fact tone,

> *"Brian, coming in here that way is disruptive. Pick up the books and let's go out to talk about what's bothering you."*

The teacher is using *reflection* to communicate recognition of Brian's disruption to the room and *redirection* to redefine the task—going out to talk about what has happened to cause Brian to be disruptive. In using these two strategies, the teacher is also providing the readiness steps for two subsequent strategies: *interpretation* of Brian's behavior and participation in the LSI process. This is a more effective alternative for fostering Brian's social-emotional growth than if the teacher reacted to the scene by confronting him with "What's the matter with you? What do you think you're doing, coming in here like that? Give back that pencil, pick up those books, and *sit down!*"

At times, reflections should be *depersonalized* ("Sometimes it's hard for students to wait") instead of using a personalized response ("Sometimes its hard for *you* to wait"). Depersonalized reflections provide psychological space between the adult and student. This is needed to insulate a student from emotional stress that cannot be handled rationally. By referring to "others" (speaking in the third person), adults convey that other students have the same feelings (or behavior) and that an incident (crisis, conflict, or mistake) is not so overwhelming or terrible that it cannot be resolved. For example:

> "Children don't like to have their hands covered with red paint."
>
> "Everyone wants other kids to like them."
>
> "Last year when a student broke a window, she made an agreement with the principal to do chores to pay for its replacement."

By looking away from a student while reflecting feelings, an adult can also ease the intensity of the focus on the student, which might otherwise result in increased defensive behavior. At other times, it is essential to personalize a reflection, especially with students who have difficulty identifying themselves. For these students, the personal pronoun is helpful in reflecting ("I see that *you* have *your* workbook").

Interpretation

Interpretation is using words to connect feelings to behavior. It is a management strategy that is not used until a student is well into Stage Three because it requires a level of cognitive development and communication skill in students that typically is not present in earlier stages of development. Interpretation continues to be a major strategy for behavior management throughout the subsequent stages of development.

When it is first used, interpretation simply reflects the feeling suggested by a student's behavior. It requires no response or action from the student. Typically, before Stage Three, students are not aware that their behavior is influenced by their own feelings or by the behavior and feelings of others. With interpretation, the intent is to first help students to understand that behavior communicates inner feelings, both positive and negative. The students then begin to recognize these connections in themselves and others. Here are several examples of this simple form of interpretation:

> "It's hard to be quiet when you have to wait."
>
> "It makes you mad when you can't get the one you want."
>
> "When things don't go right, it doesn't seem fair."
>
> "It feels good to do it right."
>
> "Look at Carol's face—is she kidding?"
>
> "When I see you walk into class like that, I know you're discouraged."
>
> "Sometimes you're not interested and you don't want to . . ."
>
> "It makes you angry when a teacher makes you take turns."
>
> "Sometimes it's scary to try something new."
>
> "It's hard to stop when the game is so much fun."
>
> "You were feeling upset, so you tried to get David into trouble."
>
> "It doesn't seem fair for the teacher to give you work others don't have."

These interpretations provide a focus to teach some very specific skills needed by students in Stage Three, such as *"to describe attributes, strengths, and problems in self," "to describe attributes of others,"* and *"to recognize the feelings of others."* Notice that an objective to focus on having students openly describe their own feelings is not included among the Stage Three objectives. Our experience has been that most students in Stage Three are able to recognize the feelings of others before they can openly acknowledge their own feelings. Learning to communicate their own feelings is a focus for students beginning Stage Four.

Although the intent in using interpretation with students in all stages is to recognize feelings that are generating behavior, the types of interpretation are quite different in form for students in Stages Three and Four. With students in Stage Three, the adult uses statements to connect a student's behavior to the feeling it suggests. With students in Stage Four, the adult asks questions that lead a student to make the connections between behavior and feelings. Here are examples of questions asked by an adult of Stage Four students to help them make their own interpretations. These questions focus on two Stage Four communication and socialization objectives, *"to spontaneously express cause-and-effect relationships between feelings and behavior in self and others"* and *"to use words to express feelings spontaneously and appropriately in a group"*:

> "Why did you feel you needed to do that?"
>
> "What were you really doing to Rick?"
>
> "How does he feel when that happens?"
>
> "As you look back on what happened, what were you feeling as she said that?"
>
> "What were some of the reasons you took it out on her?"

In Stage Five, interpretation continues to be a major strategy for assisting teens to understand their own feelings and behavior. Nondirective counseling methods, using reflection and interpretation, are helpful in expanding students' ability to understand the behavior of themselves and others in the context of emotional needs and feelings. *"To understand and respect others' feelings"* and *"to sustain group and individual relationships"* are important objectives for social-emotional development in Stage Five as teens struggle with their private feelings, sense of identity, and need to be a valued member of a group.

Verbal Interaction Between Adults

Verbal exchange between adults serves as a significant interpersonal behavior model for students learning to use words to control their behavior and to have successful interactions with others. Because of the social communication goals for students in Stages Two and Three, adult verbal interaction is a major management strategy during both stages. These goals include learning *"to use words to affect others in constructive ways"* and *"to use words to express oneself constructively in groups."*

Verbal interaction between adults is used at the beginning stages of students' development to teach social communication skills by providing basic response models for students to imitate. It also can neutralize an explosive situation, stimulate interest in an activity, teach an activity, reinforce a student's acceptable behavior, and provide a dynamic model of positive relationships between adults. This latter use is particularly effective when both a man and a woman are on the team, because many students have limited experiences observing positive, respectful relationships between men and women in general.

To be effective with this strategy, the adults on a team must be able to work together well and meet daily to discuss the way they plan to approach the management of each student the next day. They also must be able to communicate necessary refinements in the ongoing management strategies as they occur during a day. Most important, they must communicate the message that the members of the team are in complete agreement and are working together for the well-being of each student. The verbal exchange between adults should clearly convey the teamwork.

Here are examples of how verbal interaction between adults is used with students in Stages One, Two, and Three.

Example of Adults' Interactions for Stage One. Students in this stage of development have limited skills in attending and responding. They appear to be unaware or disinterested in the words of adults and the associated meanings. However, students at this stage often are absorbing more than adults realize. For this reason, almost all verbalizations by adults with Stage One students should be carefully selected to model basic verbal skills. Adults working with students in Stage One have the double challenge of teaching that the world is a verbal place while keeping the words so basic that the students begin to grasp meaning from the associations they form as they hear the words repeated frequently. This is often done by interactions between adults who reflect to each other the key words needed by the student—words that are simple in structure and that reference tangible objects, actions, and people. In this way, adults teach the associations of words to objects and actions. When the key vocabulary has been selected, it is used in precisely the same way by all adults on the team and always in reference to the same situations. As the adults talk among themselves, they use the key words with emphasis. The students hear these words from each adult, repeatedly, and in many different situations. Here is an example:

FIRST ADULT: "This is a *ball*."

SECOND ADULT: "I see the *ball*."

FIRST ADULT: (to student) "Leon, this is a *ball*."

SECOND ADULT: (to student) "What do you see, Leon?"

When Leon looks at the ball, the first adult responds, "Leon sees the *ball*," as the second adult puts the ball in Leon's hand. Although this exchange could easily be done by one adult, the benefit of two adults is that they are also modeling a verbal exchange for interacting with others.

Example of Adults' Interactions for Stage Two. Teaching students to participate in an activity verbally by modeling the expected verbal responses is a major strategy used with students in Stage Two. Students who are developmentally in Stage Two usually are unable to participate in a new activity until there is something to imitate or some connection is made to a previous success. The purpose of verbal interactions between the adults is to provide models of the responses expected of the students. Here is an example.

A group of Stage Two students becomes disorganized in the transition from one activity to another. The teacher has material for the next activity in a box, but she cannot get the students' attention to begin, so she and the aide sit down at the table together. She rattles the contents of the box, and she and the aide converse:

AIDE: "What's in that box?"

TEACHER: "It is something we used last week."

AIDE: "A week ago! Let me think . . . is it soft?"

TEACHER: "Listen." (She shakes the box.) "It sounds hard."

AIDE: "It must be something hard. Maybe you can give us a hint."

TEACHER: "Well, it has three colors."

AIDE: "Three colors!" (to student) "Help me guess, Susan. What did we use a week ago that's hard and has three colors?"

One by one the students are drawn into the guessing game that started out as a conversation between the teacher and aide. As the students respond, they quite naturally enter into full participation. (Parents can use this same approach at home when they want to involve their child in a family activity.) In contrast, had the teacher and aide tried to organize and control the students with commands such as "Get quiet," "Sit down," or "We're going to sit here until everyone quiets down," participation would have been delayed and some of the students would have been unable to organize themselves adequately to participate with success. By slipping into the role of a student to provide a verbal response to the teacher, the aide is able to model the responses expected from the students. As the students begin to imitate the aide's responses, it is important for the aide to pull back from a responding role and redirect her attention to the teacher, again modeling, but this time modeling *attending* behavior for the students. When the group begins to lose interest, the aide remotivates with this same strategy, using her facial expressions and body language to convey interest in the activity and in what the teacher is telling the students.

Example of Adults' Interactions for Stage Three. Verbal interaction between adults continues to be a major strategy for behavior management with students in Stage Three. But in this stage the interactions between adults offer models for students to learn positive interpersonal responses. The adults provide models of respect for each other, teamwork, communication, and cooperation.

Relationships between adults are watched carefully by most students in Stage Three. A considerable number of them have had disturbing experiences with adults. No small part of these experiences might have been with family members, where the student was involved as the third party. Students who have learned dysfunctional behaviors from dysfunctional families bring these strategies into class and attempt to use them with the adults on the team. When this is evident, we use verbal interaction between adults to emphasize cooperative relationships and close communication between adults on the team—and always in support of the students.

Verbal interactions between adults have also proved useful in cuing the other adults about behavioral situations that are beginning to spiral out of control during an activity. For example, as a teacher introduces a current events lesson, one student is making obscene gestures at another. The aide says, "Ms. Jones, maybe we need to talk about trying to get other students into trouble before we talk about current events." The teacher picks up on this cue and takes the aide's suggestion that the group needs to talk. In doing this, the adults are helping the students with the objectives *"to show awareness of expected conduct"* and *"to tell other, more acceptable ways to behave."*

Example of Adults' Interactions for Stages Four and Five. The major change in using verbal interaction between adults with students in Stage Four is in combining the verbal interaction of adults with *interpretation*. Here, one adult reflects a statement about a student's behavior and interprets the associated feelings to the other adult. In this way, insights about feelings and behavior can be aired without stirring vehement denials or reactions from the students. This strategy is no longer needed when students begin to acquire skills that help them to understand the connections between feelings and behavior, in themselves and others.

By Stage Five, students are generally able to talk directly with adults about themselves and others, and a second adult is no longer needed. One exception to this is the continuing need for teens to have good role models for interpersonal relationships, especially those between men and women. These opportunities should involve many adults in the students' lives, providing interpersonal models for effective verbal interaction in school, after school, in extracurricular activities, and in vocational preparation.

Rules

Rules are the expectations and procedures established to guide and regulate behavior. Piaget included practice of rules, consciousness of rules, type of morality, and views of punishment as the elements in the development of children's moral judgments. We use his stage sequence for the development of rule consciousness, involving (a) knowing and remembering rules, (b) adhering to rules, (c) understanding reasons for rules, and (d) associating consequences with rule violations (Piaget, 1932/1960, pp. 19–57). Mastery of this sequence is a gradual, developmental process extending over three stages in a child's development. An infant is without any conception of rules. Organized, solitary play becomes the forerunner of rules. Imitation and absolute adherence to unchanging rules are characteristic of the next stage of development. Increasingly, children learn to cooperate with other children and by age 12 they have learned that they can change rules by consent of the group. The fact that children at this age make and modify rules by mutual agreement implies a sense of interpersonal reciprocity and social competence. It also is the foundation for autonomous morality at higher stages of development. Piaget believed that adults' styles of punishment for rule infringement also contribute significantly to moral development or lack of it. The implication from his work is that authoritarian discipline, demanding absolute conformity and obedience from younger children, must give way to styles of discipline that encourage cooperation and reciprocity in older children as they develop these capacities in interactions with peers.

Rules

Building Rules

These rules apply to everyone on the premises.
Source of authority: the building principal at school; the senior adult at home.

Group Rules

These rules state the expectations for conduct that apply to everyone in a group. The group may be a family group, a classroom group, or a sports group.
Source of authority: the lead teacher in a classroom; a parent in a family; the coach in a sports group. (Students in Stages Four and Five assume increasing responsibility for group rules and regulation of conduct.)

Interpersonal Rules

These rules are informal codes of conduct used between individuals within a group or in a relationship.
Source of authority: the adult leader of a group in Stages One through Three; by mutual agreement between adults and children in Stages Four and Five.

Students must master cognitive processes for sequencing events and have a rudimentary understanding of cause and effect before they can take personal responsibility for adhering to stated rules. While formal and informal expectations for behavior apply to all individuals, students in Stage Three have developed sufficient cognitive and social-emotional maturity to focus on learning formalized rules as a step in learning to regulate their own behavior. For this reason, rules are a major management strategy with students in Stage Three and are used frequently with students in Stages Two and Four.[5]

We think of rules in three categories: *building rules*, which apply to everyone on the premises; *group rules*, which apply to everyone in a specific group; and *interpersonal rules*, which are applied informally among individuals within a group.

Building Rules. At school, building rules are those that apply in all places. The source of authority for building rules is the principal, and they are upheld by all adults responsible for students—the principal, secretaries, bus drivers, cafeteria workers, teachers, and all other adults working in the building. Rules should be very few, concise, simply stated, and enforced consistently among all individuals. Rules in this category could include the following:

- No one fights in this school.
- Be considerate of others.
- Furniture and books are for using, not breaking.
- Help keep the restrooms clean.
- Make the cafeteria a nice place for everyone.
- Keep our school drug-free.
- No weapons are allowed.
- On the bus, everyone sits—and stays seated.
- The edge of the playground is the limit for everyone.

When severe behavioral problems result in violations of building rules, it is important to involve the principal or appropriate school administrator in resolving the situation in ways that uphold the building rules and that are administered to all students fairly. The important message is that certain rules apply to everyone for the protection of everyone in the building, and that these rules are administered fairly by the responsible authority.

At home, the same idea applies, with building rules being the expectations for conduct that apply to everyone living in the home. The source of authority is usually the parent or other senior family member who defines the rules of conduct and is responsible for the care, protection, health, safety, and guidance of the other family members. This person also is responsible for ensuring that the rules are upheld by everyone. The following are examples of building rules that apply in children's homes:

- Be kind and show respect.
- Help with chores.
- Respect personal privacy.
- Keep the door locked.

Group Rules. These rules are formal, procedural guidelines conveying clearly the behavior expected of students as members of a group—school group, family group, sports group, neighborhood group, or church group. Group rules should be stated simply, in positive rather than negative terms, and should be as few as possible. They should be viewed as a way of creating security and trust within the group. They should also be aids to successful participation. When they are fair, clearly conveyed, and meaningful to students, these rules will be assimilated into the students' inner control systems.

Group rules are custom-designed for each group and stage of students' social-emotional development. They should also reflect an individual's program objectives. For students in Stage One, rules are concerned primarily with the expectation that students proceed through the schedule of activities, for example, "We sit on the rug for Story Time." For students in Stage Two, group rules center on procedures that help students participate with individual success in the activities, for example, "When we pass the cookies, we take only one at a time." When you are establishing group rules for students in Stage Three, consider the students as group members and begin the process of teaching the reasons for the rules and the consequences of rule violation. A typical group in Stage Three needs only three fundamental group rules:

- Be considerate of others.
- Participate.
- Follow directions.

Almost all problem behaviors can be addressed within these three broad rules, and they provide adults with room to negotiate for constructive results when violations occur, for example:

"We take turns with the computer." (*Be considerate of others.*)

"Everyone will have a chance." (*Participate.*)

"This is how it's done here." (*Follow directions.*)

By Stage Four, group rules are a product of the group process, such as "If someone makes you mad, tell him

[5]Chapter 2 contains a discussion of how responsibility for behavior gradually shifts from adults to children. Chapters 8–12 provide examples of rules designed to foster the goals in each stage.

instead of hitting him" ("There is a better way to handle your feelings and his behavior"). By Stage Five, group rules are typically the same as the building rules, because the students are working to function successfully in many varied areas of school life.

Also, because they do not have problems with impulse control, Stage Five students are not usually in need of formalized group rules, unless they might be guides such as the following:

- Be on time.
- Cooperate to make the deadline.
- Make a difference.

Life Space Intervention

Life Space Intervention (LSI) is a verbal method of supporting students in crisis while using the crisis to assist them in gaining insight into their own behavior.[6] LSI is used as a major strategy in Developmental Therapy–Developmental Teaching with students in Stages Three and Four and frequently with students in Stage Five. It is not used at all with students in Stage One and is used only occasionally with students in Stage Two, because LSI requires some amount of expressive language and conceptual ability. These skills are generally not developed sufficiently until a student is moving into Stage Three.

LSI is used to solve many different types of crises that restrict students' opportunities to mature and develop social-emotional competence. Various forms of LSI address these problem areas and have specific goals:

- to provide emotional first aid by decreasing the effects of frustration, supporting students in crisis, keeping communication channels open, regulating behavior, or conveying the dependability of adults' fairness
- to organize reality for students who do not see an event as others do, are unaware that their own behavior causes reactions in others, or are unable to interpret events in an accurate way
- to confront the unacceptable behavior of students who rely on counterproductive aggression, and who refuse to respond to alternatives except when anxiety is created about their behavior through verbal confrontation concerning the consequences that follow
- to build values that strengthen self-control by emphasizing positive attributes and that relieve the guilt of students burdened by their own failures or inadequacies
- to teach interpersonal social skills to students who lack a repertoire of acceptable behaviors
- to create awareness of exploitation in students who are singled out as scapegoats, or who are abused, isolated, or exploited by others

[6]LSI was developed by Fritz Redl and extended by David Wineman, William Morse, Nicholas Long, Ruth Newman, Stanley Fagan, and Mary M. Wood. The complete procedure is contained in Wood and Long (1991).

Steps in Conducting Life Space Intervention

Step 1. **Focus on the incident.**
Purpose: To convey support and understanding of the student's stress and to start the student talking about the incident.

Step 2. **Students in crisis need to talk.**
Purpose: To talk in sufficient detail to clarify and expand understanding about the reality of the incident and to decrease the student's emotional intensity while increasing reliance on rational words and ideas.

Step 3. **Find the central issue and select a therapeutic goal.**
Purpose: To explore the student's perception of the incident and associated feelings and anxieties until you have sufficient understanding to concisely state the central issue and decide what the therapeutic outcome should be.

Step 4. **Choose a solution based on values.**
Purpose: To aid the student in selecting a solution that the student values as beneficial and claims with a sense of genuine ownership.

Step 5. **Plan for success.**
Purpose: To rehearse what will happen and anticipate reactions and feelings (of self and others) when the chosen solution is actually put into action.

Step 6. **Prepare to resume the activity.**
Purpose: To plan with the student the transition back into the group's ongoing activity, and to close down private topics or feelings that might have surfaced during the talk.

Source: From *Life Space Intervention: Talking with Children and Youth in Crisis* (pp. 9–10), by M. M. Wood and N. J. Long, 1991, Austin, TX: PRO-ED. Reprinted with permission of the publisher.

In dealing with all of these problems, adults find LSI helpful and effective in (a) conveying understanding, (b) building relationships with students, (c) presenting a model of a fair adult authority figure, (d) resolving crises, and (e) fostering responsible behavior in students. LSI is organized into six basic steps that can be modified, lengthened, or shortened as each crisis situation requires. We summarize the steps in brief here. These steps have been helpful to parents, teachers, clinicians, coaches, and counselors who follow them as guidelines for crisis resolution. However, to become skilled in LSI with students who have severe behavioral and emotional problems, we suggest more extensive study and supervised training.

Step 1. Focus on the Incident. When you begin an LSI, think about the student. What elements are you dealing with in the situation? How upset is the student? Angry and acting out? Needing restraint? Needing emotional support? Needing firmness? Be calm and put the pieces together in your own mind. Most important, take your cues from the nonverbal messages you are getting from the student.

Remember, your role at this time is to be a mediator between the student and a particular issue. Remember also that LSI is not a one-time exchange between you and a student in crisis, but a series of interactions between you and the student around issues that arise while working with developmental objectives. The purpose is to help the student gain insight into the situation, the feelings that promoted the behavior, and the consequences. Ultimately, the two of you are working for changes in behavior that will promote more satisfying responses from others. To do this you have to be trusted by the student, have a developing relationship, and convey acceptance. This first step is over when the student gives you some basic response, verbally or nonverbally, and the crisis event is understood by the student ("Why are we here?" or "We are here because . . .").

Step 2. Talking About the Incident. Teachers sometimes expect a student to bring anxiety under control and talk right away. Don't push too much. Use reflection. If a student is crying or cursing, you might say sympathetically, "Things are pretty bad." Don't expect an answer. It is essential to convey dispassionate compassion. When the student's breathing and muscle tone are restored to normal, try to obtain the student's perception of the situation. Do not begin by telling what you saw. Students need this opportunity to tell it the way they see it. Sometimes you will have to start it off by reflecting what you saw or interpreting a possible feeling behind a behavior ("Something happened during juice and cookie time. Bob was trying to make you feel bad in class").

You might get the following responses from a student during this part of the LSI:

- refusing to talk
- digressing to other subjects to avoid the issue
- distorting reality
- attacking physically or verbally
- blaming others, including you, for the crisis
- regressing

During this step, your primary role is to listen, reflect, question, and enhance the student's feeling that you care and can help. Your objective is to get the student involved in talking.

Sometimes the situation will have to be reconstructed from the beginning to pin it down. At this point in the LSI, do not be concerned with uncovering "the truth"; instead, focus upon how the student sees it. Use questions. Show interest and sensitivity to feelings, but do not judge. If the student changes the subject, you might want to reflect this behavior and possibly interpret the feeling behind it. In any event, keep the exchange focusing back on the situation and keep in mind which objectives the student is working on. This will guide the direction of the LSI. Sometimes it may be necessary to arrive at a temporary resolution and stop.

Try to find out what is important to the student. You will need to listen intently; try to pick up cues from nonverbal communication and remember what seems to be important from the student's point of view. You may need to use such information later in the LSI. Many times a student will lose control during this phase because he feels bad and cannot put it in words. The student may need to lean on you for emotional strength until he can recover enough to handle it himself. Your support may be through words, physical contact, or physical proximity. If the student starts to draw back, let him. As the LSI progresses, you will find your role changing, from providing understanding to having an attitude of "we'll work on it together."

Step 3. Find the Central Issue and Select a Therapeutic Goal. The next step is to use what the student has provided and put it together in a reality context around the central issue. This may be related to a specific, obvious incident for students in Stage Three or may be a quite complex, emotional issue for students in Stage Four or Stage Five. Again, reflection and interpretation are techniques to help you. Having the student admit guilt is not the object. You want to identify what is really significant in the incident for the student's private reality as well as the observed incident. During this step, continue the process of awareness of behaviors, the feelings behind them, and the consequences. It is important that you avoid judgments or opinions.

This step ends when you have obtained sufficient understanding to (a) state the issue concisely; (b) assess the student's perceptions, insights, and motivation to change; and (c) decide on a goal or outcome.

Step 4. Choose a Solution Based on Values. If the student seems ready, move the discussion to a solution to the situation. There are many alternative responses, some more productive than others. Let the conversation consider a number of these responses, good and bad, weighing the possible outcomes. Work with the student among fairly specific choices to select an alternative that will assist in dealing more successfully with the central issue. It will be important for you to keep in mind the objectives for the student as you guide the LSI to its conclusion. Allowing students to select alternatives beyond their current abilities will certainly mark them for failure, whereas modifying an alternative to a more realistic level will help them in the process of constructive change. For example, Stage Three students may be working on a behavioral objective, *"to tell other more acceptable ways to behave."* A Stage Four student may be working on the same objective but at a higher level, *"to implement alternative behaviors."* For the Stage Three student, you may have to pose the choice; a Stage Four student can choose independently.

When students seem unable to participate in a plan to change their strategies, you will need to state the rules, provide the values to guide the selection of new strategy, and describe the probable outcome. You will have to offer the chance to choose from several specific alternatives. In such situations, set up a fairly specific circumstance and end the LSI with the idea that you and the student will continue to work together. This step ends when the student is able to tell what has been decided.

Step 5. Plan for Success. Once a solution (or resolution) has been selected, you and the student should talk about what to do and how the plan will be put into operation. The purpose in this step is to expand the student's understanding about what the selected alternative will require. Consider the question, "Will this alternative work successfully for the student?" Discuss possible negative and positive outcomes of the newly proposed solution. We use the question, "What if . . . ?" and keep in mind that the student must value the potential outcome to be willing to try a new behavior and risk failure again. All students need encouragement and practice as they begin to try out a new approach to a situation.

Step 6. Prepare to Resume the Activity. This last step provides a "cool-down," helping a student prepare for reentry and participation in the ongoing activity. You and the student should talk about what is going to happen upon return to the program. If the student does not need to talk with others (who might have been involved in the incident), you might respond with "Okay, some things are private." If the student needs to talk with others, you should see that a group LSI or a meeting with the involved adults occurs. In some situations, you may offer to talk to the others and give the student the choice of participating or not. In all circumstances, if there are consequences to the original incident, you must see that the student follows up with the agreed-upon solution or resolution.

It is important to close down private topics and feelings, so that a student does not return to the program with feelings and thoughts still raging. To do this step well, we find it important to end all discussion of the issue and refocus conversation on what will be happening as the student returns. The student should return with a sense of being empowered to demonstrate acceptable conduct and with enhanced self-esteem about being a person who can change things and make them better.

General Guidelines. Here are some final cautions about using LSI:

- Keep in mind that the student is emotionally hurting and cannot remedy the situation without your assistance.
- Too much adult talk causes a student to withdraw from freely participating in the LSI.
- Too little adult participation will result in an LSI that dissolves from lack of direction.
- Do not be judgmental.
- Choose your responses and directions from the student's nonverbal and verbal behavior.
- Be flexible.
- If you try to wind up with an appropriate resolution too soon, it will probably be wasted effort.
- Provide abundant "A's" to the student. (In LSI, an "A" is an affirmation of the student.)
- Always end on a positive note and prepare the student for reentry into the classroom activity.
- Avoid reflecting negative feelings unless you are working for symptom estrangement.
- Avoid questions that may lead a student to entrapment.
- Do not ask a student to elaborate on feelings unless the Stage Four communication objective, "to verbalize feelings spontaneously and appropriately," has been mastered.
- Stay calm and focused.
- Guard against allowing feelings of hostility or anger to develop in yourself.
- Credit a student's good intentions whenever possible.
- Maintain an ongoing positive relationship based on trust.
- Think of the LSI as two-way communication.
- Convey that change will produce satisfying results.

Control of Materials by Adults

Control of materials (supplies, equipment, and toys) by adults should systematically decrease as students mature. It begins with almost total control of materials by adults working with students in Stage One, where it is a major management strategy. Adults carefully control the distribution, use, and collection of supplies, work folders, snacks, and other materials. They introduce the guitar, walking board, puppets, and rhythm instruments. They hold the story pictures and provide each student with opportunities to participate in using the materials as independently as possible while ensuring a satisfying outcome.

Gradually, this management strategy shifts to student control of materials. Students in Stages Two and Three are given progressively more control and responsibility for getting materials, using them in acceptable ways with increasing independence, and putting them away when an activity is over. However, because their inner controls are not yet completely established, adults sometimes must reinstate control of materials to calm a group or prevent students from acting out. By Stage Four, students generally are sufficiently self-directed to choose materials and activities as a group, plan for their use and care, and be responsible for the outcomes. In Stage Five, students are expected to manage their own materials and those of the group without prompting or control by adults.

Even when there is a need for materials to be controlled by adults, at every stage of development there should be daily opportunities for students to explore materials freely. During these times, it is important to convey to students that this is their own time for using the materials. Adults should monitor themselves carefully during students' free time to avoid assisting, redirecting, commenting, or instructing to such an extent that a potentially creative, independent experience is turned into a structured lesson. We have seen adults continue to control materials long after students are ready to do it themselves. When this happens, students' development is restricted by the adults. This situation often occurs when adults work with students who have poor impulse control and need considerable structure and control of materials to be successful. As students make progress, they begin to develop inner control, and they should have opportunities to practice managing materials without as much adult control as previously needed. This is the point where adults must begin, gradually and systematically, to turn the materials over to the students.

Beginning with Stage Two students, the shift in control of materials is focused on the objective, *"to use play materials in acceptable ways."* With elementary, middle, and high school students, the transition from adult to student control of materials occurs during Stage Three and centers on program objectives such as *"to complete individual tasks"* and *"to share and take turns spontaneously without reminders."* By the end of Stage Three, students should be able to use materials successfully and independently. By Stages Four and Five, adult control of materials is no longer needed.

Physical Proximity

An adult's physical proximity is used to convey psychological support or strength. It can communicate positive messages to students, signaling encouragement, interest, and caring. It can be used to motivate, de-escalate tension, and convey authority. Adults' physical position in relation to each student in a group should be given careful attention when a behavior management plan is designed. An adult's physical nearness to students in every stage of development controls and encourages participation in an activity. It communicates care about what the students are doing.

Physical proximity can often prevent inappropriate behavior before it happens. By sitting next to an impulsive student, an adult can prevent the student's losing control and is in a position to react quickly before things get out of hand. But more important, by their physical presence, adults are telling students that one does not need to use unacceptable behavior to obtain adults' attention.

The type and amount of physical proximity needed change distinctly between Stage One and Stage Five. In most early childhood programs, and for young children at home, an adult's physical proximity is a major management strategy. Closeness and touch are used to nurture young children, to help them focus and attend to materials, to calm them down, and to communicate generally that adults like them. During Stage One, adults often keep a student in psychological contact with the activity by physical contact and touch. Patting, hugging, holding, and touching are all used by adults working with students in Stage One. In contrast, during Stage Two, body contact is used only when a student regresses or is in need of unusual amounts of nurture, whereas touch is used to a greater extent when students show a need for direct adult intervention. By Stage Three, physical contact changes to physical closeness—an arm around a student or a touch on the shoulder. Especially during Stage Three, physical nearness conveys "I am here to help, if you need me." By Stages Four and Five, physical proximity is not often needed to manage behavior, and body contact and touch are not used at all. Older students cannot tolerate being held; however, some older students still need physical proximity and respond well to this management strategy.

Occasionally there will be students, in any stage of development, who do not trust people or the world around them enough to tolerate any physical contact or touch. For these students, body contact (or even the physical proximity of another student) may trigger impulsivity and loss of control. Often, students who cannot tolerate any contact are severely emotionally deprived and associate physical nearness or contact with abuse or severe punishment. With some students, dislike of touch also may indicate that they cannot handle personal attention or the suggestion of a relationship. Adults must be careful to plan their contacts with these students in a verbal, low-key manner without personal focus. An adult might slow down while walking around the room during an arithmetic lesson and say, "Good work on that page, Dennis," then quickly go on to the next student. For such students, an adult's caring is often more effectively communicated through literature, stories, and food.

Although physical proximity usually conveys that an adult cares about what a student is doing, there are times when an adult's closeness stifles a student. If it becomes a violation of an individual's psychological space, the student will begin to lose control or engage in other forms of unacceptable behavior to get away. For example, Danielle is a student in Stage Three. Her teacher notices that she is randomly throwing her crayons across the room. He stops her, quickly but calmly, by putting his hand over hers, saying, "Crayons are for coloring, not for throwing." Danielle does not like this interference by the teacher and attempts to grab the crayon away from him. Realizing that a struggle for control of the crayon is about to occur, the teacher moves his hand away, stating with confidence, "You can put the crayons away." He then walks away, conveying confidence that she will do it. By walking away, the teacher does not challenge Danielle, but instead communicates the expectation that she will follow through. He gives her psychological space, needed by children in Stage Three, by not standing over her to be certain that she complies. Danielle picks up the crayons without further incident.

It is easy to use physical presence in a coercive way without being aware of it. Standing over a student communicates, "I am the authority around here, and I'm not going to let you get away with a thing." Unless adults need to convey this sort of power with individual students, it is better to avoid standing over them. Instead, kneel, stoop, or sit. Being at eye level with a student communicates the message, "We can handle this situation together, and I trust you not to take advantage of it." Also *avoid* using physical presence as a form of punishment ("If you two can't behave, I'm going to move your seats near mine" or "Now that I'm here, you won't be able to get into trouble").

LESS FREQUENTLY USED STRATEGIES NEEDED FOR SEVERE PROBLEM BEHAVIOR

Confrontation by Adult

Confrontation is taking a position in direct opposition to a student's behavior or words; it brings an adult and student face to face over an issue. The most commonly used form of confrontation is just saying *"No!"* When it is initiated by an adult, confrontation is a strategy that places the adult in a potentially adversarial position with a student, with the potential power to control and evoke consequences and punishments. When it is initiated by a student, confrontation is an attempt to control or test an adult's power, expertise, authority, or authenticity as a person to trust. For these reasons, confrontation is not a major behavior management strategy in Developmental Therapy—Developmental Teaching, although it is used occasionally at all stages of students' development. It is included in our list of management strategies because there is no strategy with a greater potential for producing emotional growth or psychological devastation.

Selecting confrontation as a strategy to sharply focus a student's attention on an issue, connecting behavior to natural (usually negative) consequences, can produce considerable progress toward insight and self-regulated behavior. Here are several examples:

"When you don't play by the rules, you have to leave the game."

"If you don't finish your work, you'll miss your swimming class."

"Maybe he did start the fight, but you're the one who ends up suspended."

"You want friends, but you do things they don't like."

On the other hand, if confrontation is used by an adult to respond to insignificant issues, to punish, or to get back at a student, an unnecessary conflict may be created between them. If this happens, both the student and the adult lose. The student may have no other response than to retreat or counter with more hostility, and the adult is cast in a coercive, nonsupportive role. Here are examples of confrontation that we try to avoid:

"Try that once more and you'll feel the consequences."

"You'll have to stay in time-out until you get your act together."

Confrontation is infrequently used with students in Stages One through Three. When necessary, it generally takes a physical form, in which an adult makes a student conform by physically controlling the child's actions (described in the following sections). Children in these stages generally have insufficient verbal skills or cognitive development to be able to benefit from verbal cause-and-effect connections between their behavior and natural consequences.

By Stage Three, students have functional language and are beginning to use inner controls for some self-regulation of behavior, but these controls are fragile. When adults use confrontation, these students often respond with increased physical defiance, aggression, hostility, or anger. If an adult can manage these expressions of spiraling stress and bring the confrontation to a therapeutic conclusion, this strategy can be effective with Stage Three students. Used selectively and skillfully, confrontation can help students in Stage Three to grow emotionally. The success depends upon students' seeing the adult as someone who has the ability to solve problems, manage a crisis, and help them, even if they do not trust adults.

By Stage Four, confrontation is used frequently, primarily in verbal form, to assist students in considering the potential consequences of their behavioral choices. By Stage Five, confrontation is only used occasionally, when it is needed to help a student focus on conflict resolution and problem solving. In these latter stages, students have developed enough impulse control, independence, and insight into their own needs so that confrontation, used by a respected adult, does not deteriorate into loss of control. These students also have a capacity for abstract thinking that enables them to respond to issues verbally and see relationships between feelings, behavior, and consequences. They can rationally choose between alternatives and have sufficient independence to see their own responsibility for making choices.[7]

Combining confrontation with reflection and interpretation is often highly effective with some students in Stages Four and Five. This combination of strategies can be used to connect a student's problem behavior to underlying feelings and real-world consequences when the student is working on objectives such as *"to implement acceptable alternative behaviors"* or *"to express cause-and-effect relationships spontaneously between feelings and behavior in oneself and others."* Here is an example:

> "You say you hate school [*reflection*]. Maybe that's because you don't like to fail and it makes you feel dumb [*interpretation*]. If you quit now, you'll feel the same way [*confrontation*]."

This form of confrontation often is hard for adults to use because it always produces emotional hurt to the student during the process. It stresses the adult-student relationship, and it highlights a problem. However, it may be the only way to move a student to further progress. Without it, a situation may continue to exist as a major obstacle to a student's insight and understanding.

Physical Intervention

The use of physical intervention, that is, physically moving a student through an activity or physically controlling a student, follows the same pattern as body contact—the need and use decrease the higher the stage of development. The physical movement of a young child by an adult can be used to ensure appropriate behavioral responses and outcomes. In Developmental Therapy–Developmental Teaching, great emphasis is put upon expecting appropriate responses, communicating these expectations clearly, and intervening to directly teach a response when it is not forthcoming. To permit students to participate with responses that are inappropriate to their developmental stage perpetuates or extends the period of developmental lag.

Physical intervention is a major technique for Stage One, is used frequently at Stage Two, is occasionally used at Stage Three, and is not used at Stages Four or Five.

In Stage One, the adult will bodily move a student through an activity, hold a student to keep him with the group, or physically move his arm and hand in response to materials. Such physical intervention should be accompanied by a specific word or simple statement reflecting the activity. By associating physical intervention with positive, supportive words, the student will begin building associations between words and behavior. For example, "We put away the toys. Play Time is over," is a reflective statement used by a parent of a child in Stage One as the child is physically assisted in making the proper movements to complete the activity.[8]

With students in Stage Two, the adult uses physical intervention less frequently. When a student is in a Stage Three group, direct physical intervention should be very limited. Instead, students should be able to respond to verbal intervention because they have basic language skills and are working on objectives that emphasize using words to mediate behavior and impulses. At Stages Four and Five, the strategy is not needed because students have developed sufficient skill to participate and control behavior through words.

When an adult physically moves a student to teach a new skill, stops a student from throwing materials, or holds a student through a rage, the student always must feel that the adult cares. The adult should hold the student firmly but gently and supportively. In the midst of chaotic classroom activity, it is easy to slip into a pattern of moving quickly to intervene, and too often adults may find themselves grabbing an arm or shirt. This is where physical control becomes destructive. A student's reflexive response will be to jerk away. This move adds an additional dilemma—whether to pursue or ignore the student. No therapeutic gain can be made from such an incident.

What should be done with students who seem to be physically out of control (kicking, screaming, hitting, spitting, throwing themselves on the floor, or running away)? Should they be restrained physically or should verbal strategies be used to talk them out of the crisis? Often students may seem to be out of control because they are frustrated, need attention, or are so anxious that they must test limits. If the crisis seems to be a manifestation of such an urgent, unmet need, the student may respond constructively to verbal techniques or some form of supportive physical nearness. This strategy is preferred over physical

---

[7]Confrontation used with students in Stages Four and Five is provided through the LSI strategies described previously.

[8]In early childhood special education programs, this strategy is often referred to as "motoring through a task."

contact because it allows the student to recover control without being completely dominated by the adult, which is often the result when physical restraint is used. However, if the crisis seems to have developed to the point where students seem unable to respond to changes in the situation and do not pull themselves together, physical restraint may be necessary. Some very disturbed students actually lose the ability to control themselves.[9]

If physical restraint seems to be the only way to protect violent students from themselves or each other, we use a holding procedure, standing behind a student, crossing the student's arms in front, and holding securely but supportively. This procedure should also communicate to the student that there is nothing to be afraid of because the adult can help control. The other essential element is to convey psychological security with a reassuring statement such as "It's all right. I can help you calm down." Such messages communicate to students the expectation that they can do better and the adult will help.

Be aware that many students react with increased violence to physical holding or restraint. Panic reactions often result. If this occurs, moving a student to a corner of a room or some other physically enclosed place is a more effective strategy for containment than physical restraint. By taking a position at the entrance in a supportive, nonthreatening way, the adult can contain a student and provide emotional support. Older students particularly should have access to a quiet room away from the group so that they can be contained without being held, and a verbal form of conflict resolution can be introduced as the student regains composure.[10]

Removal from the Room

Removal from the room is a temporary aid in remobilizing appropriate behavior in a crisis situation. There are times when students are so difficult to manage that they must be removed from the group. The criteria for removal are fairly clear: (a) if a student may do harm to himself or others, (b) if a topic is so private that a student cannot discuss it in front of the group but needs to discuss it alone with the adult, or (c) if the student's continued presence will cause the group to disintegrate. When students are removed, they should not be left alone in isolation because the purpose in using this strategy is to remobilize appropriate behavior following a crisis event. A student left alone after a crisis seldom can use the time alone to a constructive end. The best that can be hoped for from a student in isolation is "cooling off" and compliant reentry. More often, the result is regression, psychological withdrawal from reality, fantasizing, increased bitterness or hostility toward uncaring adults, and increased resentment toward adult authority.

In these situations, isolation increases feelings of alienation, decreases positive student-teacher relationships, and produces little, if any, long-range change. The student who returns compliantly from isolation often masks bitter, angry feelings, and such feelings inevitably surface again.

For these reasons, we suggest that an adult accompany a student from the room. A quiet place away from the group is necessary for such occasions. When you remove students from the room, do it with as little talk as possible. Be swift and firm. Plan to stay with them in order to use the crisis to help them to grow emotionally. Know which developmental objectives students are working on in order to avoid expectations beyond the developmental level. Have a prior arrangement with other adults on the team about who will be responsible for continuing the group activities and who will work through the crisis with the student.

If a student is going through a particularly turbulent period of adjustment, it is important that the same adult accompany the student to the quiet room each time. Each incident and its resolution can be used as a step in the sequence of building trust and relationship, reducing or resolving anxiety, and eventually mastering appropriate coping behaviors.

Removal from the room is not particularly useful for students in Stage One, those beginning Stage Two, or those who are well into Stage Four. Few Stage One students are invested enough in what is going on in a room for removal to be effective. In contrast, by the time students are in Stage Four, they feel that they are part of the group and that they have developed enough skills to monitor their own behavior and to talk within the group about what is bothering them.

Removal from the room is particularly effective for students in Stage Three, because they have enough skills to be successful, they have some ability to be verbal, they have capacity for some insight about themselves, and they are motivated to return to the activities of the group. Removal from the room at the time of crisis provides a good opportunity for the adult to focus the student on behavioral and communication objectives.

Often the most difficult part of removing students from the room is getting them back. A student cannot be expected to move rapidly from loss of control to model behavior. An adult must always structure the situation so that it will end positively, allowing the student to save face. The individual LSI is usually an appropriate technique for use at this point. For students with less developed communication skills, such as those in Stage Two, we use a modified LSI (Wood & Long, 1991, Chapter 12).

---

[9] The management of severely deviant and violent behavior is discussed in the last section of Chapter 5.

[10] See the discussion of LSI earlier in this chapter for the steps for doing this.

Removal from the Group (Time-Out in the Room)

Removal from the group while remaining in the room is a form of time-out in which a student can still see or hear the others and the activity as a reminder of what is being missed. Brief exclusion from participating in an activity, moving to a time-out chair or special place, is a popular management strategy used by many early childhood programs and by parents when they are trying to teach young children to control themselves. If a child's problem behavior is not severe, time alone often helps the child calm down and think about a better way to behave. However, if a child has severe behavioral problems or is otherwise limited in ability to think through the necessary behavior, it is essential that the child not be left alone. An adult is needed in order to help the child calm down and to restructure the expected behavior. Some children simply do not know how to behave in an acceptable way. For these children, time alone is generally not productive. In any case, a time-out should be brief and should result in a child's returning to the activity to participate with the expected behavior.

Brief exclusion from participating in an activity is usually effective with young children because it reestablishes the child's interest in returning to the activity. For example, a child who is being silly can be taken to an area with a teacher or parent for a very short period of time and told, "When you calm down, we can go back. You were doing well with your part of the racetrack we were building."

Removal from the group is a strategy used frequently with students in Stage Two when they enjoy participating and are developing behavioral control. It can be used to eliminate hitting, upsetting other students, "messing around," or having temper tantrums. Students beginning Stage Two often misbehave when they feel insecure or uncertain about what is expected of them. By remaining in the room, they can be reassured and remotivated to return to the activity. However, this strategy is effective only when a student has developed some amount of interest in the activity and motivation to participate. It also can provide a beginning for teaching older Stage Two students about actions and consequences. The adult says, "You're here because you hit Tommy. We don't hit because it hurts. When you calm down, you can go back to the group."

Just as in removal from the room, it is important in removal from the group for an adult to stay with a student who has severe behavioral problems. The purpose of removal is to assist the student to return to participation in the activity. The more rapidly this can be done, the more productive the time will be for the student. We keep in mind that Stage Two goals and objectives emphasize participation.

Removal from the group while remaining in the room seldom works with Stage Three students because they are aware of the group and will try to incite others to join in the unacceptable behavior. Group contagion often results. With students in Stage Four, failure to participate or engaging in disruptive behavior either is a group problem requiring LSI or is a personal problem usually better handled outside of the room. Occasionally, a variation of this strategy that is quite effective with adolescent students in a Stage Four group is the provision of a quiet corner in the room or a small adjoining room where they can choose to go on their own when they feel that a situation or feeling may get out of control. This process is sometimes called "getting space." The adult and the group members decide how the area will be used. It must be a place with furniture where a student can sit comfortably or work. The student usually initiates use of the procedure. It should never be used as a disciplinary action or be bound by set time periods. When this seems to be an appropriate strategy to use with a group of Stage Four students, it is important for the adult to unobtrusively monitor the way the area is used and the time involved. If it appears that the time a student spends removed from class activity is counterproductive, the adult should join the student in the area and use an LSI approach.

SUMMARY

When children and youth misbehave, adults who are responsible for them must respond. And when children and youth have chronic behavioral problems, the challenge for fostering responsible behavior is even greater. The task of managing their behavior is formidable. Strategies used by adults can promote students' growth or stifle it.

Most adults come equipped with the basic forms of behavior management—they can choose to ignore, punish, or reward behavior. However, the choices are much broader and more complex. Adults who are effective in managing behavior use a great number of strategies, choosing those that suit the needs of students as individuals attempting to adjust to the expectations of groups in which they are members—family groups, school groups, play groups, work groups, sports groups, and leisure groups. Effective behavior management teaches students to use behaviors that bring satisfactory results for them in every situation. The results should have long-term benefits.

In Developmental Therapy–Developmental Teaching, behavior management is an essential part of fostering social-emotional growth and responsible behavior. It is accomplished with strategies that emphasize positive actions, participation, consistency, and concern for students. It must provide experiences for students that help to alter old feelings, increase insights, and build positive attitudes in addition to changing behavior. It must enable a student to acquire needed developmental objectives, and it must respond to short-term needs while shaping long-term changes. In brief, behavior management in Developmental Therapy–Developmental Teaching is a decision-making process for selecting the management strategy for an individual student that is most effective and appropriate for the student's age, program objectives, and individual developmental needs.

This chapter is a review of the 11 positive management strategies that are most frequently used to accomplish the goals and objectives of Developmental Therapy–Developmental Teaching. *Positive feedback and praise* are at the top of the list, followed by *motivate with materials, structure, redirection, reflection, interpretation, verbal interaction between adults as models, rules, LSI, control of materials by adults,* and *physical proximity.* In the description of each strategy, we have illustrated how it is used at each stage in a student's development and how the strategy changes in frequency of use and form across the stages. Also included are 4 additional strategies that are occasionally used when a student's problem behaviors are so severe that more intensive forms of intervention are necessary. These are *confrontation, physical intervention, removal from the room,* and *removal from the group.*

PRACTICE

Using the key points in this chapter

The two vignettes at the beginning of this chapter are about students of different ages with quite different problem behaviors. They illustrate the broad range of behavioral problems that challenge the adults who care for them—their parents and teachers. Rita, a 4-year-old child with a severe developmental delay, is participating in an early childhood special education program. David is enrolled in a regular second grade but is causing such concern to his mother and teacher that he has been referred for special help. Plan individual behavior management programs for Rita and David. Use Figure 3.2 to identify the Preliminary Profile goals for social-emotional competence and the stages of social-emotional development for each child. Follow the six steps in planning, outlined in Chapter 5, and use Figures 6.1 and 6.2 to select the specific management strategies you would use with each student. Keep in mind that the strategies you select should focus the program on fostering their program goals in each of the four curriculum areas: *doing, saying, caring,* and *thinking.*

NOTES

NOTES

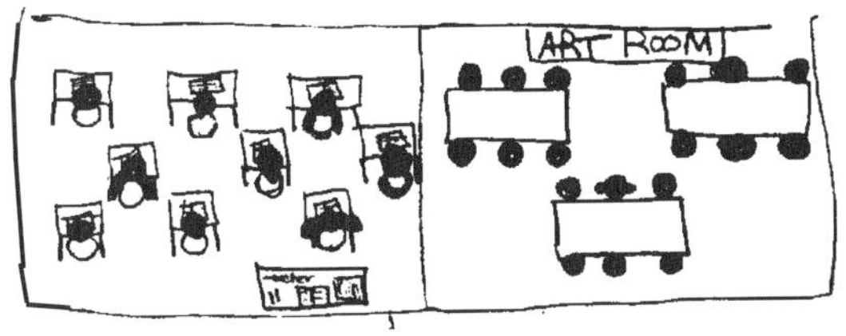

CHAPTER 7

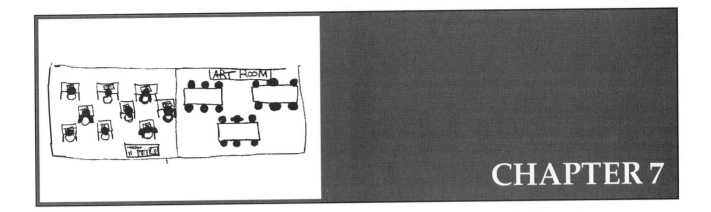

Adults as Agents for Change

Children learn what they know by following the example of adults, parents, and other kinfolk, their primary role models. They also learn by observing such secondary role models as teachers, preachers, athletes, coaches, entertainers, and even politicians.

—*UNIDENTIFIED MENTOR*

ADULTS ARE THE PIVOTAL PSYCHOLOGICAL POWER IN CHILDREN'S LIVES

The single most important component in the successful development of infants, children, and youth is the skill of the adults whom they value and trust. These adults—parents and teachers—provide the dynamic material that forms each child's world. At every stage of a child's social-emotional development, valued adults are the pivotal psychological power, shaping the child's personality and behavior by their own behavior and responses to the child. This task of fitting an adult's personal style with children's needs, in ways that foster their social and emotional development, is enormously challenging. It requires considerable insight into oneself. Most important, it requires a depth of emotional maturity, self-confidence, empathy for others, dedication, self-discipline, compassion, and understanding. It is not an easy task!

To be successful in fostering the social and emotional development of others, adults must be able to understand the realities, cultural values, expectations, motivations, drives, feelings, anger, conflict, stress, successes, and failures of others. They must be able to recognize when these powerful pressures cause reactions in themselves and in the way they respond to others. They must also learn to be the type of adult needed by children, changing strategies as a child matures. They must have a clear sense of what the goals are for every child and the steps needed to reach these goals. They must be able to recognize even the smallest accomplishment a child makes toward achieving an objective, and to know when to change strategies to expedite the child's progress toward mastery of a developmental milestone. They must learn to recognize deeper meanings in surface behavior and to use strategies that help reduce anxiety and other emotional defenses that may be standing in the way of a child's progress.

In short, the most important tool you will have for fostering social-emotional development in your children is you—what you know and how you put it into action. Consider Keith. In this illustration, Keith, a troubled boy, tries to dump his own anger onto his teacher. Her understanding of his developmental status, emotional needs, and behavior in coping with feelings guides her therapeutic responses to him. What would be your first reaction to Keith if you were his teacher? Follow the teacher's self-monitoring to see how she guards against taking Keith's

Keith

Nine-year-old Keith is receiving a Stage Two Developmental Therapy–Developmental Teaching program. He is aggressive and frequently shouts, curses, and bites. He feels bad about school and has a poor self-concept, poor socialization skills, and difficulty in reading. He is large for his age and has a poor body image. Often he has sudden mood swings, and after being physically aggressive, he becomes remorseful. Academic work is difficult for him because of his poor academic skills.

During work time, his teacher watches Keith's actions closely. She knows that reading is particularly difficult, but some success has been achieved, with encouragement from her. Keith has completed his math work and now works slowly on an initial consonant recognition sheet. The teacher reflects, "Good! The *C* matches *car*."

Several children in the class finish and go on to the next scheduled activity, Play Time. But Keith is still sitting at the table working with his assignment. As the teacher leaves the work table to join the group in the play area, she says, "Keith, your work is almost finished. I'll be waiting for you."

Noticing that he continues to sit and stare at his paper, his teacher continues, "As soon as you match the *D* and the *R* lists you will be finished."

Keith shouts, "Shut up! You have bad breath. I ain't finishing."

The teacher responds by interpreting his concern: "You wonder what will happen if you don't finish." She knows that it is difficult for him to be the last student finished. She also knows that he has the capability to finish, because he has succeeded with previous reading activities. She suspects that he may be testing limits as his frustration increases, so she makes no physical move toward him. But she conveys nonverbally that he is expected to finish his paper.

Keith's body seems to tighten. The teacher senses more frustration. He rips his paper and wads it into a ball, screaming, "Take your paper! I ain't doing it."

The teacher takes the wad of paper, reflects, and restates the expectation: "Keith, you want to see what happens if you rip up that paper. Put it back together, and then you can finish. You can do it." She is careful not to move physically toward Keith at this moment. Instead she pauses and then restructures the task for him: "There are two more items. Then you can go to Play Time."

"Ain't doing it! You're dumb. You stink! And you're ugly and your breath smells like old dirty socks!" Instead of responding to the personal attack, the teacher reminds herself that it is Keith who actually feels dumb and ugly.

As Keith stands up and moves to the other end of the table, the teacher quickly moves toward him. He is now yelling at the other children in the play area, "Hey, look at her. She's dumb! She stinks!"

The teacher puts her arm around his shoulder and moves him to a quiet area of the room. She keeps in mind that she must ignore personal comments made toward her. Keith's derogatory comments are made partially to test the teacher's responses and partially to express his own frustrations. If they are not carefully treated, the remarks can become self-derogatory and lead to more detrimental feelings about himself as inadequate and "bad." The teacher is aware that she must prevent this from happening. She keeps reminding herself that Keith feels stupid, fat, and unsavory and is projecting those feelings toward her for psychological insulation from his own feelings. She also observes that he is not yet out of control.

As she and Keith reach the quiet area, she releases her arm from around his shoulder, and without looking at him directly, she says, "Keith, you made 100 on a list like that last week—or was it the week before?"

Keith: "I ain't talking to no ugly old bitch—It was this week. I got three 100s."

The teacher, still looking away: "Last Monday we had a good conference in the principal's conference room. Remember, we decided that you were grown-up enough to talk in there? Boys who can control their behavior can talk in that room."

Keith listens. He likes the image of being associated with the adults and the conference room. The teacher has reduced his feelings of anger toward himself as a first step. Then, she aligns herself as his advocate as a second step.

The teacher, looking at her watch: "I think the people who were working in the conference room left 5 minutes ago. We can talk in there. You are in control now so we can use that room."

(*continues*)

Keith: "Yeah, I went down there Monday." His body language says he is ready to go. He appears relaxed. The teacher tells the classroom aide that she and Keith are going to the conference room, and they leave without further talk.

In the conference room they sit at a table. The teacher, in a businesslike manner, begins: "Keith, you did your math and most of your reading. Sometimes work goes slowly, and boys rip their papers to see what teachers will do."

Keith: "I was going to tape the paper back together."

Teacher: "That's an excellent idea. We may be able to get back and finish your work with a little time left to play." (This is necessary in order to alleviate any anxiety Keith may have about what happens next.)

Keith and his teacher walk back to the classroom. The teacher puts her hand on his shoulder. As they reenter she says to the assistant teacher and the group, "Keith is going to tape his paper together and will come over to play as soon as he finishes."

The assistant teacher picks up on the cue: "We need someone who can pump gas for the cars and run this gas station we've just built."

Keith responds with renewed determination to complete his academic task. He finishes his work and joins the other students.

behavior as a personal attack and how she translates her understanding of his needs into positive actions.

To be effective with the Developmental Therapy–Developmental Teaching curriculum, adults must fulfill the roles of valued and respected adults. This requirement demands continual, active headwork. It is not always the easiest curriculum to implement when it is tried for the first time. But as adults use this approach and their proficiency increases, they see their own effectiveness and the positive impact on their children's progress. Adults who have become effective in using the curriculum tell us that once they have started thinking developmentally, they always do so.

In this chapter, we review this maze of skills needed by adults who seek to foster the social-emotional development of infants, children, or teens. If you are already experienced as a teacher or parent, these skills should be fairly easy to add to your present practices. If you are new to this field, use the material in this chapter to develop self-assessment and self-monitoring strategies. For those who have used this curriculum in the past, we have refocused the material around these five topics:

- lead and support roles when two adults work together as a team
- establishing a healthy interpersonal climate
- phases of skill development for adults using this curriculum
- problems adults have with themselves
- studies of refinements in practices during in-service training

LEAD AND SUPPORT ROLES WHEN TWO ADULTS WORK TOGETHER AS A TEAM

Because programs for most children and teens are conducted in groups, and groups are a natural social structure, we begin this chapter with a focus on a fundamental concept for effectively managing any group.[1] The issue is how to keep cohesion among the group members and momentum in the group for carrying out an activity. There are several universal problems in managing a group. First, a group only functions together when the individuals in it see themselves as group members and are willing to participate. A group must offer individuals something for themselves. To see oneself as a fully accredited member is not always easy for every individual, and this is particularly true for very young children and for alienated youth.

A second universal problem in group management comes from the breakdown or isolation of an individual in a group. Disturbance by an individual member, distracting behavior, resistance, or failure of a member to participate creates a ripple of uncertainty in the psychological climate. Unless the momentum for continuing as a group is preserved, the activity will disintegrate into separate, individual units of activity, which opens the way for increased behavior management problems from the other members. This reaction can quickly grind an entire group activity to a halt, and group disintegration or chaos may result.

To maintain individual participation and group cohesion in Developmental Therapy–Developmental Teaching, the responsibilities of the adults who work on the team are defined into *lead* and *support* roles.[2] The lead role provides pivotal psychological power for the group by conducting the group activity so that each child feels recognized, successful, and safe and enjoys participating. The support role provides the necessary individual attention to each member so that maximum participation results. The reason these responsibilities are separated into two roles and

[1] In Chapter 4 we discuss grouping children for Developmental Therapy–Developmental Teaching by goals and objectives for social-emotional development.

[2] These same roles, lead and support, apply to any team that works with a group—parents and their families, coaches with their teams, therapists with counseling groups, teachers and their classes. Presland and White (1990) describe a variation of the support role used in England.

clearly communicated to children has to do with group dynamics. Someone must be the adult to whom children look for leadership, decision making, and authority; this is the *lead.* Someone must also be available to give individual attention and assistance; this is the *support.*[3]

Separating these responsibilities is particularly effective when working with groups of troubled children—those who have disabilities or who are at risk for social and emotional problems. The lead instigates the group's activities and keeps the activities flowing along smoothly in spite of any disruptions caused by an individual. The lead does not take care of a child who needs individual assistance. It is the responsibility of the support to see that a child returns to full participation in the group activity. (If a lead attends to the needs of a disruptive child, the psychological bonds that maintain group momentum and cohesion are instantly broken, and a breakdown in group behavior happens rapidly.)

Building effective lead and support roles for a team requires major attention, and it is the first focus we give in staff development. Each role has separate responsibilities, yet the success of the lead-support team comes from the extent to which they communicate with each other both verbally and nonverbally.[4] As a helpful team member, you should be able to

- anticipate where you should be physically, at a given moment;
- decide which students need immediate attention and which can be managed without individual adult support;
- select appropriate verbal and physical strategies for individual children;
- know when to interact with the other team members;
- determine which strategies are appropriate for the lead and which are appropriate for the support;
- tolerate frustration when a strategy seems to be correct but a child is not responding;
- plan ahead—anticipate when to change a strategy; and
- use open, supportive teamwork between the lead and the support.

We encourage the support person on a team to signal the lead when an individual child gives any indication that his attention or interest in participating is beginning to lag. This cue from the support allows the lead to redirect the child's attention back to the activity before his behavior becomes a problem. If redirection is insufficient, the lead will tell the support to provide the necessary type of intervention to assist the child in regaining group status as a participating member.

For this model of lead and support teamwork to be effective, children need to be aware of the attitudes, structure, and expectations established by the lead and backed by the support. The actions of the team must be carefully executed to convey the expectancy of positive outcomes. If expectations are reasonable and valued by the group, children will respond to meet them. If expectations for the outcome are low, unreasonable, ambiguous, or not valued by children, their participation will be reluctant at best (or, at worst, group chaos will erupt).

Responsibilities of the Lead Person on a Team

The lead is the psychological power position—the adult in charge. The lead initiates, conducts, and ends each activity. As defender of the collective interests, the lead also must maintain group motivation and keep the group process going. In short, an effective lead sets the general psychological climate for a group, pacing and timing every activity to maintain maximum participation and investment in every activity by all of the children. The success of the group, and of every individual within the group, depends upon the lead's ability to ensure the comfortable and successful inclusion of each individual in the group process. The lead is also in an advocacy role where each child believes the adult to be dependable in taking care of events that the child cannot handle. These responsibilities are summarized below:

Responsibilities of a Team's Lead Person

- to keep the group together and participating
- to provide for smooth transitions from activity to activity
- to involve every child in every activity
- to ensure successful or pleasant outcomes for every child in each activity
- to convey expectations and maintain them
- to provide abundant, positive feedback
- to create an accepting and supportive climate for every child
- to manage the routines and activities in ways that make each child feel psychologically secure

[3]Underlying all of these adult skills is knowledge of each child's profile of social-emotional development: (a) the milestones already acquired, (b) those that are currently a program focus, and (c) those that must be postponed until later because of the sequential nature of development.

[4]Chapter 6 includes a discussion of verbal interaction between adults, a major management strategy used with children in Stages Two and Three, where they are learning the skills to be group members. By Stage Four, adult interaction becomes a model for students to use to expand their own interpersonal skills.

If you are the lead for your team, personally greet individual children as they enter. All children want to believe that the lead is glad to see them. The lead must establish an individual connection with each child in order to be viewed as a valued adult. One way to do this is to begin the first activity of the day by locating yourself in a strategic place where you will be able to attract the children into the first activity. As they join you, motivate and hold their attention for the activity by your introduction, your demonstrations of materials to be used, and your voice quality.[5]

When you expect children to move to a new area for a change in activities, be the first into the new location to provide the motivation for them to come to the new activity. Without structuring a transition this way, there is no incentive for individual children to go to a new area. If a lead forgets this basic rule and deals with an individual child who is reluctant to end one activity and begin another, the result usually is deterioration of the group process, because there is no group leader while the lead is involved with the individual child. The resulting insecurity often causes heightened anxiety and a noticeable increase in problem behaviors in every group member.

Responsibilities of the Support Person on a Team

An effective team is an important part of a successful intervention program, and a team is most efficient when a second adult is working as support. This person might be an assisting teacher, teacher, aide, community volunteer, mental health professional, or parent. The responsibility of a support person on a team is to respond to individual children in crisis or to those who need one-to-one assistance to maintain their participation. The objective is to redirect a child back to the group activity. An effective support person complements the tone of the lead and keeps individual children involved in the activity that the lead is providing. Often a support deals with children in crisis, those who are resistant to participation, and those with special needs.[6] The support offers individual assistance when a child shows signs of floundering, thereby freeing the lead to keep the group activity flowing smoothly. The team's support person has the following responsibilities:

Responsibilities of a Team's Support Person

- to respond to individual children in crisis or to those who need one-to-one assistance
- to complement the tone established by the lead
- to keep individual children involved in participating
- to provide individual relationships and attention
- to provide appropriate response models for children to imitate when needed

A support conveys enthusiasm for the group activity to keep children's interest and involvement. In doing so, he or she serves as an appropriate response model when needed, using actions that convey expected responses for the children to imitate. It is essential also for a support to communicate attention to the lead, especially in Stages One and Two, as a model of attention and listening for children to follow.

A support must learn basic strategies, body movements, and verbalizations to accomplish this goal. Reflection, redirection, praise, and positive feedback are strategies that are easy for a beginning support to learn when working with children in any stage. Physical proximity, without direct intervention, is also an important strategy for a support to use selectively, often providing reassurance and sufficient adult presence to prevent further loss of control by a child. Movement by a support is usually around the periphery of a group. Positive, verbal redirection by the support is often all that is needed to keep the children participating. Within a group, usually about one to three children require special management plans, rather than the total group. These are the children identified by the team as vulnerable to failure in the group. Often they are also the ones who are the most troubled and who easily lose control.

One of the most frequent problems that supports have is allowing children to manipulate them into engaging in a personal exchange on some subject other than the designated activity. If this is allowed, the support undermines the message that the activity is the important focus and the expectation that the child will participate in the activity. Although supports do not intend for this to be communicated, when they respond to a child who is having difficulty, individual assistance can easily become the child's escape from responsibility. Yet there are circumstances and incidents in which it is essential to provide individual support in response to a child's needs. Determining just how much personal assistance an individual should receive in order to rejoin a group is a major issue for every support.

A support can learn to use all of the management strategies described in Chapter 6; however, this will take time, experience, teamwork, and encouraging feedback from the lead. We have found that a support often learns to use these strategies with skill by following the example of the lead, discussing together every day the strategies that worked or did not work. We call this *debriefing*. This is the time each day when all members of a team get together, preferably immediately after the children leave. The following points should be covered in the daily debriefing:

[5] Examples of effective procedures for conducting activities at all stages are included in Chapter 4. Chapters 8–12 provide additional detail about adapting strategies to students' individual stages of development.

[6] Occasionally, an experienced teacher of severely disturbed students will be the support on a team in order to provide skilled one-to-one crisis intervention, while an aide will be the team lead, providing group leadership for each activity.

- At what one time during the day were the children most successful? Why?
- What specific verbalizations did the adults use that were appropriate to achieve the desired results?
- Which strategies were most effective for each child?
- What verbal and nonverbal communication was effective?
- Were there emotional reactions from student to adult and from adult to child?
- What is the lead role conveying, and is it suited for the children's stages of development?
- Were behavioral expectations, rules, and procedures consistent, appropriate, and clear?
- If a child had to be removed from the group or the room today, what was the precipitating event? What was the therapeutic resolution?

Each team will develop its own debriefing style; however, it is the responsibility of the team's lead to ensure that debriefing occurs and to set the pace for the group process. An opportunity should be provided for ventilation of feelings during debriefing, but it should not dominate the time or the discussion. Ventilation should always be followed by problem solving. The team should work toward open discussion, where all members of the team feel comfortable about expressing ideas, feelings, and attitudes. Team members should feel enhanced by their own contributions but should also be receptive to constructive criticism and willing to try something new.

The time spent in debriefing about effective and ineffective strategies is time well spent. The result will be a highly effective team that works together like clockwork and can demonstrate significant changes in the children. These adults are viewed by their children as caring adults who respect each child and provide experiences that are meaningful, profitable, and enjoyable. In successful programs, younger children convey their enthusiasm for the adults by participating with interest each day. Older children usually make comments such as "We did some neat stuff today" or "We did a great project." From their side, the effective team communicates to each child:

> *"You are important. You are someone who can do things well."*

ESTABLISHING A HEALTHY INTERPERSONAL CLIMATE

A healthy emotional climate among individuals in a group is as complex as a healthy personality within an individual, whether the group is a classroom, a family, an after-school group, or people together for recreation or sports. A psychological climate always permeates the group. An outsider observing an adult with a group of children or teens can sense this psychological climate—the "tone" of the group. It is seen in the adult's attitude toward each child and the children's behavior toward each other. In a healthy interpersonal climate, the adults clearly convey respect and regard for the children, and the children seem to absorb these attitudes and reflect them back to each other. The adults use maximum amounts of positive statements and a minimum of negative ones. The children also make few negative comments and numerous remarks that are spontaneously enthusiastic. They convey interest in the activities and support for each other. The observer will see children smiling—a singularly important indicator of a positive interpersonal climate in a group. There will also be spontaneous social interaction between the children and the adults. The product of such a climate is a responsiveness of the children to the adults and the program. Children in this climate progress toward mastery of developmental objectives because the environment supports comfortable interpersonal relations, promotes success, and results in personal satisfaction.

A healthy interpersonal climate is not always easy to establish. It is shaped by the children's emotional needs and the adult's behavior in response to these needs (Kuykendall, 1992). Figure 7.1 illustrates this process schematically, showing the way these elements interact to produce a positive relationship that is supportive of a child's growth in social-emotional competence and responsible behavior.

In this diagram, the needs of the child are shown to be at the heart of a solid relationship, which, in turn, contributes to the eventual success of the child. First, a child's essential needs are defined by a general stage of social-emotional development, which influences the choice of general role-types the adult will convey. We then identify the child's underlying developmental anxieties, which shape the type of power choices the adult uses in the adult-child relationship. The child's specific objectives in the areas of Behavior, Communication, Socialization, and (Pre)Academics/Cognition guide us in choosing specific instructional and management strategies. The message is

> *"This adult cares about me and can help me when I cannot help myself."*

Build Relationships by Choosing Effective Social Power Bases

Social power is the ability to influence others to do something that they would not ordinarily do on their own. Most adults do not recognize that they are using forms of social power to influence others, yet everyone does so. Every adult working with children or teens, of any age, learns in a short time how to affect the interpersonal climate by utilizing social power. Consider the four univer-

Figure 7.1. Elements in building a relationship between child and adult.

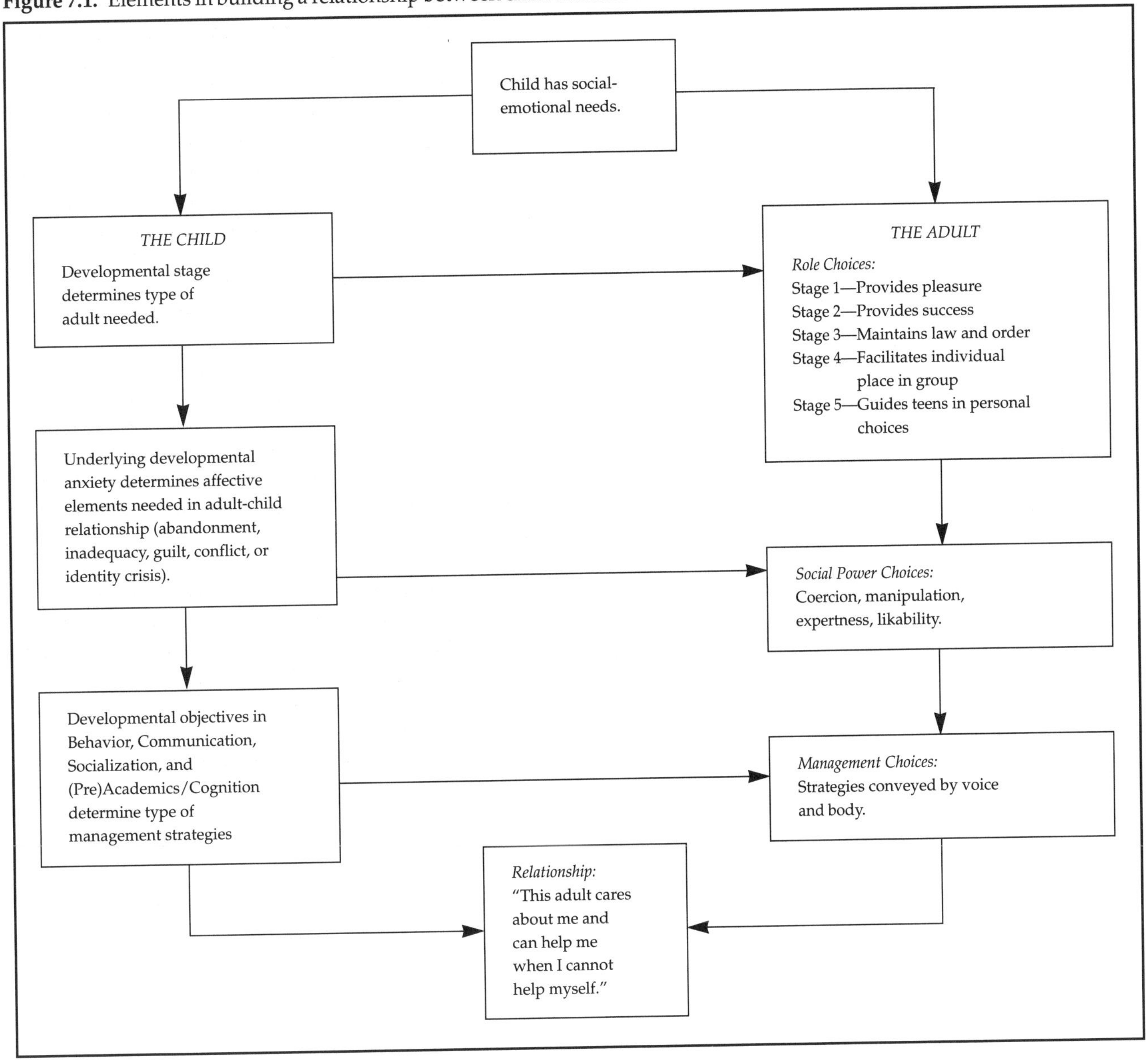

sal social power bases most frequently used by adults: coercion, manipulation, expertness, and likability:

1. *Coercion:* Verbal or physical confrontation, force, or overpowering psychological control, with an implied threat, that influences children's behavior.
2. *Manipulation:* Covert control of situations in which the results are not directly associated with the manipulator.
3. *Expertness:* Ability to help children solve problems that they cannot handle alone.
4. *Likability:* Positive personal characteristics such as warmth, mannerisms, or expressions that children admire or respect and that influence their behavior.

These forms of influence are used singly or in combination by adults in every culture, deliberately or unknowingly, to enhance or restrict each child's development. They are reviewed here in some detail because we have observed that effective adults demonstrate an ability to selectively use each of these approaches.[7] In building genuine relationships that influence the social and emotional development of each individual child, adults must be able to selectively use all of these forms of social power in ways that bring positive benefits. Experienced adults find themselves deliberately choosing between these approaches daily to meet the conditions of the moment. We review each of these strategies briefly here.

[7] Social power is also used by children. See Chapter 10 for a discussion of how social power is used by students in Stage Three and beyond.

Coercion. Coercion is a form of influence that uses verbal or physical confrontation, force, or overpowering psychological control, with some threat implied or actually stated. Many structured reinforcement systems currently in vogue for managing problem behaviors are sophisticated versions of coercion—that is, rewards are given or withheld by the powerful adult. Here are several examples: College professors use coercion in the form of grades to motivate students to study and learn. Some parents employ coercion by withholding love or approval in order to make their children employ socially acceptable behaviors. Adults working with children from neighborhoods where force is the only means of survival find the children defending themselves with violence or weapons to combat coercion with coercion. When children have learned to respond only to coercion, the adult may need to use coercion strategies as a first step in maintaining law and order.

Clearly, there is a place for coercion as a social power option in influencing the behavior of others. The important issue is when to use coercion, with whom, and for how long. Coercion always puts someone in a powerless, losing position. Children who lose repeatedly to adults accumulate negative reactions and become so psychologically well defended against further coercion that little or no growth is possible. This outcome must be weighed against the need for adults to influence the behavior of children. Children must know that they are physically safe and that the adult is psychologically in charge. A climate of safety must always be maintained, and it may sometimes be necessary to resort to coercion to establish this basic security. Verbal confrontation is another form of coercion that may be used constructively with a small number of children, particularly those in Stage Four, to help gain insight into nonproductive attitudes or behaviors. Reality therapy, based on the idea that there is little payoff in holding on to old coping strategies, is yet another form of coercion in which possibly painful natural consequences are sanctioned, although not directly administered by the adult (Glasser, 1965).

Manipulation. Manipulation is covert control of situations and people in which the results are not directly associated with the manipulator. If it is implemented positively, manipulation influences children to participate constructively and to see themselves as central players. Adults use manipulation as a social power base when they select highly motivating materials, use their voice tone to convey security, or design activities in which children participate without resistance because they know they have a good chance to succeed. The Montessori method of using materials to provide intrinsic feedback is an example of manipulation of the learning environment as a subtle form of social power. Self-correcting academic lessons also are examples of manipulation of the learning environment.

Manipulation has negative connotations for many adults. Perhaps this is why it is not used as frequently as it could be by adults as a strategy for helping children. It is a particularly effective way to influence children who have learned to distrust adults or adult authority, because the role of the adult is not evident in the situation. It is also an effective power base for teachers who have passive-aggressive children. Such children, who use manipulation themselves, are experts at outmaneuvering adults. When these children have no target to manipulate, they tend to relax their own controls and defenses.[8]

Expertness. The ability to help children solve problems that they cannot handle alone requires adult expertise. It is probably true that children prefer adults who have high levels of expertness, even if they do not have problems to be solved. But when a child feels overwhelmed with inadequacy because of failure to cope with a pressing situation, expertness on the adult's part is essential. By sifting through the waves of recriminations, remorse, panic, and anger, the adult and child together come up with a plan to cope more comfortably. A high level of trust develops, and psychological security in the entire group results.

Adults are recognized by children as having expertness when they have knowledge of subjects that interest children. Children also recognize an adult's expertness when the adult conveys an understanding of the feelings underlying problem behaviors or successfully manages a child who is out of control. When adults are effective in helping children solve their problems in positive ways, the result is trust, admiration, positive identification with the adult, more security, and positive growth.

Likability. Using positive personal characteristics to influence others is a form of social power broadly described as likability. Children respond to adults who have likable attributes such as humor, warmth, helpfulness, approval, and fairness. Often such characteristics are the very elements that promote constructive imitation of an admired adult by a child. This personal appeal is evident when an adult—perhaps a parent—says to a child, "Do this for me," or when a child calls to an adult, "Look at this . . . do you like it?" or "I made this for you."

Likability is most effective as a form of social power when it is used in combination with the other three forms of social power. It adds a personal, positive, caring dimension to the interpersonal climate of the group. But if it is used as an adult's only power base, likability can result in a level of dependency in children that restricts their emotional development. The child-adult relationship dissolves into person-to-person bonding in which the adult neither exercises authority nor allows the child the psychological space to explore independently. Separation may become extremely difficult for the adult and child. Through this sort of personalizing, both of them may

[8] See Chapter 5 for a discussion of strategies for managing children with severe passive-aggressive behavior.

come to feel that other adults (including parents) cannot provide what this adult can provide.

Social power is essential in establishing relationships between children and adults in a group. Children will respond with increased participation and progress toward mastering objectives if an adult has established social power in positive ways. This is true whether the adult is moving a child in Stage One toward a new toy or helping a student into the principal's office at school to discuss a fight on the bus. The form of social power will vary with the child and the situation. A luring type of manipulation may be needed in the first example to move the child toward the toy; in the second example, the adult's social power may take the form of an expert exchange between the adult and the student about bus regulations and what happens to a child who gets in trouble on the bus. In any event, all four social power bases should be considered as options. Every adult needs to be skillful in using all four forms of social power and in selecting the form needed for individual children and situations.

Learn To Use Social Power Options Effectively

If this idea of social power is new to you, we suggest that you first identify the typical social power strategies you use naturally in your own interpersonal relationships. This will give you an indication of the type of social power you rely on instinctively when trying to influence others. The typical form you use will probably be the one you rely on when working with children. Consider also the forms of social power you might not have used. Experiment with verbal and nonverbal ways to convey unfamiliar social power bases. Try them out first in nonexplosive, neutral situations where children will not be confused by sudden changes in your interpersonal style. Then observe the way children respond to these different social power styles. This information will help you to select the appropriate social power styles to use with each child. The intent in using social power is to encourage constructive responses from a child to the established expectations.

Behind every form of social power, the message from adults must be

"Adults care about children, and adults can be depended upon."

Adults must carefully monitor themselves to ensure that the intended messages are being clearly received by children. To communicate such messages with children of every age and stage, adults must be effective in their nonverbal forms of communication. We review three basic skills here: *body language, eye contact or avoidance,* and *voice quality.* These are powerful tools for conveying this fundamental message.

Body Language. Children rely on unspoken messages from adults' body posture, tone, gesture, and expression. With body language an adult can

- accept
- reassure
- convey security
- nurture
- redirect attention
- motivate
- intervene in a developing crisis
- decrease discomfort
- reward
- praise

In times of crisis, the deliberate choice of a relaxed body stance may convey the sense of security and confidence needed to neutralize a panic reaction in a child. Body language can communicate respect and care. Nonverbal messages may also convey an adult's own anxieties, tensions, or insecurities. By standing over a child, adults convey authority or the threat of coercion. Physical proximity or touch also can evoke feelings of closeness that some children crave and others misinterpret or cannot handle.

When body language is not conscious on an adult's part, the messages conveyed to children may not be what was intended. Adults must train themselves to monitor their own body messages and to use nonverbal communication deliberately. If an adult relies only upon words (the preferred adult mode of communication) to convey important interpersonal messages, a more effective way to communicate may be lacking. If you do not feel comfortable communicating without words, practice in private. In front of a mirror, try to communicate confidence, power, concern, and enthusiasm without using words. As you increase your confidence in your own ability to convey these messages, practice with other adults. Then try role-playing in pantomime with groups of children until you and the children are able to communicate simple ideas without any words being exchanged. This can be your most effective technique—use it!

Eye Contact or Avoidance. Eye contact serves many purposes, such as interacting nonverbally with others, enhancing verbal exchanges, and obtaining attention for an instructional task. Eye contact should be systematically used by an adult with most children throughout every activity. However, there are times when avoiding eye contact may be an appropriate strategy. In some cultures, children are taught that it is disrespectful to look directly at adults. For some children, a direct gaze from an adult is an encroachment on their psychological space; by avoiding a direct gaze, adults can provide the needed distance. Some children in crisis may therefore feel less vulnerable or less in need of maintaining a disruptive behavior when an adult is not watching. This allows for a cooling-off time while physiological processes come into balance and emotions recede. Then the child may be able to engage in communication with the adult.

Eye contact and avoidance are used to communicate with children in all stages of development. Adults should be confident in themselves and comfortable enough with children to look them straight in the eye. If a child accepts the adult, the look will be returned. If the child seeks the adult's support, eye contact will be interpreted as a personal contact—a reassurance of care and respect. Many older children are responsive to a quiet, steady gaze from an adult, and eye contact may be effective in building relationships with them.

With young children, particularly in Stage One, an adult may touch a child's chin to direct attention toward the adult. This technique is effective in helping the child attend to the adult's verbal direction or to help a child who is learning to speak by imitating lip movements. A few children in Stage One may react against this approach or avoid all contact with adults. Avoid direct eye contact with them until they begin to watch adults spontaneously. This watching often indicates that they are seeking some form of contact with the adult. They may be beginning to trust adults, yet cannot bring themselves to show it by overtly looking. In such situations, adults should make their glances brief, supportive, and nondemanding, gradually lengthening the glance into a smile and finally calling the child's name and pausing until the glance is returned. When a meaningful, motivating activity is the vehicle for such an exchange, a child often may reach out suddenly to show the adult what has been done in the activity or to call for help. A major Socialization milestone in Stage One is reached through this achievement, when a child spontaneously seeks contact with an adult.

Voice Quality. Many children rely on "reading" messages into an adult's tone of voice and voice modulation rather than on listening to the words the adult uses. Adults should be aware of the effect their voice quality can have on children and should learn to convey a range of messages through voice quality as well as words. By varying volume and tone of voice, adults are able to attract and hold children's attention. Few children can resist listening to an adult whose voice suddenly drops to a whisper, or who conveys a questioning tone with surprise or excitement in both face and voice. When a child is upset, a slow and soothing tone conveys that the adult is not upset and can be trusted. A light, happy voice reflects ease and pleasure in a situation. An emphatic, matter-of-fact voice depersonalizes the situation and communicates that the adult expects the child to respond as requested. The amount of enthusiasm and warmth conveyed by adults is directly related to children's stages of development and their need for adults to be the source of pleasure, encouragement, authority, power, leadership, or guidance.

Some children will not respond to even a simple request unless firmness is conveyed through voice tone. This does not imply shouting or demanding, but it lets the child know very clearly what is expected. If an adult does not clearly convey expectations, a child is more likely to test the adult's limits. On the other hand, a tone that is too firm or strident can inadvertently convey anger or tension, which may become the catalyst for a child's losing self-control.

Similarly, some women have a particular problem with a high pitch or a negotiating, tentative quality to their voices. The thinness of the sound seems to trigger a sense of uncertainty in some children about the adult's power and dependability. The message may be interpreted as pleading or insecurity on the adult's part, arousing greater anxiety in the children. Invariably, these adults have behavior management problems with their children. In contrast, quiet confidence, conveyed through a deep, full tone of voice, works wonders in building a healthy interpersonal environment for a group.

Effective adults are able to convey an array of techniques that complement or change the verbal and nonverbal messages as needed.[9] We use a simple series of exercises to practice this skill. Try saying "Good morning" four different ways:

as an authority figure

as kindly but distant

as absent-minded or preoccupied with something else

as intensely personal and focused

Try another familiar expression used frequently by parents and teachers: "You have to leave the table until you can get yourself together." This time, convey these nonverbal messages as you make that statement:

support and confidence that everything will be all right

toughness and authority

uncertainty that the child will leave without a fight

rejection and disgust

These simple exercises are merely the calisthenics of staying in shape for communicating attitudes toward children. You might have noticed that the words themselves are not nearly as important as how they are said. If you have sufficient control over your voice quality to convey

[9]In linguistics, these practices are sometimes referred to as *suprasegmental phonemes*.

each of these nonverbal messages with the same set of words, you have the skill necessary to convey a range of other messages that are important for children to hear as you establish your social power bases with individual children.

In short, an effective relationship depends upon an adult's ability to show children what kind of person that adult really is—and how the adult sees a particular child. This is what an effective adult should strive to communicate: a positive attitude, gentle firmness, calm logic, humor, enthusiasm, fairness, and psychological strength—attributes that contribute to an overall attitude of dispassionate compassion (sympathetic feelings conveyed without emotional intensity). The result should be a healthy interpersonal climate with mutual respect between adults and children.

As adults build relationships with children in the Developmental Therapy–Developmental Teaching program, they keep in mind the attitudes that they are conveying and the way the messages are being received. They maintain a sense of respect for each child's psychological space. In the end, they avoid creating a relationship in which a child becomes dependent on control and direction from the adult; they also avoid encouraging emotional dependence on the adult. While it is often difficult to maintain a balance between the necessity to be in control in the short run and the equally important need for eventual self-direction by the child, achieving the latter is the purpose of our efforts.

PHASES OF SKILL DEVELOPMENT FOR ADULTS USING THIS CURRICULUM

In the first six chapters, we presented the underlying philosophy, theory, and general curricular applications to effectively foster social-emotional development and responsible behavior in children and youth of all ages. If these beliefs and practices are compatible with your own, the additional skills for Developmental Therapy–Developmental Teaching will come easily to you. If you disagree with the fundamentals, you may be able to acquire the additional skills but there will be a dissonance between your beliefs and these practices. We do not recommend using this curriculum if you feel that it is not in harmony with your own orientation.

As adults begin to use the Developmental Therapy–Developmental Teaching curriculum, they often ask,

> *"What are the most important skills for me to learn for this approach?"*

Our studies of how teachers' competencies develop indicate that most teachers acquire many basic skills during their college preparation that are generic for all good teaching. Successful teachers use these skills frequently, even before being introduced to this curriculum. This natural fit makes it easy for many teachers to acquire the additional skills needed for implementing Developmental Therapy–Developmental Teaching.

Quirk (1993, p. 74) studied the skills of 25 early childhood education teachers before they began on-the-job training to use this curriculum. She found that 87% of them had previously acquired these basic practices, which are also necessary for using this curriculum with preschool children:

- Preschool or primary grade materials are adapted to meet individual needs.
- To help children organize themselves, certain areas of the room are designated for specific activities.
- The teacher encourages children to freely explore materials.
- Activities such as games are designed so that there are no losers and there is no peer competition.
- Inside play is included.
- Play equipment provides an opportunity for independent feedback.
- Snack Time and preacademic work time are included in the daily schedule.
- Opportunities to work on the social-emotional goals of the stage are provided through art, music, and play.
- The content of the material is manipulative and encourages exploration.

These practices involve the physical setup of a classroom, the schedule of activities, and the use of age-appropriate materials. By most standards for preschool education, these 9 practices are fundamental for any well-conducted program. They are also included on the DT/RITS performance assessment instrument Stage Two form included in Appendix 2.

There are three rather distinct phases in the acquisition of skills by adults using Developmental Therapy–Developmental Teaching. The *beginning phase* is best characterized as adults' learning survival skills—working with a group in an orderly and positive manner. In the *middle phase,* adults are able to provide a mentally healthy climate in which children participate willingly and their progress in achieving some of their individual program objectives is clearly noted. We have heard the same comment repeatedly from adults into their second year with this curriculum: "I know I'm being truly effective now!" Adults progressing to the *demonstration phase* are able to alleviate children's severe social, emotional, and behavioral characteristics while fostering social-emotional growth.

Some adults are able to move rapidly through all of these phases. Others find that it takes a year or more. It seems to be helpful if they receive ongoing feedback and team support as they expand their skills. Each of these phases of skill acquisition has particular practices that are important for an adult to master. When the adult concentrates on one set of skills at a time, the task does not seem quite so overwhelming. These practices are outlined below for each phase of skill acquisition.

The Beginning Phase of Skill Acquisition

Figure 7.2 outlines the important practices to focus on during the *beginning phase* in learning to use the Developmental Therapy–Developmental Teaching curriculum.[10] Because each individual child's IEP, IFSP, or ITP objectives are the basis for planning and conducting Developmental Therapy–Developmental Teaching, each objective should be understood and memorized for constant application in the program. This is the essential first step in skill acquisition for adults, because the objectives are the guideposts for planning suitable materials, activities, and management strategies. We ask adults who are in this beginning phase to prepare themselves by being able to respond to the question, "Why are you doing that?" with a statement of a specific objective that is the focus of the activity for an individual child or the group.

After learning the children's objectives, plan specific materials and activities that are motivating and meaningful to each child. These choices should directly relate to specific objectives. Many teachers tell us that they begin their planning with individual sequences for independent and group work in reading (language arts), spelling, and arithmetic. These subjects seem to be easier to translate into sequential learning experiences for most beginning teachers than objectives in Socialization, Communication, or Behavior. When teachers are selecting content and designing the sequence of steps needed to acquire an objective, students' out-of-school interests and concerns provide excellent resources for motivating them and capturing their interest in participating. When tasks feature age-appropriate interests, they are almost always received with enthusiasm. Experienced teachers expand rapidly into using art, music, storybooks, creative writing, puppetry, sports, and recreation as major motivating activities to accomplish the objectives. With older children, adult heroes and entertainment figures also provide sources for motivation.

In this first phase of skill acquisition, an adult must learn and practice the following prototype roles of adults needed by their children, according to the children's stages of social-emotional development:[11]

Roles of Adults

Nurturer and satisfier of basic needs (for students in Stage One)

Encourager of individual successes in basic social learning (for students in Stage Two)

Upholder of law and order; teacher and model for group interaction skills (for students in Stage Three)

Group facilitator; social role model and individual advocate (for students in Stage Four)

Counselor, adviser, and confidant (for students in Stage Five)

Contrast the general characteristics of each of these adult roles with your own personal preferences for style in working with children and teens, considering your natural characteristics when interacting with both adults and children. By comparing, you should see which personal style you use and which roles you must learn to expand your skills and enable you to more fully meet the range of needs of your children. A good match between your own competencies and the children's stages of social-emotional development is a foundation for program effectiveness.

Adults often ask how to select an effective role when a group is composed of children in various stages of development. This is difficult to do. Multiple roles require a broad range of responses on the adult's part and an ability to change from one set of strategies to another. Even experienced adults, including parents, may have trouble making these shifts at first. For this reason, we prefer to group children together for activities according to their social-emotional goals and objectives. This procedure minimizes the range of social-emotional goals and objectives for the children within a group and thus narrows the range of adult roles needed. It is especially helpful for adults who are learning to provide needed role models to begin with small groups of children who have similar needs. When this is not possible, we have seen adults use subgroups for brief periods, where particular children are paired with others who have similar social-emotional goals and objectives.[12]

Instant recall of every child's goals and objectives is a big help, particularly in crises—those moments when a child loses control. When the adult thinks, "What do I do now?" the answer is found in tailoring responses to the child's needs, the social-emotional goals and objectives, the child's developmental anxiety and defenses, and the needed adult role. This information about each child is essential for rapid recall, especially when working with troubled children in crisis.

These skills are not always acquired easily or rapidly. The process requires considerable personal insight and self-monitoring. Most important, it requires a depth

[10] The DT/RITS contains 212 performance items for teachers and other adults using this curriculum and is recommended as a comprehensive guide for training. It is contained in Appendix 2.

[11] These roles are described briefly in Chapters 1 and 2 and are discussed in greater depth in Chapters 8 through 12.

[12] Alternative ways to schedule groups of children are discussed in Chapter 3. Greater detail about grouping variations for each stage of development is provided in Chapters 8 through 12.

Figure 7.2. Practices to focus on in the beginning phase of skill acquisition.

- Know the developmental milestones that each child has achieved and the objectives identified for current focus in the program.
- Identify the needed adult role for each child's stage of social-emotional development.
- Prepare a group profile to identify the range of social-emotional objectives within the group, the objectives needed by all of the students, and the particular objectives needed by individual children.
- Plan program adaptations within group activities for individual children, based upon their objectives.
- Plan lead and support role strategies for the team.
- Learn the goals and milestones of development at the stages immediately below and above the current levels of functioning for each child in the group.
- Plan the daily routine and keep to it the same way every day, but change the content daily.
- Select a weekly content theme based upon the personal experiences and interests of the children.
- Plan strategic locations for each activity and store the necessary materials where they are easily accessible for each activity.
- Arrange furniture and seating in ways that promote socialization and minimize opportunities for behavioral problems.
- Meet children entering and leaving if the developmental stage of the children indicates a need.
- Learn how each child responds to stress and success.
- Assume a pleasant attitude verbally and nonverbally and use it to help children participate positively. Respond to the content of their work.
- Be physically alert, moving when needed to motivate children by proximity, to prevent a crisis from developing, or to convey interest in their work.
- Make verbal or nonverbal contact with every child in the group at least once every 5 minutes.
- Avoid asking questions that could be answered by refusal, such as "Don't you want to do your work?"
- Make positive statements that reflect the outcomes of children's behavior in positive terms.

of emotional maturity, self-confidence, and empathy for others. To help develop these skills during the beginning phase of skill acquisition, we recommend reviewing the specific competencies contained in the DT/RITS, described in the latter part of this chapter and included in Appendix 2 (Robinson, 1982). This instrument provides specific competencies that can be used as guidelines for self-monitoring. The four forms contain the practices recommended specifically for children at each of the first four stages of social-emotional development. Try doing a self-rating with the DT/RITS. This will provide a review of the practices you use already, to see how closely they match the practices recommended for this curriculum. Then you will know which of the practices you already have acquired and those you need to work on to complete the first phase of skill development in using Developmental Therapy–Developmental Teaching. This should prepare you to move ahead into the next phase of skill acquisition.

The Middle Phase of Skill Acquisition

After mastering the basics, adults often say, "There is so much to learn—what should I do next?" In response, we summarize in Figure 7.3 the practices adults should focus on during the *middle phase* of skill acquisition.

After mastering the basics, the focus for adults shifts to decoding behavior, learning to "read" behavior in order to understand the emotional needs driving each child. Adults learn to understand their children's anxieties, interests, values, sources of satisfaction, and concerns. When decoding, they look for the children's methods of gratifying their own emotional needs, ways of interacting with peers and adults, length of attention, ways of dealing with frustration, and ways of responding to interpersonal and social stresses. Adults also expand their skills by using a wide range of management strategies that clearly and effectively provide children with the adult roles needed for their various stages of development.

During this middle phase of skill acquisition, adults using Developmental Therapy–Developmental Teaching become proficient in using developmental patterns for social and emotional growth to guide program strategies. As they continue to use this knowledge, they learn to recognize, from children's words and actions, patterns of strengths and weaknesses in the sequence of development. They also become proficient in identifying a child's general stage of development from the Preliminary Profile (see Figure 3.2), using the social-emotional goals in each of the four major curriculum areas—Behavior, Communication, Socialization, and (Pre)Academics/Cognition—for program

Figure 7.3. Practices to focus on in the middle phase of skill acquisition.

- Plan lessons and activities from children's developmental objectives.
- Adjust your own style of communicating to the developmental level of each child's receptive language level.
- Use your own body to convey nonverbal messages to your children.
- Understand each child's own experiential world.
- Anticipate a child's behavior and respond within the context of the child's stage of development.
- Recognize anxieties behind observed behaviors and respond in ways that reduce the anxiety.
- Convey the necessary psychological power to ensure security for everyone in the group.
- Convey calm dependability and competence under stress.
- Make your own needs secondary to those of the children.
- Adjust your actions and procedures and alter activities as needed to foster change in children.
- Serve as an advocate for children, parents, and their programs.
- Assist other adults to ensure successful integration of your children into the general education program.
- Work with other mental health professionals and educators as a member of the interdisciplinary team effort to assist children and families.

planning. They are able to specifically address an individual child's goals and objectives and unique social-emotional needs with activities, materials, and behavior management plans.

This phase of skill expansion is also a time for expanding responsibilities for teamwork. Adults become increasingly aware of children's emotional needs that require positive experiences with adults, and they expand their strategies to provide for these experiences. To do this, it is often necessary for adults to draw on their own psychological resources—maturity and creativity—as never before. Each day represents a new challenge in planning and implementing program strategies. We call this fine-tuning the program. As they do this, adults become both increasingly capable of independent decision making and effective as members of the team, working with parents, professionals, and paraprofessionals to provide the best possible program for each child. The effectiveness of a program is directly influenced by the extent to which adults cooperate and pool team efforts for the benefit of the children as they spontaneously and independently generalize new learning into other situations.

The Demonstration Phase of Adults' Skill Acquisition

Adults who are experienced and skilled in using Developmental Therapy–Developmental Teaching are usually in the *demonstration phase* of skill acquisition. These skilled individuals provide the best possible models for others who are learning to implement the Developmental Therapy–Developmental Teaching curriculum.[13] The refinements in practices generally developed during this phase are listed in Figure 7.4.

At this point, adults are using motivation, positive management strategies, decoding behavior, and an understanding of the emotional needs of each child to anticipate needs and apply strategies in therapeutic ways. Children's emotional needs, social-emotional goals, and developmental objectives are the top priority. Adults at this phase of skill development are usually asked to demonstrate their skills as master teachers, supervisors, and consultants to general and special education programs. Their daily programs include therapeutic uses of art, music, rhythms, movement, storytelling, sociodrama, and dramatic play to touch and reshape children's emotional memories, resolve developmental anxieties, and help them experience crisis and resolution vicariously—in short, to accomplish the goals for each child. They monitor themselves and their children so carefully that every moment together is constructive, positive, and therapeutic. The children benefit from these focused adults, showing notable progress in their increasing social-emotional competence and responsible behavior.

Adults performing at this level of competency seem to be keenly aware of their responsibility to ensure their children's ability to function successfully in other places. As they reach this level of performance, they have had experience working in numerous settings to see that their children are successfully generalizing new skills at school, at home, and in the neighborhood. This is an extremely diffi-

[13]DT/RITS proficiency scores greater than 90% indicate an adult's performance with this curriculum at the demonstration level. See Appendix 2.

Figure 7.4. Practices to refine during the demonstration phase of skill acquisition.

- Use knowledge of children's basic anxieties, defense mechanisms, group dynamics, and roles in groups to plan and conduct activities.
- Use creative, expressive, and imaginative curriculum materials, such as creative writing, art, music, movement, role play, storytelling, and make-believe, as major resources for therapeutic change.
- Conduct each activity, including transitions and free time, to work on specific goals and objectives as if it were the single most important moment of the day for each child.
- Maintain a psychologically healthy climate in the room, in which you provide the necessary amount of psychological power to mobilize and sustain each child's motivation and productivity without fostering dependence.
- Monitor each child's progress carefully so that you can facilitate advancement to succeeding objectives as rapidly as possible.
- Change intervention strategies to adjust to each child's changes in development.
- Use DTORF–R profiles at each grading period to interpret progress and make changes in groups if they are needed to accelerate progress during the next grading period.

cult task, often requiring accelerated work with parents, other community agencies, other educators, policy makers, and mental health professionals. It requires expert use of the DTORF–R data to interpret children's gains (or lack of gains) in acquiring social-emotional objectives. A demonstration-level person also is required to design and implement new program initiatives with others who are involved in interdisciplinary efforts. Considerable insight about children and the emotional conditions surrounding their current situations is essential, because this understanding is the foundation for designing and implementing advanced placements as rapidly as a child shows gains.

The role of expert in managing difficult problems associated with children who have severe social-emotional disabilities is not an easy one. Administrators, policy makers, and many other adults who work with children and youth typically may have little background with mental health problems or extremely difficult children. They often lack knowledge about group dynamics, crisis intervention, management of violence, the power of anxiety, or the profound impact of adult behavior on the behavior of children. Therefore, staff development and team enrichment often become another responsibility for adults who become skilled at the demonstration level of proficiency.

To be a successful advocate requires a large amount of time, knowledge, and close communication with other parents, professionals, and paraprofessionals. An effective advocate also must have the ability to manage even the most catastrophic crises (among children, other professionals, or families) with skill and professionalism. This task calls for personal maturity, disciplined responsibility, and emotional stability. It requires empathy, interpersonal perspective-taking, and skill in crisis resolution and mediation. Those who are experienced and skilled in Developmental Therapy–Developmental Teaching often find themselves cast as parent counselor, demonstration teacher, program consultant, conflict mediator, child advocate, mental health expert, in-service provider, and friend. The expectations are endless—because the needs are enormous!

PROBLEMS ADULTS HAVE WITH THEMSELVES

Considering the severity and range of problems presented by children with social, emotional, or behavioral disabilities, it is not surprising that parents and other adults who work with them encounter many personal pressures. In addition to stress from the responsibilities of providing effectively for these troubled children and youth, adults may, from time to time, experience overwhelming personal frustrations. Fatigue, emotional intensity, pressure to be successful, fear of failure, or a sense of aloneness contribute to this stress. It is necessary for adults to keep personal feelings out of their relationships with children, and this requires considerable effort and self-monitoring.

An adult's emotional state is usually detected by children through body language and voice tone. Yet children in need themselves are not able to provide supportive responses for a troubled adult. If an adult is upset or anxious, a conscious effort must be made to convey exactly the opposite attitude to children. Mass confusion in a group, with a host of emotional and behavioral hurdles, can arise if an adult "lets down." Emotional responses, anger, unstructured or ambiguous expectations, and inconsistency by adults result in heightened anxiety and disorganization in children. These conditions may occur because of an adult's fatigue, personal problems, lack of self-discipline, or failure to recognize the need for continuing positive structure and positive feedback. When an adult has a pervasive concern about being liked, looking unattractive or overweight, being an outsider in a group, fearing invasion of privacy, or harboring hostility toward authority, such issues can so dominate the adult's perceptions and responses that an effective program for children may be impossible. There are also times when past experiences, personal attitudes, or even physical attributes can negatively influence an otherwise effective adult. When a child has similar problems to those that are unresolved in the adult who is there to help, it is not likely that the adult can help the child.

Adults must learn to manage their personal feelings and behavior in ways that allow children to function at optimum levels every day. Calm, deliberate movements instill confidence. A low, soft voice sends the message, "Everything is all right"—even if the adult is in personal turmoil. In contrast, an adult's tense, rapid speech pattern may raise anxiety in every child, and impulsive, jerky movements convey an adult who is tense and uncertain.

In this section, we have grouped problems adults frequently have with themselves into these topics: *personal style; understanding different values; housekeeping for a supportive environment; sarcasm, teasing, and slang; professional dress and appearance; and finding and accepting support from others.* These potential problems are minimized in Developmental Therapy–Developmental Teaching when adults successfully fulfill the needed prototypical adult role for a child's stage of social-emotional development and convey the forms of social power needed to foster an individual child's development. Chapters 8 through 12 describe these needed adult skills in detail. Here, we simply summarize the concerns as a reminder that we are all vulnerable to these problems and need to be alert to avoid them.

Personal Style

The most effective resource an adult has for helping children is oneself. Adult behavior usually is the model by which children learn responsible, social behavior. Adults are also models for effective relationships. Children learn responsible conduct and ways to build relationships by imitating others, usually admired adults. Deliberate use of the voice and body can also communicate simple, clear messages to children. For these reasons, adults must be extremely sensitive to their own personal style, to ensure that it represents the attributes and behaviors needed by a child. An effective adult must behave with the responses of others in mind, confine speech to developmentally appropriate verbalizations, physically move in a free and nonseductive manner, change affect and demeanor when appropriate, and convey social values that are also compatible with those in the children's own cultural environments.

Many adults who use this curriculum effectively have endured changes in voice, appearance (including clothing), manner of movement, outward affect, and personal habits to facilitate children's progress. In one particular class, a teacher possessed great understanding and many competencies that were effective with the children. She was able to perform her role adequately, but the children responded to her redirection and verbal input less and less. The program coordinator observed that although the teacher was dedicated, bright, aware, and knowledgeable, her voice was consistently soft and barely audible to children other than the one to whom she was speaking. She seemed to keep her voice low to respect each child's need for privacy. Other members of the team recognized this characteristic as part of her personal style with children, but it had not been discussed as a possible problem in her lack of influence with them.

The teacher's team was feeling increasingly uncomfortable about her lack of effectiveness with the children. They had discussed many strategies for intervening with their problem behaviors, yet they had not talked about her voice quality, to avoid hurting her feelings. This situation, if it was allowed to continue, could have had further detrimental effects on her children and their programs. When the problem was brought out into the open, the team worked out strategies to help her develop more effective verbal communication skills. Initially, she felt that she might not be able to change her voice and was self-conscious when she tried to vary her pitch and volume. But she learned, through role play and a concerted effort in the classroom, to effectively convey a number of different social power messages. Her situation illustrates that growth and change for teachers may often involve personal, and even painful, changes in an adult's style of interacting with children.

Understanding Different Values

Many problems encountered by adults are related to their inability to feel and think as others do; thus they fail to understand and anticipate behavior. These adults may have difficulty understanding and accepting the values of children and their families. They may also have problems controlling a desire to impose their own particular values on others. When this happens, they may have serious difficulties in managing children's behavior and may be unable to help them.

When an adult's own value system is opposed to a child's personal, cultural, or family values, it is hard to avoid direct conflict. Differences may include beliefs about religion, politics, sex, clothing, stealing, illegal drugs, authority, a work ethic, conduct and manners, style of dress and speech, and forms of entertainment, to mention only a few. With Developmental Therapy–Developmental Teaching, an adult must be able to understand the feelings of others and respect each individual's point of view. With this understanding, differences in values may be resolved in ways that should not present roadblocks to progress.

Frequently, children's values are a result of their own emotional needs or environmental influences and may not be in their best interest. Adults working with children in Stages Three and Four will often have children who are growing up in situations where value is attached to being physically strong, being sexually active, coercing others, using drugs, skipping school, or stealing. Through the normal process of identification, these children may adopt such behaviors to meet their developmental needs, yet the emotional drives behind these behaviors are often the developmental anxieties of abandonment, inadequacy, guilt, conflict, or identity.[14] An effective adult understands these emotional undercurrents and finds a balance between the values held by a child's family, the child's personal needs, and the values of society represented by expectations for responsible standards of behavior. It is the adult's job to recognize when these values are conflicting and to help children resolve them.

Housekeeping for a Supportive Environment

Adults who place little emphasis on housekeeping in their own lives should be careful that this trait does not carry over into their work with children and teens. A psychologically healthy environment provides a supportive climate and reflects adults' concern for the children. Neatness, arrangement of materials and equipment, displays, and an attractive atmosphere communicate caring. Displaying children's work helps them feel their accomplishment and acceptance. With children in Stages One and Two, visual cues from their environment help them to organize themselves. Order, simplicity, and organization are essential. With children in Stages Three and Four, an attractive environment conveys an atmosphere in which they are respected and valued. They sense that the surroundings are desirable, and they absorb these qualities into their feelings about themselves and others. There is an increasing sense of being empowered to control their own environment as they become more independent in their personality development. Participating in the maintenance of an orderly environment has benefits for learning personal responsibility at each stage of development.

Sarcasm, Teasing, and Slang

When adults use sarcasm, teasing, slang, or other ways of veiling messages, children are left with feelings of helplessness or confusion about how to respond. This lack of confidence in responding to adults does not foster development. Children may also take such remarks as personally derogatory or as evidence of disregard on the part of the adult. Children who have difficulty developing adult and peer relationships are particularly sensitive to how others view them. They often interpret even the most casual, unintentional comment as a statement of scorn or ridicule.

Adults who persist in using sarcasm or teasing with children often try to defend their choice by declaring that it is their natural way of relating to people. Although their intent may be the best, it shows a lack of sensitivity to how their words and actions are received by others. With Developmental Therapy–Developmental Teaching, the adult role is so critically important in fostering children's progress that when an adult's need to be "natural" overrides being the type of adult needed by a child, it may preclude progress.

However, there can be situations in which slang expressions are useful. Slang can be a casual, relaxed means of communicating if it is easily understood by a child. It can also create a camaraderie between adult and child that may foster the relationship between them, particularly during Stages Four and Five. However, subtle problems arise when adults use slang. First, children may interpret the use of slang as sloppiness. A child with this view will not accept the adult as a source of psychological security, which many troubled children must have. Also, the coequal relationship between adult and child that is conveyed through slang is inconsistent with the need for adult role models during the first three stages of social and emotional development.

Professional Dress and Appearance

Good judgment is important in choosing a wardrobe for work in any setting. It is seldom helpful to make a personal statement through dress, other than one of professionalism. One's personal appearance conveys a clear message to children, parents, and other professionals. Understandably, conditions of dress will vary with the circumstances surrounding a particular program, and many agencies have specific or implied dress codes. In some programs, adults sit on the floor with children, participate in outside play, conduct potentially messy art projects, or physically restrain children. Such activities require functional clothing and shoes that allow freedom of movement. The wrong shoes can slow you down or be dangerous. Few adults escape having juice or paint on their clothes, and anyone who has attempted to restrain a child who is out of control knows how important it is to wear durable clothes. Also, it should not be necessary to remind responsible adults to avoid seductive or revealing clothing. Children of all ages can become unnecessarily aroused by a scantily clad adult. Unfortunately, a few thoughtless adults continue to dress without considering how this will be interpreted by children.

---

[14]See Chapter 2 for a discussion of these developmental anxieties. See also Chapters 8 through 12 for a detailed review of how each anxiety forms as a natural part of social-emotional development.

Attend meetings dressed in "conventional" outfits, to convey respect for the cultural values of the group you are with. It is not necessary to make a personal statement in dress to convey a professional look. Clothes worn when attending meetings with other professionals or parents may be different from those worn when working directly with children. School personnel and parents may object if the adult who is working with their child has an unkempt, unprofessional appearance. It undermines their confidence in the ability of the agency to help the child. Adults who attempt to display themselves through dress can impede communication with parents and others who may have different standards for dress and appearance. When meeting parents or other members of the community, adults should take care that what they do, how they look, and what they say will enhance acceptance of the child and the program, not impede cooperative efforts.

Finding and Accepting Support from Others

Most problems adults have with themselves can be solved. Be open to support from others; they can often help when your own solutions do not produce positive changes or growth in children. However, accepting suggestions from others in not always easy. They may suggest procedures that have been used already with no success. Their comments may imply failure. Even practices that are effective may come under scrutiny or criticism. Many times others will inadvertently convey the attitude that what is being done is wrong. At that point it is easy to give up and become defensive or critical of others' ideas.

Adults who can overcome these feelings by understanding the source of their own anxieties and defenses will be able to use the suggestions of others with positive outcomes for themselves and their children. Supportive colleagues can help. Suggestions can grow out of discussion about what practices are effective, what emotional needs the children are expressing, what procedures need to be changed to respond more precisely to these needs, and what changes can be expected as a result. Most of all, others can provide support by conveying confidence that what is being done is effective.

A final comment may be helpful here about how much of an adult's personal reactions and feelings should be displayed to children. We believe that when an adult is responsible for fostering the social-emotional maturity of children, displaying personal emotions or reactions is not helpful to these children. A child with social-emotional needs does not need to bear the additional burden of an adult's own needs. In situations where there is uncertainty about what is appropriate or needed, a carefully calculated response is more beneficial than an impulsive, emotional one. Avoid the temptation to "let go" emotionally. Such responses put an adult into a conflict cycle with a child (Wood & Long, 1991, chap. 2). It is more constructive to focus on changing the social power base used with a child, modifying the adult role, or selecting a different management strategy. To do this and effectively communicate dispassionate compassion, an adult must be able to use a wide array of management strategies, convey understanding and any adult role that may be required for the situation, and be skilled in using each social power option. One skilled and dedicated teacher summed it up this way:

> *"Personal feelings are simply put aside for the benefit of the social-emotional growth of our children."*

STUDIES OF REFINEMENTS IN PRACTICES DURING IN-SERVICE TRAINING

The first research studies of adults' performance in using this curriculum occurred in the 1980s when the DT/RITS was constructed and shown to be a reliable and valid instrument (Robinson, 1982). In subsequent studies over a number of years, the DT/RITS has been used continually to assess the performance of adults—teachers, aides, parents, clinicians, volunteers, and others. The DT/RITS is the instrument used in all of our performance-based evaluations of adults. This instrument defines the basic practices necessary for each of the first four stages of the Developmental Therapy–Developmental Teaching curriculum. It includes performance items to assess adults' use of materials, activities, and strategies suitable for the children's stages of development. The standards we originally established when using the DT/RITS continue to be helpful guidelines in evaluating adults using Developmental Therapy–Developmental Teaching and in conducting research into the ways these adults acquire advanced skills with this curriculum. We review several of the studies here, highlighting teachers' and aides' skill acquisition and their retention of skills following in-service training. The following standards were used in evaluating adults' performance:[15]

1. Assessment of an adult's competency is based on observed performance while working with children at an identified stage of social-emotional development.
2. The instrument used to assess an adult's performance has reliability and validity for the children's stages of social-emotional development.

[15]Alan Kaufman provided invaluable assistance and consultation in the development of these standards and the resulting performance instrument, the DT/RITS. These standards are adapted from Robinson, Wood, and Combs (1982). The DT/RITS is included as Appendix 2 with permission of the authors and publisher and may be reproduced for use in staff development programs.

3. Criteria used for assessing competencies are provided to the adult before the assessment.

4. Competencies are defined and adult roles specified.

5. Evaluation of performance includes both high-inference and low-inference rater judgments.

6. Evaluation provides both qualitative and quantitative information on the adult's performance while actually working with children.

7. The evaluation procedure is part of the staff development process and program monitoring.

Wood, Combs, and Walters (1986) investigated a number of variables that might influence the in-class performance of elementary school special education teachers and aides of children who have severe emotional and behavioral disabilities. The staff development program was designed to assist the staff in adding Developmental Therapy–Developmental Teaching to their existing curriculum. The in-service program included 37 hours of seminar instruction and an additional 21 hours of individual follow-up, in-class consultation, and individual feedback. The 45 teachers and aides were rated on the DT/RITS in their classrooms at the beginning and again at the end of their training. Data were also collected using the *Developmental Therapy Administrative Checklist.* This instrument contains 41 items generally considered desirable for educational programs serving children with severe emotional and behavioral disabilities.[16] The checklist provided an administrative support score for each participant's school, which was entered into a stepwise multiple regression analysis along with hours of seminar instruction, hours of field supervision and in-class feedback, years of prior teaching experience in special education, years of prior teaching experience in general education, highest educational degree earned, and preparation in the specialized area of children with emotional and behavioral disabilities. The DT/RITS classroom performance score was the dependent variable.

Results indicated that the participants achieved specified proficiency levels in using the curriculum in their classrooms. The results also showed that the participants' proficiency levels were related to the amount of administrative support in their individual schools. Administrative support was the only variable that entered the regression model, suggesting that conditions in a school play a significant role in the skill with which teachers and aides conduct their programs. The lack of significant contributions by the other variables to the performance scores suggests that prior experience and educational level may not be the critical elements in predicting the classroom proficiency of adults participating in a staff development program that provides seminars, individual observations, and consultation in classroom follow-up.

More recently, in a series of statistical and qualitative analyses, Quirk investigated 63 teaching practices contained in the DT/RITS to identify skills acquired by 25 teachers of young children with emotional and behavioral disabilities after participating in their first in-service staff training program in Developmental Therapy–Developmental Teaching (Quirk, 1993). The teachers were in 13 schools in six states; 88% were female and 12% were male. The group included first-year teachers and those with many years of experience; however, none had prior experience with this curriculum. Following a standard introductory 3-day workshop on this approach, the teachers were observed in their classrooms and then rated on the preschool form of the DT/RITS, constructed for working with children in Stage Two. At that time, 20% of the teachers were rated as less than adequate, 36% were in the adequate range, 40% were in the effective range, and 4% were in the highly effective range.[17]

The staff development instructors then periodically followed each participant individually throughout the school year. They observed the teachers' performance and provided both oral and written anecdotal feedback about their progress in acquiring the recommended curriculum practices. At the end of the school year, the teachers were observed and rated again with the DT/RITS. To analyze the changes, Quirk (1993, p. 67) used a series of one-tailed t tests comparing mean performance on each item from pretraining to posttraining. She identified the following 17 skill items that improved significantly:[18]

1. Activities are conducted to encourage participation by each child in the group. (1)

2. (Pre)Academic tasks focus on each child's specific academic objectives. (15)

3. Activities requiring physical movement are interspersed with those that are less active. (20)

4. Materials are used to stimulate individual skills and success. (27)

5. Materials provide opportunities for individuals to participate successfully. (29)

6. Classroom structure is used as a major technique. (31)

7. Children know the behaviors expected for each activity. (32)

---

[16] The *Developmental Therapy Administrative Checklist* is included as Appendix 3 and may be reproduced for use in staff development programs with permission of the Developmental Therapy Institute and the publisher.

[17] DT/RITS quality performance levels were established in a previous study by Wood and Combs (1981) at the time of validation for the National Diffusion Network. See the DT/RITS in Appendix 2 for these performance criteria.

[18] Table 1.7 in Appendix 6 contains the mean performance scores and t values for the skill items that improved significantly after an in-service program in Developmental Therapy–Developmental Teaching. Numbers in parentheses refer to item numbers in the DT/RITS.

8. Expectations are meaningful to children and reflect developmental objectives. (35)
9. Expectations focus on helping children be successful. (37)
10. Structure is consistent but not static. (38)
11. Adults' voice and facial expressions are used effectively. (41)
12. Control of materials is used frequently. (43)
13. Rewards and token reinforcements are not used or are minimized. (45)
14. The process of doing is recognized and used as a reward. (47)
15. Redirection is used as a major strategy to manage behavior. (56)
16. Redirection or reflection is used. (60)
17. Physical intervention is used when needed to assist children in participating. (75)

More than three-fourths of the participants achieved mastery on all of these skills by the end of the in-service training. Six of these skills were mastered by 100% of the participants, whereas none of the skills had been mastered by all of the participants at the beginning of the training. This study led Quirk to conclude that an in-service staff development program can help teachers acquire the fundamental practices needed for a well-managed program that enhances children's successful participation.

Quirk's findings also support the notion that some practices may be too difficult to acquire during a 6- to 7-month training period. In her study, the following eight difficult-to-master or volatile practices were not mastered by most of the participants (Quirk, 1993, p. 77). She defined difficult-to-master practices as those not mastered by more than half of the teachers during the training, and volatile practices as those that the teachers gained briefly and then lost during the training period. The eight difficult-to-master and volatile practices were as follows:

1. Snack Time provides an opportunity to stimulate children's communication and socialization skills.
2. Some activities involve simple role-playing and use of make-believe.
3. Activities are not allowed to extend beyond the "peak" of the children's motivation to participate.
4. Classroom rules are few and stated positively.
5. Verbal interaction between the lead and the support is a frequently used, major management strategy.
6. The support is a response model, encouraging children to participate in acceptable ways.
7. Reflection is used frequently to put simple experiences into words.
8. The adult depersonalizes issues to reduce a child's defensiveness.

Such skills may require longer periods of time to acquire and refine, but they are important for effectively promoting responsible behavior in children. These practices are not achieved without a great deal of self-confidence, self-monitoring, and awareness of one's impact on others. They require personal attributes, verbal skills for interacting with children, and effective interactions with other adults.

Continuing this line of inquiry, Quirk then used qualitative research procedures to study the impact of supervisors' written feedback on the performance of the in-service teachers who were learning to use Developmental Therapy–Developmental Teaching in their classrooms. In 830 observations of 36 practices contained in the preschool, Stage Two, form of the DT/RITS, three experienced in-service instructors provided 404 written feedback references to the teachers they had observed and rated. Their written feedback was coded as either *direct* (feedback about a practice cited as in need of work) or *indirect* (a positive comment about a practice that was observed). The instructors gave repeated feedback on 25% of the observed practices, using direct feedback (citing a skill in need of work) more frequently than indirect, positive feedback.

The instructors' ratings of teachers at the end of training revealed a two-to-one greater acquisition of skills referenced in the written feedback than for skills not referenced, suggesting that instructors' or supervisors' written feedback can play an important part in acquiring the specified practices.

These studies add to our growing data base about how adults achieve proficiency in using this curriculum. The data suggest that adults beginning the program can become proficient within a school year and, with prior experience, can acquire the additional skills needed to increase their proficiency. There may also be a particular sequence in skill acquisition that teachers can use to guide themselves as they begin to acquire skills, keeping in mind that some practices will be too difficult to acquire during the first year they are using the curriculum. Perhaps most important, adults who want to implement this curriculum should use the DT/RITS as a guide. With observation and guided feedback from another team member or a supervisor, proficiency can be achieved.[19]

[19]The complete DT/RITS (four forms corresponding to the first four stages of social-emotional development) is included in Appendix 2. The DT/RITS is also discussed in Chapter 1 in the section on model effectiveness. Chapters 3, 4, and 5 describe the general curriculum practices, and Chapter 6 describes the management strategies included on the DT/RITS.

SUMMARY

In Developmental Therapy–Developmental Teaching, the adult is the agent for change—the fixed point of reference from which children and youth draw strength, motivation, and a view of themselves. In order to be this catalyst for growth, adults must first master themselves. It may be a slow, gradual process, but it will produce individuals who respond to children and youth as skilled listeners and observers, aware of their own impact on children. Acquiring these skills, which are necessary for being proficient in using this curriculum, is a process of monitoring one's own feelings and actions toward others. It is a process of learning to convey the adult qualities needed by each child. It means using verbal and body language with clarity and adjusting responses to the developmental needs of each child.

The personal characteristics of effective adults are more difficult to define than knowledge to be acquired or curriculum practices; however, they generally appear to be the same as for effective adults anywhere. Certain adult attitudes seem to foster excellence: respect for each child, genuine liking, and confidence in children to do their best. Other important characteristics include flexibility in thought and responses, intelligence, warmth, cheerfulness, honesty, objective self-understanding, a desire to succeed, empathy with children and adults, a personal sense of security, self-discipline, and a positive outlook.

If children are troubled or have social and emotional disabilities, parents and teachers will also be dealing with behavior that is taxing both physically and emotionally. They must prepare to face personal attack, failures, and frustrations. When this happens, personal feelings must be controlled and constructive responses mobilized so that these children keep moving toward mastery of the goals and objectives established for them. In short, adults must

be responsive—but keep focused!

As adults increase in proficiency using this curriculum, they will find that being effective is a mental process requiring active engagement. They will recognize that they have an expanding repertoire of effective responses that are tailor-made for accuracy in meeting the needs of each child and every situation. This framework for normal social-emotional development provides the appropriate mind-set and guides the interpretations of what is heard, observed, and concluded about a child. This developmental perspective also shapes how adults respond and determines the type of adult that will be provided to a developing child or teen. Here are some of the key concepts for effectively putting the curriculum into action:

- the typical process for social-emotional development
- individual children's patterns of development
- children's attitudes, feelings, and anxieties about themselves and others
- each child's goals and objectives for social-emotional growth
- group dynamics—in the family, neighborhood, and school
- children's views of adults and authority
- strategies that build adult-child relationships
- strategies that encourage children's participation
- forms of social power
- personal attributes that convey needed adult roles

PRACTICE

Using the key points in this chapter

It takes practice to think developmentally. It also takes practice to put theory into action. These quick anecdotes should give you a chance to try out your skills. Although they are extremely brief, they open the door to a voluminous amount of knowledge that an adult must have (and use) in moment-to-moment decision making. For each episode, answer these questions:

1. What do you think this child is feeling?
2. What developmental anxiety do you suspect may be influencing the child's behavior?

3. Based on the probable developmental anxiety, which type of adult social power will you select in responding?
4. Which management strategies will you try first?
5. What message will you be conveying to the child through your choice of social power and the strategies? Will your message address the child's feelings and developmental anxiety?

Lia

Out on the playground, Lia refuses to play any group games. She says the kids are stupid and she would rather read storybooks. In the past, enforced participation has always led to a confrontation between Lia and her teacher.

Catrece

Catrece sets off an aggressive classmate by deliberately knocking over a jar of paint and pretending it was an accident. Discussing the incident with the support teacher, Catrece repeatedly shouts, "Why are you talking to me? He's the one who messed up my picture. You should be talking to him. You just don't like me! You're always picking on me!"

Eugene

As a result of a fight on the school bus, Eugene has been out of his group and with the support teacher in a quiet room, where he is raging about the injustice and beating the walls with his fists. After 30 minutes, Eugene finally calms down. As the support begins talking to him, Eugene curls up on the floor and does not respond.

Evan and Latanya

Evan arrives late and the group is already playing together, building a fort out of blocks. As Evan comes in he runs past the teacher, kicks the blocks, and begins pounding Latanya. Evan is pulled away by the support and taken to a time-out area to get himself under control so that they can talk about the problem. To everyone's surprise, Latanya quickly destroys her own section of the fort that she had been so carefully building.

PART III

The "Stage Chapters" from Stage One Through Stage Five

CHAPTER 8

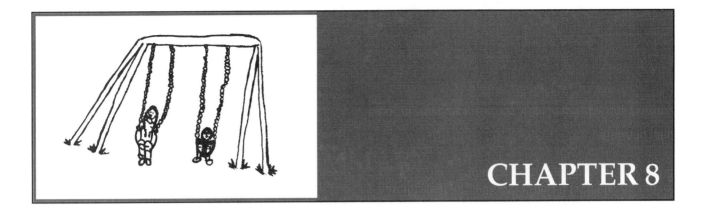

Stage One: Responding to the Environment with Pleasure

I am what I am given.
—E. H. ERIKSON, 1959/1980, P. 87

IN THE BEGINNING: THIS MUST BE A SATISFYING PLACE TO BE

Children who are developmentally in Stage One have not yet acquired completely functioning sensorimotor systems or expressive language—the basic tools needed to participate in human events. They are totally dependent upon adults for care and emotional security. Whether they are typical infants, young children at risk, or teens with severe developmental delays, children in Stage One must rely totally on others to help them become social beings. They need assistance to learn that the world is a satisfying place to be and that people can be trusted to make this happen for them.

When typical infants and very young children have needs, they may not know how to communicate except through vocalizing, body language, and tantrums. A few older children, whose development has been delayed in Stage One, also communicate this way or may have imaginary worlds that dominate them to the point where nothing else exists. Other older Stage One children seem to exist with no world at all, either imaginary or real. They seem to be saying, "If I don't see you, I won't be confused by what your look intends for me to do." Distorted fears and extreme disorganization characterize most older

Stage One Children in Brief

Program goal:	Responding to the environment with pleasure (trusting adults)
Central concern:	Comfort; being cared for; expressing impulses
Motivating values:	Comfort, security, and pleasure
Developmental anxiety:	Abandonment; helplessness; deprivation; uncertainty
Approach to problems:	Impulsive reactions; "fight-or-flight"; no problem-solving skills
Source of authority:	Psychological parent (caregiver)
Type of adult needed:	Adult who provides care and nurture
Effective strategies:	Physical proximity and nurturing touch from adults; repetition of learning experiences; uncomplicated, predictable order and structure in daily activities
Materials, activities, and content themes:	Sensory-based learning that brings pleasure; familiar materials that allow simple physical movements and sensory stimulation; themes of nurturing and care

Stage One children, and there is a pervasive feeling of floundering and futility. In short, they have little or no trust of themselves, others, or the world around them.

The Developmental Therapy–Developmental Teaching program can begin at home during the first year of life with the Stage One curriculum. With young children, it can be provided in the most natural educational setting—an early childhood or Head Start program. Sue is an example of a young child who will benefit from the Stage One curriculum in the day care center.

For older students who are still in Stage One in social–emotional development, the curriculum is offered as a part of an inclusive or special education program in the schools. Older students in Stage One are organized and redirected to new responses that bring them pleasures and recognition from valued adults. Dysfunctional behaviors that are detrimental to themselves and others are not the focus; instead, the students are motivated by the pleasure of the experiences they have in their programs and with the adults. They acquire the fundamental milestone skills as they respond to the environment with pleasure. Edward is an example of an older student who also is in need of a Stage One program as part of his special education.[1]

In whatever setting the curriculum is provided, the goals and objectives for Stage One include the social–emotional milestones of development that are typically acquired during the first 2 years of life. The program focuses on providing children with experiences with adults and the world around them that are arousing, yet supportive and reassuring. It teaches them to trust that the world can be a comfortable, pleasing place. Children in Stage One are dealt with so consistently and so warmly that they begin to trust the adults and the daily program to bring satisfactions and pleasures. This fundamental psychosocial attitude is the foundation for all subsequent social–emotional development. The Stage One program stimulates children to respond to those around them and guides their learning as they begin to grow.

The overall social–emotional goal for Stage One is to learn to respond to the environment with pleasure. Trust in oneself and others is the key to accomplishing this goal, and sensory experiences that bring comfort are the major motivation for learning. The Stage One program provides a place that is so attractive that even the most reticent children are enticed into responding. As children master the

[1]We refer readers who are interested in more details about how the Developmental Therapy–Developmental Teaching curriculum is adapted for children with autism to four references: Bachrach, Mosley, Swindle, and Wood (1978); Newman and Romack (1981); Hendrick (1981); and Wood, Hendrick, and Gunn (1983).

Sue

Sue is almost 3 years old and goes to a day care center. Her teachers and foster mother are concerned about her. The teachers comment about her "strange" behavior, her tendency to daydream, and her lack of response to her surroundings or to people. Her foster mother is concerned because Sue never looks at people even though she seems to be aware of them. She will take her mother's hand or push at her to turn on the TV. Her facial expressions change rapidly, from a flat, serious look to inappropriate grinning for no apparent reason. Her foster mother is also concerned because Sue is not affectionate and becomes rigid when attempts are made to hug or comfort her.

Sue was neglected by her natural mother, who is said to have used drugs often and was extremely withdrawn. Sue's foster mother believes that Sue had a typical early development, but Sue's grandmother reports that she was slow and had strange behavior. Teachers at the day care center also convey concern about Sue's early development. According to them she never cried as an infant but grinned constantly. At 18 months she walked, but in an unusual way.

Now, Sue continues to walk on her toes. Her large-muscle development is delayed, she still needs assistance on stairs, and she is not toilet-trained. Her eating habits are erratic and she cannot, or will not, hold a spoon. She laughs inappropriately at times, frequently stares for extended periods, and avoids looking directly at people. She looks at objects but seldom seeks them. She responds to very few directions but seems to understand her own name because she comes when called. She makes no attempt to imitate the movements or vocal sounds of others but vocalizes sounds with no apparent connection to any object or event.

Sue will benefit from a Stage One program—at home and in the day care center.

Edward

Edward is 14 years old and is an only child. His parents, who welcomed his birth, strive in every way to make life happy for him. Edward is able to perform many hand movements that seem to please him. He laughs for reasons unknown to others, and he resists intrusion or direction from adults. Because he is overweight, he does not enjoy running, climbing, or riding bikes. He communicates with sounds that do not approximate words. His parents and teachers can interpret the meaning of many of his sounds, and they have tried facilitative communication methods with mixed success. When they speak to him with simple, familiar words, he is able to respond to requests, but he does not attempt to use the words himself.

As a young child, Edward spontaneously entertained himself by handling and turning the pages of books and magazines. His teachers used this interest to motivate him to look at the pictures for details. At home, his parents found that Edward enjoyed picture postcards; later, he discovered the pleasure of photographs of family members and familiar people. From these interests, teachers and parents helped him learn skills for keeping postcard collections and photograph albums. In turn, sharing his collections became a source of satisfaction, and Edward began communicating with other students and visitors at home about his collections.

Now, Edward is able to locate and begin at the top of a page in his scrapbooks, follow the order down the page, turn the page when he reaches the end, and begin again at the top of the next page. He looks at details in the pictures and points to selected details. The materials are not unlike those of typical teens, and they provide a source for mental stimulation and pleasure during his leisure time at home.

Edward will benefit from a Stage One program at school and home as he continues to acquire skills that prepare him for the next stage of social–emotional and behavioral development.

sequence of developmental milestones in the Stage One curriculum, social–emotional development is occurring. In the area of Behavior, spontaneous and constructive responses are mobilized. Children learn to respond in organized, purposeful ways to play materials and the routine of activities. In Communication, they are motivated to begin using words to obtain needs. In Socialization, they learn to trust adults sufficiently to watch them, seek them out spontaneously, and accept their touch. In (Pre)Academics/Cognition, they expand their understanding of the immediate world around them and master fundamental cognitive skills—remembering, discriminating, and classifying—expressed with increasing eye-hand and body coordination.

In this chapter we describe the Developmental Therapy–Developmental Teaching curriculum for children who are socially and emotionally in Stage One by considering these topics:

- typical social–emotional processes developing during Stage One
- goals and objectives for children in Stage One
- how the program meets the needs of children in Stage One
- activities designed to accomplish the goals and objectives for Stage One

TYPICAL SOCIAL–EMOTIONAL PROCESSES DEVELOPING DURING STAGE ONE

A significant preamble to social and emotional growth occurs in Stage One that involves basic sensorimotor processes. Beginning at birth (or before), sensory perceptions and awareness are formed by touch, taste, sound, temperature, sight, and body-in-space sensations—major processes that provide the foundations for development and shape a child's future. Figure 8.1 highlights these key processes.

Early sensorimotor experiences rapidly become the foundation for an infant's learning and the subsequent development of children's feelings and attitudes about themselves, the environment, and the adults who provide these experiences (Piaget, 1952). Such experiences produce global feelings of comfort and discomfort that permeate children's perceptions. They begin to know what and who bring pleasure and pain. In the stages of development that follow, these perceptions probably can be reversed and reconstructed, but the foundations are clearly laid at this earliest stage.

For children in Stage One, associating one significant person, the *psychological parent*, as the comforting provider is the first step in normal social–emotional development

Figure 8.1. Key processes of typical social–emotional development in Stage One. The dotted lines indicate the inner life—thoughts and feelings.

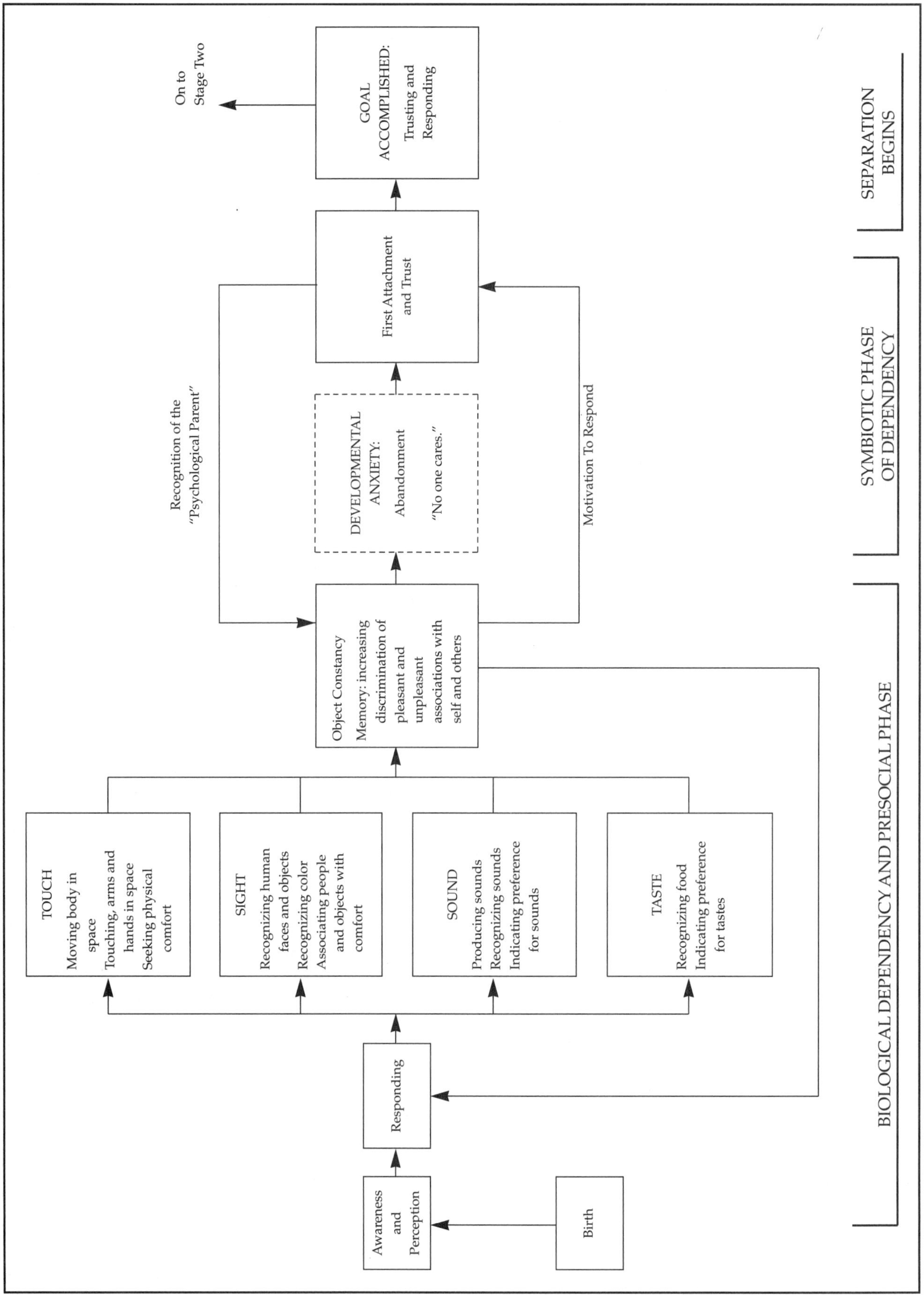

(Mahler, Pine, & Bergman, 1975). For infants and very young children, this natural dependency creates a bond of attachment and trust that is the foundation for all future caring relationships with others. Kegan describes this process as "the incorporated self" (Kegan, 1982, chap. 4). Every Stage One child must have these nurturing experiences in order to develop emotionally. A first developmental milestone is accomplished when an infant looks at the caregiver. This awareness leads to recognition and association of the provider with pleasure. The result is a primary form of relationship called the *first attachment* (Ainsworth, 1973; Bowlby, 1982, 1988; Maccoby, 1980; Mahler, 1968/1987). This first attachment is the foundation for self-esteem and for the later capability to develop interpersonal relationships, a step that finally culminates in the ability to form mature love relationships as an adult (Bretherton, 1987).

The origin of the first relationship can be traced back to the earliest, presocial phase of development in which an infant makes no differentiation of self or others from inanimate objects. Mahler and others have called this the "autistic interpersonal style" (Loevinger, 1976, p. 15). Biological dependency is characteristic of this phase. An infant beginning Stage One does not differentiate self, objects, and others. Physical, sensory, and psychological nurturance are the primary ingredients for continued development. Usually, these are provided by the person who satisfies the child's day-to-day biological needs while providing stimulation through social contact. Parents, teachers, or other caregivers can provide these nurturing experiences.

As the relational bond is established between an infant and the psychological parent, the second phase begins. The bond becomes intense and excludes others. Margaret Mahler, Anna Freud, and Jane Loevinger identify this phase as *symbiotic*—a phase of dependency in which there is an egocentric progression from total dependency to eventual independence from total reliance on the caregiver as the source of all pleasure and comfort. This progress is seen in several universal activities of infancy: feeding (from nursing to weaning and self-feeding), wetting and soiling (to bladder and bowel control), and play (from biological unity with the adult to interactive play with the adult and independent play with objects) (Mahler, 1968/1987; A. Freud, 1973; Loevinger, 1976).

With a basic pleasure-pain response system in place, an infant develops feelings and attitudes about self (one's own body) and about others as sources of comfort. Jean Piaget conceptualized this period of development as the *sensorimotor* period (Piaget, 1952, 1972). Although Piaget originally prepared his model to describe the sensorimotor phase of cognitive development, it is a useful way to think about all forms of early psychological development, including social–emotional development.[2] Piaget describes the mechanism through which development occurs as a process of *equilibration* (Piaget, 1977)—balancing inner needs and outer stimuli so that a child assimilates, accommodates, internalizes, and adapts to the parts of a new experience that bring comfort.

At this stage of development, infants and very young children receive most of their pleasure from comfort in sensory experiences involving their own bodies and other people (Greenspan, 1992). They learn to respond to the environment with pleasure through these sensorimotor experiences, each with the potential for bringing comfort or discomfort (Maslow, 1987). These experiences include eating, touching, and moving their arms, legs, and mouth (sucking, chewing, mouthing, randomly vocalizing, blowing). In a typical infant these behaviors are appropriate, but when they are seen in a severely delayed 12-year-old, the same behaviors evoke feelings of frustration or dismay from adults. However, if they are viewed as indicators of comfort-seeking in a developmental context, these behaviors can provide important keys for motivating a child to begin gradual developmental expansion.

Loevinger cites Piaget's work in *The Construction of Reality in the Child* (1937/1954) as particularly relevant to this phase of development. To form a satisfying, healthy emotional attachment, a child must first be able to recognize the existence of the caregiver as separate from self (Howes, Rodning, Galluzzo, & Meyers, 1988). To do this, early in Stage One, infants typically develop a mental process associated with memory and visual discrimination called *object constancy* (the ability to maintain a stable mental image of an object or person) (Edward, Ruskin, & Turrini, 1992). Loevinger clarifies the significance of this process for subsequent social–emotional development by saying, "The progress out of the [developmental] autistic stage appears to require confidence in the stability of the world of objects. Even symbiotic interpersonal relations imply the existence of another person" (Loevinger, 1976, p. 177). This ability clearly separates the earlier presocial phase of the neonatal period from the later phase of attachment during Stage One, where intense interpersonal dependency, a natural step in development, occurs as a result of consistent physical care and emotional nurturance.

Trust, formed from a satisfying first attachment, is the basis for relationships. It also is the essential ingredient for responding to life's experiences and continuing social–emotional development. Eric Erikson (1959/1980) has built his psychosocial theory of life stages on the emergence of this basic trust during the first stage of life. Trust, he believes, implies not only that individuals have learned to rely on the sameness and continuity of their providers, but also that they may trust themselves.

As young children develop a greater ability to discriminate between what is pleasant and unpleasant, their typical developmental anxiety during this stage emerges— concern about abandonment or deprivation. The psychological parent, the provider of care, nurture, and comfort, is the source of emotional security—the buffer that protects young children from

[2]Jane Loevinger (1976) suggests that these sensorimotor foundations are as relevant to future ego and affective development as to intellectual development.

the developmental anxiety that *no one cares.* If a Stage One child's essential support systems from the caregiver break down from neglect, abuse, illness, or denial of affection, the child is at risk and vulnerable to experiencing *aloneness* or *abandonment* (helplessness and deprivation). This is the first in the series of developmental anxieties all children experience.

When a first attachment fails to develop, infants and young children become vulnerable and at risk for social–emotional problems. If this begins to happen, the child's sensorimotor energies are redirected toward survival instead of expanding outward toward the environment and people (Bowlby, 1973, 1982; Brody & Axelrad, 1970; A. Freud, 1942; Rutter, 1981). Relationships with adults, if they are formed at all, are fragile. These at-risk children are often upset and anxious about anything that is new or changed. There is an absence of constructive, self-directed activity, rage reactions are typical, and resistance to participation in any new activity is common. Such responses are sensorimotor expressions of fundamental emotional insecurity. These early forms of breakdown in social–emotional development also have a detrimental effect on developing intellectual systems, and cognitive concepts are often formed in fragmentary, unrelated bits and pieces (Bretherton, 1987; Edward, Ruskin, & Turrini, 1992).

Trust is the essential foundation for the successful completion of Stage One. Trust—in self and others—must be established prior to the emergence of the two major social–emotional themes that dominate the subsequent psychological development of a child throughout childhood and adolescence: *dependence* and *independence.* The dynamic interplay between these two competing forces permeates the successful accomplishment of each subsequent stage of social–emotional development (Erikson, 1956, 1950/1963; Honig, 1990). The psychological foundations of trust are in place as a child acquires the goals and milestones that complete development for Stage One. Writing to parents, but equally relevant for the Developmental Therapy–Developmental Teaching curriculum, T. Berry Brazelton summarizes the importance of this first stage this way: "A child's expectations and attitudes are formed in the very first months and years of life, . . . and . . . encouragement and stimulation are the second most important gifts that parents can provide their children. Love comes first. But parents also need to understand how their actions can help generate the confidence, the curiosity, the pleasure in learning and the understanding of limits that will make their children expect to succeed and help them do so" (Brazelton, 1994, p. v).

GOALS AND OBJECTIVES FOR CHILDREN IN STAGE ONE

The Goal: *Responding to the environment with pleasure*

There is a basic guideline for conducting an effective program for children of any age who are developmentally in Stage One: Provide sensorimotor experiences in which the children associate adults with comforts and pleasures, and design activities to evoke responses from children that bring them pleasure and satisfaction. This guide is the result of selecting program goals for objectives that are the milestones in social–emotional development that typical infants and young children acquire during the first 2 years of life.

The Developmental Therapy–Developmental Teaching curriculum divides the key milestones of doing, saying, caring, and thinking into the four curriculum areas of Behavior, Communication, Socialization, and (Pre)Academics/Cognition. Although each of the developmental milestones for these curriculum areas can be further analyzed into smaller steps for teaching and learning during Stage One, we find it helpful to begin program planning with a focus on the key milestones. In this way adults are able to identify the key characteristics of individual children and to offer programs, activities, materials, and intervention strategies that are matched directly to milestone teaching objectives for fostering social–emotional growth.[3]

The previous descriptions of Sue and Edward, two vastly different children, illustrate the similarities in the characteristics of social–emotional and behavioral development seen among Stage One children of different ages and types of disabilities. In the following review of major milestones for this stage, look for these characteristics in Sue and Edward.

Behavior Milestones for Stage One

In the curriculum area for Behavior during Stage One, the general goal for children is to learn *to trust their own body skills.* Program objectives begin with simple levels of awareness, to be sure that the sensory channels are receiving stimuli. At this basic level, responses that indicate attention to any stimulus are encouraged, even a fleeting moment of attention to an event or person. If infants, young children, or older children with severe delays in development show little awareness or response to their environment, their program should begin at this point. Here we teach the most fundamental milestones that will mobilize them to interact with adults and the environment. It is through this interaction that they begin to respond to people and events around them. When this behavior begins to occur more frequently (more than might be considered a reflex response to a sensation), the emphasis shifts to evoking consistent motor responses for specific activities. Eventually, these skills blend into more complicated motor responses, with increasingly complex environmental interactions that include attempts at self-

[3]Our analysis of the content in these four curriculum areas is contained in Appendix 4 and includes the processes directly related to the curriculum in Stage One.

Stage One
Behavior Milestones

Goal: ***To trust one's own body skills***
Indicate awareness of sensory stimuli.
React to stimuli with sustained attending.
Respond to stimuli with a motor behavior (intentional behavior).
Respond to complex environmental and verbal stimuli.
Independently respond to play materials.
Spontaneously move from area to area, indicating recall of routine, without assistance.

Source: Abstracted from *The Developmental Teaching Objectives for the DTORF–R,* by Developmental Therapy Institute, 1992, Athens, GA: Developmental Therapy Institute.

help and sensorimotor play with toys. The final milestones to complete the goals and objectives for the Behavior sequence are the indications that a child recalls routines, the location for each activity, and simple behaviors associated with participating in the activities.

Communication Milestones for Stage One

In the curriculum area of Communication during Stage One, the general goal for children is to learn *to use words to gain needs.* The primary task is to learn to communicate intent—in other words, to understand that language has meaning and can be used to meet needs. It is important to realize when working with Stage One curriculum that development of speech may be unrealistic for some children because of disabilities, but that all children must be enabled to use some communication system.[4]

The first milestone for development in the Communication area of the curriculum emphasizes vocalizations, to indicate that the speech apparatus is operative and to stimulate vocalization as a means of interacting with the environment.[5] As children learn to recognize caregiving adults, there should also be vocal exchanges between the adults and children.[6] These vocalizations are indications that an infant or child is ready to learn to associate sounds with people, events, and objects. Developmental progres-

[4] Several alternative and augmentative communication systems are available to use in conjunction with the Developmental Therapy–Developmental Teaching curriculum. For example, manual communication, communication boards, facilitative communication, and electronic devices may be effective in assisting some students to acquire a communication system. We recommend working closely with a specialist when considering these approaches with Stage One children.

[5] For students who are learning alternative communication systems, lack of control over hand and finger movements (or eye movements) may require supplemental objectives in the area of Communication.

[6] Although some infants and young children do not appear to look directly at adults when they are in the beginning of Stage One, they often are aware of adults and attend to the sounds made around them, following the adults' movements visually without appearing to do so. This veiled watching is also evident in defensive older children and teens.

Stage One
Communication Milestones

Goal: ***To use words to gain needs***
Produce sounds.
Attend to the person speaking.
Respond to verbal stimuli with a motor behavior.
Respond to verbal cues with recognizable word approximations.
Use recognizable word approximations (or words) spontaneously to describe, label, or request.
Produce recognizable single words to obtain desired actions from adults.
Produce recognizable single words to obtain desired responses from peers.
Produce meaningful sequences of words to obtain desired responses from others.

Source: Abstracted from *The Developmental Teaching Objectives for the DTORF–R,* by Developmental Therapy Institute, 1992, Athens, GA: Developmental Therapy Institute.

sion along several Communication dimensions occurs rapidly at this point, with children beginning to understand spoken words (receptive language) and to make sounds (and eventually words) to communicate their needs to others (expressive, intentional language). During this time, they make the transition from prompted, cued language to spontaneous language, beginning with single word approximations and gradually expanding to recognizable word sequences and sentences. As social communication skills grow, the final milestone in the Communication area for Stage One is the use of meaningful sequences of words to obtain desired responses from others.

Socialization Milestones for Stage One

In the curriculum area for Socialization during Stage One, the goal for children is to learn *to trust an adult sufficiently to respond.* To successfully foster socialization of children in Stage One, the curriculum assists them in learning to play, acquiring language and communication skills, and responding to adults. Milestones of development in the area of Socialization during Stage One focus first on being aware of others and learning to respond to others. These skills expand a child's capacity to learn by imitating and interacting with others, leading to organized—although still solitary—sensorimotor-based play. As a child's positive experiences with adults increase, the child is increasingly responsive to closer relationships, greater participation, and more active learning by imitating the valued adult. Often, children indicate that this is happening by responding willingly when adults call them or make requests of them. The last milestones for Socialization in Stage One include the spontaneous participation of a child in parallel play with peers, indicating awareness of others and the desire to participate. The final milestone is spontaneous contact with familiar adults.

Several developmental processes become apparent as the Stage One Socialization milestones are acquired: First, as a child indicates awareness of others, watches the behavior of others, and responds when spoken to, there is an evolving sense of self as a separate being, apart from the adults and objects in the environment. This is an important first step in social–emotional maturity. It allows for the further development of attention and organized interactions with adults, activities, and play materials.

During this process, there are signs of awareness and interest in other children (Beckman & Lieber, 1992). Although play during Stage One is primarily sensorimotor, it is beginning to take shape as a social activity in parallel play, when a child indicates awareness of a peer and shows interest in imitating the other child's play or using the same toys. Although early solitary, parallel play is a necessary step in the process of sensorimotor learning, exploration, and self-organization, play should also begin to expand gradually into interactions with other children. Increasing communication skill is the new tool children use for play and exploration of toys and materials as they advance through Stage One (Goncu, 1987).

A second major Socialization theme during Stage One is a growing relationship between the child and adult. Early in this stage a child is almost completely dependent upon adults.[7] Stage One children are learning that adults meet needs and provide protection, care, and comfort. They learn that adults make it possible for them to achieve satisfaction from exploration and activity. They also learn that adults protect them from injury, hurt, and discomfort.

[7] This dependency is described by some theorists as a symbiotic relationship in which both child and adult benefit emotionally from the relationship.

Stage One Socialization Milestones

Goal: ***To trust an adult sufficiently to respond***

Indicate awareness of others.
Attend to others' behavior.
Respond to adult when name is called.
Engage in organized, solitary play.
Interact with adult nonverbally (or verbally) to meet needs.
Respond to adult's verbal and nonverbal requests to come.
Demonstrate understanding of single verbal request or direction.
Convey a beginning awareness of self.
Participate spontaneously in parallel play (with awareness of peers).
Spontaneously seek contact with familiar adults in several environments.

Source: Abstracted from *The Developmental Teaching Objectives for the DTORF–R,* by Developmental Therapy Institute, 1992, Athens, GA: Developmental Therapy Institute.

This learning gradually shapes a sense of themselves as separate from others, and with this awareness come increasing amounts of independence.

Assertions of independence are a significant step toward the Socialization goal for Stage One: learning to trust adults sufficiently to respond to them. Such assertions signify trust in themselves and trust in adults to guarantee that an action will have a satisfying outcome. In the following chapter, we discuss the expansion of this trust in the social–emotional development of young children during Stage Two. And we recognize that children are ready for the next stage when we hear them say,

"I want to do it myself!"

(Pre)Academics/Cognition Milestones for Stage One

In the area of (Pre)Academics/Cognition during Stage One, the goal for children is *to respond to the environment with mental processes of classification, discrimination, basic receptive language, and body coordination.* Preacademic skills achieved during Stage One aid a child in developing basic cognitive processes leading to mental organization. The earliest preacademic skills are sensorimotor and memory processes with people and objects, the same skills needed for development in the curriculum areas of Communication, Socialization, and Behavior. These fundamental milestones in (Pre)Academics/Cognition emerge from coordinated development of skills in the physical, language, and behavioral areas. Similarly, development in all domains is dependent upon a basic level of mental awareness and attention to relevant stimuli. This achievement is followed by physical exploration and interaction with the environment, essential for early mental development. Fine- and large-muscle movements (associated with the development of 18-month-old children) are necessary for learning during this stage and are therefore included in the sequence of (Pre)Academics/Cognition for Stage One. (Motor skills continue to expand during subsequent stages.)

Another critical milestone for children in Stage One is the ability to imitate the physical actions of adults and other children. Much subsequent learning depends upon this skill. Other fundamental skills that must be acquired to achieve the goal for (Pre)Academics/Cognition in Stage One include understanding the names of familiar objects; using verbal approximations (or words) spontaneously to label, describe, or request objects or events; visually discriminating between objects and their spaces; and matching objects with identical, similar, and different characteristics. As children progress through Stage One they become able to transfer sensorimotor learning and memory into symbolic learning—from objects to pictures. They are able to name details in pictures and can match pictures as they previously had matched objects. They learn the concepts of *same* and *different* and achieve the last (Pre)Academics/Cognition milestone in Stage One when they produce recognizable single words (or phrases) to label simple pictures of familiar objects, animals, or people. These foundation skills prepare them for continuing progress in all areas of the social–emotional curriculum, including (Pre)Academics/Cognition, during the next

Stage One (Pre)Academics/Cognition Milestones

Goal: ***To respond to the environment with intentional body movements and basic mental processes of memory, classification, and receptive language***

Note: The first two milestones are the same as the beginning milestones for the area of Behavior.

Show spontaneous short-term memory for people and objects.
Respond through imitation with body movements to complex environmental and verbal stimuli.
Spontaneously imitate simple, familiar actions of adult.
Show rudimentary fine and large motor skills associated with an 18-month developmental level.
Indicate understanding of names of familiar objects.
Respond verbally to adult cues with recognizable word approximations.
Use recognizable word approximations (or words) spontaneously to label, describe, and request objects or events.
Match shapes of objects with corresponding space.
Identify own body parts (at least four).
Recognize simple details in pictures.
Sort two types of similar objects with slightly different attributes.
Produce recognizable single words to label simple pictures of familiar objects, animals, or people.

Source: Abstracted from *The Developmental Teaching Objectives for the DTORF–R,* by Developmental Therapy Institute, 1992, Athens, GA: Developmental Therapy Institute.

stage of development. When children come to an adult spontaneously to share their ideas, we recognize that they are beginning the transition into cognitive thinking for Stage Two. This is when we may hear them saying,

"Look what I did! This is a . . . "

HOW THE PROGRAM MEETS THE NEEDS OF CHILDREN IN STAGE ONE

In planning a Developmental Therapy–Developmental Teaching program for children in Stage One, continually be aware of the goals and developmental objectives that the program must foster. Because children in Stage One have very short attention spans and few skills, an effective Stage One program must not lag in stimulating—and restimulating—the children's motivation to respond. Activities must mobilize their basic processes of awareness, response, sustained attention, comfort, and trust. In each activity, involve every sensory channel: tasting, touching, hearing, smelling, and seeing. Encourage children to develop preferences for simple choices and to communicate their preferences in productive ways. Teach them to use language—at first using simple sound approximations, later linking words into phrases. Always choose activities and materials that encourage development across all four curriculum areas, and stimulate eye-hand coordination and control of the large muscles of the body. Focus on the sensory channels of learning, and emphasize positive behaviors that bring pleasure.

At its most basic level, the Stage One program can be viewed as a stimulus-response paradigm. A potentially useful random response from a child should be followed by repetitions of the stimulus that can evoke the response repeatedly. These repetitions should be continued until the response becomes a part of the child's existing sensorimotor response network. At that point, the response can be freely generalized into new situations by pairing the learned response with a new stimulus. Here is an example: A child beginning Stage One vocalizes randomly, with nonspecific sounds. Vocalizing itself is the source of stimulation and pleasure. The parent or teacher then selects one or two of these sounds, puts them together into a pattern, and uses them during Snack Time (sensory pleasure) as a way to relate and for vocal play (people pleasure). Soon the sounds become a way for the child to attract the adult's attention and for the adult to catch the attention of the child. This exchange is a basic unit for learning in the developmental hierarchy but it rapidly becomes too simplistic. (The steps we follow to teach this basic procedure are summarized in a following section.)

The next phase of this sensorimotor learning process is one of elaboration and expansion of a basic response into many new ones. This phase represents a much more complex level of development, an indication that the basic stimulus-response has been expanded for new uses and adaptations. Expansion of a child's skills requires using existing responses, however limited, and building new, more complex skills from them. With new stimuli the child can develop new responses and greater adaptation somewhat independently. This is the time to provide Stage One children with child-centered activities.

Organization and Structure as Sources for Psychological Security

For emotional security—to develop and learn—most infants, very young children, and older children with or without developmental delays need order and predictability in their lives. Because most Stage One children lack the rudiments of organized behavior, they must be provided with order and organization through their daily experiences. Although most have acquired the basic processes for responding to sensory stimuli, almost all Stage One children require environments that are orderly, organized, and predictable. These conditions foster the cognitive processes necessary for organized, self-directed behavior and self-confidence. It is no wonder that these children often appear restless or seem to fail to pay attention. If their environments are unpredictable or chaotic, they have even less chance for emotional security than they would in stable environments. Dysfunctional environments lack predictability and this is destabilizing to young children. They may have difficulty with sustained attention, organizing their bodies in space, sequencing experiences, associating, classifying, discriminating, and recognizing cause and effect. To complicate the problem, they frequently have difficulty with relationships, which require understanding and using language.

The Stage One program uses structure as one means of providing psychological security. *Structure* refers to the elements of organization in an environment that foster each child's internal organization.[8] Structure—both implied and obvious—conveys order, predictability, and security. The schedule itself, followed consistently every day, provides the basic framework around which activities are planned and rules and expectations for individual children are conveyed. The expectations (rather than rules) for Stage One children of all ages are as follows:

Expectations for Stage One Children of all Ages (Rules)

- There is a defined place to do each activity.
- All children participate.

[8]See Chapter 6 for a discussion of structure as a behavior management strategy.

- Certain behaviors must be used to obtain materials and participate.
- After an activity, materials are put away in a specific place.
- When one activity ends, another begins.
- Words (or sounds) are part of every endeavor.

Obviously, not all children will respond to these expectations in the same way. Some will participate spontaneously; others will resist or ignore attempts to engage them in an activity. Some will request materials using well-articulated words or phrases; others will make random sounds or no sounds at all. Some will seek the adults and materials, whereas others may have to be physically assisted (moving them through the movements) for rudimentary participation. The important point is that there are established expectations for each child as an individual, and all children must meet those expectations, even if it is necessary to assist them. In meeting expectations, young children experience comfort and pleasure. This structure is a powerful source for emotional stability.

Continuity across activities with a unifying content theme, the schedule of activities, routine procedures, rules for expected behaviors, and the amount of adult control are parts of structure. The same routine repeated day after day fosters development of *sequencing*—anticipation of what comes next and a sense of knowing what activity and expected behaviors are to occur with every activity during the day. When adults repeat each activity many times to increase children's familiarity with the process, always in the same physical space, the children are given further cues to aid them in learning specific behaviors for particular activities.

The idea that there is a beginning and an ending to an activity must be taught. A motivating beginning prepares children for the organization within an activity. A defined ending is equally important because it prepares them to "let go" of one endeavor and shift their mental focus to something new, which will always be pleasant in a Stage One program. An effective ending also expands memory by reflecting positively on the steps just completed. Ending with a review prepares the children for advanced cognitive skills that will be developed in subsequent stages and that will enable them to review, summarize, and evaluate an experience.[9]

Guidelines for Choosing Activities and Materials for Stage One

The essential ingredients for expanding development are motivating and developmentally appropriate activities and materials. Provide not only a variety of materials and activities that stimulate adaptations of basic sensory responses, but also experiences that expand the children's current preferences into new skills. In selecting activities and materials, it is important to consider the characteristic needs of Stage One children: *pleasure, organization,* and *functional language.*[10]

Pleasure in doing is the focus. Be sure that every material and activity will bring a satisfying outcome for the children. Definitely forget skilled performance as an outcome. Here are some general guidelines we use to be certain that we are choosing activities and materials that capture their attention and sustain participation:

- Use materials and activities that stimulate the senses and have pleasure-producing feedback.
- Select materials that can be easily manipulated.
- Plan for repetition of simple, pleasurable activities and favorite materials.
- Be aware of ways to motivate each individual.
- Use group activities that provide opportunities for social interaction.
- Fill the program with communication opportunities.

Materials and Activities Stimulate the Senses, with Pleasure-Producing Feedback.[11] Most pleasurable feelings of children in Stage One involve their sensory systems. They have definite preferences between the sensory systems, with unique strengths and weaknesses in certain of the sensory modalities. For this reason, it is important to choose activities and materials that incorporate as many of the sensory modalities as possible every day. In that way, if one sensory system is underdeveloped or damaged, other systems can be tapped, so that growth and learning will continue. Examples of materials high in positive sensory stimulation are shaving cream as an art material, jack-in-the-boxes, water (especially warm water), sand, feather dusters, fragrances, simple instruments for making musical sounds, and food. We avoid associating food with negative experiences because it is the most basic, intrinsic form of nurturing. For this reason, we seldom withhold food as a behavioral contingency. Rather, we view food as an essential part of a caring environment.

A detrimental aspect of using sensory activities and materials with some Stage One children concerns behaviors they may have that are perseverative, self-stimulating, or nonproductive. These behaviors can present major

---

[9] Chapter 4 describes procedures for introducing and ending activities at every stage of development.

[10] Younger Stage One children benefit from activities planned around unit themes such as "Water Play," "What Is It?" "Listen," "Touch," "Do This," and "Baby Animals." For older Stage One students, unit themes and activities such as "My Room," "The Kitchen," "Using a Mirror," "Going Out To Eat," and "Tools" prove to be developmentally motivating when they are also age-appropriate.

[11] Appendix 5 contains a summary of numerous motivational systems from theorists, including those with applications for Stage One children.

blockades to successful intervention. Two strategies useful in dealing with these types of behavior are (a) to substitute an entirely different behavior for the nonproductive behavior and (b) to modify the form of the behavior so that it enables a child to become involved in a more meaningful activity.

The first strategy—substitution of an entirely different behavior for a nonproductive behavior—is often effective with children who are so occupied with a particular form of self-stimulation that they would engage in this activity most of the time if left to their own devices. These children are often functioning with very few apparent skills. For example, consider Caren.

Caren

Caren spends all of her waking hours rubbing paper between her fingers. She has no language and no play skills and shows little response to sensory stimuli other than paper. When her paper is removed, she has a tantrum. If she is aware that any paper is nearby, she protests until she obtains it. Once the paper is in her hands, no other stimuli can break through her self-absorption with the paper.

It is apparent that Caren cannot learn any new skills until she learns to respond to some other source of stimulation than paper. Her teacher uses the first approach, removing all paper and providing alternative forms of stimulation that arouse her. Once this occurs and Caren is convinced that there is no paper to be found, learning can occur. Her teacher hopes to tap into some of the same sensory modalities—in this case, tactile stimulation—as substitute sources of the pleasure that rubbing paper provided. Gradually, Caren learns to roll clay, assemble simple jigsaw puzzles, put animals in a barn, open containers, and look for hidden objects to put in the containers. As she learns the movements for each of these activities, she is also experiencing alternative tactile stimulation, and her need for self-stimulation, rubbing paper, is reduced dramatically.

Sally's parents and teachers use the second approach—modifying her self-stimulating behavior by expanding her current love of twirling into new movements using different muscles and new patterns for twirling and spinning.

Sally's preoccupation with visual and vestibular stimulation provides an easy way for her parents and teachers to blend new movements into the old ones that gave her so much pleasure. When she comes home from school, one of her parents picks her up and gives her a "Hello Dance," around and around. At school, her teachers do the same thing, with circle games such as "Ring Around the Rosy" and circle dances added to Music Time. Sally is then taught to discriminate between acceptable and unacceptable times for "going around in circles."

Sally

Sally loves to twirl objects with her hands. She attempts to twirl anything she touches, continuously spinning the objects in circular motions. She is so visually alert and so physically active that she is seldom still. Her restless, constant motion and determination to find objects to twirl exhausts her family and her teachers in their efforts to keep her from hurting herself or destroying everything around her.

Effective use of either of these strategies is dependent on their occurrence in the context of warm, pleasurable interaction between the teacher and the child. In fact, the success of the entire Stage One program relies on this relationship.

Materials Can Be Easily Manipulated. Abstract ideas, many pictures, and words are often very difficult or impossible for children in Stage One to understand. It follows, then, that their attention is more easily cultivated when they are presented with concrete material that can be easily manipulated to obtain a desired sensory experience. Real objects and real experiences are better than pictures. When children become involved with materials and activities, they begin to learn the associations between doing something and achieving results. This is why it is so essential for the results to bring pleasure. When the experience is also functional and accompanied with associated spoken words, understanding expands and the actions take on meaning. For example, the word and concept of *cup* take on meaning for a child when the word is used in combination with the act of drinking, especially when the cup contains something that the child enjoys.

There Is Repetition of Simple, Pleasurable Activities and Materials. Repetitive action offers many possibilities for increasing sustained attention to tasks. Simple activities that have been done before (and repeated frequently) are preferred. One caution, however, is that an activity or material must be motivating to a child, or repetition will be nonproductive at best, or possibly destructive. Activities and materials involving pleasurable sensorimotor movements are generally welcomed by children if they are familiar and associated with pleasure, not frustration or confusion. It always seems to surprise adults that children in Stage One often choose the same activity or toy over and over again. It is through repetition that children explore all of the possibilities of the material, and they do so with decreasing need to rely on an adult to show them how to do it.

With children beginning Stage One, it is appropriate to repeat the same activity day after day for weeks at a time. Progress can be slow with some children, and repetition can help them to develop a history of successful experiences so that they become sufficiently comfortable to participate in group activities using the same materials. As new ways to use these materials are introduced, learning is consolidated and then generalized.

Examples of simple activities with repetitive actions to stimulate beginning awareness and increased attention are dipping and splashing children's hands in water, blowing bubbles, ringing bells, and dropping clothespins in a can. Activities with the same elements for attention, but with increased complexity for older children and those younger ones who have advanced in Stage One, include simple storytelling using toys and objects (rather than pictures); washing dishes in water; blowing different sizes of bubbles; repeating rhythms to match a rhythm model on a tape; stirring food while cooking; sorting fruits, vegetables, or eating utensils by size or use; and raking leaves. Many activities that are functional in nature have this type of repetition and should be included in the program if they are equally motivating.

As such activities become increasingly familiar, they should be linked together into simple unit activities around a unifying theme.[12] In this way, Stage One children learn other related skills such as fine- and large-muscle coordination, simple relationships, and sequencing. They also are learning to associate words, objects, people, and actions. Without such skills, these children have few available avenues for increasing productive behavior and social–emotional competence. However, with newly learned skills that bring them pleasure, they see activities and materials as more meaningful. They have learned productive ways to participate and bring about desired results. They naturally begin to pay greater attention, respond more freely, and participate with increasing spontaneity. Thus, a productive cycle begins where attention fosters development of new skills, which in turn increases attention, producing more skills and new understandings. As Stage One children progress through this cycle of learning and development, their capacity for attending to complex stimuli is increased for longer periods of time.

Ways Are Found To Motivate Each Individual. Pleasure in participation results from doing things that bring pleasurable results. Many Stage One children's sources of pleasure come from sensorimotor stimulation. For this reason the program must focus on arousal of the senses (touch, taste, sight, hearing, and body-in-space). Another important source of pleasure comes from children's enjoyment of interactions with adults. Activities that combine these basic motivators are most effective. For example, variations of pat-a-cake and peek-a-boo involve nonverbal interaction with others. For older children in Stage One, taking turns with adults in simple games or household activities offers opportunities for social interaction and is a motivator for children to participate. As Stage One children interact with adults, they associate the adults with comfort, protection, and good feelings. An added benefit of the interaction between adult and child during the Stage One program is the experience of social reciprocity. These associations become the basis for the development of Stage One children's trust in others.

Each child must value the task to be done. As we have discussed previously, the attention an individual gives to an activity will depend upon the value that individual places on it. We look for any positive indication or movement toward a material or activity as a possible indication of interest. Some children explore materials by touching or looking. Others actively engage in using a material or moving it in repetitive ways. Others may be able to sustain interest for long periods of time. The problem with all this variability in interest and attention span is that adults often select materials, plan activities, and establish an arbitrary standard for performance that is not uniquely suited to each child and that may result in resistance, disinterest, or negative behavior from several children in a group. Too often adults blame the children, identifying them as troublemakers or blaming their disability for their lack of participation, whereas in fact, it may be the task itself that caused the unacceptable behavior and lack of participation. In an effective Developmental Therapy–Developmental Teaching program, boredom and task frustration should never happen.

Group Activities Provide Opportunities for Social Interaction. Activities and materials at all stages of development should involve others. Even during Stage One, it is essential for the program to provide abundant opportunities for satisfying interactions with others, both peers and adults. Without such skills, social–emotional competence and responsible behavior never emerge.

Genuine group activity is almost impossible for beginning Stage One children. Their own needs drive their participation. Individual, parallel activities for very short periods of time may be helpful to them as they begin to independently explore ways of using a material or activity. However, watch closely to see that an independent activity holds a child's interest and fosters mental organization. Unstructured independent time should not disintegrate into repetitive motions that reinforce meaningless,

[12] See Chapter 4 for a discussion of unit themes and their contributions to the curriculum's effectiveness.

unacceptable behavior. Even though they may be engaged in individual activities suited to their own interests and skills, beginning Stage One children, left to "play" alone, generally display little constructive, purposeful behavior. Alert adults should maintain contact with each child to ensure that the independent activity is providing what is intended for the child's continuing progress.[13]

In addition to opportunities for independent exploration, children in Stage One also need to bring these skills and interests into interaction with others. At first, these group exchanges are very brief and carefully guided by adults to see that everyone maintains an interest and has an opportunity to participate. Waiting for turns is seldom a focus in a Stage One activity. (It is downtime for all except the one child who has the turn.) We prefer to see group activity that evokes simultaneous participation by all of the children. Everyone can participate together in activities such as chants, unison responses, and imitation of rhythm movements, with the adult providing the model. In this way, children have maximum amounts of participation and are not waiting around, doing nothing, while others have their turn. A unison activity is also more psychologically comfortable for many children because it allows them to participate without a direct focus being placed on them.

Play has unlimited opportunities for both individual and group activities that stimulate a wide range of skills in Stage One children, in all four areas of the curriculum. Even though it may look unstructured and free, it is a mistake to adopt a laissez-faire attitude toward play. Play and the playground provide many productive ways to assess a student's independent, purposeful behavior in independent play. Social interactions are also stimulated during play. The playground arouses the senses. Children usually want to run wild, yell, chase, and climb. While adults may want to use this time to catch their own breath, they should not fail to use it to benefit the children. With careful planning and selection of suitable activities, play and playgrounds provide great opportunities to teach and learn socialization and interpersonal skills, especially during Stage One.

Body management skills (fine- and large-muscle movements) are acquired during play and on the playground during Stage One. We systematically include a sequence of learning activities every day, indoors and out-of-doors, to foster locomotion skills and sensory integration, including crawling and creeping, walking and running, climbing, ascending steps, jumping, and hopping. Nonlocomotion skills such as bending, stretching, and leaping are also included, both indoors and on the playground. Manipulation of objects is another essential physical skill for Stage One children to acquire. We particularly like to focus on these skills using balls and beanbags during indoor play and on the playground: rolling, catching, throwing, bouncing, kicking, pulling, pushing, and lifting.

We also consider carefully the effect of play toys and equipment on individual children. If a child needs to acquire interactive play skills, we find it necessary to first provide two sets of the same preferred toy, so that one child can imitate another who is at play with the same toy. With the accomplishment of parallel play, it is usually not long before the first child shows some interest in interactive play, reaching out to take the other child's toy or bringing the two sets of toys together. A rocking chair in a classroom and the merry-go-round on a playground are other examples of equipment that can attract children. The rocking chair may be an effective way for adults to nurture some young Stage One children, and the merry-go-round may keep children occupied for extended periods of twirling. However, if such equipment is used by children to retreat and isolate themselves, it becomes detrimental to progress. The equipment should be removed until the children find alternative activities that are both satisfying and more developmentally productive. Another example of the individual ways children use toys during Stage One is that of a bouncing toy, which may increase repetitive, nonproductive, isolated behavior in some children, while it may provide an appropriate physical outlet for another child with restless, aggressive behavior.

The Program Is Filled with Opportunities for Communication. Development of language and communication skills cuts across all four curriculum areas and is especially significant for children throughout Stage One. Language is so intimately connected with self-awareness, behavioral control, cognitive development, and social interactions that language delay or dysfunction can be profoundly detrimental to the overall development of a child (Goldstein & Gallagher, 1992; Kagan, 1982). In the Developmental Therapy–Developmental Teaching curriculum, language learning is a part of every activity. Development of functional, social language by Stage One children is the most important skill to be developed. It is a major program effort during Stage One, providing abundant opportunities for children to learn communication skills. Children are taught to use language as it is intended to be used—for requesting, regulating behavior in others, expressing feelings, and conveying information.

Very early language, including new words, imitations, or syntactic constructions, is taught to children beginning Stage One through a controlled vocabulary and by adult models.[14] For every activity, we establish a consistent vocabulary that describes the procedures and routines the children are expected to learn (even though, at first, they

[13]Even during free play, we suggest that adults scan the group constantly and make some form of contact with each Stage One student at least every minute.

[14]See Chapter 6 for a description of how adults verbally interact, using controlled vocabulary with children in Stage One. Children must learn during Stage One that the world is a verbal place and that words have associations with real events.

may not be able to produce the words themselves). We call this process *building a controlled vocabulary.* We have been asked if it is not a contradiction to emphasize an environment abounding with opportunities and encouragement to communicate while controlling the vocabulary. This is a perceptive question and reflects the subtlety and skill needed by adults working with children in Stage One. Adults must provide both conditions—creating meaningful communication and language exchange as a part of every activity while controlling the words that are used so that children do not have word overload.

Many children in Stage One cannot or will not talk. The essential ingredients needed to begin this process are a need to communicate and trust in the person with whom the communication will be made. Many children with severe disabilities in Stage One need abundant prespeech experiences (sounds exchanged in an interactive way with another person). When they begin to use the same sound repeatedly for the same purpose we introduce the next steps in communication. The steps are as follows:

1. Begin with a desire on the child's part for something (a cookie, a toy, your attention).
2. Provide a single word consistently in association with the desired object.
3. Catch the child's attention as you say a word.
4. Encourage the child to imitate the sound. (This may be done by providing another adult as the response model, by providing the word yourself and then imitating it yourself, or by catching the child making a similar sound and responding by imitating the child.)
5. Convey that you are listening for the word (or an attempt at the sound) so that the child can obtain the desired object.
6. Provide the desired result when an attempt is made. The child's IEP or IFSP should specify the quality of the speech communication that is expected.[15]

Each of these steps contributes to a learning sequence to help a child learn to use words. Try using all of the steps in a sequential way. However, if a child does not progress, there has been a breakdown somewhere in these steps. When it is located, focus on that particular step until it seems to be successful. Then go back and try the sequence of steps again. They should produce results.[16]

We have found that if children in Stage One are exposed to a vast selection of words for every experience, they tend to retreat from the overload and confusion. They often block out the noise or simply retreat from making an attempt to select those that make sense to them. Such a simple expression as "Let's have dinner" may become enormously confusing if a child hears adults use different words to describe the same event. Here is an example of ineffective efforts by three adults—the teacher, aide, and parent—to communicate to one very young child in a preschool program:

TEACHER: "It's lunchtime."

AIDE: "What do you want to eat?"

PARENT: "Let's eat."

PARENT: "I have your favorite dish today."

TEACHER: "It's hot dogs on the menu today."

AIDE: "Food!"

These expressions were all used by the adults when they talked with the child about lunch. It is not surprising that he appeared to ignore them all and did not show interest (or understanding) of what was about to happen in his program. They were using 24 different words for the same event! We recommended that they agree upon a phrase to use consistently. They chose "It's time to eat!"

With a controlled vocabulary, specific, functional words, phrases, or sentences are carefully chosen and used by all of the adults involved with a child, in any setting. The child is expected to learn the meaning of these expressions and eventually to use the words spontaneously. The words have direct reference to the activities and materials being used (*go, stop, put, milk, cookies, paste, Play Time*). We use an individualized, controlled vocabulary with each child in Stage One who is having difficulty mastering the fundamentals of social communication. In this way, the adults' simple, consistent language patterns serve as models for the children to imitate. We actually post the vocabulary we are teaching on the wall in the particular activity areas where the words apply, to remind the adults that they must use the selected words as models for the child. In this intensive approach to communication, the curriculum's emphasis is on social, functional language. Children always respond to this strategy and begin to learn the associations between events and sounds—the idea that there is a particular sound that should be used for each situation.

It is important to embed language experiences in social context, because language implies social interaction. Social relationships and feelings toward others have a powerful motivating effect on developing language. There is no doubt that infant games such as peek-a-boo and pat-a-cake and simple exchanges of objects have a role in teaching children the pleasure of social interaction.

---

[15] See also the sequence of Communication milestones in Stage One specified on the DTORF–R.

[16] Children with autism and those challenged by hearing disabilities will have a particularly difficult time acquiring speech. It has been suggested that children with autism cannot make progress in speech until they can attend to the speaker's face, especially the mouth. We have found that both attention and motivation (through relationship and a desired result) are important factors in their progress.

Adults should keep in mind that, with prelanguage children, communication programs should focus on forming social bonds, fostering the children's awareness of each other using verbal interactions, and encouraging them to take turns by modeling simple activities such as taking turns dropping objects in a box. Here is an example:

> The adult looks at the child and says, "Put in," demonstrates the action, and then says, "Your turn." The child looks at the adult and then drops an object in the box, thus simulating the reciprocal turn-taking that occurs as part of this communication. As this pattern is repeated with looks and nonverbal exchanges, the child begins to imitate the verbal exchange as well as the action, usually selecting "Your turn" for the preferred communication to control the adult's action.

Once the necessary socialization experiences are incorporated into a program, children are more prone to be motivated to use language functionally; in other words, social experiences give reasons for a child to communicate. And, just as social experiences provide the motivation for communication, cognitive processes provide the material children will talk about. It is important that, as a language program is set in motion, adults realize that language is dependent on the development of cognitive processes and on social relationships. Object constancy, matching, discriminating, sequencing, and classifying are among the cognitive skills that must develop to provide the support necessary for language production. In short, cognitive objectives should be seen as part of a good language program.

The Adult's Role: Caring, Nurturing, and Organizing

The major responsibility for adults working with children who are developmentally in Stage One is to assure them that their responses to the environment can be pleasurable. This goal is achieved as they learn to trust the use of their own bodies, to trust adults, to meet their needs with language, and to develop a basic level of cognitive organization. Adults who are successful in teaching these goals are masters of arousal and enticement, understanding the primary importance of providing pleasant sensory experiences, and maintain predictable, secure, comfortable environments.

Adults who are effective in fostering the development of children in Stage One arouse and mobilize them to respond to materials, people, and activities in predictable, pleasure-producing ways. These adults are quick to recognize the sensory preferences of each child and use materials and activities that tap into these preferences. These adults are bubble blowers, bearers of wonderful aromas, music makers, touchers, people who dazzle with color, movement, and sounds. These adults introduce materials that are soft and hard, cold and hot, fuzzy and smooth. They whisper, nurture, burst with excitement, or display infinite calmness and patience.

The quality of a child's response is not of concern at first. What is initially important is for each child to simply respond to the adult and the material, and for the response to bring pleasure. The relationship that develops from these exchanges between adult and child is warm and responsive, providing comfort and pleasure in interaction. At the same time, the adult is equally careful to pull back when a child indicates sustained, independent attention to an activity. When a pattern of interaction between child and adult is established, the child begins to make rapid gains in acquiring the key developmental milestones for social–emotional competence needed for continuing development at the following stage.

Most Frequently Used Strategies That Foster Development in Stage One

The strategies adults use with children who are in Stage One can mean the difference between a child's "tuning in" or "tuning out."[17] Teachers, parents, and other professionals who are effective in working with Stage One children must be certain that the strategies they use stimulate responses, participation, satisfactions, and pleasures for every child. We have found that eight strategies are used frequently by adults who are effective in working with these children. Although these strategies are discussed at length in Chapter 6, we review them briefly here with a focus on those we have observed to be uniquely effective in fostering social–emotional development during Stage One.

Positive feedback and praise	Pleasure from positive sensory experiences; nurturing, caring adults (warm voice, soft touch)
Motivate with materials	Familiar and pleasure-producing; sensory-based manipulative materials; nurturing content themes
Structure and organization	Familiar routines; controlled vocabulary
Redirection	Usually a physical touch combined with a verbal cue

[17]The Stage One form of the DT/RITS in Appendix 2 contains performance items to assess the use of materials, activities, and strategies by adults working with children in Stage One.

Reflection	Controlled vocabulary mirroring action, needs, people, or objects
Control of material by adults	Beginnings to introduce materials; endings to review and put materials away with adults' help
Physical proximity	Nearness; eye-level contact; body contact; touch
Physical intervention	Patterned repetition of needed movement; moving through an action with help from an adult; protective holding

We have gone into considerable discussion throughout this chapter about the first three strategies—*positive feedback* through pleasing sensory experiences, *motivating materials* that are manipulative and have nurturing effects, and *structure* through familiar routines and controlled vocabulary. Several other strategies have unique applications in Stage One.

To rekindle failing attention or to guide children away from nonproductive behavior into participating in meaningful activity, we frequently use *redirection* in Stage One programs. With children beginning Stage One, redirection is physical and is often combined with moving a child through the motion. This might involve turning the child's head toward the focus of the task or moving the child's hands into a substitute motion that approximates the self-stimulating motion but applies to the specified task. This strategy requires a gentle touch that conveys assurance and is in no way invasive.

As children progress through Stage One, simple verbal redirection is paired with physical redirection, eventually becoming almost entirely verbal. Care is needed that the verbal cues, paired with the physical assistance in responding, are simple, direct, and with clear meaning to a child.

Reflection is also an effective strategy to teach fundamental associations between actions, objects, and words. It provides the verbal cues, applying words to events. It is through this strategy that functional language becomes a part of a child's repertoire. Our discussion about controlled vocabulary cautions adults to be selective in the words used in the Stage One environment. It is essential to keep this in mind when using reflection.[18]

Adults' *physical proximity* is one of the most effective strategies for arousing and redirecting children. For a child who will not respond to verbal arousal or to highly exciting materials, we find strategies that bring the child in close physical proximity to a valued adult to be particularly effective. Nearness, eye-level contact, and touch often mobilize a child to pay attention. A brief caress, a touch on the cheek, or a whisper next to the ear often arouses a child to look at the adult or the material. When attention is not forthcoming, we also may put a hand gently under a child's chin and turn the child's face to obtain visual attention. When we do this, it is essential for the result to bring pleasure to the child.[19]

Another strategy with a unique application in Stage One is a type of *physical intervention,* in which a child is assisted in moving physically through an activity (called *motoring* by some early intervention specialists). Physically moving a child's hands to pattern a motion or touch a material is used to stimulate a response, increase the child's awareness, teach a new response, or increase participation.[20] The quality of the response is not the focus. An example would be moving a child's arm to assist in shaking a tambourine to the rhythm of music. In this way the child is aroused by the touch of the adult and the patterned repetition of the movement. This repetitive patterning enables the child to eventually perform the activity without assistance.

We close this section on strategies with an extended illustration of a typical indoor Play Time with Stage One children in an early intervention preschool program. Because play is so important in every child's development, we selected this particular example to illustrate how play skills can be taught if children do not already have them. This example illustrates the role of the adults and emphasizes the importance of stimulating social language as a part of play. It also illustrates how participation is obtained, the use of controlled vocabulary by the adults, sensory-based manipulative materials, and the need for continued physical intervention and proximity of the adults to maintain meaningful attention and participation of five children who would otherwise be unable to sustain attention and interact independently with the play materials.

ACTIVITIES DESIGNED TO ACCOMPLISH THE GOALS AND OBJECTIVES FOR STAGE ONE

For very young children and those with severe developmental delay, we plan activities that are each about 5–10 minutes long. The length of time is extended as children gain skills, motivation to participate, and understanding

[18]See Chapter 6 for further discussion of how these strategies are used with children in Stage One.

[19]Some children react to a stimulus with a delayed response. For them, direct stimulation may be overwhelming, and they often retreat from responding further.

[20]When using any form of physical intervention, touch, or moving a child physically through a motion, be certain that the child does not fear adult touch. Children conditioned by past experience to fear touch do not usually discriminate between adults they can trust and those they cannot trust. In these situations, avoid the use of strategies requiring physical contact

Playtime in Stage One for Donald, Carla, Sammy, Emily, and Foster

It is the first day of school in the fall. Donald attended the summer program but the other children are all new to the teachers and the room. The teacher reports:

"As the students enter, I move down on my knees and into their line of vision, announcing with animation, 'It's Play Time!' Donald is familiar with the room and routine from the summer program, so he moves over from the door with Carla, Sammy, Emily, and Foster, who are all greeted individually with touches and smiles and the phrase, 'Carla's here,' 'Sammy's here,' 'Foster's here.' Sammy allows a quick hug, then sits on the rug. Carla pulls away from the hug but tolerates my hand on her back. Emily is still cowering by the door with her head down and her fingers in her mouth. My aide, Peg, stoops to Emily's level, puts an arm around her, and tells her quietly about a doll in the cabinet. With her arm gently around the student, Peg begins to move her over to the play area.

"The play area is designated by the red shag rug. Except for a small wooden jungle gym and a large barrel on a wooden frame, most of the toys are in the toy cabinet. Foster begins to wander away from the play area, rocking from foot to foot, jabbing one hand into the other, and making a throaty noise. I call his name, but he doesn't seem to hear, so I move to him, put my hand on his back, and lead him gently back to the play area, saying, 'Play Time is on rug.' When we pass near the jungle gym, I move his hands out to touch it, saying, 'You can climb.' He starts climbing.

"Peg has finally moved Emily to the toy cabinet, and she encourages her to open the cabinet. After several unsuccessful attempts, Peg puts the student's limp hand on the knob and pulls with her. When Emily sees the doll, she squeals and shakes her arms aimlessly but doesn't reach for it. Peg brings the doll close to Emily and says, 'Doll. This is a doll.' Finally Emily reaches for the doll, and Peg then says, 'Say *doll*, Emily.' After several repetitions Emily attempts 'daw,' and immediately Peg gives her the doll and a big hug, saying, 'Emily has *doll*.'

"Carla is now sitting on the floor, staring at the wall. I move over to her and emphatically say her name while I rub her back. She still doesn't seem to hear me, so I blow in her face. She is startled and looks at me. I am still calling her name. Then I say, 'It's Play Time.' I put a fuzzy white ball in her hands, whispering, 'This is a ball. It feels soft." She starts rubbing the ball and begins to roll it around.

"As I turn my head, I see Sammy giving Emily a big push into the cabinet door. Emily starts to cry. I comfort her. Then I take Sammy's hands firmly, saying, 'Sammy, push the pig to Emily.' I move him over to a big stuffed animal and help him push the toy across the room.

"Donald is lying on the floor, his eyes half open, repeating bits and pieces of a TV commercial, completely oblivious to anything outside of his own body. I intercept him immediately, saying, 'Donald, sit up. Look at the barrel.' I take his hands to give him encouragement but not to do the task for him completely. Once he is sitting, he is aware of me but needs motivating to begin to respond to the toys. I say, 'Donald, do you want to play in the barrel?' He nods his head, and I say, 'Tell me.' He then says, 'I want to play in the barrel' and moves to the toy. I've been working on helping him refer to himself as 'I' during the summer program. I do not give him what he wants or let him do what he wants until he uses the right pronoun because I know he can do this. I supply him with the words he needs if he can't say them."

of the expectations set for them. In this section we briefly describe activities we have found to be highly motivating and effective in enabling children to acquire their individual goals and objectives for social–emotional competence and behavioral responsibility during Stage One within a group setting.[21] The following list shows activities modified for younger and older children. Those marked with an asterisk should be included in an abbreviated program where other programs provide the remaining activities.

[21]See also Chapter 4 for a description of activities and instructional practices and how they change in this curriculum to reflect the developmental changes of children in each stage.

Very Young Children	Older Children in Stage One
Play*	Hello*
Hello	Work*
Work (Readiness)*	Play*
Wiggle	Story*
Story	Art
Art	Music
Bathroom (self-help)	Self-Help
Snack*	Outside (exercise)
Outside (exercise)	Snack*
Surprise (imitation)	Special
Table (more readiness)	Special (imitation)
Music	Good-bye*
Good-bye*	

Although the length of each activity will be extended as children's ages and attention spans increase, the same basic types of activities are used whether the children are very young or are older students still in Stage One. The schedule of activities provides a balance between quiet and active learning experiences. It also offers broad opportunities for the acquisition of the needed developmental milestones. In all of these activities for Stage One, we prefer that there be little or no waiting for turns.

Activities should foster participation by all of the children in the group. Unison activities are often the most effective for this stage. Waiting for extended periods, while another child has a turn, increases downtime and reduces opportunities to acquire skills through involvement and practice. There is ample opportunity in the next stage of development to learn to take turns. Unison activity promotes imitation—an effective way to acquire new skills. There are three primary types of imitation, most of which can be taught in unison activities: imitating use of materials, imitating physical movements, and imitating sounds.

Generally, the lead teacher serves as the model for imitation when the activity is conducted as a group. (See the example below during Surprise Time. We also call the activities "'Do This' Time.") Individual children will respond with varying degrees of imitative ability. Some may respond spontaneously to previously learned actions but will have difficulty generalizing to new actions. Others will have no imitative ability at all and will have to be moved through the motions of the activity by the support teacher.[22]

"Going on a Picnic"—A Unit for Stage One

To illustrate how we use a single content theme to unify the activities during a day or week, we summarize "Going on a Picnic" here. In these brief descriptions, we indicate the curriculum focus that may receive the greatest attention in each activity. Readers may find it helpful to identify the specific social–emotional milestones (presented in a previous section of this chapter) that could be used as specific instructional objectives for each activity.

Play in Activity Centers. During this time, children are encouraged to interact freely with materials and with the teachers, as long as their responses are purposeful. If not, the teachers aid them in interacting with a material by modeling its use, luring them with the material's sensory appeal, moving them through use of the material, or giving verbal redirection.

At this particular Play Time for the Picnic theme, teachers have put play materials in the activity centers related to a picnic, such as baskets, tablecloths, napkins, kitchen utensils, food containers, dishes, and plastic foods. These materials are new and have been added to familiar materials such as a Nerf basketball and hoop, building blocks, musical instruments, a cash register, play money, magazines, puzzles, a rocking chair, a record player, and records. This activity keeps the adults as busy as the children, to ensure that their play is purposeful and satisfying to them. Behavior, Communication, and Socialization skills are emphasized during this time.

Hello Time. This first structured activity is used to help children organize themselves in a designated area and to develop awareness of themselves and the other children in the group. During this time, activities involve greeting the children by name and encouraging them to look at one another or greet them with a handshake. (In some programs, Hello Time is used before Play Time if the children seem to need additional help in organizing themselves for purposeful behavior in the play areas.)

Each day this week, for Hello Time, a large, simple picnic scene is placed on the wall. The lead teacher brings in a box that contains a mirror and laminated photographs of each child. The teacher greets the children by name as each one looks in the mirror. She then holds up each photograph in turn and asks, "Who is this?" The child is encouraged to answer with any appropriate response, even as little as "Me," or a gesture. Other children are also encouraged to look at and identify the photograph. The children take their photographs to the board and place them on the picnic scene, usually with the help of the support teacher. Communication and Socialization skills are the focus for this activity.

Work Time. The children generally work individually at a table, sitting together as a group. The primary emphasis is on developing Stage One preacademic skills. The activities are individualized to each child's IEP objectives for readiness skills. Materials and activities include scissors, simple puzzles, busy-boxes, putting objects in containers, matching objects or simple pictures, discrimination and

[22] See Chapter 6 for a discussion of lead and support interaction and Chapter 7 for a description of the distinct roles of lead and support on the team.

classification tasks, and tasks involving fine motor skills. In addition to individual tasks, children work together in unison as a group. For example, a good way for teaching color discrimination would be to put a large pan of blocks in the middle of the table and have the children choose between red and blue blocks. Once they each have made the correct choice, they put their blocks back in the pan in unison. (A second Work Time may be added as needed during the day. See Table Time, below.)

For the Picnic unit, children have individual preacademic tasks prepared in picnic boxes. Individual assignments are planned for work on their specific objectives in sensorimotor and readiness skills. Some tasks are designed to use real objects and simple pictures related to the theme (using a can opener, sorting eating utensils, folding napkins, and matching food pictures). This further reinforces the concepts and vocabulary involved in the Picnic theme.

Wiggle Time. The primary focus of this activity is exercise—to develop large-muscle skills, a sense of the body in space, imitation skills, and the ability to follow simple directions. Exercise time may include activities like being swung in a blanket, doing simple body movements to a rhythm, crawling through a tunnel, walking over a beanbag, or running through a sprinkler on a hot summer day (Goldman, 1981).

In another area of the room, or in the gym, the tablecloth from the picnic is used to play a modified parachute game. Children hold the edges of the tablecloth and move it up and down while the teacher chants, "Up and down, up and down . . ." in a rhythmical sing-song. The children are encouraged to sing along. They also go "under" and get "on" the tablecloth. The emphasis here is on Behavior, (Pre)Academics/Cognition, Socialization, and Communication skills.

Story Time. This is the time to foster Socialization, Communication, and (Pre)Academics/Cognition. It is a time for abundant nurturing by closeness with adults. Sometimes physical closeness and touch are carefully planned as a part of the strategies needed for individual children. At other times the closeness is simply a natural part of the relationship between adults and children.

With children who are beginning Stage One, books and pictures are not used for Story Time. Manipulative objects such as dolls, cars, farm animals, puppets, toy dishes, or balloons might be used to tell a simple story and to increase involvement and active participation by the children themselves. Story lines are extremely simple and involve themes such as putting a baby to bed, putting farm animals inside fences or barns, making puppets say "Hello," make-believe cooking, or blowing up balloons. Advanced Stage One children respond to very simple pictures, but story lines are simple: "Look—a cat. The cat says meow!" We find teacher-made storybooks to be most effective in evoking responses and maintaining the attention of Stage One children (Hendrick, 1981).

For the Picnic theme, the teachers use a tablecloth (the same color and pattern as the one in the picnic scene at Hello Time), a picnic basket, cups, an empty milk carton, paper plates, and play food (pictures of food or small amounts of real food are used if they are more motivating). For the next few days, the teacher tells a story about going on a picnic and leads a very simple role play of the story line. Later in the week, the teacher introduces a simple teacher-made book using photographs of the children going on a picnic—a repeat of the same story line they played out in previous Story Times. The emphasis during this activity is on Communication and (Pre)Academics/Cognition skills.

Art Time. Art Time can be particularly effective in providing Stage One children with pleasurable tactile and visual stimuli that encourage responses and sustained attention. Materials such as finger paints, scented Magic Markers, preglued stickers, tinfoil, cotton, and colored macaroni for pasting are successful. Because movements are not refined, these children cannot be restricted to a limited working space such as a single sheet of paper. Instead, the entire table is covered with butcher paper as a work area for the whole group (Williams & Wood, 1977).

Bathroom Time. This is a time for development of self-help skills. Toileting, zipping, buttoning, and washing hands are important skills to learn. Because the activities are time-consuming, it is important to have other activities available for the children who are waiting their turn. For some groups, we have ongoing play in the activity centers at this time with one teacher supervising self-help skills and the other involved with the play. Self-help skills are also taught, in context, within the natural events during the day. For example, removing and putting on jackets when entering and leaving the room, removing shoes before jumping on the trampoline, and brushing teeth after lunch are prime teaching opportunities. Keep in mind that self-help objectives in Developmental Therapy–Developmental Teaching emphasize participation in the process of learning rather than requiring skilled accomplishment of a task.

Snack Time. Snack Time is used to provide children with the nurturance implicit in providing food. It is also a major time for stimulation of social language. Children are expected to communicate their interest in receiving the snack. Some children will be able to give only fleeting eye contact as a response, whereas others will be able to use words to meet their needs. The IEP specifies the level of performance that will be acceptable for each child. In spite of their levels of performance, all children receive snacks. Eating may be the only activity sufficiently motivating to mobilize basic behavioral and language processes in some children who are beginning Stage One.

(With some groups, as many as three time slots have been allotted to eating activities.) As the children develop more skill, less time needs to be allocated for this type of activity (Bachrach, Mosley, Swindle, & Wood, 1978).

Everything needed for a picnic is in a picnic basket for Snack Time this week. As the teacher brings out cups, napkins, sandwiches, paper plates, and milk, she asks the children to name or describe each item. Then they eat together, with Communication objectives emphasized.

Outside Time. Outside play is primarily devoted to the development of large-muscle skills, but it obviously also has an impact on the development of social, language, and behavioral skills. Games of chase, swinging, sliding, climbing, and sand play, as well as ball handling and riding on tricycles or wagons, are effective. We also like to bring some indoor activities out-of-doors when the weather is nice and the children are ready to handle the shift in setting. Music rhythms, stories, and snacks make easy transitions and prepare children for generalization of learning to new settings (Paget & Stueck, 1981).

The children follow the teacher on a hike around the playground looking for a special spot for their picnic. The teacher brings the picnic basket and asks each child to assist in carrying it for part of the hike. On the hike, they are led up and down a "mountain" (a steep incline at the edge of the playground), over a bridge (a balance beam), through a "tunnel" (a large cement culvert on the playground), and the "lake" (the basketball court). When they reach the picnic spot, the teacher spreads the cloth on the ground and they all sit down to rest. Communication and (Pre)Academics/Cognition skills are emphasized throughout this activity.

Surprise Time. Surprise Time is an activity devoted to teaching imitation skills—that is, repeating old actions with new applications. Many cognitive concepts and actions (body parts, large-muscle skills, and language) can also be taught, even though imitation is the focus of this particular activity. For example, touching various body parts, jumping, "Simon Says," "Follow-the-Leader," "London Bridge," bubble-blowing, and coloring—in fact, almost any Stage One activity—can be an imitative activity as long as the teachers provide a model for use of the materials, actions, or language (Wood, Hendrick, & Gunn, 1983).

For this unit, each day Surprise Time focuses on self-help skills associated with the Picnic theme. One day, the children use their experiences with the art materials in the previous activity to refine their sandwich-making skills. When the sandwiches are made, they participate in wrapping and packing them in the picnic basket. Behavior skills are the focus for this activity (Newman & Romack, 1981).

On other days, Surprise Time involves dance. Simple dance and rhythm movements offer motivating opportunities to imitate others' movements. Dance and movement also hold children's attention for extended periods of time. Walking, hopping, swaying, clapping, stomping, leaning, and skipping are all effective rhythmic movements. Resistant children, seeing the others having so much fun, usually loosen up and respond. And confused, disoriented children often use imitation of another person's movement to orient themselves. These activities also contribute to large-muscle coordination, eye-hand movements, social awareness, and knowledge of body parts. Circle activities are particularly effective during dance time. Dancing and singing around a particular child is an example of socialization as a part of this type of activity. Picking up young children and dancing to music with each in turn is another pleasurable alternative. When this is planned, the others will need to be guided into a parallel dance movement and not expected to simply wait (Purvis, 1981).

Table Time. This is a second Work Time for this particular group. The teacher has prepared a rebus chart illustrating the procedure for making a bacon, lettuce, and tomato sandwich. Children are given precut forms representing each item and are assisted in making sandwiches that are then pasted on paper plates (Pre)Academics/Cognition and Behavior skills are emphasized.

Music Time. Almost all Stage One objectives can be learned through musical experiences. Often overlooked, but extremely important, are the gains in Socialization from musical experiences. Children become aware of other children, often for the first time, as they are drawn together by a musical activity (Purvis, 1981). Drums, rattles, cowbells, and other rhythm band instruments arouse children, keeping them involved and participating. Songs and vocal sounds stimulate basic language processes. With songs, all of the following Communication milestones for Stage One can be practiced:

- vocalizing with others (in unison)
- vocalizing by imitating others
- vocalizing in response to others
- using verbal approximations
- using single words and sequences
- using words to get something from another person

Two music activities are specifically designed for the Picnic unit. The first utilizes the picnic basket, which contains small pieces of food. The children are seated in a circle. With a popular tape playing in the background, the teacher helps them pass the basket around the circle. When the music stops, the child holding the basket is encouraged to look in the basket, name the food, reach in the basket, and take some out. The second activity, sung to the tune of the Campbell Soup song, focuses on using words to label pictures. While holding up pictures of various foods, the teacher sings, "Mmm, mmm, good; Mmm, mmm, good; Sammy tell me what is . . . Mmm, mmm, good." Play foods, food containers, or actual foods could also be used. The focus during this period is on Communication and Socialization skills.

Good-Bye Time. This ending to the day's activities is a time to organize the children at the table as the program ends. Again, children's names might be the focus as each is given a personal good-bye from the others in the group, in unison. A good-bye song like this is particularly effective in signaling the end of the program and reemphasizing that others are all a part of the pleasurable Stage One experience (Williams & Wood, 1977).

Back at the table, the teacher leads the children in a simple review of the day's activities. Communication skills are emphasized. As the Picnic theme is repeated throughout the week, pictures and objects are reviewed at each Good-Bye Time to assist children in linking activities and meanings. At the end of the review, the teacher says good-bye to each child by name, encouraging each to respond to another child with a similar

"Good-bye. See you tomorrow!"

SUMMARY

For children of any age, with or without disabilities, who are in Stage One of social–emotional development, almost all significant experiences occur through sensory channels, producing physical comfort or discomfort and psychological pleasure or pain. They cling to sources of pleasure and retreat from potential discomfort and psychological pain. This is why most of the intentional actions of infants and young children during Stage One (as well as the actions of older children and teens with severe disabilities who are still in Stage One) are directed toward increasing comfort and pleasure and reducing physical and psychological discomfort and pain. At times, their sources of pleasure may seem strange or disconcerting to adults, but to ignore sensory pleasure as a motivation is to ignore a most important force in early human development. The quest for pleasant, satisfying results can be channeled into productive responses that bring comfort. This process is the foundation for a child's motivation to respond and to trust.

Mastery of this first stage of social–emotional development requires mobilization of a child's rudimentary ability to respond, pay attention, participate, communicate, and spontaneously interact with people, objects, and activities. Adults using the Stage One curriculum encourage new responses from very young children, with sensitivity to their need for comfort, stimulation, organization, and pleasure. Underlying this priority to provide pleasurable outcomes for children participating in the Stage One experience is an understanding of the equally important need they have for an organized, familiar, secure environment.

Children in Stage One—whether they are progressing in a very normal way through the first year of life or are older students acquiring developmental skills at a slower rate—are dependent on others for any progress they make. Experiences provided by others aid them in the development of organizational concepts such as body-in-space, impulse control, attention, communicating, relating, remembering, discriminating, sequencing, and generalizing, to name only a few. It is the adult's responsibility to provide organization and structure for these experiences within the context of stimulating pleasurable activities that facilitate emergence of these basic skills. Consistency and structure help both in organizing the children and in providing them with a sense of psychological security.

Adults create the emotional foundation for all subsequent social–emotional development to occur in a child's life. A child's feelings about people, relationships, and the world originate in these earliest relationships and from the experiences they have with those who provided for them. With care and nurture, and predictability in routines, adults provide the satisfying results that encourage a child to respond with trust. Adults must guide children to respond intentionally in ways that bring them comfort and pleasure. The resulting trust in people and the world around them is the foundation necessary for progress during the next stage.

Accomplishment of the goals and milestone objectives of Stage One prepares a child with the foundation for social–emotional competence and for progress in the next stage of development, where skills become more organized and increasingly complex. The basic elements for constructive behavior are mobilized: awareness, attention, responding, remembering, and trusting one's own responses. It is the adults who make all of this possible.

We summarize the essentials of the program for children in Stage One with these guidelines for teaching activities in a Stage One program that you may find helpful:

- Plan for the systematic transfer of learning. The same communication and motor skills learned in one activity should be used in other activities. A simple weekly unit theme helps in planing for these connections.
- Provide activities that arouse the sensory modalities and evoke communication responses. Try to incorporate several senses in every activity.

- Conduct each activity so that it has a clear, consistent beginning and ending. Announce when a previous activity is over and a new one is beginning: for example, "Work Time is over! Now it's Yum-Yum Time."
- There should be little or no waiting during a Stage One activity, unless the material is so arousing that it really commands all the children's attention.
- Continually stretch the activity to a maximum for productive involvement, then draw back and end the lesson before interest and motivation lag.
- Expect every child to participate in cleaning up after each activity. The cleanup directions consist of only four words: "Time to clean up." You may have to teach the actual physical motions employed in bending, reaching, grasping, and putting things away.
- Continually be alert to the children's smallest responses in an activity.
- Carefully sequence each small step in the learning process. When any material is shown and a response is expected, many small steps are needed. Because Stage One children usually cannot accomplish these steps spontaneously, you may find it necessary to physically move children through the process.
- Know when to accept a particular response and when to expect a higher-level response. This knowledge comes from knowing how the sequences of milestones for social–emotional development apply with individual students.
- Provide the motivation and leadership for every activity. In times of crisis continue the group activity, drawing children back to the materials, while your aide responds to the individual child who is diverted from the group.
- Make some form of contact with each child each minute. Without such psychological arousal, the children may rapidly become disoriented or lose touch with reality, often reverting to meaningless behavior.
- Discover what to do to help a child in crisis. Be alert to recognize the child's anxiety or feeling, then communicate the necessary warmth and reassurance that the situation is under control.

PRACTICE

Using the key points in this chapter

Donald is a 3-year-old with a disability who is beginning an early intervention program. Imagine that you will be his teacher. As you and his parents plan an IEP for Donald at the preschool and an IFSP for his parents at home, consider the following information about Donald. After reviewing this brief information, think about how you will answer these questions, which will be raised during the IEP meeting with Donald's parents.

1. What social–emotional goals and developmental milestones should be emphasized for Donald in each curriculum area—Behavior, Communication, Socialization, and (Pre)Academics/Cognition?
2. What appears to be Donald's major emotional need?
3. What does he appear to value and what will be sources of satisfaction that might be used to motivate him to respond to the environment?
4. Which developmental anxiety seems to be present, and is another emerging?
5. What type of adult role will you try to convey to Donald when he joins your group of young children at school?
6. What management strategies will you use to convey this role and to assist Donald in acquiring the identified milestones at the preschool and at home?
7. What activities and materials might provide Donald with the best opportunities to respond and participate, at home and at school?

Donald

Donald wanders around the room for a while and then sits and blankly stares. He does not seem to be aware that there is anyone or anything else in the room. Occasionally he repeats TV commercials or makes bizarre, meaningless statements. His mother demonstrates her attempts to engage him in interactions with her by calling his name and asking him to bring her a toy. He gives her only fleeting glances and ignores the suggestion and coaxing to bring her a toy. She says he is afraid of some stuffed animals and any new people. Even with his parents, Donald is unresponsive and rarely touches them. Both parents are discouraged about their lack of progress with Donald, and they tend to leave him alone now—watching out only for his physical needs, as best they can.

His parents identify a number of concerns they have about Donald's behavior, including these:

- makes strange, ritualistic hand movements
- echoes the words and phrases of others
- ignores and resists discipline
- seldom looks at them
- uses toys in a careless and disorganized way
- seems to be unaware of what goes on around him
- lacks understanding of what they tell him
- avoids other children and adults
- makes unusual sounds and does not seem to listen

Donald will be a handful for his early childhood teachers, but using a Stage One program, they should be able to help him stay in touch in an organized way and learn with comfortable results. With parallel programs by his parents at home and his teachers at school, expect progress!

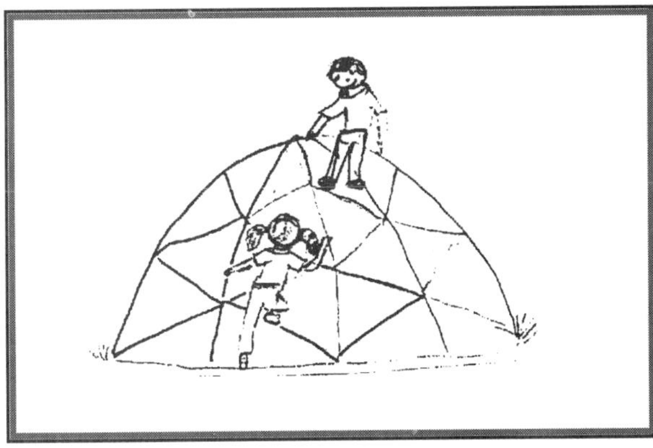

CHAPTER 9

Stage Two: Responding to the Environment with Success

I am what I will.

—E. H. ERIKSON, 1959/1980, P. 87

THE STAGE TWO EXPERIENCE: FULL OF EXPLORATION AND LEARNING

Stage Two is a time when a child's limited skills are expanding with new behaviors that bring increased success. It is a dynamic time—full of exploration and learning. This second stage of Developmental Therapy–Developmental Teaching includes the social-emotional milestones usually associated with development from about 2 through 5 years of age. Typical Stage Two children are in day care, preschool, kindergarten, or Head Start. The curriculum helps each child experience success by learning to explore, talk, think, relate, and play in new ways. It emphasizes learning individual skills for successfully organizing information, participating in daily routines, exploring new environments, and testing others to verify newly formed perceptions about oneself. These new skills bring success and increased self-confidence. Successful Stage Two children begin to believe in themselves, and we often hear them saying,

"I can do it!"

Pleasing adults is a central concern of children in Stage Two. In fact, they value the attention and approval of

Stage Two Children in Brief

Program goal:	Responding to the environment with success
Central concern:	Measuring up to please adults
Motivating values:	Adult approval; avoiding punishment; seeking recognition and praise
Developmental anxiety:	Inadequacy; failure to be approved or accepted by adults
Approach to problems:	Wants and needs to justify acts; adults are responsible for order and problem resolution
Source of authority:	All-powerful adults; supernatural forces (magic, make-believe)
Type of adult needed:	An adult who approves; one with skill to solve problems, admire student, and ensure success
Effective strategies:	Encouragement and praise for individual accomplishments; positive reflection of words and actions; motivate with activities and materials; redirection; adults as response models
Materials, activities, and content themes:	Movement, exploration, and imagination; good-conquers-bad; make-believe; animals; children as invulnerable; adults care for children and admire them

adults so totally that this motivation shapes most of their behavioral responses. They seek adults for emotional strength, security, and a sense of feeling good about themselves. When they cannot cope with new challenges or have unsatisfying ways of responding to the world around them, they need adult help. Encouragement, successful mastery, and recognition from adults are the cornerstone elements that foster their continuing social-emotional development during this stage.

Most children begin Stage Two with little self-confidence or self-esteem, a limited awareness of cause and effect, and ineffective responses to adults and peers. New activities often cause anxiety and resistance, so they tend to cling to whatever is familiar. Impulsive behavior is characteristic and frustrations are usually directed toward adults. Kegan calls this phase of development "the impulsive self" (Kegan, 1982, pp. 134–135). Yet, paradoxically, children in Stage Two crave adult reassurance and recognition. They see adults as all-powerful. Valued adults are those who are able to solve their problems and to provide for their needs. Encouragement from adults, coupled with a program that creates success, motivates children to participate, alleviates failure, and gives order to disorganization. Stage Two children are then able to mature socially and emotionally.

Although Stage Two children are not yet able to see themselves as members of a group, simple group experiences with peers are essential for accomplishing individual objectives. They may be members of several groups—their family groups, church groups, school groups, and play groups. Within each of these groups, their receptivity to change must be sensitively directed by adults into new, successful experiences. As they progress through the Stage Two curriculum, they begin to rely less on adults and more on their own good feelings about themselves. For all of this to happen, adults must remain alert to each small sign of growth and allow children to use their own resources as they emerge.

During Stage Two, children with or without disabilities face major developmental challenges as they mature in their capacity to function successfully in their environment. Although they have developed speech, they are limited in communication skills. They need abundant opportunities to communicate. And because they are also restless, have short attention spans, and are generally disorganized, their materials and activities must be uncomplicated while encouraging action and exploration. With all that must be accomplished during Stage Two, we find it helpful to consider the seven emotional foundations of school readiness suggested by The National Center for Clinical Infant Programs (1992, p. 7)—characteristics that must be developed before a child leaves Stage Two for first grade, prepared "with the knowledge of how to learn":

1. confidence
2. curiosity
3. intentionality
4. self-control
5. relatedness
6. capacity to communicate
7. cooperativeness

Individual children respond to the challenges of this stage in quite different ways, depending upon their chronological age, prior experiences, and the behaviors they have already learned for coping with the world around them. Children without disabilities between the ages of 2 and 6 will acquire the Stage Two milestones of development in a fairly predictable sequence and will be ready for first grade with the basic characteristics for successful school performance. However, if they are vulnerable, at-risk children, Stage Two is often a difficult time for them. They frequently show signs of stress that have an impact on their subsequent development. Elizabeth is an example of such a child, for whom Stage Two milestones for social-emotional development will be difficult to acquire without encouragement and special help.

Older children with social, emotional, or behavioral problems and those with mild to moderate delay between 6 and 8 years old lack many of the same Stage Two skills that 4-year-old Elizabeth is struggling to acquire. Six-year-old José is an example of a first-grade child whose anxieties and lack of social-emotional skills will keep him from successfully participating in typical first-grade activities with peers.

There are many Stage Two children like Elizabeth (see p. 203) and José (see p. 205) in early childhood programs who can benefit from Developmental Therapy–Developmental Teaching. Many have been told again and again, "Don't act so stupid," "You're a bad kid," or "How can you be so ugly [or mean, or no good, or a nothing]." The fewer skills they have for social-emotional competence, the more they receive these comments from others, and the more vulnerable they become to fulfilling these messages. The Stage Two program is designed to turn around such self-defeating concepts of inadequacy into beliefs of themselves as adequate, successful, and esteemed individuals.

Older school-age children and teens less frequently lack Stage Two skills unless they have severe and chronic problems of adjustment, psychosis, depression, autism, or aggression. Little that they do produces success. Without success, they feel bad about themselves. They frequently communicate by kicking, screaming, cursing, resisting adults, and destroying property. Sometimes they turn inward—masking their feelings, talking very little, avoiding others, or passively resisting. These are responses of students who do not like themselves or the world around them. For them, a Stage Two program focusing on success and self-esteem offers opportunities to turn their negative responses around.

The most important goal to keep in mind for all Stage Two children is that they must experience success abundantly. Without success their self-esteem fails to develop, and self-esteem is essential for developmental progress. It is adults' responsibility to provide situations that foster success. The material in this chapter reviews the Developmental Therapy–Developmental Teaching approach to providing success for children of any age who are in Stage Two. We illustrate applications for young, preschool children as well as for older students with disabilities who need to achieve the Stage Two goals and objectives for social-emotional competence. We organize the information around these four topics:

- typical social-emotional processes developing during Stage Two
- goals and objectives for children in Stage Two
- how the program meets the needs of children in Stage Two
- activities designed to accomplish the goals and objectives for Stage Two

TYPICAL SOCIAL-EMOTIONAL PROCESSES DEVELOPING DURING STAGE TWO

During Stage Two, children with and without disabilities are moving from the safety and protection of attachment and dependency provided by adults in the previous stage to psychological initiative by the end of this stage. Figure 9.1 highlights the key processes necessary for the development of all preschool children—and older children who have delays in social, emotional, or behavioral development.

There are two predominant developmental themes during Stage Two: (a) physical exploration, which leads to increased skill, greater independence, and decreased dependence, and (b) the need for adult approval and attention, which leads to self-confidence. Children in Stage Two learn to explore successfully while relying on adults to satisfy their dependent needs.

As a very young child begins this process, passing psychologically from Stage One to Stage Two, the changes are subtle and scarcely noticed at first. When a toddler's attachments are secure and satisfying, successful experiences foster separation and individuation, in which a child begins to freely separate from the adults with whom attachment bonds have been built (Mahler, 1968/1987). Healthy psychological separation gradually occurs as the child's emotional dependency on adults diminishes. It must come from within the child, and it happens gradually, as the child becomes increasingly aware of the successes and pleasures that can be experienced with independent action. (Separation anxiety, in which an infant or very young toddler shows distress when a significant adult leaves, is a signal that this process of separation is under way but not yet complete.)

This paradoxical combination of the two processes—protection by adults and small amounts of successful independence—produces *individuation* (Bretherton, 1987; Mahler, 1968/1987). Individuation is the process of differentiating oneself from others—being a separate person. Separation and individuation are successful when there is a solid foundation of attachment that children can carry in their emotional memory. In this way, they can take the comfort of attachment with them vicariously as they begin to explore the world around them. This is the beginning of the struggle between dependence and independence, which continues for a lifetime in ever-changing forms.

When the first processes of separation and individuation are successful, a toddler progresses into a phase called *autonomy*. Eric Erikson described autonomy this way: "Autonomy is the phase of personality development when the individual has developed a sense of self with

Elizabeth

Four-year-old Elizabeth's Head Start teachers are concerned. For attention she likes to crawl up into their laps. At other times she hangs onto their legs, clinging so tightly that they cannot move away. When adults or children approach, she pushes them away, emphatically shouting, "No!" Her attention span is approximately 5 minutes, when a teacher stays nearby, but alone, she seldom involves herself in the activity centers. Her constant thumb-sucking, staring, and chewing on her clothing also concern her teachers.

Elizabeth likes food, dolls, cuddly toys, and physical activities. She usually participates in activities if she is encouraged, or if the activity involves materials that are manipulative in nature. But when she is frustrated or cannot have her way, she withdraws or runs away.

Figure 9.1. Key processes of typical social–emotional development in Stage Two. The dotted lines indicate the inner life—thoughts and feelings.

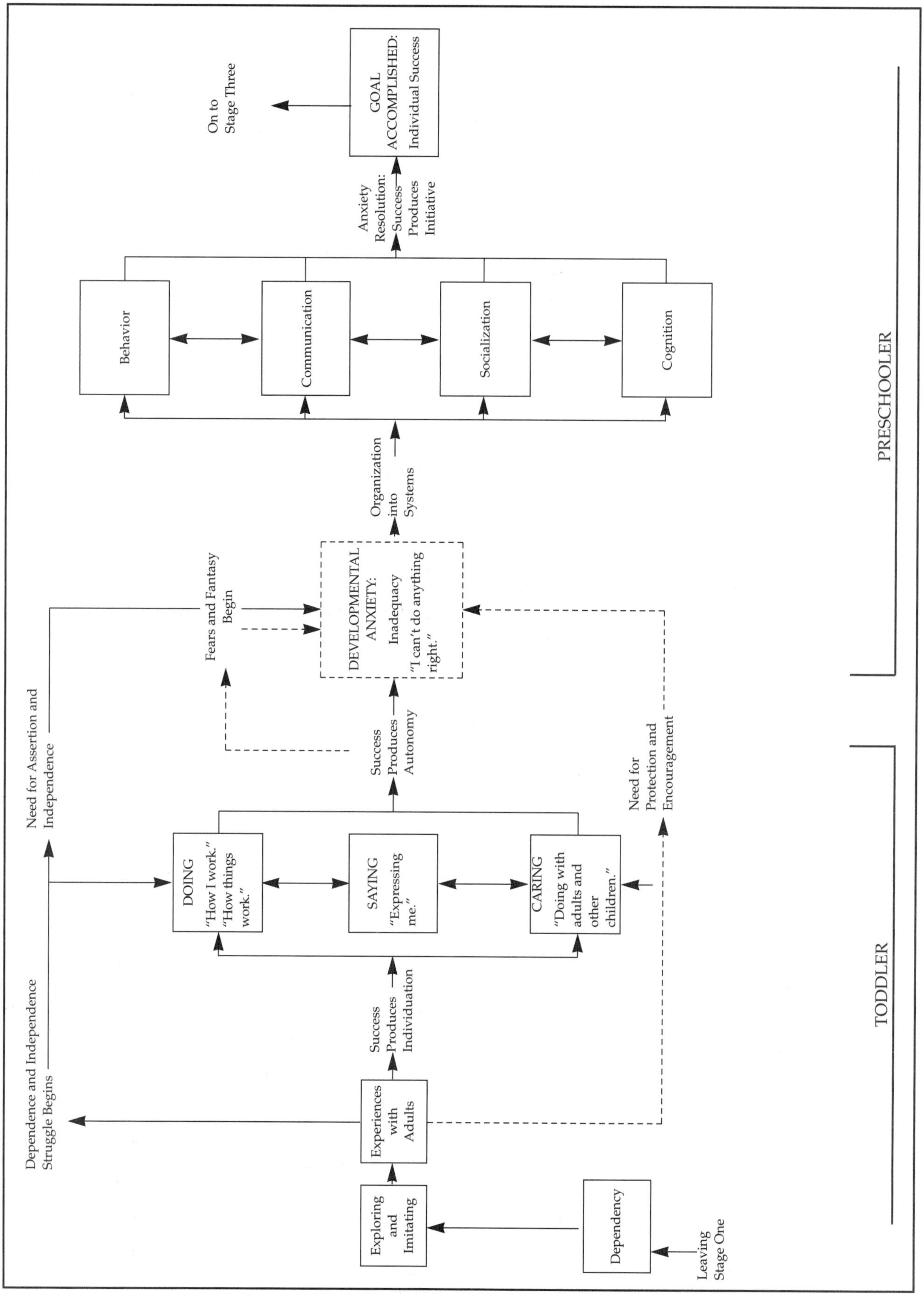

José

When José was enrolled in the first grade it was a disaster. The teacher and principal were concerned because he would not enter the classroom without panic—crying as he was pushed into the room by a bigger brother, wetting his pants, losing control, and running out of the room. When he was brought back, he pleaded with the adults not to make him go to school. He cried without stopping for almost an hour. Finally, they called his mother, who could not explain why he was so upset but suggested that she would take him home with her and try again the next day.

José returned two days later. He cried all the way to school and again erupted into a violent panic, pleading with his mother and teacher not to make him enter the building. This time, his mother physically carried him, whimpering, into the room. There he broke into a tantrum. The first-grade teacher held him, firmly but gently, and showed him the activity areas in the room. The important message was that he was there to stay, that the teacher liked him, and that there were things in the room that he could do.

As he went home at the end of the day, José turned to his mother and said,

"You know, I didn't think they wanted me there, but they do!"

some basic capacity to accomplish and master simple situations" (personal communication, February 1985).[1]

To develop autonomy, the efforts of young Stage Two children are directed toward exploration and self-assertion. Although these actions are essentially physical, the children's mental development is also rapidly growing as a result. Thinking and memory permeate their exploration. At the same time, they are learning to rely on adults and to trust them to encourage them in these endeavors. Success in *doing, saying,* and *caring* brings *autonomy*—a sense of being capable of mastery and control of simple situations. We briefly review each of these developmental processes here, with particular attention to those that are incorporated into the Developmental Therapy–Developmental Teaching program for Stage Two.

The early foundations for thinking are built from sensorimotor learning in the previous stage. Now, thinking becomes functional, when the early sensorimotor perceptions take on meaning through language acquisition and memory. Early in this stage, one of the most significant foundations for thinking is formed—*object permanence,* the idea that people or objects exist in memory even if they disappear from view. This process originates in Stage One but continues early in Stage Two when a toddler is able to remember people or objects even when they are no longer present. In contrast to an infant in Stage One, who is interested in visually tracking the movement of people or objects and who believes that what has disappeared can be found, a Stage Two child can keep the memory but give up the search in the immediate surroundings. Cognition and memory are clearly developing into organized systems. Basic memory and thinking processes continue to expand rapidly throughout the stage as motor skills allow a child to explore, experience, and think about all that is happening. For this reason, Piaget (1952) described this period of intellectual development as one of *sensorimotor learning.*[2] With expanded thinking and language skills, the developing child has the fundamental tools for acquiring social-emotional competence at this stage of development.

Doing

Children in Stage Two explore their immediate world and the many complex objects within it through large and fine muscles. Skills for *doing* give them the tools to learn about themselves and provide the equipment to cope with new demands from others. They learn to master impulses and find out about themselves in relation to their parents, other adults, and other children (Mussen, Conger, Kagan, & Huston, 1990, chap. 5). Large muscles help Stage Two children learn to coordinate their own bodies and express themselves through motion: *"how I work."* Movement is perhaps the most significant part of large-muscle experiences during this stage. Body-in-space movements are refined and become tools for success. Rhythmic motions are particularly attractive. During exploratory and rhythmic experiences, Stage Two children learn to organize their body sensations and to connect what is felt to things seen, heard, and tasted. Significant muscle coordination skills include throwing, catching, and kicking a ball, swinging, sliding, going up and down stairs, balancing, and learning to ride a tricycle or pedal a go-cart. In short,

[1]For further reading on autonomy and how it develops, we recommend Erikson's classic work, *Childhood and Society (1950/1963).*

[2]See Chapter 8 for a review of the foundations of mental development that occur during the first 2 years of life. Because mental development is dependent upon sensorimotor development, we intersperse milestone objectives for motor development throughout the curriculum in the (Pre)Academics/Cognition area of the curriculum and continue to include related milestones for school-age children, weaving physical and psychological elements together for social-emotional competence.

body movement and large-muscle activities provide effective ways for exploring surroundings with success.[3]

Fine muscles are used by children early in Stage Two to explore *"how things work."* There are many sensorimotor, perceptual, and manipulative activities that are also indicative of developing social-cognitive (functional) behavior, such as those that include self-help skills, stringing beads, turning pages of books, stacking six to eight blocks, imitating horizontal and vertical lines with simple crayon strokes, using a spoon and cup, filling containers and emptying them, and assisting in dressing, toileting, and washing hands. As they progress through Stage Two, children's fine motor skills become increasingly refined. They are eventually able to copy a circle, hold a crayon with fingers rather than a fist, snip with preschool-sized scissors, and unbutton clothing. All of these skills, when successful, add to their expanding sense of independence and competence.

Saying

Stage Two children are intent on expressing themselves and attempting to explore and influence their environments with words. Learning and remembering functional words facilitates their attempts to describe experiences, to command, and to convey intent. *"Me"* and *"mine"* are typical expressions early in this stage. This focus on self is an attempt at self-validation; they are trying to find out exactly who and what they are (Kagan, 1982).

Stage Two children add words rapidly to their speaking repertoire, including verbs, pronouns, adverbs, adjectives, prepositions, the possessive form, and plurals. As their skills in communicating increase, they delight in stories that describe them and use their names. They use three to four phrases at a time to demand, elaborate, and communicate needs. They talk about their experiences spontaneously with adults and other children and are able to describe their characteristics and those of others (Howes, Droege, & Phillipsen, 1992). They can follow several directions at a time, particularly those involved with moving objects from one place to another. They know the uses of objects and the names of body parts, and they are able to look at details in pictures, associate certain words with the pictures, and eventually sequence the pictures.

Caring

The focus of typical Stage Two children is on doing things with adults who provide care, security, and approval. Most activities enjoyed by Stage Two children are enhanced when they are done with valued adults—those upon whom they depend. They learn to care for others by being cared for themselves (Lickona, 1985). They learn by imitating adults, from the simplest responses to complex patterns of responding. They imitate adults' expressions of emotions such as anger, frustration, fear, and uncertainty. From adults they also learn ways to interact with others, to express affection, and to care.

Gradually, during Stage Two, children become increasingly interactive with other children, and this sequence of socialization is most evident in play. Their play typically begins with solitary play or parallels the activity of other children. As self-confidence and communication skills increase, socialization skills expand, bringing great pleasure from play and social exchange with others (Erikson, 1972; Guralnick, 1992; Parten, 1932; Piaget, 1951/1962). Throughout Stage Two, however, these social efforts center on their own needs and they have only one point of view—their own (Selman, 1980).

The Need To Be Assertive and Aggressive in Stage Two Children

The more confident Stage Two children become about themselves, the more they tend to explore and assert themselves. This assertion is directed primarily toward their families and to a lesser extent toward other adults and peers. Earlier forms of assertion and aggression are evident in biting others, refusing certain foods, ignoring adults, and resisting toilet training, which sometimes occur in children as they complete Stage One. Assertion of will is often expressed in negative statements and is misinterpreted by adults as a negative period or the terrible twos (sometimes carried over as the terrible threes). However, assertion within boundaries is an important step forward for children during Stage Two to validate themselves and their own autonomy (Ilg, Ames, & Baker, 1981/1992).

When assertion and willfulness are contained within clearly defined boundaries by adults and redirected into acceptable behavior, these potentially negative forces are shaped into initiative and behavior that bring about the desired results from adults—approval and affection. This positive transformation of assertion offers the fuel for continuing social-emotional development along healthy lines. If they are not well managed, natural assertion and aggression become sources for future conflict, oppositional behavior, and social-emotional immaturity (Anthony, 1976; Greenspan, 1992).

Looking back to the beginning of Stage Two, it is easy to understand why children can be caught up in resistant, controlling behavior. In Stage One they developed minimal skills to obtain what they wanted from adults in the immediate world around them. Jane Loevinger describes their effort as demanding immediate gratification—with people seen as the providers (Loevinger, 1976). So the next obvious step for children during Stage Two is to learn about controlling themselves and others in new situa-

[3]For the detailed sequences of skill development, see the DTORF–R. See also Appendix 4, which contains the content analysis charts of these four areas of social-emotional development, and Appendix 5 for a summary of motivational systems.

tions. Because they are developing proficiency in motor and communication skills, they are able to take on these challenges. For this same reason adults sometimes think of this behavior as aggressive or difficult to manage. But aggression, properly channeled, is often indicative of unpolished initiative that is emerging.

Developmental Anxieties of Children in Stage Two

The typical developmental anxiety during this stage comes from expectations placed on children that they fear they cannot meet. Parents and other adults set the expectations. When they set standards for proficiency in performance beyond a child's capability for success, a sense of inadequacy develops.[4] Their behavior begins to convey the message:

"I can't do anything right."

During this phase of development, children are bombarded with many new expectations that often produce stress and uncertainty about their own adequacy. For example, they must respond to

- expectations of adults for acceptable conduct that restrains impulses
- expectations of adults about proficiency in performance
- their own need for acceptance by valued adults
- their own need to explore and be assertive
- their own need to find acceptable ways to control and express their feelings

As pressures for better performance increase and their own self-awareness grows, children's anxiety about personal adequacy becomes a paramount concern. Fears and fantasies about all that could happen grow as a result of their increased mental awareness. They can remember and imagine good and bad, in themselves and others.[5] They understand that pretend and reality are different, yet they have difficulty detaching themselves from fears. Children gradually find relief from these fears and anxieties as they learn to rely on caring and competent adults or other powerful forces they trust. Many children at this stage transfer their concerns and the burden of fears and anxieties vicariously through imagination, fantasy, and make-believe. With these forms of pretend, children can

- blame others
- love
- express drives
- experience fears
- control evil
- gratify themselves
- express uneasy feelings

Through imagination, fantasy, and make-believe, all of the terrible possibilities that might occur can be safely considered. Imaginary friends and other fantasies, whether people, animals, heroes, or characters from make-believe, provide private ways for Stage Two children to meet emotional needs vicariously. Fears, concerns, and problems can be resolved to the satisfaction of Stage Two children by powerful forces beyond themselves. Denial, make-believe, and fantasy are used to cope with these concerns. Magic is believable, and other supernatural forces have legitimacy as sources of ultimate authority and protection. Fictional characters like Peter Pan, Santa Claus, the tooth fairy, Peter Rabbit, Mickey Mouse, and Barney all have credibility with young Stage Two children as sources for meeting needs, as do parents and teachers. With older students in Stage Two, fears and fantasy are sometimes dealt with through imaginary friends, supernatural forces for good and evil, larger-than-life heroes, or imaginary events the students admire.

From their daily experiences—if they are successful and reassuring—and with supportive relationships with adults, children form the secure belief that they are safe. The terrors and fears of the unknown are diminished. Their increasing mental abilities help them to understand and predict what will happen. They begin to see themselves as successful and able to meet the expectations of those around them. When preschool children accomplish these milestones, they have acquired a Stage Two level of social-emotional competence. They are able to overcome anxiety and master fears. As this gradually happens, they are reinforced in their hope that the world is still a secure place.

Organization of Developmental Processes into Systems

During the latter part of Stage Two—usually when children are 3–5 years of age—the developmental systems become organized as distinct pathways, while also becoming completely interdependent. These are the preschool and kindergarten years, when learning becomes a focus and increases at an amazing rate. The *behavioral system* organizes sensorimotor learning into functional social behavior, providing the tools for Stage Two children to explore, participate, and assert themselves, with control over objects and a degree of influence over others. The *communication system* offers children a more sophisticated method of asserting themselves by using words to evoke desired

[4]Sometimes adults set expectations that a child could actually meet, but the child does not have that same confidence. The result is the developmental anxiety we call *inadequacy*. See Chapter 2 for a discussion of the developmental anxieties across all five stages of development.

[5]Some clinicians call this *object anxiety*. See also A. Freud (1942).

responses from others. By asking "Why?" Stage Two children expand their understanding of the world around them. They also are developing an interactive method of relating to others in a rational way. The *socialization system* expands their understanding of the expectations of others and the skills needed to interact in ways that bring recognition and acclaim from "best friends," peers, and family. The *cognitive system* offers them ways to understand their environment and begin to resolve earlier fears as they start to associate new ideas with old concepts. They learn to categorize, connect cause and effect in events, develop spatial concepts, and form limited ideas about the past and future. Together, these four systems, successfully developed, produce confident children prepared for the next stage of development and full of

initiative!

GOALS AND OBJECTIVES FOR CHILDREN IN STAGE TWO

The Goal: *Responding to the environment with success*

An effective program for children of all ages in Stage Two can be summed up in one simple guideline: It provides abundant opportunities for successful participation. The Developmental Therapy–Developmental Teaching program for Stage Two provides structure, consistency, routine, and predictability while also encouraging children to explore, create, and use new skills. Each experience is carefully planned, with opportunities to work on needed skills for social-emotional competence and responsible behavior. The end result must always be satisfying and successful. Stage Two experiences should leave children with a sense of themselves as individuals with some capacity to accomplish and master what is expected of them by others. They should complete their Stage Two programs with a sense of confidence that their world is manageable and that they can be successful in it.

The milestones of typical social-emotional development for children in Stage Two provide the sequence of goals and objectives for their programs in Developmental Therapy–Developmental Teaching. In reviewing these major milestones below, we summarize the subgoals and objectives for each of the four curriculum areas. As students acquire these milestones, they achieve a sense of autonomy, a positive outlook about themselves and the world around them, and the initiative to begin assuming responsibility for their own behavior.

Behavior Milestones for Stage Two

In Developmental Therapy–Developmental Teaching, the Behavior goal for Stage Two is *to participate in routines and activities with success.* Children beginning Stage Two have learned in the previous stage that there are routines to be followed, although they cannot always follow through without occasional redirection or physical intervention by adults ("motoring them through a task"). They also begin Stage Two with some ability to follow simple verbal directions and often imitate the actions of adults with the assistance of cues and occasional physical intervention. During Stage Two, the program builds on these skills and assists the children in learning to participate more fully and successfully in activities without physical intervention by adults.

Beginning Stage Two children show an interest in using play materials or equipment on their own, although they may not know how to use the materials appropriately or successfully at first. This expectation to use play materials appropriately is the first Behavior milestone in Stage Two. The same expectation exists whether a child is using materials inappropriately because of a failure to develop this skill, disinterest, or an emotional need (resistance, defiance, or inability to discriminate reality from make-believe). It is important to understand that Stage Two children should not be judged on the skill with which they use materials or equipment, but on appropriate participation. Success is defined as being a part of the activity and participating in acceptable ways. We are not concerned with proficiency during this stage, because a typical child in Stage Two has little skill in any area; the developmental priority is to instill sufficient confidence to spark initiative for spontaneous participation.

Because children beginning Stage Two have considerable difficulty with impulse control, waiting is difficult, even for short periods of time. This milestone is the first in a series of developmental steps concerned with increasing attention span and participation. Having a child wait for an extended period of time is not the object; rather, it is the idea that the child can wait for materials or a turn for even a brief period, given verbal support by an adult. The remaining milestones in Behavior for Stage Two continue this focus on students' participation by waiting, listening, and following directions without physical intervention by adults. This sequence includes participation in (a) quiet activities such as sitting at a table or in a chair, (b) activities requiring physical movement with less structure, and (c) spontaneous participation in all activities without physical intervention by adults. Mastery of this basic sequence does not include independent participation in the transition from one activity to another, because transitions require self-regulatory behavior beyond the level of many children in Stage Two. The final milestone for Behavior in Stage Two is the ability to accept praise for successful participation without inappropriate behavior or loss of control. This last milestone indicates that self-esteem is growing. Children have accomplished the Behavior sequence for Stage Two when they participate spontaneously in the planned activities without needing adults' physical assistance or intervention.

Communication Milestones for Stage Two

Communication milestones for children during Stage Two focus on basic speech acts for social communication. In Developmental Therapy–Developmental Teaching, the Communication goal for Stage Two is *to use words to affect others in constructive ways*. In Stage Two, children learn that words can be effective tools for interacting with others successfully, by requesting objects, requiring action, making assertions and denials, and stating information.

The first milestone in this sequence is basic interactive speech between a child and another person (child or adult). This milestone skill is applicable for children who do not want to speak (because of uncertainty, insecurity, or distrust) and those who have not learned to speak. Keep in mind that, though the milestone—needing to talk—may be the same, the strategies for achieving it will be individualized for each student. In this milestone, the emphasis is on the occurrence of the interactive speech act itself; the content does not have to be particularly accurate or positive.

As the receptive vocabularies of children beginning Stage Two increase, their ability to grasp social meanings expands. To determine if a child's receptive vocabulary is sufficient for continuing social-emotional development, we use the arbitrary guideline that a child of any age or intelligence level with a receptive vocabulary 2 years or more behind age peers lacks mastery of this fundamental skill.[6] The idea is that continuing development of social-emotional competence requires a fundamental understanding of the words that others use.

The remaining sequence of Communication milestones in Stage Two focuses on using words and word sequences rather than physical actions to influence others. These communication skills involve sharing information spontaneously with adults and then with other children. Some young children and many troubled teens resist talking with adults. For them, this milestone is often quite difficult to acquire, while spontaneously talking with other children is quite easy. A few children will have the reverse pattern; they are quite at ease in sharing information spontaneously with adults, but find it difficult, if not impossible, to talk with other children. Equally difficult for almost all Stage Two children is describing simple, tangible characteristics of themselves and others. Most children learn to describe the characteristics of others before they are able to describe themselves. However, the reverse may also occur, especially with children who have had limited experience with other children and more experience in talking with adults about themselves. Mastery of this milestone represents a benchmark for the later development of social understanding and interpersonal perspective-taking. Spontaneous social communication with other children is the final Communication milestone for Stage Two, completing the skill sequence preparatory to the next stage.

[6]A number of standard instruments are currently available for assessment of receptive vocabulary to provide a guide to the acquisition of this developmental milestone.

Socialization Milestones for Stage Two

In the curriculum area for Socialization during Stage Two, the goal is to learn *to participate successfully in activities with others*. To successfully foster socialization, the curriculum's focus is on play, communication, and interaction between children, in both organized and unstructured situations. The sequence of Socialization milestones for Stage Two parallels those for Behavior. In Behavior the emphasis is on doing the expected activity, and in Socialization the emphasis is on participating with others, primarily in one-to-one interactions within group activities. The Socialization emphasis in Stage Two also prepares children for the next stage, where the emphasis is on the social skills needed to be a successful member of a group.

The first Socialization milestone in Stage Two is spontaneous imaginative play. In the previous stage, children

Stage Two Behavior Milestones

Goal: ***To participate in routines and activities with success***

Use play materials appropriately.
Wait without physical intervention by an adult.
Participate in sitting activities without intervention.
Participate in movement activities without intervention.
Spontaneously participate verbally and physically in activities without intervention.
Accept praise or success without inappropriate behavior or loss of control.

Source: Abstracted from *The Developmental Teaching Objectives for the DTORF–R*, by Developmental Therapy Institute, 1992, Athens, GA: Developmental Therapy Institute

Stage Two Communication Milestones

Goal: ***To use words to affect others in constructive ways***
Answer questions or requests with relevant words.
Indicate comprehension of others' words (receptive vocabulary).
Spontaneously use simple word sequences.
Spontaneously use words to share information with an adult.
Describe simple, tangible characteristics of oneself and others.
Spontaneously use words to share information with other children.

Source: Abstracted from *The Developmental Teaching Objectives for the DTORF-R,* by Developmental Therapy Institute, 1992, Athens, GA: Developmental Therapy Institute.

learned to respond independently to play materials, but the quality of the play was not an issue. However, during Stage Two, play becomes increasingly complex. In Behavior the focus is simply on using play materials in purposeful ways, as they are intended to be used (as opposed to destructively), whereas in Socialization the focus is on the ability of a child to add imaginative expansions to play, eventually seeking adults and other children to share in imaginative play.

Socialization milestones, then, focus on a child's ability to wait for materials, equipment, or a turn without intervention by an adult. This milestone is the first major point where children must acknowledge the existence of the needs of other children. Once this milestone has been achieved, they move fairly quickly through the remaining sequential milestones: initiating social exchanges with other children; sharing toys, materials, or equipment when asked to do so by adults; spontaneously participating with another child in organized play unstructured by adults; and cooperating independently with peers during activities or play that an adult has organized. This final Socialization milestone in Stage Two is a bridge to the emphasis on group activities and social interaction in the next stage.

(Pre)Academics/Cognition Milestones for Stage Two

In the area of (Pre)Academics/Cognition during Stage Two, the goal is *to participate in activities with self-help, motor coordination, language, and the mental processes of discrimination, sequencing, and numeration.* The 17 milestones in the Stage Two (Pre)Academics/Cognition area of the curriculum include these key readiness skills: self-help, language concepts, visual perception, fine- and large-muscle coordination, and numeration. This sequence of milestones spans a period of rapid intellectual growth in developing children. Because of this, each child's Developmental Therapy–Developmental Teaching program includes at least one milestone for each of these key skill areas during the same time period. The importance of individualizing each child's program in the area of (Pre)Academics/Cognition cannot be overemphasized. It is essential to have a detailed assessment of a child's thinking skills and current achievements. This will indicate exactly which milestones a child has previously acquired and which need to be included in a current program. We use the DTORF–R for a child's profile in acquiring these milestones. However, other preacademic readiness tests and developmental inventories can provide similar information.

These milestones must be sequenced into smaller steps for gradual mastery.[7] A sequence of small steps offers the optimal opportunity to adjust the program to the unique learning styles, strengths, skills, and interests of each individual. For this reason, the curriculum does not specify the smaller steps, preferring instead to allow maximum flexibility in how each child's individual program is planned to provide a sequence of steps toward mastery of a milestone.

The milestones for the (Pre)Academics/Cognition area of the Stage Two curriculum are organized to correspond to well-known, age-related performance, documented by many developmental psychologists, readiness achievement tests, and early childhood educators.[8] The milestones include sequences of basic thinking skills associated with egocentric, prelogical learning. Through motor activity and manipulative materials, the milestones increasingly provide for comprehension, memory, decision making, problem solving, and creative thinking. Recognizing that thinking skills are also fostered through different sources of information, they reflect the use of spoken words, objects,

[7] Task analysis procedures are helpful in outlining the sequence of small steps to follow for mastery of a milestone. See also Figure 4.2 for our approach to how this process should be structured for an instructional objective.

[8] In examining content validity of these processes as contained in the DTORF–R, an item-by-item comparison was made with five other early childhood inventories and curricula. This process is described in Chapter 3, and the content grids outlining these thinking processes are in Appendix 4.

Stage Two Socialization Milestones

Goal: To participate successfully in activities with others

Initiate imaginative play spontaneously.
Wait without physical intervention by adults.
Initiate appropriate social movement toward peers.
Participate in sharing activities, when asked to do so by adults.
Participate in interactive play with peers.
Cooperate with peers independently during organized activity and play.

Source: Abstracted from *The Developmental Teaching Objectives for the DTORF–R,* by Developmental Therapy Institute, 1992, Athens, GA: Developmental Therapy Institute.

pictures, letters, numbers, and shapes. The milestones include several well-established, age-related benchmarks. These include fine- and large-muscle development at the 3-year-old level and eye-hand coordination, body coordination, and memory skills at the 5-year-old level. Interwoven throughout are increasingly complex skills for visual discrimination of similarities, differences, and details, requiring matching, classifying, categorizing, and sequencing.

Teachers of older students who are socially, behaviorally, or emotionally in Stage Two ask how to plan for them when they are achieving academically beyond the (Pre)Academics/Cognition area of the curriculum. Examples of activities in the following section illustrate how academic work can be included in the time allocations for these older students who are participating in a Stage Two program.[9] A reverse problem also occurs for older students who have learning disabilities that require work on Stage Two preaca-

[9] Chapter 10 illustrates how to adjust academic programs for students who are in Stage Three in social-emotional development but in Stage Two in (Pre)Academics/Cognition because of a learning disability.

Stage Two (Pre)Academics/Cognition Milestones

Goal: ***To participate in activities with self-help, motor coordination, language, and the mental processes of discrimination, sequencing, and numeration***

Recognize uses of familiar objects.
Perform simple body coordination activities at the 3-year-old level.
Match identical pictures.
Perform fine-motor-coordination activities at the 3-year-old level.
Recognize objects that are alike or different.
Understand concepts of simple opposites.
Categorize pictures that are different but have similar characteristics.
Count by one-to-one to 4.
Identify colors and shapes.
Respond to shifts in verbal directions to find pictures that are alike or different.
Count by one-to-one to 10.
Perform eye-hand coordination activities at the 5-year-old level.
Discriminate between numerals, designs, and uppercase letters.
Perform body coordination activities at the 5-year-old level.
Recognize groups of objects to 5 without counting.
Demonstrate rote memory skills at the 5-year-old level.
Sequence three simple pictures that tell a story.

Source: Abstracted from *The Developmental Teaching Objectives for the DTORF–R,* by Developmental Therapy Institute, 1992, Athens, GA: Developmental Therapy Institute.

demic skills while their general social-emotional development may be well into Stage Three or beyond. Chapters 10 and 11 provide examples of these adaptations.

As the Stage Two milestone skills for (Pre)Academics/ Cognition are acquired, children have an increasing sense of adequacy. They show self-confidence and begin to believe that schoolwork is something they can do successfully. With a foundation of solid thinking skills, they are ready for beginning reading, writing, language arts, and arithmetic programs in the next stage of development.

HOW THE PROGRAM MEETS THE NEEDS OF CHILDREN IN STAGE TWO

Success is the springboard for an effective program during Stage Two. The Developmental Therapy–Developmental Teaching program in Stage Two provides this success abundantly, with an environment and a curriculum free from failure and competition. To do this, activities are planned in ways that emphasize successful individual participation, usually in a small-group setting. Why is success so important for the social-emotional development of children during Stage Two? Because it is essential to a sense of self-confidence. Stage Two is a period of development in which all children experience a major threat to their sense of self as being adequate in the eyes of others, especially adults.

Success can be difficult to define and even more difficult to implement. The program must balance children's developmental needs for activity, exploration, and success against their limited skills for achieving it. For Stage Two, success must be a major part of every activity every day. Plan carefully, anticipate children's responses, understand what they value, and guide each of them in ways that bring a personal sense of accomplishment.

The downside of this priority for success is the possibility that one child's success becomes another child's failure. Because this must not happen in a Stage Two program, we completely avoid activities or materials that require competition between individuals or groups.[10] Children in Stage Two need to develop a sense of their own adequacy without having to achieve it at the expense of another's failure.

Perhaps the most important characteristic of children during this stage is their limited views of adults and other children. They have the belief that adults are responsible for everything and seldom see other children as unique individuals. They do not recognize that the behavior of others is often a result of their own actions. Their behavior is guided by their own needs, and they do not yet see that they are responsible for their actions. This shortsighted view makes them vulnerable to mistakes and failures. It also frequently makes them the source of friction and conflict with others. They believe that problems should be solved by adults, while their chief concern is to gain acclaim or recognition from adults and avoid punishment for failure. These characteristics also may make it difficult for some individuals in Stage Two to be successful in a group with other children without special assistance from adults.

To be successful, when they have such limited skills, children depend upon considerable encouragement and guidance from adults, and to avoid failure, they usually respond positively to organization, structure, and predictability. The Stage Two program must provide this environment to allow the child to believe,

"I can really do this!"

Success Through Participation

Because participation is the focal point of a successful program, expectations and rules established for children in Stage Two center on participation that brings success to every individual in the group. A typical Stage Two group needs only three rules:

1. Participate.
2. Do what adults say.
3. Make others feel good.

These expectations are sufficiently broad to encompass almost any situation that may arise during a well-planned program for Stage Two children of any age. They are simple and easy to remember and can be recalled by the children. As they learn that they can be successful when they participate and follow directions, they also learn that they can be successful by being considerate of the needs of others.

Some adults may question the second rule—obedience to adults. While we recognize that there are adults in our contemporary society who abuse children, we also recognize that a fundamental emotional need of children in Stage Two is to believe in adults. They need adults to encourage and guide them to successful participation. Therefore, the burden for a child's success in Stage Two falls almost entirely on an adult's skill in ensuring that every child participates successfully. For this to happen, students must also give something of themselves. They are able to fully and freely participate when they know the expectations and believe that they can meet them successfully. This is the key to a child's sense of successful participation. The message becomes

"Look what I can do!"

---

[10] Because our society is so competitively oriented, keeping competition out of a Stage Two program can be difficult. Stage Three is the time to gradually introduce healthy competition between groups rather than between individuals.

Success Through Organization and Structure

The organization of the room and the structure of each activity in a program for children in Stage Two defines the expectations for successful participation. The room does not need to be large, but it must be carefully organized. A well-organized room helps children organize themselves. Work tables and chairs are preferred over individual desks, which are seldom used because of the children's need to physically move, explore, and learn social interaction skills. There is a designated place in the room for every activity. For some activities requiring more behavioral controls, an area may be marked off with masking tape on the floor or a special area rug used to convey the boundaries for the activity.

A schedule of daily activities is placed so that it is easily seen by the children. Picture cues and clear lettering on the schedule help them to learn and recall the sequence of activities. Individual folders for paperwork are placed within their reach so that they are able to get to them independently. Frequently used supplies such as pencils, scissors, and crayons are arranged in separate boxes. For a beginning Stage Two group, each child will have a personalized box of materials, and the adult will distribute them when needed. However, if the children are ready to learn to participate in cooperative activities with others, the individual boxes are replaced with single boxes of materials that are shared. Similarly, games, toys, and play materials are kept in boxes that are stored out of sight in cabinets until they are needed for an activity. This orderly control of materials protects children from overstimulation and confusion about where to focus their attention. As their ability to be successful with materials and other children increases, adult control over materials is relaxed and the children are encouraged to explore activities and materials independently with each other.

Carefully consider how to display students' products and manage everyone's work in ways that avoid competitive comparisons or criticism from other students. Work displayed too long does not attract attention; neither does work that must compete for attention with a great amount of other displayed material. Some children in Stage Two are distracted by an abundance of visual material around a room. Examples of work, art, teaching tools, and other visual aids may not always enhance learning or create a sense of pride in what they have done. We find that simplicity is generally more effective in displays of children's work. We change it regularly and usually involve the children in planning how it will be displayed. Each piece should be a work that a child is pleased with and the child must not object to the work's being seen. When work is displayed, it should be neatly arranged and not allowed to become old and tattered before it is removed.

Some children are in the habit of destroying their own work. We do not let children destroy their own work. It perpetuates failure. If a child is known to do this or to destroy the work of another child, the adults intervene and compliment the work as it is completed (before the child has time to destroy it). Then it is stored in the child's folder for protection, conveying what the child does is of value to the adults. If adults show that the things children make are valued and protected, the children sense this and feel,

"I did something of value."

The Adult's Role: Encouraging, Motivating, and Problem Solving

Adult approval is a profoundly powerful source for motivating children who are in Stage Two of social-emotional development. Their sense of responsibility to adhere to adults' expectations comes from a belief in adults as all-powerful and the ultimate source of authority. This translates into the child's view that

"I do what I'm told, so they will like me."

The responsibility for adults working with these children is to ensure that they participate in activities in ways that are satisfying and highly successful. Providing a program for children whose social-emotional development is in Stage Two, whether in a preschool, elementary school, or high school, is demanding. The adults must be the predictable point of reference—encouraging, expecting appropriate responses, motivating, reflecting success, and holding limits while guiding successful exploration.

Considerable physical proximity and individual attention on an adult's part may be necessary to accomplish successful participation in the activities by all of the children in a group that is beginning Stage Two. The children may frequently revert to earlier, counterproductive coping behaviors. At such times it is important to redirect each one to participate in acceptable ways and to reduce opportunities for regressive or other unacceptable behavior to a minimum. The optimum arrangement for accomplishing this is to have two adults work as a team, one as *lead* and the other as *support*. We describe these roles in Chapter 7. With teamwork, one adult conducts the activities of the group and the other provides individual attention as needed to redirect children into participating.

The key to progress in Stage Two is the relationship between adults and children. This relationship is a simple one from a developmental perspective—each child must learn that adults care. Stage Two children must be certain that adults approve and that they are powerful (not overwhelmed themselves by events they cannot control). It is also natural for Stage Two children to depend upon adults to make good things happen. The adults must be convincing; they must guarantee success and convey that they really like the children as individuals. Accomplishing this relationship is not easy, because children in this stage frequently test adults, often with immature, primitive, or unpredictable forms of behavior. Adults must recognize these emotional needs as well as a child's skills that can be used to encourage a cycle of success. Elizabeth, described at the beginning of this chapter, is an example of a Head Start child at risk for emotional problems. She needs a relationship with a skilled and caring adult to support and mobilize her to successful participation in events. Similarly, Richard is a bright, extremely troubled kindergarten child who will probably make little or no progress without intensive assistance.

The task for adults working with troubled and at-risk children like Elizabeth and Richard is to provide a relationship with them that turns around their frightened, almost desperate view of the world. To accomplish this, adults must instill in these youngsters a sense of confidence in their own adequacy and the belief that the world can be a satisfying place. With encouragement, they will become increasingly successful with activities, materials, and the other children. In this way, the goals and objectives for their social-emotional development will eventually be achieved and their participation will become more spontaneous, successful, and self-confident.

Management Strategies That Foster Success in Stage Two

Adults use a number of strategies to build relationships and help children become successful during Stage Two.[11] Among the major ones are encouragement through positive feedback and praise, the use of highly motivating materials, structure for organization of the activities, positive verbal redirection, supportive reflection of feelings and successes, and verbal interactions between adults on the team to provide positive response models. Here are strategies that are frequently used:[12]

Positive feedback and praise	For individual participation
Motivating with materials	Noncompetitive; successful; exploratory; imaginative
Structure	Clear expectations easily achieved; limits; familiar predictable routines
Redirection	Verbal cues from adult to remotivate participation
Reflection	Mirroring positive participation and successes
Verbal interaction between adults	Adults as response models
Rules	Expectation that child will participate with others in acceptable ways
Control of materials	Gradual reduction in adult management
Physical proximity and touch	Eye contact; nearness; limited touch
Physical intervention	Physical containment to prevent hurting oneself or others when out of control
Removal from the group	Time-out to remobilize controls for continuing participation

Rules are not included in this list of major management strategies because they are not a central focus for guiding behavior at this stage; adult authority is the primary guide. Therefore, the rules are brief, focus on being successful, and reflect adult authority. Here are examples of rules as we communicate them to children in Stage Two:

Expectations for Stage Two Children
(Rules for Success)

- Follow directions.
- Be helpful.
- Be kind to others.
- Do your best.

Children at this stage of development typically accept obedience to adult authority as a major regulator of their behavior. They have not yet developed to the point where they question adult authority (as they do during the existential crisis occurring in the next stage).[13] Thus, young children understand that they must obey. Values that regulate their behavior are simply those of right and wrong, good and bad, as defined by adults. If young children have not previously had successful relationships with adults to provide psychological security by setting limits, their behavior is often out of control. They resist adult direction and defy suggestions. These habits are old responses to uncertainty about whether they are supposed to be in charge or can trust adults sufficiently to depend upon them. (This concern may be an unresolved remnant from the previous Stage One anxiety—fear of abandonment by the psychological parent.) The following values (attitudes about authority) regulate the behavior of Stage Two children:

Values that Regulate Behavior
(Attitudes About Authority)

- "Adults are to be obeyed"
- "Adults will manage things"

---

[11] The Stage Two form of the DT/RITS in Appendix 2 contains performance items to assess the use of materials, activities, and strategies by adults working with children in Stage Two.

[12] See Chapter 6 for a further discussion of these management strategies with Stage Two children.

[13] Chapter 2 contains a discussion of the existential crisis from a developmental perspective, in which preschool children are preexistential. Chapter 10 also describes the existential crisis for children during the early years of elementary school.

Richard's Puppets

The students are making hand puppets. Richard makes a tall cylinder puppet with angel wings and silk fringe hair. He calls her "Mother." He makes another puppet, a faceless creation, from an old sock with holes. This is "Father."

While other children are finishing their puppets, Richard carries his puppets to the windowsill. The father puppet spanks the mother puppet and imaginary children. Richard says, "Father has to spank the children—and spanks and spanks and spanks and spanks!

"The children are put in jail but escape by climbing out.

"They go home, and Mother and Father are put in jail. Mother stands at the bars, and Father escapes by climbing up Mother. Then Mother says, 'Oh, oh, I better jump out and escape too!'

"Then the family gets back together on the boat. The boat is sinking. Help, help. Mother is tall enough to escape and drags Father out, because he is holding on to the base of Mother.

"The boat is under water. It's painted 'I love you' and all decorated fancy, but the paint washes off."

- "I do what adults tell me to do."
- "Good people obey"
- "Bad people deserve to be punished"
- "Adults punish if you are bad"

When management strategies are used skillfully with a two-person team that conveys caring but firm attitudes, a Stage Two program will move smoothly, even with extremely difficult children in the group. We find that effective adults selectively use all of these strategies, as needed, to meet the program goal for each child's successful participation. We also find them using all four forms of social power—coercion, likability, manipulation, and expertness—to convey the needed adult role. *Coercion* conveys power that must be obeyed, *likability* communicates personal qualities of caring, *manipulation* allows the environment to be structured so that success is inevitable, and *expertness* sends the message to children that the adults can help them solve their problems and protect them.[14] These are the messages children in Stage Two need to hear from the adults who are significant in their lives.

Activities and Materials for Success in Stage Two

Another major source of success for children in Stage Two is well-chosen activities and materials. When well matched to children's developmental and emotional needs, activities and materials can

- stimulate the desire to participate
- touch fears and anxieties stored in emotional memory
- provide vicarious resolutions to fears and anxieties
- enhance feelings of success
- build self-confidence
- provide models for successful behavior
- create understanding about how others behave

When selecting materials and activities to foster the mastery of individual IEP goals and objectives in children in Stage Two, it is important to consider their individual interests, ages, anxieties, and physical and mental maturation. The unique characteristics of each child will influence the selection and design of activities. Following are guidelines we have found to be useful in choosing suitable materials and activities for a Stage Two program:

- Use materials and activities that encourage active exploration and creative imagination.
- Choose materials with no-failure qualities.
- Match materials to individuals' skills and interests.
- Design activities to foster interactions between children.
- Select content that reflects children's everyday experiences.
- Include content dealing with good and evil, in which good prevails.
- Find materials that embody the fears and anxieties of each student.
- Design content to resolve these concerns vicariously.

[14] A discussion about forms of adult social power used to influence the behavior of children is provided in Chapter 7.

Activities and materials used in Stage Two are more demanding of children than those in Stage One.[15] In the previous stage, the children learned to respond, and now, during Stage Two, their responses to activities and materials must bring them not only satisfaction with the results but also a sense of success.

An effective material or activity in Stage Two must be interesting and arousing, or children may not put forth the effort to get involved. It should provide opportunities to imitate the successful behavior and problem-solving strategies of others. The people the children imitate are peers, parents, teachers, fictional characters, and other adults who embody their own concerns and interests. Activities and materials with content qualities that touch their concerns and anxieties will catch their interest and almost always evoke involvement. When content also offers reassuring solutions, it is often imitated, with outcomes that satisfy the children and engender feelings of success.

Language arts activities are particularly effective for providing content that encourages participation. Storytelling, dramatic play, puppets, storybooks, role play, and pretend games are natural parts of the language arts programs for typical children in Stage Two. Readiness activities for creative writing can also be effective in encouraging children to use spoken words and sentences to describe pictures, experiences, and ideas. These readiness skills for self-expression equip children in Stage Two with essential tools for continuing to explore and succeed. When content is adjusted to age-appropriate interests of older students who are still in Stage Two, these same activities continue to be highly effective.

Content that catches the imagination and motivates children to participate can be woven into every activity and each skill area. Figure 9.2 contains examples of content themes with qualities that have been effective with Stage Two children. These examples were taken from various areas of the academic curriculum to illustrate how emotional and dramatic content can be included in all curriculum areas. When a single theme is carried out through an entire week of activities, it serves as a mental organizer and a connection for the learning that is occurring in each of the activities.[16]

A child's successful involvement in materials and activities must provide satisfaction as an outcome of participation. Satisfaction and success are influenced, in large part, by the expectations set by adults. When adult standards for success match children's ability to participate and their standards for satisfaction, the chosen materials and activities will be effective. The children see themselves as benefiting from participating, and social-emotional growth continues. Although successful materials and activities for older and younger Stage Two students may differ in presentation, visual format, and level of sophistication, the essential message for students of any age in Stage Two is the same:

"The world is full of bad things, but they can be overcome. Good things happen . . . and good things can happen to me."

ACTIVITIES DESIGNED TO ACCOMPLISH THE GOALS AND OBJECTIVES FOR STAGE TWO

In this section we briefly describe activities found to be highly motivating and effective with children in Stage Two. We do not specify the length of the daily program, because the options are extensive and schedules must reflect the ages, skills, and needs of the children. The time constraints of the program must also be considered. However, the minimum activities that must be included to prepare a child for mastery of the Stage Two milestones for social-emotional development include a Play Time, Story Time, Snack Time, and Preacademic (Readiness) Time. Although these four activity areas do not necessarily need to be called by these names, the activities that are provided must include the same essential content. They provide multiple opportunities to focus on the four curriculum areas—Behavior, Socialization, Communication, and (Pre)Academics/Cognition. Most Stage Two programs, however, provide more extensive opportunities, typically including about ten activities each day.[17] The following list shows activities for a typical program. The activities marked with an asterisk should always be included at this stage.

Activities for a Typical Stage Two Program

Hello Time

Work Time (preacademic readiness)*

Play Time*

Story Time*

Art Time

Music Time

Outside Time (physical skills)

Snack Time*

Special Time

Good-bye Time

[15]See the section on selecting effective activities and materials in Chapter 4 for general guidelines for all stages of Developmental Therapy–Developmental Teaching, including Stage Two. Chapter 4 also contains a summary of steps for structuring a creative writing lesson for students in Stage Two and beyond.

[16]Chapter 4 contains an illustration of a unit for Head Start children in Stage Two that integrates all of the daily activities around the unifying theme of "Bears."

[17]Chapter 4 contains a discussion of the activities, materials, and schedules used in Developmental Therapy–Developmental Teaching. Table 4.1 in that chapter summarizes the types of activities usually used for typical preschool children and those with special needs.

Approximately 25% of the time is specifically for individual activities; the remaining time is used for group activities that have an individually designed focus. In this way, each child has many opportunities to participate and learn skills for interacting successfully with others. For toddlers just beginning Stage Two and older students with developmental delay, we plan activities that last about 10–15 minutes each. The time allocated for each activity is increased gradually as their age, skills, and enthusiasm for participating increase. The time planned for an activity also depends upon the nature of the content and materials—some activities and materials hold students' attention and involvement for longer periods than others.

Adaptations of the basic program of activities for older students in Stage Two usually contain many of these same activities. They are stated in different age-related words and interests but are adapted for individual needs, IEP objectives, time requirements, and physical skills. Here is an example of activities for older students in Stage Two, following a similar pattern of activities, but using different words to describe the general content of the activity:

Activities Adapted for Older Students Still in Stage Two

The Daily Report (Hello Time)

Reading (Work Time, part 1)

Writing (Work Time, part 2)

Recreation Time or "Break" (Play Time)

Literature (Story Time)

Art and Graphics (Art Time)

Music (Music Time)

Physical Education (Outside Time—physical skills)

Break (Snack Time)

Special Project (Special Time)

Wrap-Up (Good-Bye Time)

The two programs are essentially the same; however, the words used to describe each activity and the academic content are changed to reflect the advanced ages, interests, and mental maturation of older students. Another difference is the inclusion of more individual time in the program for older students. They generally are much more reticent to become involved in activities requiring them to interact with others. Typically "loners," these students seem to need more individual time early in their programs. It enables them to organize themselves and to focus on tasks. Individual time also helps many older students in Stage Two learn to manage their reactions when they believe they are encroached upon by others. But as they begin to experience success in their Stage Two program, the need for extended amounts of individual time gradually diminishes. In subsequent stages, less individual time and more group time is scheduled.

An Early Childhood Program for Children in Stage Two

In the following descriptions of activities, we focus them for early childhood, preschool, kindergarten, and Head

Figure 9.2. Examples of content themes for children in Stage Two.

Themes from Natural Science and Social Science

Monsters of the Deep	Bears
The First Rainbow	Dinosaurs
Our City	Teddy the Forgotten Frog
Alligators	Island Castaways
The Greatest Jet	The Sad Caterpillar

Themes from Literature and Language Arts

King Nellie	Five Elves
The Magic Beanstalk	The Gnome Train
Pirates	The Dragon and the Treasure
Secret Kingdom	The Crying Clowns
Princess Ellen	The Flying Carpet

Themes from Food, Health, and Physical Education

Cooking for Fun	Bionic Buddies
Refrigerator Mystery	Superman Meets the Cookie Monster
The Hungry Children	Escape to Chocolate Mountain
Apple Jack	The Day Snack Disappeared

Start programs, which have most of the children in need of a Stage Two program in Developmental Therapy–Developmental Teaching. However, we have found that older Stage Two children in the primary grades of elementary school and special education programs also benefit from these same activities.[18]

Hello Time. Hello Time, also called Talk Time, serves several purposes: The adult establishes psychological control as the person in charge and makes personal contact with every child in the group. The children are introduced to the events to come, motivated to participate, and encouraged to be a part of social communication.[19]

This first 5-minute activity brings the children together at a table. It usually begins with some sort of roll call, "Hello," or recognition of each child present. Some teachers sing a "Hello Song" for younger Stage Two children that is repeated each day so that the children can begin to imitate and join in. Sometimes Hello Time involves comments about the day, calendar, or weather from each child. As their memory skills increase, the teacher may ask the children to remember who is missing that day.

For children who are resistant to adults or choose not to talk, hand puppets have been used to encourage responses in Hello Time. Puppets can prepare children for an activity to come, review the steps for the next activity, or motivate them to participate. A puppet can serve as a response model for the children by answering the teacher's questions and also can be the teacher, asking questions of the children.

Work Time (for Preacademic Readiness Skills). After Hello Time, teachers with children in Stage Two move into Work Time or Story Time, depending on the age of the children, the length of their attention span, their thinking skills, and their individual IEP objectives. It often is the second activity of the morning because children are fresh and able to spend time focusing on activities and tasks that stimulate thinking skills. For individual paper-and-pencil tasks, each child has a folder or "work box" containing the materials to be used during this activity. If worksheets are used, they are often teacher-made and designed individually to directly target each child's preacademic objectives.

There are numerous commercial early childhood curriculum materials with readiness activities that can be used to acquire the specific milestones of the (Pre)Academics/Cognition area in Developmental Therapy–Developmental Teaching. A great amount of electronic equipment also is available commercially to assist in individualizing each child's preacademic program. We have found many computer software programs to be effective. There are also several devices for alternative communication that are helpful to some children during this preacademic work time. While children work independently on their individual tasks at a table, with a computer, or with other electronic equipment, the adults provide individual preacademic instruction as needed.

Some preacademic instruction in Stage Two is conducted with the children as a group, but typically, there is minimal group interaction. Initially, for group work, the teacher leads the activities and encourages the children to participate in unison. When they all are participating in unison activities, they are encouraged to take turns responding and participating. Later, to encourage more interaction, the children themselves may take turns playing the role of teacher.

A tape recorder is useful for a number of preacademic activities in a Stage Two program. Begin with recording sound effects until the children become skilled in hearing sounds and identifying the objects that make the sounds. Use crackling paper, emery boards or sandpaper, rice, cereal, or beans dropped in a tin can or a plastic cup. Encourage the children to think of what makes the sound or what idea the sound might convey. Most Stage Two children will also think of new sounds to make and ways to reproduce them. By combining sound effects with role-playing activities, conveying character and feeling through changes of voice, the group can eventually role-play a familiar story sequence and even add musical activities at the beginning and ending of the tape.

A chalkboard can solve a multitude of problems related to the transition from Work Time to the next activity. Because children often work at varying rates and complete their individual tasks at different times, provision must be made for attractive, supplemental activities while some are waiting for the others to finish. No child should be asked to do another assignment after completing an assignment early. A chalkboard provides excellent opportunities for supplemental preacademic and socialization activities for one or two students. With a chalkboard, they can move around and organize themselves for informal games of "school," "teacher," tic-tac-toe, mazes, dot-to-dot pictures, or drawing pictures collaboratively. Computers offer similar opportunities to interact informally with another child. Numerous software games and readiness programs provide excellent practice for eye-hand coordination, memory, matching, and categorizing.

Many preacademic milestones can be achieved by group games at the end of each Work Time. A modified treasure hunt is an example. The teacher hides parts of a large picture around the room, one piece for each child (a house, car, bicycle, motorcycle). As the group sits at the table, she gives a "clue" to each child in turn, telling the child where to walk and where to turn to find a part of the "treasure." As the group speculates on what the picture will be, each child has a turn. When the picture is put together, all the children have contributed to the whole, and they paste the results on

[18] This follows the sequence of Stage Two activities outlined in Table 4.1.

[19] Examples of introductions and step-by-step instruction are included in Chapter 4 in the section, "The Essentials of Effective Instruction."

another large sheet of poster paper for display. The ending brings the children together to consider their collaborative effort. This practice should be followed at the end of every preacademic time, giving ample attention to the successful participation of each student.[20]

Play Time. Play encourages exploration, spontaneous behavior, creativity, and independent practice. It is the natural activity of most children in Stage Two. Socialization and Behavior milestones are the major focus during Play Time, and functional social language is also emphasized.[21] For children beginning Stage Two, play involves many manipulative toys. Gradually, play becomes increasingly imaginative, social, and interactive. Play is usually planned for about 10–15 minutes and may be unstructured or structured, depending upon the ability of the members of the group to use play materials in purposeful and satisfying ways.

Free play seems to be difficult for most Stage Two children, perhaps because of the lack of structure and the fact that they must use their own resources and controls. During the first weeks of a beginning Stage Two program, free play may be an explosive, anxiety-producing activity and may cause the rest of the day to go badly. Children may withdraw, destroy materials, avoid meaningful play, or exhibit extreme aggressiveness. When this occurs, it may be better to begin with structured play or group games instead of free play. In this way, adults can gradually teach the children how to play with materials in appropriate ways.

One teacher provided a dramatic play situation for the children to arouse their interest and provide more structure at the beginning of each day. The story line was presented during Story Time, and each following morning they were encouraged to repeat the same dramatic theme with spontaneous improvisations. The teacher played the lead role in these dramas and in this way provided structure and set limits while motivating each child to respond. One of the first successful dramas centered around the "mean old witch," who was constantly stealing children from a little house in the woods. The crisis was resolved when they were rescued by the "good witch." The theme was deliberately chosen because many of the children in the group had been abused and were terrified of adults. This simple, dramatic play not only touched their deepest anxieties but provided a symbolic way to overcome their fears. It also stimulated reluctant children to become involved and brought some immediate organization and success to their play. The play skills they developed with this teacher's involvement were later used independently in spontaneous, unstructured play where they repeated the theme again and again, with the heroes changing form with each Play Time but always saving the children.

Make-believe with a box of hats or dress-up costumes is an excellent way to give younger children in Stage Two needed socialization experiences during Play Time. The teacher may bring out a supply of hats for particular characterizations, such as a cowboy hat, football helmet, firefighter's hat, police officer's hat, army helmet, hard hat, motorcycle helmet, old lady's hat, or baby bonnet. Such activities require alert adults who can move into the play to restructure it if it falters and then pull back to encourage independent exploration as the children catch on. It is also important to be alert to those who are not yet able to play this way or who are reticent about participating. A considerable amount of subtle play structuring may be necessary to encourage interaction with others.

If a child does not play with others, determine what is holding his interest when he is playing alone. By using materials that a child prefers, the groundwork can be laid for future interactive and cooperative play. This is done by encouraging another, more outgoing child to become involved with similar, parallel play and then gradually structuring interactions between the two children. There are a number of ways in which adults can structure interactive play during Play Time to teach children how to play with others. Here are two examples:

- Children playing alone with blocks or trucks are asked to "deliver the mail" to others who are involved in playing "dress-up."
- Two students with toy cars are both encouraged to follow a highway marked off by chalk on the floor. Then the adult adds, "Do you run the gas station, Steven? Susan's car is almost out of gas. Susan, ask Steven to fill 'er up."

The ending of Play Time is as important as the play activities themselves. Carefully structure cleanup and see that every student participates in putting materials or toys away. As they clean up, provide reflective statements about each child's contribution. Also, begin the transition to the next activity by a motivating statement concerning the next event on the schedule. This helps to convey that something equally interesting is about to happen, making it less difficult for the children to leave an enjoyable activity for something new.

Story Time. Story Time can be planned for any time in a schedule, depending upon when children need a quiet change from activities requiring physical movement and upon how the story content is to be used as part of a unit theme in other activities. It is held in a place where children and adults can be physically close. Story Time should be a pleasant, quiet contrast to the many physical activities needed during the day for an effective Stage

[20] Endings are an important part of every activity in Developmental Therapy–Developmental Teaching. See Chapter 4 for examples of effective endings and transitions for Stage Two activities.

[21] We sometimes begin a Stage Two program with play when the children arrive at different times. This allows the children the opportunity to orient themselves individually to the program and the adults before the more structured group activities begin.

Two program. It is also a contrast to the organized, structured activities—a time when children settle down and receive much-needed nurturance and reassurance. A considerable amount of physical touch can be used with children beginning Stage Two if they seem to respond positively.

Stories should be well illustrated and should not tax the children's attention span. Alternatives to reading from a book include telling the story or using flannel boards, film strips, or records; involving children in telling the story; and creating homemade storybooks. When a story becomes familiar and the group is spontaneous in responding to the sequence in the story line, child drama is an effective expansion of the story, encouraging creativity, spontaneous communication, and socialization among the children.

Perhaps even more effective than reading a story to children in Stage Two is telling a story with simple sentence structure, feeling tone, and animation. The adult storyteller can stop in the middle of a sentence and encourage the children to respond with a missing word or idea or questions such as "And then what happened?" or "What should they do now?" Eventually, the storyteller can give portions of the storytelling role to each of the children in turn.

Whatever form Story Time takes, it should involve children in active communication and socialization. It should fire their imaginations and teach them to follow the sequence in a dramatic event that leads to a satisfying conclusion. It should also provide content with characters who have feelings or problem situations similar to their own. This is an opportunity to help them vicariously experience and resolve the fears and anxieties they dread the most.

The essential criterion when selecting a story is that it lead to a satisfying ending. This is especially necessary for children who are at risk and those who are vulnerable to emotional problems and developmental anxieties. It is not always as easy as it sounds to select stories with satisfying endings. Often a storybook will have characters (sometimes animals) representing good and evil, or a plot in which good things happen to some of the characters but not to others. The standard resolution is for good to conquer evil. Unfortunately, many troubled children identify with the evil character or the one to whom misfortune falls. When this character is annihilated in the conclusion, the child experiences the same emotional annihilation vicariously, resulting in reinforcement of the developmental anxieties of abandonment or inadequacy. As in all activities for Stage Two children, Story Time should end with a sense of satisfaction, comfort, and success in becoming involved.

Art Time. Because most children in Stage Two are able to use basic art supplies and like to use art as an expressive outlet, it is an activity in which each child can participate with satisfaction. The art reflects the children's environment, visually and verbally, with color, lines, and shapes. As they work, they typically offer ideas and describe the art process as it unfolds. Early in the stage, they use *controlled scribbling,* which is an important step in gaining fine motor skills and dexterity in using the materials. These works may be "unreadable," but the children can usually talk about what they had in mind. It may also be necessary to accept this early work without much comment except to admire color, lines, and shapes. As the children become increasingly confident, they repeat and then elaborate on shapes, lines, and patterns that have been successful and pleasing to them. Toward the end of Stage Two, their pictures become *preschematic,* where shapes and meaning emerge and they can explain the idea they have reproduced and what they are doing with the materials (Lowenfeld & Brittain, 1970; Williams & Wood, 1977).

Art should be fun! To ensure that it is, we keep two guidelines in mind: First, provide materials that all of the children in the group can use with pleasure and satisfaction. Second, at the beginning of the activity, demonstrate the art process very simply and briefly. Art activities should be varied, to encourage flexibility in materials, creativity, and opportunities to express oneself. We give each child individual art supplies in the beginning of Stage Two. Gradually, we move the children toward sharing art materials with a partner, eventually expanding this by providing groups of supplies to share. We introduce the word *"cooperation"* as the signal that it is desirable to have a partner and work with another child. Similarly, we begin with activities that are individual art projects and eventually move the children to successfully collaborating on a mural or similar project in which each student makes an individual art contribution as part of a bigger scene (such as murals of a flower garden, a basket of vegetables, or a box of toys).

Stage Two children may be able to work at art projects designed for their interests and skill levels for up to 15 minutes (usually within 8–10 minutes). They can cut, color, draw, and create their own artwork. Sometimes they will need assistance with outlines or designation of the area they should work in. They also benefit from adult proximity and positive comments about the process. Sometimes redirection and restructuring of the project helps a child elaborate or experiment in new ways.

Watch carefully for the right moment to begin the ending segment of an art activity. Because of the need to bring closure and acclaim to each individual's work, followed by cleanup, this can be among the most difficult activities to end. Transitions often become chaotic if adults are not experienced in pacing, timing, and management. We look at the progress and attention level of each individual and then begin to end the activity with reflections about the children's successes. We make a comment to each child about what should be done to end the project. Acknowledgment and acceptance of each artistic effort is essential to each child's continuing participation and development.

Music Time. Music reaches almost everyone. Truly a universal language, music is an activity that few children try to resist. Also, musical activities foster the development of milestones in all four of the Developmental Therapy–Developmental Teaching curriculum areas for Stage Two. Because musical activities are easily adapted within a single group activity to individual skills, ages, and intellectual differences, they should be included every day. Following are guidelines adapted from Purvis (1981, pp. 63–65) for conducting musical activities with Stage Two children:

- Be familiar with the musical selection before using it.
- Carefully prepare the materials and organize the sequence of steps so that the activity flows smoothly.
- Allow children to decide for themselves what the music means, without preconceived ideas from adults.
- Try all types of musical materials; unfamiliar materials often spark children's creativity.
- Keep selections brief.
- Provide ways for children to hear their musical efforts replayed.
- Be flexible—the unexpected often is a creative leap.
- Avoid trying to explain what music means or how it makes them feel.
- Minimize the words used to introduce and close the musical activity. The pleasure is in doing.
- Minimize prerecorded music. It may restrict creativity and independent exploration of musical sounds and rhythms.
- Expect Music Time to be noisy.
- Make it fun, satisfying, and successful!

As with most activities in a Stage Two program, musical activities are conducted with an individual focus but in a group setting. Here are examples of a variety of musical activities that have been effective with Stage Two children, illustrating how the simultaneous participation of all group members in the activity fosters the acquisition of specific skills for development of social-emotional competence:

- Using instruments in a rhythm band to give a signal to other instruments to begin playing gives nonverbal, nonassertive children opportunities to influence and command others.
- Taking turns clapping a beat for others to follow provides opportunities for a student to be the music teacher and lead others.
- Making and using musical instruments such as tambourines, drums, and shakers builds enthusiasm for participating as a member of a group.
- Marching, clapping, moving, or dancing in pairs encourages Socialization skills for cooperative activity with others.
- Asking questions through a song requiring a unison chant or physical response, such as "If you're happy and you know it . . . ," brings individual children into group participation.
- Selecting favorite songs for the group to sing gives reticent children an opportunity to be assertive.
- Contributing a word, sentence, or refrain to a song creates a sense of making a worthy contribution.
- Singing a "color song" and raising a card when that color is mentioned stimulates attention as children watch and listen for their turn.
- Moving from one activity area to another with rhythms, clapping, or marching helps structure transitions.

Musical activities also can be effectively combined with every other activity in the program. For example, *Musical Play Time* uses rhythm instruments such as tambourines, triangles, rhythm sticks, bells, and maracas along with autoharps, resonator bells, glockenspiels, xylophones, and drums of various sizes to encourage children to explore sound and rhythm and manipulate the music materials creatively. Similarly, *Musical Art* encourages children in Stage Two to finger paint, draw, or color with felt-tipped pens, while listening to brief musical selections, to express "how the music sounds," even when they cannot describe it or tell what the music is conveying. In *Musical Make-Believe,* music provides emotional tone and creates a framework—or boundaries—for imagination, role play, or dramatic play, whereas in *Musical Storytelling,* children tell original stories while listening to musical selections. *Musical Composition* is yet another way to provide Stage Two children with opportunities for creative exploration. Almost all children in Stage Two enjoy creating songs with new words to familiar melodies, and learning to answer adult questions asked through song with a similar melody, patterning their answer to the adult's musical refrain (Purvis, 1981).

Outside Time (Physical Skills). Outdoor play offers an opportunity for physical activity and for acquiring movement skills, which are essential to progress in Stage Two. It also provides a change of scenery with different expectations for behavior. If possible, several Outside Times should be scheduled during a day. There should also be an alternative place indoors for daily work on physical skill development, if the outdoors cannot be used. Gyms or large activity rooms are also excellent alternative spaces.

Development of movement and socialization skills is the focus during Outside Time. Stage Two children need to acquire locomotion skills such as sliding, galloping, skipping, leaping, and jumping rope. They need to learn ball manipulation skills—throwing and catching, kicking, trapping, and striking a ball. Stunts and tumbling should also be part of the Stage Two program for developing physical skills, including make-believe movements and balancing skills.

Although adults traditionally think of Outside Time as "recess," or as free time to use the playground, in Developmental Therapy–Developmental Teaching, Outside Time is a very significant time for working on specific social-emotional milestones and responsible behavior. To achieve the goals and objectives for Stage Two, Outside Time must be designed skillfully and actively involve adults with the children. Physical movement activities are such an essential part of children's development in this stage that they need to have numerous movement activities interspersed throughout their day. In addition to the planned activities described here to encourage the development of needed physical and social skills, we also plan Outdoor Times when children have unstructured time to play, by themselves or with others. However, when children are at risk or troubled, they often do not know how to use free play time purposefully; the program must first focus on teaching them how to engage in outside activities so that they will be able to use free play successfully.[22]

Sometimes, adults hesitate to take Stage Two children outside because the freedom of space encourages impulsivity and out-of-control behavior. However, if the activity is carefully planned and structured, this does not have to be a problem. One effective Stage Two strategy centers around using make-believe themes that are so motivating that they overcome the children's impulses to run away. Here is an example of make-believe in a week-long unit on race cars that is highly effective in rechanneling children's running behavior into acceptable participation and successful outcomes. The children make cardboard steering wheels and racing helmets out of old rubber balls cut in half (during Art Time). A racetrack is roped off outside where the children are able to run their "cars." Green flags, checkered flags, stop signs, pit stops, and an adult in charge of the races are all devices used to structure the activity. It works, and in subsequent weeks the roped-off area becomes a horse pasture, farmyard, house, and camping hideout. Eventually, as the children begin acquiring some of the Stage Two developmental milestones in Behavior for participating in movement activities without intervention by adults, the rope will not be needed. The children should be able to use their own behavioral controls and stay with the group.

Always plan an alternative indoor movement activity for inclement weather. There are any number of group games for children in Stage Two that can be played inside, encourage cooperation, and do not have competition with winners and losers. Several classic examples are "Follow the Leader," "Mother, May I?" "Hot Potato," and "Cat and Mouse." Such games provide practice with Stage Two milestones in Behavior and Socialization. Younger children in Stage Two like "travel" games that work well indoors (these can also be used during Play Time). Using butcher paper on the floor for roads, the children and adults plan a trip and identify a particular destination (a store, swimming pool, lake, mountains, picnic, home). They also plan what they will see along the way (stop signs, mountains, railroad crossings, forests, bridge, stores). The children travel the road with a predetermined plan. Crossroads are added later; then children make maps to guide them to the destination. When combined with role play or child drama, these roads add structure, providing a dramatic story line and a role for each child along the way. This activity works well if children are particularly reticent about interacting with others or have difficulty keeping a story line going. A variation of this activity also works as a transition to the next activity. If space permits, a "road" can be marked off permanently with masking tape from a work table to the place where supplies are kept. A child is selected to get materials for the group, "travels" this road, and returns with the supplies for the next activity. If the child is given a "supply list" illustrated with pictures or written with basic words, another activity for (Pre)Academics/Cognition skills is added.

"Treasure Hunt" is another indoor game, offering opportunities for older children in Stage Two to focus on (Pre)Academics/Cognition, Behavior, and Socialization milestones. Children are given paper bags and individual lists with pictures of objects hidden in the room. When they complete their own list, they bring it to an adult to be checked and then return to the game to help another child.

As the ending of Outside Time draws close, it is helpful to alert children that the end is approaching. Look for the right time to break in with the signal to stop. Provide directions about where to gather the group together for the ending to this activity. There should be a designated place to gather, usually with some sort of evident boundary—a bench, fence, wall, tree, or corner of a building. As they gather, convey the expectation that it is time to become quiet, to rest and catch their breath. Use the group ending to discuss the activity and the positive contributions made by each member. They will quiet down to hear how they have been recognized. Then begin the transition to the next activity by briefly talking about what is to follow.

Snack Time. Because being outdoors may cause a difficult transition for some children in returning to the building, it is important for a very attractive indoor activity to follow. Because most children love Snack Time above all other activities, they willingly leave outdoor play if Snack Time is next.[23]

The enjoyment of food and supportive contact with adults during this time makes it an excellent opportunity

[22]Some troubled children are so tense and anxious that it may be helpful to include a preliminary relaxation or warm-up activity at the beginning of this Outside Time. We have seen great benefits, such as increased behavioral controls and positive participation, when such programs are used.

[23]Occasionally Snack Time may be held out-of-doors, as part of a special activity such as a picnic, a birthday celebration, or a Special Time project. However, such variations often create unsettling feelings in very troubled Stage Two children or may result in some children losing control and having an unsuccessful experience. Therefore, we generally do not recommend these outdoor variations in the Stage Two program for Snack Time, preferring instead to introduce the change gradually into the Stage Three program. (See Chapter 10.)

to focus on Communication and Socialization milestones. Snack Time should always be a time for talk and discussion between the children and adults. Adults often must guide the topic and encourage contributions from each child. The content of discussions should center around topics that every group member can speak about. Talk can also include a discussion to prepare the children for the next activity of the day. When role play or story dramatization follows, the adult can use Snack Time to review the familiar story that will be used in that activity.

At first, snacks should be distributed by the adults. Later, a chart designating a "leader" or "cook-for-the-day" can be used. If children progress rapidly in sharing materials, they should be encouraged to pass snacks among themselves. Eventually, they are ready to participate in an organized, cooperative activity to prepare the snack, especially pizza, cookies, sandwiches, or other nutritional snacks.

Participation in Snack Time is never withheld as a consequence of previous misbehavior or failure to accomplish another task. It is considered a scheduled activity in which all children are expected to participate every day. If a child is out of control or shows signs of using unacceptable behavior, the same management strategies are used during Snack Time as for other activities; the purpose is to redirect the child to participate in the activity and not allow disruption for the other children who are participating in the Snack Time activity.

Another problem that sometimes arises in Snack Time is when a child wants (or needs) special food. It is difficult to be sure that children feel that Snack Time has been personally successful and satisfying if other children have some sort of preferential treatment. Unless all the children are allowed to have something different that they especially like, we discourage giving special snacks. We prefer instead to focus on cooperative sharing, in which each child receives as much as she wants of the same wholesome snack. Because food has such symbolic meaning for so many young children, it can become a source of regression or a focal point for conflict with adults. To guard against this, the focus is shifted away from the food, and the social communication aspects of the activity receive the emphasis.

As with all other activities in Developmental Therapy–Developmental Teaching, Snack Time closes with an ending that includes having the children clean up the materials or supplies that were used. The adult brings the children back together again as a group, reducing excitement and getting their attention for the transition to the next activity.

Special Time (Creative Activities). Special Time is a creative period that uses material from the unit theme for the week's activities or from Story Time. It often is effective when it follows directly after Story Time or when it is used to combine art, music, role play, or drama. Creative activities offer children ways to express themselves and explore new ideas.

Children in Stage Two gravitate to activities and materials that permit them to influence, assert, and command in ways that are acceptable and bring approval from adults. By involvement in a creative play activity, they may act out a portion of their life experience that they can never express in words. Creative activities in Special Time provide acceptable ways to express feelings and experience alternative solutions—*doing to,* rather than *being done to.* Left alone, almost all children will resort to imaginative play of one sort or another. We find that by including creative, dramatic play in the program, all of the Stage Two milestones for social-emotional development can be encouraged. This also becomes a powerful way to help all children, especially those who are troubled or who are at risk, to resolve developmental anxieties and concerns.

Role play is a natural outgrowth of storytelling and is an important phase of creative expression and dramatic play. Although we have mentioned role play previously in the discussion of Play Time, it is such an important part of the Stage Two program that we recommend its use during Special Time at least twice a week, if not daily. Stage Two children love to role play how to behave and what to do in familiar situations. Characters or events are selected from stories, music, pictures, TV, or actual experiences of the children. Because role play in Stage Two is first done in unison (all children play the same role at the same time), the topic is most effective when all of the children have the same prior experience or familiarity with it. This is why stories heard by the children during Story Time are particularly useful to repeat in role play during Special Time.

When role play is first introduced to children in Stage Two, the adult (or a puppet) serves as a model. The adult initiates the situation and sets the tone. The characters and the play are developed by the children without any props or preplanning. The adult defines the action by role-playing the central figure. Here is an example: The adult plays a student struggling to put on a coat. She asks the group, "What shall I say?" or "What shall I do?" The children contribute solutions that the adult then role-plays. Next, the children think of another situation and they all participate in unison. Eventually, they become sufficiently comfortable to role-play individual characters.

When the adult assumes a leadership role, in character (the chief of a "tribe," the head of a household, the captain of a group), events can be kept moving dramatically and under control. This provides a sense of security and a behavioral response model for inexperienced children. In such a role, the adult can create a sense of drama and excitement and can also avoid loss of control by a child who might otherwise be carried away by the excitement.

After a group has some success with role play, the adult pulls back from direct participation except to set the tone or to move in as a character when a child indicates that unacceptable behavior or loss of control is imminent. By stepping in and out of a role, as needed, the adult is able to make remarks that encourage the children's characters, move the story line along, and manage an ending that brings satisfaction to everyone.

Although it is important to anticipate problems that might occur while role-playing an incident, be prepared for changes that occur spontaneously while the children role-play. Follow their new leads as long as the role-playing situation remains relevant to the chosen topic. And, as in all Stage Two activities, the conclusion or ending must be positive; all of the students must end the role play feeling satisfied with their own participation and the success of their particular character.

Good-Bye Time. The ending to each daily program is critical. The children are gathered together in an area where they can sit quietly and participate in a social communication activity that very briefly reviews the day's events. This is the time when high activity levels are reduced, relationships between adults and children are strengthened, and the successes of the day are the focus. The purpose is to have each child leave with a sense of organization and personal satisfaction in having participated.

We do not review misbehavior, recount negative behavior, or criticize during Good-Bye Time. The adults make all of the children feel good about their individual contributions. Even the smallest success or progress may be praised, verbally and through body language. We sometimes refer to this as the time for giving "A's"—*attention, affirmation, approval,* and *admiration.* Here are several ways to do this:

- Look with approval and comment about the way a child put the puzzle pieces together.
- Smile in a way that conveys a compliment about how two children designed a city made of blocks.
- Comment about the best thing each child did with another child.
- Reflect some thoughtful action by a child toward another child.
- Affirm the child's work by saying, "Give me five—that's your best work ever!"

Examples of Role Play and Dramatic Play
for Children in Stage Two

Situations

What happens when you
- go to the store?
- go to the dentist (or doctor)?
- go to a ball game?
- have an accident?
- visit a friend?
- have visitors come to school (or home)?

Characters

- Animals with human characteristics
- Characters from favorite books (*The Wild Things, The Cat in the Hat*)
- Family roles (grandparent, parent, sibling, neighbor)
- Community helpers (teacher, police officer, store clerk)
- TV characters (the Muppets, *Sesame Street,* Barney)

Themes

- A magic toy shop where all the toys come to life
- Traditional fairy tales
- Adventures of a make-believe family
- Taking care of children with accidents or illness
- Looking for hidden treasure
- Protecting the fort (castle, ship) from pirates
- Characters running away from home
- Finding a magic wand (bottle, shoe, stick)

If a child does not talk during Good-Bye Time, the adult uses strategies to obtain some minimal social communication and exchange of ideas. This may require giving the child the words or phrases to use, or providing another adult to model verbal responses that reflect on the positive aspects of the day. Good-Bye Time can be very upsetting to some troubled children. If they have had great emotional support and comfort from adults in the program and have had satisfying successes by participating in the day's activities, they may be reluctant to leave. Children who are emotionally at risk may participate and cooperate fully throughout the day and then lose control during the final Good-Bye Time. This signals that the security they feel in the program is meeting an emotional need, and they often require personal time with the adults to provide memory links that will sustain them until the next day. Each day must end with the children feeling good about what happened and eager to return.

"All Aboard Our Train"—A Week-Long Unit for Stage Two

This week-long unit was designed for preschool and young primary-age children in Stage Two who are participating in an early childhood special education program that includes two hours of Developmental Therapy–Developmental Teaching daily. Figure 9.3 gives the weekly plan, following the general sequence of activities outlined previously.[24]

The activities for Monday are described in some detail below. For the remainder of the week, there is little variation in the routine, organization, or procedures. Each of the daily activities is an elaboration of those presented on Monday. In this way, concepts and skills are coordinated. With *repetition* and *variation,* both success (from familiarity) and interest (from curiosity) contribute to an expanding proficiency in participating in these activities as the week progresses.

Hello Time. The children enter the room and are greeted warmly by the teacher, who is wearing a train conductor's hat. She calls "All aboard our train!" and directs them to the table (the "train") for Talk Time. The teacher asks the children about the blue engine posted on the wall in front of the daily schedule constructed of train cars: "What color is it? Who is sitting in the engine?" The emphasis is on Communication objectives. The focus shifts to Behavior objectives for participation and (Pre)Academics/Cognition objectives for perceptual motor skills when the teacher brings out a box of large snap-together blocks and demonstrates how to build an engine. Each child is given the same number of blocks and builds an engine like the teacher's. The conductor's hat is passed around, and each child, in turn, calls, "All aboard," like the conductor. At the end of Talk Time, the teacher, in the conductor role, directs the children to "park" their engines in the box ("train station") and calls, "All aboard for Story Time!"

Story Time. In the story corner, the children sit on the floor facing the teacher. The teacher presents the book *The Little Engine That Could* and tells the story. On subsequent days the teacher adds movements to the story and eventually moves the children into simple role play. The unit culminates at the end of the week in a movement experience where the children, all in the role of the little blue engine, help the circus engine back to the town (the table).

Work Time. Each child has a folder of worksheets focusing on individual (Pre)Academic/Cognition objectives. On each folder is the child's name and a cutout of the little blue engine. The children work independently, while the teacher contacts each one frequently to give encouragement and help. As the children complete the specified work, the teacher checks each child's work and suggests a free-time activity in the play area.

Play Time. In the toy cabinet are toy trains, train tracks, conductor's hats, blocks, people, animals, toy buildings, the snap-together trains from Hello Time, and the storybook. The teacher encourages play about the story line and interaction among the children. Socialization objectives are the focus. When the end of Play Time is announced, the children are directed to drive their trains to the station (toy cabinet).

Special Time. At Special Time, the teacher uses art experiences to reinforce the train story, the theme concepts, and the vocabulary. Each child makes a train car by pasting together precut shapes and adds pictures of food and toys as the freight. When the train cars are completed, they are collected and displayed on a bulletin board behind the little blue engine on the wall. Objectives for Behavior and (Pre)Academics/Cognition are the emphasis here.

Music Time. The teacher and children sit on a rug for Music Time. Several music activities, designed specifically for this unit, are used throughout the week. The children play sand blocks to a tape recording of "I've Been Working on the Railroad." They stop and start along with the music. While singing "The Wheels on the Train Go 'Round and 'Round" (modified from "The Wheels on the Bus"), the children take turns taping precut and laminated parts onto a laminated picture of a train engine. At the end of Music Time, the children form a train behind the teacher and return to the table, singing, "This train is going to the table, this train . . ." (modified from "This Train Is Bound for Glory"). The emphasis in this activity is

[24]This unit was designed by Bonnie McCarty. Chapter 4 includes another example of a unit for a Stage Two preschool group—"Bears."

Figure 9.3. "All Aboard Our Train"—a week-long unit for Stage Two.

Daily Schedule	***Monday***	***Tuesday***	***Wednesday***	***Thursday***	***Friday***
Hello Time	Who's on our train?	Make a train like mine!	Build your own train	Park your train in the station	Fix the broken train
Story Time	*The Little Engine That Could*	*The Little Engine That Could*	All aboard our pretend train	All aboard our pretend train	All aboard our pretend train
Work Time	Jobs at the train station: Count the trains	Jobs at the train station: Which train is different?	Jobs at the train station: Find all of the blue engines	Jobs at the train station: The alphabet train	Jobs at the train station: Help the train stay on the track
Play Time	All aboard for fun with trains	All aboard for fun with trains	All aboard for fun with trains	All aboard for fun with trains	All aboard for fun with trains
Special (Art) Time	Load up your trains!	All aboard for a trip!	Make your own train station	Little engine story: "Wheels"	Let's make "engine cookies"
Outside Time	Follow the engine	Climb the mountain	Train tricks	The great train relay race	Don't fall off the track!
Snack Time	Power punch and toy crackers	"I-think-I-can" pudding	Power punch and toy crackers	Power punch and toy crackers	Power punch and "engine cookies"
Music Time	Moving down the track	All aboard our train	The stop-and-go train	This train is going to the station	Working on the railroad
Good-Bye Time	What did we take on our train?	What did we see on our trip?	What can our train do?	Where did our train go today?	How did we help the little engine?

on Behavior objectives for participation and on Socialization objectives for cooperative interactions.

Outside Time. The teacher stands at the door and calls "All Aboard." The children line up to go outside. Large snap-together climbing cubes are set up as a train. The children take turns being conductor in the "engine." The others are the passengers. Playground monkey bars become the "mountain" the little engine has to climb. The children and teacher make believe that they are chugging up the mountain on the bars, saying, "I think I can, I think I can." Objectives for large motor skills are the focus.

Snack Time. Snack Time includes toy-shaped cookies, oranges, and apples—a repeat of the make-believe freight. On other days of the week, during the Special Time activity, the children make "engine pudding" by taking turns shaking a jar of instant pudding while everyone chants, "I think I can, I think I can." On Friday, the children make cutout "engine cookies." These cooking products are used for snacks, providing Communication and Socialization experiences in discussions about each child's participation.

Good-Bye Time. During Good-Bye Time, the teacher leads the children in a review of the day's activities. The children are given a brief preview of coming attractions, the "Good-Bye Song" is sung using each child's name, and the children line up at the door to go to the bus with their teacher. Communication objectives for describing experiences are the focus in this final activity.

SUMMARY

Preschool children who are progressing in a typical way through early childhood are in Stage Two of social-emotional development. Programs that are intended to foster their continuing development in social-emotional competence and responsible behavior use the Developmental Therapy–Developmental Teaching curriculum to focus on achieving the goals and milestones. Similarly, older children with developmental challenges that have limited their development of social-emotional competence may also be in need of a Stage Two program to acquire the necessary milestone skills. The overall goal for all children in Stage Two, with or without disabilities, is to learn to respond with success to the environment and expectations set for them by adults.

When children are in Stage Two, their dominant concern is to obtain the approval of adults so that the adults will be pleased with them. The behavior of Stage Two children reflects this concern. They seek adult recognition and praise while going to great lengths to avoid failure or punishment. They typically view adults as omnipotent—all-powerful—and responsible for solving problems and maintaining order. This view is such a pervasive part of their development that it shapes almost all that they do and learn. Adults who provide them with the four "A's"—attention, affirmation, approval, and admiration—foster continuing development. Without this significant relationship with adults, Stage Two children are caught in circumstances that put them at risk for emotional and behavior problems. Failure to obtain the necessary adult support also may introduce a cycle of failure in which the typical developmental anxiety—inadequacy—emerges as a powerful and detrimental block to further development.

In the Developmental Therapy–Developmental Teaching program for Stage Two children, adult roles are defined specifically to provide the necessary adult support that enables a young child to become increasingly independent and successful. Activities focus on exploration and imagination. The curriculum's content provides opportunities to deal with fears and anxieties symbolically, with good conquering bad. The content also provides the comforting reassurance that good behavior is rewarded by adults. In this way, the program reassures children that adults can be depended upon to see that children are successful, that adults hold limits, and that good things happen in children's lives. Initiative, confidence, and responsible behavior are the products of these effective interactions with adults and the world around them. The overall goal for the Stage Two curriculum is achieved as children spontaneously participate, communicate, seek out others, and respond in positive ways to people, materials, and activities in their immediate environments. We summarize this approach by the following guidelines:

- Insist on the participation of every child in every activity.
- Design activities so that every child in the group will enjoy participating and will feel successful.
- Avoid activities requiring long waits for a turn and have unison activities for children beginning Stage Two so that they do not have to wait for turns to participate.
- Redesign games and activities if necessary so that there are no losers.
- Select activities and materials that the children's age-peers are using and redesign them as needed to guarantee success.

- Design every activity with many opportunities for every child to talk, and convey the expectation that talking is part of participating.
- Provide brief and simple demonstrations of each activity or material so that the children have a model to imitate successfully.
- Encourage children's involvement with each other by pairing them for some activities.
- Select content themes in which characters are children or animals in situations that are close to the personal experiences of each child in the group.
- Always ensure that there is a satisfactory resolution at the end of a story or creative play.
- Be flexible, improvise, and redesign a planned activity when children's responses indicate that it is not sufficiently motivating or is too difficult to ensure success.

PRACTICE

Using the key points in this chapter

Evan is a child whose unmet emotional needs so dominate his preschool situation that he is beginning to show delay in all areas of development. His timely referral for an early childhood special education program may prevent further delay. Review this report on Evan, considering that you will be his teacher.

Using Figure 3.2 and the milestones in each curriculum area outlined in this chapter, identify Evan's social-emotional profile and the milestones he needs to acquire in each area of development in order to achieve the goals for social-emotional competence in Stage Two. With that in mind, answer the questions below.

1. What social-emotional goals and milestones should be emphasized for Evan in each curriculum area?
2. What appears to be Evan's central concern?
3. What does he appear to value?
4. Which developmental anxieties seem to be established and which seem to be emerging now?
5. What might be provided to reduce Evan's anxieties?
6. What type of adult role would you try to convey to him?
7. What management strategies would you use when he attempts to sabotage a group activity with negative verbal comments?
8. What content themes might catch his interest and ensure his participation?
9. Which activities and materials would provide optimal opportunities to help him participate successfully?

Evan

Five-year-old Evan has had a very difficult time in his preschool program. He ignores the other students and pushes them away when they try to play with him. He reacts by hitting any child who attempts to take his toys or looks at his projects. He refuses to share and destroys materials when he is allowed to spend time by himself in the activity centers. When he is asked to be a leader he laughs inappropriately, acts silly, and runs away from the activity. The teachers have great difficulty coaxing him to participate in any organized activity.

Evan shows much ambivalence toward his teachers. Sometimes he accepts their attention; at other times he regresses into infantile behavior—ignoring their attempts to talk with him, lying down, and sucking his thumb. Or, unpredictably, he may strike out at the adults by kicking and biting.

The staff was so concerned about his behavior that they suggested to Evan's parents that they seek special assistance. The assessment team for a local early childhood special education program met with Evan's parents and together they identified their concerns and Evan's needs. After the assessments, they met again and agreed that Evan has achieved most of the milestones for social-emotional development in Stage One, but only a few in Stage Two. They also agreed that he will benefit from intensive Developmental Therapy–Developmental Teaching in the early childhood special education program, to focus on acquiring the Stage Two milestones he needs. Evan's IEP will be reviewed every 10 weeks to evaluate progress on these milestones and to add a similar Developmental Teaching program to his regular preschool program.

CHAPTER 10

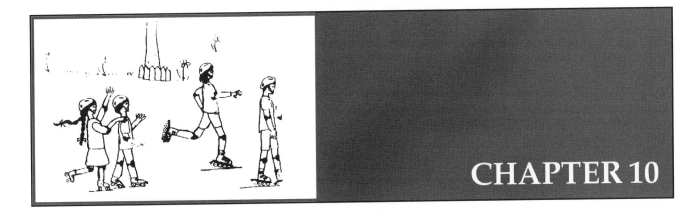

Stage Three: Learning Skills for Successful Group Participation

I am what I can imagine I will be.
—E. H. ERIKSON, 1959/1980, P. 87

STAGE THREE: GIVING UP TO GAIN

The major accomplishment in social-emotional development during Stage Three is the formation of a sense of adequacy in each student as a successful participant in group activities.[1] Children typically begin Stage Three about the time they start first grade in school, and they make the transition to the next stage within three years. Throughout this stage, they are learning to regulate their own impulsivity so that fewer outside controls are needed. They are also learning to use verbal skills rather than physical and behavioral responses to express themselves. They are struggling to overcome anxieties of inadequacy and guilt, created by events, people, and feelings that they cannot control, or by expectations of others that they cannot fulfill.

Most children beginning Stage Three must learn to participate in organized group activities without adult control. Although they have previously been introduced to many basic group activities in early childhood programs, students entering first grade begin to take part in many more organized activities requiring group skills such as taking turns, sharing materials, contributing to group planning, accepting suggestions from other students, developing simple friendships, participating when another student is leader, and recognizing the characteristics and needs of others. They rely on rules and routine for security and find it hard to accept changes. They express great concern over nonconformity of others and want adult authority to be used to maintain the rules with fairness. Beneath this concern for an orderly group, however, is the concern of children for their own rights and security as individuals.

The paradox for children during this stage of development is that even as they begin to give up personal demands so that they will be accepted by their peers, they also need experiences where their new skills and ideas result in personal acclaim. They need to feel individually important while looking good in the eyes of others. It is a slow process to understand that there are personal benefits in giving up a totally self-oriented view when participating as a member of a successful group.

The Developmental Therapy–Developmental Teaching curriculum for Stage Three provides experiences that help students learn to make friends, control impulsivity, and participate in planning group procedures and rules, and, in general, learn that social cooperation and communication are pleasurable and desirable. The curriculum content focuses on simple real-life situations that allow for abundant success in group endeavors. Themes that are personally and culturally relevant to every member in the group catch their attention and encourage spontaneous,

[1]As we move into Stage Three, we arbitrarily shift between using the terms *children* and *students* as a reminder that, while they are still children, they are also members of groups in school, and school is a major element in their development during this period.

Stage Three Students in Brief

Program goal:	Successful group participation
Central concern:	Looking good to others
Motivating values:	Recognition by others; fairness; law and order
Developmental anxiety:	Guilt over failure to meet the expectations of others
Approach to problems:	Self-protective; desire to justify acts; adults are responsible for order and problem resolution
Source of authority:	Rules; important, powerful adults
Type of adult needed:	Fair but strong leader who keeps others in line while recognizing individual's good points
Effective strategies:	Positive feedback and praise for individual contributions to group; reflection of positive events; motivating material; interpretation; verbal redirection; adult models; rules; Life Space Intervention
Materials, activities, and content themes:	Group focus; courage; heroes; epic adventure; good versus evil; right and wrong

sustained participation. Heroes and bigger-than-life characters, and stories in which good overcomes evil and right wins out over wrong, are the content themes to which students in Stage Three respond with enthusiasm. This content allows them to identify with winners and the forces of good. By vicariously identifying with heroes who win, they reduce their own fear of failure and their own guilt about being inadequate in the opinion of others.

With mastery of the program for Stage Three, students have the basic skills for successful group participation. They are able to regulate their own behavior with decreasing need for outside controls. Behavior and expression of emotion have fallen under greater self-direction. Words become a substitute for physical reactions to stress or crisis. Increasingly, students are able to talk with adults about ways to handle conflict and solve problems. Students finishing Stage Three recognize that the group has some value and are willing to commit themselves in small ways to its success. They have discovered that social cooperation and communication can be pleasurable. Facilitating these accomplishments are the students' increased abilities to use symbols for representation of personal experiences and an expanding capacity to understand social situations from others' perspectives.

In our review of the Stage Three portion of Developmental Therapy–Developmental Teaching, we organize the material around these topics:

- typical social-emotional processes developing during Stage Three
- goals and objectives for children in Stage Three
- how the program meets the needs of children in Stage Three
- group dynamics and group conflict in Stage Three
- activities designed to meet the goals and objectives for Stage Three

TYPICAL SOCIAL-EMOTIONAL PROCESSES DEVELOPING DURING STAGE THREE

Social-emotional development during Stage Three can be characterized as a drive for self-esteem, acquired through an expanding sense that others approve and culminating in success as a member of a group. This self-esteem develops through children's *initiative, industry,* and *activity* within ever-expanding social contexts (Erikson, 1950/1963; 1959/1980). Although interactions with others continue to be seen from a self-protective viewpoint during this stage, children develop control of their impulses and are able to conform to the expectations, standards, and rules established by adults (Loevinger, 1976; Selman, 1980). While they learn to enjoy the results of group membership, they continue to operate throughout this stage from a self-protective, self-gratifying frame of reference, in which they are increasingly vulnerable to fears and anxieties about failing in the opinion of others. Figure 10.1 portrays these key processes for social-emotional development during Stage Three.

Children begin Stage Three with basic intellectual, social, emotional, and physical skills and an emerging sense of self-worth. They have intellectual and sensorimotor systems that give them the capacity to translate preferences and feelings into constructive actions. They are able to see their world and themselves in organized ways, and their awareness of the relationship between cause and effect is developing. This expanding capacity for more abstract thinking also fosters the expansion of values that they use in making choices. The key values for children during Stage Three are *fairness* and *right brings rewards.* For them, this means fair treatment for themselves. They also expect to see the reward of good behavior and the punishment of wrongdoing.

Two major forces have an effect on their psychological development during Stage Three: *self-protection* and *the*

Figure 10.1. Key processes of typical social–emotional development in Stage Three. The dotted lines indicate the inner life—thoughts and feelings.

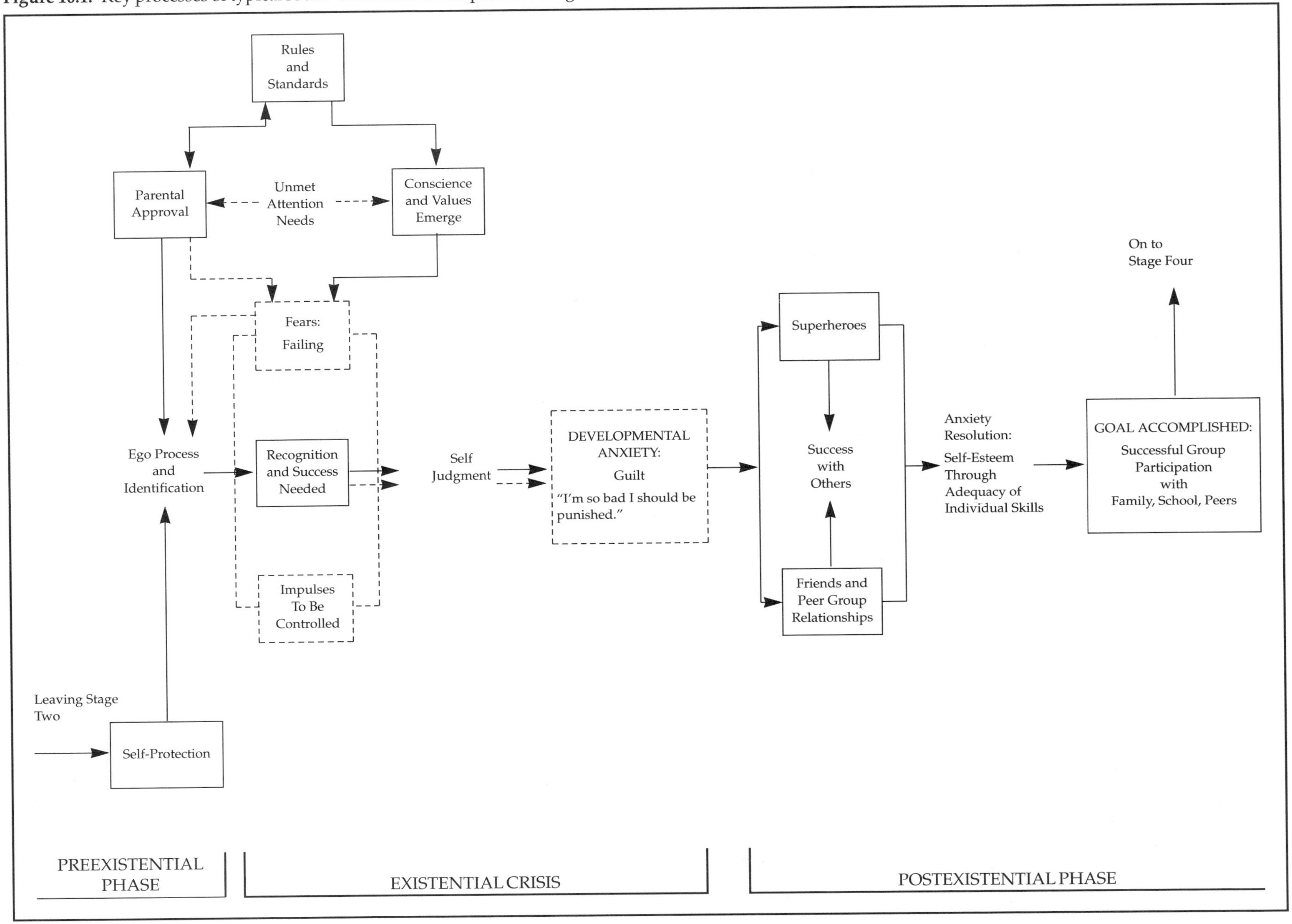

need for adult approval. Kegan called this phase "the imperial self" (Kegan, 1982, chap. 6). Even as their skills expand in ways that gratify their own drives and protect their emotional needs, these children continue to see adults as the source for protection. At the beginning of Stage Three, while they rely on parents and other adult authority figures to solve problems, they also believe in magical solutions, fantasy, make-believe, and wishes. But, increasingly, they identify with the standards adults have established and assimilate these standards as their own. The need for increased competence to meet these expectations brings about greater impulse control and self-regulated behavior. Control of their own behavior and solutions to problems become governed by rules based in reality, bringing them recognition and success. As the rules and social expectations of adults become their own, children in Stage Three are learning what is expected of them as group members—in their family, school, neighborhood, and church.

New attitudes, feelings, and behaviors are formed during Stage Three by the process of identification with valued adults, in which children assimilate the characteristics of parents and other significant adults (A. Freud, 1973). This is perhaps the most dynamic force at work during development in Stage Three. The boundaries provided to developing children by their parents, and parental accessibility to their children, seem to be necessary for the process of identification to occur. In the previous stage, children imitated their parents' behavior to obtain security, protection, and acceptance. But in Stage Three, they mentally assimilate their parents' attitudes, characteristics, and values. If the parents are available to their children; if parental rules, standards, and emotional responses are mature and reasonable; and if parents deal with children in helpful and approving ways, then children take on many of their parents' positive characteristics. These characteristics and values contribute to the formation of children's personalities, beliefs, and behaviors (Coopersmith, 1967). They shape conscience development and values used by children to regulate their own behavior with peers, in groups, and with other significant adults.

There is abundant research on parents' personality traits and how they influence children's developing personalities. When parents deal with their children aggressively, a model for aggression is provided. The result may be imitation: A child assimilates a parent's aggressive patterns of behavior and evokes a similar response from the parent, eventually alienating the child from the parent. Anger and rejection of a parent leaves a child without needed approval and love, producing more resentment and anger. Historically, this anger has not been openly directed toward a neglectful or inaccessible parent. Direct physical aggression toward parents or teachers was practically absent in children under 10 years of age and among young teens (Mussen, Conger, Kagan, & Huston, 1990, chaps. 9–10). Recently, however, national statistics show a clear change in this pattern, suggesting that the bonds created by parental approval and love may not be adequate in these instances to overcome the self-centered needs and drives of some children. Although the causes for this are not clear, some psychologists suggest that parental neglect—emotional or physical—or the lack of boundaries for a developing child are root causes of the failure to develop emotional controls, responsible behavior, and social-emotional competence (Anthony, 1976; Coopersmith, 1967).[2]

Some children in Stage Three cannot openly show their disappointment or anger toward valued adults for fear of retaliation or losing adult approval. Other children use verbal aggression, including cursing and profanity, as a substitute for more physical forms of conveying their anger. This is a way for a child to feel relief from hostile feelings toward his parents, teachers, or other adults without actually losing control and succumbing to physical aggression. Passive aggression is another way for children to respond to adults who have failed them. Because they are afraid of losing a valued adult's approval by open opposition, they retaliate in covert ways, such as lying, hoarding, stealing, using sex words, or failing in school.[3]

Fear of Failing

Because they have assimilated standards that adults have set for their behavior, children in Stage Three experience many fears and feelings that cannot be expressed openly or fulfilled. They are aware of the expectations and rules and invest considerable energy in winning approval and explaining away their mistakes with "I forgot" or "I don't know." They worry about feelings and forces that cannot be controlled and mistakes they might make. Their fears and anxieties are the result of this struggle for impulse control and their attempts to meet the standards of others. Following are sources of children's fears and anxieties during Stage Three:

- a sense of the need to meet standards
- the possibility of letting out hidden secrets or unacceptable drives
- concern that others will disapprove
- frustration over unfulfilled feelings, often the need for nurturance and love
- hostility toward a parent, often because of unmet love needs or "unfair" discipline
- the impact of the irreversible nature of death and adults' inability to control it

[2]There are discussions in Chapter 2 about the attachment-separation process between parent and child and also about teachers as stand-ins for other adults in a child's life.

[3]Chapter 5 contains a discussion of ways to use this curriculum with children who have severe passive aggression or other forms of severely troubled behavior.

The shape and form of fears usually depend upon past experiences and relationships with adults, ego processes, cognitive maturation, and conscience development. Characteristically, fears of children during Stage Three are expressed in nightmares, school-related fears, death fears, obsessions, compulsions, symbolic play, art, or other creative activities. Their fears usually take several forms:

Realistic fears	"It could happen."
Remote fears	"It might happen."
Mystical, symbolic fears	"Wouldn't it be awful if it happened?"

Many fears of young children in Stage Three can be resolved by parental support and psychological strength that reassures them about their own adequacy and guides them in resolving their fears. However, at some point during Stage Three, all children come face-to-face with the realization that adults are not all-powerful and are not always in control. This new awareness creates an *existential crisis*. The term is used to describe the frightening revelation that adults will not always be able to solve all problems and meet all needs. This leads children to question who will provide security and to wonder if they must be the ones to then take on the burden of coping with problems. This threatening possibility is almost always anxiety-producing and increases fears. The natural existential crisis is intensified by experiences with death, divorce, perceived abandonment by an absent parent, parental alcohol and drug abuse, or hearing and observing the catastrophic reactions of adults who are in crisis themselves.[4] Without a sense of self-confidence and a stable parent—as a model for coping with stress—a child will have difficulty resolving the existential crisis and may become vulnerable to a sustained period of anxiety.

Guilt: The Developmental Anxiety of Children in Stage Three

In addition to developmental anxieties about abandonment and inadequacy that are sometimes carried over from previous stages, children in Stage Three are vulnerable to a newly emerging developmental anxiety—*guilt*. Feelings of guilt typically are acquired by age 6 or 7 and continue to develop during this stage (A. Freud, 1965). Guilt is a developmental anxiety that results from a child's sense of failing to meet parents' standards, a reaction to severe punishment and blame turned inward, or failure to obtain parental love. It is associated with high levels of conscience development. Carried to an extreme, it results in an overly anxious, superego-dominated child whose autonomy, self-esteem, and self-reliance are severely impaired (Ausubel, Sullivan, & Ives, 1980).[5]

The most dynamic aspect of guilt is a child's self-judgment of failure to meet adults' standards and expectations—inability to be the person they are expected to be. This anxiety permeates development during Stage Three and frequently continues to be evident in Stage Four. As a buffer from the psychological pain of guilt, some children and teens become alienated. It is easy to see how a child (or a teen still in Stage Three), striving to obtain or keep parental approval and identifying with adults' values, can react negatively when parental behavior is abusive or discipline is overly harsh and unfair. Severe discipline and abusive behavior by parents are assaults on children's intense need for parental approval. It is very difficult for them to identify with these parents. Yet, paradoxically, a child at this age often takes on the responsibility for abuse; the guilt that can arise from this may be enormous. These children may come to feel extremely inadequate in the eyes of their parents and blame themselves.

The sense of failure and inadequacy among Stage Three children is quite different from that of children during Stage Two, where the concern was being successful to receive praise or avoid criticism. In contrast, during Stage Three, children self-judge. They identify with valued adults whose standards and values then become their own. If these adults see them in a negative light, the children's self-image will be a similar one—of failure and inadequacy. It is a view of themselves that carries over into school and their relationships with peers, teachers, and other adults.

Peer Relationships in Stage Three

As a counterbalance to the power and pressures from adults, peer relationships begin to develop during Stage Three as a way for children to increase their sense of independence and affirm themselves with others. "Looking good" in front of peers is essential to expanding self-esteem, and failure in front of peers reinforces feelings of inadequacy. Yet these restrictions on personal expression are not yet under control during Stage Three. Brown and Gilligan, in their studies of the psychological development of young girls, clearly illustrate this process as it occurs during Stage Three—the burden of trying to please others for relationships and personal affirmation (Brown & Gilligan, 1992, p. 45). These characteristics of peer relationships change dramatically from the beginning to the end of Stage Three. Selection of a "best friend," small groups of friends, and enemies is characteristic of typical 6- to 8-year-olds and also of older children in Stage Three. These alliances shift frequently, but by the end of Stage

---

[4] Chapter 2 contains a discussion of the existential crisis and the developmental processes before and after this period, which typically occurs during Stage Three.

[5] Although the developmental anxiety of guilt typically occurs during Stage Three, it can emerge earlier in children whose life circumstances force an early existential crisis. Similarly, life experiences shape a child's motivations. See Appendix 5 for a summary of motivational systems.

Three, peer groups and relationships become more tolerant and stable.

Attitudes about how rules should apply to other children also change dramatically during this stage. For children beginning Stage Three, rules represent order, security, and the only way to govern the actions of others. Rules are absolute and come from adult authority, which is also viewed as absolute. To illustrate the way these children strive to adhere to rules as guidelines for behavior, Brown and Gilligan (1992, pp. 74–75) describe an 8-year-old girl in their study who, with her mother's help, prepared a notebook of advice to "Think before you act!"

Tattling is another common characteristic. It is a way for children to communicate their need for reassurance that adults will maintain security through order, even in the face of possible transgressions by other children. Between the ages of 8 and 10, Stage Three children typically become concerned about cheating by others. This infraction threatens their own sense of security and adequacy. Similarly, the nonconforming behavior of others is stressful to many children in Stage Three, who are not yet able to understand the reasons for behavior, relationships between the behavior of one person and the reactions of another, alternative ways of responding, or new ways to use rules (Piaget, 1932/1960).

Quarreling among children in Stage Three is typical and represents their concerns with right, wrong, and fair treatment for themselves. These values coincide with their level of cognitive maturation, social knowledge, and self-esteem (Kohlberg, 1981; Kohlberg & Turiel, 1971). As children mature during Stage Three, quarreling tends to drop off. But boasting and winning out over others seems to continue as a different manifestation of the same maturational need to promote individual self-esteem. Carried to extremes, children sometimes tell great, exaggerated tales or lies to protect themselves from feeling the Stage Three anxiety of guilt over being inadequate in meeting standards.

Proficiencies or deficiencies in motor skills influence children's acceptance by peers and views of themselves as esteemed and competent. Children also seem to need a fairly high level of physical activity during this period. It may be that their uneven growth spurts are major culprits in producing many classroom behavioral problems typical of this stage, such as restlessness, hyperactivity, lethargy, or apathetic attitudes. As Stage Three children become increasingly successful in their physical, communication, and social skills, they are able to identify with a group. Friendships become increasingly important and the need to promote themselves over others is increasingly sublimated. As the stage is fully mastered, self-protective characteristics are gradually replaced by team pride, loyalty to friends, and group identification (Loevinger, 1976).

Throughout this period of development, children experience a significant increase in their ability to use words for social power. They use words for shock effect with their families and to gain status with their peers. The school, too, is a fertile ground for the shock effect of words. The words children choose and the ways they are used seem to be generated by their prior experiences, cultural standards, current models, and level of cognitive development. As they mature during this stage, they are able to perform more complex mental tasks using symbolic forms for communicating and are increasingly better equipped intellectually for participating in social exchanges and interpersonal problem solving. With successes based on these skills, their need to shock with words and actions seems to diminish. They show an increasing ability to influence others in constructive ways as they distinguish differences in how others think and behave (Lickona, 1985; Piaget, 1932/1960; Selman, 1980; Turiel, 1983, 1994). However, even at the end of Stage Three, many children are not always able to anticipate the consequences of their actions. This remains a challenge for mastery during the next stage of social-emotional development.

GOALS AND OBJECTIVES FOR CHILDREN IN STAGE THREE

The Goal: *Learning skills for successful group participation*

The Developmental Therapy–Developmental Teaching program for students in Stage Three is a vehicle for helping them achieve specific milestones for social-emotional competence and the overall Stage Three goal. In the previous stage, children learned to value themselves and to see themselves admired as successful individuals by adults. Now, in Stage Three, they must go beyond the singular concern for their own needs and successes and become involved in regulating their own behavior, individually and in groups. Self-control and self-confidence are the fundamentals of successful participation in groups during this stage. Students who do not have these qualities will fail without a carefully implemented program. Therefore, programs must help them achieve a sense of themselves as successful group members and unique contributors to the group. The outcome of an effective program in Stage Three should be progress toward mastery of the milestones, increased self-esteem, and a sense of worth as a group member.

Here are two students, of different ages and circumstances, whose social-emotional development puts them right in the middle of Stage Three. Vance, at age 8, is a student at risk; whereas 11-year-old Kathy, an older student whose social-emotional development is still in Stage Three, is already in crisis socially and emotionally.

Vance's and Kathy's Developmental Therapy–Developmental Teaching programs must catch their attention and motivate them to participate in their groups in ways that bring success and increased self-esteem. This is the Stage Three goal, which is accomplished as students acquire the milestones in each of the four curriculum areas—Behavior, Communication, Socialization, and Aca-

Vance

Vance is 8 years old and beginning third grade. His teacher is concerned. He is extremely restless, roaming aimlessly around the room whenever the students have an unstructured activity. Sometimes he stares into space for long periods of time. When his teacher or other children speak to him, Vance twitches his neck and shoulders and then mutters something under his breath that no one else understands.

During the previous school year, his second-grade teacher was concerned about Vance's excessive daydreaming and lack of participation with the other children on the playground and during free time. She brought this to the attention of the social worker in the child protection agency, which has placed him in a stable foster home because of abuse by his natural mother. As a preschool child, Vance was hospitalized for burns, bruises, and a dislocated shoulder.

Somehow, Vance has maintained adequate academic achievement. His reading comprehension, oral reading, numerical concepts, and spelling scores are at grade level, while his achievement with numerical operations is about a half-grade below expected level.

Because of his teacher's concerns, Protective Services arranges for Vance to receive another psychological evaluation that confirms their previous information that he is well within the average intellectual range. The assessment also confirms his high distractibility and anxiety, as well as his difficulty completing tasks where concentration, memory, and psychomotor speed are needed. His projective stories portray vicious authority figures transforming themselves into werewolves. Themes of deprivation, punishment, and cruelty dominate his responses. The solutions he offers for these symbolic crisis events are typical of younger children dealing with stress—destruction of evil by gasoline explosions set off by werewolves from space.

For Vance, a Stage Three Developmental Therapy–Developmental Teaching program could be the turnaround, converting anxiety into self-confidence.

demics/Cognition.[6] In the following review of the developmental milestones that are the objectives for Stage Three, keep Vance and Kathy in mind. Consider how necessary it is for both students to master these milestones.

[6]Appendix 4 contains our content analysis for these four curriculum areas, including the processes directly related to the curriculum in Stage Three.

Behavior Milestones for Stage Three

The goal for students in the curriculum area for Behavior in Stage Three is *to apply skills for individual success as a group member.* Students beginning Stage Three have the basic intellectual, social, emotional, and physical skills to participate in activities with some degree of success. The goal for them now is to learn ways to behave and interact

Stage Three Behavior Milestones

Goal: ***To apply skills for individual success as a group member***

Complete individual tasks independently.
Understand the rules that regulate behavior.
Understand the reasons for the rules and behavioral expectations.
Describe alternative ways to behave.
Respond acceptably to choices for leadership in a group.
Refrain from unacceptable behavior when others are losing control.
Maintain acceptable physical and verbal behavior in a group.

Source: Abstracted from *The Developmental Teaching Objectives for the DTORF–R,* by Developmental Therapy Institute, 1992, Athens, GA: Developmental Therapy Institute.

Kathy

Eleven-year-old Kathy's fifth-grade teacher describes her as being very aggressive, constantly fighting with peers, and verbally abusive to teachers. She was suspended from school four times last year for bringing weapons to school and fighting. The school guidance counselor met with her several times and suggested a referral for psychotherapy or special education, but Kathy's parents would not agree to either. The following episode on the first day of the new school year reopens the referral issue.

Kathy is working on an assignment in current events but finds it too complex and frustrating. Her teacher recognizes her frustration and tells her that he will help as soon as he finishes assisting another student. While Kathy sulks and fidgets in her chair, another student, Robert, calls out to Kathy, "Stupid" and "First Grader!"

Kathy yells back, "Shut up, you bastard!"

Robert laughs and taunts her, "Retard!"

At this, Kathy stands up and threatens Robert with a chair. He continues laughing, taunting, and running away from her. Kathy throws a chair at Robert, hitting another student instead and injuring him seriously.

When they meet with Kathy's parents to talk again about a referral for psychotherapy or special education, Kathy's teachers identify the following major problems, in addition to their concerns about her academic problems in reading, arithmetic, written communication, and spelling:

- *demands excessive attention*
- *resists discipline*
- *denies feelings*
- *cries easily*
- *daydreams*
- *tells lies*
- *forgets frequently*
- *seems inattentive*
- *loses interest quickly*
- *lacks confidence*
- *steals others' belongings*
- *complains of others' actions*

The challenge is to turn Kathy's cycle of conflict and failure into a cycle of success.

Can it be done without a special education program? And can it be provided in an inclusive setting? These are the questions facing Kathy's parents and teachers.

successfully as group members. The milestones in Behavior begin with the ability to work independently for a brief time period and complete a task. The next two milestones concern the expectations established for acceptable behavior—the rules. Students in Stage Three are expected to learn the rules by simply stating them, and then learn the reasons for these rules and expectations. It is not necessary for students to always behave in acceptable ways for these two early Stage Three milestones to be acquired. These are simply the first steps in the sequence of learning—to describe acceptable behavior (the rules of conduct) even if it is not always possible to do what is expected.

The sequence of milestones in Behavior then continues to expand students' understanding of acceptable alternative behaviors, although some students will not be able to do more than talk about other ways to behave. However, during this sequence, they are expected to learn to participate in group activities when another student is chosen as the leader, and to refrain from losing control themselves when the behavior of others is unacceptable. These milestones are particularly difficult for troubled children and those who have grown up around aggressive, volatile adults. The final milestone in Behavior for Stage Three focuses on acquiring the ability to maintain acceptable verbal and physical control during all scheduled activities, including transitions between activities. It is this last area of participation that may take students the longest time to achieve. Transitions always involve change and disruption. They are confusing for some and stressful for others. For this reason, learning to make smooth transitions becomes important in a Stage Three program.

Communication Milestones for Stage Three

The goal for students in the area of Communication in Stage Three is *to learn to use words to express themselves constructively in groups.* Beginning Stage Three students are already

Stage Three
Communication Milestones

Goal: ***To use words to express oneself constructively in groups***
Spontaneously describe personal experiences and ideas.
Show positive and negative feelings appropriately.
Participate in group discussions without being disruptive.
Show pride in work, activity, and oneself.
Describe attributes, strengths, and problems in oneself.
Describe characteristic attributes of others.
Recognize feelings of others.
Express pride in group achievements.

Source: Abstracted from *The Developmental Teaching Objectives for the DTORF–R*, by Developmental Therapy Institute, 1992, Athens, GA: Developmental Therapy Institute.

using words functionally and with some social meaning. Early in this stage, their Communication objectives focus on communicating about themselves to others in acceptable ways—what they are doing, thinking, and feeling in the social context. They learn to describe their own experiences, ideas, and feelings appropriately with members of their group. And they learn to use communication skills to contribute to the group effort. These milestones are often difficult for troubled students and those with social, emotional, and behavioral disabilities. For such students, this area of development may be one of the slowest to show progress. It is not too difficult to express thoughts and feelings in unacceptable ways, but vastly more difficult to do so appropriately with a group of peers or with family members.

Even though students in Stage Three are encouraged to describe *what* they feel, they are not asked to explain *why* they feel as they do. This latter level of insight into themselves should follow after they become fluent in sensing their own feelings and describing them. This is a very difficult milestone for troubled students to acquire. Typically, this skill becomes a focus during the next stage of social-emotional development.

During Stage Three, it is important that students learn to openly express pride in themselves and what they do. Some students may have such feelings long before they are consciously aware that they are doing well. Others bear such burdens of inadequacy or guilt that they will not admit success to themselves. With this milestone, they are able to openly "own" the feeling of success, putting it into words for others to hear.

In the process of mastering the remaining milestones for Communication in Stage Three, students expand their observations about the characteristics of themselves and others. They begin to see and describe their own attributes as well as their difficulties. They also learn to describe the characteristics and feelings of others. For some students, focusing on others seems to be easier than talking about themselves. But in either situation—describing oneself or others—the focus needs to be on positive characteristics that contribute to the expectations for this stage of development: expressing oneself constructively in a group.

Socialization Milestones for Stage Three

In the curriculum area for Socialization during Stage Three, the goal for students is to learn *to find satisfaction in group activities.* Beginning Stage Three students are usually still seeking unilateral gratification of their own needs and look to adults to provide authority, protection, discipline, and rewards. During this stage, they learn the social expectations created by being a member of a group and learn to enjoy the results of group membership. In order to do this, they must be taught basic group skills such as taking turns, sharing materials, and accepting suggestions from other students.

This shift from a self-centered to a social orientation requires students to be sufficiently aware of peers to observe and imitate acceptable behavior that brings desired, successful results. This process is called *decentering* by some psychologists (Piaget, 1951/1962, pp. 285–290), and it may be one of the most difficult milestones for troubled students or those with severe social, emotional, and behavioral disabilities to achieve. Students who are oppositional, vulnerable to losing behavioral control, or communicate through aggression generally imitate unacceptable behavior, because it often expresses what they are feeling (Anthony, 1976). It is much more difficult for them to identify and then imitate the successful behaviors of their peers, because it is something they have not learned to do. Another dimension to Socialization during this stage is recognizing that certain values (right and wrong, fair and unfair, good and bad) can be applied to situations involving others. As a part of the process of learning to discriminate between successful and

Stage Three
Socialization Milestones

Goal: To find satisfaction in group activities
Share materials and take turns spontaneously.
Imitate appropriate behavior of peers spontaneously.
Use value statements to describe simple social situations (right and wrong).
Lead or demonstrate for a group activity.
Participate in activities suggested by peers.
Describe one's own experiences in a sequence of events.
Develop a friendship with a peer.
Spontaneously seek assistance from a peer.
Spontaneously assist others in conforming to rules.

Source: Abstracted from *The Developmental Teaching Objectives for the DTORF–R*, by Developmental Therapy Institute, 1992, Athens, GA: Developmental Therapy Institute.

unsuccessful behavior—acceptable and unacceptable conduct—many students need to learn how to recognize and describe these basic values in their own social situations.

The Socialization sequence for Stage Three also includes milestones for basic group social interactions—leading or demonstrating for the group, participating in activities suggested by others, following others' leadership (also a Behavior milestone), telling others about experiences, developing friendships, and seeking the assistance of others. The final milestone for Socialization in Stage Three is acquired when students spontaneously assist others in conforming and participating in the group. This milestone is a signal that a student is maturing in interpersonal perspective-taking and social responsibility. It alerts adults that the student's social-emotional development is beginning to move into the next stage, and that a distinct sense of caring about others is beginning to emerge.

Academics/Cognition Milestones for Stage Three

In the area of Academics/Cognition during Stage Three, the goal for students is *to participate in an academic group successfully, using primary academic skills, language concepts, and symbolic representation of experiences.* This area of Developmental Therapy–Developmental Teaching emphasizes basic reading, writing, and arithmetic skills that can be used to foster social-emotional development during Stage Three. The milestones correspond to the steps for academic achievement in the primary school, grades one through three, grouped roughly into skills associated with first-grade, second-grade, and third-grade achievement. The first group of milestones focuses on the eye-hand skills and on beginning to read, write, and do numerical operations. As students begin to read, they first learn to remember facts and understand the sequence of events they have read about. They then learn to explain the behavior or actions of the characters in their reading. This skill supports corresponding skills developing in the areas of Socialization and Communication, expanding their social knowledge.

As progress is made in acquiring thinking skills and the primary academic tools, students are encouraged to apply them in communicating their own ideas in symbolic form—written words and sentences. They also use these tools for solving practical problems with relevance to their daily lives. Throughout Stage Three, these skills continue to be refined, because they are powerful means for increasingly putting emotions and behavior under rational management.

Because schoolwork and academic proficiency is such an integral part of every student's self-esteem, it is extremely important in Stage Three to give them every help necessary to master the fundamental academic tools. It becomes quite complex when students also have learning disabilities that require special methods for achieving these skills. Similarly, students with developmental disabilities need special help to acquire the basic milestones. Because these programs are planned and adapted for individual differences, they must also take into account a student's chronological age. Interests and motivation, as well as social-emotional stage of development, also must be considered to determine what proportion of students' academic activities should be group or individual instruction. This is discussed in greater detail in the last section of this chapter.

HOW THE PROGRAM MEETS THE NEEDS OF CHILDREN IN STAGE THREE

Success among peers in a group is the purpose of an effective program during Stage Three. Children in this stage are dis-

Stage Three
Academics/Cognition Milestones

Goal: ***To participate in an academic group successfully, using primary academic skills, language concepts, and symbolic representation of experience***

Perform eye-hand coordination activities at the 6-year-old level.
Perform body coordination activities at the 6-year-old level.
Read at least 50 basic primary words.
Recognize and write numerals for groups to 10.
Write 50 basic primary words from memory.
Listen to and understand facts and sequences of events in stories.
Explain the behavior of others in stories, pictures, or experiences.
Read primary sentences with comprehension.
Calculate numerical operations 1 through 9.
Identify illogical elements in simple situations.
Write simple sentences to answer questions about a story.
Perform physical skills in games with age-peers.
Use basic rules of punctuation in creating simple written sentences.
Use numerical concepts of addition and substraction involving time and money.
Read and explain words for quantitative measurements of time, length, and liquid volume.
Use place value, regrouping, multiplication, and simple seriation to solve problems of size and relationship.

Source: Abstracted from *The Developmental Teaching Objectives for the DTORF–R*, by Developmental Therapy Institute, 1992, Athens, GA: Developmental Therapy Institute.

tinctly different in actions, conceptual abilities, and social perceptions from children in previous stages of social-emotional development. They have some sense of themselves as important, although this sense of self is typically so fragile that it requires enormous amounts of self-protecting behavior. The characteristic that most clearly distinguishes Stage Three students from those in previous stages, and that affects the nature of their program, is their *active awareness of each other.* They are excruciatingly aware of peers, going to elaborate lengths to be admired while appearing to be indifferent. They seek larger-than-life models to imitate. Heroes from books, television, and films often fill their need to be powerful, but Stage Three students have limited skills and expertise to be effective themselves. What they dream of doing is often not doable, and many of their attempts to solve their own problems in everyday life fail.

The typical response of a student in Stage Three is self-protection at any cost. Many of the problems these students have result from this need to protect themselves from further exposure of their inadequacies, and many of their behavioral problems result from attempts to insulate themselves from their own sense of guilt about failing to meet the standards of others. This need for self-protection is particularly evident in students who are at risk and in those with social, emotional, and behavioral disabilities. These students whose social-emotional development is in Stage Three can be found in elementary schools, middle schools, or high schools. They can exhibit more acceptable behavior and more outrageous, rebellious behavior than students at any other stage. Their shyness or sophistication often misleads adults and other students into believing that the behavior they see represents the "true" child. They also can mislead people into thinking of them as totally primitive, with the rawest behavior imaginable. To their parents, teachers, and acquaintances, they are frustrating paradoxes of good and bad. For instance, they make up rules then ask to be personally exempted from them. They reject overtures of friendship and then seek to repair the same relationships. They refuse to tell you when they are upset but will tell the student sitting next to them. This happens at home, at school, and in their neighborhood groups.

Stage Three students, whether they have enormous problems or are typical students who are going through the stage in a fairly predictable way, all change dramatically as they progress from the beginning to the end of this stage. The differences between students beginning Stage Three and those at the end of this stage are so great that we have been asked why we do not subdivide this curriculum stage into two separate stages. However, we have maintained the stage as a whole because these developmental changes are the very characteristics that define the uniqueness of this stage—an orientation from self-as-the-center to self-in-relation-to-others. We summarize these distinct changes in Figure 10.2.

These characteristics tend to make programs for students in Stage Three somewhat volatile, from day to day

Figure 10.2. Changes in students during Stage Three.

Interests

Beginning Stage Three students are more like advanced Stage Two children with an interest in fantasy and play, all-powerful forces that control destiny, magical solutions, and wish fulfillment.
Advanced Stage Three students are interested in undertaking real tasks and developing academic and social competencies. They want to participate in the real world of adults and their own age groups.

Response to Rules and Expectations

Beginning Stage Three students accept rules as an unchangeable representation of adult authority, order, and security.
Advanced Stage Three students view rules as guides to their own behavior, needing outside authority but flexible in rule making and rule changing.

Imitation and Identification with Others

Beginning Stage Three students imitate parents, teachers, and superheroes, accepting adults' views as true and adults as all-powerful.
Advanced Stage Three students test themselves against other students and adults, identifying with real-life heroes, admired adults, and peers whom they respect as friends or team members.

Thinking

Beginning Stage Three students' thinking is functional, subjective, and related to their own needs.
Advanced Stage Three students begin to see connections between events, can understand that there are several ways of looking at a problem, and can generalize ideas to solve problems.

Relationships

Beginning Stage Three students see others from a self-centered, superficial, and exploitative view as providers of needs and are not able to see others' needs or points of view.
Advanced Stage Three students recognize the influences of feelings on the behavior of themselves and others and are interested in being recognized by peers and adults.

or from moment to moment, depending upon their needs. Some days will be productive and successful; others will be a series of disasters and crises. A poet might write beautifully of these students' paradoxical natures—projecting an image of isolation, struggling to become esteemed by others, and attempting to fit into a society composed of various groups with different rules and expectations. But parents and the adults who work with Stage Three children will see this as a time for unpredictable responses. At one time the children will be models of acceptable, cooperative behavior, then, equally unpredictably, their behavior and emotions will deteriorate and different needs become a priority.

Helping students with such characteristics requires considerable sensitivity, understanding, flexibility, tolerance, sincerity, time, and hard work. Teachers and parents find themselves needing each other for support, sharing information, resolving crises, and keeping in touch about what students' need. Teachers and school social workers establish communication between home and school. They may aid their students if they have difficulties with juvenile court, often serving as mediators or advocates. They assist their students in integrated settings as they attempt to adjust to a general school curriculum. And they support them with crisis intervention when they lose control and regress again. These activities are all part of providing an effective Stage Three program of Developmental Therapy–Developmental Teaching, in any location.

With persistence and understanding, such efforts produce results. Somehow, just about the time adults begin to doubt themselves and the program strategies, Stage Three students begin to change in positive ways. The changes are small at first and often are overlooked unless adults are watching carefully for the small positive indicators of progress. They begin to see signs of group cohesion and teamwork among students in the group. They document the acquisition of some of the Stage Three milestones and, often in a surprisingly short period of time, they have students who are ready for the curriculum in Stage Four.

The Adult's Role: Praising, Enforcing, and Problem Solving

Adults represent authority and a source of authentication for children in Stage Three as they seek to be recognized as valued people. An effective adult embodies the adult characteristics needed by children to ensure their individual success. Students in Stage Three look to valued or powerful adults to solve the many problems they cannot handle. They seek recognition and praise, yet will continually test adult power, authority, expertise, and personal characteristics. They do this because they are anxious to verify an adult's credibility as someone who can be relied upon in a crisis. They also need a psychologically powerful adult as a model for group participation and problem solving. They expect adults to recognize and reflect real success and they depend upon redirection in case they falter in a group activity.

A major responsibility for adults working with students in Stage Three is to help them understand the connections between what they do and what happens to them. This understanding is a gradual process, going on throughout Stage Three. In the process, students must have many experiences with others, accompanied by discussions about what is happening and why. It is the adult who must lead these discussions and guide the students to new insights. Small groups provide more opportunity for this social learning than do large groups and are essential for a Stage Three program to be effective. Here is an example of a fairly basic Stage Three group discussion, guided by a skilled teacher.

During this conversation, the teacher is aware of each student's vulnerable spots and provides the structure to guide the conversation to a positive conclusion for each member. Kendra's verbal participation is minimal, reflecting her lack of communication skill. Attempts to ask questions and to draw her into the group are not usually successful because she feels rejection from the group. Often Kendra looks to Maria for approval and help. Lewis, as usual, tests the limits, requires verbal redirection, and devours verbal and nonverbal attention as if he never receives enough. Because of Kendra's lack of involvement, the teacher asks her a question he knows she can answer. He speaks directly to her and lightly touches her arm to interrupt her staring episode.

This illustration also emphasizes that the group must offer something in return for participation—personal recognition, success, or esteem. It is the adult's role to see that these experiences result in reassurance that there is a place in the group for each individual. What makes this difficult to manage is the limited ability of Stage Three students in a group to contribute for the benefit of others. Each individual's self-protective priorities produce a group that scarcely functions independently during Stage Three. (When it does the group members are beginning the passage to the next stage, and the program must begin to shift into Stage Four.) For this reason, adults who work with Stage Three students are always faced with the necessity of using the dynamics of a group and the attractions of a highly motivating activity to involve the students. It is equally necessary for the adult to serve as

A Snack Time Discussion

VICTOR: "I used to play on a baseball team, and one day I hit a home run that went 500 miles. No one ever found the ball, it went so fast. I hit a couple of other home runs in that game, too."

MARIA: "You can't hit a ball 500 miles."

TEACHER: "Victor, it looks like you made a couple of good catches today for our ball game."

VICTOR: "Yeah, I caught three fly balls."

BRAD: "You got that high ball Maria kicked!"

VICTOR: "Well, you have to keep your eye on the ball. My father told me that. I'll show you how to do it tomorrow."

LEWIS: "He can't even catch a ball if it's right to him."

TEACHER: "Maybe with some coaching he can. Everyone made some good catches today, and our team had a very high score. Does anyone remember the score?"

LEWIS: "It was 17. I know. I kept count!"

TEACHER: "Right! And what was yesterday's score, Kendra?"

KENDRA: "Eleven."

TEACHER: "This group gets better every day!"

As the group finishes the snack, the teacher moves to conclude it: "Two minutes left." He scans the group, making visual contact with each momentarily. He asks Maria to remove the remaining graham crackers from the table.

Brad flicks his milk carton across the room. The teacher responds to Brad by reflecting previous progress: "Brad, for three of the four days this week you put the carton in the wastebasket. Four out of four would be a perfect record!" Brad gets the milk carton and puts it in the trash container. The teacher praises Brad and moves near him as the students begin a discussion about the next activity.[7]

[7] This example was used by C. Cook and O. Jennings in the first edition of *Developmental Therapy*. It is reprinted here with permission of the publisher.

group leader to ensure that each student participates successfully with the others.

Many older students in Stage Three resist participating. They react vocally—and negatively—to every suggestion because they have faced failure or rejection so many times they resist exposing themselves again. This makes it difficult for them to spontaneously join a group. When this happens, it is the adult with power and persuasion and the activity with intrinsic attraction that, together, break the deadlock and get things moving in a group.

It is typical to hear Stage Three students complaining about a proposed activity. They frequently deny any interest and just as frequently demand to get started without sufficient information to be successful. This is the time when the adult must persist in a brief, clearly structured introduction to each activity, often demonstrating with visual examples how the students can use the materials in successful ways and establishing expectations for the steps involved. The temptation is to skip over the introduction to an activity, especially when students are very vocal with their comments:

"Let's get started!"

"I can do that."

"I did that before."

However, it is essential for the adult leading a group activity to always go through a brief introduction. For all their protestations about already knowing how to do something, students in Stage Three frequently fail unless they receive a carefully organized introduction that prepares them for each step.[8]

When things go badly in a group, which frequently happens in the beginning of Stage Three, adults must guide, restructure, and intervene before an activity begins to disintegrate into failure for a student. The dynamics within each group will influence the frequency and level of volatility. Students with high sensitivity to failure and those with poor behavioral controls can set off a group rapidly as a way to deflect attention from themselves and their own stress. Adults must be alert to signs of such stress and use verbal forms of intervention to reduce anxiety or redirect a student's efforts to the ongoing activity. (The importance of understanding group dynamics is discussed in a following section.) Some students will show their stress by picking on another student, whereas others choose the activity or the adult as their target. They may make complaints like these:

"This is a dumb thing to do."

"I don't like this."

"Why are you asking us to do this?"

Even when they do like an activity and feel pride in what they are doing, Stage Three students may proclaim loudly that they dislike it. Adults must remind themselves that Stage Three students may not give accurate feedback about their personal reactions to what is happening. Their distortions in perception are not always deliberate. Many times, they are simply indicating a reaction; they have not yet learned to accurately recognize positive feelings or reveal them to others.

Personal rights are a priority for many older students who are still in Stage Three. On the one hand, an adult must have a sufficient relationship with each individual student in the group to convey recognition to each one as a respected individual. On the other hand, the adult must also be convincing as a fair but strong leader who can keep others in line for the protection and benefit of the individual. This balancing act requires considerable personal strength on the part of adults working with these students.

Management Strategies That Foster Success in Stage Three

Adults use a number of strategies to foster success for individuals and the group during a Stage Three program.[9] The most frequently used behavior management strategies are these:

Strategies Adults Frequently Use for Behavior Management
(with Students in Stage Three)

Positive feedback and praise	About individual's contribution to the group
Motivating with materials	Personally relevant, enhancing individual in eyes of peers
Structure	Predictable procedures for law and order by adult as authority
Redirection	Verbal cues to remotivate
Reflection	Words, actions, and feelings
Interpretation	Feelings behind behavior
Verbal interaction between adults	For group process model
Rules	Applied with fairness to all
Life Space Intervention (LSI)	Talking through a crisis for resolution and greater understanding of oneself and others
Removal from the room	An opportunity for LSI and crisis resolution

[8]Chapter 4 contains a discussion and examples of introductions, step-by-step procedures, and endings for activities at each stage of the curriculum.

[9]The Stage Three form of the DT/RITS in Appendix 2 contains performance items to assess the use of materials, activities, and strategies by adults working with students in Stage Three.

These strategies are all used in ways that emphasize positive group processes—words, actions, and feelings—and convey understanding of how a situation is affecting the individual members of the group. Physical intervention may occasionally be necessary to establish authority early in a Stage Three program. However, always consider physical intervention as a last resort.[10] Materials, the structure of the program, verbal skills of the adults, and their interactions as models for successful social exchange stimulate group participation. The result of these strategies must be participation and a successful ending to each activity for each student. This expectation is conveyed through rules that come from adult authority and are applied fairly to all:

Expectations for Behavior of Students in Stage Three
(Rules)

- Be part of the group.
- Follow directions.
- Be helpful to others.
- Show respect.
- Take care of property.

Crisis, conflict, physical aggression, and loss of control are at a peak during Stage Three. Children in earlier stages generally have not yet developed sufficient skills or interest in how other students view them to be a powerful force for disrupting others. In the later stages of social-emotional development, children have gained sufficient maturity and understanding of themselves and others to regulate their own behavior. But during Stage Three, all of these forces merge, usually with conflict and without corresponding skills for successful coping among group members.

During this volatile phase, it is essential that adults manage their own feelings and behavior in acceptable ways.[11] Verbal skills, control of the group, and a sense of direction are necessary. This is why the adult in the team's lead role focuses on keeping an activity moving along with the entire group while the support person on the team responds to an individual student who may need adult assistance to continue in the group activity.[12] If the adult is not in control, the behavior and emotions of the students will control the group. Adult emotions and loss of control have no place in a Stage Three program. Physical interventions should be a last resort, used only when a student is so out of control that others may be hurt, or when a student is so disruptive that the group cannot function without his removal from the room.

Individual Life Space Intervention (LSI) is a major strategy to assist individual students in increasing their understanding of themselves and others, and to solve their crisis events. LSI is also an essential way to strengthen the adult's relationship with each student.[13] Every adult working with students in Stage Three needs to be proficient in LSI and also skilled in the therapeutic management of physical aggression.

The power an adult has to influence the behavior of students in groups during Stage Three comes from the same four general types of social power described in Chapter 7: coercion, manipulation, likability, and expertness.[14] *Coercion* conveys the message that everyone conforms to the rules, and punishment for breaking rules is fair and justified. *Manipulation* achieves the participation of all the members of the group through selection of content that catches their imagination, touches the relevant concerns of each individual, and presents opportunities to be successful in the eyes of others. *Likability* attracts students into imitating the adults because of personal qualities admired by them. These qualities fulfill the students' own need to be respected and liked. *Expertness* establishes confidence in the ability of the adult to keep everyone under control, to solve problems that the student cannot handle alone, and to provide psychological security for the group. The message is

"No one is hurt here, and no one is allowed to hurt others."

GROUP DYNAMICS AND GROUP CONFLICT IN STAGE THREE

Becoming a secure group member is the essential accomplishment of development in Stage Three. Yet almost all students who are socially, emotionally, or behaviorally disturbed have enormous difficulty with this process. Verbal and physical forms of aggression among students toward each other are the most typical indicators that they do not feel secure about themselves as individuals and their place as group members. When this occurs, group conflict invariably arises. These students go to many extremes to be noticed by their peers and to obtain the reassurance that they have legitimacy in the group. Unfortunately, the other members of the group are equally ill equipped to provide positive or constructive social responses because of their own deficits and needs in

---

[10] See Chapter 6 for a review of behavior management strategies with Stage Three students.

[11] There is a section in Chapter 7 on problems adults often have with themselves. Many of these problems are manifested most acutely during Stage Three because of the stresses adults experience in working with troubled children in this stage of development.

[12] See Chapter 7 for an elaboration of the roles of lead and support on a Developmental Therapy–Developmental Teaching team.

[13] See Chapter 6 for a description of how LSI is used and the steps to follow.

[14] See Chapter 7 for a discussion of social power as a means for adults to influence students' behavior.

this area. This paucity of skills for socialization among group members in Stage Three leaves the adult with the responsibility for building a functioning group in which individuals feel secure and successful with their peers. It also leaves group conflict as one of the most difficult, challenging, and long-range problems to be overcome during this stage.

Conducting effective groups is an essential part of implementing a Developmental Therapy–Developmental Teaching program for students who are sufficiently concerned with others to be influenced by group membership. We include a discussion about group dynamics and managing group crisis here, for Stage Three, because of the power of a group to influence the progress of each individual in the group. However, adults providing programs for students who are making transitions between stages, into or out of Stage Three, should also find this information applicable.

It is a sensitive and complicated endeavor to observe, analyze, and change individuals' roles and interactions in groups. Considerable information is needed to implement changes in the behavior of students in a group, and in the group's structure and functions. By managing group dynamics and the roles of students in a group, it is possible to foster new behaviors, new interactions, and new roles. An effective Developmental Therapy–Developmental Teaching program can assist students in acquiring skills that can be generalized, by concentrating on the Socialization and Communication milestones outlined previously. The result will be positive changes by individuals that enable them to function more effectively as members in their various groups.[15]

Group Dynamics

In addition to knowing what role (or roles) a student fulfills in a group, it is equally important to identify who influences whom in the group. The pattern of relationships—actions and reactions in which individuals attempt to meet their own emotional and social needs through others—is called *group dynamics.* We work with several aspects of group dynamics to bring about changes in group behavior. The concepts we use are organized below into five steps: (1) level of Socialization, (2) the roles of students in a group, (3) the type and amount of social power each student uses, (4) an analysis of positive and negative interactions occurring between group members (a sociogram), and (5) ways to use information to change group dynamics.

Step 1. Verify the Specific Stage of Socialization for Each Student. As interactions begin to develop between the members of a group, we review all possible information that helps us to specify which stage and milestones in Socialization the student has acquired or lacks. We find it helpful to refer again to the Preliminary Profile (Figure 3.2) to verify the Socialization stage because it may not always be the same as a student's overall stage of social-emotional development.[16]

During the latter phases of Stage Two and the early phases of Stage Three, distinct signs of interest in other students become evident. A student may boldly confront an adult and then turn to see if a friend is watching. A student also may refuse to sit by one student in order to sit by another. Sometimes one student will encourage another to do something unacceptable in the classroom. Students may give indications like these of an awareness of differences in individual work assignments and preferential treatment (real or imagined):

"It's not fair."

"He gets all the good stuff."

"I want one like hers."

"I want to sit at his table."

"This is too easy. Give me some hard stuff."

These are signs that the students are beginning to develop Stage Three characteristics. With this growth comes a new force for adults to deal with—increasing self-assertion and independence from adult authority, with a coinciding realignment with peers. This will affect group behavior dramatically. This information about a student's stage of Socialization also helps us to understand whether the student's attitude toward adult authority is still in a preexistential phase or if the student is going through the existential crisis. (See the discussion at the beginning of this chapter about the development of the existential crisis during Stage Three.)[17] If a student is postexistential, it may be possible to successfully encourage a productive, leadership role within the Stage Three group.

Step 2: Identify the Role of Each Student in the Group. Perhaps the most difficult part of effective group management is to identify each student's current role in a group (as perceived by the student and by the group).[18] Each individual in a group will have a role. Sometimes the role is assigned by group consensus; at other times the student seeks it. A student's role in a group will remain fairly consistent until membership in the group changes, or until the adult uses strategies that change the relationships between the group members through planned changes in the behavior of individuals. A child's membership in vari-

[15]Skills acquired in a Stage Three group usually do not conflict with skills needed by students to be successful in other groups, such as family or friends, neighborhood gangs, sports groups, or cultural, religious, and ethnic groups.

[16]The DTORF–R is also used to provide this specific information about the Socialization stage. See Chapter 1 for a description.

[17]The existential crisis is also discussed in the theory section of Chapter 2.

[18]Step 3 in Chapter 5 contains a description of the typical roles of students in groups.

ous other groups—family, recreational, sports, neighborhood—does not always produce the same role; however, the dynamics of emotional need that form an individual's position in one group often are the same forces that shape that person's roles in other groups. This is because the role of a group member is a product of an individual's own emotional needs and the emotional needs and behavior of the other group members.

Among the most common roles in any group are nine that occur frequently in groups of students in Stage Three: instigator, leader, group conscience, bully, clown, isolate, scapegoat, baby, and follower. As soon as group interactions occur during Stage Three, we begin to watch for these various roles to emerge. Some roles will be quite evident; others will never be seen. Some roles will change as membership in a group changes (as when a new student is enrolled, or when a student who is frequently absent returns). Others will remain consistently the same.

During the time when group roles are emerging, a group will be difficult to manage. There will seem to be little or no cohesion, considerable strife between members, and frequent, unpredictable outbursts. This apparently unfathomable behavior occurs because students are venturing into the social climate, testing themselves against each other. As the group settles down, sometimes after several weeks together, the roles will emerge consistently. Then it is possible to see which roles are going to be a positive influence for group success and which will be destructive and counterproductive. Sometimes the adult can intervene with individual students during this fluid period to change their roles by helping them to see that changes in their behavior will change others' behavior toward them. This usually results in a change in roles, usually for the better. However, many students in Stage Three are not yet able to see these connections and to make the needed behavioral changes, so the group roles become somewhat fixed.

Step 3. Assess the Type and Amount of Each Student's Social Power. *Social power* is the ability to influence others and to get them to do what they might not ordinarily think of or do by themselves.[19] We briefly review the concept of social power here, as exercised by students in Stage Three. Four forms of social power are typical:

Coercion:	Physical force or its threat to control others' behavior
Likability:	Personal characteristics that influence others
Expertness:	An individual's ability to solve problems that others cannot handle
Manipulation:	Covert (undercover) behavior that seduces others, unaware, into behavior

[19]For an overview of social power for adults, see Chapter 7. See also the previous discussion about the forms of social power used by adults working with students in Stage Three.

- *Coercion or intimidation:* This is the use of force or threats to make other students (or adults) do what they might not otherwise choose to do. It is perhaps the most ineffective, yet the most common, form of social power used by Stage Three students. The most obvious example of coercion is physical force. When it is used by students, it is often called *aggression* or *unsocialized behavior.* (When it is used by adults it is called *corporal punishment.*) Examples of students' use of coercion include bullying, destroying the property of others, using verbally abusive language, fighting, threatening, and defying others. It is undeniable that coercion can force other students, teachers, and parents to respond. Yet the results of coercion seldom bring the full benefits desired by the student.

- *Likability:* This form of social power has "personality" overtones—it is the ability to have other students and adults respond because of personal qualities. Likability has many positive aspects, such as promoting friendliness and interpersonal bonds. It may also have negative consequences when it is used by a student to gain attention through the chronic use of nonconstructive roles such as being the class clown, displaying genitals to the class, or attempting to buy friendship with gifts or favors. Although positive personal attributes are an important form of social power for students, they are insufficient in themselves. A group cannot rely on the selected personal characteristics of one member or a few members for effective functioning.

- *Expertness:* This form of social power is based on the ability to solve the problems of others. It is possibly the most effective form of social power, particularly when it is combined with likability. Yet Stage Three students seldom have either form in adequate amounts. Because all groups of students in Stage Three need expertness to solve their problems, a student or adult who is expert in solving individual and group problems has considerable influence and social power. Expertness in students must be channeled into positive efforts or the student expert can become a gang leader who sets the agenda and controls the behavior of others in destructive ways.

  A group of students who are well into Stage Three needs to begin developing expertness within the group. Too often, adults who are expert in problem solving tend to keep their skills as their own; that is, they continue to be the major source for crisis management in a group, even after individual students begin to show the ability to begin to assume responsibility for crisis resolution. This requires an important change in a teacher's management strategy. Because students beginning Stage Three have few skills to qualify them as experts, they cannot contribute to the solution of individual of group problems. It is the adult who must exercise social power through expertness. But soon, Stage Three students must develop individual expertness for crisis resolution and responsible choices in behavior—and the adults must foster it.

- *Manipulation:* This form of social power is a covert strategy students use to influence others when they want to

> avoid direct confrontation. Manipulation is an undercover approach and creates an impression of hidden agendas, in contrast to the openness and direct attack that are seen in coercion. When a student uses manipulation in a group, the others generally do not understand why certain social interactions are occurring. The group does not function smoothly or openly. No one knows where the manipulator stands in relationship to the others. The result is distrust among the group members, anger toward the adult for failing to provide a predictable environment, and insecurity within the manipulator because the boundaries of power are not clearly defined. Group cohesiveness and success are seldom achieved in this climate.

Step 4. Chart the Positive and Negative Contacts Occurring Between Group Members. With the information about each student obtained in the previous steps, we identify whom each student interacts with or attempts to influence. These interactions are sometimes referred to as *bonds* when they occur consistently. Bonds can be constructive or destructive. Some bonds link students positively to each other, whereas others are built through active dislike or emotional need. A few are neutral or expedient. Social psychologists call the procedure for such an analysis a *sociogram*—it is a way to illustrate the structure of a group's interactions.

As an example of a Stage Three sociogram, consider the group dynamics between the students in Figure 10.3. Their teacher charted the information about each one as she followed the steps outlined above. She observed their interactions for several days and made notes about the contacts between them. Then she completed the sociogram shown in Figure 10.4.

The solid lines in Figure 10.4 denote positive movements between the students and the broken lines denote negative movements. The arrow indicates the direction of the movement, pointing away from the student who initiated the contact and toward the recipient. From this information, several situations are evident: There is no clear leadership in the group. Roger, Tom, and Sam have considerable power to influence some members of the group, but not always in positive ways. No one interacts negatively with Tom, but Sam and Roger interact negatively with each other. Tom uses negative strategies only with Sam and Helen. It is reasonable to assume that Roger is not particularly eager to fight with Tom, so he ignores him. Roger, Tom, and Sam use positive approaches only with Alan, whereas Helen and Donna receive no positive approaches from any of the students.

Step 5. Use the Information To Plan for Changes in Group Dynamics. What is done with the information gathered in the preceding steps? We use it to reduce group conflict and enhance group cohesiveness, by targeting changes in certain roles, types of social power, and bonds (interactions between the students). We first determine who should, realistically, become the group leader. Sometimes the decision is that the existing leader is the one to remain in that position, but that changes are needed in the type of social power used by the leader. (Frequently, coercion should be changed to expertness.) When this decision is made, it shapes how we respond to the student in the role of leader. If the decision is to have another student fill the leader role, the existing leader must be helped into a new role while the new leader is encouraged to become more active in social interactions. Such changes are sometimes necessary when the existing leader is firmly entrenched in using coercion as the power base—keeping the group members terrified and unable to become a secure group. We also have had some success in shifting a strong leader to a social power base of expertness—the student's concern for others grow extensively and the others respond with increasing respect.

For each group member, we identify what alternative sources for social power need to be learned and decide which new type of power can be learned most readily. Then we assess ways to build new, positive bonds between group members and ways to reduce negative

Figure 10.3. Examples of roles and social power in a Stage Three group.

Student	*Roles in Group*	*Forms of Social Power*	*Amount of Power*
Roger	Clown, instigator, bully, leader	Likability, manipulation, coercion, expertness	Medium to high
Donna	Follower, scapegoat	Manipulation	Low
Sam	Leader, instigator, bully	Manipulation, coercion	Medium
Helen	Conscience, scapegoat	Manipulation	Low
Tom	Leader, instigator, bully	Coercion, manipulation	Medium to high
Alan	Follower	Likability	Medium

Figure 10.4 Sociogram illustrating the relationships (bonds) between members of a Stage Three group.

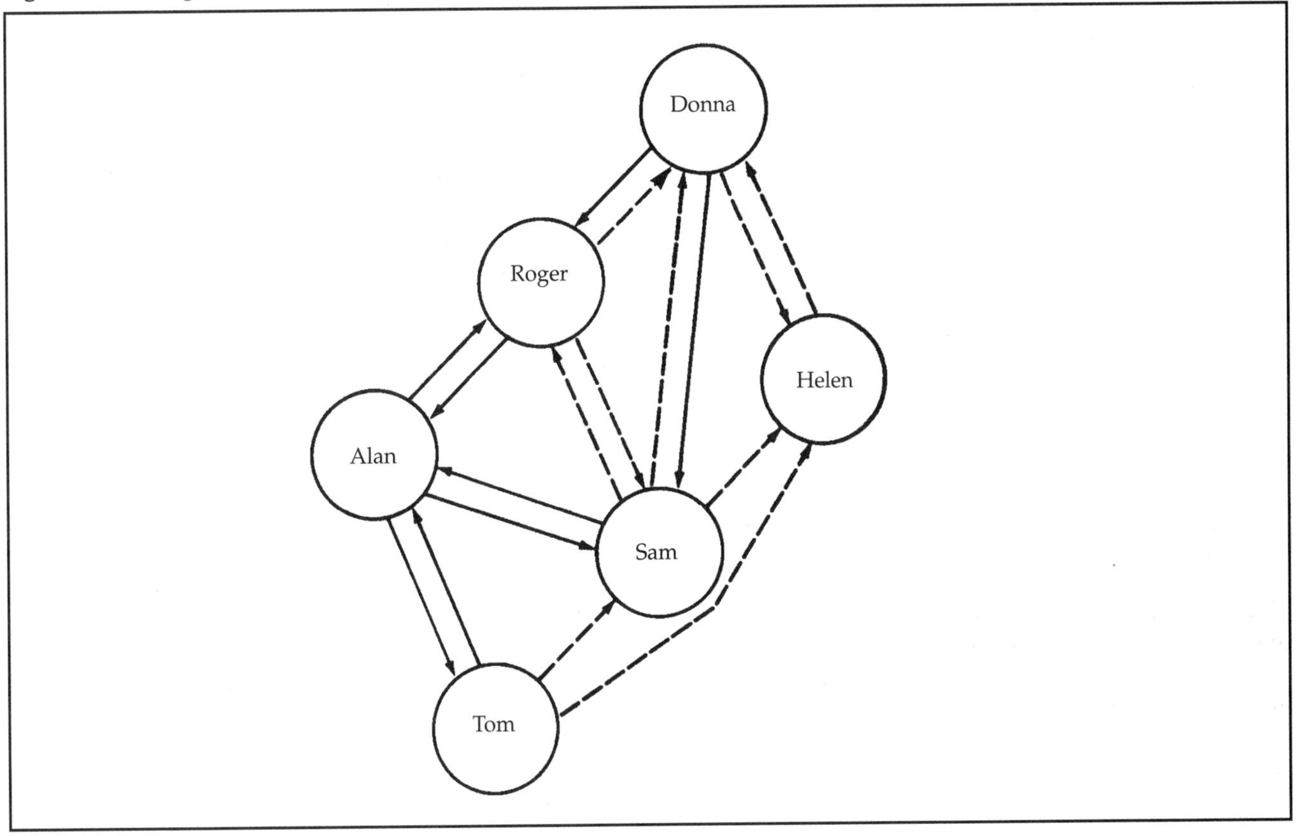

bonds. This is done by identifying the student who initiates most of the negative bonds (the disruptive student) and determining what that individual will respond to in positive ways. Using this information, we encourage the students receiving the negative bonds to change their behavior in ways that produce positive responses from students who previously initiated the negative bonds.

Changing group behavior is a slow and deliberate process. Yet it is a systematic way to bring about changes in the social competence of Stage Three students. To summarize the process: First, outline your expectations for an improved group structure—that is, to reduce group conflict and enhance group cohesiveness. Students also must have a sense of the group mission. This means that you must work with them to develop group activities and performance standards for those activities. Give them an idea of what the completed project or task will be and provide a sense of the potential benefits and emotional hazards before the task is undertaken. Give periodic feedback on the progress the group makes in achieving the mission. Be abundant in your praise when it is deserved. Be careful with your criticism—keep it task-related and avoid personal innuendo. Recognize each student's role in the progress being made. Finally, have a time for individual private exchanges with each student concerning that individual's changing role in the group. In this way, students know that they can receive personal attention from the adult without having to use unacceptable behavior to obtain it.

Managing Group Behavior for Successful Participation by All

Increased peer interaction between students (both positive and negative in form) is an early indication of emerging interest in a group. Age, maturation, and prior experience determine the point when casual interest in peers changes into an intense involvement with one or more individuals in a group. At this point, group conflict generally appears.

In most Stage Three groups, there will be one or two students who have not yet acquired some Stage Two milestones for Socialization and Behavior. A close look at these students often reveals that their social exchanges with other members of the group are rare. Their interactions are primarily with the adult. When they do interact with other members of the group, it is usually through the adult's structure and planned activities. The structure of activities is designed especially for Socialization milestones to encourage interaction and cooperation with others. (Chapter 9 contains a number of suggestions for promoting such social interactions between students in Stage Two.) Without considerable structure, these students will have minimal exchanges with others and may become group isolates or scapegoats. Adults must direct, encourage, and shape student's interactions with others. Adults must also create opportunities for group members to interact spontaneously. Although such exchanges will be fairly limited, they are essential readiness steps as a foundation for merging these students into their group with others who are already in Stage Three.

To be cohesive, a group must have a leader. Because it is rare to have a student with positive leadership skills in a beginning Stage Three group, the adult must be the group leader until skills are developed within the group. The adult must maintain a posture as a strong group leader—a fair but not overwhelming presence—to guarantee that law and order will prevail. As a group leader, an adult should be aware of a number of elements that influence a group's structure and functions. Marshall and Kurtz (1982, p. 327) suggest several principles that are helpful in keeping a group on track. These guidelines have been adapted for use with students in a Stage Three group:

- Emphasize the value of the group.
- Emphasize noncompetitive attributes of individuals.
- Clarify the individual member's responsibility in the group.
- Encourage group verbal interactions (Communication skills).
- Maintain expectations (structure, goals, objectives, contracts).
- Reflect students' positive behaviors toward each other.
- Minimize negative labeling.
- Protect individuals' psychological space.
- Encourage constructive self-disclosure.
- Stop destructive self-disclosure.
- Reflect feelings conveyed by talk or behavior (interpretation).
- Reflect constructive content (interpretation).
- Confront group interactions that have negative consequences (reality).
- Guide the group in positive evaluation of individuals' efforts in the group.

Reflecting the progress and accomplishments of individuals as a group is necessary to reduce group conflict to a minimum. It is essential to also be able to structure the timing of activities, drop back to a Stage Two type of management when regression sets in, and consistently but flexibly set limits and convey expectations. Continually revise estimates of each student's ability to interact and systematically plan activities and procedures that foster greater interaction between group members.

Perhaps the most difficult part of managing a Stage Three group is being able to adjust the structure to accommodate individual problems without losing credibility about being fair with other group members. Individual assertion of oneself is the basis for group conflict in Stage Three. Frequently, assertion is in the form of manipulation, hostile comments, and aggressive actions directed toward adults and other students. As this happens, react in a manner that is nonjudgmental and fair. View the student's behavior as a sign of emerging independence. Hold to the established expectations for behavior, and restructure the student for positive participation in the group. Convey understanding and dependability while maintaining the position that the group is important and each member can thrive within the group.

As the Stage Three group develops, a few group problem-solving skills emerge. Students begin to make comments that indicate appreciation for others' positive characteristics and contributions. These reflections about others indicate mastery of several of the Socialization and Communication milestones in Stage Three. This happens because the adult has reflected frequently on the positive effects a student has on the group—and the benefits to everyone from a successful group.

ACTIVITIES DESIGNED TO ACCOMPLISH THE GOALS AND OBJECTIVES FOR STAGE THREE

In this section we describe a core of daily activities needed for students in Stage Three to make progress in acquiring milestones in all four curriculum areas—Behavior, Communication, Socialization, and Academics/Cognition. These daily activities can include a group meeting, an academic session that may include reading, a total language approach, current events, social science, natural science, math, and history; a group project with stories, creative writing, art, music, and role play; time for physical movement and skill development, preferably outside; a Snack Time for socialization and communication; and a group review to wrap up the daily activities with an appraisal of progress. The two latter activities can be combined for some Stage Three groups; however, this is not always successful. Some Stage Three students cannot handle both activities well and tend to become preoccupied with the snack. For them, the group wrap-up tends to be difficult and their stress may precipitate behavioral problems during Snack Time.

For students who have abbreviated programs in Developmental Therapy–Developmental Teaching, activities may be as few as a group discussion, an academic time, a group project, and Snack Time with a wrap-up as part of it. The major milestones in the four curriculum areas for

Stage Three can be addressed in these activities. In contrast, students served in all-day programs or residential programs will have a full array of activities. There will be a number of academic periods for individual and group instruction, interspersed with several total language activities, creative projects, movement activities, and other group projects of daily living. The following activities are part of a typical Stage Three program:

- Group meeting
- Academic work
- Group project
  - story
  - creative writing
  - art
  - music
  - role play
- Outside (physical skills)
- Snack
- Group Review

We do not specify the amount of time for a Stage Three program because the needs of each student and program will vary considerably.[20] Some students will be in totally inclusive settings where the Developmental Therapy—Developmental Teaching activities are woven into the regular education program throughout the day. Others will be in special education pull-out programs that vary from an hour or two of intensive intervention up to full-day and residential programs. However, in general, a typical activity for students beginning Stage Three should be about 12–18 minutes long, whereas students completing the stage can sustain their attention for as long as 15–25 minutes for each activity. Although some activities may be shorter and some longer, these seem to be the typical times needed for most Stage Three activities.

Up to 50% of the total time is typically spent in academic tasks, individually and in groups (current events, reading, language arts, science and arithmetic). Independent work provides for learning at each student's individual pace and encourages personal academic achievement. The group academic activities are organized to provide opportunities for group instruction and collaborative group projects using academic as well as creative skills. Decisions about the portion of time to be allotted for individual and group instruction are guided by the readiness of the students to benefit from a group emphasis and the extent of each student's need for individual learning programs. Every activity involves work on specific milestones for social-emotional development, including the academic portion of the program. The activities also require traditional, independent, in-seat behavior such as sitting quietly to listen, following directions, working quietly, and answering questions when called upon. Activities also require appropriate group interactions that promote group socialization and communication skills. Such systematic planning and structure is necessary for students in Stage Three because of problems they frequently have in regulating their own behavior, particularly with unstructured situations in locations such as the playground, cafeteria, bus, restroom, gym, and halls.

Activities and Materials for Success in a Stage Three Group

With activities and materials that result in successful participation, Stage Three students' confidence in themselves grows. They begin to see themselves as accepted and successful members of a group. This is the pivotal concept in the program—activities are designed to promote an emerging sense of individual contribution to the group effort. At all times the adults encourage group involvement and individual contribution to mutual effort. Yet there is an implicit assurance that the adults will not expect more than individual members of the group can handle comfortably. This confidence is the basis for students' building trust in the adults, in themselves, and in the program. When students in Stage Three have confidence that the adults will not set expectations too high, and when the activities are relevant to their concerns and interests, they will participate with increasing enthusiasm.[21]

Considerable structure is needed for beginning Stage Three students to be sure that each activity has a successful outcome. School materials and equipment are already familiar to the students. However, their memories are often of failure and frustration. For this reason they frequently resist participating. To reduce resistance and to avoid spiraling anxiety about possible failure in an activity, the purposes, goals, and expectations are clearly communicated before each activity begins. By always "talking through" an activity in abbreviated form before beginning, adults ensure that each student understands the events to come. This process is crucial to the success of every activity for a Stage Three group.

Selecting specific materials and activities for Stage Three is much like the selection process in the previous stage, with one important difference. Stage Three students can assimilate abstract concepts; can identify with admired heroes; are concerned with right and wrong, fairness and unfairness, and good and evil; and can generalize

[20] Chapter 3 contains several sample time schedules for students in Stage Three—in elementary school (Figure 3.6) and in middle school (Figure 3.7).

[21] See the section on selecting effective activities and materials in Chapter 4 for general guidelines for all stages of the curriculum, including Stage Three.

to their own experiences. Therefore, it is essential that Stage Three activities have age-appropriate and culturally relevant elements that can be generalized to personal experience, while maintaining exciting or dramatic qualities that appeal to students in this stage. When selecting materials and activities for students in this stage, we find the following guidelines to be helpful:

1. Select materials and activities that can be used by all members of the group.
2. Adapt as needed for individual successes with peers.
3. Use regular school materials and activities that are age-appropriate.
4. Choose content that is relevant to students' own experiences.
5. Select materials and activities that increase individuals' effectiveness in the group.
6. Introduce culturally and personally relevant themes.

To counter the preexisting notions of many students that all schoolwork is dull or irrelevant, select materials with highly dramatic content that touches the real interests and concerns of the students. Unit themes provide this opportunity. The content of themes and units should lend itself to a group emphasis while still providing abundant opportunities for individual success. For some older students and those who are making progress in Stage Three, themes may be carried over for 2 weeks or longer.

When choosing a content theme, keep in mind the specific concerns and interests of individual students as well as their general social and emotional characteristics. Effective themes generally have some convincingly real aspects but are bigger than life and involve dramatic events such as good versus evil, right versus wrong, achievement and acclaim, or courageous characters in epic adventures. Figure 10.5 contains examples of content themes for units of study that have proven highly motivating.

Role Play in Stage Three

To bridge the distance for Stage Three students between the need to have the world (and themselves) as they wish it would be and the way it actually is, we find stories and role play to be highly effective. Role play allows children to practice new ways to behave and to experience real concerns without having to confront them directly. Through role play or reading about characters from literature, personal feelings can be dealt with symbolically, and often in more meaningful and less uncomfortable ways than by simply trying to talk about them.

Sometimes role-playing evolves spontaneously from students during unstructured play. This is a natural way for many typical students in Stages Two and Three to learn. Adults should not intrude as long as this play is purposeful and positive. If it breaks down, structure is needed from an adult who must step in to ensure group success. This may be done in several ways, including taking on a character's role or stepping into the play scenario as the real adult or teacher. Here is an example.

Several 8- to 10-year-olds are playing "Space Battle" with toy space figures. Considerable action and imagina-

Figure 10.5. Examples of content themes for students in Stage Three.

Themes from Natural Science and Weather

Mr. Night	The Ivy Castle	The Eye of the Storm
Star Wars	Jungle Evils	The Snowmobile Squad
Mission Possible	Space Heroes	Adventures in the Wild
Dinosaur Days		The Evil Empire

Themes from Social Science and Current Events

Detectives	Rock Review
Rescue Squad	Dazzle
The Five Pioneers	The Time Machine
Mystery Clues	The Junkyard Club
Cowboys of the West	The Roadway

Themes from Health, Sports, and Physical Education

The Supergroup	Winners	Superpowers
Cooks in Our Town	Best of the Best	Workout
Olympic Stars	The Superteam	Fact or Fiction?
The Game Plan		

tion are involved in this play, but it begins to show signs of rampant impulsivity. Two students are particularly aggressive in their play and one throws a space figure at another. The alert teacher intervenes immediately in the play in a character's role. As "traffic control headquarters," she broadcasts over the space waves:

> *"Attention, space pilots! Attention, space pilots. This is traffic control headquarters. There is a summit meeting for all experienced pilots at headquarters. Please return your spacecraft to the satellite and report to the space terminal now. Over and out."*

In this role, the teacher, as traffic control headquarters, conveys authority, law, and order. She enters the students' pretend world as a participant in the make-believe and is prepared, if necessary, to continue the role for a successful outcome. Her voice quality conveys someone in control (expertness) and provides the firmness needed to deescalate the intensity of the play. The teacher's command to "experienced pilots" to return for a "summit meeting" appeals to the students' own need to be respected (manipulation), making it easy for them to calm down without being put down.

With advanced Stage Three students, the teacher might follow this play with a discussion about space war and conflict resolution. The exchange might go like this:

TEACHER:	"When fighting and battles happen, there are ways to end the war. The leaders of the flight group must make the decision. What can they do?"
FIRST STUDENT:	"Wave a white flag?"
SECOND STUDENT:	"That's surrender!"
FIRST STUDENT:	"Not if you just want to talk."
SECOND STUDENT:	"They might trick you."
TEACHER:	"Maybe they want a truce."
SECOND STUDENT:	"Yeah. Maybe they're tired of getting beat up."
TEACHER:	"After battles there are peace talks and negotiations. Let's get our experienced pilots together to talk about the war and how to eliminate war in space."

The teacher and students then go on to discuss what transpired in the space battle, how they helped each other, and what happened. The students are encouraged to make observations about their own actions as pilots in the space war and the ways their flight crew can become the peacekeepers in space. This entire exchange came about spontaneously from creative group play, yet it culminated in a group discussion that focused on many of the Stage Three milestones in Socialization and Communication.

The adult also has an essential contribution to make with students who are unfamiliar or reserved about role-playing, creating believability in the situation and providing structure for the characters and their characteristics. Clarity, simplicity, and repetition help students learn to role-play. For example, a group of students beginning Stage Three is involved in learning about rules. The teacher reads a story about a young Native American boy who wants to be a brave warrior. The story deals with the boy's struggle to go through the tribal rites that will enable him to become a man. After the story the teacher takes the role of the chief, and the students, simultaneously, all take on the role of the boy learning the rules of the tribe. Each student puts an individual interpretation on this simple play to get into the character of the boy.

In addition to stories as a source for role play, the adult may set the scene for an imaginary event that might occur within the experience of every student in a group by asking, for example:

- "What will we do when we go to the movies?" (set up chairs; make and buy tickets; make and sell popcorn; show a film, preferably a videotape of the group itself involved in a culminating activity for a week-long project)
- "What will we do when we go shopping?" (use costumes, clothes, wallets, pocketbooks, hats, play money or student-made money; make several departments in a store for groceries, shoes, food, books, toys, sports equipment, clothes; price objects and make appropriate signs)
- "What will we do when we go to a restaurant?" (include fast food drive-ins or other familiar spots; make signs; make menus; make clay hamburgers and French fries; for a real snack make peanut butter cookies, popcorn, or cupcakes; set prices; an adult may serve as cashier unless one group member has advanced skills for adding money)

The students discuss what they actually have done in such situations. The adult makes a list of the activities and assigns each student a part. The purpose is to re-create the event so that the students can explore the range of behaviors, expectations, and rules they may encounter from others in these situations.

Ideas for role-playing often come from the students themselves in advanced Stage Three groups. For example, as a result of a discussion about rules and procedures for a planned field trip, a group of volatile, aggressive students decide on their own, and with minimal guidance from their teacher, to stage a demonstration of appropriate and inappropriate ways to conduct themselves on the field trip. The role play unfolds with a series they call "The Wrong Way," followed by "The Right Way." The negative practice, followed by the acceptable alternatives, is fun for the students and effective in helping them learn to make deliberate behavioral choices. The unit continues to be expanded by the group into creative writing on a script, art projects for background, and a culminating videotaping session in which the students become a rock group with a rhythm band and extemporaneous dialogue. In typical Stage Three style, they call themselves

"Mr. Wrong and Mr. Right."

"Supergroup"—A Week-Long Unit for Stage Three

To illustrate how a weekly content theme is translated into daily Stage Three activities, we use the sample schedule and the theme "Supergroup," illustrated in Figure 10.6.[22]

"What's happening?" (Group Meeting). The primary purpose of a Group Meeting is to develop socialization, communication, listening, planning, and organizing skills. The formation of rudimentary group cohesion also is under way. The proposed activities for the day are presented and connections are made to the students' previous activities and accomplishments. Equally important for students with social, emotional, and behavioral disabilities, this is a time for settling in, when they can relax their initial defensiveness as they join the group. In the "Supergroup" theme, the teacher introduces the theme and leads a discussion about their ideas about Superfriends. As the theme progresses during the week, other ideas are discussed, including attributes of others, group pride, and responsible behavior in a group.

News. This current events activity emphasizes skills in communication and thinking. Newspapers, magazines, and television provide the resources. The topic selected each day focuses on an aspect of the overall weekly theme. In this example, individual acts of friendship, acclaim, and acts of group collaboration are emphasized in contrast to negative images of notoriety (the *Scums*). These topics allow for work on milestones concerning skills for participating in group discussion, listening and comprehension skills, reading, and logical analysis.

Language Arts. This activity is a *whole language* approach, divided into two parts. First, a teacher-made storybook creates the dramatic tone for the weekly theme by setting up a conflict between story characters—the good guys in the Supergroup and the bad guys, the Scums. By making the simple storybook, the teacher is able to design characters who are accessible to every student in the group, create a brief and swiftly paced series of events leading to a crisis, and construct a resolution allowing the characters to achieve victory with advice from a wise and caring adult character. The teacher-made storybook also allows the teacher to adapt the vocabulary and syntax to the students' exact academic levels and provides a common, shared experience for the many group projects to follow. Versions of the story, with the same characters, are used each day for a series of increasingly complex events that often develop into role plays. The second part of this language activity involves work on individual writing skills such as spelling, punctuation, sentences, and creative writing. The daily assignments are taken from the story. Students are asked to prepare reports, write an ending, solve a problem, and write descriptions for a television script and news release, all about "Supergroup Versus the Scums."

Art and Music. This project is intended to emphasize work on Behavior, Communication, and Socialization objectives. Art is scheduled on Mondays and Wednesdays and music on Tuesdays and Thursdays. Friday is used as the day for a culminating activity that blends the two together into a highly acclaimed accomplishment. The "Supergroup" theme in art begins on Monday with each student designing a personal logo to be printed on a T-shirt. The guide for the students' designs is "Keep it simple; make it strong." These shirts are used on Friday for the Supergroup Show. Specific milestones that receive focus during the activity include completing an individual task, accepting success, expressing feelings in acceptable ways, sharing materials and taking turns, and participating as a leader and as a follower. On Wednesday for the art activities, the students design massive shapeless Scums, using Magic Markers and a long roll of butcher paper. These shapes become the mural backdrop for the show on Friday.

During the week, music activities with bongos, tambourines, and xylophones are used to create rhythm patterns. The patterns are coded to represent activities of the Supergroup and the Scums. The story from the teacher-made book is translated into a musical story using the instruments. When the musical story is developed to the group's satisfaction, the teacher makes an audiotape of their creative effort. Thursday's music activity is to create lyrics for the music and the story. On Friday the activities culminate in Show Time. If self-confidence and group confidence are evident, the teacher will videotape the show and play it back for the students to review themselves and their group effort.

Outside (Physical Skills). Stage Three students need abundant opportunities for physical movement and a sys-

[22] Chapter 4 contains another example of content theme, "Superheroes," illustrating the use of dramatic characters for Stage Three students in a special education program.

Figure 10.6. "Supergroup"—a week-long unit for Stage Three.

Daily Schedule	***Monday***	***Tuesday***	***Wednesday***	***Thursday***	***Friday***
What's Happening?	Let's talk about Superfriends	What makes a friend Super?	What makes a Scum?	What makes a Supergroup?	Why are we a Supergroup?
News	Super Event of the Day	Superhero of the Day	Scum of the Day	Supergroup Spotlight	News releases for the Supergroup Show
Language Arts	*Story:* "Supergroup Meets the Scums" *Writing:* The Supergroup Reports	*Story:* "Supergroup Meets the Art Thieves" *Writing:* Write the Ending	*Story:* "Return of the Scums" *Writing:* How To Handle Scums	*Story:* "Supergroup on Stage" *Writing:* Scripts for the Supergroup Show	Rehearsal for the Supergroup Show
Art and Music	Supergroup symbols (designing personal logos)	Supergroup coded musical messages	Famous Scums in art	Supergroup lyrics "Conquer the Scums"	Supergroup Show Time "Supergroup Versus the Scums"
Break	Superbreak	Superbreak	Superbreak	Superpause	"Take 5"
Physical Education	Tests of Skill and Courage	Superific Relays	Impossible Mission Against the Scums (obstacle course)	Superteam Relays	More Tests of Skill and Courage
Snack	Superpunch and protein packets	Colossal cookies	Kryptonite crackers and atomic juice	Superbounty	Supergroup feast
Math	Decoding messages	Electronic mail	Supercalculators	Supershow: Time studies	Estimating future Supergroup plans
Wrap-Up	Supergroup meeting	Supergroup meeting	Supergroup meeting	Supergroup meeting	Supergroup report

tematic program to increase their coordination skills in group games.[23] Physical fitness activities can be conducted indoors or outside. Movement, manipulative games, and low-organization games are easily adapted to either setting, even if an indoor activity room or gymnasium is not available. Tumbling, balance stunts with partners, and activities with group movements are examples of the skills that contribute to progress in this stage. Students also need to increase their ball-handling skills, including the underhand throw, the overhand throw, and dribbling.

Group games are also used extensively to bring Stage Three students together, both indoors and outside. Relays and tag games are particularly well suited for students in Stage Three, especially when they are played in teams. If the rules are simple and the opportunities for both success and failure are controlled, the students gain a very important sense of "groupness" without personal failure or loss. They learn that their own success can come from being a part of a team. They also learn that to have a turn they must wait their turn, and that rules help to hold others in line as well as themselves.

When using games in a Stage Three program, emphasize group processes and group product. The process is the excitement of action and participation with others. The product is the group output. Avoid performance elements that break down into individual competition and rivalry. Redefine the games so that scores apply to the whole group rather than to an individual. This groupness ensures success for every member. Because the group's performance on one day can be compared with its performance on another day, competition is between the group and itself.

The Stage Three physical education program for the "Supergroup" theme is conducted daily, sometimes indoors and sometimes out-of-doors. In addition to work on specific physical skills, this time provides for work on many Behavior and Socialization objectives for individual and group skills. As with the other scheduled activities, the theme is carried into all of the activities throughout the week. On Monday, Tests of Skill and Courage focuses on individual skills. Tuesday uses Superific Relays to introduce group game skills for interaction and building team spirit. Physical stamina in an obstacle course is the activity for Wednesday, with the theme, Impossible Mission Against the Scums, and on Thursday the teams again compete against their own records in relays. Friday concludes the week with a repeat of the first lesson to assess individual and group progress.

[23]If a school has its own physical education schedule, a Developmental Therapy–Developmental Teaching program can be integrated into it, or an adapted physical education program can be used within this curriculum. For individual students, these scheduling decisions are made during the IEP conference at the time of placement.

Snack. A major purpose of the daily snack activity is to provide opportunities for learning acceptable behavior and group social communication skills in a fairly subdued but highly motivating situation. A second purpose is to provide psychological nurturing, conveying that adults care. As mentioned previously, for abused, deprived, and emotionally disadvantaged students of all ages, food may be one of the few forms of expressing caring that they can accept.

Snack Time is an effective activity for encouraging the imitation of other students' acceptable behavior, sharing, participating in group discussions, describing attributes in others, and discussing appropriate behaviors and reasons for rules. Although it is not essential to carry out the weekly theme during Snack, a theme can aid disorganized students and can provide discussion topics that lead into expanded discussions about what students have been doing. In the "Supergroup" theme, snack activities have been given names that interest the group members and stir their imaginations.

Math. This second academic activity of the day provides both group and individual instruction in quantitative operations and concept building. Numeration, computation, and problem solving are Stage Three tasks in arithmetic. The Behavior emphasis is on completing individual tasks, and the Communication emphasis is on participating in group discussions. The "Supergroup" theme adds interest and motivation to the math tasks. On Monday, the teacher uses the Supergroup characters from the original story to present math problems to be solved in pursuit of the Scums (decoding messages). Tuesday's activities include individual work on computers and math worksheets done by pairs of students in which they exchange numerically coded messages (electronic mail). On Wednesday, the students have a group table game similar to "Jeopardy" in which each student solves individual computations for a team score (Supercalculators). Math for Thursday and Friday involves a group study estimating time and effort in preparation, rehearsal, and production of Supergroup Show Time.

Wrap up. The Supergroup meeting at the end is used to synthesize the events of the day, to evaluate progress, and to plan for the next day. Social communication skills are emphasized. Students particularly learn to accept success and praise appropriately; express pride in group achievements; recognize values inherent in the behavior, decisions, and accomplishments of the day; and praise each other. The tone is positive and success-oriented. The daily wrap-up helps to clarify new ideas that may emerge. Changes are discussed, plans modified, and mistakes resolved. Perhaps most important of all, each student leaves with a sense of success as a group member. And this is the overall goal for Stage Three students.

SUMMARY

The outcome of an effective program in Stage Three is evident in the progress students make toward mastery of the milestone objectives that result in increased self-esteem and a sense of self-worth as group members. With success in group activities, Stage Three students' confidence in themselves grows. They begin to see themselves as accepted by their peers and as successful members of a group. This is the pivotal concept at work in a Stage Three program.

The activities and materials used in the Stage Three curriculum are designed to promote an emerging sense of individual contribution to the group effort. At all times, the adult encourages group involvement and individual contribution to mutual effort. Yet there is an implicit assurance that the adult respects the student and will not expect more than an individual member of the group can comfortably handle. This confidence is the basis for building trust in the adult, the program, and each other. When Stage Three students have confidence that the adult will not set expectations too high to be met successfully and will not embarrass them in front of the other group members, they become more spontaneous in their group participation. And when the activities are personally relevant, each student will participate with increasing enthusiasm, involvement, and self-confidence. We summarize this Developmental Therapy–Developmental Teaching approach with students in Stage Three in the following guidelines:

- Focus on individual benefits that result from group participation.
- Design group activities so that every student in the group will participate and feel successful.
- Plan activities requiring short waits and taking turns, as students learn that each person will have a turn and be treated fairly.
- Redesign games and activities so that teams, rather than individuals, win and compete against their own previous record.
- Select activities and materials that students' age-peers are using, and redesign them as needed to guarantee success.
- Design every activity so that there are many opportunities for every student to contribute successfully to the group effort.
- Provide brief and simple demonstrations of each activity or material so that students have a model to imitate successfully.
- Encourage the students to communicate with each other in group discussions about topics in which they share a common interest or experience.
- Select content themes in which successful heroes have feelings that students recognize as their own, or in which children triumph over evil when they collaborate.
- Establish a few basic rules that apply in most situations, are stated positively, and are applied with fairness to everyone.
- Be flexible, improvise, and redesign a planned activity when students' responses indicate that it is not sufficiently motivating or is too difficult to ensure success.

PRACTICE

Using the key points in this chapter

Danny is an example of a typical student beginning a Developmental Therapy—Developmental Teaching program in Stage Three. His overall IEP program goal is to learn skills for successful participation in groups. In order to accomplish this, Danny must master a sequence of developmental milestones for social-emotional development that leads to the goals in each curriculum area for Behavior, Communication, Socialization, and Academics/Cognition. After reviewing this brief description of Danny, answer the questions below.

1. What are the general social-emotional goals for Danny in each curriculum area? (Refer to the Preliminary Profile guide, Figure 3.2.)
2. Which milestones of social-emotional development has he acquired, and which ones seem to be missing?
3. What appears to be Danny's central concern?

4. What does he appear to value?
5. Which developmental anxieties seem to be established and which seem to be emerging now?
6. What situations might be provided to reduce Danny's anxieties?
7. What type of adult role would you try to convey to Danny?
8. What behavior management strategies would you use with Danny?
9. What unit themes might catch his interest and ensure his participation?
10. What activities and materials would provide the best opportunities to help him accomplish the curriculum goals for increasing his social-emotional competence and responsible behavior?

Danny

Danny's current age is 9 years 6 months. His current school assignment is in a fourth-grade program for gifted students. Danny's teachers report that he talks incessantly and cannot sit still or stay at his desk. He argues with them and seldom carries out an assignment in class. He uses obscene language continuously and is verbally abusive to other students. He likes to be the center of attention and tries relentlessly to control others. However, they are afraid of him and try to ignore him. Danny shows considerable skill in writing and telling original stories that are highly imaginative but usually end with the destruction of the hero. He has not completed any homework assignment this year and does little academic work in class.

These problems were evident during the previous school year and his parents have been to many school conferences to discuss his situation. His parents believe that he has always had these problems. They tell the teachers that even by age 2 he was "hard to love," "hard to discipline," "headstrong," and "willful." During kindergarten, he was reported to have been cruel to animals and frequently walked around the playground with a stick, beating the bushes and commenting, under his breath, "I hate my mother. I hate her. I hate her!" His mother explains that she is the family disciplinarian and that is why he resents her so.

Danny's parents were so concerned and frustrated that they asked for a psychological evaluation while he was in third grade. The results indicate that Danny has a full-scale IQ of 133, about evenly distributed between verbal and performance skills. He has superior verbal concept formation and range of information and works well with abstractions. His perceptual-motor skills are superior, especially the ability to identify and arrange components of objects. His academic achievements are at expected age levels, except in reading, which is at seventh-grade level. His greatest intellectual weakness is a lack of ability to concentrate and apply himself to tasks. The report also indicates that Danny is experiencing excessive anxiety and psychomotor tension, has low ego strength, and has a moderately severe psychoneurotic anxiety reaction. According to the report, severe alienation from his peers and parents is heightening his anxiety. His excessively high psychomotor and verbal activity appears to consist of poorly formed attempts to cope with anxiety. The report recommends psychotherapy, counseling with his parents, and participation in a Stage Three Developmental Therapy group for 2 hours daily, coordinated with Developmental Teaching in his regular fourth-grade classroom for the remainder of the day.

CHAPTER 11

Stage Four: Investing in Group Processes

I am what I can learn.

—E. H. ERIKSON, 1959/1980, P. 87

STAGE FOUR: HAPPINESS COMES WITH BELONGING

Social-emotional development and responsible behavior typically flourish during Stage Four if all has gone well in a student's previous development. This is the stage of the Developmental Therapy–Developmental Teaching curriculum associated with typical students in upper elementary school, usually between the ages of 9 and 12. These years can be the "golden age" of childhood or a time of agonizing conflict for them as students change from dependence on adults to greater independence, from narcissism to group conformity, from seeking acclaim to valuing friendships, and from self-doubt to acceptance—belonging in a peer group.[1]

Such distinct changes can produce considerable anxiety in these preadolescent students about their own increasing opportunities and responsibilities for independent behavior and belonging. This concern is first expressed through intense preoccupation with their own

[1] We are particularly appreciative of the fieldwork and research contributions to the Stage Four curriculum by Bonnie C. McCarty, who has used Developmental Therapy–Developmental Teaching with both typical and troubled preadolescents and adolescents. Her contributions to our applications of interpersonal perspective-taking have also been particularly useful.

Stage Four Students in Brief

Program goal:	Investing in group processes, with concern for others
Central concern:	Belonging; meeting expectations of peers and adults
Motivating values:	Personal qualities that meet standards of others
Developmental anxiety:	Conflict over independence and dependence
Approach to problems:	Responsibility for self; to conform or not
Source of authority:	Others' expectations and approval
Type of adult needed:	A supportive adult who approves and facilitates
Effective strategies:	Positive feedback; interpretation; Life Space Intervention
Materials, activities, and content themes:	Real-life experiences and successes with peers; acclaim from significant adults and peers

personal qualities—their desire to look, talk, and behave like others. It shows in their interest in how others handle their lives. Their values are focused on acquiring personal qualities for meeting standards they admire and value in others. Stage Four students seek independence but fear that they may fail at it. They have some skills for at least minimally effective group participation, as both contributors and followers. They have increased awareness of themselves, have expanded communication skills, and are learning to understand others' point of view. They also can be characterized as vacillating between extremes. They attempt to conform and in the process may revert to old strategies of self-protection and noncompliance.

It is not unusual to see beginning Stage Four students happy one minute and distraught the next. They struggle with the conflict between finding acceptable outlets for expressing their independence and securing the acceptance of friends and peers. Put another way, their typical developmental anxiety is the conflict between compliance and noncompliance, independence and dependence. This conflict can be minimal or devastating, depending upon the intensity of their feelings, their skills for managing these feelings constructively, and their experiences with friendships and group membership.[2]

Jerome is a typical fifth-grade student in Stage Four, who is at risk for developing social-emotional problems. His personal circumstances are creating problems for him that have not yet been seen as serious by his teachers. However, his social-emotional needs are rapidly becoming a central issue, and the way they are dealt with will shape his future. At the center of the potential risks for Jerome is his isolation from other students. Whether this is self-imposed or is a role thrust on him by his peers, Jerome is at a point where he can swing either way. He is typical of students who are attracted to gang membership or who submit to delinquent peers because they offer alliance, affirmation, and belonging.

Most Stage Four students, with and without disabilities, and especially those with social, emotional, and behavioral disabilities, begin this stage with a self-protective orientation toward success in a group. They usually

[2]Brown and Gilligan (1992) vividly describe this typical conflict in preadolescent girls. See their narrative of Jessie in *Meeting at the Crossroads*, pp. 58–62.

Jerome

Jerome is a tall, attractive 11-year-old, enrolled in the fifth grade. His parents have been divorced for 5 years. He lives with his mother and three sisters in a small rural community. His mother seeks help at the mental health center because she is not able to control him at home and she is concerned about his academic performance at school. She describes the high-priority problems she has observed with Jerome:

- demands attention
- does not follow directions
- resists discipline
- cries easily
- reads poorly
- fails deliberately
- has low frustration level
- does not tell the truth
- loses his temper easily
- complains about every thing
- lacks confidence
- is immature for his age
- seems moody and suspicious
- seems to lack understanding

The school sees Jerome in a quite different way. His teachers see him as a good student with average abilities and no special problems in conduct. Their only concern is his excessive talking, problems paying attention, and isolation from other students. They express concern that he may be seen by others as a "nerd."

The psychologist, school guidance staff, and teachers met with Jerome's mother, at her request, to review her concerns and plan for ways to help in her parenting role. According to the psychologist, Jerome sees himself as a victim in fights with peers. Religious teachings have instilled in him the belief that fighting is wrong, and the level of aggression among his peers at school is difficult for Jerome to handle. As a result of this conflict, he seems to have the fatalistic attitude that he is going to be destroyed.

Jerome's mother is eager to continue weekly meetings with the psychologist to discuss Jerome's behavior, appropriate expectations for a boy his age, and management strategies that will help to improve his behavior at home. She also responds to the emotional support she receives as a single parent from these meetings.

can see themselves as participating members and have learned that they receive benefits from participation with a group of friends. In contrast to students in lower stages, they spontaneously seek each other rather than adults. This is a key characteristic that differentiates Stage Four students from those in the previous stage; it is particularly evident when they have accomplished something they feel good about.

Tanya is a 12-year-old sixth-grade student who is also receiving special education. She is making the transition from Stage Three into Stage Four. Her social-emotional development has been marked by extremely slow progress in acquiring responsible, self-regulated behavior. Like Jerome, her personal circumstances are contributing in major ways to her current problems, but their severity and long-standing presence in her life have left her with fragile coping skills even though she, too, looks to peers rather than adults for attention and reassurance. Tanya needs every possible form of assistance.

Sometimes students are mistakenly judged to be in Stage Three when they actually are ready to begin Stage Four. This may happen because an adult reacts to a Stage Four characteristic by thinking, "This student cannot possibly do that." In Developmental Therapy–Developmental Teaching, several key changes in characteristics alert us to a student's need for program changes from Stage Three to Stage Four to accommodate new developmental needs, goals, and milestones.

The student is ready for Stage Four strategies as Stage Three milestones are acquired and new Stage Four milestones are needed.[3] We keep in mind that when students begin a particular stage of social-emotional development, they are not expected to have mastered the milestones for that stage, but they should have achieved most of the previous stage milestones and should exhibit a few of the characteristics of the new stage.

Adults also may have difficulty differentiating students who are ready for a Stage Four program from those

[3]We use the DTORF–R to assess each student's individual mastery of these milestones for social-emotional development. See Chapter 1 for a review of its development and Chapter 3 for a description of its use.

Tanya

Twelve-year-old Tanya is proving to be quite a disruptive force in the sixth-grade classroom. During particularly aggressive episodes, her teachers find it hard to bring her under control. She goes to any length to get attention from the other students and the teachers. She has stolen personal items from her teacher's desk several times and has been accused by other students of taking things from their book bags.

Because her mother has disappeared, Tanya lives with a great-aunt in extreme deprivation and poverty. This elderly lady is frail and somewhat incompetent herself. She is not able to help the school with Tanya's problems. She does know, however, that Tanya's older sister is in the adolescent unit of the state mental hospital. Two younger brothers are receiving aid to the disabled and are in other foster homes.

Tanya seems to be able to learn, but her achievement scores are about 2–4 years behind expected grade level for her age. She frequently refuses to do the assigned work at school and has never come to school with her homework completed. As Tanya's disruptive behavior becomes more frequent, her teachers seek help. The evaluation team reports that severe socioeconomic, psychological, and cultural deprivation are all contributing factors. She is enrolled in a special education program for behavioral disorders with a daily 2-hour, intensive Developmental Therapy program. Her initial placement was with a Stage Three group, but after the first semester, Tanya showed sufficient gains to join a newly formed group of students at her elementary school who were making the transition from Stage Three into Stage Four.

The Developmental Therapy–Developmental Teaching team spends many hours reviewing realistic setting of limits, workable management strategies, and feasible consequences for her unacceptable behavior—in her regular fourth-grade class, in the special program, and at home. They arrange for Tanya to participate in a remedial reading group at her school. They also spend time each week with her great-aunt, helping her to obtain needed social services and extending Developmental Therapy–Developmental Teaching strategies into Tanya's after-school environment. Eventually, they are able to find a community volunteer as a mentor for Tanya for weekend guidance. This mentor is able to continue the focus, guiding Tanya in acquiring her program milestones in Stage Four, including personal habits of hygiene and behavior that make her increasingly attractive.

Key Characteristics Differentiating Students in Stage Four
from those in Stage Three

In Stage Three, students learned	Now, in Stage Four they are learning
how to obtain approval from adults	that peers' approval is important
that adults have authority to set and enforce rules of conduct	that behavior is a personal responsibility
that there are rules of conduct that must be followed	that some rules can be made and changed by group consensus
that positive behavior produces respect from others	that others deserve fair treatment and consideration
that personal views make a contribution	that others may have views different from one's own
how to make choices that bring benefits	that there are many choices to be made with varied consequences
how to be accepted by peers	how to make and keep friends
how to participate positively in a group	how to be a valued friend and group member

needing a Stage Three program if they mistakenly associate behavioral *levels* with developmental *stages*. Although some elements are comparable, this comparison does not consistently carry over. In a system with levels, students with noncompliant behavior begin at level 1 and progress through the levels as they exhibit increasing behavioral control and compliant behavior. In contrast, in a stage model, the first stage is defined by characteristics and skills that are typically acquired during the first year of life. Each subsequent stage increases and expands skills and abilities as a function of maturation and development. Thus, older students have acquired many age-related skills although they may also have some noncompliant behaviors. Incremental progress in compliant behavior (or, as in the case of Tanya, *lack* of compliant behavior) is not the key indicator of stage progression. Students typically mature and change in their social-emotional orientation even as they still exhibit noncompliant behavior from time to time under stress. Students enter a Developmental Therapy–Developmental Teaching program at the developmental stage that best describes the skills they are ready to acquire.[4]

A shift in focus from adults to peers is the single best indicator that a student is moving into Stage Four. Then, during Stage Four, personal responsibility and thinking of others become central in the curriculum. These priorities frequently require students to restrain gratification of their own wants and needs as they acquire a working social knowledge, learning how others feel, think, and behave.

Adults do not rescue students in Stage Four, even though they are supportive, provide guidance, and facilitate the group processes. It is the students who are learning to take on personal responsibility, making choices and anticipating consequences. The adults help them to gain insights and understanding about themselves and others. Adults offer direction about reality and the natural consequences of actions. But the students in Stage Four must learn how to experience failure constructively and take personal responsibility for correcting their own mistakes. They also must develop skills for social problem solving and for communicating effectively with others for crisis resolution. It is not unusual to hear a student in Stage Four saying,

"I hope I can make the right decision when the time comes."

When students make such remarks, it is a clear indication that they are beyond the existential crisis experienced by most students at some time during the previous stage of social-emotional development.[5] It is also a signal that the program must respond to this powerful but subtle change, which indicates that a student is ready to learn personal responsibility for individual actions—to fail and then to solve the problem, instead of leaving it as someone

[4] See Chapter 3 for a review of the beliefs that are the theoretical foundation for this approach. A student who has acquired most of the Stage Three milestones will show considerable compliant behavior as a result. However, compliancy alone is not the program's focus but, rather, responsible behavior and social-emotional competence. This may require a push into Stage Four before some students have demonstrated full and consistent compliance during Stage Three.

[5] There is a discussion of the existential crisis in Chapter 2 and a description in Chapter 10 of how students in Stage Three go through this phase. Its resolution is a key concept for identifying a Stage Four student.

else's responsibility. When this is accomplished, even with marginal proficiency, the Stage Four goal for social-emotional competence is achieved.

In this chapter, the Developmental Therapy–Developmental Teaching curriculum for students in Stage Four is discussed in some detail. It includes applications for typical 9- to 12-year-olds, as well as for older students in special education, middle school, or high school who are making the transition from the previous stage into Stage Four. The material is organized into four sections:

- typical social-emotional processes developing during Stage Four
- goals and objectives for typical preadolescents in Stage Four
- how the program meets the needs of students in Stage Four
- activities designed to accomplish the goals and objectives for Stage Four

TYPICAL SOCIAL-EMOTIONAL PROCESSES DEVELOPING DURING STAGE FOUR

Typical social-emotional development occurring during Stage Four can be characterized as a movement toward increasing conformity to peers and social conventions (Ausubel, Sullivan, & Ives, 1980; Loevinger, 1976). This process is not without anguish and conflict. The price is conflict between a strong need for independence and an equally strong dependence on approval and acceptance by others. As students seek social acceptance and approval, they learn to conform to the rules and standards of others and minimize their own inner needs. Yet the need to be an independent individual is a strong drive, often expressed as

> *"They're making me, and I don't want to"* or *"I want to, but I'm not allowed to."*[6]

This developmental anxiety, *conflict*, experienced by typical students during Stage Four, is quite different from the type of conflict associated with students in the previous stage. Lack of compliance in a Stage Three student represents an external, observable conflict between the student's self-protective behavior and the expectations set by adults. When the typical anxiety for Stage Four is developing—personal conflict—students wage an inner war about whether to be independent or dependent, whether to entrust themselves to peers and valued adults or to trust only themselves. This is an internal conflict about whose standards should govern behavior and where loyalty should be placed.

The anxieties of Stage Four are expressed in many ways, with great variability in how severe they will be. Many typical Stage Four students balance the demands with great success and have a comfortable period of 3–4 years in which they enjoy increasing friendships and group memberships. Other students find the period one of difficulty, alienation, and frustrating rejection by peers. The relative successes or failures they experienced during the previous stage of development contribute immensely. The dynamic forces at work during this stage include

- intensity of emotional needs;
- extent of demands made by adults, friends, and peers;
- coping skills for dealing with these demands;
- previous successes (or failures) with peers and adults; and
- self-confidence (or lack or self-confidence).

The culmination of successful social-emotional development during Stage Four is resolution of this conflict in favor of conformity to social and cultural norms and satisfaction in belonging to a group. Students who have learned to value themselves in previous stages and have peer role models who exemplify these values seem to be able to resolve this conflict more successfully than those who lack either self-esteem or desirable peer role models (Coopersmith, 1967; Buhrmester, 1990; Mussen, Conger, Kagan, & Huston, 1990). Figure 11.1 illustrates this complex and dynamic process.

Opinions of friends, significant adults, and real-life heroes are important influences in the social-emotional development of students during Stage Four. Role models are real people, in contrast to the superhero, larger-than-life idols from previous stages. However, parents still play a major role in influencing the behavior and development of Stage Four students. It is not unusual for these students to seek help from a parent and then denounce the parent for that very same assistance. This vacillation is also transferred to teachers and other valued adults. It is only one manifestation of the anxiety they experience in the conflict over asserting independence from adults. Preadolescents want to be independent and sophisticated, but they often cling to the security of their own previous childlike behaviors. They dream great dreams of accomplishment, but the limitations of their abilities defy those dreams. They may fantasize notions of an ideal self but are faced with accepting themselves as they are seen by peers and adults. The important point is that the friendships and role models for preadolescents in Stage Four must be people with personal characteristics they admire and can

[6]See Chapter 2 for a review of the developmental anxieties occurring in typical social-emotional development between birth and age 16. Troubled students in Stage Four may be experiencing any of the previous developmental anxieties in addition to *conflict,* which is typical for this stage. Similarly, the motivational forces that shape their behavior will be influenced by prior experiences. See Appendix 5 for a review of motivational systems.

Figure 11.1. Key processes of typical social–emotional development in Stage Four. The dotted lines indicate the inner life—thoughts and feelings.

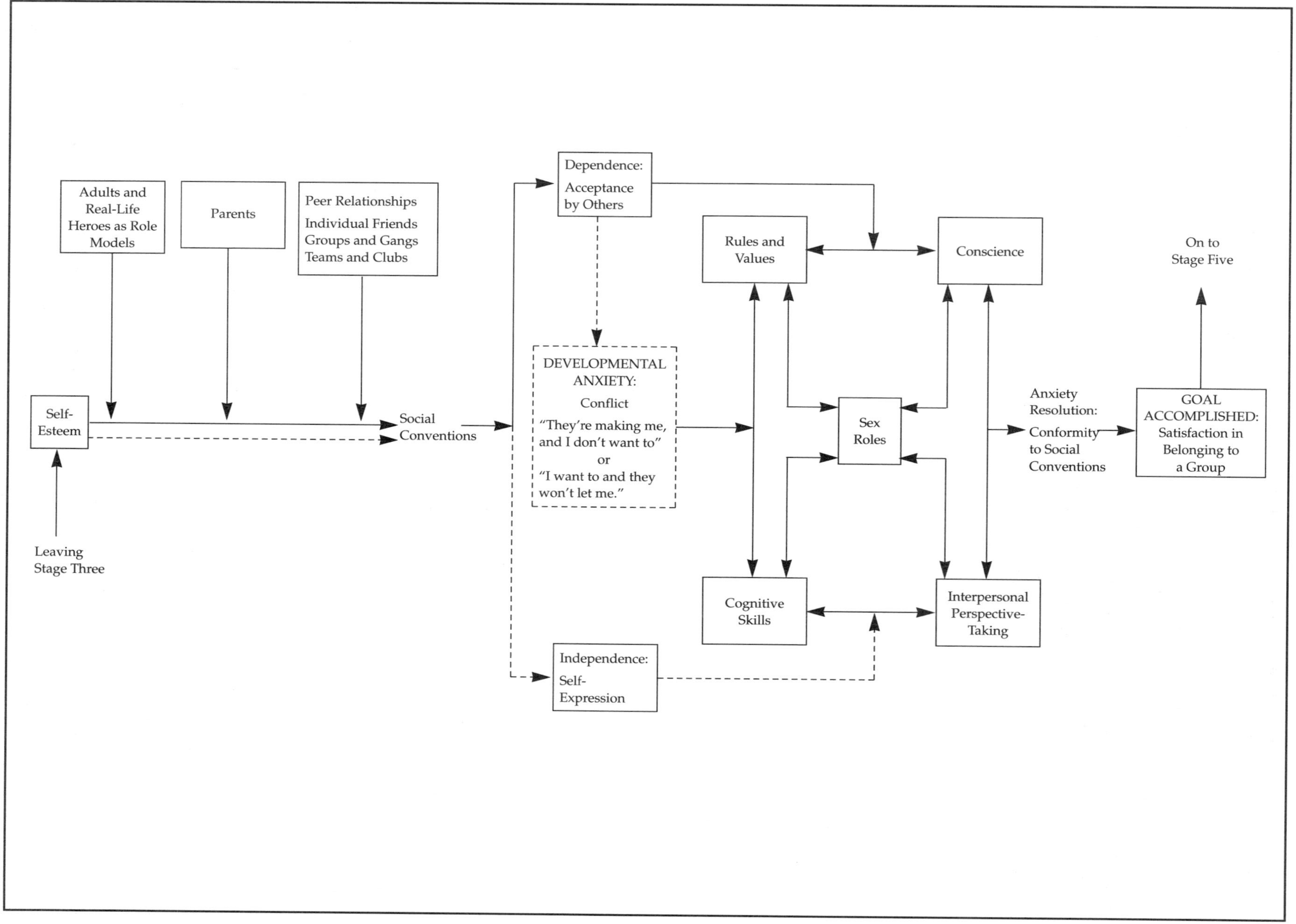

emulate (Aronfreed, 1968). These people also must openly acknowledge the value of the student and provide needed acclaim for independent successes (Bandura, 1977; Rosenhan, 1972; White, 1963).

Most Stage Four preadolescents depend heavily upon acceptance by peers. In the previous stage, they learned the necessity for yielding their will to that of the peer group. They also learned to abide by the rules of a group, understand that there are reasons for rules, and understand the consequences when rules are broken (Kohlberg, 1981; Piaget, 1932/1960). Now, in Stage Four, they learn to put this knowledge into practice. They are reaching a point in development where they are eager to participate and begin to value the participation. As they mature during this stage, quarreling and demands for competitive testing against each other tend to diminish. Relational conflicts are diminished in favor of social order and acceptance. Brown and Gilligan (1992, pp. 91–94) illustrate this preadolescent change in Stage Four girls with their description of Gail in *Meeting at the Crossroads.* Group spirit and comradeship increasingly predominate over individual expression. These preadolescents are learning to solve their interpersonal differences through verbal exchanges, listening to others' points of view, and considering the rights of others (Loevinger, 1976). They begin to modify rules to suit the needs of the group. Group membership, team pride, and winning for the group are the capstones of Socialization in Stage Four.

Cognitive skills and problem-solving abilities are also powerful components of development during Stage Four. Students are typically able to use cognitive processes to increase their social knowledge and understanding of others' ways of looking at things. Units of abstract thinking such as *images* (mental representations), *symbols* (whole and parts), and *rules* (order serialization and multiple classes) are all part of the complexity in rational approaches to social understanding. The following cognitive processes contribute to the increase in social knowledge during Stage Four:

Comprehending	Interpreting ("encoding")—a form of advanced perception and understanding
Remembering	Storing memories of experiences and observations of others
Producing ideas	Generalizing; problem solving with inductive, inferential, and creative approaches
Evaluating	Considering the quality of one's own thinking
Reasoning	Deducing; using rules to solve problems

When these processes are sufficiently developed, preadolescents are able to carry out abstract thinking and can put their behavior and feelings under rational management. These rational processes also allow them to apply principles and values in solving social situations with others. They are then able to see reasons, relationships, cause and effect, alternatives, and new ways to use rules.

As a part of these cognitive advances, most Stage Four students develop a fully operational value system with an active conscience at the center (Kohlberg, 1981; Lickona, 1985, 1991). These Stage Four values typically include

- kindness
- leadership
- friendship
- consideration of others
- living up to others' expectations

Students in Stage Four learn to use these values to guide their friendships, form personal goals, assume personal responsibility, and regulate their own behavior. At the core of values for these preadolescent students in Stage Four is the belief that fairness and justice apply to all—not just to themselves, as in the previous stage of development.

Heightened awareness of sex-role differences occurs with preadolescents as they develop cognitive abilities for classifying and differentiating people on increasingly complex dimensions. Stage Four students carefully study gender differences. They observe and imitate physical attributes, behavioral characteristics, emotional expressions, problem-solving strategies, interests, feelings, attitudes, and motivations. Their own understanding of sex-role behaviors (what it means to be a girl or a boy, a woman or a man) seems to occur as they make these differentiated perceptions. These observations shape their own sex-role behaviors through their experiences with friends and peers, and by the behavior and standards of the adults they admire (Spence & Helmreich, 1978).

Interpersonal perspective taking comes into bloom during Stage Four and dramatically changes the way students think. Research has shown that before the age of 8 or 9, students do not understand that another person may have a point of view different from their own (Buhrmester, 1990; Selman, 1980). During the next 3–4 years, preadolescent thinking about friendships, parent-child relationships, shared feelings, and reciprocal relationships increases steadily (Damon, 1988; Selman & Schultz, 1990). This dramatic change is eloquently expressed (Brown & Gilligan, 1992, p. 92) by a preadolescent girl who says,

> *"I'm not always right, they could have been just as right and they have their thoughts too."*

Forms of interpersonal perspective-taking (also called *social cognition, social role taking,* and *social reasoning*) contribute to a student's ability to understand the behavior, thinking, and feelings of others.[7] With an expanded capacity for interpersonal understanding, more mature dimensions of personality develop, such as altruism, empathy, and moral development (Turiel, 1983). These qualities enable students to anticipate the consequences of their own actions for themselves and for others. These capacities also contribute to the preadolescent's eventual resolution of the independence-dependence conflict in favor of conformity.

Interpersonal perspective-taking develops in generally incremental patterns during this preadolescent period, with differences that probably are influenced by emotional disturbance. Research findings about these patterns typically include measures of a student's views about individuals, close friendships, parent-child relationships, and peer group organization (Selman & Jaquette, 1987). Development tends to progress in each of these areas, but not always with consistent correspondence. Early studies indicated that deficits in interpersonal perspective-taking are associated with antisocial (noncompliant) behavior. However, withdrawn characteristics tend to be associated with lesser abilities for social reasoning (Selman, 1976). In preadolescents with severe emotional disturbance, impaired social reasoning has been shown to be significantly correlated with students' ideas about parent-child relationships, while their views about close friendships are more advanced than their ideas about individuals. There also appears to be a significantly reduced level of interpersonal perspective-taking when these students come from single-parent homes (McCarty, 1992).

This body of research has a direct implication for programs concerned with social-emotional competence and the development of responsible behavior during the preadolescent years (Stage Four). Family experience continues to be a significant factor in the development of children and their subsequent passage into adolescence. There also continues to be a necessary contribution from effective social support systems—peers, family, neighborhoods, sports groups, and churches. These groups provide adults who can be effective role models for preadolescents even as they pursue peer relationships with vigor.

The successful conclusion of Stage Four produces a young person on the brink of adolescence who takes personal responsibility for behavior and conforms to accepted standards of conduct. The developmental conflict between independence and dependence is temporarily resolved as students recognize that being a valued member of a group can also enhance their own independence and self-esteem (Erikson, 1959/1980, 1968). Family, valued adults, friendships, and peer groups are all significant forces in this process. By sifting through their own concerns and those of others, preadolescent Stage Four students have become aware that there are differing values and points of view. But even as they learn more about others and these differing points of view, they learn more about themselves. And if their friendships and adult role models have been positive, constructive ones, they derive satisfaction in conforming to accepted cultural standards.

The level of social understanding, social competence, and responsible behavior preadolescents are able to achieve during these Stage Four years directly influences how they will respond to the stresses of adolescence during the next developmental stage. In short, if they have developed a comfortable, temporary balance between inner needs and the expectations of others, they are prepared for adolescence—and Stage Five. Near completion of Stage Four, we frequently hear students making statements such as these:

"What do others think of me?"

"Everybody does it."

"I don't want to be left out."

"People who like you will help you."

"You can have a friend by being a friend."

"It's important for people to like you."

GOALS AND OBJECTIVES FOR TYPICAL PREADOLESCENTS IN STAGE FOUR

The Goal: *Investing in group processes*

The goals and objectives of social-emotional development in each curriculum area of Developmental Therapy–Developmental Teaching reflect the dynamic developmental changes under way in preadolescents during Stage Four. Students are developing an increased capacity to direct their own lives in constructive and satisfying ways, and this requires successful friendships and membership in groups. While reviewing the milestones that are needed during Stage Four, readers may find it helpful to remember that milestones are seldom acquired evenly across the domains of development. A student may be accelerated in one area and delayed in another. By Stage Four, these patterns may be quite extreme in some students and can sometimes mislead those who are planning for the student. We find that if a program can target a student's overall stage (the average of development in the four curriculum areas of Behavior, Communication, Socialization, and Academics/Cognition), it can be effective in accelerating progress.[8] On the other hand, if a program targets the lowest area of performance, it tends to keep the student in a plateau, with little progress in any area. Such a

[7] For readers not familiar with the characteristics of interpersonal understanding, we suggest a review of the developmental milestones in the following section, as most of them are examples of this process.

[8] Appendix 4 contains our content analysis for these four curriculum areas, including the processes directly related to the curriculum in Stage Four.

program "ceiling" may actually encourage regression to a less mature level of performance. We use the following rule: *As a student begins to acquire a milestone, refocus the program to emphasize ways to acquire the next milestone.*

Behavior Milestones for Stage Four

In the curriculum area for Behavior during Stage Four, the general goal for students is *to learn to contribute individual effort to group success.* Students beginning this stage already can describe behavioral expectations, know the reasons for the rules and standards, and can participate, at least minimally, in group activities without losing control. These are skills they acquired during the previous stage of development. The Stage Four goal places an increased emphasis on thinking of others in the group and behaving in ways that will be helpful to the peer group.

During Stage Four, the behavioral goal is achieved as students acquire an increased ability to contribute to a positive outcome of the group effort. To do this, they must first be able to self-monitor, appraising themselves realistically and viewing themselves from a perspective of improvement over time. In the process of doing this, Stage Four students need many opportunities to make behavioral choices. Then they need frequent opportunities for realistic feedback about the results of these choices. Individual goal setting and frequent review are essential for this process. In addition to daily group evaluation sessions, weekly individual conferences with a teacher or parent help students acquire this ability to monitor their own behavior. Individual students in Stage Four can rate themselves on the DTORF–R to select the program objectives they need to work on, with guidance from an adult in the rating process.[9] This rating provides the frame of reference for guiding them through Stage Four experiences and teaches them to monitor their own progress, as well as that of others in their group.

For students to achieve social competence in this stage, they must learn group process skills—planning together, establishing behavioral expectations for the group members, changing the group procedures when it will benefit the group effort, and mutually sharing in the group's accomplishments. They then need practice in applying these skills successfully in new situations that might have evoked stress or loss of control in a previous stage. To achieve this milestone, students must be able to discern, select, and implement needed behaviors in new situations that challenge self-control. This emphasis on personal responsibility for behavior is in sharp contrast to Stage Three group dynamics, which are controlled and often initiated by an adult.

The milestone accomplishments indicating achievement of the Stage Four curriculum goals in Behavior occur when students accept responsibility for their own actions and attitudes. When they can do this, they are also able to respond to group and interpersonal problems with a rational, problem-solving approach rather than with the inappropriate, defensive maneuvers so typical of students' behavior at previous stages.

Communication Milestones for Stage Four

In the curriculum area for Communication during Stage Four, the general goal for students is *to learn to use words to convey understanding of feelings and behavior in self and others.* Communication milestones in Stage Four emphasize the effective use of words to mediate between the students' own needs and the demands of others. The most pressing need for students beginning this stage is to find acceptable ways to express their feelings. Their awareness of their own feelings has increased during the previous

[9]Chapter 1 contains a report of this instrument and its use in documenting the progress of students in Developmental Therapy–Developmental Teaching programs. Chapter 3 describes the curriculum model that implements the goals and objectives contained in the DTORF–R (see also Wood, 1992a, 1992b).

Stage Four
Behavior Milestones

Goal: ***To contribute individual effort to group success***
Indicate awareness of one's own progress.
Be flexible in changing procedures for the needs of the group.
Participate in new activities with control.
Implement acceptable alternative behaviors.
Respond to provocation with control.
Accept responsibility for actions and attitudes.
Respond with constructive solutions to individual and group problems.

Source: Abstracted from *The Developmental Teaching Objectives for the DTORF–R*, by Developmental Therapy Institute, 1992, Athens, GA: Developmental Therapy Institute.

Stage Four
Communication Milestones

Goal: ***To use words to convey understanding of feelings and behavior in oneself and others***
Channel feelings through creative media.
Explain how behavior influences others.
Express feelings spontaneously and appropriately in the group.
Initiate communication for relationships with peers and adults.
Spontaneously use words to praise and support others.
Express cause-and-effect relationships between feelings and behavior.

Source: Abstracted from *The Developmental Teaching Objectives for the DTORF–R*, by Developmental Therapy Institute, 1992, Athens, GA: Developmental Therapy Institute.

stage, and now they must have acceptable outlets for self-expression. Because creative media and words are universally used to convey personal experience, attitudes, and feelings, the program puts an emphasis on teaching students to use creative media. In doing so, students also acquire another milestone for Communication during this stage—to accurately explain how their own actions influence the actions of others.

The milestones for Communication that follow build skills for communicating spontaneously with both peers and adults. It is often difficult for shy students, those who are at risk, and those with social, emotional, and behavioral disabilities to initiate contact with others spontaneously. Many have spent their lives avoiding others or behaving in ways that communicate their distress through actions. Their interpersonal skills are often extremely limited, and many avoid relationships of any kind. It may take these students longer than usual to make progress in acquiring these particular milestones.

By the end of Stage Four, students' verbal skills and understanding of themselves have expanded considerably from the previous stage. They are able not only to recognize how their feelings are connected to their behavior but also to communicate this understanding and to recognize these relationships in others. This skill represents the last milestone in Stage Four for Communication, and a new level of interpersonal perspective-taking.

Socialization Milestones for Stage Four

In the curriculum area for Socialization during Stage Four, the goal for a student is *to learn to participate spontaneously and successfully as a group member.* Socialization in Stage Four emphasizes the sort of spontaneous investment in the group that occurs when individual members see the group as enhancing to themselves—something to be valued beyond the individuals themselves. To achieve this attitude, Socialization objectives focus on a gradual

Stage Four
Socialization Milestones

Goal: ***To participate spontaneously and successfully as a group member***
Identify with adult heroes.
Describe group experiences in a time sequence.
Spontaneously suggest appropriate activities for the group.
Express awareness of others' actions.
Listen to others' ideas and opinions.
Express an interest in peers' opinions of oneself.
Suggest solutions to interpersonal and group problems.
Recognize opposite values in social situations.
Draw inferences from social situations.

Source: Abstracted from *The Developmental Teaching Objectives for the DTORF-R*, by Developmental Therapy Institute, 1992, Athens, GA: Developmental Therapy Institute.

change from self-protection and identification with adult values (as seen in Stage Three students) to understanding others as being different from themselves.

Socialization in Stage Four begins with students' identifying with the characteristics of valued adults—parents and sometimes other adult heroes. Simultaneously, they are becoming members of numerous groups, and experiences in these groups become increasingly complex as Socialization skills continue to develop. The program milestones focus heavily on social communication: describing group experiences, spontaneously making suggestions to the group, and listening to others' ideas and opinions. These processes are the tools for increasing social knowledge and understanding others.

A key milestone in Stage Four is evident when students seek the perceptions and opinions of their peers about themselves. At this point they are well on their way to accomplishing the overall Socialization goal of Stage Four—being a successful and valued member of a group. This milestone indicates an ability to value others' points of view. Students who have acquired this significant milestone have a tool for establishing and maintaining friendships. They can use this tool to monitor how their own behavior is received by others, and they can make changes in themselves to conform to group standards and values. Even as awareness and respect for others increase in students during Stage Four, it is equally important that they maintain a sense of their own contributions in a group. This milestone encourages them to contribute to interpersonal and group relationships. A big part of this process is contributing constructive solutions to interpersonal and group conflict. These skills aid them in establishing friendships.

Acquisition of the final milestone for Socialization in Stage Four results in a student who is in need of little further special assistance from adults. As they complete this stage, students are able to learn from experience and can draw inferences from the behavior of others. These are attributes they can use to foresee the outcome of actions and to regulate their own behavior responsibly.

Academics/Cognition Milestones for Stage Four

In the area of Academics/Cognition during Stage Four, the goal for students is *to use academic skills for successful social group experiences.* Academic and thinking skills achieved during Stage Four aid students in their real-life interests and problems. Most students beginning Stage Four have already mastered basic skills in reading comprehension, mathematics, and writing at the third-grade level or better. The Stage Four milestones encourage them to apply these basic skills in solving problems to enhance themselves and their group membership.

For students who have achieved the milestones in the previous stage, program objectives focus on acquiring milestones that allow them to use rational, cognitive processes and thinking skills in expanding their understanding of others and the world around them. These milestones also aid them in seeing the practical use of academic tools for solving their own problems and communicating with others effectively in symbolic forms—essays, diaries, logs, opinion letters, and the like. The milestones include all written forms of communication and reading for pleasure and information about others and their values. Similarly, milestones in mathematics emphasize solving problems with logic, advanced computation skills, and elementary, functional economic principles.

One of the most challenging jobs for teachers of students in Stage Four involves adjusting academic instruction to the individual academic achievement levels of each student, while maintaining age-appropriate content. It is not unusual to have students in a Stage Four group working on Stage Three academic milestones (primary-grade-level academic work). Many streetwise students are

Stage Four Academics/Cognition Milestones

Goal: ***To use academic skills for successful social group experiences***
Write to communicate information, events, and feelings.
Solve multiplication and division problems to 100.
Read for pleasure and personal information.
Compute values for money to $10.00.
Describe characters and explain the motives of fictional characters on television, in reading, or in movies.
Use grammatical rules in writing sentences, paragraphs, short essays, prose fiction, and poetry.
Use units of measurement (time, length, liquid volume) and other quantitative concepts to solve problems of logic.

Source: Abstracted from *The Developmental Teaching Objectives for the DTORF–R,* by Developmental Therapy Institute, 1992, Athens, GA: Developmental Therapy Institute.

effective problem solvers but have limited academic skills. Other students in special education with learning disabilities have progressed in their social-emotional development to near-age-appropriate levels but are significantly behind in academic skills. An individualized approach to academic instruction is essential for such students.

Every academic program must be designed with topics, materials, and activities that reflect the actual chronological-age interests and developmental qualities needed by individual students whose social-emotional characteristics put them in Stage Four. Yet it is equally necessary to see that their IEP or ITP includes opportunities for application of these skills in groups, so that social-emotional competence can develop along with academic skill and thinking ability. Keep in mind the Stage Four goal for Academics/Cognition: to use academic skills for successful social group experiences.[10]

HOW THE PROGRAM MEETS THE NEEDS OF STUDENTS IN STAGE FOUR

A Developmental Therapy–Developmental Teaching program for students in Stage Four should stimulate individual involvement and commitment to group endeavors. Students in Stage Four need a reality-oriented, less structured curriculum and a less protected environment than at previous stages. The task to be accomplished during Stage Four is one of enlarging the students' capacity to understand themselves and others and to function effectively with peers and adults under the ordinary rules, constraints, and consequences all students face.

The organization of the Stage Four program can be best described as a flexible, student-focused approach. In the previous stage, students learned basic individual skills for participating in group activities with success, given adult guidance. Now, less structure is required to elicit successful participation. When a student in the previous stage had difficulty participating in a group activity, one adult maintained the structure of the activity to keep it going, while another adult on the team worked with the student in crisis to rejoin the group. Now, in Stage Four, when there is difficulty within a group, the adult stops the activity to address the problem issue, usually one that is fairly subtle, but that is undermining the overall group spirit. As they recognize undercurrents detrimental to group cohesion, we hear adults saying:

"Let's stop this activity, to take care of what's going on."

"What's happening here?"

"Why is this not working?"

"Do you like what's going on?"

"Do you want to say something to him?"

"There's another issue that we need to attend to first."

The emphasis is on responding to others and to each event with rational consideration of what is involved. While maintaining a "now" orientation, the Stage Four program also deals with the recent past. Students are encouraged to recall recent events and the behavior of others. They also link these recollections to present situations. At times discussion can be carried on fairly independently by the group members, with only marginal, intermittent participation by an adult to guide the direction of a group discussion. At other times a group's lack of leadership and direction will require active leadership by the adult. The overall strategy involves the transfer of behavioral regulation from adult authority to self-direction by students, guided by their expanding value systems.

Students in Stage Four are encouraged to develop and maintain their own group rules, regulations, and enforcement procedures (consequences). "Say 'Yes' Instead of 'No'" is an example that illustrates how a program involves the students in learning self-regulation.

This approach to rule making is effective by having both negative and positive rules to choose between: "things we can do" and "things we can't do." The students begin to see opposite solutions within the same set of circumstances and have opportunities to make these choices. Yet the choices are still within the framework of what is allowable. Students are still expected to conform to the expectations for acceptable behavior.

The Adult's Role: Group Facilitator, Individual Advocate, or Role Model

Students in Stage Four do not look to the adult for solutions to problems as often as they did in previous stages. They test adults less frequently and usually accept guidance readily, if they see the adult as someone who represents fairness and justice for all. However, as group leader there are times when the adult may have to set limits. This is done in a way that involves students in decision making, yet maintains the boundaries of what is possible and acceptable.

Adults as Group Facilitators. The major responsibility for an adult during Stage Four is that of group facilitator, reflecting reality and guiding the group members. Such an adult is needed by students in Stage Four to help resolve conflicts between individual needs and those of the group. As students learn how to plan activities, rules, and procedures for the group, the adult is the bridge to help them consider their decisions in relation to each other, and to the

[10] Proficiency in academic skills often can be used to enhance a student's social power with peers by Stage Four, when the skills are used in solving individual or group problems. See Chapter 10 for a review of expertness as a form of social power used by students to influence others.

Say "Yes" Instead of "No"

It was the first day of class. The teachers and students were planning classroom procedures and rules. The group decided to write these rules on a large piece of construction paper and post it in their room. Here are the first procedures and rules they came up with, all negative in tone, but realistic:

No fighting, kicking, or cursing on the bus.

Don't run or talk in the hallways.

No fighting, kicking, or spitting in class.

Don't talk back to the teacher.

Don't call anybody bad names.

In the past, these students had heard adults state rules over and over again in negative terms: "You can't do that," "That's not allowed," "Don't run in the halls," "No, you can't go outside now!" "Don't talk back to your teacher." Through the years they had internalized these negative approaches to behavior regulation and now were using them as the basis for regulating their own group processes and classroom organization (identifying with adults). They viewed school as a place where they have to go, and where they have to do things that others tell them to do. School and group activity represented constraints defining what they could not do.

Being aware of these attitudes, their teacher asked them during the next class meeting to review the rules to see if they wanted to make any changes. At first they said they could find nothing wrong with the rules and felt them to be appropriate. A discussion ensued concerning their group goal for the 10-week period—"learning to work and play together." In their own words, this goal had real meaning for them. They talked about how rules should help them accomplish it. The teacher then asked if they could make another list of rules that said "yes" instead of "no." The students thought it was a challenge to write rules without using the words "don't" and "no," and they responded with enthusiasm. They called their new list of rules, "Things To Remember for a Good Day":

Things To Remember for a Good Day

Listen while others talk.

Be polite.

Ignore trouble.

Stick to the point.

Talk when it's your turn.

Do something friendly every day.

Stay with the group.

Both lists were posted on the wall for the next few weeks, side by side. The teacher and the class referred to both lists when planning an activity or solving a problem. When situations arose in which the group needed to refer to the rules, both lists were read and the group would select the rule that sounded most appropriate. In situations where there had been a fight or where the class activity fell apart because of disagreements in the group, the students usually agreed upon the first list as the most appropriate for the situation. However, when the group discussed plans for a special project or field trip, they would always decide on the second list of rules. The teacher pointed this out to the class and, as time passed, the group chose the second list more and more often.

At the end of two weeks, the group decided to take down the first, negative list of rules and use only the second, positive list. They felt that it was better to have rules that reminded them of what they could do than to have rules about what they could not do. The students also recognized that if they followed the list of positive rules, there would really be no trouble in the room, whereas with the first list it was almost inevitable that trouble of some sort would occur and punishments would be imposed.

real, natural consequences. The adult reflects reality for the group to consider, suggests experiences, and assists the group in utilizing the abilities of each member. Less structure and control are required from the adult during these group processes except in instances when the group fails to function constructively or fails to benefit an individual student. Here is an example:

> *"There is just no way we can use the art room this week. Other classes have already reserved it. Shall we reserve it for early next week?"*

Adults as Individual Advocates. There are numerous opportunities for an adult to come to the aid of individual students in a Stage Four group. These students have skills they need in order to feel good about themselves, but they must be recognized for those skills by significant adults. Each student must be provided with as many opportunities for independence as can be managed successfully. Situations will also arise where students must talk things out—realistically. They need to know that adults will give them straight answers. Here is an example:

> *"You may be right that the bus driver was grouchy this morning, but do you think it helped matters when you started making all that noise? Have you ever felt grouchy?"*

Adults working with students in Stage Four who are at risk for emotional problems and those who are socially, emotionally, and behaviorally disabled will be confronted with unanticipated defensive behaviors from time to time that are disruptive to progress. This should not be a deterrent from continuing the Stage Four program, but it is a time for individual support and advocacy from a valued adult. It indicates that some previous developmental anxiety has not been fully resolved. Stressful situations can trigger a flood of unresolved anxiety that breaks out as immature, disruptive behavior, and it can usually be recognized as a defense mechanism.[11] When these old, self-protective responses occur, the adult must be ready to provide increased structure and support, temporarily resorting to proven Stage Three strategies. Yet, because of their age, these students also have typical age-related needs and an interest in being treated like their peers.

Adults as Role Models. No stage makes greater demands upon an adult to be an effective person. Adults are observed by students in Stage Four for characteristics that represent the sort of person the student would like to be. The behavior and attitudes of adults toward students and other adults provide interpersonal, social, and gender role models. With heightened sensitivity toward others, the students look closely at how adults behave and at the relationships between adults. They also watch the ways adults deal with other students. More comfortable than ever before with themselves, students in this stage are able to identify with the actions and reactions of adults as models for their own behavior and relationships.

Because these students cannot be fooled by empty praise and condescending encouragement, adults need to be authentic in praise and feedback. If the adult is someone in whom the students can believe, it should be received as genuine respect when adults say things like

> *"You know, I really like that story you wrote about your trip to the mountains. It was very interesting!"*

The adult role with students in Stage Four has several new dimensions that are not paramount in previous stages. Although personal characteristics associated with expertness and likability are powerful influences on the behavior of these students, integrity and genuine respect are essential attitudes to convey. Without these characteristics, adults cannot effectively influence the development of social-emotional competence or the responsible behavior of students in this stage. Adults who are effective with them convey these qualities by recognizing the students' contributions. These adults respond to the students by seeking their ideas, listening, and incorporating their suggestions into the daily program. This requires taking a minor role in the group and allowing the students to have decision-making responsibilities, while still providing direction and guidance as needed. Here is a response by an adult that illustrates how this can be communicated:

> *"I guess you're right. This game isn't as much fun as I thought it would be; how should we change it?"*

In their attempt to be the type of adult needed by a student, some adults carry their role in a Stage Four group to a point where they convey a peer status, or they may break the boundaries of their own privacy and personal life. These are mistakes that can prove disastrous. Adults with appropriate social power are still needed by Stage Four students because adults represent the source for identification with desired characteristics. Students must believe that adults can help them during situations when they are not successful and when unfamiliar events or stress overwhelm them. They do not need to be exposed to the personal life or feelings of the adults responsible for their programs. Developmentally, they are still learning to be competent themselves. The adult responsible for helping them must not use them for personal reassurance, to be liked, or to have a "friend."[12]

---

[11] See Chapter 2 for a discussion of defense mechanisms and how they change as a function of development. Chapter 4 also includes a discussion of emotional memory and its impact on learning.

[12] Chapter 7 contains a discussion of these problems that adults may have with themselves.

Management Strategies That Foster Successful Group Processes in Stage Four

The nature of development associated with typical students from ages 9 through 12 requires a diminishing presence of the adult as the central figure in the program dynamics. Management strategies, following this need, are fewer, less obvious, and more facilitative than in past stages.[13] The following are the most frequently used:[14]

Positive feedback and praise	From peers and adults
Motivating with materials	Real-life; age-appropriate; culturally relevant; personally enhances individual with peers
Interpretation	Adult helps student recognize feelings behind behavior
Rules	Group develops rules and changes them when necessary
Life Space Intervention (LSI)	Individual and group talk, through conflict and crisis, for resolution and students' greater understanding of themselves and others

The manner in which adults use these strategies with students in Stage Four is of utmost importance. The first two strategies emphasize the positive benefits to individuals of their successful contributions to the group. Because peer acceptance and belonging are so essential, the benefits are intrinsic if participation is successful. However, success in Stage Four does not come through the contrivances provided by skilled adults or activities that always end in success, as in previous stages. Now, success comes from personal choices for behavior that result in acceptance by peers, which is not always a pain-free process.

Students need considerable help in recognizing when they make poor choices that result in rejection by others. They also need help in understanding why they make the choices they do—often because of feelings they are beginning to recognize in themselves or because of beliefs or ideas they have. Although these insights are an important part of their development early in Stage Four, their views must broaden during this stage to understand that others may have feelings and ideas quite different from their own. This knowledge of oneself and others is fostered by adults using interpretation and LSI daily in their work with Stage Four students.

Effective use of both of these strategies requires sorting out which behaviors are a student's superficial responses to stress and which mask personal, psychological pain. With the former, behaviors can be changed by the students themselves as they gain insight into themselves and others, or as they experience the real consequences of their choices, both positive and negative. With the latter, students must develop understanding of their own feelings and emotional needs, as well as learn positive ways to meet these needs through responsible behavioral choices. They seldom can accomplish this without adult understanding and guidance through the LSI process. It is a difficult but essential strategy if students are to learn to break their own cycle of conflict and failure with others. Because such changes may also involve changing a student's role in a group or the type of social power a student relies upon, adults working with students in Stage Four must be familiar with group dynamics and know how to use these concepts to assist students. We include an extended discussion of this process in Chapter 10, because group processes are central in an effective Stage Three program. Readers who are not familiar with the process or who have students making the transition between stages should refer to that chapter for group management strategies.

In the following example, the teacher of Len, a typical Stage Four student, uses LSI and interpretation to focus on increasing his understanding of how and why other people behave as they do. Had Len been in Stage Three, the teacher would have used interpretation and LSI to sensitize him as to how his own behavior resulted in consequences that worked against his own best interests. She would also have introduced the idea that his own feelings and motivation for fighting on the bus might be a part of the problem. The solution would have been for Len and the teacher to consider alternatives that would have been better for him to make in response to provocations on the school bus. Now, Len is in Stage Four. His teacher continues to use interpretation and LSI, but with a different focus—to expand his understanding of others' motivations and to make his own interpretations about his and others' behavior.

At this point, Len has described the event in cause-and-effect terms. He has connected the behavior of others with their feelings. He also has shown understanding of his own needs and how his behavior reflects those needs. The teacher then concludes the LSI by turning the discussion to the school rules ("No fighting on the bus").[15] She and Len discuss the reality of the events—Len was the one who lost control and started the actual fight. In fact, he had fallen for the setup by the other students because of his own feelings. In Stage Four, this understanding of motivation, although it is an important insight for a student's continuing development, does not expiate the student's responsibility for his own behavior. As a follow-up of the *individual LSI* between Len and his teacher, the other boys involved in the incident are brought together for a

[13]The Stage Four form of the DT/RITS in Appendix 2 contains performance items to assess the use of materials, activities, and strategies by adults working with students in Stage Four.

[14]Chapter 6 describes these management strategies in detail, with illustrations of how they are adjusted for use with students in each stage.

[15]There is a discussion in Chapter 6 of the several categories of rules and how they are adapted to the stages of development.

Len

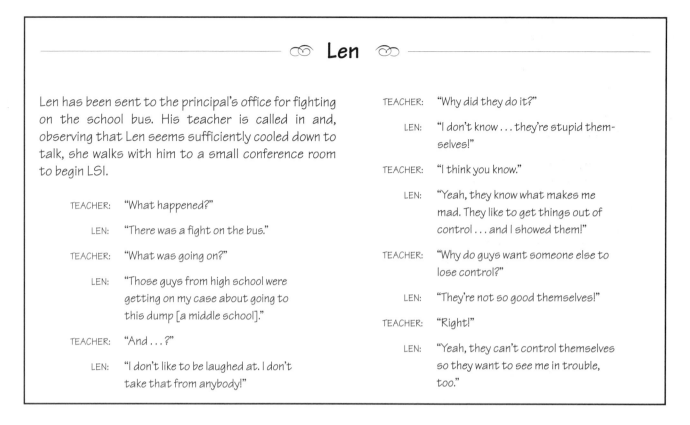

Len has been sent to the principal's office for fighting on the school bus. His teacher is called in and, observing that Len seems sufficiently cooled down to talk, she walks with him to a small conference room to begin LSI.

TEACHER: "What happened?"

LEN: "There was a fight on the bus."

TEACHER: "What was going on?"

LEN: "Those guys from high school were getting on my case about going to this dump [a middle school]."

TEACHER: "And . . . ?"

LEN: "I don't like to be laughed at. I don't take that from anybody!"

TEACHER: "Why did they do it?"

LEN: "I don't know . . . they're stupid themselves!"

TEACHER: "I think you know."

LEN: "Yeah, they know what makes me mad. They like to get things out of control . . . and I showed them!"

TEACHER: "Why do guys want someone else to lose control?"

LEN: "They're not so good themselves!"

TEACHER: "Right!"

LEN: "Yeah, they can't control themselves so they want to see me in trouble, too."

group LSI with Len, the principal, and the teacher. The principal is included because the incident involved a schoolwide rule for which the principal has authority and responsibility. The group LSI centers on the responsibility borne by the other boys in inciting a fight. The same process for expanding insight into others' behavior is used with the group, and fair, equal disciplinary action is given to all of them by the principal at the conclusion.

It is clear in this illustration that the students are *post-existential;* that is, they have developed to the point where they want to see themselves as being in charge of their own lives.[16] Yet Stage Four students depend upon skilled adults, whose opinion is of crucial and significant importance to them. In previous stages, adults' power to influence the behavior of students required using all forms of social power—coercion, manipulation, expertness, and likability.[17] By Stage Four, only the latter two forms are used extensively by adults, because of the developmental dynamics of this stage.

Students usually value adults with *expertness* because of (a) the insights adults can provide into the reasons why others behave as they do and (b) the objective perspective adults can offer into the consequences that may befall a student if the student chooses one course of action over another. *Likability* as a form of social power for adults to use with students in Stage Four can be effective if it is carefully depersonalized. An adult's personal characteristics that a student likes will be those most frequently imitated and internalized. In the previous discussion of roles filled by adults for Stage Four students, we emphasized the many forms of likability—cultural qualities, sex-role attributes, management of emotions, and values of fairness, respect, helpfulness, and friendliness. There are also many superficial mannerisms of speech, dress, and behavior that may be admired by students in this stage. To use likability as a form of social power with Stage Four students, an adult must fully understand what each student values and portray personal characteristics that serve to guide that student into responsible behavior. As mentioned previously, the Developmental Therapy–Developmental Teaching program is not the place for adults to express their own personal needs or characteristics, especially those that may not be therapeutic for students.

These strategies help students in Stage Four to navigate through the conflicted sea of dependence versus independence. Adults and peers make them aware of their unique abilities and affirm them as a necessary, integral part of a peer group. Group acceptance and group belonging are the vital ingredients for a successful program with students at this stage, and these kinds of strategies are necessary to get the social connections going successfully. This is the way students achieve a sense of social competence—by belonging.

[16] Chapter 2 contains a discussion of the existential crisis and its impact on a student's view of authority and personal responsibility. See also the discussion in Chapter 10 about the existential crisis typically experienced by students during Stage Three.

[17] Chapter 7 contains a discussion of the forms of social power used by adults. Chapter 10 explains the way these forms are conveyed to students in Stage Three.

ACTIVITIES DESIGNED TO ACCOMPLISH THE GOALS AND OBJECTIVES IN STAGE FOUR

In this section we describe the core activities that offer opportunities for students to acquire the goals and milestones for social-emotional competence and responsible behavior to successfully complete State Four of Developmental Therapy–Developmental Teaching. These activities may include a group planning time for discussion, group and individual academic work sessions, a group project that involves the creative arts (music, art, creative writing, or sociodrama), a time for expansion of physical skills, and a final group review of the activities each day. In contrast to schedules for students in previous stages, snack and the group wrap-up can be conducted as one activity for students in Stage Four. This reflects their increased proficiency in integrating group communication and socialization skills with the activities of daily living. Academics can be incorporated in all of these activities, while students also work on acquiring developmental milestones for social-emotional competence. The following list shows the activities for a typical Stage Four program:

- Group meeting
- Academic work
- Group project
  - field trip
  - creative writing
  - art
  - music
  - role play and creative dramatics
- Outside (physical skills)
- Snack
- Group review

Typical students in Stage Four respond to these activities with enthusiasm, especially when they are naturally enjoyed by the students and chosen by them. Even insecure students, those who are at risk for emotional problems, and those with social, emotional, and behavioral disabilities will respond with confidence when there is sufficient adult guidance to ensure successful acceptance by their peers.

We do not attempt to prescribe the amount of time a student should participate in an intensive, focused intervention program each day because it is such a uniquely individual matter. Some students receive a Developmental Therapy–Developmental Teaching program that is fully integrated into their regular school or after-school programs; others have as little as one 45-minute period of Developmental Therapy daily in an intensive, scheduled session. Between these extremes there are as many variations as there are students with unique needs. For example, there may be 2-hour programs, residential programs, small groupings within an inclusive program, special mental health groups, or counseling sessions that are either informal or scheduled. However, in any setting, we find that these core activities provide maximum opportunities for students to acquire the targeted milestones.

Activities that are generally between 20 and 30 minutes long will hold the sustained attention of students in Stage Four. Of course, some activities will be briefer and others can extend for longer periods of time. In general, for a 2-hour period, six different activities can be scheduled, averaging 20 minutes each. We encourage students as a group to review time allocations as part of their involvement in planning how group activities will be conducted. Timing also becomes a topic for evaluation in the group wrap-up at the end of the activity.

Group projects are the backbone of the Stage Four curriculum. Because of their motivation to participate successfully and to be accepted by their peer group, students are often willing to risk themselves in group activities to continue the good group feeling. Through group discussion and planning, students themselves participate in selecting the activities. This also provides motivation for them to maintain control when provoked by others. One typical example was heard when a student spontaneously turned to another and said,

> *"You stayed cool when Nicole pushed your chair. We didn't have to stop things, so we kept going with our plans for the trip."*

Group projects provide for new experiences that a student might have avoided previously. Projects can also be effectively individualized for optimum participation by individual students through the use of computer software, interactive video computers, camcorders, videotapes, and VCR equipment. There are many opportunities in such projects for expanding social roles when selecting teams, project partners, and group leaders. Members of a Stage Four group feel secure when they know that they will have many opportunities to be acclaimed as a leader and recognized as a successful participant with a peer.

Choosing Activities and Materials for a Stage Four Program

Stage Four activities and materials generally are more sophisticated than those used for students in lower stages. Curriculum and text materials from the regular school program are used and are adjusted to accommodate the individual academic needs of each student. Each activity has sufficient flexibility to individualize academic content, with about a third of the time spent in independent, individual activities, or as specified in students' IEPs and the general academic curriculum for the school. Following are the general guidelines we use in selecting materials and activities for students in Stage Four:

- Select materials and activities that provide a vehicle for social understanding.
- Involve students in choosing and adapting materials and activities for group success.
- Use materials and activities that are age-appropriate.
- Use culturally and personally relevant themes.
- Choose content that aids students in understanding others.
- Select materials and activities that increase the individual's effectiveness as a valued group member.

Authentic and highly motivating content is necessary for obtaining maximum involvement from students in Stage Four. It is essential to draw curriculum materials from current trends and styles that are popular with students. This may mean that the adults need to watch the TV shows and movies that the students are talking about. Visits by the adults to children's neighborhood recreation spots in the afternoons and evenings also will bring them in closer tune with students' actions, cultural values, and age-related preferences.

Almost all activities and materials in a Stage Four program should provide a means for expanding social reasoning, thinking about friendships, and understanding others' points of view (Shure & Healey, 1992). Students are naturally developing these processes between 9 and 12 years of age, and a curriculum that guides this growth will simultaneously promote increased social competence and personal responsibility. Central to these goals in Stage Four is academic success. Other frequently used activities that are effective include creative writing; role play, creative dramatics, and sociodrama; and field trips. Although these particular activities can be effective in limited ways with students in the previous stage, they are extremely productive during Stage Four, especially when integrated into academics through careful unit planning. Opportunities to acquire key milestones for social-emotional competence and responsible behavior during Stage Four encourage independent thinking and involvement from every member of the group. Successful group activities also require thought about others' points of view. This skill is needed by students for satisfying personal and group relationships and for expanding their social knowledge.

Academics. The academic phase of the Stage Four program is most effective when it is woven into a group project. Both individual assignments and collaborative group work are included. Individualized work is kept to a minimum but does have a place in the schedule, allowing each student to continue progressing on individual academic objectives. It also provides opportunities for personal expression and achievement independent of the group. Computer software offers a range of individual topics to assist in the independent aspect of the academic program. Also, individual work folders have proved effective for use with Stage Four students. The folder can include a daily or weekly plan for individual academic work, usually developed jointly by the teacher and student. A weekly plan is particularly helpful, because it allows a student to plan how to regulate work independently. The folder can contain regular class assignments when it is necessary to use a portion of academic time for remediation, catch-up, or stay-up. Close coordination with teachers of academic subjects is essential if this is to be useful in the limited time available.

The group aspect of academics requires every student to participate and should ensure successful accomplishment by everyone. Group discussions are essential to every group academic session. Such activities, centered around a selected academic topic, help to expand thinking skills and stimulate social communication. Group academic activities might include group storytelling; writing and producing plays, newspapers, and magazines; or constructing props (including math estimates, signs, charts, and backdrops). Chalkboard work also can be used for group focus if the board material has provisions to accommodate individual academic differences.

One popular group game that encourages vocabulary building and communication of ideas is the Instant Word Game: A one-word topic is given to the group, and each member in turn gives the first, brief idea that comes into his mind concerning the topic. Certain ground rules are developed by the group concerning the length of time any one person may speak on the topic (1 minute is recommended at the beginning). The group also decides on the order in which turns will be taken, and whether or not group members will be permitted to engage in unstructured responses and rebuttals to each other's ideas. Here are a few examples of topics that have stimulated expansive ideas from Stage Four students: *Stop, Hide, Indebtedness, Runaway, Lost, Imperial, Experience,* and *Secrets.*

As they become proficient in conversation about topics, Stage Four students are usually eager to expand their discussion. Frequently these topics become a major part of the Stage Four program and a valuable source for the students to gain insight into themselves and others. These extended topics can be included in almost every activity in the curriculum for students at this stage.

As emotional maturity begins to emerge, students in Stage Four often exhibit a new eagerness for assistance with academic difficulties. There is openness to acknowledge real academic interests as well as difficulties, and a determination to achieve. Regular academic studies and remedial work are pursued with new interest and are frequently used as a way to communicate independent ideas.

Examples of Topics for Discussion with Students in Stage Four

"No money"

"Why do people write checks that bounce?"

"What happens when they do this?"

"What other ways can they handle the situation?"

"Nothing to do"

"Why does this happen?"

"How do you feel?"

"What can you do about it?"

"Left alone"

"What is it like?"

"What do you do?"

"How do you feel?"

"What can you do about it?"

"Nobody likes me"

"What gives you that idea?"

"Why does it happen?"

"How do you feel?"

"What can you do about it?"

"Feeling dumb"

"What happens to make you feel dumb?"

"What can you do about it?"

"How does it end?"

Creative Writing. During Stage Four, most students' skills in independent writing have increased.[18] They are using rules of grammar, spelling, and punctuation. However, these skills are not taught as part of creative writing activities. The focus is on expanding students' ability to organize ideas and feelings into cohesive units of thinking and then communicate them to others.

Creative writing should be a part of every unit of study planned for students in Stage Four. It can be included in reading, language arts, natural science, social science, math, and current events. Writing is a medium for expressing oneself during Stage Four. The greater the range of writing forms students are exposed to, the more tools they have for using creative writing independently in the next stage. In addition to writing news reports, essays, opinion statements, biographies, book reports, and position descriptions, students also enjoy writing verses, song lyrics, poetry, cartoons, letters, diaries, autobiographies, and logs. These personal forms of communicating should be carefully reviewed before sharing them with the peer group so that content that is too emotional, personally destructive, or extreme will not be shared with others, but will be handled privately between the adult and the student. The description of Tony's reaction to a creative writing assignment illustrates the potential usefulness of creative writing with troubled students.

Another example of a simple, personal form of writing was a well-structured activity at the beginning of each day for a group of students in special education making the transition from Stage Three into Stage Four. The teacher took a Polaroid photograph of each student and used the photographs to make the covers for a 10-page booklet for each student, put together ahead of time by the teacher. The cover was titled *My Life*. The photograph was mounted below the title and a line was added at the bottom for the student's signature. At the end of each day the last activity was making a personal statement to add to the book. The student wrote the statement on regular lined paper, which was glued into the book at the end of the assignment. This was important because a student with poor control might have wanted to recopy messy work before adding it to the book. Each daily assignment was mounted on a separate page. At the end of the 10-day period, the booklets were used as the basis for a personal conference between each student and the teacher to explore ideas together. Invariably, the booklets became tangible evidence of progress.

Before this stage, few students have the ability to put their feelings into cohesive written expression. But as their skills increase, it is important to encourage them to put personal feelings into written form. This should be done with a good bit of structure and sensitivity. Few students will be able to handle the task independently at first. Always allow for some psychological distance in such assignments. Word association games are a good preparation for this sort of writing. The teacher writes one word on the chalkboard. This is the "title"—for example, *Fire, Bug, Color, Tears, Air, Life, Time, Forever, Never, Delicious, Gruesome, Kindness,* or *Love.* The students copy the title at the top of their papers. Then they are told to write anything they want to about the title in 3 minutes. Students who "can't think of anything to say" are encouraged to write down anything that comes

[18] Figure 4.7 contains an overview of creative writing as it is used in Stages Two through Five. A list of the general steps we use in conducting a creative writing lesson at any stage is included in the same section.

Tony

Tony is a gifted 11-year-old with a consuming anger toward peers and adults. He admits to liking no one, needing no one, and caring about nothing. He has learned to out-talk and outmanipulate adults. He is disdainful of participating in any classroom activity.

Each day, Tony's teacher assigns the group a topic for a descriptive essay. The assignment is to make a drawing of anything or any idea related to the topic assigned that day. Then they are to write a description of their picture. One day, their writing assignment is an essay called "A Psychological Study."

"What's that mean?" ask several students.

One student responds, "That means crazy."

The teacher explains, "*Psychological* means 'ideas in your head,' and to study them means to 'see how ideas and behaviors are connected.'"

Several students, including Tony, proclaim vehemently that they cannot write something about something like psychology. For Tony to find himself a vocal member of a peer group, all with the same concern, is a new experience. The teacher uses this motivation to foster group discussion about ways to modify the assignment. Tony argues, "How do you know what people are thinking?"

Another student suggests, "Everyone has a right to act different and think different."

The teacher pulls the suggestions together and redefines the task: "Why not simply describe two different people you know. Tell how they are different. This will be part of a psychological study describing different characteristics."

Tony completes the assignment rapidly but refuses to add a title. The teacher comments, "I'm keeping each person's work in a private folder. These are called your Private Papers. It will be important to have a title and a date on each paper so that when you and I go over them, we can trace the progress you have made."

The teacher verbally reflects the original topic and Tony agrees that the teacher can add that title.

into their minds. After the time is up, the writers are stopped, wherever they are in the process, and they use the notes they have made to put together a group story. The teacher is the recorder, using the chalkboard, and each student makes a contribution.

Simple pictures or drawings of feelings of others are also used to begin this process. Students are asked to write one sentence that describes the feeling of the person in the picture. Sometimes a caption is provided by the teacher, and the student writes three sentences to elaborate on the portrayed experience and feelings. Unfinished sentences are yet another way to help structure these writing experiences early in Stage Four. The teacher provides the stem and leaves the ending of the sentence to the student to complete.

When students have been successful with the more structured assignments in creative writing, a diary or personal journal becomes an extremely effective means for self-expression. Several ground rules should be established with the students before this type of assignment is undertaken. First, discuss whether the students want to use this written form to communicate with the teacher privately. If so, set up an exchange system. For example, every Friday the students turn in their diaries for the teacher to read over the weekend. Next, decide how the students want the teacher to respond. The teacher can write a letter to each student in response, which should be ready on the following Monday for meaningful feedback. Another way is to write notes to the students in the margins of their diaries. This activity is an extremely effective way to communicate with a troubled student who is also bright and skilled in writing. It allows more time for sharing private thoughts than is often available during a school day. With students who are particularly suspicious of others or hostile toward their family or peers, providing a diary with a lock and key ensures privacy, especially if it is kept at school and reviewed with the teacher alone.

Letters of advice written as newspaper columnists are particularly popular with older Stage Four students, even those with limited academic skills. They all have ideas about how problems should be handled and like to share their ideas with others. The important point is to enhance the students' confidence in themselves as potential problem solvers rather than as individuals who have problems they cannot solve.

Lyrics and poetry also are extremely effective forms of writing for students in this stage. One Stage Four group had a special time each week called "The Songwriters' Association." The group voted on the top audiotape of the week and then wrote a new title for it. The teacher served as recorder for the group and wrote the title on the chalkboard. Then the teacher numbered down the chalkboard for the number of lines the students needed to rewrite the refrain. They composed their own ideas, line by line. When they finished, they sang along with the music on tape, using their new verse.

Role Play, Creative Dramatics, and Sociodrama. These three forms of drama are highly effective activities for creative problem solving with students in Stage Four.[19] They offer endless opportunities to promote social-emotional development and interpersonal perspective-taking. Many students in this stage have difficulties that result from their inability to handle situations involving interpersonal and group conflict. Creative dramatics, sociodramas, and role plays help them learn personal and social problem-solving strategies. Such activities allow them to span time and anticipate how they might respond in future situations. They can express emotions, make mistakes, and fail—and then retrace their actions as they think of better ways to handle a situation.

The emphasis in dramatic activities is on feelings, situations, or events that have been experienced mutually by the members of the group. Sometimes the focus will be on a group issue; at other times it will be on individual's conflict that the others have also experienced. The goal is to find and try out alternative ways of solving the problem using dramatic techniques.

Drama may be used to clarify a problem, propose alternative solutions, and evaluate outcomes. New behaviors can be practiced, evaluated, and changed to improve results. With new insights, students begin to see their own potential for expanded relationships with others (Wood, 1981). For example, some students may be involved in drugs. The group enacts a situation in which several members try to convince another student to join them in trying drugs. Several group members may have the role of the student who is being recruited. Others have the roles of recruiters. The assignment in the drama is to think of ways to say "No." The emphasis is on the mutual problem they have in saying "No" to any form of wrong behavior, rather than focusing on the "bad behavior" in this particular situation.

Although many techniques exist for involving students in creative dramatics and sociodrama, there are eight general steps for creative problem solving that we find helpful when using drama with students in Stage Four (Canfield & Wells, 1994; Osborn, 1963; Parnes, 1992; Torrance, 1981).

1. *Define the topic:* Use discussion to stimulate understanding of the situation.
2. *Establish the conflict:* Narrow the focus to a specific, believable conflict.
3. *Cast the characters:* Encourage participation as "actors" (several students may be the same character).
4. *Brief actors and observers:* While actors spend time planning the scenario together, warm up the observers for ways to view what will occur.
5. *Act out the conflict:* Without clues for direction to solutions, encourage continuing action if needed, or "cut" if conflict gets out of hand.
6. *Cut the action:* Do this when the incident comes to a conclusion or actors fall out of role or are unable to continue to a solution.
7. *Discuss what happened:* Analyze the situation, the behavior, and the ideas produced.
8. *Plan for uses of ideas:* Use them in subsequent sessions or transfer ideas to different projects.

The adult creates the attitude that conflict can be useful rather than destructive. Everyone is taken seriously and group cohesiveness is encouraged. At the beginning, the adult may heighten a sense of conflict to simulate reality and stimulate involvement. Then, as tensions increase and students warm up to the situation, the adult may interject relief from the stress to allow them to produce creative solutions. The last step is as important to the success of the process as any of the preceding steps. It is through this discussion that understanding is expanded, new ideas are generated, and new behaviors become possible (Z. T. Moreno, 1959; J. L. Moreno, 1972; Yablonsky, 1976).

Here are two conflict scenarios that lend themselves to creative problem solving through either role play, creative dramatics, or sociodrama:

"Chicken"

This scene gives students practice in taking roles. One student is taunting another to steal something from the teacher's desk. The second student does not want to steal but is embarrassed by being called "weak," "chicken," and a "coward." Have two students act out this scene, in which one taunts the other to steal some object. Stop the drama before a solution is found. Ask the students to share their thoughts and feelings while being taunted or trying to entice the student into wrongdoing. Then have the audience share their ideas and experiences about what has happened. Bring the entire group into the discussion about alternative ways to resolve such experiences.

[19] We are indebted to E. Paul Torrance for his creative contributions to the Developmental Therapy–Developmental Teaching curriculum model over the years. In particular, his analysis of the applications for sociodrama in this curriculum have been uniquely helpful and are summarized here.

"It's Not Fair"

A student is angry about the choice the group has made for a game and complains loudly, "It's not fair! We never play what I want to play!" And with that, the student tears the game into pieces.

Assign roles, with one student as the antagonist and several others as the protagonists. Begin the drama by describing the setting—school, playground, or recreation center. Then let the students play out the conflict, stopping the drama when they seem to have carried it as far as they can spontaneously. Reverse the roles and reenact the drama with another child playing the role of antagonist.

Stop the drama again, and have each participant contribute ideas about the event and the feelings involved. Then have the entire group offer suggestions for solutions. Sometimes they will want to continue the drama, acting out several solutions to resolve the conflict.

Field Trips. Field trips are particularly effective with Stage Four students. When used as a culminating activity after several weeks on a language arts project, a field trip can provide students with new experiences and opportunities to experiment with new behavior in new situations. Because field trips can be a major means of helping students generalize new skills beyond the program, the trips should be carefully preplanned by the students, well rehearsed through role play, and with several follow-up activities for evaluation and generalizations about the benefits gained. Field trip activities might include simple or elaborate projects, but they should expand the students' social knowledge for understanding themselves and others. Here are several ideas for trips that have been productive for Stage Four students:

- a local radio station
- the kitchen of a fast-food chain
- a local newspaper
- a television studio
- an artist's or potter's studio
- the Post Office mailroom
- a hospital emergency section
- a campsite for a picnic or cookout
- a historical home open for tours
- a professional sports team
- a museum
- a police department
- the mayor's office
- a bank

In one highly successful group, the field trips were planned by the students to include doing something for those whom they were visiting. This was an unusual approach, as field trips are standard for most programs when students are studying community helpers. With each visit, the students planned to do something for those they visited. When they visited the airport, they wanted to help by washing down an airplane—which was arranged. Before they visited the police station, they baked cookies at school as a "thank you" and then left them at the police desk, much to the surprise of those on duty. When they visited the fire station, they brought flats of spring flowers and planted them at the entrance. The firefighters were touched and amazed. They told the students that in all the years of visits by schoolchildren, none had ever done something for them in return. These exchanges of services pleased the students, too. They understood the value of these reciprocal acts and explained the give-and-take this way:

> *"They do things for us, and we do things for them."*

Content Themes. In all of these activities, the content of the activities and materials must be relevant to students' developmental interests, personal and cultural preferences, anxieties, and concerns, while also being age-appropriate. As we identify areas of intense interest and concern to students in a Stage Four group, we formulate several themes that can be developed into group projects. Then, we involve the students in progressively more active ways, planning how the themes should be carried out. Week-long unit themes are effective for unifying the many diverse activities needed by the students as they attempt to generalize newly learned skills into real-life settings. Themes can be carried over several weeks and can be expanded as students become increasingly interested and knowledgeable about a topic. The themes should bridge outside interests and academic content areas. Figure 11.2 provides a list of content themes from academic areas that have been effective with Stage Four students.

If a student's anxiety is unresolved during a previous stage of development, it will continue to influence the student's behavior and social understanding during Stage Four. This is frequently the situation with an abused or psychologically deprived child who continues at age 9 or older to struggle with a sense of abandonment that has been unresolved since Stage One. The program must counter this emotional memory with some symbolic, age-

Figure 11.2. Examples of content themes for students in Stage Four.

Themes from Natural Science and Weather

The Supernova Mystery	Eye of the Storm
Clash of the Titans	Lightning Bolts
Trail Adventure	Space Odyssey
Acid Rain	The Human Machine
Future Worlds	Endangered Species

Themes from Social Science and Current Events

Station WILD Radio Show	Sly and Shy
Prime Time	On the Road Again
Ladder to the World	The Evil Empire
Crime Report	The Human Side
Runaways	The Martin Luther King Story

Themes from Health, Sports, and Physical Education

Sports Dramas	National Heroes
Spotlight Success	The 10K Event
Track and Field	Dirt Bikes
Winners	Walkman
Sports Highlights	Fitness and Strength

Themes from Economics

Why Work for Money?	In Search of Treasure
The Million-Dollar Man	Costs and Rewards
The Price is Right	Not Enough To Go Around
Rich Man, Poor Man	Who's in Charge?
The Money Tree	Make a Trade

appropriate form of nurturance in the content themes or the activities. Frequently food, cooking, and fictional stories and characters dealing with attachment, affection, kindness, and friendship are substitutes that ameliorate some of the psychological pain and are acceptable to these older students.

"Track and Field"—A Week-Long Unit for Stage Four

As an example of the authenticity, flexibility, and real-life focus needed in programs for Stage Four students, we include a week-long unit using the theme "Track and Field" (see Figure 11.3).[20] This unit was designed for students with behavioral disorders in a special education, middle school program of Developmental Therapy–Developmental Teaching. Students spend 2 hours each day in an intensive Stage Four session and the remainder of the day in an inclusive setting where Developmental Teaching is used. This example illustrates the balance needed between individual and group activities, alternating quiet and active times, and weaving of the theme for continuity throughout the activities.

Group Planning. This first activity is a time set aside each day for students to plan and discuss strategies for the day—listening, contributing, and organizing. It also provides for work on Socialization, Communication, and Behavior milestones. During the week, it is not unusual for this planning period to take longer as a group project develops. It is a time that affords opportunities for social exchanges, expression of feelings, and both group and individual problem solving. This group planning time should promote spontaneity of expression by making students feel comfortable. They are encouraged to contribute ideas and ask questions about the proposed activities, saying what they know about the subject and what they want to do with it. They are also encouraged to express any reservations or concerns they may have. There is an open understanding that verbal rather than physical expression of feelings is preferred by all. Group members are encouraged to anticipate potential problem situations

[20] Chapter 4 contains another example of a unit for a group in Stage Four—"Flashlight."

Figure 11.3. "Track and Field"—a week-long unit for Stage Four.

Daily Schedule	***Monday***	***Tuesday***	***Wednesday***	***Thursday***	***Friday***
Group Planning	"Meet the Athletes"	"What Makes a Winner"	"What Makes a Winning Team"	"The Decathlon Challenge"	"Bringing Home the Gold"
Current Events	Interviews with track athletes (audio/news)	"The Life of Gwen Torrance, Olympic Star"	World-class athletic teams (video clips)	The ten events	Field Day: Warm-Up practice for events
Journalism and Group Projects in Art and Drama	*Writing:* Biographical "Questions and Answers" *Role Play:* Athletes and interviewers *Art:* Designing a track-and-field bulletin board	*Writing:* Essay about the life of Gwen Torrance *Role Play:* "Her Best Moment. Her Worst Moment." *Art:* Continue track-and-field bulletin board	*Writing:* Short story "What it Means to Lose" *Role Play:* Losing situations of famous teams *Art:* Begin track-and-field events mural for room	*Writing:* Sports writing "The Ten Events" *Role Play:* Sports announcing *Art:* Continue track-and-field events mural for room	Competition with other class teams
Math	Conversions: Distance and time	Conversions: Distances in kilometers	Estimating times and distances	Calculating fractions	Calculating individual and team times
Physical Education and Music	Warm-up with Walkman for stretching (to pop music)	Warm-Up with Walkman for relays	Warm-Up with Walkman for broad jump	Warm-Up with Walkman for shotput	Writing a group report of the event for the bulletin board
Snack and Wrap-Up	Locker room wrap-up	Locker room wrap-up	Locker room wrap-up	Locker room wrap-up	Locker room wrap-up

that may arise as a result of the group plans and the feelings in others that may result.

Some groups plan to keep individual *learning logs* as a way of recording their personal experiences, ideas, and impressions during the progress of the unit. They may decide to keep these journals private, sharing them only with the adult, or they may prefer to use them as part of the wrap-up, evaluation sessions. In either case, the decision about how logs will be used is determined before the activity begins. That way, the students know who their reader will be and can decide for themselves what they will record.

The "Track and Field" theme in this example is introduced to the students on Monday as a way to prepare the group for a schoolwide field day at the end of the week. During the group planning activities, the theme variation for each day is introduced, setting the focus for the day. For Tuesday, the topic is analyzing the qualities that make a sports winner. On Wednesday, they consider the qualities of winning teams, preparing to collaborate for the team effort on Thursday. And on Friday, the field day occurs and the group is ready as a team.

Current Events. The world beyond the classroom is of vital interest to Stage Four students as they tentatively explore their own emerging independence. If time allows, a daily current events activity, related to their own experience, should be included in every weekly theme. This is essential if motivation for the theme and participation in the activities are to be sustained. Material for current events can be drawn from the regular academic curriculum that students are expected for follow—for example, health, civics, political science, natural science, or vocational education. Or resources can come from TV news, discussion sessions, magazines, or newspapers or from visiting public figures, sports stars, or other people admired by the students, such as a scuba diver, musician, dancer, artist, or police officer.

On Monday, the "Track and Field" theme uses an audiotape, prepared by the teacher from interviews with locally known athletes by a professional newscaster. The intent is to stimulate communication and socialization skills and provide content for the academic portion of the next activity. On Tuesday a biographical video of a sports hero is used to begin the exploration of individual feelings at the best and worst moments of life. For Wednesday the teacher prepares a series of VCR segments showing winning athletic teams. The purpose is to explore the elements of personal courage and skill that produce winning teams. The current events discussion on Thursday is centered on photos from sports magazines illustrating the events the students are working on and the ten events that compose a decathlon. The Friday field day becomes the current event. The field day also illustrates the flexibility possible in scheduling, while still maintaining the theme of the week and the same general activities.

Journalism Project. Written communication activities are a major element for every Stage Four program.[21] In Figure 11.3, a journalism project is used in a whole language approach to the language arts. The content is unified to emphasize group Socialization and Communication milestones. Throughout the week, the "Track and Field" theme provides many opportunities for work in reading, writing, art, role play, and sociodrama. In reading and writing activities, students prepare written answers to written questions based on the audiotape interview of local athletes used in the preceding current events activity. They write biographical or autobiographical essays growing out of the discussion about the qualities of life. They create short stories around the theme of losing and prepare sports reports describing the decathlon events. After the field day on Friday, the students collaborate on a group news report of the event.

Art. Art projects carry out the creative visual aspects of a language arts project. They can involve any materials or ideas students find interesting. Art supplies are restricted only by the budget, facilities, and students' interests. Students are able to attempt fairly sophisticated art projects such as batiks, acrylics, model building, carving, printing, and three-dimensional construction. Silk-screening T-shirts is a particularly popular activity. Stage Four students tend to want to express themselves and the world around them in naturalistic art forms but generally lack the skill to meet their own standards. Because of this they frequently tend to degrade their own art expressions. For this reason, color, design, feelings, and expression of symbolic elements in students' art projects should be emphasized (Williams & Wood, 1977, pp. 82–83, 90–91).

The weekly art activities for "Track and Field" involve a series of group projects that are all related to the weekly theme. On Monday the group plans the layout for a school bulletin board about the track-and-field events, and on Tuesday the students complete the project. Each student contributes to one part of the design, which includes a lettered title and stylized designs illustrating aspects of the event (hurdle, high jump, shotput, flag relay, track shoes, shorts, T-shirt, scoreboard, the track, bleachers). On Wednesday and Thursday the students design and execute a classroom mural depicting a famous team receiving gold medals at a judges' stand. The art content is drawn from the students' own creative writings and discussions in the previous activities.

Drama. In the "Track and Field" unit, role play and dramatics are the outgrowth of the current events material and the students' own creative writings. On Monday, using an audiotape recorder, students "try on" the roles of sports announcer, interviewer, commercial announcers, and sports heroes. On Tuesday they use material from the

[21] See Chapter 4 for a review of creative writing activities and how we structure these lessons step by step.

sports video to explore imaginary moments from the sports hero's life—the best moment and the worst. This interviewing theme is continued on Wednesday with the topic of losing situations of famous teams, and on Thursday each student role-plays a sports announcer responsible for one of the decathlon events the students described in the writing assignments. These role-playing situations provide opportunities for the students to work on Communication and Socialization milestones, with an emphasis on understanding others' points of view, values, and feelings.

Physical Education. Sports and games for students in Stage Four offer great possibilities for work on Behavior and Socialization milestones. These activities foster physical skill building, use of the body, and development of skills in individual and team sports. Depending upon available resources, these activities are conducted outside on the playground, on the athletic field, in the gym, or in the classroom. The teacher can be a coach, physical education teacher, recreation therapist, or another adult on the team.

It is helpful to think of these activities in three categories: *team sports, individual sports,* and *group indoor activities.* We plan a program with a balance between all three opportunities. Team sports include familiar games with established rules and competition. Games such as touch football, softball, basketball, volleyball, modified soccer, flag tag, and relay races are particularly good for Stage Four groups. Individual sports should emphasize flexible rules and team competition. Included in this category might be dodgeball, whiffleball, shooting baskets for points, running and standing broad jumps, shotput, softball throw, running distances, tetherball, swimming, tumbling, and badminton.

It is necessary to have indoor activities as alternatives during inclement weather. These generally require greater impulse control, a longer attention span, and more cognitive skill than do outside activities. In this category would be calisthenics, aerobics, dancing, and quiet games for socialization rather than for sports skills development. Games we have found particularly effective are card games such as Spades, Rummy, Spoons, Hearts, Uno, and Crazy Eights and group activities such as beanbag games, Ping-Pong-ball blow, pool, marble roll, a water gun with a candle flame as the target, horseshoes, and charades. Commercial games such as The Ungame, Word Bingo, and modified Monopoly are also popular. Games requiring long periods of time to complete and those that emphasize winning over everyone else are seldom appropriate because students lose the sense of social exchange, which is an essential requirement for Stage Four activities. For this reason such games as Checkers, Scrabble, Chess, or Monopoly played by the regular rules usually are not effective in accomplishing the Stage Four goal of investment in the group.

Sports and games in the Stage Four program have elements of normal competition, and game rules generally are not modified. Through these experiences, Stage Four students are learning to bring impulsivity and behavior under greater inner control. They are encouraged to support others as well as to accept support themselves. With a greater awareness of the viewpoints of others and the causes and effects of behavior in themselves and others, and with acceptance of each individual by the group, Stage Four students are able to tolerate greater stresses in competition. They also learn to solve problems that arise in game situations with greater maturity and insight.

Although music and movement are usually included in a language arts project, it seems effective for the "Track and Field" unit to use popular, rhythmic music, familiar to all of the students in the group, as a motivation for warm-up calisthenics and stretching activities. Physical skill activities consist of practice each day for a different event, including relays, broad jumps, and the shotput. The choices are made by the students from the list of events for the school field day on Friday.

Music. Through music, Stage Four students can work on almost every Stage Four milestone. In rhythmic movements, dance, and body movement activities, many Stage Four students find a source of recognition and success that is generally not otherwise available to them. Patterns of dance movements, reverse or mirror movements, shadow dancing, interpretive movements, symbolic and dramatic dance stories, line dancing, square dancing, and other forms of social dancing all require expression of self. When dancing is performed in a group or in pairs, the Stage Four Socialization goal of participating successfully as a group member is easily accomplished.

Stage Four students also enjoy planning and creating their own individual musical instruments, playing them as a group, and taking turns as bandleader. They eventually learn to appreciate the possibilities in instruments for expressing themselves and being understood by others. Songs also can be effective vehicles for them to communicate their own feelings and recognize the feelings of others. They have definite preferences for songs that touch them, and this avenue of communication is very effective in expanding their understanding of themselves and others. By writing new lyrics to songs or designing their own raps, students explore new experiences vicariously. In this way many new feelings and situations can be experienced within the framework of a supportive peer group.

Math. The math period provides both group and individual work in quantitative problem solving and computations. Brain teasers can be used to begin each math period with group effort and connection to the unit theme. Mathematical content is linked to the "Track and Field" theme each day as students work with distance, time, metric measures, and fractions. Math activities are adjusted to each student's specific math skill levels and IEP objectives. By the end of the week, all the students are able to understand and use the concepts and operations in their own team field events.

Snack and Group Wrap-Up. Snack contributes considerably to an unspoken sense of comfort and caring in the program. As discussed previously, Snack is particularly effective in reaching older Stage Four students who have been severely deprived or abused. It also provides a climate of relaxation in which students are less defensive, less self-protective, and more open to new ideas and positive social exchanges. Snack is often combined with the wrap-up session in Stage Four. However, it should be secondary to the feedback aspect of the wrap-up session.

Each day, the lead teacher guides the group in an exploration of the results of the day, including feelings, behaviors, and outcomes. The discussion identifies the strengths of group members, with the adult providing a social role model for the students in learning to praise and support each other. Many beginning Stage Four students find this activity uncomfortable if they must talk about themselves. Instead, after the adult has modeled positive feedback several times, the students are asked to do the same by identifying one good thing that another student did. For this process to be effective, every student must be recognized for a positive accomplishment. This procedure rapidly catches on and becomes a major positive force in producing group cohesion. As group members develop skill in evaluative conversation and gain understanding of the perspectives of others that are different from their own, longer discussions on sensitive topics are encouraged.

After a positive tone is well established, it may be necessary to bring up problems that have not been thoroughly resolved during the day (group confrontation). Group LSI techniques are useful. The students can handle this sort of discussion constructively if the resolution becomes positive and they leave feeling good about their contributions to solving the problem.

SUMMARY

The focus of Developmental Therapy–Developmental Teaching for preadolescents during Stage Four is to acquire the milestones that help them to become invested group members, with concern for others as well as themselves. This is the developmental stage when a student's central concern is meeting the expectations of friends, peers, and admired adults. The standards by which students are judged (and judge themselves) often create the developmental anxiety for typical preadolescence we have labeled *conflict*—needs within themselves conflicting with loyalty to others. This private, inner conflict between independence and dependence dominates this preadolescent phase of development. Stage Four is also a time when students are receptive to thinking about values to live by. Their newly acquired mental capacity to see others' points of view and to understand that others have ideas different from their own enables them to establish and maintain friendships. These abilities also help them to resolve their own conflicts, generally in favor of friends and those who belong to their own group.

Providing an effective program for expanding preadolescents' social-emotional competence and responsible behavior during Stage Four requires adults who guide, encourage, inspire, and then pull back and affirm students in their efforts to speak out and express their individual uniqueness. The program must empower students to be responsible for themselves. Personal responsibility also requires social responsibility. To achieve this, students must be a part of group goal setting, planning, conflict resolution, evaluating, and affirming. Adults working with Stage Four students must be expert in group dynamics and must be sensitive to providing insights when needed while allowing the natural consequences of students' actions to unfold. Finally, adults must be responsive to students but stay focused on the boundaries of what is acceptable and valued.

We summarize the guidelines for an effective Developmental Therapy–Developmental Teaching program for preadolescents who are in Stage Four here, bearing in mind that some troubled preadolescents will need a Stage Three program first. (See Chapter 10 for those guidelines.) Similarly, some older, troubled teens may be either in Stage Four or Stage Three. A careful assessment of each student's profile of social-emotional development is necessary before beginning a program at any stage. The guidelines are as follows:

- Expect that every student will participate in every activity.
- Involve students as a group in designing and conducting activities so that every student has input and feels successful with individual contributions to the group effort.
- Encourage students to make choices that have natural consequences, but help them anticipate outcomes before choices are made.
- Involve students in individual goal setting.

- Involve students in individual and group appraisal of results.
- Provide activities and materials that reflect students' cultural and age-related interests.
- Plan daily activities for expanding students' friendships and peer relationships.
- Mutually plan with students ways to enhance the group's accomplishments.
- Encourage students to support and recognize each other's progress.
- Select content themes that represent students' real-life concerns.
- Involve the students in developing rules to guide their own behavior and that of the other group members.
- Be flexible; encourage the group to improvise, and redesign a planned activity when it is not as successful as they would like it to be.

PRACTICE

Using the key points in this chapter

Helene is an example of a student whose social-emotional competence is in the earliest phase of Stage Four. At risk for more serious problems than she is currently exhibiting, Helene is troubled in many different ways—with her peers, family, school, neighborhood, and herself. The overall Developmental Therapy–Developmental Teaching goal of Stage Four—investing in the group—is one that she appears to be actively seeking. However, she is having great difficulty acquiring the skills to accomplish this goal. To genuinely belong she must be accepted in the several groups of which she is a part. Without acquiring the skills for social-emotional competence associated with this stage of development, Helene will not successfully complete it. After reviewing this brief description, answer the questions below.

1. What are the general social-emotional goals for Helene in each curriculum area? (Refer to the Preliminary Profile guide in Figure 3.2.)
2. Which milestones of development in Stage Four has she acquired and which ones are lacking?
3. Are there milestones remaining in Stage Three that she needs to acquire as well?
4. What appears to be Helene's central concern?
5. What does she appear to value?
6. Which developmental anxieties seem to be established and which seem to be emerging now?
7. What situations might be provided to reduce her anxieties?
8. What type of adult role would you try to convey to Helene?
9. What behavior management strategies would you use with her?
10. What unit themes might catch her interest and ensure her participation?
11. What activities and materials would provide the best opportunities to help her accomplish the curriculum goals for increasing her social-emotional competence in Stage Four?

Helene

Ten-year-old Helene is in the fifth grade. She is frequently tardy or does not come to school at all. Her mother is aware of this but does not know where she goes or what she does when she fails to come to school. She tries without success to make Helene behave and go to school. Helene's mother works a night shift and sleeps during the day. Her father is in prison. Helene says she misses him and he was "pretty good" to her. However, she tries to change the subject when he is discussed. Helene's mother has told the teacher that Helene's father was abusive to everyone in the family. Helene is the oldest of four girls and seems to get along with them fairly well. Their grandmother lives with them and provides the meals for the family.

At school, Helene tries to be pleasant and cooperative but seems anxious and somewhat withdrawn. She tells her teachers that she likes them, but she complains to them about the other students and the children in her neighborhood. She says she does not like them because they fight and argue. In school she tries to create an image of knowing everything and tries to be a friend to the students who are the social leaders. However, her overtures toward them are seldom well received, as she is viewed by the others as somewhat "strange" and someone to be avoided. Helene has one friend with whom she spends time regularly after school. Together they play with dolls, try new hairstyles, or paint their nails. They talk about how much they dislike the other girls, watch television, and play cards together. Sometimes they attend an after-school program for swimming or basketball, but Helene's attendance there is as erratic as it is for school. When other students discuss vacations and trips they take, Helene talks about going to the mall. She seems to spend considerable time there, because she can take the bus there by herself. Her teachers suspect that she may be shoplifting but have no specific evidence of this.

Helene's academic skills are at the third-grade level. She says she does not like to read because it is so hard. When she attempts to draw, she is usually displeased with the results and throws her work away. When she is writing, she frequently erases until she has worn a hole through her paper. As she works, she often makes negative comments about what she is doing and expresses disgust at the assignment and the behavior of others.

Her teachers are concerned. Helene willingly participates in the school activities during the morning, if she attends, but by the afternoon her behavior deteriorates and she becomes resistant, quarrelsome, and negative. She does not seem to be able to pay attention for long periods of time, gets up from her desk frequently, talks excessively, and seldom completes her assignments. She frequently incites other students by making negative comments or encouraging them to break rules. When her teachers remind her of the rules or attempt to bring the students together for a discussion about a group conflict, Helene seems unwilling to see events as they really happen or people as they really are.

CHAPTER 12

Stage Five: Applying Individual and Group Skills in New Situations

I am "One who will be able to stand on his own feet."
—E. H. ERIKSON, 1950/1963, P. 235

STAGE FIVE: "WHO AM I, AND WHAT WILL I BECOME?"

A typical student entering Stage Five is characteristically self-confident and comfortable with others. Emotional security has developed from belonging and conforming during the past years. However, any complacency rapidly dissolves as students enter puberty and are forced to respond to the dramatic changes associated with adolescence. They must cope with new dimensions of themselves—mentally, physically, and sexually. The uniqueness of each personality is rapidly unfolding. On one side is the expanding need for expressing individuality; on the other side is the continuing need for approval from others. Experimentation and identification with new roles, new ideas, new values, and new behaviors are the catalysts for this stage of social-emotional development. The major accomplishment during this stage is resolution of the adolescent quest for a comfortable status in which a new, inner person discovers acceptable outlets for self-expression and recognition from valued individuals in many new situations.

Beginning around age 12, adolescence is a period in which some of the most dynamic changes occur in the

Stage Five Students in Brief

Program goal:	Using individual and group skills in new situations
Central concern:	Being oneself while being valued by others
Motivating values:	Justice; independence to choose; individual rights; responsibilities of friendship
Developmental anxiety:	Identity; self-doubts; multiple roles and value systems
Approach to problems:	Finding one's own solutions by experimenting with alternatives
Source of authority:	Values of right and wrong; others' expectations and approval
Type of adult needed:	Role model for desired personal attributes; counselor; adviser
Effective strategies:	Positive feedback and recognition; interpretation; Life Space Intervention about values that guide conduct; analysi s of salient aspects of events in universal and personal context
Materials, activities, and content themes:	How people behave and communicate in a pluralistic society; how institutions regulate people (families, governments, schools, churches, military, employers, sports, social groups)

entire course of social-emotional development.[1] Among the many changes occurring in adolescents during Stage Five are these:

- physical growth
- sexual maturity
- competing moral values
- advanced mental development
- enhanced self-awareness
- pending entrance into the adult world

It is not unusual for a teen to have problems adjusting to these many changes. If previous stages of development have been completed successfully, Stage Five can be an exciting, robust adventure, with new happenings, many disappointments, and many achievements. But these challenges can also become so stressful that students may regress to previous stages of development. Even those with no prior history of social, emotional, or behavioral problems may show signs of regression from time to time. Some adolescents experience a gradual, subtle decline in their capacity to cope effectively during the first 3 or 4 years of adolescence. In their previous stages of social-emotional development, what appeared to be rather typical development in elementary school might actually have had a marginal quality underlying some of the key developmental processes. With the stresses of adolescence and the pressures of the complex environments in which they now find themselves, these students may simply collapse in their ability to sustain higher-level functioning.

Sidney is an example of a teen who is at risk, struggling with the fundamental anxiety of those beginning Stage Five and asking

"Who am I?"

Sidney's situation illustrates how essential adult guidance will be throughout his school year. Without positive adult support and clear evidence of progress, Sidney's chances of achieving a successful adjustment to adolescence are greatly reduced. These two critical elements, *adult support* and *evidence of progress,* are essential for all teens, troubled or not. Parents who have established solid communication links with their children during previous stages of development can provide the necessary support, positive feedback, and guidance needed by teens. When they are not able to provide this help, teachers, school counselors, mentors, or coaches can be of considerable assistance. If this support is not available, teens experiencing stress may fail to make progress or may even regress to Stage Four concerns and coping strategies.

Most troubled adolescents are not functioning in Stage Five. If typical students in their teens begin to exhibit characteristics more like those of Stage Four students—or of even earlier stages—it may indicate that they are having increasingly severe adjustment problems, or that support systems are either not present or insufficient. If they have failed to master the goals and milestones for social-emotional competence at previous stages, their problems will persist. The examples of John and Elka illustrate two different paths to teenage adjustment difficulties. John is a 15-year-old with severe emotional and behavioral disabilities who has received special education since fourth grade. He lacks the skills for social-emotional competence and behavior that are acquired in Stage Three by typical children as they complete third grade, at about age 9. Yet at age 15, John is still without some of these skills. He will be unable to develop more complex, age-appropriate skills until he acquires the basic skills for participating successfully as a group member. Elka, in contrast, probably had typical, age-appropriate skills and abilities at some previous time in her life, but drugs and alcohol have caused her social-emotional competence to deteriorate to a level of behavior associated with children just beginning Stage Two, who need to learn how to participate with success.

Developmental Therapy–Developmental Teaching offers the framework for providing students like these the programs they need. Whether through special education, counseling, vocational education, or related community mental health services, this curriculum focuses on helping them acquire the skills for social-emotional competence. Because it focuses their programs on their current stages of development, within the context of adolescence programs for teens must be designed around their individual social-emotional goals for milestones they need to acquire. Adolescents may be grouped by goals for social-emotional development that range from Stage Two through Stage Five.[2] Sometimes, students in several stages are grouped together; for others, small groups of peers needing similar skills provide the most effective environment for acquiring the needed skills. But whatever grouping or setting is used, students' individual programs must be conducted with maximum attention to acquiring the targeted skills and goals.

Adolescents generally respond quite rapidly when they are in small groups with intensive Developmental Therapy–Developmental Teaching. As they acquire the milestones of social-emotional competence specified in their IEP or ITP, it is necessary that their programs be responsive to these developmental changes. Regrouping with peers who have greater social-emotional skills is

---

[1] Biological adolescence begins at approximately age 12 for girls and a few years later for boys. However, psychological adolescence is a function of previous experience. We rather arbitrarily refer to age 12 for the chronological division between Stages Four and Five; however, there is much variation around this age point. We find it more helpful to consider the milestones of social-emotional competence acquired during Stage Four than age to determine if a student is prepared to begin a Stage Five program.

[2] Chapter 1 contains a discussion of the cumulative effect of disability on development. As age increases, the impact becomes increasingly debilitating without amelioration.

Sidney

A high school sophomore, Sidney spends every minute he can playing video games or drinking beer with other boys in a downtown parking lot. He has many physical complaints, possibly because of his weight problem. Eating is his main outlet when he is frustrated. He also is on medication to control epilepsy. His mother sets high expectations for him and hopes that he will become a lawyer. She sees him as shy and dependent, yet she expects him to shoulder most household tasks, including care for two younger brothers. According to Sidney, his mother likes his younger brothers more. He thinks that she is ashamed of him because of his epilepsy and his lack of athletic skills. She is a sports fan and makes frequent disparaging remarks about his lack of physical skills.

Problems with weight and lack of athletic skills also affect Sidney's appeal to his peers. Their attitude that epilepsy makes him different adds to his problem of lowered self-esteem. The real Sidney fails to meet his image of an ideal self. The strongest element working in his behalf is a capacity to talk about these concerns with some amount of realistic insight. But it is clear that Sidney will need guidance through this maze of feelings and attitudes that he holds about himself and how others view him.

Sidney has managed to get by during his first year in high school, but his preoccupation with his own situation, present and future, is beginning to interfere with the academic demands of the high school program. He has a fair amount of insight into what is happening to him and feels comfortable talking with the school guidance counselor about it. Together, they identify specific milestones that Sidney feels he does not have but needs for a happier life. The objectives that he and the counselor select include (a) developing a positive role with a group at school (for the area of Behavior); (b) learning to express his own values, ideals, loyalties, and beliefs with others (for the area of Communication); (c) building some successful friendships with others; and (d) making personal choices in social situations based on his own values and principles (for the Socialization area). One of the strategies they talk about is using television movies, current films, and favorite books to analyze how others make friends and relationships (for the Academics/Cognition area).

Sidney and the guidance counselor plan his schedule to include one period each week when they can review his experiences and appraise the strategies he is using to achieve the objectives. The counselor includes a physical fitness course in his schedule, with a coach who is supportive of individual students. They also choose several elective courses that include students Sidney knows, where he believes he can cultivate friends.

often helpful in encouraging students to achieve similar results. Such reassignments are tangible evidence for the students of their own progress and successes.

In this chapter, we select general principles that guide the applications of the curriculum in Developmental Therapy–Developmental Teaching for adolescents. The material is relevant for those who are typical teens, those who are at risk, and those with serious delays in their social-emotional development. Because much of the material in Chapters 8 through 11 is applicable for adolescents if their stage of development is delayed, it is not necessary to repeat it all here. What modifies the applications for adolescents is their age-related characteristics. Whatever stage of development they may be in, they also have lived and experienced more than a decade of life, and this living has shaped them in distinct ways. Their program must be responsive to these age-related needs as well as to their developmental accomplishments. We organize this approach to Stage Five around these topics:

- typical social-emotional processes developing during Stage Five
- goals and objectives for typical adolescents in Stage Five
- how the program meets the needs of adolescents in Stage Five
- activities designed to accomplish the goals and objectives for Stage Five

TYPICAL SOCIAL–EMOTIONAL PROCESSES DEVELOPING DURING STAGE FIVE

A typical adolescent beginning the teen years is making the transition from Stage Four, in which conformity produces approval by others, to Stage Five, with uncharted passages where emerging physical, mental, and sexual maturity

John

Here is an incident that occurred recently in a large inner-city high school. The setting is a resource room for severely emotionally and behaviorally disabled students. Seven students are working on their individual assignments. One very large student, John, is not working, has not asked for help, and is rocking back and forth in his chair. The teacher asks John if he understands the assignment. John responds, "I ain't going to do this." The teacher responds, "What can I do to help?"

With that, John gets up, grabs another student around the neck, and chokes him. Then he stands on his desk, reaching up to swing on the ceiling pipes for the sprinkler system, kicking at anyone within reach and yelling obscenities. When the school security guard is called, John threatens to kill the teacher, the security guard, and nearly everyone else with whom he comes in contact.

John is nearly 15 years old, yet he is working on specific milestones for social-emotional competence and responsible behavior in Stage Three. He has not yet achieved the overall Stage Three goal of learning skills for successful group participation. Specific milestones that are critical for John to acquire include (a) completing individual tasks independently and maintaining acceptable physical and verbal behavior in a group (in the area of Behavior); (b) showing positive and negative feelings appropriately (in the area of Communication); and (c) imitating appropriate behavior of other students spontaneously (in the area of Socialization).

An intensive program in Developmental Therapy and Developmental Teaching can assist John in acquiring these Stage Three milestones for social-emotional competence. With these skills, John has a chance to develop in age-appropriate ways. Without them, his future looks bleak.

must be factored into the personality equation. The preadolescent child that *was* is rapidly being reshaped into a teen that *is*. Through experimentation with multiple roles, new ideas, new values, and new behaviors, adolescents gradually acquire a sense of identity that conveys their unique nature and potential for success with others as esteemed members of society (Erikson, 1956; A. Freud, 1942, pp. 149–152; Loevinger, 1976, p. 19). The essential question arising from these rapid changes is the developmental anxiety faced by all teens during this stage of development—*identity*, or

"Who am I?"

Surprisingly, many of the psychological processes of Stage Five adolescents are repeats of those experienced when young, preschool children in Stage Two attempt to establish autonomy and become individuals who can be successful.[3] But for adolescents, life is vastly more complicated and sophisticated. Behavior, sexual maturity, language, thinking, and the boundaries of their social environments are expanding dramatically (Blos, 1979). Yet the fundamental question asked by Stage Five adolescents is the same as that pursued by the young ones in Stage Two. Eric Erikson (1950/1963, p. 261) explains this return to the old quest for autonomy, in the new form of identity, this way:

> In puberty and adolescence all sameness and continuities relied on earlier are more or less questioned again, because of a rapidity of body growth which equals that of genital maturity. The growing and developing youths, faced with this physiological revolution within them, and with tangible adult tasks ahead of them are now primarily concerned with what they appear to be in the eyes of others as compared with what they feel they are.

Figure 12.1 illustrates this process and the forces that influence the social-emotional development of typical adolescents during Stage Five. These characteristics are the foundation for the Developmental Therapy–Developmental Teaching curriculum used for typical adolescents who are in Stage Five and struggling with problems of psychosocial adjustment and social-emotional competence.

Among the factors that complicate the development of adolescents are the large number of individuals, groups, and institutions that have an impact on their lives. In addition to parents, relatives, mentors, friends, peers, and members of the many groups in which they participate, teens also continue to be influenced by public figures, sports

[3]See Chapter 9 for a review of the psychological processes at work in establishing the autonomy of early childhood.

Elka

In contrast to John and Sidney, consider Elka, a 16-year-old who has been in a private psychiatric hospital for a year, including treatment for drug abuse. She has just been released and will be participating in an inclusive program of special education in her high school. On an individual intelligence test, she scores in the intellectually superior range, despite her severe emotional problems. Her parents have high aspirations for her, but she has a record of school failure and alcohol and drug abuse, and has been a discipline problem since fourth grade. Elka is frequently sick, complaining of stomachaches and nausea. She has a high absence rate and often walks out of school after a few hours. When asked where she goes, she mumbles, "Just around" or "I don't know . . . I just need air." Over the years Elka has been in many private schools and treatment programs, some aimed at increasing her motivation to learn and reducing her negative behavior, others dealing with her alcohol and drug problems.

Now, released and in high school, Elka tunes out or daydreams most of the time. She does not read anything and forgets most details, such as when lunch money is due, what her schedule is, or what day it is. She cannot or will not give answers to questions asked by teachers in class. She looks at assignments and says, "I don't know" or "I can't do it." Rarely does she do a class assignment or homework. Her only recreation is listening to rock and space age music. She has no contact with peers and avoids her family, eating her evening meal in her room and listening to tapes.

At some time in her life, Elka might have had more sophisticated behaviors than John or Sidney, but these are not evident now. She is socially, emotionally, and behaviorally in Stage Two, and in need of a program that will help her relearn individual skills for basic participation. The essential milestones of Stage Two needed by Elka are (a) learning to spontaneously participate verbally and physically in activities; (b) sharing minimum information with adults and other students; (c) describing her own characteristics and those of others; (d) initiating minimum movement toward other students; and (e) sharing and interacting with others in both organized and unstructured activities.

heroes, and prominent entertainers. Every contact brings with it certain experiences, expectations, associations, and results that have considerable impact on their developing personalities, both negative and positive (Cooper & Cooper, 1992). Sifting through each experience for meaning and personal relevance takes an adolescent a number of years and many encounters with many people (Mussen, Conger, Kagan, & Huston, 1990, chaps. 13, 14). According to research findings, parents have a great role in this process, whether the issue for an adolescent is political opinion (Gallatin, 1980), values and moral development (Arnold, 1984; Eisenberg, Miller, Shell, McNalley, & Shea, 1991; Hoffman, 1980), social knowledge (interpersonal perspective taking) (McCarty, 1992; Selman, 1989), occupational choice (Kandel & Lesser, 1969), or parent-youth relationships (Lam, Powers, Noam, Hauser, & Jacobson, 1993; Patterson, 1988).

Researchers seem to agree also that conflict between adolescents and parents may not typically reflect a schism in the relationship as much as vast differences in the demands of their age-related roles, aspects of lifestyle differences, and the pending inevitability of independence in the lives of teens (Allison & Lerner, 1993). The implications of this view are that teens are apt to listen when adults communicate with them on the big issues. In a survey of over 8,000 young adolescents in fifth through ninth grades, Benson, Williams, and Johnson (1987) found that parents' behavior and family atmosphere were the foundations for teens' fears, worries, concerns, and hopes. Characteristically these young people were building friendships, showing empathy for others, valuing parents and family, and struggling with issues of independence and dependence, racial discrimination, hunger, and poverty. These researchers concluded: "In the majority of cases, what parents say and do is important, and the example they set is even more significant. Both the parent modeling and the family atmosphere have measurable impact on what young adolescents value, believe, and do" (Benson, Williams, & Johnson, 1987, p. 11).

Matt Williams, producer of *The Cosby Show* on television, put these findings to successful use in writing the script to portray contemporary family life with preteens and teenage children. This successful series demonstrated that parents who can bridge communication and cultural gaps can help their teenage children through difficult times of dissonance and anxiety, by actively guiding them through this period of development. Williams's purpose was to illustrate the responsibilities and values that can be gained by parental involvement: "I created positive male

Figure 12.1. Key processes of typical social–emotional development in Stage Five. The dotted lines indicate the inner life—thoughts and feelings.

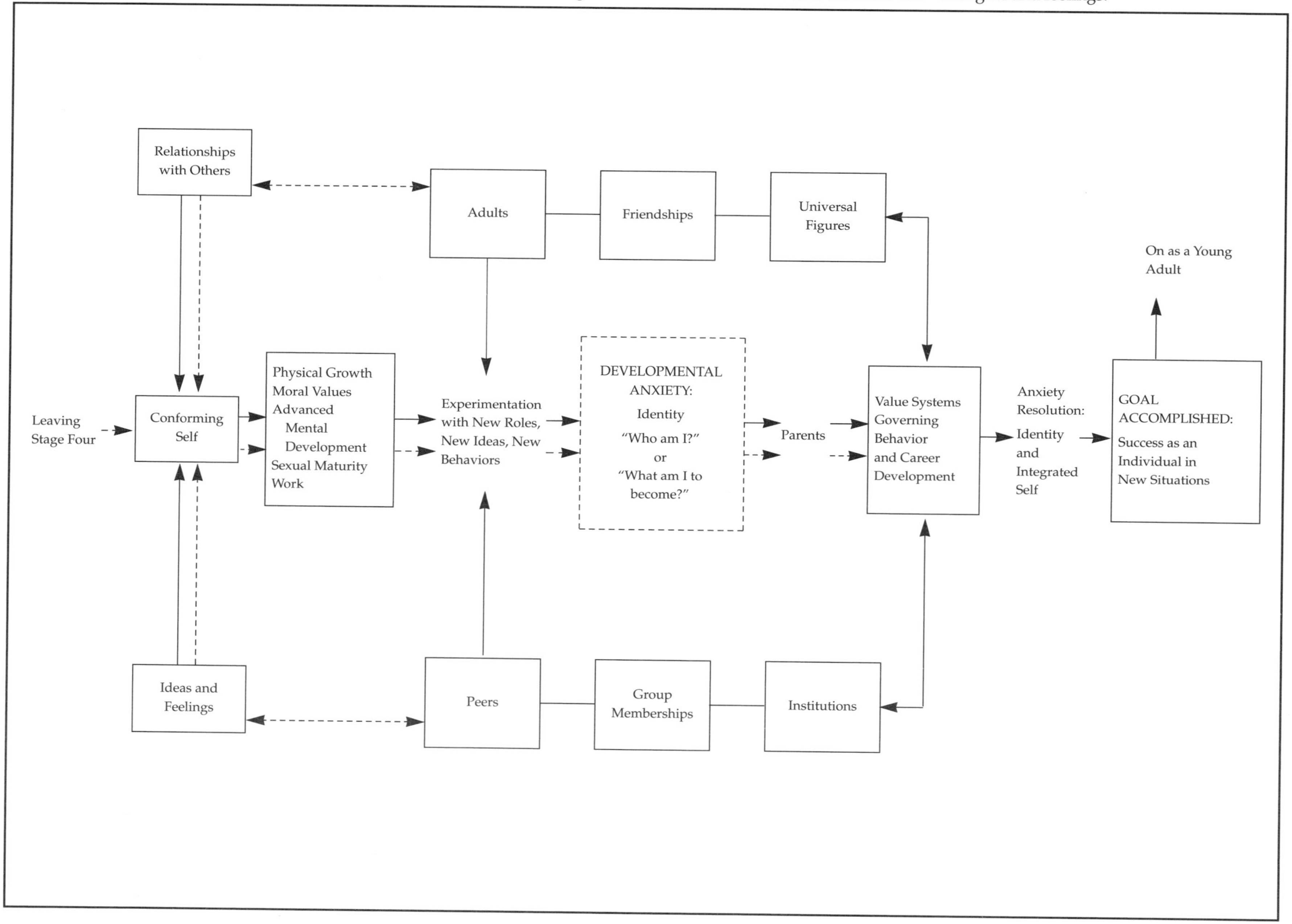

role models to break down color barriers and teach children to respect their elders. . . . We also celebrated the educational process and the fact that parents are smarter than their children" (Williams, 1994).

This formidable task seems quite contrary to some current social trends in which parents go one way and teens go another. If research is correct, parental abdication of responsibility to counsel and guide teens may be a major factor in today's national epidemic of teen violence and aggression. Research is beginning to closely examine family climates and parent-teen relationships as these factors are related to the adjustment and social behavior of disturbed adolescents (Margalit, Weisel, Heiman, & Shulman, 1988; Ramsey & Walker, 1988; Robins & Rutter, 1990).[4]

There is no question, however, that adolescent behavior is also influenced powerfully by peers and cultural trends. Research suggests that peer influence may be greatest in forming a physical, social, and sexual identity and for meeting affectional needs, whereas parents and society have greater influence in the areas of long-range career goals, the ideal self, emerging values, and moral and ethical characteristics (Brittain, 1968; Feather, 1980; Kohlberg, 1981; Larsen, 1972; Selman, Beardslee, Schultz, Krupa, & Podorefsky, 1986).

These conclusions are supported by longitudinal research that has looked at change and stability in characteristics during adolescence.[5] Selman studied these developmental changes in relationships, friendships, and interpersonal negotiating strategies of young teens. Selman reports two processes evident as these young people attempt to define themselves in relation to others. First, there is a need for intimacy to share experiences with others, and a second need is for autonomy to negotiate one's own goals and needs with others (Selman, 1989, p. 412). Similarly, Brown and Gilligan (1992, p. 183) described the same tensions in the needs of adolescent girls as "a political struggle which is anchored relationally rather than ideologically, psychologically rooted in girls' desire to be in genuine connection with others. . . . Most girls we listened to showed signs of this struggle, and its legacy reaches far into women's lives." They concluded that the relative successes of adolescence will eventually merge into a career selection that directly reflects the extent of a student's self-esteem and identity.

Super and Crites developed a hierarchy of tasks and behaviors in adolescence related to vocational development. One significant aspect of their work is the suggestion that career direction does not occur until the twenties or early thirties and can be expected to change and expand into vocational expertise beyond the midthirties (Super, 1980; Super & Crites, 1974). Similarly, Ginzberg (1972) proposed a sequence of changes in adolescents' approach to vocational choice beginning at about age 11 and continuing until about age 25:

- fantasy about careers
- interest in many different careers
- self-appraisal used as a guide
- use of values to guide career alternatives
- transition from high school work opportunities to higher education opportunities
- realistic exploration of life's work

There are others who argue that vocational directions begin much earlier. According to Vondracek (1993), vocational identity of some teens may already be formed by adolescence and they will be fairly advanced in career ideas and attitudes, whereas others will be delayed. His review of research findings suggests that individual differences in developmental domains such as political ideologies, religious beliefs, gender role, family roles, and values contribute to this wide fluctuation in identity development. Values that emerge during typical development in Stage Five are reflected in an expanding emphasis on personal goals, personal responsibility, social responsibility, fairness, and justice for everyone (Benson, Williams, & Johnson, 1987; Kohlberg, 1981). As students in Stage Five become increasingly concerned with moral issues, we hear them make these statements:

"The system should protect everyone."

"Be a responsible person for society."

"Live by a creed."

"Fulfill obligations."

"Think for yourself about others' needs."

The actions of typical teens who are acquiring these values reflect their concern about these standards. They see themselves as moral and responsible—for themselves and those less fortunate. They are attracted to like-minded people who also speak out on moral issues, and they tend to criticize and avoid those who fall short of the standards they have set. In contrast, adolescents who have not fully acquired the milestones for interpersonal perspective-taking during previous stages will be less motivated by concern for others or standards of conduct. Like students in Stage Four, they may still attend to priorities that emphasize responsibility for their own conduct without responding to the needs of others. Or, like students in Stage Three, they may still be concerned over the

[4]Chapter 1 contains a discussion of current psychosocial trends that affect the emotional health of today's children and youth.

[5]Coopersmith's (1967) classic study of determinants of self-esteem in fifth graders ages 8–10 (Stage Four students) expands our understanding of the trajectories of development that become so apparent in adolescents in Stage Five. He reports the powerful effect of parental influence, shown when parents' respect and acceptance for their child's actions are combined with clearly defined limits and the willingness to enforce them.

issue of fairness for themselves, with the parallel attitude of "do to others what they do to you" (Kohlberg, 1981).

Friendships are increasingly important to adolescents and directly reflect their level of social-emotional adjustment (Buhrmester, 1990). Those with increased interpersonal skills—greater social-emotional competence—have more stable adjustment and close, supportive friendships. Researchers emphasize that parent-child relationships are not typically severed as their teenage children increase their skills with friends. Researchers also point out that there are differences between the concepts of *friendships, popularity,* and *peer relationships*. The latter two represent peer nomination (being known) and influence (social power), whereas friendships represent individual relationships and interpersonal skills (Parker & Gottman, 1988). Principles and values, such as fairness and mutual respect, tend to regulate friendships (Youness & Smollar, 1985). Friends share activities, communicate, and see themselves as under obligation to support each other. Girls have more same-sex friends and emphasize friendships that are supportive when they are needed, whereas boys also expect friends to be loyal and supportive.

Adolescent friends view each other as equals and work at maintaining the friendship by negotiating differences. They provide the means for teens to share intimate thoughts and concerns. They also assist each other with problems and advice. Topics most frequently shared between same-sex friends include sex, dating, family, and their futures. When friendships go wrong, teens tend to explain the breakdown as caused by untrustworthy acts, lack of attention, disrespect, or unacceptable behavior. They tend to resolve differences by apologizing, talking it over, making restitution, not resolving the differences, forgetting their differences, or accepting them (Youness & Smollar, 1985).

Teenage girls experience enormous conflict within themselves when what they know and experience is in opposition to relationships they value and seek to maintain. According to the findings of Brown and Gilligan (1992), relationships are maintained by young adolescent girls at a high personal cost. If girls capitulate to maintain relationships, they become less able to articulate feelings and express their ideas openly. Those who resist going "underground" with their feelings demonstrate psychological courage—"an act of relational heroism"—at the cost of relationships. These researchers summarize the dilemma for adolescent girls this way (pp. 183–184):[6]

> For some the resistance remains open and turns political; for some it moves underground—into a political underground where feelings and thoughts are secretly shared, or into a psychological underground where feelings become "nothing that anyone can see" and thoughts become private and protected. But once girls remove themselves from relationships, they begin to have difficulty articulating their feelings. Finding themselves in relationships that are not psychologically real, that are not psychological or emotional connections, they can no longer say what they know.

These studies of adolescents' relationships clearly emphasize the importance of successful friendships in developing social-emotional competence. Without close friendships, adolescents feel themselves "powerless and all alone" (Brown & Gilligan, 1992, p. 217). The findings about how close friendships are made and maintained also contribute to our understanding of how intervention programs can assist troubled adolescents, who frequently have dysfunctional families and few friendships.

Learning to communicate one's own viewpoints and feelings must be balanced with learning to establish and maintain relationships—to be a friend and to have a friend. A teen's social-emotional competence depends upon achieving a comfortable balance between these many psychosocial and inner forces. Teens must achieve a belief in the adequacy of their own ideas, empathetic understanding of others' perspectives, and close friendships that may require giving in order to receive.

The resolution of the conflict in favor of one's own beliefs, feelings, and values, with an inner confidence in one's own choices, results in a successful adjustment to adolescence. Just as in previous stages of social-emotional development, successful accomplishment of these Stage Five goals requires a blending of skills in Behavior, Communication, Socialization, and Academics/Cognition. As the developmental milestones for social-emotional competence are acquired, a student achieves the overall goal for this stage—the capacity to be effective in new situations requiring both individual and group skills. In the process, an adolescent begins to unravel the universal human question that continues with the young adult.

"Who am I? And what will I become?"

GOALS AND OBJECTIVES FOR TYPICAL ADOLESCENTS IN STAGE FIVE

The Goal: *Applying individual and group skills in new situations*

Typical adolescent students need assistance from adults in acquiring Stage Five goals and milestones as they face the new and often difficult situations of the teen years. The goal for this stage is to help adolescent students help them-

[6] These conclusions about teenage girls have validity with developmental theory that shows the adolescent quest for identity as a resolution of the conflict between the drive to be oneself and the desire to find one's place in the world. We have not located parallel studies of teenage boys to validate the presence of this same conflict; however, we suspect it is a similar phenomenon.

selves. They must learn to recognize and use values and skills they already have acquired for building and maintaining satisfying friendships and relationships with others. The Developmental Therapy–Developmental Teaching curriculum goals and objectives reflect this overall Stage Five goal of integrating adolescents' complex personality dimensions with the sophisticated and demanding situations they face as they prepare to become young adults. These goals and milestones that are the Stage Five program objectives in each curriculum area—Behavior, Communication, Socialization, and Academics/Cognition—are summarized in this section.[7]

Behavior Milestones for Stage Five

In the curriculum area for Behavior during Stage Five, the general goal for students is to learn *to respond to life experiences with constructive behavior*. This behavioral goal for students in Stage Five reflects the challenge they face as they are confronted by the demands of a sophisticated and diverse society. On the brink of adulthood, they cannot know what lies ahead, but they do see employment as one of the rites of passage. The other regulators of their behavior are their own value systems and cognitive skills forming around ideas about friendships, rational problem solving, and justice.

The first milestone in Behavior for Stage Five concerns expanding personal, social, and work-related skills. This often is the first objective for students as they make the transition from the previous stage. A student's relationships with friends, roles with peers, and inclusion in other valued groups are the focus. Adolescents in Stage Five are also learning to regulate their own actions by making choices about their own behavior based on values and principles of universal good, law, order, and compassion.

[7]Appendix 4 contains our analysis of the content of these four curriculum areas and the developmental processes directly related to social-emotional development from birth through early adolescence. See also Developmental Therapy Institute (1992).

The last milestone for this stage in Behavior concerns a student's ability to solve personal problems using a rational, logical approach, and to maintain close friendships using interpersonal understanding.

Communication Milestones for Stage Five

In the curriculum area for Communication during Stage Five, the general goal for students is to learn *to use words to establish and enrich relationships*. Students in Stage Five have already developed fundamental skills for social communication during previous stages. The Communication milestones for Stage Five emphasize social reciprocity in interpersonal relations and friendships.

The first milestone of Communication concerns expanded verbal skills to aid students in dealing effectively with complex situations and often abstract ideas. Language facility is emerging as a major interpersonal tool and is a priority if students are to learn to use their verbal skills for conciliatory purposes in times of crisis. Positive interpersonal relationships are the concern of the remaining Communication milestones in Stage Five. Language skills are the means by which students understand, assist, and support others. Expression of personal values, ideals, beliefs, and loyalties is a milestone closely associated with a parallel one in the curriculum area for Behavior, in which students learn to be responsible for their own behavior using their values as guides. The final milestone in Communication for students in Stage Five emphasizes all of the facets of communication that go into sustaining successful interpersonal relationships and friendships once they have been established.

Socialization Milestones for Stage Five

In the curriculum area for Socialization during Stage Five, the goal for students is to learn *to initiate and maintain effective interpersonal relationships independently*. To be valued by others is a driving need among students in Stage Five.

Stage Five Behavior Milestones

Goal: ***To respond to life experiences with constructive behavior***
Seek new personal habits and work skills.
Seek desired, positive roles in groups.
Understand and accept law and order in the school and community.
Participate in group self-governance.
Solve personal problems.

Source: Abstracted from *The Developmental Teaching Objectives for the DTORF–R*, by Developmental Therapy Institute, 1992, Athens, GA: Developmental Therapy Institute.

Stage Five
Communication Milestones

Goal: ***To use words to establish and enrich relationships***
Use complex, figurative statements.
Use conciliatory verbal responses to provocation.
Support others by recognizing their contributions.
Describe multiple motives and values in social situations.
Express values and ideals spontaneously.
Use communication skills to sustain positive interpersonal and group relationships.

Source: Abstracted from *The Developmental Teaching Objectives for the DTORF–R,* by Developmental Therapy Institute, 1992, Athens, GA: Developmental Therapy Institute.

They begin this stage with a fairly well developed value system and sense of self. But these successes are undermined during adolescence as a result of the widening awareness of others' feelings, values, and behavioral choices. These adolescent changes make Socialization the most critical and often most painful of the four curriculum domains for Stage Five students.

The first objective in Socialization is to acquire the milestone for interpersonal understanding necessary for empathetic feelings toward others and understanding of others' points of view. Learning to adapt to the expectations of others in a variety of roles and settings requires students to put their expanded social knowledge into practice. Whereas these first Socialization milestones in Stage Five aid students in expanding their understanding of the experience of others, the remaining milestones aid students in refocusing on themselves, for a sense of a new, more adult self in answer to the question, "Who am I?"

Students learn to make personal choices in social situations based upon their own values and principles. The fairly common adolescent concerns of self-doubt and self-judgment must be addressed and resolved in positive ways. The final Socialization milestone represents the accomplishment for this entire developmental period when a student can sustain satisfying interpersonal and group relationships with self-confidence and without depending on special help.

Academics/Cognition Milestones for Stage Five

In the area of Academics/Cognition during Stage Five, the goal for students is *to use academic skills for personal enrichment*. Academic skills and thinking processes achieved during Stage Five aid a student in coping effectively for personal enrichment and with the demands of living. In Stage Five, as in the previous stages of social-emotional development, the Academics/Cognition curriculum milestones also emphasize cognitive skills to assist students in successful acquisition of the milestones in the other three curriculum areas.

The first Stage Five milestone in Academics/Cognition parallels the process of interpersonal understanding being emphasized in the other curriculum areas at the same time. This milestone is designed to help students seek out other opinions concerning contemporary issues, with

Stage Five
Socialization Milestones

Goal: ***To initiate and maintain effective interpersonal relationships independently***
Understand and respect the feelings and beliefs of others (empathy).
Interact successfully with others in various roles.
Make personal choices based on values and principles.
Indicate self-understanding by describing goals and characteristics.
Sustain group and individual relationships.

Source: Abstracted from *The Developmental Teaching Objectives for the DTORF–R,* by Developmental Therapy Institute, 1992, Athens, GA: Developmental Therapy Institute.

Stage Five
Academics/Cognition Milestones

Goal: ***To use academic skills successfully for personal enrichment***
Seek others' opinions of current issues.
Discriminate fact from fiction.
Recognize and explain illogical, inconsistent behavior of others in social situations.
Solve word problems involving fractions, decimals, and negative numbers.
Use academic tools independently as a citizen and worker.

Source: Abstracted from *The Developmental Teaching Objectives for the DTORF–R*, by Developmental Therapy Institute, 1992, Athens, GA: Developmental Therapy Institute.

direct reference to current events in the social sciences and natural sciences. It also is relevant to other academic course offerings in a high school curriculum. Steps in this sequence culminate with milestones concerned with rational (cognitive) processes used to solve personal problems, including the logical pursuit of fact versus opinion and logical versus illogical ideas. The capstone for Academics/Cognition in Stage Five is accomplished as a parallel milestone in Behavior is achieved. Cognition and rationality triumph over impulsivity in solving personal problems. Academic skills, particularly those involving reading and applied mathematics (such as computing taxes, converting proportions, budgeting, or understanding salaries, medical costs, banking, and insurance), are used to prepare Stage Five students with academic survival skills as they enter the work force.

HOW THE PROGRAM MEETS THE NEEDS OF ADOLESCENTS IN STAGE FIVE

In planning a Developmental Therapy–Developmental Teaching program for adolescent students in Stage Five, the most difficult aspect is adjusting their programs to their teenage maturity and their social-emotional immaturity. While they may be in Stages Two, Three, or Four in their social and emotional development, they are physically, mentally, and sexually teenagers. The similarities such adolescents share with younger students are the general developmental milestones they need to acquire for increased social-emotional competence. Yet the differences are also great—experiences, language proficiency, academic achievement, age interest, and developmental anxieties. It is this juxtaposition of their chronological adolescence with delayed social, emotional, and behavioral development that makes working with these students such a challenge.

Adolescents' statements often provide clues that alert us to the possibility that their social-emotional development may be below their actual teenage years. Their ideas about values and issues often indicate their level of interpersonal perspective-taking and moral development.[8] And their comments about others, themselves, and the type of concerns they have very often suggest developmental anxieties from previous stages that are not yet resolved. Here are a few examples of statements made by young, typical teens that reflect their concerns about justice, individual rights, and their personal solutions to others' expectations:

> "Why not? Everyone else does."
>
> "I don't see any use in doing that."
>
> "Politicians don't care if development is destroying the earth."
>
> "It isn't fair to keep 19-year-olds from drinking."
>
> "Frankly, you can shove it."

In contrast to the content in these statements, consider the following remarks made by other teens. The words are those of teenagers, but the emotional content reflects the concerns and coping strategies of earlier stages of social-emotional development.

Stage Four developmental anxiety—conflict:

> "Tough! You can't make me do this."
>
> "He better leave me alone or I'll kill him."
>
> "If I go to church Sunday, it'll make up for what I'm doing now."
>
> "If I don't do it, they'll talk about me."

Stage Three developmental anxiety—guilt:

> "There's no point in trying. I'll just get it wrong again."
>
> "I guess the world doesn't need people like me."

[8] See Chapter 2 for a discussion of interpersonal perspective-taking and the development of values across the stages of social-emotional development. See also Lerner (1993) for a comprehensive overview of the issues surrounding adolescent personality development. Appendix 5 summarizes the motivational systems that may be operating in adolescents.

"I knew we wouldn't win. I jinx everything."

"He got what he deserved—I guess I did, too."

Stage Two developmental anxiety—inadequacy:

"I can do that work, but I don't feel like doing it now."

"I don't care if I can't read."

"If the cops come, I'll bust 'em up."

"Get out of my way, or you'll be flying."

Stage One developmental anxiety—abandonment:

"I'm going home, there's nothing here."

"You're always sticking up for them—you don't really like me."

"What's the point? I'm on my way out."

"Nobody cares for nobody."

"You gotta expect it. They'll shaft you, too."

From a developmental viewpoint, these remarks illustrate a decreasing capacity to cope effectively. With each lower stage, there is less use of values to regulate behavior and increased domination by impulses and inner needs over cultural expectations. Each of these statements is also a defensive maneuver—an attempt by students to protect themselves from anxieties.[9] The subtle—and not so subtle—struggles teens have with these unresolved anxieties often make it difficult for adults to help them. In addition, their adolescent search for identity and their place in society compounds the problem. If adults ask whether troubled adolescent students should be expected to assume responsibility for their own behavior, they are asking the wrong question, because teens should always act in a responsible way, although they sometimes do not. The reasons can frequently be found in their social-emotional development. We find that we can more fully understand what is needed when we identify the milestones of social-emotional development students have acquired and those that they have not yet mastered. This gives us an understanding of their stages of development.

A question often asked by high school teachers is this: "If troubled adolescents are in need of Developmental Therapy–Developmental Teaching for Stage Two, Three, or Four, are there any students in need of a program for Stage Five?" The answer depends upon the students with whom the teachers work. Typical teenage students who are progressing through adolescence without extraordinary stress or trauma will be acquiring these Stage Five milestones of social-emotional competence in the natural course of development—if they receive responsible guidance from valued adults. For students who have social, emotional, and behavioral difficulties, Developmental Therapy–Developmental Teaching provides programs focusing on their social-emotional needs in Stage Two, Three, or Four. The IEPs and ITPs for these students provide this curriculum through special education, community mental health programs, or vocational education (Bullis & Gaylord-Ross, 1991). The curriculum has been adapted for use in adolescent hospitals and residential schools. It also can provide a framework for support and assistance in inclusive high school settings as students with psychiatric disabilities return to general education programs.

However, many troubled adolescents and those who are at risk are not receiving special programs. They often gravitate to guidance counselors, coaches in a physical education department, or particular teachers who serve as mentors and take an interest in their development. For adults who assist these students, the Stage Five curriculum serves as a guide. It allows them to organize a program focused on the necessary milestones for social-emotional competence. Not surprisingly, as adults get to know the students, they discover that specific skills for coping effectively are lacking.

The program described in this section addresses the need of typical adolescents to acquire age-appropriate competencies for effective social-emotional adjustment and responsible behavior. This information can be helpful in adjusting individual assistance to the specific needs of each teen, usually resulting in a blend of Stages Four and Five programs.

The Adult's Role: Counselor, Adviser, and Confidant

Adolescent students in any stage of development are in quest of new ways to behave. As they experiment with new mannerisms, new images, and new experiences, they are observing others intently, even if they do not appear to do so. The passage through adolescence exposes them to an ever-widening range of adultlike behavior. In this process, adolescents tend to seek out particular adults who have qualities they admire. Adults working with Stage Five students are subject to this appraisal of personal qualities. This is not to say that adults must be "likable" in the sense of being attractive to adolescents. It means that adolescent students will seek adults with qualities they value. With Stage Five adolescents, adults with social power are those who have likability—characteristics that attract students. Students admire friendliness, sociability, looks, style, mannerisms, warmth, or power, among a number of traits.[10] They are also particularly responsive to adults who have expertness and share

[9] Chapter 2 contains a discussion of developmental anxieties and the defense mechanisms that students use to protect themselves from anxiety.

[10] Chapter 7 contains a discussion of personal characteristics of adults that are effective and ineffective in working with troubled students. Included in this discussion is a review of forms of adult social power that can influence the behavior of students. For a discussion of how students use social power to influence peers and adults, see Chapter 10.

it with them. Adults with insight into the psychology of human behavior are seen as experts, as are adults who have work-related skills, creative talents, sports skills, or social skills desired by teens. Adults who can teach them to play a guitar or drive a car, help them to find a summer job, or reveal some of the mysteries of relationships with the opposite sex are also valued as experts. Adolescents also respond to coercion and manipulation, as do most individuals in every stage of human development, but negatively. These two forms of social power in adults do not generally facilitate the adults' influence with adolescents' social-emotional growth during this stage.

To be helpful to students in Stage Five, adults must first be accepted by students as someone they respect. To the extent that they are respected and admired, they can influence students. These adults are imitated, becoming personal role models and mentors. This relationship also puts an adult in the role of counselor—one to whom the student will confide and listen. When such a relationship is established, it becomes the foundation for the guidance and counseling aspects of the adult's role with students in Stage Five.

A mistake that some adults make with adolescents in Stage Five is misunderstanding the nature of this adult-student relationship (teacher, coach, mentor, parent, relative, counselor). The fact that an adult is identified by a student as someone special, to respect and emulate, does not imply a desire for a peer-to-peer type of relationship. An adult with admired qualities can guide and help when needed, but the line must be maintained that separates the student from the adult. The important characteristics needed by an adolescent from a helping adult must remain those that convey respect, recognition of potential, and encouragement. When this adult-student relationship is established with these supportive dimensions, a student will be accessible to the adult and will be open to guidance.

Brown and Gilligan, in their study of the psychological development of girls, conclude that both girls and women seek "authentic relationships with one another and an appreciation of . . . working out such relationships appropriately." These researchers also observe that adolescent girls, "sensing women's fear about showing themselves in relationships, . . . often were willing to withhold their feelings and thoughts in order to have 'relationships' with their teachers" (Brown & Gilligan, 1992, p. 231). Although their interpretation is that this restraint on the part of students may be undesirable, it may also indicate the potential value that can result from carefully built adult-student relationships. Similar conclusions may be assumed for relationships between men and boys, but parallel studies have not yet been undertaken.

It has been our observation that the difficulty for most adults working with troubled teens is to determine what constitutes an appropriate relationship. It is difficult to be an effective role model and establish adult-student relationships when an adult's own needs are interjected. At the same time, developing adolescents need the benefit of experience and insight offered by adults. They also need the affirmation of themselves that comes when an adult likes them.

Guidance Strategies That Foster Independent Responsibility in Stage Five

Adolescents who are genuinely in Stage Five of social-emotional development need very little management by adults, but they need considerable guidance. For this reason, adult accessibility is vital, and intervention typically focuses on the content of issues. Adults often find that listening and reflecting is sufficient for teens who are working to solve their own dilemmas.[11] The viewpoint of adults and shared ideas are the strength of this process. For this reason, we list only four frequently used strategies here:

Positive feedback and praise	From peers, adults, and oneself
Interpretation	About sense of identity, private feelings, and values
Rules	Values and principles that guide individual choices
Life Space Intervention	Individual focus on personal issues and relationships with others

However, if an adolescent is still in a previous stage of social-emotional development, the management strategies applicable for that stage would be used.[12]

The major guidance strategy used by adults and counselors of Stage Five students is interpretation. This strategy differs in Stage Five from previous stages in several respects. First, the adult uses reflection to highlight particular aspects of a situation that might have been overlooked or avoided by a student. Then the student is asked to make the interpretation and consider the relevance of this view of the situation. In this use of the strategy, the student is guided into making the interpretation.

Interpretation is essential to assist Stage Five students in forming their own sense of identity, recognizing their private feelings and values, and translating these insights into actions. Self-monitoring and self-analysis, independent of guidance from others, is the long-range purpose in interpretation. The intent is to facilitate insight and a heightened grasp of the complexities involved in most social situations. This is somewhat similar to the Stage Four application of interpretation, in which a student is helped to connect personal feelings with behavior and results. The difference is in the content and the broader

[11] Reflection is a strategy used with students in all stages. See Chapter 6 for a discussion of the way it is adapted for each stage of the curriculum.

[12] See Chapter 6 for a description of these management strategies and how they are adapted for each stage of development.

scope of the interpretation. In Stage Five, a student is not blatantly structured to make the associations, as may be necessary for students in previous stages.

A second aspect of interpretation with Stage Five students involves an analysis of a situation by the adult. The intent here is to put salient points in a broader context than the student might have considered before. This strategy expands the student's awareness of multiple viewpoints, values, and feelings in a diverse society and provides a universal perspective on a personal situation.

Rules for students in Stage Five are those associated with the natural and inevitable results of their own actions and the reactions of others. Rules are not presented as restrictions but, rather, are developed as connections between what a student wants to happen, the responses needed, and the principles or values the student wants to embrace in the process of making things happen. In this context, rules are decision guides, generated by students' own aspirations and empowering them to be responsible for their own lives. During adolescence, students are able to see that there are expectations for conduct that vary from situation to situation.[13] However, they also begin to understand the need to formulate their own, personal guides to choices, reflecting their own, independent uniqueness. In deliberately making these choices, natural consequences are put in the context of their own values and principles, which they deliberately use in making their individual choices.[14] The following are the values and principles of typical adolescents:

Expand personal goals.

Emphasize personal ideas.

Assume personal responsibility.

Be a moral person.

Act in ways that express beliefs.

Think for yourself.

Think of others' needs.

Choose friends with similar views.

Be trustworthy.

We recall several notable examples of rules developed by Stage Five students. A group of older, typical teens used the words of the Reverend Martin Luther King, Jr., as part of a unit on leadership:[15]

"Make a Difference"

Meditate daily.

Remember . . . seek justice and reconciliation—not victory.

Walk and talk in the manner of love . . .

Pray daily.

Sacrifice personal wishes.

Observe . . . the ordinary rules of courtesy.

Seek to perform regular service.

Refrain from violence of fist, tongue, or heart.

Strive to be in good spiritual and bodily health.

Follow the directions of the movement and of the captain.

Another special education group of Stage Five teens developed rules for their special group. They called them "Rules to Live By":

"Rules to Live By"
(Written by Stage Five Students)

- "Be on time."
- "Cooperate to make the deadline."
- "Do a kindness for someone else."
- "Live with yourself."

ACTIVITIES DESIGNED TO ACCOMPLISH THE GOALS AND OBJECTIVES FOR STAGE FIVE

The Stage Five milestones that serve as program objectives are a balance between those requiring active interpersonal efforts on the part of a student and those focusing on the student's private pursuit of self-respect and self-understanding. The milestones are also a balance between skills for sustaining individual relationships and skills needed to be an effective, contributing person in a broad, diverse culture. None of the milestones requires a special group for adolescents who are progressing through social-emotional development in Stage Five. Typical teen groups, recreational programs, and regular education settings are the natural environments for adolescents, and these are all settings in which Developmental Therapy–Developmental Teaching can be used.

If an adolescent needs a special education program for achieving increased social-emotional competence, it may be provided in a high school, community clinic setting, or residential school. A high school Developmental

[13] The curriculum does not endorse situation ethics; however, many adolescents need to learn to use analytic processes for critically discriminating between issues in a situation.

[14] Glasser's *Reality Therapy* (1965) is applicable for the crises of many typical adolescents in Stage Five. It is an approach that helps them understand the *conflict cycle* and the *cycle of success*. See Chapters 3 and 6 for further discussions of how the curriculum aids students in obtaining these insights. (See also Glasser 1989; Zeeman, 1989; Wubbolding, 1988.)

[15] These are excerpts from pledges signed by volunteers in Birmingham, Alabama (King, 1987, p. 74).

Therapy–Developmental Teaching program can be provided in any flexible place for scheduling these services—a counseling room, resource room, or activity room. However, our general guide is that every special program should be considered a supplement, not an attempt to replace a high school curriculum.

The question is sometimes raised about whether a Stage Five high school student should receive a Developmental Therapy–Developmental Teaching program in a special education class or in an inclusive, general education program. In Figure 3.6, we outlined an example of how two classrooms are used to schedule both special education and inclusive programs in a high school. This same schedule can be adapted for students who are not already enrolled in a special education program, but who are in need of special help to make an adjustment in the school or community. These two schedules can also be adapted to the needs of various special education programs and agencies. The example illustrates how two resource classrooms are used in a high school for the flexibility to shift groups as students acquire advanced skills. One classroom is for adolescents who need to acquire goals and milestones for social-emotional competence in Stages Two and Three. The second classroom is designed as a resource room to assist adolescents in Stage Four or Five. Students like John and Elka would be scheduled with groups in the first classroom and students like Sidney with a group in the second classroom.[16] Then, as progress is made, students are regrouped. The room and the Developmental Therapy teams follow the same time schedule used in the general education program. Some students participate for only one class period each day. Others are scheduled for two-period blocks—some, once a day; others, twice a day. Students completing the program may be scheduled for only once a week or on a drop-by-basis.

Typical activities for one high school class period of Developmental Therapy might include a time for individual assignments ("Learning Lab"); a group exchange of ideas, issues, and solutions ("Town Meeting"); a group activity for exploring values, beliefs, and attitudes ("What Counts"); and an informal wrap-up that could include a snack, a cooking project, or simply a review of highlights of the period. While adolescents can stay focused and involved in an activity for 45 minutes to an hour, it is important to systematically provide a variety of opportunities for acquiring needed milestones. Following are activities in a typical Stage Five program with related academic subjects:

Learning Lab (independent assignments and academic work)
- Literature
- Creative writing
- History
- Mathematics
- Art
- Music

Group-Values Clarification **("What Counts")**
- Philosophy
- Psychology
- Social science
- Ethnic diversity
- Cultural diversity
- Gender diversity

Current Issues and Events **("Town Meeting")**
- Natural science
- Environmental science
- Political science
- Economics and money
- Family and consumer science
- Culture
- Entertainment and sports

Group Wrap-Up
- Nutrition and health (snack and cooking)

If only one hour is available daily, at least four essential activities are included. About a third of the time is spent in independent work and another third is used for discussion of values by members of the group. These are two essential activities for the continuing development of Stage Five skills. We find that about 20 minutes at a minimum should be spent in independent assignments, and about 20 minutes in group, values clarification. The remaining time is divided between the other activities, current events issues and wrap-up.

A well-designed, 1-hour schedule can provide considerable help to troubled students in Stages Four and Five. Because the daily program includes time for students to participate as a small group as well as time for independent focus, goals for personal and social growth can be achieved. Small groups foster exchanges of ideas and different points of view. They also provide opportunities for interpersonal skills to be refined. Many times, these special peer groups are the means for students to "find themselves"—to validate their new, emerging identities. They also provide opportunities for dealing with remnants of old developmental anxieties that may have remained unresolved in the past.

It is important to recognize that these small-group resource room assignments do not take the place of the natural friendships and peer relationships that are typically developing in high school during adolescence. There is insufficient time in a resource room schedule to build a

[16] For high school students who are delayed in development and who need a program to achieve developmental milestones in Stages Two or Three and for those who are beginning Stage Four, we refer you to Chapters 9, 10, and 11.

genuinely cohesive group. Students' close friendships and other significant relationships probably will occur within other groups (homeroom groups, other classes, clubs, home, neighborhoods, and sports and leisure groups). The relationships established in a resource room program are usually on an interim basis but are an important step in practicing new skills for relationships. However, the unguided experiences that occur naturally in the high school and community provide the climate for actual achievements of the goals and milestones of Stage Five. Because these experiences are not always successful, it is important for the Developmental Therapy team assigned to a resource room to also be available for crises and have a drop-in arrangement for students seeking advice or guidance.

Guidelines for Choosing Activities and Materials for Stage Five

The activities and materials for the Developmental Therapy–Developmental Teaching curriculum in Stage Five draw directly from the high school academic curriculum and from students' daily experiences and interests. The content most important for Stage Five students is one that expands their understanding of other people and themselves. They need information concerning human behavior and the institutions that regulate it. Many high school curricula include such material in studies of literature, history, current events, ecology, vocational and career education, economics, drug and alcohol abuse, human physiology and sexuality, health and nutrition, introductory psychology, ethics, driver education, and child care. The specified milestones for social-emotional development can be found embedded in all of this subject material. The guidelines we use for Stage Five are as follows:

1. Select materials and activities that draw from students' daily experiences.
2. Use materials and activities to explore human issues.
3. Use culturally and personally relevant themes.
4. Choose content that concerns human behavior and the institutions that regulate it.
5. Select materials and activities that expand the students' understanding of other people and themselves.
6. Use symbolic content.
7. Emphasize values and principles.

To expedite the progress of individual students in mastering specific milestone objectives, a considerable amount of content for the Stage Five program comes directly from the students themselves—from their own experiences and their own ideas about these experiences. We try to use the interests expressed by the students. If they are limited in their personal interests or experiences, the program should provide themes that are pertinent to typical adolescents. We have used a brief questionnaire, "How Is It With You Today?" at the beginning of the daily program to assess individual interests, daydreams, preoccupations, or concerns. The information provided by the students often helps the adults select content with immediate relevance. We also find that real-world activities stimulate their involvement. We draw ideas for activities from current happenings around the world and in the lives of prominent individuals whom the students admire.

Examples of Activities of Interest to Students in Stage Five

Preparing news reports (sports, social events, and community events)
Field trips
Volunteer activities (Red Cross, hospital, political campaigns, Scouts)
Travel
Camping
Vocational and prevocational experiences
Driver education
Building and construction
Cooking
Music
Hobbies
Future problem solving
Space colonization
Living in domed cities—the Biosphere
Hypnosis
Extrasensory Perception

Even though individual experiences are the focus in a Stage Five program, we find that units with content themes provide continuity from period to period and day to day. The content should also be a balance between material from the regular academic program and material selected explicitly to provide individual relevance. The individual experiences of students enrich and expand unit themes, which often can be used for a month or longer. Figure 12.2 contains ideas for Stage Five content themes that integrate academic subject matter with social-emotional goals and objectives, using the interests and personal experiences of the students.

These suggestions only tap the surface of adolescents' interests. With some groups, content themes take on a distinctly academic tone, whereas with other groups, the content reflects personal concerns, anxieties, and issues of immediate relevance to everyday events. Some teens will seek trendy content; others will prefer third-person, abstract, distant subjects that require less confrontation on personal issues. However, for all Stage Five programs, planning must keep the content focused on the milestones to be accomplished by each individual and integrate these objectives to achieve students' goals for each curriculum area—Behavior, Communication, Socialization, and Academics/Cognition.

Creative Writing as a Bridge from Academics to Personal Concerns

Creative writing is used in Stage Five as a major means for self-understanding and conflict resolution.[17] It also is a tool for adolescents to explore the questions,

> *"Who am I?"*
>
> *"Where do I fit?"*
>
> *"What will I become?"*

Every day, written forms of communication should be used by adolescents to explore and expand their understanding of complex human nature and the cultures in which they live. Their values, attitudes, experiences, beliefs, and feelings can all be woven into the fabric of creative writing. Used effectively, creative writing is an effective way to increase social knowledge and one's boundaries.

Creative writing tasks are organized with both *structured* and *unstructured* dimensions for Stage Five students

[17] See the section on creative writing in Chapter 4 for a general overview of language arts and creative writing applied to all stages of the curriculum.

Figure 12.2. Examples of content themes for students in Stage Five.

From the Language Arts Curriculum

The Veracity of Folklore	Music with Messages
Mythology in the Twentieth Century	Fathers and Sons
Parables	Mothers and Daughters
Docudrama	Heaven in Lyrics
Fiction as Truth	Short Stories
Pathos in Poetry	

From History and Political Science

The Miranda Decision	Events That Change the World
Biographies	People Who Change the World
Autobiographies	Unsung Heroes
Guns or Butter	Power in the Ballot
Roots	Revolution

From Economics and Vocational Education

Poverty and Wealth	Why Work?
Who Controls the Money?	How to Become a Millionaire
What's the Price?	International Gourmets
Winners and Losers	The News Behind the News
Worldwide Hunger	Careers

From Natural Science and Health

Space Colonization	Brain Waves
Hypnosis	Dreams and Sleep
Extrasensory Perception	Here's My Advice
Diseases That Destroy	Body Building
Test-Tube Babies	The Human Engine

and can be offered as a course for credit or not, as needed. The structured aspects of creative writing are provided to encourage a student to use a wide range of writing forms. The unstructured part comes in the content (subject selection). Figure 12.3 is a model we find helpful in planning creative writing assignments.

All forms of creative writing are suitable for high school students to use. The column on the left in Figure 12.3 contains traditional writing forms that might be included in any high school creative writing curriculum, with the exception of the first item, "Group discussions and brainstorming." Extensive work in creativity by Paul Torrance and others suggests that group problem solving through brainstorming techniques produces a great number of alternative, workable solutions to problems (Torrance, 1979). For Developmental Therapy–Developmental Teaching, group problem solving through brainstorming offers an excellent means of addressing the overall Stage Five goal of applying individual and group skills in new situations. The group warm-up focuses on interactive problem solving with others while the individual writing that follows provides for individual applications.

There should be daily opportunities for students to experiment with new topics and new forms to express their ideas. These processes expand alternatives and broaden each student's views about the topics under consideration. The amount of structure needed by individual students to do this will vary enormously. Some students in Stage Five will respond independently when encouraged to "think about it in a different way" or "say it like it's never been said before."

This emphasis on originality dictates a looseness on the part of a teacher in defining the task. On the other hand, there are students in Stage Five who still need assistance. For them, a certain amount of structure makes it possible for them to do the task successfully. Whether it is structured or unstructured, the writing assignment should be made in a climate open for considering new ideas. Group discussion and brainstorming do this.

When using the outline in Figure 12.3, think of it as a grid, and systematically plan to include a writing topic for each unstructured content area within each writing form. This planning procedure provides the outline for a yearlong curriculum in creative writing. Begin with group discussion around a topic that is related to the unit theme. Prepare questions and statements that involve one or more dimensions from the Unstructured Content Topics column on the right-hand side. For example, if the topic is "What will happen if the world's air supply runs out?" the first discussion might involve identifying as many scenarios as possible (identify problems). Then the discussion might shift to possible solutions. After group brainstorming on this topic, the writing assignment shifts to an independent assignment that might use any of the structured forms in the left-hand column.

Here are several suggestions for topics that have been effective with adolescents and that encouraged their experimentation with numerous writing forms while stimulating them to think for themselves:

1. Imagine you are an old, old person living after the natural air supply runs out. Write one page as if you were telling your grandchild about the experience. (imagine what has never been/autobiographical/science fiction)
2. Write a one-page TV news bulletin to alert the world to the coming disaster. (highlight the essence/TV news script)
3. Write an ad for a car you are selling in the year 2001. (produce something new/commercial)
4. You are the president of the United States. Prepare a speech to the people that presents the problem and several solutions. Make your own views strong. (express emotion/argumentative essay)
5. Write a rebuttal to your own presidential speech as if you were the opposing presidential candidate. (imagine the opposite/critique of others)
6. Write a description of a city built after the natural air supply fails. (guess the future/expository)
7. Use your description of the city as the location for a story about people who want to save the city and their fight against those who want to destroy it. (elaborate/science fiction)

Notice that each topic is a combination of a particular structured writing form with some unstructured content. The possible combinations are endless. However, it is important to explore each theme with several combinations of writing forms and content topics. These multiple approaches in thinking and written communication help students synthesize, organize, and generalize. These variations also give them an expanding information base and a variety of points of view about the same general theme.

It is helpful to keep a record of the combinations selected for creative writing assignments. Otherwise, the same forms of writing tend to be used repeatedly. Sometimes this repetition is helpful to students who are just beginning to use creative writing. For others, repetition creates a stereotyped activity, the purpose is defeated, and creative social-emotional growth tends to stop.

Even with teens who have limited academic skills, creative writing can be successful. We provide help to them by putting a spelling list of key words on the chalkboard before they begin writing. We also have a procedure for encouraging students to add to these key words as they begin their work and find the vocabulary that is needed to expand the ideas they are working with. We also frequently find it necessary to teach outlining and paragraph construction. This is fairly easy to do, even with students who have academic difficulties, if they are highly motivated by the topic under discussion. Following is a guide to outlining and paragraph construction:

Figure 12.3. Planning for unstructured content within structured writing forms. The ideas in the right-hand column are used with the permission of E. Paul Torrance, who identifies them as among the elements that compose the essence of creativity. For a guide to conducting these activities, see Torrance (1979).

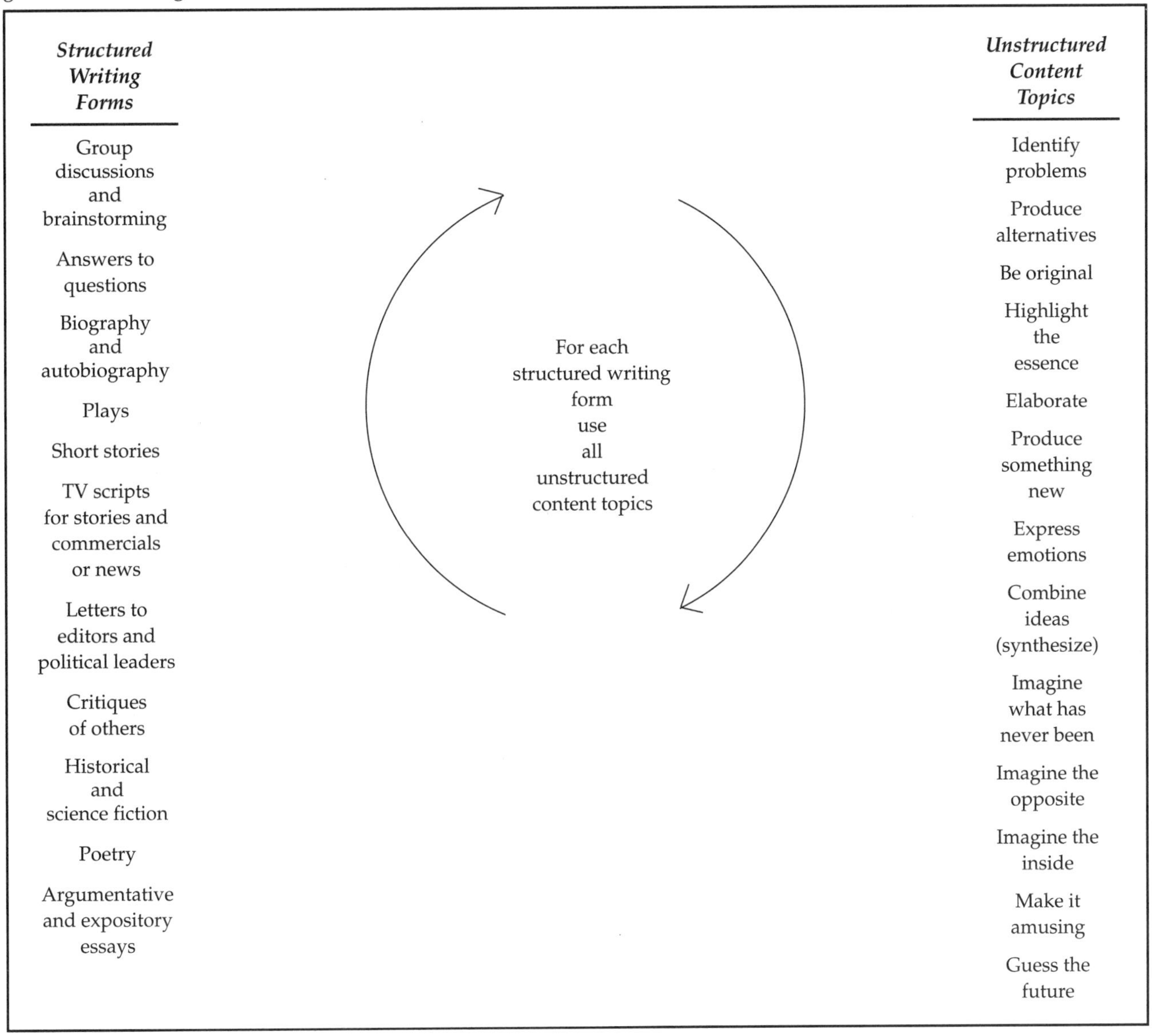

Structured Writing Forms
Group discussions and brainstorming
Answers to questions
Biography and autobiography
Plays
Short stories
TV scripts for stories and commercials or news
Letters to editors and political leaders
Critiques of others
Historical and science fiction
Poetry
Argumentative and expository essays
For each structured writing form use all unstructured content topics
Unstructured Content Topics
Identify problems
Produce alternatives
Be original
Highlight the essence
Elaborate
Produce something new
Express emotions
Combine ideas (synthesize)
Imagine what has never been
Imagine the opposite
Imagine the inside
Make it amusing
Guess the future

1. *The title:* Tells it all in brief.
2. *What:* The first paragraph—introduces the situation and characters.
3. *Who:* The second paragraph—describes the characters.
4. *Where and when:* The third paragraph—describes the place and time.
5. *The point:* The next paragraphs—tell the point and punch line.
6. *The meaning:* The last paragraph—wraps up your idea.

Of course, there are several forms for outlining and a technically correct format for each writing style. It is important for students who can to refer style manuals to use the correct forms. These forms can be taught as a part of the general academic curriculum. However, if too much emphasis is placed on the form, creative content may be jeopardized, thus defeating the purpose in using creative writing for social-emotional growth.

Eventually, adolescents become quite comfortable using creative writing forms. When writing skills and self-confidence are sufficiently developed, a student will be able to create highly personalized forms of expression and problem solving through writing. When this change first occurs, it is time to change the format and deemphasize sharing their writings with each other. Eventually, they will want to bring their personal thoughts back to the group. But at first, provide privacy for personal expression in writing. As they become proficient, also decrease the amount of structure used in making the creative writing assignments and increase the amount of free time allocated for independent writing. Remember that increased proficiency requires increased time for writing; students have more to say and the skills to communicate.

"Poverty and Wealth"—A Week-Long Sample Unit for Stage Five

To illustrate how a unit them is designed for a Stage Five schedule, we selected *economics* as the topic and applied it to the 1-hour resource room schedule described above. Figure 12.4 illustrates how weekly planning for the four daily activities integrates a single theme around many different academic areas and human situations.[18]

Learning Lab (Individual Assignments). With this schedule students begin the daily period with independent work. This is planned to provide a "settling in" time, when the teacher circulates for maximum private exchanges with each student. This activity constitutes about a third of the scheduled time. The assignments can be remedial, instructional, or creative in nature. Computer software and interactive videos are particularly effective here. Creative writing or other individual creative projects are also scheduled during this time. Although each student works independently and demands for group interaction are not present, the adult is available for personal issues.

Students begin individual work when they arrive. The assignments are outlined in a weekly notebook to permit them to pace themselves. The theme in this unit, "Poverty and Wealth," is highlighted in their notebooks and on the chalkboard: "What would you do with $100,000?" Individual academic assignments are adapted to each student's level. Topics throughout the week include budget planning (for $100,000), computing costs and planning purchases using spreadsheets, preparing monthly and annual time lines, projecting future results, and ending the week with computations involving taxes.

Current Issues and Events ("Town Meeting"). The second activity, Current Issues and Events, moves the group members into direct discussion with each other about contemporary issues of interest to them. This activity uses news media accessible to students to make the important bridge between classroom content and the world beyond. These topics can be effectively brought to the classroom with newspapers, magazines, and VCR tapes.

With this activity second in the sequence, students are less likely to be as reticent to share their opinions as they are at the beginning of the class period. Less time is scheduled initially for this activity, because it may be difficult for students who have limited daily contact to interact or participate in direct discussions. In time, the proportion of group members' involvement with each other may need to be expanded. This decision often depends upon the extent to which each student has significant group relationships elsewhere. (It is seldom appropriate for relationships in a Stage Five program to supersede students' relationships in other groups in school, the community, home, or work.)

For the "Poverty and Wealth" unit, video recordings are used to bring content issues to the group. During the week, the students consider big spenders, local economic conditions, job values, and definitions of relative poverty and wealth. As their analytic skills increase, they are encouraged to increase their skills in communicating their points of view to the others in the group.

Group-Values Clarification ("What counts"). In this third activity, the students as a group deal with problems of other people or events that are also of concern to them: that is, values are explored through the study of other people with similar problems. This focus on interpersonal problem solving and values clarification as a group allows students to get involved without violation of their own psychological space. This group activity uses about a third of the allotted time.

For the "Poverty and Wealth" unit, this activity explores economic topics in terms that are directly applicable to the students' concerns. On Monday, the issue is scarcity: "Why can't everyone have everything they want?" On Tuesday, the ethics of making money are explored: "What is [the value of] money?" The students' grasp of fundamental economic concepts grows during the week as they consider the following labor production and income distribution issues: "Why do people work for money?" "What happens when there isn't enough to go around?" and "How does the supply affect the demand?"

Group Wrap-Up. The wrap-up activity provides group members with the opportunity to reflect on individual contributions to the topics of the day. It also teaches self-evaluation and self-monitoring skills. Even though the daily time is brief, the cumulative effect of this activity can produce mastery of many of the objectives of high Stage Four and Stage Five.

For the "Poverty and Wealth" unit, each period ends with a review of the issues and solutions generated by the students. During the week, the daily wrap-up summarizes supply functions, money and banking, production, economic responsibility, and how economic factors influence the students directly. Although the general topics for summary are related directly to the unit of study, the discussion follows the students' appraisal of their own thinking about the subjects. Differing viewpoints are respected, and attitudes supportive of other students are fostered.

[18] As a reference for the teacher, we recommend the scope and sequence guidelines, K–12, from the National Council on Economic Education (Saunders & Gilliard, 1995).

Figure 12.4. "Poverty and Wealth"—a week-long unit for Stage Five.

Daily Schedule	*Monday*	*Tuesday*	*Wednesday*	*Thursday*	*Friday*
Learning Lab (Independent Assignments)	"What would you do with $100,000?" • goal setting • budget planning	Budget planning continues	Computing time lines	Estimating and projecting for the future	Computing taxes
Current Issues and Events ("Town Meeting")	*People* magazine for how celebrities spend big bucks	Local newspapers for indicators about the local economy	*Newsweek* magazine for review of high- and low-paying jobs	*USA Today* and *Wall Street Journal* for reports on poverty and wealth	Media week in review
Group-Values Clarification" ("What Counts")	"Why can't everyone have everything they want?" • scarcity of goods • scarcity of money	"What is money?" • currency • checks • bank notes • credit	"Why do people work for money?" • resources • labor • production	"What happens when there isn't enough to go around?" • income distribution • income redistribution	"How does the supply affect the demand?" • losers and winners
Group Wrap-Up	Review the issues and answers: Supply functions	Review the issues and answers: Money and banking	Review the issues and answers: Production	Review the issues and answers: Whose responsibility?	Review the issues and answers: How does the economy affect us?

A successful week with this unit, with typical Stage Five students, should produce considerable progress in acquiring the milestones for social-emotional competence and responsible behavior. With success, these experiences will result in the eventual achievement of the Stage Five goal,

Applying individual and group skills successfully in new situations.

SUMMARY

The critical issue in planning a program for adolescents in need of increased social-emotional competence, including those with social, emotional, or behavioral problems, is the individual's pattern of development. Each profile should be viewed against the backdrop of what is happening to typical students as they travel through this new developmental territory called adolescence. A well-planned program must first determine the extent to which the student is functioning with age-appropriate skills and the degree to which lower-level skills are lacking. If an adolescent is in need of a Developmental Therapy–Developmental Teaching program at lower stages, the program's principles described in previous chapters apply, with adaptations for the age-related interests and physical, mental, and sexual maturity of the student. For adolescent students who actually are functioning in Stage Five, we summarize the program guidelines here:

- Involve students in individual analysis of attributes and goal setting.
- Encourage students to identify personal values to use in decision making.
- Design programs with new experiences to broaden horizons.
- Provide opportunities each day for expansion of students' skills in effective social communication.
- Encourage group planning for activities that foster interpersonal skills and successes with age-peers.
- Provide opportunities for every student to develop individual, creative ideas.
- Guide students to broaden their understanding of people and the relational implications in situations.
- Encourage students to take personal responsibility for themselves and others, using the values they have chosen.
- Provide content that helps students make connections between academic content and their own real-life anxieties and concerns.
- Be available for support, reflection, and affirmation.
- Share knowledge, expertness, and insights as a mentor and advocate.

PRACTICE

Using the key points in this chapter

Review this brief description of Lewis. Imagine that he has just been recommended for your high school special education program in Developmental Therapy–Developmental Teaching. Using this description, answer the following questions, and then consider whether you will schedule Lewis with a group of students for a Stage Four program, with a group for a Stage Five program, or for individual sessions with you on a scheduled basis.

1. What are the general social-emotional goals that should be emphasized for Lewis in each curriculum area? (Refer to the Preliminary Profile guide, Figure 3.2.)
2. What are the milestones for social-emotional competence that Lewis has failed to develop?
3. What appears to be Lewis's central concern?
4. What does he seem to value?
5. Which developmental anxieties seem to be established and which seem to be emerging now?
6. What situations might be provided to reduce Lewis's anxieties?
7. What type of adult role would you try to convey to Lewis?

8. What management strategies would you use when Lewis attempts to sabotage the group activity with negative verbal comments?
9. What unit themes might catch his interest and ensure his participation?
10. What activities and materials would provide the best opportunities to help Lewis accomplish the curriculum goals for increasing his social-emotional competence and responsible behavior?

Lewis

In the ninth grade in high school, 15-year-old Lewis reacts poorly to both home and school expectations. A low tolerance for frustration and a high level of anxiety continue to plague and isolate him. Attractive in appearance, Lewis is highly verbal and seemingly self-confident. He is self-conscious about his clothes and defensive about his problems in academic areas. He achieves generally at the sixth-grade level in reading and at the fourth-grade level in math. His attempts to avoid schoolwork are frequent.

Lewis is an enigma to his teachers. When he is angry with himself, he verbally lashes out at other students or adults trying to help him. He often attempts to sabotage the success of a group. Other students fear his potential for disruptive behavior and his verbal attacks. His verbal skill makes him an influential, negative leader in his group. Students watch him and respond when he makes a remark. Yet he usually conveys detachment and an apathetic attitude toward others and organized school activities.

Lewis's mother sometimes suffers periods of severe depression requiring hospitalization. She has raised him alone with the general attitude that tomorrow may not be any better than today. She expresses concern that she cannot control him and particularly worries about his late nights out on the streets. She says she does not know what he does, but she fears that he has gotten involved with a gang whose members use drugs and steal to supply themselves.

At his mother's request, Lewis is referred to the school psychologist. At the time he is referred, Lewis's mother and teachers identify these problems:

- does not follow directions
- resists discipline
- seems moody and restless
- acts irresponsibly
- uses obscene language and curses
- tries to control others
- has no friends
- lacks interest in school
- is immature for his age
- reads poorly
- criticizes others
- is preoccupied with clothes

Epilogue

With the conclusion of Stage Five in the Developmental Therapy-Developmental Teaching curriculum, a young person has traveled from birth to the brink of adulthood.

If the goals and milestones of each stage have been achieved, we will see a socially competent, responsible individual who is well equipped to face the unknown challenges that the future holds.

This will be an individual who has acquired a sense of self-respect and an optimistic confidence that he or she can make a personal contribution that will bring satisfaction and purpose to life. As one student put it,

"The end is the beginning!"

APPENDIX 1

Publications Documenting the Developmental Therapy–Developmental Teaching Movement During Three Decades

In Chronological Order

Original Model Development

Wood, M. M., & Fendley, A. (1971). A community psychoeducational center for emotionally disturbed children. *Focus on Exceptional Children, 3,* 9–11.

Wood, M. M., Quirk, J. P., & Swan, W. W. (1971). *Comprehensive services to children with serious emotional and behavioral problems.* Report to the Governor's Commission to Improve Services for Mentally and Emotionally Handicapped Georgians. Atlanta: Georgia Archives.

Wood, M. M. (Ed.). (1972). *The Rutland Center model for treating emotionally disturbed children* (Unpublished Prototype Report). Athens: University of Georgia.(Sections reprinted in J. Platt (1973), *Exemplary programs for the handicapped* (Vol. 3, pp. 1–25. Cambridge, MA: Abt Associates.

Huberty, C. J., Quirk, J., & Swan, W. W. (1973). An evaluation system for a psychoeducational treatment program for emotionally disturbed children. *Educational Technology, 13,* 73–80.

Wood, M. M. (Ed.). (1975). *Developmental Therapy: A textbook for teachers as therapists for emotionally disturbed young children.* Baltimore, MD: University Park Press.

Hoyt, J. H. (1978). Georgia's Rutland Center. *American Education, 14,* 27–32.

Wood, M. M. (1982). Developmental Therapy: A model for therapeutic intervention in the schools. In T. B. Gutkin & C. R. Reynolds (Eds.), *A handbook for school psychology* (pp. 609–629). New York: Wiley.

Wood, M. M. (1986a). Developmental Therapy. In C. R. Reynolds & L. Mann (Eds.), *Encyclopedia of special education* (Vol. 3, pp. 499–500). New York: Wiley.

Wood, M. M. (1886b). *Developmental Therapy in the classroom* (2nd ed.). Austin, TX: PRO-ED.

Wood, M. M. (1989). Lessons learned and insights garnered. In S. Braaten, F. H. Wood, & G. Wrobel (Eds.), *Celebrating the past: Preparing for the future* (pp. 59–97). Minneapolis: Minnesota Council for Children with Behavioral Disorders and Minnesota Educators of Emotionally/Behaviorally Disordered.

Schuh, D. (1992, December). Peg Wood on today's children. *Athens Magazine,* pp. 78–85.

Instrument Development

Wood, M. M. (1979). *The Developmental Therapy objectives: A self instructional workbook* (3rd ed.). Austin, TX: PRO-ED. (Portions reprinted in *A user's manual for the structured learning center behavioral classroom* (1984). Portland, OR: Portland Public Schools.

Developmental Therapy Institute. (1982). *Developmental Therapy Rating Inventory of Teacher Skills (DT/RITS)* Athens: University of Georgia, Developmental Therapy Institute.

Robinson, J. S. (1982). Construction of an instrument to assess the classroom skills of teachers who use Developmental Therapy with emotionally disturbed students (Doctoral dissertation, University of Georgia, 1982). *Dissertation Abstracts International, 43,* 1932A.

Robinson, J. S., Wood, M. M., & Combs, M. C. (1982). *Technical report on the Developmental Therapy Rating Inventory of Teacher Skills (DT/RITS).* Unpublished manuscript, University of Georgia, Developmental Therapy Institute, Athens.

Weller, D. L. (1991). Application of a latent trait model to the developmental profiles of SED/SBD students (Doctoral dissertation, University of Georgia, 1990). *Dissertation Abstracts International, 51,* 3388A.

Developmental Therapy Institute. (1992). *The Developmental Teaching Objectives for the DTORF–R: Assessment and teaching of social-emotional competence* (4th ed.). Athens, GA: Author.

Wood, M. M. (1992a). *Technical report for the Developmental Teaching Objectives Rating Form—DTORF–R.* Athens, GA: Developmental Therapy Institute.

Wood, M. M. (1992b). *User's manual for the Developmental Teaching Objectives Rating Form—DTORF–R.* Athens, GA: Developmental Therapy Institute.

Documentation of Effect and Model Validation

Kaufman, A. S., Paget, K., & Wood, M. M. (1981). Effectiveness of Developmental Therapy for severely emotionally disturbed children. In F. H. Wood (Ed.), *Perspectives for a new decade* (pp. 176–188). Reston, VA: Council for Exceptional Children.

Wood, M. M., & Combs, M. C. (1981). *Inservice training in Developmental Therapy.* Research report submitted to the Joint Dissemination Review Panel of the National Institute of Education, U.S. Department of Education, and approved for national dissemination.

American Psychiatric Association. (1993). Significant achievement awards. Clinical and special education services for severely disturbed children: Developmental Therapy Program, Rutland Psychoeducational Services, Athens, Georgia. *Hospital and Community Psychiatry, 44,* 994–996.

Davis, K. R. (1994). Rutland Developmental Therapy model. In *Educational programs that work: The catalogue of the National Diffusion Network* (20th ed., p. 12.12). Longmont, CO: Sopris West.

Interventions and Curriculum Expansions

Developmental Music, Movement, and Play

Graham, R. M. (1975). Music education for emotionally disturbed children. In R. M. Graham (Ed.), *Music for the exceptional child* (pp. 111–129). Reston, VA: Music Educators National Conference.

Graham, R. M., Swan, W. W., Purvis, J., Gigliotti, C., Samet, S., & Wood, M. M. (1975). *Developmental music therapy.* Lawrence, KS: National Music Therapy Association. Sections reprinted in *Developmental music therapy conference reports.* Developmental Music Therapy and Special Education Conference. Tempe, AZ: Arizona Department of Education and Arizona State University Music Department, 1975. Sections also reprinted as A developmental curriculum for social and emotional growth. In *The interdisciplinary use of art, music, and literature* (1979, March). Madison, WI: Wisconsin Department of Public Instruction.

Purvis, J., & Samet, S. (Eds.). (1976). *Music in Developmental Therapy.* Baltimore, MD: University Park Press.

Wood, M. M. (Ed.). (1981a). *Developmental Therapy sourcebook: Vol. 1. Music movement and physical skills.* Baltimore, MD: University Park Press.

Wood, M. M. (Ed.). (1981b). *Developmental Therapy sourcebook: Vol. 2. Fantasy and make-believe.* Baltimore, MD: University Park Press.

Developmental Art Therapy

Williams, G. H., & Wood, M. M. (1977). *Developmental art therapy.* Austin, TX: PRO-ED.

Life Space Intervention (LSI), Behavior Management, and Discipline

Wood, M. M., Combs, M. C., & Lomax, A. (1976). *Strategies for managing severe problem behavior while fostering emotional growth* (CEC Early Childhood Education Institute Series). Reston, VA: Council for Exceptional Children [Instructional material and training manual].

Wood, M. M., & Weller, D. (1981). How come it's different with some children? A developmental approach to Life Space Interviewing. *The Pointer, 25,* 61–66.

Wood, M. M., & Long, N. J. (1991). *Life Space Intervention: Talking with children and youth in crisis.* Austin, TX: PRO-ED.

Wood, M. M., & Quirk, C. A. (1993). The "Talking into the Air" LSI. *Journal of Emotional and Behavioral Problems, 2,* 45–53.

Hyman, I. A. (in press). *Teacher variance: A multidimensional approach to school discipline.* Needham Heights, MA: Allyn & Bacon.

Age Extensions

Early Childhood

Wood, M. M. (1975). A developmental curriculum for social and emotional growth. In D. L. Lillie (Ed.), *Early childhood education* (pp. 163–182). Chicago: Science Research Associates.

Wood, M. M., & Hurley, O. L. (1977). Curriculum and instruction. In J. B. Jordan, A. H. Hayden, M. B. Karnes, & M. M. Wood (Eds.), *Early childhood education for exceptional children* (pp. 132–157). Reston, VA: Council for Exceptional Children.

Wood, M. M. (1978). The psychoeducational model. In N. J. Enzer (Ed.), *Social and emotional development: The preschooler.* New York: Walker.

Wood, M. M., & Swan, W. W. (1978). A developmental approach to educating the disturbed young child. *Behavioral Disorders, 3,* 197–209.

Knoblock, P. (1982). *Teaching emotionally disturbed children* (pp. 110, 215–216, 233–235). Boston: Houghton Mifflin.

Geter, B. A. (1991). Longitudinal study of preschool handicapped children (Doctoral dissertation, University of Georgia, 1991). *Dissertation Abstracts International, 52,* 879A.

Zabel, M. K. (1991). *Teaching young children with behavioral disorders.* Reston, VA: Council for Exceptional Children.

Geter, B. A. (1992). Longitudinal cost study of preschool children with severe emotional disabilities. *GPN Research Report, 5,* 17–30.

Adolescents and Preadolescents

Braaten, S. (1979). The Madison School program: Programming for secondary level severely emotionally disturbed youth. *Behavioral Disorders, 4,* 153–162.

Brown, G., McDowell, R. I., & Smith, J. (1981). *Educating adolescents with behavior disorders* (pp. 148–149). Columbus, OH: Merrill.

Braaten, S. (1982a). *Behavioral objective sequencing.* Minneapolis: Minnesota Public Schools, Special Education Program.

Braaten, S. (1982b). A model for assessment and placement of emotionally disturbed students in special education. In M. M. Noel & N. Haring (Eds.), *Progress or change: Issues in educating the emotionally disturbed* (Vol. 1). Seattle: University of Washington, Program Development System.

Rich, H. L. (1982). *Disturbed students, characteristics and educational strategies* (pp. 292, 294–295). Baltimore, MD: University Park Press.

Shea, T. M., & Bauer, A. M. (1987). *Teaching children and youth with behavior disorders* (2nd ed., pp. 222, 272–274). Englewood Cliffs, NJ: Prentice-Hall.

Rizzo, J. V., & Zabel, R. H. (1988). *Educating children and adolescents with behavioral disorders: An integrative approach* (pp. 80–81, 276–282). Needham Heights, MA: Allyn & Bacon.

McCarty, B. C. (1992). The effect of race, socioeconomic status and family status on the interpersonal understanding of preadolescents and adolescents with severe emotional disturbance (Doctoral dissertation, University of Georgia, 1992). *Dissertation Abstracts International, 54,* 485A.

Disability Extensions

Autism and Developmental Delay

Bachrach, A. W., Mosley, A. R., Swindle, F. L., & Wood, M. M. (1978). *Developmental Therapy for young children with autistic characteristics.* Austin, TX: PRO-ED.

Wood, M. M., Swan, W. W., & Newman, V. (1981). Developmental Therapy for the severely disturbed and autistic. In R. L. McDowell, G. W. Adamson, & F. H. Wood (Eds.), *Emotional disturbance* (pp. 264–299). Boston: Little, Brown.

Wood, M. M., Hendrick, S. W., & Gunn, A. L. (1983). Programming for autistic students: A model for the public schools. In C. R. Reynolds & J. H. Clark (Eds.), *Assessment and programming for children with low incidence handicaps* (pp. 287–318). New York: Plenum Press.

Gunn, A. L. (1985). A comparison of behaviors and developmental ratings between mentally retarded autistic and mentally retarded non-autistic children (Doctoral dissertation, University of Georgia, 1984). *Dissertation Abstracts International, 45,* 2835A.

Language Delay

Lucas, E. V. (1978). The feasibility of speech acts as a language approach for emotionally disturbed children (Doctoral dissertation, University of Georgia, 1977). *Dissertation Abstracts International, 38,* 3646A.

Staff Development

Wood, M. M. (1971). *Rutland Center staff training: Exemplary early childhood centers for handicapped children* (Staff Training Prototype Series, Vol. 2, No. 10) (U.S. Office of Education, Bureau of Education for the Handicapped; Project Number OEG-0-70-4815-613). Austin: University of Texas at Austin.

Wood, M. M. (1977). The Developmental Therapy teacher training program: Review of the components for teachers of children with autistic characteristics. In F. H. Wood (Ed.), *Proceedings of a conference on preparing teachers for severely emotionally disturbed children with autistic characteristics.* Minneapolis: University of Minnesota, Advanced Institute for Trainers of Teachers for Seriously Emotionally Disturbed Children.

Wood, M. M., Skaar, C., Mayfield, G., Morrison, K., & Gillespie, F. (1984). *Psychoeducational computer simulation series for teachers of emotionally handicapped students,* Lessons 1 & 2 [Computer program]. Apple IIE software with accompanying workbook. Athens, GA: Developmental Therapy Institute.

Wood, M. M., Combs, M. C., & Swan, W. W. (1985). Computer simulations: Field testing effectiveness and efficiency for inservice and preservice teacher preparation. *Journal of Educational Technology Systems, 14,* 61–74.

Wood, M. M., & Gunn, A. (1985, May). *Technical assistance to principals, administrators, and teachers in the Portland, Orgeon school system for replication of the Developmental Therapy curriculum.* Unpublished report to the school district, Portland, OR. Reprinted in the CASE national newsletter, Fall 1985.

Wood, M. M., Combs, M. C., & Walters, L. H. (1986). Use of staff development by teachers and aides with emotionally disturbed and behavior disordered students. *Teacher Education and Special Education, 9,* 104–112.

Quirk, C. A. (1993). Skill acquisition in in-service teachers of students with emotional and behavioral disabilities (Doctoral dissertation, University of Georgia, 1993). *Dissertation Abstracts International, 54,* 2116A.

Quirk, C. A., Wood, M. M., & Davis, K. R. (1995). *Skill acquisition of early childhood personnel: Developmental findings.* Manuscript submitted for publication.

Quirk, C. A., Wood, M. M., & Hoy, C. A. (1995). *Influencing teachers' skill acquisition through written feedback of classroom performance.* Manuscript submitted for publication.

Cultural Diversity

Wood, M. M. (1975). *Terapía evolutiva* [from *Developmental Therapy,* A. Alegría-Martín, Trans.] Trujillo, Peru: Escuela Especial Carlos A. Manucci. Reprinted also as *Revisión por Programa de Educación Especial,* Departamento de Instrucción Pública, Hato Rey, Puerto Rico, 1976.

Marsé, A. (1980). *Recherche en musecotherapie de developpement.* Unpublished master's thesis, École de Musique, Université Laval, St. Damien, Quebec, Canada.

Wood, M. M. (1981). *Terapía de desarrollo* (from *Developmental Therapy,* I. Cudich, M. del C. Gonzalez, & M. I. Stinga, Trans.). Buenos Aires, Argentina: Editorial Médica Panamericana S.A.

Chowdhry, M. (1982). *A study of the programs of some selected institutions for handicapped children in the United States and their relevance to India.* Unpublished master's research report, University of Georgia, Athens.

Wood, M. M. (1986). *Developmental Therapy in the classroom* (2nd ed.). Austin, TX: PRO-ED. Sections translated into Chinese by Wu Jiajin (1988), Anhui Normal University Library, Wuhu City, Anhui Province, China.

Wood, M. M. (1989, February). What will become of the "Chinese princess"? *Women of China* (pp. 24–25, 44). Beijing, China: Women of China.

Wood, M. M. (1993). *Entwicklungstherapie im Klassenzimmer.* Kettwig, Germany: Sonderpädagogisches Förderzentrum für Erziehungshilfe (Translation of *Developmental Therapy in the classroom* by M. Bergsson).

Benkmann, K.-H., & Bergsson, M. (1994). Der entwicklungstherapeutische Ansatz einer Pädagogik für Kinder und Jugendliche mit Verhaltensstörungen. In K.-H. Benkmann & K. Saueressig (Eds.), *Fördern durch flexible Erziehungshilfe* (pp. 73–93). Vds Landesverband Nordrhein-Westfalen e. V., Fachverband für Behindertenpadagogik.

Outreach, Replications, and Service Delivery Applications

Wood, M. M. (1971). A case study in replication. *TADSCRIPT Newsletter.* Expanded in 1976, in L. Gunn (Ed.), *Outreach: Replicating services for young handicapped children* (pp. 133–136). Chapel Hill, NC: University of North Carolina, Technical Assistance Development System.

Wood, M. M. (1972). Case study 2: An example of program development and the replication process. In D. W. Davis, B. Elliot, & R. R. DeVoid (Eds.), *Replication guidelines* (pp. 28–36). Chapel Hill: University of North Carolina Technical Assistance Development System.

Dillard, J. W. (Ed.). (1974). *Steps in decision making for teachers of disturbed children, and representative objectives rating handbook.* Tuscaloosa: West Alabama Children's Center, Alabama Department of Education.

Wood, M. M. (1974). The Georgia Psychoeducational Center Network. In F. R. Crawford (Ed.), *Exploring mental health parameters* (pp. 194–203). Atlanta, GA: Paje.

Swan, W. W. (1975). *An outreach process model* (Tadscript No. 8). Chapel Hill: University of North Carolina, Technical Assistance Development System.

Orange County School District. (1976). *An educational model for autistic children* (Vol. 3, pp. 71–83, 92–106). Orange County, FL: Gateway School.

Swan, W. W., & Wood, M. M. (1976). Rutland Center supplemental services to day care programs. *Educational programs that work.* U.S. Office of Education, Division of Education for the Disadvantaged. San Francisco: Far West Laboratory for Research and Development. Reprinted in D. Pefley & H. Smith (Eds.), *It's Monday morning: A history of twenty-seven handicapped children's early education projects* (pp. 20–22). Chapel Hill: University of North Carolina, Technical Assistance Development System.

Wood, M. M. (1977). Interagency response to a troubled child. *Teaching Exceptional Children, 9,* 86–88.

EDGE. (1979). *Expanding developmental growth through education* [Curriculum guide]. Coon Rapids, MN: Anoka-Hennepin School District No. 11, Special Education Department.

Crimm, W. L. (1980). *An investigation for a prototypical school: The Rutland Center for Developmental Therapy.* Unpublished master's thesis, University of Pennsylvania, Philadelphia.

Davis, K. (1983). *Rutland Center Developmental Therapy Outreach Project: 1982–1983 Annual Report.* (Grant # G008200730). Washington, DC: U.S. Department of Education.

Davis, K. (1985). *Rutland Center Developmental Therapy Outreach Project: 1984–1985 Annual Report.* (Grant # G00840193). Washington, DC: U.S. Department of Education.

Swan, W. W., Wood, M. M., & Jordan, J. A. (1991). Building a statewide program of mental health and special education services for children and youth. In G. K. Farley & S. G. Zimet (Eds.), *Day treatment for children with emotional disorders: Vol. 2. Models across the country* (pp. 5–31). New York: Plenum Press.

Swan, W. W., & Brown, C. L. (Eds.). (1992). *GPN Research Reports.* Atlanta: Georgia Psychoeducational Program Network, Georgia Department of Education.

Davis, K. R. (1994). *Developmental Therapy Outreach Project annual report.* (Grant # HO 24 D90014). Washington, DC: U.S. Department of Education, Office of Special Education Programs, Early Education Programs for Children with Disabilities.

Wood, M. M., Davis, K. R., & Swindle, F. L. (1995). *Developmental Therapy–Developmental Teaching: Documentation of program effectiveness.* Unpublished research report, University of Georgia, Developmental Therapy Projects, Athens.

APPENDIX 2

Developmental Therapy Rating Inventory of Teacher Skills (DT/RITS)

Stages One Through Four

Developmental Therapy Rating Inventory of Teacher Skills*

The Developmental Therapy Rating Inventory of Teacher Skills (DT/RITS) is a systematic observational rating process for rating teacher skills after an extensive classroom observation period of between one and two hours. The inventory contains 304 skill items. These items are divided into four rating forms with a separate form for each of the stages in Developmental Therapy. Within each rating form the items are organized into three subsections: (1) activities, (2) materials, and (3) teacher techniques. The DT/RITS is to be used by observers who have received training in its use or by teachers for self-monitoring purposes.

Recording Procedure

The format used to record the observed teacher skills is a modification of the present-absent format. The rater observes the entire class and then rates the teacher using the appropriate stage rating form. A five-choice rating format requires the rater to make judgments about the presence or absence of the skills, and also, the degree to which the skills are used effectively. Thus, the ratings can be used to differentiate between the teacher who demonstrates a skill effectively and consistently from one who demonstrates the skills but is less effective or inconsistent.

There are five rating categories for the DT/RITS:

Yes (Y)	The activities, materials or techniques are being used.
No (N)	The activities, materials or techniques are not being used.
Partially (P)	The activities, materials, or techniques are being used but are not being used consistently with all the children or are not used all of the time with the group.
Not Needed (NN)	The activities, materials, or techniques are not used because they are not needed for that child or group during that specific time.
Not Seen (NS)	The activities, materials, or techniques are not seen due to the physical absence of the evaluator.

Scoring Procedure

The teacher's effectiveness is determined by tallying the total number of skills rated "Yes" and dividing this number by the total number of skills that were rated. This number is then multiplied by 100 to obtain the teacher's effectiveness percentage score. The step-by-step procedures are as follows:

1. Count the number of skills that are rated "Yes" (Activities, materials, or techniques are being used). This number is labeled *Y.*
2. Count the number of skills that are rated "No" (Activities, materials, or techniques are not being used). This number is labeled *N.*
3. Count the number of skills that are rated "Partially" (Activities, materials, or techniques are being used but are not being used consistently). This number is labeled *P.*
4. Compute the teacher's effectiveness percent, using the following formula:

$$\frac{Y}{Y+N+P} \times 100$$

Note that the No (N) and Partially (P) are both in the denominator, which means that the teacher is only given credit for skills used effectively. Not needed (NN) and Not Seen (NS) are not included in the score.

Effectiveness categories translate the teacher's score into different levels of teacher effectiveness:

Effectiveness Percentage	Effectiveness Category
.91–100	Highly Effective
.71–.90	Effective
.51–.70	Adequate
.31–.50	Less than Adequate
.16–.30	Poor

*For information on instrument development, validity, and reliability see Chapter 3.

Check One of the Following:

Pre ______

Post______

Reliability______

Other______

DEVELOPMENTAL THERAPY
RATING INVENTORY OF TEACHER SKILLS
DT/RITS

STAGE ONE

Lead Teacher: ____

Support Teacher: ____

Others Working on Team: ____

____

Children (first names only): ____

____

____

Length of Observation:

Full Time–Beginning: ______________________ Ending: ______________________

or

Partial Time–Beginning: ______________________ Ending: ______________________

If partial, list activities observed.

____

____

Rater: ____

Date: ____

Agency: ____

©1981, Copyright by J. Stafford Robinson and the Developmental Therapy Institute. All rights reserved. Permission is given to reproduce this form for educational purposes.

STAGE ONE

ACTIVITIES AND SCHEDULES FOR STAGE ONE

Directions:
Circle "Yes" if the following activities and schedules are used.
Circle "No" if the activities and schedules are not used.
Circle "P" (Partially) if the activities and schedules are used but are not used consistently with all children or are not used all the time with the group.
Circle "NN" if the activities or schedules are not needed.
Circle "NS" if the activities or schedules are not seen.

1. Activities are conducted to encourage the participation of each child in the group.	Yes	No	P	NN	NS
2. Activities provide success and promote pleasure-producing responses from the children.	Yes	No	P	NN	NS
3. Activities require no waiting for turns.	Yes	No	P	NN	NS
4. Inside play is included.	Yes	No	P	NN	NS
5. Play equipment is used to stimulate communication.	Yes	No	P	NN	NS
6. Play equipment provides opportunity for socialization.	Yes	No	P	NN	NS
7. Play time is planned to stimulate organization and solitary play.	Yes	No	P	NN	NS
8. Play equipment provides sensory stimuli for arousal and awareness.	Yes	No	P	NN	NS
9. Play equipment stimulates child to activity.	Yes	No	P	NN	NS
10. Story time is included (or some form of symbolic communication activity).	Yes	No	P	NN	NS
11. Story time provides opportunity for physical nurturance with children.	Yes	No	P	NN	NS
12. Material and content are on an appropriate level that the children can understand.	Yes	No	P	NN	NS
13. Opportunity is provided for child to work on indirect communication objectives (e.g., attending to story, producing sounds or words).	Yes	No	P	NN	NS
14. Snack time is included.	Yes	No	P	NN	NS
15. Snack time provides opportunity to stimulate communication and socialization skills.	Yes	No	P	NN	NS
16. Snack time is designed to be motivating and pleasurable.	Yes	No	P	NN	NS
17. Preacademic work time is included.	Yes	No	P	NN	NS
18. Work time tasks include activities planned to focus on children's specific (pre)academic objectives.	Yes	No	P	NN	NS
19. Work time is designed to produce pleasure and be motivating.	Yes	No	P	NN	NS
20. Activities are included such as art, music, and play, which provide the opportunity to work on the overall goals for the stage.	Yes	No	P	NN	NS

ACTIVITIES AND SCHEDULES FOR STAGE ONE
(Continued)

21. Average activity time is 10 minutes or less.	Yes	No	P	NN	NS
22. Activities requiring physical movement are interspersed with those which are less active.	Yes	No	P	NN	NS
23. Teacher has an alternate activity or "back up" planned to substitute . for an unsatisfactory activity.	Yes	No	P	NN	NS
24. Activity does not extend beyond "peak" of motivation. (Circle "Yes" if activity *does not* extend beyond peak.)	Yes	No	P	NN	NS
25. Before activity begins, teacher demonstrates the activity, when necessary, so each child will understand the task.	Yes	No	P	NN	NS

MATERIALS FOR STAGE ONE

Directions:

Circle "Yes" if the following criteria are used in selecting materials.
Circle "No" if the criteria are not used.
Circle "P" (Partially) if the criteria for selecting materials are used but are not used consistently for all children or are not used all the time with the group.
Circle "NN" if the materials are not needed.
Circle "NS" if the materials are not seen.

26. Classroom materials are used for a specific purpose and are chosen as vehicles for the accomplishment of objectives.	Yes	No	P	NN	NS
27. Content of the materials is concrete, sensory.	Yes	No	P	NN	NS
28. Materials are special, arousing.	Yes	No	P	NN	NS
29. Materials are used for individual mobilization.	Yes	No	P	NN	NS
30. Materials provide opportunity for each child to pleasurably participate in an independent way.	Yes	No	P	NN	NS
31. Materials allow for exploration.	Yes	No	P	NN	NS
32. Materials provide opportunity to develop eye-hand coordination and control of large muscles of the body and to use language.	Yes	No	P	NN	NS
33. Focus of materials is for child's pleasure-of-doing.	Yes	No	P	NN	NS

TECHNIQUES FOR STAGE ONE

Directions:
Circle "Yes" if the following techniques are used.
Circle "No" if the techniques are not used.
Circle "P" (Partially) if the techniques are used but are not used consistently with all children or are not used all the time with the group.
Circle "NN" if the techniques are not needed.
Circle "NS" if the techniques are not seen.

34. Body contact and touch are used in a positive, nurturing way and are major techniques (i.e., patting, hugging, holding, touching and physical nearness).	Yes	No	P	NN	NS
35. Classroom structure is used as a major technique.	Yes	No	P	NN	NS
36. Teacher has a consistent schedule of activities to follow each day.	Yes	No	P	NN	NS
37. Expectations are "meaningful" and reflect developmental objectives.	Yes	No	P	NN	NS
38. Classroom expectations are stated positively.	Yes	No	P	NN	NS
39. To help children organize themselves, certain areas of the room are designated for certain activities.	Yes	No	P	NN	NS
40. Children are prepared for transition time from one activity to another (e.g., "Play time is almost over.").	Yes	No	P	NN	NS
41. Voice modulation and facial expression are effectively used (e.g., calm, quiet voice; animated voice and expression; emphatic, matter-of-fact voice; eye contact; nurturing tones).	Yes	No	P	NN	NS
42. Rewards and token reinforcements are avoided completely or minimized. (Circle "Yes" if rewards or tokens are not used.)	Yes	No	P	NN	NS
43. Interpersonal forms of praise and rewards are used frequently (e.g., body contact, hugging, touching, positive statements rather than negative statements).	Yes	No	P	NN	NS
44. Teacher controls the materials during structured activity periods as needed.	Yes	No	P	NN	NS
45. Verbal interaction between lead and support teachers is used occasionally.	Yes	No	P	NN	NS
46. Two teachers are able to work together well.	Yes	No	P	NN	NS
47. Support teacher complements lead teacher, keeping children involved and redirected to the activity lead teacher is conducting.	Yes	No	P	NN	NS
48. Lead teacher is clearly leading.	Yes	No	P	NN	NS
49. Redirection (usually physical) is used frequently.	Yes	No	P	NN	NS
50. Reflection is used frequently. Teacher reflects actions of children.	Yes	No	P	NN	NS
51. Interpretation is not used. (Circle "Yes" if interpretation is not used.)	Yes	No	P	NN	NS
52. Teacher's verbal techniques are adapted to encourage each child's individual communication objectives (i.e., controlled vocabulary; simple phrases and sentences).	Yes	No	P	NN	NS
53. The teacher removes the child from the group to calm him or for inappropriate behavior when needed.	Yes	No	P	NN	NS
54. Time away from the group is very short.	Yes	No	P	NN	NS

	Yes	No	P	NN	NS
55. The teacher does not use removal from the room as a technique. (Circle "Yes" if removal from the room is *not* used.)	Yes	No	P	NN	NS
56. Physical intervention is used in a positive, nurturing way and is a major technique (i.e., bodily moving a child through an act; holding a child to keep him with the group; physically moving his arm and hand in response to material when needed).	Yes	No	P	NN	NS
57. Physical intervention is accompanied by a specific word or simple statement related to activity (e.g., "We pick up toys at the end of play time," as teacher moves the child through the activity).	Yes	No	P	NN	NS
58. When physical intervention is used, teacher holds child firmly but gently and supportively.	Yes	No	P	NN	NS
59. Teacher's voice generally expresses a warm, comforting tone.	Yes	No	P	NN	NS

Check One of the Following:

Pre ______

Post______

Reliability______

Other______

DEVELOPMENTAL THERAPY
RATING INVENTORY OF TEACHER SKILLS
DT/RITS

STAGE TWO

Lead Teacher: ____

Support Teacher: ____

Others Working on Team: ____

____

Children (first names only): ____

____

____

Length of Observation:

Full ____Time–Beginning:____________________ Ending:____________________

or

Partial ____Time–Beginning:____________________ Ending:____________________

If partial, list activities observed.

____

____

Rater: ____

Date: ____

Agency: ____

©1981, Copyright by J. Stafford Robinson and the Developmental Therapy Institute. All rights reserved. Permission is given to reproduce this form for educational purposes.

STAGE TWO

ACTIVITIES AND SCHEDULES FOR STAGE TWO

Directions:

Circle "Yes" if the following activities and schedules are used.
Circle "No" if the activities and schedules are not used.
Circle "P" (Partially) if the activities and schedules are used but are not used consistently with all children or are not used all the time with the group.
Circle "NN" if the activities or schedules are not needed.
Circle "NS" if the activities or schedules are not seen.

1. Activities are conducted to encourage the participation of each child in the group.	Yes	No	P	NN	NS
2. Activities provide success and promote pleasure-producing responses from the children.	Yes	No	P	NN	NS
3. Activities such as games are designed so that there are no losers and no peer competition.	Yes	No	P	NN	NS
4. Teacher avoids materials which require long waits for a turn and preferably selects materials which do not require turns.	Yes	No	P	NN	NS
5. Inside play is included.	Yes	No	P	NN	NS
6. Play time provides opportunity for communication (receptive and expressive).	Yes	No	P	NN	NS
7. Play time equipment provides opportunity for independent feedback.	Yes	No	P	NN	NS
8. Story time is included.	Yes	No	P	NN	NS
9. Story time provides opportunity for communication (receptive and expressive).	Yes	No	P	NN	NS
10. Story time provides opportunity for nurturance with children.	Yes	No	P	NN	NS
11. Snack time is included.	Yes	No	P	NN	NS
12. Snack time provides opportunity to stimulate communication and socialization skills.	Yes	No	P	NN	NS
13. Snack time is designed to be motivating and pleasurable.	Yes	No	P	NN	NS
14. Preacademic work time is included.	Yes	No	P	NN	NS
15. Work time tasks include activities planned to focus on children's specific (pre)academic objectives.	Yes	No	P	NN	NS
16. Some activities involve simple role-playing and use of make-believe.	Yes	No	P	NN	NS
17. Activities are included such as art, music, and play which provide the opportunity to work on the overall goals for the stage.	Yes	No	P	NN	NS
18. Opportunities are provided for each child to produce newly learned responses on his own.	Yes	No	P	NN	NS
19. Average activity time is 10–15 minutes.	Yes	No	P	NN	NS
20. Activities requiring physical movement are interspersed with those which are less active.	Yes	No	P	NN	NS
21. Teacher has an alternate activity or "back up" planned to substitute for an unsatisfactory activity.	Yes	No	P	NN	NS
22. Activity does not extend beyond "peak" of motivation. (Circle "Yes" if activity *does not* extend beyond peak.)	Yes	No	P	NN	NS
23. Before activity begins, teacher "talks through" or demonstrates the activity, when necessary, so each child will understand the task.	Yes	No	P	NN	NS

MATERIALS FOR STAGE TWO

Directions: Circle "Yes" if the following criteria are used in selecting materials.
Circle "No" if the criteria are not used.
Circle "P" (Partially) if the criteria for selecting materials are used but are not used consistently for all children or are not used all the time with the group.
Circle "NN" if the materials are not needed.
Circle "NS" if the materials are not seen.

24. Classroom materials are used for a specific purpose and are chosen as vehicles for the accomplishment of objectives.	Yes	No	P	NN	NS
25. Content of the materials is semiconcrete, exploratory.	Yes	No	P	NN	NS
26. Materials are adapted from regular preschool or primary grade materials as needed.	Yes	No	P	NN	NS
27. Materials are used to stimulate individual skills and successes.	Yes	No	P	NN	NS
28. Teacher assists child in control of materials.	Yes	No	P	NN	NS
29. Materials provide opportunity for each child to successfully participate.	Yes	No	P	NN	NS

TECHNIQUES FOR STAGE TWO

Directions: Circle "Yes" if the following techniques are used.
Circle "No" if the techniques are not used.
Circle "P" (Partially) if the techniques are used but are not used consistently with all children or are not used all the time with the group.
Circle "NN" if the techniques are not needed.
Circle "NS" if the techniques are not seen.

30. Body contact and touch are used frequently as needed. (Touch is used to a greater extent than direct body contact.)	Yes	No	P	NN	NS
31. Classroom structure is used as a major technique.	Yes	No	P	NN	NS
32. Children know the behaviors expected in each activity.	Yes	No	P	NN	NS
33. Teacher has a consistent schedule of activities to follow each day.	Yes	No	P	NN	NS
34. A schedule of activities is posted in order for the children to anticipate the activities and know the routine.	Yes	No	P	NN	NS
35. Expectations are "meaningful" and reflect developmental objectives.	Yes	No	P	NN	NS
36. Classroom rules are few and are stated positively.	Yes	No	P	NN	NS
37. Classroom expectations focus on helping children be successful.	Yes	No	P	NN	NS
38. Classroom structure is consistent but not static.	Yes	No	P	NN	NS
39. To help children organize themselves, certain areas of the room are designated for certain activities.	Yes	No	P	NN	NS
40. Children are prepared for transition time from one activity to another (e.g., "Play time is almost over.").	Yes	No	P	NN	NS
41. Voice modulation and facial expression are effectively used (e.g., calm, quiet voice; animated voice and expression; emphatic, matter-of-fact voice; eye contact).	Yes	No	P	NN	NS
42. Each child is frequently contacted by the lead teacher (either through verbal or non-verbal techniques).	Yes	No	P	NN	NS
43. Control of materials is used frequently.	Yes	No	P	NN	NS
44. Teacher allows opportunities for children to freely explore materials.	Yes	No	P	NN	NS
45. Rewards and token reinforcements are avoided completely or minimized. (Circle "Yes" if rewards or tokens are not used.)	Yes	No	P	NN	NS
46. Interpersonal forms of praise and rewards are used frequently (abundant verbal praise accompanied by physical contact).	Yes	No	P	NN	NS
47. Process of doing is reward.	Yes	No	P	NN	NS
48. Teacher uses praise and positive statements rather than negative statements.	Yes	No	P	NN	NS
49. Punishment is not used. (Circle "Yes" if punishment is not used.)	Yes	No	P	NN	NS
50. Small accomplishments are recognized.	Yes	No	P	NN	NS
51. Teacher conveys personal recognition of child as an important individual.	Yes	No	P	NN	NS
52. Verbal interaction between lead and support teachers is used as a major technique.	Yes	No	P	NN	NS
53. Two teachers are able to work together well.	Yes	No	P	NN	NS
54. Support teacher is a "response model" encouraging children to participate in an activity.	Yes	No	P	NN	NS
55. Lead teacher is clearly leading.	Yes	No	P	NN	NS

TECHNIQUES FOR STAGE TWO
(Continued)

56. Redirection is used as a major technique. (Physical redirection is combined with verbal redirection to help child respond to verbal cues when needed.)	Yes	No	P	NN	NS
57. Reflection is used frequently to put simple experiences into words.	Yes	No	P	NN	NS
58. Interpretation is used only occasionally (when appropriate).	Yes	No	P	NN	NS
59. Teacher's verbal techniques are adapted to encourage each child's individual communication objectives (i.e., controlled vocabulary; simple phrases and sentences).	Yes	No	P	NN	NS
Teacher uses the following techniques to insure participation:					
60. Teacher uses redirection or statements.	Yes	No	P	NN	NS
61. Teacher does not ignore a child's behavior when the child is in "crisis" and is in need of teacher support. (Circle "Yes" if teacher does *not* ignore child in crisis.)	Yes	No	P	NN	NS
62. Teacher depersonalizes the issues to reduce a child's defensiveness.	Yes	No	P	NN	NS
63. Removal from the group but remaining in room is used when needed.	Yes	No	P	NN	NS
64. Teacher stays with the child when he is away from the group.	Yes	No	P	NN	NS
65. Time away from the group is as brief as possible.	Yes	No	P	NN	NS
66. Teacher structures the removal so that the child understands why he was removed.	Yes	No	P	NN	NS
67. The interpersonal exchange between the child and the teacher is constructive and ends on a positive note.	Yes	No	P	NN	NS
68. Removal from the room is used occasionally when needed.	Yes	No	P	NN	NS
69. Support teacher removes child from the room.	Yes	No	P	NN	NS
70. Child is removed because he is out of control and may harm himself or others or a topic is so private that a child cannot discuss it in front of the group. (Circle "Yes" if the teacher removes the child for appropriate reasons.)	Yes	No	P	NN	NS
71. Teacher stays with the child when he is out of the room.	Yes	No	P	NN	NS
72. Time away from the group is as brief as possible.	Yes	No	P	NN	NS
73. Teacher structures the removal so that the child understands why he was removed.	Yes	No	P	NN	NS
74. The interpersonal exchange between the child and the teacher is constructive and ends on a positive note.(Child returns to group and participates.)	Yes	No	P	NN	NS
75. Physical intervention is used frequently.	Yes	No	P	NN	NS
76. When physical intervention is used, teacher holds child firmly but gently and supportively.	Yes	No	P	NN	NS
77. Teacher uses calm, quiet voice to reflect feelings and to reassure child.	Yes	No	P	NN	NS
78. Teacher allows child to be verbally aggressive by ignoring his remarks and redirecting to a constructive topic or activity.	Yes	No	P	NN	NS
79. Teacher terminates holding when child indicates self control.	Yes	No	P	NN	NS
80. Teacher uses reflection to provide simple descriptive statements of the central issue.	Yes	No	P	NN	NS
81. Teacher sets up minimal expectations or responses which child must make in order for him to return to the group.	Yes	No	P	NN	NS
82. Teacher structures situation so it will end positively.	Yes	No	P	NN	NS
83. Life Space Intervention (LSI) is not used unless it is appropriate for a particular child. (Circle "Yes" if LSI is used appropriately.)	Yes	No	P	NN	NS

Check One of the Following:

Pre ______

Post______

Reliability______

Other______

DEVELOPMENTAL THERAPY
RATING INVENTORY OF TEACHER SKILLS
DT/RITS

STAGE THREE

Lead Teacher: ______________________________

Support Teacher: ______________________________

Others Working on Team: ______________________________

____

Children (first names only): ______________________________

____

____

Length of Observation:

Full Time–Beginning: ______________ Ending: ______________

or

Partial Time–Beginning: ______________ Ending: ______________

If partial, list activities observed.

____

____

Rater: ______________________________

Date: ______________________________

Agency: ______________________________

©1981, Copyright by J. Stafford Robinson and the Developmental Therapy Institute. All rights reserved. Permission is given to reproduce this form for educational purposes.

STAGE THREE

ACTIVITIES AND SCHEDULES FOR STAGE THREE

Directions: Circle "Yes" if the following activities and schedules are used.
Circle "No" if the activities and schedules are not used.
Circle "P" (Partially) if the activities and schedules are used but are not used consistently with all children or are not used all the time with the group.
Circle "NN" if the activities or schedules are not needed.
Circle "NS" if the activities or schedules are not seen.

1. Activities are conducted to encourage the participation of each child in the group.	Yes	No	P	NN	NS
2. Activities provide success and promote pleasure-producing responses from the students.	Yes	No	P	NN	NS
3. Activities such as games are designed so that there are no losers and no peer competition.	Yes	No	P	NN	NS
4. Teacher selects materials that require students to wait for *short* time periods for their turns.	Yes	No	P	NN	NS
5. Academic work time is included.	Yes	No	P	NN	NS
6. Work time tasks include activities planned to focus on students' specific academic objectives.	Yes	No	P	NN	NS
7. Group project or game time is included.	Yes	No	P	NN	NS
8. Activity provides opportunity to develop skills in socialization and communication.	Yes	No	P	NN	NS
9. Snack time is included.	Yes	No	P	NN	NS
10. Snack time provides opportunity to stimulate communication and socialization skills.	Yes	No	P	NN	NS
11. Activities are included such as art, music, and play which provide the opportunity to work on the overall goals for the stage.	Yes	No	P	NN	NS
12. Each student has opportunities for successful participation.	Yes	No	P	NN	NS
13. Activities requiring physical movement are interspersed with those which are less active.	Yes	No	P	NN	NS
14. Teacher has an alternate activity or "back up" planned to substitute for an unsatisfactory activity.	Yes	No	P	NN	NS
15. Activity does not extend beyond "peak" of motivation.(Circle "Yes" if activity does not extend beyond peak.)	Yes	No	P	NN	NS
16. Before activity begins, teacher "talks through" or demonstrates the activity, when necessary, so each student will understand the task.	Yes	No	P	NN	NS

MATERIALS FOR STAGE THREE

Directions: Circle "Yes" if the following criteria are used in selecting materials.
Circle "No" if the criteria are not used.
Circle "P" (Partially) if the criteria for selecting materials are used but are not used consistently for all children or are not used all the time with the group.
Circle "NN" if the materials are not needed.
Circle "NS" if the materials are not seen.

17. Classroom materials are used for a specific purpose and are chosen as vehicles for the accomplishment of objectives.	Yes	No	P	NN	NS
18. Content of the materials is semiabstract.	Yes	No	P	NN	NS
19. Materials are regular school materials adapted if needed.	Yes	No	P	NN	NS
20. Materials are used to stimulate individual skills for success in the group.	Yes	No	P	NN	NS
21. Group is allowed to control the materials with teacher assistance.	Yes	No	P	NN	NS
22. Teacher selects materials which have opportunities for both small successes and small failures.	Yes	No	P	NN	NS
23. Materials emphasize group processes and are motivating.	Yes	No	P	NN	NS

TECHNIQUES FOR STAGE THREE

Directions: Circle "Yes" if the following techniques are used.
Circle "No" if the techniques are not used.
Circle "P" (Partially) if the techniques are used but are not used consistently with all children or are not used all the time with the group.
Circle "NN" if the techniques are not needed.
Circle "NS" if the techniques are not seen.

24. Body contact is used occasionally as needed (physical closeness or touch).	Yes	No	P	NN	NS
25. Classroom structure and rules are used frequently.	Yes	No	P	NN	NS
26. Students know the behaviors expected in each activity.	Yes	No	P	NN	NS
27. Teacher has a consistent schedule of activities to follow each day.	Yes	No	P	NN	NS
28. A schedule of activities is posted in order for students to anticipate the activities and know the routine.	Yes	No	P	NN	NS
29. Expectations are "meaningful" and reflect developmental objectives.	Yes	No	P	NN	NS
30. Classroom rules are few and are stated positively.	Yes	No	P	NN	NS
31. Classroom rules focus on helping students be successful.	Yes	No	P	NN	NS
32. Consequences for breaking rules are stated constructively and provide for constructive solutions.	Yes	No	P	NN	NS
33. Classroom structure is consistent but not static.	Yes	No	P	NN	NS
34. To help students organize themselves, certain areas of the room are designated for certain activities.	Yes	No	P	NN	NS
35. Students are prepared for transition time from one activity to another (e.g., "Game time is almost over.").	Yes	No	P	NN	NS
36. Voice modulation and facial expression are effectively used (e.g., calm, quiet voice; animated voice and expression; emphatic, matter-of-fact voice; eye contact).	Yes	No	P	NN	NS
37. Each student is frequently contacted by the lead teacher (either through verbal or non-verbal techniques).	Yes	No	P	NN	NS
38. Control of materials by teacher is used to calm a group or prevent a student from acting out.	Yes	No	P	NN	NS
39. Rewards and token reinforcements are avoided completely or minimized. (Circle "Yes" if rewards or tokens are not used.)	Yes	No	P	NN	NS
40. Interpersonal forms of praise and rewards are used frequently (verbal praise and group activities).	Yes	No	P	NN	NS
41. Teacher uses praise and positive statements rather than negative statements.	Yes	No	P	NN	NS
42. Punishment is not used. (Circle "Yes" if punishment is not used.)	Yes	No	P	NN	NS
43. Small accomplishments are recognized.	Yes	No	P	NN	NS
44. Teacher conveys personal recognition of student as an important individual.	Yes	No	P	NN	NS
45. Verbal interaction between lead and support teachers is used as a major technique.	Yes	No	P	NN	NS
46. Two teachers are able to work together well.	Yes	No	P	NN	NS
47. The lead and support teachers use verbal exchanges to provide models for interpersonal responses.	Yes	No	P	NN	NS
48. Lead teacher is clearly leading.	Yes	No	P	NN	NS
49. Redirection is used as a major technique. (Mainly verbal redirection; minimal physical redirection.)	Yes	No	P	NN	NS
50. Interpretation is used when appropriate and does not require a response from the student.	Yes	No	P	NN	NS

TECHNIQUES FOR STAGE THREE
(Continued)

51. Confrontation is used only when there is certainty of a therapeutic outcome.	Yes	No	P	NN	NS
Teacher uses the following techniques to avoid confrontation:					
52. Teacher uses redirection or statements rather than questions.	Yes	No	P	NN	NS
53. Teacher appropriately ignores a student's behavior when the student is merely "testing" a teacher to elicit a reaction.	Yes	No	P	NN	NS
54. Teacher does not ignore a student's behavior when the student is in "crisis" and is in need of teacher support. (Circle "Yes" if teacher does *not* ignore student in crisis.)	Yes	No	P	NN	NS
55. Teacher responds to a student's inappropriate request with a question.	Yes	No	P	NN	NS
56. Teacher depersonalizes the issues to reduce a student's defensiveness.	Yes	No	P	NN	NS
57. Teacher uses humor to neutralize the situation.	Yes	No	P	NN	NS
58. Teacher reflects on the positive qualities in a student.	Yes	No	P	NN	NS
59. Removal from the group but remaining in the room is used occasionally when appropriate.	Yes	No	P	NN	NS
60. Removal from the room is used frequently when needed.	Yes	No	P	NN	NS
61. Support teacher removes student from the room.	Yes	No	P	NN	NS
62. Student is removed because he is out of control and may harm himself or others or a topic is so private that a student cannot discuss it in front of the group. (Circle "Yes" if the teacher removes the student for appropriate reasons.)	Yes	No	P	NN	NS
63. Teacher limits her talk and is swift and firm while removing the student.	Yes	No	P	NN	NS
64. Teacher stays with the student when he is out of the room.	Yes	No	P	NN	NS
65. Teacher structures the removal so that the student understands why he was removed.	Yes	No	P	NN	NS
66. The interpersonal exchange between the student and the teacher is constructive and ends on a positive note. (Student returns to group and participates.)	Yes	No	P	NN	NS
67. Physical intervention is used occasionally.	Yes	No	P	NN	NS
68. When physical intervention is used, teacher holds student firmly but gently and supportively.	Yes	No	P	NN	NS
69. Teacher uses calm, quiet voice to reflect feelings and to reassure the student.	Yes	No	P	NN	NS
70. Teacher verbalizes to student that she is holding him to help him gain control.	Yes	No	P	NN	NS
71. Teacher allows student to be verbally aggressive by ignoring his remarks and redirecting to a constructive topic.	Yes	No	P	NN	NS
72. Teacher gives verbal cues to student as to what is expected of him before terminating physical holding.	Yes	No	P	NN	NS
73. Teacher terminates holding when student indicates self control.	Yes	No	P	NN	NS
74. Teacher limits her talk and is positive.	Yes	No	P	NN	NS
75. Teacher structures situation so it will end positively.	Yes	No	P	NN	NS
76. Life Space Intervention (LSI) is used as a major technique with individual students.	Yes	No	P	NN	NS
77. Reflection is used to "ready" a student for the LSI.	Yes	No	P	NN	NS
78. When the student's physiological processes are restored (breathing, muscle tone), the teacher obtains the student's perception of the situation.	Yes	No	P	NN	NS
79. If the student is having difficulty talking, teacher reflects what was observed or interprets feelings behind behavior.	Yes	No	P	NN	NS
80. Teacher finds out what is important to the student.	Yes	No	P	NN	NS
81. Teacher uses what the student has given and puts it together in a reality context around central issue, using reflection and interpretation.	Yes	No	P	NN	NS
82. Teacher is not judgmental.	Yes	No	P	NN	NS
83. If the student is ready to consider changing his responses, teacher discusses with the student alternative ways to respond to a situation.	Yes	No	P	NN	NS
84. Teacher helps the student select alternate response which he can successfully accomplish.	Yes	No	P	NN	NS

Check One of the Following:

Pre ______

Post______

Reliability______

Other______

DEVELOPMENTAL THERAPY
RATING INVENTORY OF TEACHER SKILLS
DT/RITS

STAGE FOUR

Lead Teacher: ____________________

Support Teacher: ____________________

Others Working on Team: ____________________

____

Children (first names only): ____________________

____

____

Length of Observation:

Full Time–Beginning: ______ Ending: ______

or

Partial Time–Beginning: ______ Ending: ______

If partial, list activities observed.

____

____

Rater: ____________________

Date: ____________________

Agency: ____________________

©1981, Copyright by J. Stafford Robinson and the Developmental Therapy Institute. All rights reserved. Permission is given to reproduce this form for educational purposes.

STAGE FOUR

ACTIVITIES AND SCHEDULES FOR STAGE FOUR

Directions: Circle "Yes" if the following activities and schedules are used.
Circle "No" if the activities and schedules are not used.
Circle "P" (Partially) if the activities and schedules are used but are not used consistently with all children or are not used all the time with the group.
Circle "NN" if the activities or schedules are not needed.
Circle "NS" if the activities or schedules are not seen.

1. Activities are conducted to encourage the participation of each child in the group.	Yes	No	P	NN	NS
2. Activities provide success and promote pleasure-producing responses from the students.	Yes	No	P	NN	NS
3. Academic work time is included.	Yes	No	P	NN	NS
4. Work time tasks include activities planned to focus on students' specific academic objectives.	Yes	No	P	NN	NS
5. Some academic work is conducted in groups.	Yes	No	P	NN	NS
6. Academic activities include content of specific interest to the students.	Yes	No	P	NN	NS
7. Group project or game time is included.	Yes	No	P	NN	NS
8. Socialization and communication are emphasized during group times.	Yes	No	P	NN	NS
9. Snack time is included.	Yes	No	P	NN	NS
10. Communication and socialization are emphasized during snack time.	Yes	No	P	NN	NS
11. Unstructured activities are included which provide opportunities to "try out" newly learned responses independently and successfully (e.g., games, projects, and outside play).	Yes	No	P	NN	NS
12. The daily schedule is consistent and provides for group meetings at the beginning and ending of the day.	Yes	No	P	NN	NS
13. Group planning and feedback are a part of every activity.	Yes	No	P	NN	NS
14. Teacher permits deviation from the schedule when appropriate.	Yes	No	P	NN	NS
15. Students contribute ideas for the selection of activities.	Yes	No	P	NN	NS
16. Teacher has an alternate activity or "back up" planned to substitute for an unsatisfactory activity.	Yes	No	P	NN	NS
17. Activity does not extend beyond "peak" of motivation. (Circle "Yes" if activity does not extend beyond peak.)	Yes	No	P	NN	NS
18. Before activity begins, teacher "talks through" or demonstrates the activity, when necessary, so each student will understand the task.	Yes	No	P	NN	NS

MATERIALS FOR STAGE FOUR

Directions: Circle "Yes" if the following criteria are used in selecting materials.
Circle "No" if the criteria are not used.
Circle "P" (Partially) if the criteria for selecting materials are used but are not used consistently for all children or are not used all the time with the group.
Circle "NN" if the materials are not needed.
Circle "NS" if the materials are not seen.

19. Classroom materials are used for a specific purpose and are chosen as vehicles for the accomplishment of objectives.	Yes	No	P	NN	NS
20. Content of the materials is abstract, symbolic, and complex.	Yes	No	P	NN	NS
21. Materials reflect real-life interests of students.	Yes	No	P	NN	NS
22. Materials are used to stimulate group processes.	Yes	No	P	NN	NS
23. Students have considerable responsibility for control of materials.	Yes	No	P	NN	NS

TECHNIQUES FOR STAGE FOUR

Directions: Circle "Yes" if the following techniques are used.
Circle "No" if the techniques are not used.
Circle "P" (Partially) if the techniques are used but are not used consistently with all children or are not used all the time with the group.
Circle "NN" if the techniques are not needed.
Circle "NS" if the techniques are not seen.

24. Body contact is used, as needed.	Yes	No	P	NN	NS
25. Classroom structure is used frequently.	Yes	No	P	NN	NS
26. Classroom rules are few and are stated positively.	Yes	No	P	NN	NS
27. Teacher encourages group members to develop or modify rules and procedures as needed.	Yes	No	P	NN	NS
28. Reflection of established procedures and/or expectations is used to provide students with behavioral guidelines.	Yes	No	P	NN	NS
29. Consequences of breaking rules are stated constructively and provide for constructive solutions. (Punishment is not used.)	Yes	No	P	NN	NS
30. To help students organize themselves, certain areas of the room are designated for certain activities.	Yes	No	P	NN	NS
31. Voice modulation and facial expression are effectively used (e.g., calm, quiet voice; animated voice and expression; emphatic, matter-of-fact voice; eye contact).	Yes	No	P	NN	NS
32. Control of materials by teacher is seldom used. (Circle "Yes" if control of materials is used appropriately.)	Yes	No	P	NN	NS
33. Rewards and token reinforcements are avoided completely or minimized. (Circle "Yes" if rewards or tokens are not used.)	Yes	No	P	NN	NS
34. Teacher uses praise and positive statements rather than negative statements.	Yes	No	P	NN	NS
35. Teacher conveys personal recognition of each student as an important individual.	Yes	No	P	NN	NS
36. Praise and recognition for individual and group interactions are authentic in quality.	Yes	No	P	NN	NS
37. The adult-student relationships depict genuine respect and openness for each other.	Yes	No	P	NN	NS
38. Teachers are completely honest in their interactions with the students.	Yes	No	P	NN	NS
39. Verbal interaction between lead and support teachers is used occasionally.	Yes	No	P	NN	NS
40. Two teachers are able to work together well.	Yes	No	P	NN	NS
41. Lead teacher is clearly leading (when adult leadership is needed).	Yes	No	P	NN	NS
42. Redirection is used occasionally. (A verbal reminder is usually sufficient.)	Yes	No	P	NN	NS
43. Reflection is used occasionally to help students recognize and express feelings in themselves and others.	Yes	No	P	NN	NS
44. Interpretation is used when appropriate and does not require a response from the student.	Yes	No	P	NN	NS

TECHNIQUES FOR STAGE FOUR
(Continued)

Teacher uses the following techniques to avoid confrontation:					
45. Teacher uses redirection or statements.	Yes	No	P	NN	NS
46. Teacher responds to students' anger or hostility by ignoring verbally aggressive remarks, reflecting feelings, redirection, or interpretation of behavior and feelings.	Yes	No	P	NN	NS
47. Teacher does not ignore a student's behavior when the student is in "crisis" and is in need of teacher support. (Circle "Yes" if teacher *does not* ignore student in crisis.)	Yes	No	P	NN	NS
48. Teacher clarifies situation rather than giving commands.	Yes	No	P	NN	NS
49. Teacher uses humor to neutralize the situation.	Yes	No	P	NN	NS
50. Teacher reflects on the positive qualities in a student.	Yes	No	P	NN	NS
51. Removal from the group but remaining in room is rarely used.	Yes	No	P	NN	NS
52. Removal from the room is used frequently when needed. (Removal is often voluntary and centered around the student's need to discuss an issue in private.)	Yes	No	P	NN	NS
53. Teacher limits her talk and is swift and firm while removing the student.	Yes	No	P	NN	NS
54. Teacher stays with the student when he is out of the room.	Yes	No	P	NN	NS
55. Teacher structures the removal so that the student understands why he was removed.	Yes	No	P	NN	NS
56. The interpersonal exchange between the student and the teacher is constructive and ends on a positive note. (Student returns to group and participates.)	Yes	No	P	NN	NS
57. Physical intervention is not used unless a student regresses. (Circle "Yes" if physical intervention is used when appropriate or otherwise is not used.)	Yes	No	P	NN	NS
58. When physical intervention is used, the student is taken to a private area as quickly as possible.	Yes	No	P	NN	NS
59. When holding a student, teacher limits own talk but conveys positive support.	Yes	No	P	NN	NS
60. When physical intervention is used, teacher structures situation so that the issue is resolved positively for the student.	Yes	No	P	NN	NS
61. Life Space Intervention (LSI) is used as a major technique with individual students.	Yes	No	P	NN	NS
62. Reflection is used to "ready" a student for the LSI.	Yes	No	P	NN	NS
63. When the student's physiological processes are restored (breathing, muscle tone), the teacher obtains the student's perception of the situation.	Yes	No	P	NN	NS
64. If the student is having difficulty talking, teacher reflects what was observed or interprets feelings behind behavior.	Yes	No	P	NN	NS
65. Teacher finds out what is important to the student.	Yes	No	P	NN	NS
66. Teacher uses what the student has given and puts it together in a reality context around central issue using reflection and interpretation.	Yes	No	P	NN	NS
67. Teacher is not judgmental.	Yes	No	P	NN	NS
68. If the student is ready to consider changing his responses, teacher discusses with the student alternative ways to respond to situation.	Yes	No	P	NN	NS
69. Teacher helps the student select alternate response which he can successfully accomplish.	Yes	No	P	NN	NS
70. Life Space Intervention (LSI) is used as a major technique with the group.	Yes	No	P	NN	NS
71. Teacher clarifies the purpose of the discussion for the group.	Yes	No	P	NN	NS
72. If the group is having difficulty talking, teacher reflects what was observed or interprets feelings behind behavior.	Yes	No	P	NN	NS
73. Teacher finds out what is important to the group.	Yes	No	P	NN	NS
74. Teacher uses what the group has given and puts it together in a reality context around central issue, using reflection and interpretation.	Yes	No	P	NN	NS
75. Teacher is not judgmental.	Yes	No	P	NN	NS
76. If the group is ready to consider changing its response, teacher discusses with the group alternative ways to respond to situation.	Yes	No	P	NN	NS
77. Teacher helps the group select alternate response which can be successfully accomplished.	Yes	No	P	NN	NS
78. The interpersonal exchange between group and teacher is constructive and ends on a positive note.	Yes	No	P	NN	NS

APPENDIX 3

The Administrative Support Checklist

ADMINISTRATIVE SUPPORT CHECKLIST

The Administrative Support Checklist contains 41 items needed within a school for administrative support of teachers using Developmental Therapy–Developmental Teaching.

This rating form is completed after reviewing program descriptions and student IEPs and talking with the teacher/treatment teams and administrators. Because a unique opportunity exists in each school building to mount a highly therapeutic program, a separate rating should be done for each individual building which houses Developmental Therapy groups.

There are four possible rating choices.

Yes—The procedure is being used.

No—The procedure is not being used.

P (Partially)—The procedure is being used but not consistently with all the children and by all teaching/treatment teams.

INA (Information not available)—It was not possible to obtain sufficient information to make a judgment.

Circle each item as indicated.

An administrative support score is obtained by a simple count of items marked "Yes." The maximum score obtainable is 41. The following criterion levels were established, using the checklist at 28 sites replicating the Developmental Therapy–Developmental Teaching model:

26–41 items present—Demonstration Level (exemplary practices with elements successfully implemented.)
16–25 items present—Adoption Level (sufficient number of elements to implement model)
10–15 items present—Minimum Level (basic elements used)

ADMINISTRATIVE SUPPORT CHECKLIST

Rater: ______________________________

Date: ______________________ Name of School: ______________________

Administrative Head of School: ______________________________

Title: ______________________________

Name of Person Responsible for the Daily Implementation of the Developmental Therapy–Developmental Teaching Program in this School: ______________________

Number of Developmental Therapy–Developmental Teaching Groups in this School: ______________________

Total Number of Children Enrolled in the Developmental Therapy–Developmental Teaching Program: ______________

Names of Lead Teachers in Developmental Therapy–Developmental Teaching Program: ______________

____

Names of Support Teachers (Aides): ______________________________

____

Names of Others Working as Resources to the Teams: ______________________________

____

How Was This Rating Obtained? (Check All That Apply)

Talking with Administrators ______________________________

Talking with Teachers ______________________________

Talking with Resource People/Parents ______________________________

Reading Program Description ______________________________

Observation of Program ______________________________

Self-Rating by School Personnel ______________________________

(Names: ______________________________

______________________________)

©1981, Copyright by J. Stafford Robinson and the Developmental Therapy Institute. All rights reserved. Permission is given to reproduce this form for educational purposes.

THE TEACHING/TREATMENT TEAMS

1. There is more than one Developmental Therapy group (teacher) in a building.	Yes	No	P	INA
2. The Developmental Therapy group has a lead and a support teacher (or aide).	Yes	No	P	INA
3. The support teacher or aide is an actively involved, constructive part of the team.	Yes	No	P	INA
4. Adequate time is allocated for team planning and preparation.	Yes	No	P	INA
5. Adequate time is allocated for team debriefing each day.	Yes	No	P	INA
6. Adequate time is allocated for team to provide mainstream follow-through as needed.	Yes	No	P	INA
7. Adequate time is allocated for school and parent contacts.	Yes	No	P	INA
8. Consultation (support and feedback) is provided to the teams on a scheduled, consistent basis.	Yes	No	P	INA
9. The teams perceive administrative support for their work.	Yes	No	P	INA

SCHOOL LIAISON, MAINSTREAMING, AND INCLUSION

10. Appropriate inclusion or mainstreaming placements are available.	Yes	No	P	INA
11. All children have some concurrent placement in a parallel school setting (mainstreaming or inclusion).	Yes	No	P	INA
12. Teacher in child's regular school placement is involved with the team in planning.	Yes	No	P	INA
13. An educational planning conference including the regular teacher and the Developmental Therapy teacher is held to present results of testing, recommendations, and to plan a supportive mainstream program for the child (at the IEP conference or shortly thereafter).	Yes	No	P	INA
14. The principal is included in the mainstreaming program planning and implementation.	Yes	No	P	INA
15. Weekly contact is made with the child's regular school teacher to exchange information (e.g., telephone and/or classroom visit).	Yes	No	P	INA
16. Child's regular teacher has visited the Developmental Therapy classroom.	Yes	No	P	INA
17. Child's regular teacher has observed the Developmental Therapy team, when teaching.	Yes	No	P	INA
18. A teaching/treatment team member is available for crisis intervention in the regular education program with children from the Developmental Therapy program.	Yes	No	P	INA

SERVICES TO PARENTS

19. A parent worker is assigned to each child and family.	Yes	No	P	INA
20. A parent planning conference is held to communicate to the parents the test results and to jointly plan the programs to be conducted at home, in the Developmental Therapy class, and in the mainstream.	Yes	No	P	INA
21. Parents are involved with the treatment team in ratings or reviewing the child on the DTORF–R.	Yes	No	P	INA

SERVICES TO PARENTS (continued)

22. Parent planning conferences are held as a part of or following the scheduled DTORF–R ratings.	Yes	No	P	INA
23. Opportunities are available for parents to observe Developmental Therapy classes when needed, with a professional person knowledgeable about their child's Developmental Therapy program.	Yes	No	P	INA
24. Home visits are made by a team member or parent worker when needed.	Yes	No	P	INA

DEVELOPMENTAL TEACHING OBJECTIVES RATING FORM–REVISED (DTORF–R)

25. DTORF–R objectives are utilized to ascertain children's levels of functioning and to plan experiences, materials, and strategies.	Yes	No	P	INA
26. The lead teacher, support teacher, parent and/or parent worker/monitor work together as a treatment team to rate the child.	Yes	No	P	INA
27. In using the rating form, at least *one* objective and no more than *four* objectives are used in each of the 4 curriculum areas.	Yes	No	P	INA
28. Objectives are rated sequentially with mastery of previous objectives being necessary before new objectives are initiated. If exception, brief explanation is needed on rating form.	Yes	No	P	INA
29. Each child's appropriate stage is identified according to his general stage of therapy as determined by his average stage of development in the 4 curriculum areas.	Yes	No	P	INA
30. Each child is placed with a developmentally comparable group of children according to DTORF–R ratings and stages.	Yes	No	P	INA
31. Sizes of groups are appropriate to developmental needs of the children (groups of eight or less).	Yes	No	P	INA
32. The DTORF–R is completed for the 1st time after the child has participated in the program for 8 days in order to obtain the child's developmental baseline.	Yes	No	P	INA
33. The DTORF–R is completed on each child on a predetermined schedule.	Yes	No	P	INA
34. The DTORF–R is completed on each child at least three times during the year.	Yes	No	P	INA
35. The DTORF–R is completed on each child at the end of the school year or at termination.	Yes	No	P	INA
36. Children are regrouped on the basis of DTORF–R results after each scheduled rating.	Yes	No	P	INA
37. A summary DTORF–R on each child is available to assess and document progress of child.	Yes	No	P	INA
38. A class DTORF–R is designed to clearly emphasize group objectives and individual differences to facilitate planning activities.	Yes	No	P	INA
39. Each child generally appears to have mastered the objectives that have been checked on the DTORF–R and is working on objectives that have been marked as goals.	Yes	No	P	INA
40. The DTORF–R is used as the basis for program and/or curriculum.	Yes	No	P	INA
41. The children are together in a group for at least two hours a day.	Yes	No	P	INA

APPENDIX 4

Theoretical Foundations: Content Analysis Charts for Behavior, Communication, Socialization, and (Pre)Academics/Cognition

Behavior Content Grid

Stage	Behavioral Style	Physical Skills	Behavioral Motivators and Regulators	Behavioral Processes	Rule Governing Behavior and Play
Stage One	Affectomotor Impulsive Unorganized	Body Management Manipulation of hands Balance, locomotion, coordination	Sensory Stimulation Impulses Pleasure Nurture	Impulsive Repetitive movement Motor limitation Fleeting attention span	No Awareness of Rules
Stage Two	Motor, Language, and Imagination Expression of personal experience	Basic Movement Skills Ball manipulation Eye-hand coordination Directionality Spatial awareness (body-in-space) Stunts and tumbling	Adults and Physical Gratification Punishment orientation to conforming Simple control of impulse	Motor-Verbal Exploration Imitation of social behaviors of adults Limited interaction with peers Limited attention span	Games Played with No Rules or Simple Ones Winning not a priority
Stage Three	Vacillation Between Self-Expression and Conformity	Body Coordination Skills in Simple Group Games Ball manipulation Low-organized games Manipulative games Body movement (rhythm) Laterality	Self-Expression and Expectations of Adults Some inner controls Self-protection Language used to mediate behavior Adult power through approval	Patterns of Simple Group Behavior Feelings expressed with minimal restraints Adults and heroes modeled Increased attention span	Rules Represent Authority Elaborate rules Inflexible rules Rules to serve own interest Fairness in taking turns Winning is important Losing is intolerable

Behavior Content Grid (cont.)

Stage	Behavioral Style	Physical Skills	Behavioral Motivators and Regulators	Behavioral Processes	Rule Governing Behavior and Play
Stage Four	Conformity to Demands	Basic Skills for Sports Team sports Group games Intermittent growth spurts	Peer Groups and Adults Representing Standards of Society Models mannerisms of peers and adults Identification with values Mediates behavior	Tolerates Delayed Results and Distant Goals Cause and effect Identification with others Recognizes roles of leaders and followers Group social interaction skills	Basic Law-and-Order Orientation Rules can change to suit group Personal justice Equality Golden rules Group winning important Losing is tolerated
Stage Five	Integration of Personal Behavior into a Value System	Personal Fitness Group and individual sports skills Major physical-sexual changes	Individual and Group Values Personal acclaim by others Valued by others Work role	Experimentation with New Experiences Sexual activities Sex-role mannerisms Vicarious experiences satisfy	Rights and Contracts Orientation Universal justice Rules developed and modified in response to need

Communication Content Grid

Stage	Social-Communication Style	Social Purpose	Social Communication
Stage One	Preverbal and Beginning Speech	Meeting Physical Needs Expressing Drives	Basic Receptive Language Nonverbal Language Eye following Body movement Gestures Vocalizing Word approximations Vocal imitation Labeling Word sequences
Stage Two	Spontaneous Language	Verbal Assertions Thinking aloud Organizing world with words and concepts	Egocentric Monologues Verbal language Action statements Intention statements Exchanging information
Stage Three	Socialized Language	Sustained Individual Exchanges and Inner Language	Social Expression Group discussions Describing experiences Expressing pride Describing characteristics of self and others
Stage Four	Self-Expressive Rational Language	Extended Group Social Exchanges	Social-Affective Expression Elaboration of experiences Expressing feelings of self Praising Expressing feelings of others
Stage Five	Abstract, Idea-Oriented Language	Expanded Friendships Among Peers	Ideological and Interpersonal Expression

Socialization Content Grid

Stage	Major Interpersonal Focus	Predominating Developmental Anxieties	Ego Functions
Stage One	Recognition and Trust Relational bonds with adult Dependency Primary identification and separation	Abandonment Aloneness Separation The unknown Deprivation	Undifferentiated Presocial Instincts and Drives
Stage Two	Individuation and Autonomy Measuring up and being successful to please adults Beginning independence and initiative through self-assertion	Inadequacy (anxieties from previous stage plus . . .) Fears loss of acceptance and approval Concern for obtaining needs (physical and emotional) Management of body impulses and drives Restrictions from adults Fear of being caught Fear of punishment	Impulsive Identity formed Organization of external cues Emotional security from adults Minimal expression of inner life
Stage Three	Self-Esteem and Social Uniformity Acceptance and appreciation by others Measuring up to self-standards set by peers and adults Self is worthy or unworthy "Looking good" in the eyes of others Self-protective in response to others Cooperation Independence tested	Guilt (anxieties from previous stages plus . . .) Fear of loss of love or approval because of personal failings Fear of failure Death fears; fatalism Fear of the unknown Realistic fears ("It could happen . . .") Remote fears ("It might be possible . . . ") Mystical fears ("Wouldn't it be terrible if . . . ?")	Self-Protective Superego formed Ego ideal emerges Others help solve conflicts Desires and needs expressed View of reality reconstructed to control feelings
Stage Four	Social Self Conforming to Social Rules Acceptance in gruops Interest in helping others Independence-dependence conflict temporarily resolved	Conflict (anxieties from previous stages plus . . .) Balancing complex inner drives and needs with outer demands of peers and adults Fear of not being accepted by the group versus expressing self Anxiety over responsibility for independence and making decisions	Conformist Self is obscured Feelings modified to others' expectations
Stage Five	Identity "Who am I" (in relationship to modified social standards) Personal convictions and values Security in belonging Goals and ideals Desire for independence Emotional self-reliance	Self-Image (anxieties from all previous stages plus . . .) Concern for body Sex-role doubts Sexual expressions Obtaining affection Doubts of future role and earning capacity Conflict about values governing behavior and decision making	Conscientious and Individualistic Feelings expressed within social-cultural framework Inner controls Formalized affect Instinctual anxieties intellectualized

Socialization Content Grid (contd.)

Characteristic Play	Moral Values	Interpersonal Perspectives and Friendship	Problem-Solving Approach
Sensory-Based Experiences Awareness Pleasure Sameness Touch Imitation Abundance Repetition	Premoral Conscience not yet emerged	Unaware of Separate Self Adults provide for needs Security comes from objects (toys and people)	None
Symbolic Play About People and Animals Play is for self Make-believe Imitation of other children Desires, fears, and impulses projected into play and resolved happily Simple story sequences Creative imagination Imitation of adults	Preconventional/Heteronomous Simple schemata, good versus evil Own needs justify actions Fear and respect of adults	Ego-Centered One-way relationships Affection for adults as need satisfiers Adult authority dominates Adults imitated Personal characteristics of adults not recognized Best friends change frequently	Problems Solved by Adults and Other Powerful Sources Magic Pretend
Organized Social Play Group participation and cooperation Concern over nonconformists Attempts to win games Fairness Experiments with direct power (control) over others Dramatic elaboration Imaginative group play Interactions with other children (parallel and interactive play)	Hedonistic Conscience development Fairness for self Adults' values internalized	Differentiated, Subjective Perspective Friends are close with mutual interests Sympathy for others Adults seen with undimensional characteristics Adults provide hero image for imitation and identification	Problems Solved by Others (Adults, Heroes) Conforming to rules reduces problems Winning enhances self
Group Interactions Group predominates over child's need to control	Conventional Good behavior Rules internalized Fairness and justice for others Law and order	Self-Reflective Perspective Friends are partners Interest in roles of others Sympathy and awareness of others' needs Second-person reciprocity Altruism Adults seen as multidimensional	Problems Solved by Self and Peers
Experiments with Alternatives Changes physical style via dress, mannerisms, eating, drinking, and drug experimentation Daydreams Dates (role–playing relationships) Talking about others Cliques, clubs, and groups Imitation of societal roles via TV, movies, magazines, and sports	Justice Justice in social relationships Social contract orientation Individual rights	Multiple Perspectives Empathy Mutual respect in relationships Friends are autonomous but interdependent Awareness of pluralistic social groups Personal characteristics of adults recognized	Problems Solved by Self and Close Friends

(Pre)Academics/Cognition Content Grid

Stage	Cognitive Style	Symbol System	Reasoning Process	Schematic Style
Stage One	Sensorimotor Kinetic feedback Use of simple objects as tools Association of motor movements to environment by labeling Imitative	Concrete Tangible objects and familiar persons	Simple Perceptions Matching similar objects Object permanence (memory forming)	Unorganized Random movements Scribbling Imitative movements
Stage Two	Egocentric, Prelogical Learning through motor experience and concrete materials Representative imitations	Animistic Simple concrete symbols (toys) representing direct experience and images Anthropomorphic	Egocentric Causality Categorizing Visual perceptual skills Sequencing Simple concepts of past and future, relating parts (memory)	Preschematic Simple form recognition Human figure forms Concepts defined by use Organization of parts
Stage Three	Concrete Operations Organization of parts into whole Relational concepts, rigid constructs Decentering begins	Semi-Abstract Pictures Words Numerals Ludic play	Organized Seriation Simple conservation Simple abstraction Classification Numerical operations Simple time-telling	Schematic Organized spatial relationships Basic line appears Colors used to approximate realism Primitive human forms
Stage Four	Expanded Concrete Operations Systems and relationships Generalizing	Abstract Symbols and images organized in systems	Complex Conservation processes Understands consequences of actions Cause and effect Written expression of experience Concepts of distance, time, and volume Rules used to solve problems Sex-role concepts Evaluating ideas	Drawing Realism Realistic interpretation Use of simple perspective Skyline disappears Attention to detail Human forms elaborated
Stage Five	Formal Operations How things work Values assimilated into cognitive style Decisions Producing ideas Metacognition Evaluation	Conceptual Complexity Ideological "causes" Logical relations Principles	Combining Systems Distinguishing process from outcome Group logic and ethic Writing to communicate informal ideas and feelings Inductive processes	Naturalistic Natural surroundings Proportion Detailed perspective Color for variations

APPENDIX 5

Summary of Major Motivational Systems

Applied to Developmental Stages

Stage One

Sensorimotor equilibration (*Piaget, 1972*)

Id drives, instinctual energy, pleasure (*A. Freud, 1942; S. Freud, 1920/1955; Erikson, 1956*)

Attachment (*Bowlby, 1982, 1988*)

Model warmth, loss, prosocial imitation, nurturing bonding (*Mahler, 1968/1987; Maccoby 1980; Rutter, 1981*)

Anxiety preparedness (*Brody & Axelrad, 1970*)

Temperament (*Thomas & Chess, 1977; Kagan, 1989*)

Physiological and safety needs (*Maslow, 1976, 1987*)

Stage Two

Avoidance of anxiety (*Sullivan, 1953*)

Reality demands (*S. Freud, 1920/1955*)

Belongingness and love needs (*Maslow, 1987*)

Individuation (*Mahler, Pine, & Bergman, 1975*)

Tension reduction (*Rapaport, 1960*)

Autonomy (*Erikson, 1968*)

Egocentricity (*Piaget, 1932/1960*)

Stage Three

Initative, fears, guilt (*Erikson, 1968*)

Internalization through identification (*A. Freud, 1973*) or through observational modeling (*Bandura, 1977, 1986*)

Heteronomous needs (*Kohlberg, 1981; Piaget, 1932/1960*)

Esteem needs (*Maslow, 1976, 1987*)

Self-protection (*Loevinger, 1976, 1987*)

Stage Four

Competence (*White, 1963*)

Industry and self-esteem (*Erikson, 1968, 1977*)

Conformity (*Loevinger, 1976*)

Law and order (*Kohlberg, 1981*)

Vicarious rewards, empathy for a positive effect on another (*Aronfreed, 1968; Bandura, 1977*)

Empathy, resulting from either intrinsic or extrinsic rewards (*Rosenhan, 1972*) or from reciprocal role taking (*Selman, 1980*)

Search for meaning (*Fingarette, 1963; Ausubel, 1971*)

Stage Five

Interpersonal conformity (*Kohlberg, 1981*)

Self actualization (*Maslow, 1987*)

Conscientious conformity (*Loevinger, 1976, 1987*)

Ideal self as pacer (*Loewald, 1962*)

Identity through society's rituals (*Erikson, 1977*)

APPENDIX 6

Efficacy Data

Tables 1.1–1.4: Children's Gains in Acquiring Social–Emotional Milestones

Tables 1.5–1.6: Parents' Ratings of Changes in Children's Problem Behaviors

Tables 1.7–1.8: Adults' Practices That Changed Significantly After an In-Service Program in Developmental Therapy–Developmental Teaching

TABLE 1.1
Mean Postprogram Scores (in Months)

Site	n		Behavior	Communication	Socialization	Academics	Total
Demonstration Site	20	Actual:	91.80	83.15	83.70	90.55	89.30
		Predicted:	80.64	70.18	74.28	83.92	78.91
Replication Site 1	33	Actual:	44.39	34.88	32.48	31.30	34.42
		Predicted:	26.73	23.00	19.74	17.35	19.92
Replication Site 2	18	Actual:	105.30	90.83	87.56	98.56	96.50
		Predicted:	80.87	68.32	64.04	86.79	78.65
Replication Site 3	16	Actual:	94.94	79.31	79.12	86.62	84.62
		Predicted:	78.73	71.49	67.99	83.41	77.46
Replication Site 4	16	Actual:	75.94	64.50	61.06	49.81	60.37
		Predicted:	52.10	49.07	44.04	32.53	41.18
Replication Site 5	9	Actual:	79.33	51.67	53.33	38.89	50.33
		Predicted:	57.13	35.20	37.41	28.82	36.03
Total	112						
		Actual:	77.18	64.42	62.90	63.85	66.36
		Predicted:	58.55	50.34	48.38	52.93	52.44

Note. Predicted score is theoretical achievement if pre-intervention rate of development had continued during the intervention period.

TABLE 1.2
Mean Proportional Change Indexes (PCIs)

			PCI				
Site	Average Program Time (Months)	n	Behavior	Communication	Socialization	Academics	Total
Demonstration Site	19	20	2.153	2.827	2.014	1.671	1.972
Replication Site 1	10	33	9.162	7.786	11.370	11.320	10.690
Replication Site 2	18	18	3.217	3.074	4.377	2.523	2.632
Replication Site 3	16	16	5.237	3.628	4.907	2.630	3.197
Replication Site 4	7	16	7.331	5.757	5.018	6.444	5.869
Replication Site 5	11	9	4.009	3.743	4.351	3.444	3.441
Total		112					
Average PCI			5.719	4.934	6.180	5.611	5.496
Average Program Time	13						

TABLE 1.3
Average Pre- and Postprogram Scores

	Behavior	***Communication***	***Socialization***	***Academics***	***Total***
Pretest Scores (in months)	50.06	43.19	41.40	45.36	44.90
SD	31.81	29.70	28.15	36.75	31.32
Posttest Scores (in months)	77.18	64.42	62.90	63.85	66.36
SD	36.93	37.68	35.79	39.95	36.75
t value:	11.70	11.01	11.08	13.06	15.02
p value:	0.0000	0.0000	0.0000	0.0000	0.0000
Average program time = 13 months					

TABLE 1.4
Actual and Predicted Mean Postprogram Scores (in months by age group)

	Developmental Age at Post-Test		
	Up to Age 6 n = 26	***Ages 6–9 n = 62***	***Ages 10–12 n = 24***
Actual	24.62	66.29	111.7
SD	17.56	25.74	17.92
Predicted (without intervention)	15.83	48.22	103.50
SD	14.23	23.61	14.57
t value	6.10	9.66	2.59
p value	.0000	.0000	.0165

Note. Predicted score is theoretical achievement if pre-intervention rate of development had continued during the intervention period.

TABLE 1.5
Comparison of Children's Severe Problem Behaviors Before and After Their Developmental Therapy Programs
($N = 37$)

	Number of Problems Before		Number of Problems Directly After		t of Difference Between Means
	Mean	SD	Mean	SD	
Problem Area					
Behavior	8.4	4.2	3.0	3.8	7.98**
Communication	3.0	2.3	1.1	1.7	5.55**
Socialization	2.2	1.8	0.8	1.1	5.01**
Academics/Cognition	1.3	1.8	1.3	1.8	0.09
Factor Area					
I. Aggressive/Hostile	5.5	3.4	2.3	3.2	4.33**
II. Inadequacy/Immaturity	3.6	2.6	1.2	1.8	7.17**
III. Anxiety/Withdrawal	2.2	1.8	0.8	1.2	4.47**
Total Number of Severe Problems	14.9	7.5	6.2	6.2	7.75**

Note. Mean time in program was 11.5 months ($SD = 6$ months).
** $p < .005$.

TABLE 1.6

Comparison of Children's Severe Problem Behaviors Before and 2 Years After Their Developmental Therapy Programs Ended ($N = 36$)

	Number of Problems Before		Number of Problems 2 Years After		*t* of Difference Between Means
	Mean	***SD***	***Mean***	***SD***	
Problem Area					
Behavior	7.0	4.1	3.4	4.5	4.12**
Communication	3.0	2.4	1.4	2.0	3.59**
Socialization	2.2	1.8	1.0	1.7	3.17**
Academics/Cognition	1.3	2.0	0.8	1.4	1.34
Factor Area					
I. Aggressive/Hostile	4.8	3.3	2.3	2.9	4.62**
II. Inadequacy/Immaturity	3.4	2.5	1.5	2.5	3.53**
III. Anxiety/Withdrawal	2.1	1.8	1.2	1.7	2.41*
Total Number of Severe Problems	13.4	7.8	6.6	8.6	4.23**

Note. Ratings of problem behaviors for this sample were obtained an average of 25.6 months after program completion (*SD* = 9.2 months). Because this group participated for an average of 10.0 months, the length of time between the two sets of ratings shown here was an average of 35.6 months.

*$p < .05$. **$p < .005$.

TABLE 1.7

DT/RITS Skill Items That Changed Significantly After an In-Service Program in Developmental Therapy–Developmental Teaching

	Teachers	Pre		Post		Dif			
Item Number[a]	*n*	*M*	*SD*	*M*	*SD*	*M*	*SD*	*t value*	*p value**
1	25	2.76	0.44	3.00	0.00	0.24	0.44	2.75	0.01
15	21	2.52	0.60	2.86	0.36	0.33	0.58	2.65	0.02
20	25	2.72	0.54	2.96	0.20	0.24	0.44	2.75	0.01
27	25	2.80	0.41	3.00	0.00	0.20	0.41	2.45	0.02
29	25	2.76	0.44	3.00	0.00	0.24	0.44	2.75	0.01
31	25	2.76	0.44	3.00	0.00	0.24	0.44	2.75	0.01
32	25	2.72	0.46	3.00	0.00	0.28	0.46	3.06	0.01
35	24	2.46	0.51	2.88	0.34	0.42	0.58	3.50	0.00
37	24	2.54	0.51	2.83	0.38	0.29	0.62	2.29	0.03
38	24	2.63	0.65	2.88	0.34	0.25	0.53	2.30	0.03
41	24	2.36	0.57	2.76	0.44	0.40	0.71	2.83	0.01
43	24	2.67	0.48	2.96	0.20	0.29	0.55	2.60	0.02
45	25	2.76	0.52	2.96	0.20	0.20	0.41	2.45	0.02
47	25	2.68	0.56	2.96	0.20	0.28	0.54	2.58	0.02
56	25	2.52	0.51	2.80	0.41	0.28	0.54	2.58	0.02
60	23	2.52	0.59	2.83	0.39	0.30	0.63	2.30	0.03
75	10	2.60	0.52	3.00	0.00	0.40	0.52	2.45	0.04

[a]Item numbers correspond to performance items on the Stage Two form of the DT/RITS found in Appendix 2.

*$p < .05$.

TABLE 1.8

Percentage of Change for Ratings of Items Responsive to Training

Item Number[a]	DT/RITS % Ratings						% Change	
	"No"		"Partial"		"Yes"			
	Pre	Post	Pre	Post	Pre	Post	no change	+ change
1	0	0	24	0	76	100	76	24
15	5	0	38	14	57	86	57	43
20	4	0	20	4	76	96	76	24
27	0	0	20	0	80	100	80	20
29	0	0	24	0	76	100	76	24
31	0	0	24	0	76	100	76	24
32	0	0	28	0	72	100	72	28
35	0	0	54	13	46	87	50	50
37	0	0	46	17	54	83	54	46
38	8	0	21	13	71	87	79	21
41	4	0	56	24	40	76	48	52
43	0	0	33	4	67	96	63	37
45	4	0	16	4	80	96	80	20
47	4	0	24	4	72	96	76	24
56	0	0	48	20	52	80	64	36
60	4	0	39	17	57	83	65	35
75	0	0	40	0	60	100	60	40

[a]Item numbers correspond to performance items on the Stage Two form of the DT/RITS found in Appendix 2.

APPENDIX 7

Sample Developmental Teaching Objectives Rating Form–Revised (DTORF–R)

Name ______________________ Date of Birth ______________ Date of Rating ______________

Raters ______________________ Class Stage ______________

CHECK ONE: Referral ☐ Interval ☐ Baseline ☐ Final ☐

DTORF-R
DEVELOPMENTAL TEACHING OBJECTIVES RATING FORM

Stage I

BEHAVIOR

- ☐ 1. Indicates Awareness
  - __ Tactile __ Aud. __ Motor
  - __ Taste __ Visual __ Smell
- ☐ 2. Reacts by Attending
- ☐ 3. Responds by Sustained Attending
- ☐ 4. Responds to Simple Stim./Motor Behav.
- ☐ 5. Responds to Complex Stim.
- ☐ 6. Assists in Self-Help
- ☐ 7. ▲Responds Independently/Play Materials
- ☐ 8. ▲Indicates Recall of Routine

COMMUNICATION

- ☐ 1. Produces Sounds
- ☐ 2. Attends to Speaker
- ☐ 3. Responds/Verbal Stim./Motor Behav.
- ☐ 4. Responds/Cues/Word Approx.
- ☐ 5. ▲Use Word Approx. Spon.
- ☐ 6. Uses Word/To Adult
- ☐ 7. Uses Word/To Peer
- ☐ 8. ▲Uses Word Sequence/No Model

SOCIALIZATION

- ☐ 1. Indicates Awareness/Others
- ☐ 2. Attends/Other's Behavior
- ☐ 3. Responds to Name
- ☐ 4. Engages/Solitary Play
- ☐ 5. Interacts Non-Verbally/Adult
- ☐ 6. Responds/Request/Come
- ☐ 7. Dems. Underst./Request
- ☐ 8. Same as C-6
- ☐ 9. Begins Emergence/Self
- ☐ 10. ▲Participates/Parallel Play
- ☐ 11. Same as C-7
- ☐ 12. ▲Seeks Contact/Familiar Adults

Stage II

BEHAVIOR

- ☐ 9. Uses Play Material Appropriately
- ☐ 10. Waits/No Intervention
- ☐ 11. Participates/Sitting/No Intervention
- ☐ 12. Participates/Movement/No Intervention
- ☐ 13. ▲Participates Spontaneously
- ☐ 14. ▲Accepts Praise, Success with Control

COMMUNICATION

- ☐ 9. Answers with Recog. Words
- ☐ 10. Exhibits Receptive Vocabulary
- ☐ 11. ▲Commands, Questions/Word Sequence
- ☐ 12. ▲Shares Minimal Information/Adult
- ☐ 13. Describes Characteristics/Self, Others
- ☐ 14. ▲Shares Minimal Information/Peer

SOCIALIZATION

- ☐ 13. ▲Demonstrates Imaginative Play
- ☐ 14. Same as B-10
- ☐ 15. ▲Initiates Social Movement/Peer
- ☐ 16. Participates/Directed Sharing Activity
- ☐ 17. Participates/Interactive Play
- ☐ 18. ▲Cooperates/Peer/Organ. Times

Stage III

BEHAVIOR

- ☐ 15. ▲Completes Individual Tasks Independently
- ☐ 16. Conveys Awareness/Expected Conduct
- ☐ 17. Gives Reasons for Expectations
- ☐ 18. Tells Other Appropriate Behavior
- ☐ 19. ▲Responds Approp./Leader Choice
- ☐ 20. ▲Refrains Behavior/Others Lose Control
- ☐ 21. ▲Maintains Acceptable Behavior in Group

COMMUNICATION

- ☐ 15. ▲Describes Personal Experiences
- ☐ 16. Shows Feeling Responses Approp.
- ☐ 17. Participates Approp./Group Discussion
- ☐ 18. ▲Indicates Pride in Self
- ☐ 19. Describes Attributes/Self
- ☐ 20. Describes Attributes/Others
- ☐ 21. Recognizes Others' Feelings
- ☐ 22. Verbalizes Pride/Group Achievement

SOCIALIZATION

- ☐ 19. ▲Shares Material, Takes Turns
- ☐ 20. ▲Imitates Approp. Behavior
- ☐ 21. Labels Situation/Values
- ☐ 22. Leads, Demonstrates for Group
- ☐ 23. Participates/Activity Suggested by Peer
- ☐ 24. Sequences Own Experiences
- ☐ 25. Indicates Developing Friendship
- ☐ 26. ▲Seeks Assistance, Praise/Peer
- ☐ 27. ▲Assists Others/Conforming

Stage IV

BEHAVIOR

- ☐ 22. Indicates Begin. Awareness/Own Progress
- ☐ 23. Indicates Flexibility/Procedures
- ☐ 24. Participates/New Experience With Control
- ☐ 25. Implements Alternative Behaviors
- ☐ 26. ▲Responds/Provocation With Control
- ☐ 27. Accepts Responsibility/Actions, Attitudes
- ☐ 28. ▲Suggests Interpersonal & Group Solutions

COMMUNICATION

- ☐ 23. Channels Feelings/Creative Media
- ☐ 24. Same as B-22
- ☐ 25. Explains/Behavior Influences Others'
- ☐ 26. ▲Verbalizes Feelings Approp. in Group
- ☐ 27. ▲Initiates Positive Relationship Verbally
- ☐ 28. ▲Praises, Supports Others Verbally
- ☐ 29. ▲Expresses Cause-Effect/Feelings, Behavior

SOCIALIZATION

- ☐ 28. Indentifies with Adult Heroes
- ☐ 29. Sequences Group Experience
- ☐ 30. ▲Suggest Activ./Peer Group
- ☐ 31. Expresses Aware./Others' Different Actions
- ☐ 32. Listens to Others' Opinions
- ☐ 33. Expr. Inter./Peer Opinion of Self
- ☐ 34. Suggests Solutions to Problems
- ☐ 35. Discrims. Opposite Social Values
- ☐ 36. Draws Infer. from Social Situations

Stage V

BEHAVIOR

- ☐ 29. ▲Seeks New Work Skills
- ☐ 30. ▲Seeks Desired Group Role
- ☐ 31. Understands, Accepts Law & Order
- ☐ 32. Participates/Group Self-Governance
- ☐ 33. Solves Personal Problems

COMMUNICATION

- ☐ 30. Uses Complex, Figurative Statements
- ☐ 31. ▲Uses Conciliatory Verbal Responses
- ☐ 32. ▲Recognizes, Includes Others' Contribu.
- ☐ 33. Describes Multiple Motives, Values
- ☐ 34. ▲Expresses Values, Ideals
- ☐ 35. Sustains Interpersonal, Group Relations

SOCIALIZATION

- ☐ 37. ▲Understands, Respects Others
- ☐ 38. ▲Interacts Successfully/Multiple Roles
- ☐ 39. ▲Makes Personal Choices/Values
- ☐ 40. Indicates Self Understanding/Goals
- ☐ 41. ▲Sustains Relationships

▲ = Student must do this spontaneously for item mastery, without direct adult cues or control to elicit the behavior.

©1981, Copyright by J. Stafford Robinson and the Developmental Therapy Institute. All rights reserved. Permission is given to reproduce this form for educational purposes.

ACADEMICS/COGNITION

Stage I

- ☐ 1. Same as B-2
- ☐ 2. Same as B-3
- ☐ 3. ▲Shows Short Term Memory
- ☐ 4. Same as B-5
- ☐ 5. ▲Imitates Acts of Adults
- ☐ 6. Shows Fine, Gross Motor/18 months
- ☐ 7. Knows Names/Objects
- ☐ 8. Same as C-4
- ☐ 9. ▲Same as C-5
- ☐ 10. Matches Shapes, Objects with Spaces
- ☐ 11. Identifies Body Parts (4)
- ☐ 12. Recognizes Detail/Pictures
- ☐ 13. Sorts Objects
- ☐ 14. Labels Pictures

Stage II

- ☐ 15. Recognizes Use of Objects
- ☐ 16. Performs Body Coord./3 year
- ☐ 17. Matches Identical Pictures (of 3)
- ☐ 18. Performs Fine Motor Coord./3 year
- ☐ 19. Recognizes Different Object (of 3)
- ☐ 20. Understands 3 Opposites
- ☐ 21. Categorizes Diff. Pictures/Similar Assoc.
- ☐ 22. Counts to 4 (1 to 1)
- ☐ 23. Identifies 4 colors, 3 shapes
- ☐ 24. Alternates Same, Different Pict. or Object
- ☐ 25. Counts to 10 (1 to 1)
- ☐ 26. Performs Eye-Hand Coord./5 year
- ☐ 27. Discrims. Num., Designs, Upr. Case Letters
- ☐ 28. Performs Body Coord./5 year
- ☐ 29. Recognizes Groups to 5
- ☐ 30. Dem. Rote Memory/5 year
- ☐ 31. Sequences 3 Pictures

Stage III

- ☐ 32. Performs Eye-Hand Coord./6 year
- ☐ 33. Performs Body Coord./6 year
- ☐ 34. Reads 50 Primary Words
- ☐ 35. Recogs., Writes Numerals/Groups 1-10
- ☐ 36. Writes 50 Primary Words/Mem., Dictation
- ☐ 37. Listens/Story/Comprehension
- ☐ 38. Explains Others' Behavior
- ☐ 39. Reads Sentences/Comprehension
- ☐ 40. Adds, Subtracts/1-9
- ☐ 41. Identifies Illogical Elements
- ☐ 42. Writes Sentences About Story
- ☐ 43. Performs Physical Skills, Games/Elem.
- ☐ 44. Writes Simple Sentences
- ☐ 45. Adds, Subtracts/Time/Money
- ☐ 46. Reads, Explains Meas. Words
- ☐ 47. Reads, Tells About Stories
- ☐ 48. Uses Place Value, Regroup, Mult., Seriation

Stage IV

- ☐ 49. Writes to Communicate
- ☐ 50. Multiplies, Divides to 100
- ☐ 51. ▲Reads for Pleasure, Information
- ☐ 52. Computes Money to $10.00
- ☐ 53. Explains Fiction Characters
- ☐ 54. Uses Grammatical Rules/Writing
- ☐ 55. Same as S-35
- ☐ 56. Solves Measurement, Logic Problems

Stage V

- ☐ 57. Seeks Others' Opinions/Current Issues
- ☐ 58. Discriminates Fact/Opinion
- ☐ 59. Recognizes, Explains Illogical Behavior
- ☐ 60. Solves Word Problems/Fractions, Decimals
- ☐ 61. Same as B-33
- ☐ 62. ▲Uses Academic Tools/Citizen, Worker

NOTES

____
Parent's Signature

____
Family/Services Coordinator Signature

____
Teacher's Signature—General Education

____
Teacher's Signature—Special Education

DTORF-R SUMMARY (sum √s=items mastered)

- Behavior items mastered: _____
- Communication items mastered: _____
- Socialization items mastered: _____
- Academics/Cognition items mastered: _____

Total DTORF-R items mastered: _____

- Developmental stage: _____
- Chronological age at rating: _____

References

Ainsworth, M. D. S. (1973). The development of infant-mother attachment. In B. M. Caldwell & H. N. Ricciuti (Eds.), *Review of child development research* (Vol. 3, pp. 1–94). Chicago: University of Chicago Press.

Allison, K. W., & Lerner, R. M. (1993). Integrating research, policy, and programs for adolescents and their families. In R. M. Lerner (Ed.), *Early adolescence* (pp. 17–22). Hillsdale, NJ: Erlbaum.

Alpern, G. D., Boll, T. J., & Shearer, M. S. (1986). *The Developmental Profile–II.* Los Angeles: Western Psychological Services.

American Psychiatric Association. (1993). Significant achievement awards. Clinical and special education services for severely disturbed children: Developmental Therapy Program–Rutland Psychoeducational Services, Athens, Georgia. *Journal of Hospital and Community Psychiatry, 44,* 994–996.

Anthony, E. J. (1976). The genesis of oppositional behavior. In E. J. Anthony & D. C. Gilpin (Eds.), *Three clinical faces of childhood.* New York: Spectrum.

Arllen, N. L., Gable, R. A., & Hendrickson, J. M. (1994). Toward an understanding of the origins of aggression. *Preventing School Failure, 38,* 18–23.

Arnold, J. (1984). Values of exceptional students during early adolescence. *Exceptional Children, 51,* 230–234.

Aronfreed, J. (1968). *Conduct and conscience: The socialization of internalized control over behavior.* New York: Academic Press.

Arwood, E. L. (1991). *Semantic and pragmatic language disorders* (2nd ed.). Gaithersburg, MD: Aspen.

Ausubel, D. P. (1971). Motivational issues in cognitive development. In T. Mischel (Ed.), *Cognitive development and epistemology* (pp. 357–361). San Diego, CA: Academic Press.

Ausubel, D. P., Sullivan, E. V., & Ives, S. W. (1980). *Theory and problems of child development* (3rd ed., pp. 79–81, 285–290). New York: Grune & Stratton.

Bachrach, A. W., Mosley, A. R., Swindle, F. L., & Wood, M. M. (1978). *Development therapy for young children with autistic characteristics.* Austin, TX: PRO-ED.

Bailey, D. B., & Wolery, M. (1992). Promoting social competence. In D. B. Bailey & M. Wolery (Eds.), *Teaching infants and preschool children with disabilities* (2nd ed., pp. 257–297). New York: Merrill.

Bandura, A. (1977). *Social learning theory.* Englewood Cliffs, NJ: Prentice-Hall.

Bandura, A. (1986). *Social foundations of thought and action: A social cognitive theory.* Englewood Cliffs, NJ: Prentice-Hall.

Bandura, A., & Walters, R. H. (1963). *Social learning and personality development.* Troy, MO: Holt, Rinehart & Winston.

Barbour, N. H., & Seefeldt, C. (1993). *Developmental continuity across preschool and primary grades.* Wheaton, MD: Association for Childhood Education International.

Barnett, D. W., Macmann, G. M., & Carey, K. T. (1991). Early intervention and the assessment of developmental skills: Challenges and directions. *Topics in Early Childhood Special Education, 12,* 21–43.

Battelle Developmental Inventory Screening Test. (1988). Allen, TX: DLM Teaching Resources.

Bayley, N. (1969). *The Bayley Scales of Infant Development* (2nd ed.). San Antonio, TX: The Psychological Corporation.

Beckman, P. J., & Lieber, J. (1992). Parent-child social relationships and peer social competence of preschool children with disabilities. In S. L. Odom, S. R. McConnell, & M. A. McEvoy (Eds.), *Social competence of young children with disabilities* (chap. 3). Baltimore: Paul H. Brookes.

Benkmann, K.-H., & Bergsson, M. (1994). Der entwicklungstherapeutische Ansatz einer Pädagogik für Kinder und Jugendliche mit Verhaltensstörungen. In K. H. Benkmann & K. Saueressig (Eds.), *Fördern durch flexible Erziehungshilfe* (pp. 73–93). Vds Landesverband Nordrhein-Westfalen e.V., Fachverband für Behindertenpadagogik.

Bennett, W. J. (1993). *The book of virtues.* New York: Simon & Schuster.

Benson, P. L., Williams, D. L., & Johnson, A. L. (1987). *The quicksilver years: The hopes and fears of early adolescence.* New York: HarperCollins.

Bergsson, M. (1993). *Entwicklungstherapie im klassenzimmer.* Kettwig, Germany: Sonderpädogogisches Förderzentrum für Erziehungshifle.

Bettelheim, B. (1977). *The uses of enchantment.* New York: Vintage Books.

Blos, P. (1979). *The adolescent passage: Developmental issues.* New York: International Universities Press.

Bowlby, J. (1973). *Attachment and loss: Separation, anxiety, and anger* (Vol. 2). New York: Basic Books.

Bowlby, J. (1980). *Attachment and loss: Loss, sadness, and depression* (Vol. 3). New York: Basic Books.

Bowlby, J. (1982). *Attachment and loss* (Vol. 1, 2nd ed.). New York: Basic Books.

Bowlby, J. (1988). *A secure base: Parent-child attachment and healthy human development.* New York: Basic Books.

Bowlby, J. (1989). *The making and breaking of affectional bonds.* London: Routledge.

Bowman, B. T., & Stott, F. M. (1994). Understanding development in a cultural context. In B. L. Mallory & R. S. New (Eds.), *Diversity and developmentally appropriate practices* (chap. 6). New York: Teachers College Press.

Braaten, S. (1982a). *Behavioral objective sequencing.* Minneapolis: Minnesota Public Schools, Special Education Program.

Braaten, S. (1982b). A model for assessment and placement of emotionally disturbed students in special education. In M. M. Noel & N. Haring (Eds.), *Progress or change: Issues in educating the emotionally disturbed* (Vol. 1). Seattle: University of Washington, Program Development Assistance System.

Brazelton, T. B. (1994). Preface to *Heart Start: The emotional foundations of school readiness* (p. 5). Zero to Three Project, National Center for Clinical Infant Program, Children's Hospital Medical Center, Boston, MA.

Bredekamp, S. (Ed.). (1987). *Developmentally appropriate practice in early childhood programs serving children from birth through age 8.* Washington, DC: National Association for the Education of Young Children.

Brendtro, L. K., Brokenleg, M., & Van Bockern, S. (1990). *Reclaiming youth at risk: Our hope for the future.* Bloomington, IN: National Educational Service.

Bretherton, I. (1987). New perspectives on attachment relations: Security, communication, and internal working models. In J. D. Osofsky (Ed.), *Handbook of infant development* (2nd ed., pp. 1061–1100). New York: Wiley.

Brigance, A. H. (1991). *Brigance Diagnostic Inventory of Early Development, revised.* North Billerica, MA: Curriculum Associates.

Brittain, C. V. (1968). An exploration of the bases of peer compliance and parent compliance in adolescence. *Adolescence, 2,* 445–458.

Brody, S., & Axelrad, S. (1970). *Anxiety and ego formation in infancy.* New York: International Universities Press.

Brown, L. M., & Gilligan, C. (1992). *Meeting at the crossroads.* Cambridge, MA: Harvard University Press.

Buhrmester, D. (1990). Intimacy of friendship, interpersonal competence and adjustment during preadolescence and adolescence. *Child Development, 61,*(4), 1101–1111.

Bullis, M., & Gaylord-Ross, R. (1991). *Moving on: Transitions for youth with behavioral disorders.* Reston, VA: Council for Exceptional Children.

Canfield, J., & Wells, H. C. (1994). *100 ways to enhance self-concept in the classroom* (2nd ed.). Needham Heights, MA: Allyn & Bacon.

Cardillo, J. E., & Smith, A. (1994). Psychometric issues. In T. J. Kiresuk, A. Smith, & J. E. Cardillo (Eds.), *Goal attainment scaling: Applications, theory, and measurement* (chap. 9). Hillsdale, NJ: Erlbaum.

Carta, J. J., Schwartz, I. S., Atwater, J. B., & McConnell, S. R. (1991). Developmentally appropriate practice: Appraising its usefulness for young children with disabilities. *Topics in Early Childhood Special Education, 11,* 1–20.

Children's Defense Fund. (1994). *The state of America's children yearbook, 1994.* Washington, DC: Author.

Clark, T. C. (1989). *Home-based services for infants, toddlers and preschool age deaf-blind, multihandicapped sensory impaired.* Logan, UT: SKI HI Institute.

Cooper, C. R., & Cooper, R. G. (1992). Links between adolescents' relationships with their parents and peers: Models, evidence, and mechanisms. In R. D. Parke & G. W. Ladd (Eds.), *Family-peer relationships: Modes of linkage* (pp. 135–158). Hillsdale, NJ: Erlbaum.

Coopersmith, S. (1967). *The antecedents of self-esteem.* San Francisco: W. H. Freeman.

Cramer, P. (1990). *The development of defense mechanisms.* New York: Springer-Verlag.

Damon, W. (1988). *Self-understanding in childhood and adolescence.* New York: Cambridge University Press.

Davis, K. R. (1983). *Rutland Center Developmental Therapy Outreach Project, 1982–1983 annual report.* (Grant No. G008200730). Washington, DC: U.S. Department of Education.

Davis, K. R. (1985). *Rutland Center Developmental Therapy Outreach Project, 1984–1985 annual report.* (Grant No. G00840193). Washington, DC: U.S. Department of Education.

Davis, K. R. (1994a). *Developmental Therapy Outreach Project annual report.* (Grant No. H0 24 D90014). Washington, DC: U.S. Department of Education, Office of Special Education Programs, Early Education Programs for Children with Disabilities.

Davis, K. R. (1994b). Rutland Developmental Therapy model. In *Educational programs that work: The catalogue of the National Diffusion Network* (20th ed.). Longmont, CO: Sopris West.

Developmental Therapy Institute. (1992). *The Developmental Teaching Objectives for the DTORF–R: Assessment and teaching of social-emotional competence* (4th ed.). Athens, GA: Author.

Dubow, E. F., Huesmann, L. R., & Eron, L. D. (1987). Childhood correlates of adult ego development. *Child Development, 58,* 859–864.

Edward, J., Ruskin, N., & Turrini, P. (1992). *Separation/individuation: Theory and application* (2nd ed.). New York: Brunner/Mazel.

Eggert, L. L. (1994). *Anger management for youth: Stemming aggression and violence.* Bloomington, IN: National Educational Service.

Eisenberg, N., Miller, P. A., Shell, R., McNalley, S., & Shea, C. (1991). Prosocial development in adolescence: A longitudinal study. In B. Puka (Ed.), *Moral development* (Vol. 7, pp. 1–7). New York: Garland.

Erikson, E. H. (1950/1963). *Childhood and society* (2nd ed.). New York: W. W. Norton.

Erikson, E. H. (1956). The problem of ego identity. *Journal of the American Psychoanalytic Association, 4,* 56–121.

Erikson, E. H. (1959). Identity and the life cycle. In G. S. Klein (Ed.), *Psychological Issues* (Vol. 1, pp. 18–171). New York: International Universities Press.

Erikson, E. H. (1959/1980). *Identity and the life cycle.* New York: W. W. Norton.

Erikson, E. H. (1964). *Insight and responsibility.* New York: W. W. Norton.

Erikson, E. H. (1968). *Identity, youth and crisis.* New York: W. W. Norton.

Erikson, E. H. (1972). Play and actuality. In M. W. Piers (Ed.), *Play and development* (pp. 127–167). New York: W. W. Norton.

Erikson, E. H. (1977). *Toys and reasons.* New York: W. W. Norton.

Feather, N. T. (1980). Values in adolescence. In J. Adelson (Ed.), *Handbook of adolescent psychology* (pp. 247–294). New York: Wiley.

Fingarette, H. (1963). *The self in transformation.* New York: Basic Books.

Flavell, J. H., Miller, P. H., & Miller, S. A. (1993). *Cognitive development* (3rd ed.). Englewood Cliffs, NJ: Prentice-Hall.

Freud, A. (1942). *The ego and the mechanisms of defence.* London: Hogarth Press.

Freud, A. (1965). *Normality and pathology in childhood: Assessments of development.* New York: International Universities Press.

Freud, A. (1973). The concept of developmental lines. In S. G. Sapir & A. C. Nitzburg (Eds.), *Children with learning problems* (pp. 19–36). New York: Brunner/Mazel.

Freud, S. (1920/1955). *Beyond the pleasure principle* (Standard ed., Vol. 198). London: Hogarth Press.

Freud, S. (1936). *The problem of anxiety.* New York: Psychoanalytic Quarterly Press and W. W. Norton.

Gallatin, J. (1980). Political thinking in adolescence. In J. Adelson (Ed.), *Handbook of adolescent psychology* (pp. 344–382). New York: Wiley.

Gesell, A., & Amatruda, C. (1975). *Developmental diagnosis* (3rd ed.). New York: HarperCollins.

Geter, B.A.B. (1992). Longitudinal cost study of preschool children with severe emotional disabilities. *Georgia Psychoeducational Network (GPN) Research Report, 5,* 17–30.

Ginzberg, E. (1972). Toward a theory of occupational choice: A restatement. *Vocational Guidance Quarterly, 20,* 169–176.

Glasser, S. W. (1965). *Reality therapy.* New York: HarperCollins.

Glasser, S. W. (1989). Control theory. In N. Glasser (Ed.), *Control theory in the practice of reality therapy* (pp. 1–15). New York: HarperCollins.

Goals 2000: Educate America Act (1994, March 31). Senate Bill S.846. Washington, DC: U.S. Department of Education.

Goldman, E. G. (1981). Activities for physical skills development. In M. M. Wood (Ed.), *Developmental Therapy sourcebook* (Vol. 1, chap. 5). Austin, TX: PRO-ED.

Goldstein, H., & Gallagher, T. M. (1992). Strategies for promoting the social communicative competence of young children with specific language impairment. In S. L. Odom, S. R. McConnell, & M. A. McEvoy (Eds.), *Social competence of young children with disabilities* (chap. 8). Baltimore: Paul H. Brookes.

Goncu, A. (1987). Toward an interactional model of developmental changes in social pretend play. In L. G. Katz (Ed.), *Current topics in early childhood education* (Vol. 7, pp. 108–125). Norwood, NJ: Ablex.

Greenspan, S. (1992). *Infancy and early childhood: The practice of clinical assessment and intervention with emotional and developmental challenges.* Madison, CT: International Universities Press.

Gunn, A. L. (1985). *A comparison of behaviors and developmental ratings between mentally retarded autistic and mentally retarded nonautistic children* (Doctoral dissertation, University of Georgia, 1984). *Dissertation Abstracts International, 45,* 2835A.

Guralnick, M. J. (1990). Social competence and early intervention. *Journal of Early Intervention, 14,* 3–14.

Guralnick, M. J. (1992). A hierarchical model for understanding children's peer-related social competence. In S. L. Odom, S. R. McConnell, & M. A. McEvoy (Eds.), *Social competence of young children with disabilities* (chap. 2). Baltimore: Paul H. Brookes.

Head Start Program Performance Standards. (1995). (45-CFR 1304). Washington, DC: U.S. Department of Health and Human Services.

Hendrick, S. W. (1981). Teacher-made stories: A bridge for basic communication and social skills with autistic children. In M. M. Wood (Ed.), *Developmental Therapy sourcebook* (Vol. 2, chap. 3). Austin, TX: PRO-ED.

Hoffman, M. L. (1980). Moral development in adolescence. In J. Adelson (Ed.), *Handbook of adolescent psychology* (pp. 295–343). New York: Wiley.

Holland, S. H. (1991). Positive role models for primary-grade black inner-city males. *Equity and Excellence: The University of Massachusetts School of Education Journal, 25,* 40–44.

Honig, A. S. (1990). Infant/toddler education issues: Practices, problems, and promises. In C. Seefeldt (Ed.), *Continuing issues in early childhood education* (chap. 4). Columbus, OH: Merrill.

Howes, C., Droege, K. D., & Phillipsen, L. (1992). Contributions of peers to socialization in early childhood. In M. Gettinger, S. N. Elliott, & T. R. Kratochwill (Eds.), *Preschool and early childhood treatment directions* (pp. 113–150). Hillsdale, NJ: Erlbaum.

Howes, C., Rodning, C., Galluzzo, D. C., & Meyers, L. (1988). Attachment and child care: Relationships with mother and caregiver. *Early Childhood Research Quarterly, 3,* 403–416.

Hoyt, J. H. (1978). Georgia's Rutland Center. *American Education, 14,* 27–32.

Hyman, I. A. (in press). *Teacher variance: A multidisciplinary approach to school discipline.* Needham Heights, MA: Allyn & Bacon.

Ilg, F. L., Ames, L. B., & Baker, S. M. (1981/1992). *Child behavior.* New York: HarperCollins.

Ivey, A. E. (1986). *Developmental therapy.* San Francisco: Jossey-Bass.

Ivey, A. E. (1994). *Intentional interviewing and counseling* (3rd ed.). Pacific Grove, CA: Brooks/Cole.

Journal of Emotional and Behavioral Problems. (1993). International Year of the Family, 2(4) [entire issue].

Journal of Emotional and Behavioral Problems. (1994). Inclusion of Troubled Children, 3(3) [entire issue].

Kagan, J. (1982). The emergence of self. *Journal of Child Psychology and Psychiatry and Allied Disciplines, 23,* 363–381.

Kagan, J. (1989). *Unstable ideas: Temperament, cognition, and self.* Cambridge, MA: Harvard University Press.

Kandel, D., & Lesser, G. (1969). Parental and peer influence on vocational plans of adolescents. *American Sociological Review, 34,* 213–223.

Kauffman, J. M. (1993). *Characteristics of emotional and behavioral disorders of children and youth* (5th ed.). New York: Merrill.

Kauffman, J. M., & Hallahan, D. P. (Eds.). (1995). *The illusion of full inclusion.* Austin, TX: PRO-ED.

Kaufman, A. S., Paget, K. D., & Wood, M. M. (1981). Effectiveness of Developmental Therapy for severely emotionally disturbed children. In F. H. Wood (Ed.), *Perspectives for a new decade* (pp. 176–188). Reston, VA: Council for Exceptional Children.

Kegan, R. (1982). *The evolving self.* Cambridge, MA: Harvard University Press.

King, C. S. (1987). *The words of Martin Luther King, Jr.* New York: Newmarket Press.

Kiresuk, T. J., Smith, A., & Cardillo, J. E. (1994). *Goal attainment scaling: Applications, theory, and measurement.* Hillsdale, NJ: Erlbaum.

Knoblock, P. (1982). *Teaching emotionally disturbed children* (pp. 110, 215, 233–235). Boston: Houghton Mifflin.

Kohlberg, L. (1981). *The philosophy of moral development: Moral stages and the idea of justice. Essays on moral development* (Vol. 1). New York: HarperCollins.

Kohlberg, L. (1984). *The psychology of moral development: Moral stages and the life cycle. Essays on moral development* (Vol. 2). New York: HarperCollins.

Kohlberg, L., & Hersh, R. H. (1977). Moral development: A review of the theory. *Theory into Practice, 16,* 53–58.

Kohlberg, L., & Turiel, E. (1971). *Research in moral development: The cognitive developmental approach.* Troy, MO: Holt, Rinehart & Winston.

Kuykendall, C. (1992). *From rage to hope: Strategies for reclaiming Black and Hispanic students.* Bloomington, IN: National Educational Service.

Lam, M. S., Powers, S. I., Noam, G. G., Hauser, S. T., & Jacobson, A. M. (1993). Parental moral stage and adolescent moral development. In J. Demick, K. Bursik, & R. DiBiase (Eds.), *Parental development* (pp. 75–85). Hillsdale, NJ: Erlbaum.

Larsen, L. E. (1972). The influence of parents and peers during adolescence: The situation hypothesis revisited. *Journal of Marriage and the Family, 34,* 67–74.

Lerner, R. M. (Ed.). (1993). *Early adolescence.* Hillsdale, NJ: Erlbaum.

Lewis, M. (1990). Challenges to the study of developmental psychopatholoy. In M. Lewis & S. Miller (Eds.), *Handbook of developmental psychopathology* (pp. 30–31). New York: Plenum Press.

Lewis, M. (1993). The emergence of human emotions. In M. Lewis & J. M. Haviland (Eds.), *Handbook of emotions* (pp. 223–235). New York: Guilford Press.

Lewis, M., & Rosenblum, L. A. (Eds.). (1978). *The development of affect.* New York: Plenum Press.

Lickona, T. (1985). *Raising good children.* New York: Bantam Books.

Lickona, T. (1991). *Educating for character: How our schools can teach respect and responsibility.* New York: Bantam Books.

Loevinger, J. (1976). *Ego development.* San Francisco: Jossey Bass.

Loevinger, J. (1987). *Paradigms of personality.* New York: W. H. Freeman.

Loewald, H. W. (1962). The super-ego and the ego ideal. II: Superego and time. *International Journal of Psycho-Analysis, 43,* 264–268.

Lowenfeld, V., & Brittain, W. L. (1970). *Creative and mental growth* (5th ed.). New York: Macmillan.

Maccoby, E. E. (1980). *Social development.* Orlando, FL: Harcourt Brace Jovanovich.

Madsen, K. B. (1968). *Theories of motivation* (4th ed.). Kent, OH: Kent State University Press.

Mahler, M. S. (1968/1987). *On human symbiosis and the vicissitudes of individuation: Infantile psychosis* (Vol. 1). Madison, CT: International Universities Press.

Mahler, M. S., Pine, F., & Bergman, A. (1975). *The psychological birth of the human infant.* New York: Basic Books.

Maloney, F. P., Mirrett, P., Brooke, C., & Johannes, K. (1978). Use of the goal attainment scale in treatment and ongoing evaluation of neurologically handicapped children. *American Journal of Occupational Therapy, 32,* 505–510.

Margalit, M., Weisel, A., Heiman, T., & Shulman, S. (1988). Social skills and family climate of behaviorally disordered adolescents. *Behavioral Disorders, 13,* 253–262.

Marshall, E. K., & Kurtz, P. D. (1982). *Interpersonal helping skills.* San Francisco: Jossey-Bass.

Martens, B. K., Peterson, R. L., Witt, J. C., & Cirone, S. (1986). Teachers perceptions of school-based interventions. *Exceptional Children, 53,* 213–223.

Maslow, A. H. (1976). *The farther reaches of human nature.* New York: Penguin.

Maslow, A. H. (1987). *Motivation and personality* (3rd ed.). New York: HarperCollins.

McCarty, B. C. (1992). The effect of race, socioeconomic status and family status on the interpersonal understanding of preadolescents and adolescents with severe emotional disturbance (Doctoral dissertation, University of Georgia, 1992). *Dissertation Abstracts International, 54,* 485A.

McCollum, J. A., & Blair, H. (1994). Research in parent-child interaction. In B. L. Mallory & R. S. New (Eds.), *Diversity and developmentally appropriate practices.* New York: Teachers College Press.

Moreno, J. L. (1972). *Psychodrama* (Vol. 3, 4th ed.). New York: Beacon House.

Moreno, J. L., & Moreno, Z. T. (1969). *Psychodrama* (Vol. 3). New York: Beacon House.

Moreno, Z. T. (1959). A survey of psychodramatic techniques. *Group Psychotherapy, 12,* 5–14.

Morgan, S. R. (1991). Responses to feelings and emotional wellbeing. In S. R. Morgan & J. A. Reinhart (Eds.), *Interventions for students with emotional disorders* (chap. 6). Austin, TX: PRO-ED.

Mussen, P. H., Conger, J. J., Kagan, J., & Huston, A. C. (1990). *Child development & personality* (7th ed.). New York: HarperCollins.

Myers, J. (1993). Curricular designs that resonate with adolescents' ways of knowing. In R. M. Lerner (Ed.), *Early adolescence* (pp. 191–205). Hillsdale, NJ: Erlbaum.

Myles, B. S., & Simpson, R. L. (1994). Understanding and preventing acts of aggression and violence in school-age children and youth. *Preventing School Failure, 38,* 40–46.

National Center for Clinical Infant Programs. (1992). *Heart Start: The emotional foundations of school readiness.* Boston: Children's Hospital Medical Center, Zero to Three Project.

Neel, R. S., & Cessna, K. K. (1993). Behavioral intent: Instructional content for students with behavioral disorders. In K. K. Cessna (Ed.), *Instructionally differentiated programming: A needs-based approach for students with behavior disorders* (pp. 31–39). Denver, CO: Colorado Department of Education.

New, R. S., & Mallory, B. L. (1994). Introduction: The ethic of inclusion. In B. L. Mallory & R. S. New (Eds.), *Diversity and developmentally appropriate practices.* New York: Teachers College Press.

Newborg, J., Stock, J. R., Wnek, L., Guidabaldi, J., & Svinicki, J. (1984). *Battelle Developmental Inventory Screening Test.* Allen, TX: DLM–Teaching Resources.

Newman, V. S., & Romack, C. (1981). Leisure time activities for autistic adolescents. In M. M. Wood (Ed.), *Developmental Therapy sourcebook* (Vol. 1, chap. 7). Austin, TX: PRO-ED.

Odom, S. L., McConnell, S. R., & McEvoy, M. A. (1992a). Peer-related social competence and its significance for young children with disabilities. In S. L. Odom, S. R. McConnell, & M. A. McEvoy (Eds.), *Social competence of young children with disabilities* (pp. 3–37). Baltimore: Paul H. Brookes.

Odom, S. L., McConnell, S. R., & McEvoy, M. A. (Eds.). (1992b). *Social competence of young children with disabilities.* Baltimore: Paul H. Brookes.

Osborn, A. F. (1963). *Applied imagination* (3rd ed.). New York: Charles Scribner's Sons.

Ostrosky, M. M., Skellenger, A. C., Odom, S. L., McConnell, S. R., & Peterson, C. (1994). Teachers' schedules and actual time spent in activities in preschool special education classes. *Journal of Early Intervention, 18,* 25–33.

Paget, M., & Stueck, L. (1981). The playground as a classroom. In M. M. Wood (Ed.), *Developmental Therapy sourcebook* (Vol. 1, chap. 4). Austin, TX: PRO-ED.

Parke, R. D., Burks, V. M., Carson, J. L., Neville, B., & Boyum, L. A. (1994). Family-peer relationships: A tripartite model. In R. D. Parke & S. G. Kellam (Eds.), *Exploring family relationships with other social contexts* (pp. 115–145). Hillsdale, NJ: Erlbaum.

Parke, R. D., Cassidy, J., Burks, V. M., Carson, J. L., & Boyum, L. A. (1992). Familial contributions to peer competence among young children: The role of interactive and affective processes.

In R. D. Parke & G. W. Ladd (Eds.), *Family-peer relationships: Modes of linkage* (pp. 107–131). Hillsdale, NJ: Erlbaum.

Parker, J. G., & Gottman, J. M. (1988). Social and emotional development in a relational context: Friendship interaction from early childhood to adolescence. In T. J. Berndt & G. W. Ladd (Eds.), *Peer relations in child development* (pp. 188–205). New York: Wiley.

Parnes, S. J. (1992). *Source book for creative problem-solving: A fifty year digest of proven innovation processes.* Buffalo, NY: Creative Education Foundation.

Parten, M. (1932). Social participation among preschool children. *Journal of Abnormal and Social Psychology, 27,* 243–269.

Patterson, G. R. (1988). Family processes: Loops, levels, and linkages. In N. Bolger, A. Caspi, G. Downey, & M. Moorehouse (Eds.), *Persons in context: Developmental processes.* New York: Cambridge University Press.

Piaget, J. (1932/1960). *The moral judgment of the child.* New York: Free Press.

Piaget, J. (1937/1954). *The construction of reality in the child.* New York: Basic Books.

Piaget, J. (1951/1962). *Play, dreams, and imitation in childhood.* New York: W. W. Norton.

Piaget, J. (1952). *The origins of intelligence in children.* New York: International Universities Press.

Piaget, J. (1967). *Six psychological studies.* New York: Random House.

Piaget, J. (1972). Some aspects of operations. In M. W. Piers (Ed.), *Play and development* (pp. 15–27). New York: W. W. Norton.

Piaget, J. (1977). *The development of thought: Equilibration of cognitive structures.* New York: Viking Press.

Pianta, R. C., & Nimetz, S. L. (1992). Development of young children in stressful contexts: Theory, assessment, and prevention. In M. Gettinger, S. N. Elliott, & T. R. Kratochwill (Eds.), *Preschool and early childhood treatment directions* (pp. 151–185). Hillsdale, NJ: Erlbaum.

Presland, J., & White, P. (1990). Preparing teachers for a support role in dealing with adjustment problems in secondary schools. In R. M. Gupta & P. Coxhead (Eds.), *Intervention with children* (pp. 76–93). London: Routledge.

Purvis, J. (1981). The language is music. In M. M. Wood (Ed.), *Developmental Therapy sourcebook* (Vol. 1, chap. 3). Austin, TX: PRO-ED.

Quirk, C. (1993). Skill acquisition of in-service teachers of students with emotional and behavioral disabilities (Doctoral dissertation, University of Georgia, 1993). *Dissertation Abstracts International, 54,* 2116A.

Ramsey, E., & Walker, H. M. (1988). Family management correlates of antisocial behavior among middle school boys. *Behavioral Disorders, 13,* 187–201.

Rapaport, D. (1960). The structure of psychoanalytic theory. In G. S. Klein (Ed.), *Psychological issues* (Vol. 2, pp. 7–158). New York: International Universities Press.

Rasch, G. (1960). *Probabilistic models for some intelligence and attainment tests.* Copenhagen: Paedogogiske Institute.

Reinhart, J. A. (1991). Management of instruction. In S. R. Morgan & J. A. Rinehart (Eds.), *Interventions for students with emotional disorders* (chap. 5). Austin, TX: PRO-ED.

Rich, H. L. (1982). *Disturbed students, characteristics and educational strategies* (pp. 292–295). Baltimore, MD: University Park Press.

Rizzo, J. V., & Zabel, R. H. (1988). *Educating children and adolescents with behavioral disorders* (pp. 80–81, 276–282). Needham Heights, MA: Allyn & Bacon.

Robins, L. N., & Rutter, M. (Eds.). (1990). *Straight and devious pathways from childhood to adulthood.* Cambridge, MA: Cambridge University Press.

Robinson, J. S. (1983). Construction of an instrument to assess the classroom skills of teachers who use Developmental Therapy with emotionally disturbed students (Doctoral dissertation, University of Georgia, 1982). *Dissertation Abstracts International, 43,* 1932A.

Robinson, J. S., Wood, M. M., & Combs, M. C. (1982). *Technical report on the Developmental Therapy Inventory of Teacher Skills (DT/RITS).* Unpublished manuscript, University of Georgia, Developmental Therapy Institute, Athens.

Rogers, D. E., & Ginzberg, E. (Eds.). (1992). *Adolescents at risk: Medical and social perspectives.* Boulder, CO: Westview Press.

Rosenhan, D. L. (1972). Learning theory and prosocial behavior. *Journal of Social Issues, 28,* 151–163.

Rostetter, D. (1994). Starting small: Inclusion and early childhood education. *Inclusive Education Programs, 1,* 3–5.

Rutter, M. (1981). *Maternal deprivation reassessed* (2nd ed.). New York: Penguin.

Rutter, M., & Rutter, M. (1993). *Developing minds: Challenge and continuity across the life span.* New York: Basic Books.

Sanford, A. R., & Zelman, J. G. (1981). *Learning accomplishments profile—LAP* (rev. ed.). Chapel Hill, NC: Training Outreach Project.

Saunders, P., & Gilliard, J. (1995). *A framework for teaching basic economic concepts.* New York: National Council on Economic Education.

Selman, R. (1976). Toward a structural analysis of developing interpersonal relations concepts: Research with normal and disturbed preadolescent boys. In A. Peck (Ed.), *Tenth Annual Minnesota Symposium on Child Psychology.* Minneapolis: University of Minnesota Press.

Selman, R. (1980). *The growth of interpersonal understanding.* San Diego, CA: Academic Press.

Selman, R. (1989). Fostering intimacy and autonomy. In W. Damon (Ed.), *Child development today and tomorrow* (pp. 409–435). San Francisco: Jossey-Bass.

Selman, R., Beardslee, W., Schultz, L. H., Krupa, M., & Podorefsky, D. (1986). Assessing adolescent interpersonal negotiating strategies: Toward the integration of structural and functional models. *Developmental Psychology, 22,* 450–459.

Selman, R., & Jaquette, D. (1987). *The development of interpersonal awareness: A working draft model.* Unpublished scoring manual, Harvard-Judge Baker Social Reasoning Project, Harvard University, Cambridge, MA.

Selman, R., & Schultz, L. H. (1990). *Making a friend in youth: Developmental theory and pair therapy.* Chicago: University of Chicago Press.

Shea, T. M., & Bauer, A. M. (1987). *Teaching children and youth with behavior disorders* (2nd ed., pp. 222, 272–274). Englewood Cliffs, NJ: Prentice-Hall.

Shores, R. E., Gunner, P. L., & Jack, S. L. (1993). Classroom management strategies: Are they setting events for coercion? *Behavioral Disorders, 18*(2), 92–102.

Shure, M. B., & Healey, K. N. (1992). *I can problem solve: Interpersonal cognitive problem solving. A program for preschool, primary, and intermediate grades.* Champaign, IL: Research Press.

Simeonsson, R. J., Bailey, D. B., Huntington, G. S., & Brandon, L. (1991). Scaling and attainment of goals in family-focused intervention. *Community Mental Health Journal, 27,* 77–83.

Simeonsson, R. J., Huntington, G. S., & Short, G. S. (1982). Individual differences and goals: An approach to the evaluation of child progress. *Topics in Early Childhood Education, 1,* 71–80.

Smith, A. (1994). Introduction and overview. In T. J. Kiresuk, A. Smith, & J. E. Cardillo (Eds.), *Goal attainment scaling: Applications, theory, and measurement.* Hillsdale, NJ: Erlbaum.

Snyder, S., & Sheehan, R. (1992). The Rasch measurement model: An introduction. *Journal of Early Intervention, 16,* 87–95.

Spence, J. T., & Helmreich, R. L. (1978). *Masculinity and femininity: Their psychological dimensions, correlates, and antecedents.* Austin: University of Texas Press.

Sullivan, H. S. (1953). *The interpersonal theory of psychiatry.* New York: W. W. Norton.

Super, D. E. (1980). A life-span, life-space approach to career development. *Journal of Vocational Behavior, 16,* 282–298.

Super, D. E., & Crites, J. O. (1974). *Measuring vocational maturity for counseling and evaluation.* Washington, DC: National Vocational Guidance Association.

Swan, W. W., & Brown, C. L. (Eds.). (1992). *GPN research reports.* Atlanta: Georgia Psychoeducational Program Network, Georgia Department of Education.

Swan, W. W., & Wood, M. M. (1975). Making decisions about treatment effectiveness. In M. M. Wood (Ed.), *Developmental Therapy* (chap. 3). Baltimore, MD: University Park Press.

Swan, W. W., Wood, M. M., & Jordan, J. A. (1991). Building a statewide program of mental health and special education services for children and youth. In G. K. Farley & S. G. Zimet (Eds.), *Day treatment for children with emotional disorders* (Vol. 2, chap. 1). New York: Plenum.

Thomas, A, & Chess, S. (1977). *Temperament and development.* New York: Brunner/Mazel.

Tobin, T. J., & Sugai, G. (1993). Intervention awareness: Educators' perceptions of the need for restrictions on aversive interventions. *Behavioral Disorders, 18*(2), 110–117.

Torrance, E. P. (1979). *The search for satori and creativity.* Buffalo, NY: Creative Education Foundation.

Torrance, P. H. (1981). Use of sociodrama in teaching emotionally disturbed children. In M. M. Wood (Ed.), *Developmental Therapy sourcebook* (Vol. 2, pp. 137–158). Austin, TX: PRO-ED.

Turiel, E. (1983). *The development of social knowledge.* Cambridge, England: Cambridge University Press.

Turiel, E. (1994). The development of social-coventional and moral concepts. In B. Puka (Ed.), *Fundamental research in moral development.* New York: Garland.

U.S. Department of Education. (1975). Joint Dissemination Review Panel. Washington, DC.

U.S. Department of Education. (1981). Joint Dissemination Review Panel. Washington, DC.

U.S. Department of Education. (1990). *Twelfth annual report to Congress on the implementation of the Education of the Handicapped Act.* Washington, DC: Author.

Vondracek, F. W. (1993). Promoting vocational development in early adolescence. In R. M. Lerner (Ed.), *Early adolescence: Perspectives on research, policy, and intervention* (chap. 16). Hillsdale, NJ: Erlbaum.

Weller, D. L. (1991). Application of a latent trait model to the developmental profiles of SED/SBD students (Doctoral dissertation, University of Georgia, 1990). *Dissertation Abstracts International, 51,* 3388A.

White, R. W. (1963). Ego and reality in psychoanalytic theory. In G. S. Klein (Ed.), *Psychological issues* (Vol. 3, pp. 517–649). New York: International Universities Press.

Williams, G. H., & Wood, M. M. (1977). *Developmental art therapy.* Austin, TX: PRO-ED.

Williams, M. (1994). *The responsibility of the storyteller.* Charter Lecture delivered at the University of Georgia, May 1994.

Wolery, M. (1983). Proportional change index: An alternative for comparing child change data. *Exceptional Children, 50,* 167–170.

Wood, F. H. (1981). Individualized Education Programs for seriously emotionally disturbed adolescents. In G. Brown, R. L. McDowell, & J. Smith (Eds.), *Educating adolescents with behavior disorders* (pp. 148–149). Columbus, OH: Charles E. Merrill.

Wood, M. M. (1975). *Developmental Therapy: A textbook for teachers as therapists for emotionally disturbed young children.* Baltimore, MD: University Park Press.

Wood, M. M. (1979). *The Developmental Therapy Objectives: A self-instructional workbook* (3rd ed.). Austin, TX: PRO-ED. Portions reprinted in 1984 in *A user's manual for the structured learning center behavioral classroom,* Portland, OR: Portland Public Schools.

Wood, M. M. (Ed.). (1981). *Developmental Therapy sourcebook. Vol. 2: Fantasy and make-believe.* Austin, TX: PRO-ED.

Wood, M. M. (1986). *Developmental Therapy in the classroom* (2nd ed.). Austin, TX: PRO-ED.

Wood, M. M. (1989). Lessons learned and insights garnered. In S. Braaten, F. H. Wood, & G. Wrobel (Eds.), *Celebrating the past: Preparing for the future* (pp. 59–75). Minneapolis: Minnesota Council for Children with Behavioral Disorders and Minnesota Educators of Emotionally/Behaviorally Disordered.

Wood, M. M. (1992a). *Technical report for the Developmental Teaching Objectives Rating Form–Revised—DTORF–R.* Athens, GA: Developmental Therapy Institute.

Wood, M. M. (1992b). *User's manual for the Developmental Teaching Objectives Rating Form–Revised—DTORF–R.* Athens, GA: Developmental Therapy Institute.

Wood, M. M., & Combs, M. C. (1981). *Inservice training in Developmental Therapy.* Research submitted to Joint Dissemination Review Panel of National Institute of Education, U. S. Department of Education.

Wood, M. M., Combs, M. C., & Swan, W. W. (1985). Computer simulations: Field testing effectiveness and efficiency for inservice and preservice teacher preparation. *Journal of Educational Technology Systems, 14,* 61–74.

Wood, M. M., Combs, M. C., & Walters, L. H. (1986). Use of staff development by teachers and aides with emotionally disturbed and behavior disordered students. *Teacher Education and Special Education, 9,* 104–112.

Wood, M. M., & Gunn, A. (1985). *Technical assistance to principals, administrators, and teachers in Portland, Oregon school system for replication of the Developmental Therapy curriculum* (Unpublished report to the school district). Athens: University of Georgia, Developmental Therapy Institute. Reprinted in CASE National Newsletter, Fall 1985.

Wood, M. M., Hendrick, S. W., & Gunn, A. L. (1983). Programming for autistic students: A model for the public schools. In C. R. Reynolds & J. H. Clark (Eds.), *Assessment and programming for children with low incidence handicaps* (pp. 287–318). New York: Plenum Press.

Wood, M. M., & Hurley, O. L. (1977). Curriculum and instruction. In J. B. Jordan, A. H. Hayden, M. B. Karnes, & M. M. Wood (Eds.), *Early childhood education for exceptional children* (pp. 132–157). Reston, VA: Council for Exceptional Children.

Wood, M. M., & Long, N. J. (1991). *Life Space Intervention: Talking with children and youth in crisis.* Austin, TX: PRO-ED.

Wood, M. M., Peterson, R. L., Combs, M. C., & Quirk, C. A. (1987). *Crisis in classroom behavior management: A developmental issue.* Paper presented at the 67th annual international conference of the Council for Exceptional Children, Chicago.

Wood, M. M., Skaar, C., Mayfield, G., Morrison, K., & Gillespie, F. (1984). *Psychoeducational computer simulation series for teachers of emotionally handicapped students, Lessons 1 & 2* [Computer program]. Apple IIE software with accompanying workbook. Athens, GA: Developmental Therapy Institute.

Wood, M. M., & Swan, W. W. (1978). A developmental approach to educating the disturbed young child. *Behavioral Disorders, 3,* 179–209.

Wood, M. M., Swan, W. W., & Newman, V. (1981). Developmental Therapy for the severely disturbed and autistic. In R. L. McDowell, G. W. Adamson, & F. H. Wood (Eds.), *Emotional disturbance* (pp. 264–299). Boston: Little, Brown.

Wood, M. M., & Weller, D. L. (1981). How come it's different with some children? A developmental approach to Life Space Interviewing. *The Pointer, 25,* 61–66.

Wubbolding, R. E. (1988). *Using reality therapy.* New York: HarperCollins.

Yablonsky, L (1976). *Psychodrama: Resolving emotional conflict through role playing.* New York: Basic Books.

Youness, J., & Smollar, J. (1985). *Adolescent relationships with mothers, fathers and friends.* Chicago: University of Chicago Press.

Zabel, M. K. (1991). *Teaching young children with behavioral disorders.* Reston, VA: Council for Exceptional Children.

Zeeman, R. (1989). From acting out to joining in. In N. Glasser (Ed.), *Control theory in the practice of reality therapy* (pp. 16–33). New York: HarperCollins.

Acknowledgments from the 1986 edition of *Developmental Therapy in the Classroom*

We wish to acknowledge the important contributions made to this revision of *Developmental Therapy* by the many talented school administrators and teachers throughout the United States who have worked with us in staff development at replication sites for over a decade and have created educational environments where innovation, evaluation, and revision are welcomed with enthusiasm and understanding. The contributions of these individuals have been enormous, each implementing a significant application of the Developmental Therapy model and participating in the evaluation of effectiveness. Through these efforts, more than 12,000 educators have participated in field applications of Developmental Therapy, and we have been able to study the entire range of effects resulting from widespread implementation of the model with more than 10,000 students. This second edition of *Developmental Therapy* reflects the refinements we have been able to make as a result.

The Developmental Therapy Institute at the University of Georgia has been the focal point for advanced leadership training, material development, field applications, program evaluations, and model adaptations during the 10-year period since the first edition was published. The Institute staff deserves special recognition for their sustained and creative talents in providing the nuclear energy for this revision, especially Julie Hendrick, Michael Hendrick, Bonnie McCarty, Rosalie McKenzie, Joey Thomas, and Constance Quirk.

Similarly, since 1975 the Rutland Center–Developmental Therapy National Technical Assistance Outreach Project, under the able direction of William Swan, Anthony Beardsley, and Karen Davis has provided major leadership in assisting educators and mental health professionals in replicating the model. The Outreach Project staff and consultants, Mary Beussee, Susan Galis, Joyce Garrett, Ann Long, Faye Swindle, and Sara Jo Williams at the University of Georgia; and Mary Bross, University of Wisconsin, Whitewater; Bonnie Eninger, San Diego, California; Mary Leiter, Myrtle Beach, South Carolina; Jennie Purvis-Band, Waynesville, North Carolina; Barbara Reid, Eastern Illinois University; and Geraldine Williams, Ohio University, have provided the fieldwork and outreach activities during this decade.

Both the Institute and the Outreach Project received funding from the U.S. Department of Education, Special Education Programs, and the National Diffusion Network. This support has enabled us to continue the model evaluation, personnel training in preservice and in-service, leadership training, instructional material development, and replication assistance to schools and agencies at 102 different sites in 30 states. We are deeply appreciative of the support received from our colleagues who have, through the grant review process, given us approval and sustained encouragement in this effort during the 10-year period. This second edition of *Developmental Therapy* reflects the refinements we have been able to make as a result.

The Rutland Psychoeducational Center in Athens, Georgia, has continued as the original demonstration and training site for Developmental Therapy since its beginning in 1969. We especially acknowledge the contributions of its director, Robert Jacob, the Clarke County School District, and the talented, supportive staff who have been partners with us for more than 15 years of program development at the original field-based demonstration site. They also have collaborated in the training of countless numbers of student interns and Institute trainees through the years. In all of this, the Rutland Center staff has maintained a standard of service to severely emotionally disturbed students and a dedication to exemplary demonstration of the model components. Several Rutland Center staff members have been with us since the first model demonstration 15 years ago. They are Leroy Dowdy, James Flanagan, Ruby Ann Free, Barbara Geter, the late Diane Perno, Jacqueline Smith, Patricia Stovall, and Faye Swindle. We have traveled together a long distance!

We are particularly appreciative of the sustained support and encouragement of E. Paul Torrance, University of Georgia; Frank Wood, University of Minnesota; Peter Knoblock, Syracuse University; Kathleen Paget, University of South Carolina; Larry Grantham, Western Carolina University; Gene Plank, Emporia State University, Kansas; and Cecil Reynolds, Texas A&M University. Alan and

Nadeen Kaufman, Lynda Walters, and William Swan, University of Georgia; and Joby Robinson, Columbia, South Carolina, aided us substantially in the difficult tasks involving the evaluation of treatment effects.

Special appreciation is extended to Dorothy Chambers of the Portland, Oregon, school system for her imaginative and dedicated leadership. Her insightful questions pushed us to find answers. In the follow-up work we did with her colleagues Pat Bungcayo, Bob Gettel, Judy McArdle, Stephanie Newcomer, and Eileen Uland, we continued the exciting process of seeking classroom applications of developmental theory.

To our many talented and creative colleagues in Georgia who have been supportive and encouraging over the years we extend a special thanks, especially to Joan Jordan, director of Georgia's special education programs; Robert Gordon, director of the South Metro Psychoeducational Programs in Atlanta, and program coordinators Dan Burns and Linda Dickson; George Andros, director of the Dalton Psychoeducational Programs, and program coordinators Muncie Cooper and Steve Davis; Juanda Ponsel, director of the Griffin Area Psychoeducational Program; Wayne Moffett, director of the Alpine Psychoeducational Programs; Patsy Hinely, director of the Chatham-Effingham Psychoeducational Program in Savannah, Georgia; the late Bob Clarke; and the late Jim Hall.

In the preparation of this manuscript, we are deeply indebted to Marilyn Perkins, who provided the leadership and adopted this book as her own. Without her determination to bring the finished product to press, it might not have been done. We also wish to acknowledge our appreciation of Libby Johnson, Joyce Oliver, and Isabel Clark who provided typing, editing, and cheerful encouragement. For the secretarial assistance to our projects over the years, we thank Harriet Elder and Joyce Davis, and for expert management of our grant accounts, Connie Morse.

Acknowledgments from the 1975 edition, *Developmental Therapy: A Textbook for Teachers as Therapists for Emotionally Disturbed Young Children*

The material for this text has evolved over a period of 6 years. During that time, many people have contributed to planning, implementing, evaluating, and modifying the various components of Developmental Therapy. To the families of these many individuals, the authors extend their deepest appreciation for providing a climate where each personal contribution had enthusiastic backing and understanding.

The project has had four consultants who have maintained long, loyal relationships to the effort: James Flanagan, MD, in child psychiatry; Carl J. Huberty, PhD, in research design and evaluation; Arthur E. Alper, PhD, in clinical psychology; and David R. Levine, PhD, in social work. Their contributions have influenced every aspect of Developmental Therapy.

The advice, expertise, and assistance of a number of outside consultants have also influenced the philosophy and practices of Developmental Therapy as it emerged at the Rutland Center. The time and interest of these consultants is gratefully acknowledged: Norbert Enzer, MD, and Sam Rubin, MD, in psychiatry; William Frankenberg, MD, and William Bonner, MD, in pediatrics; Robert Lange, PhD, and Herbert Quay, PhD, in research design and evaluation; Frank Wilderson, PhD, Ida Wilderson, PhD, and Dorothy Campbell, PhD, in special education; Laura Fortson, PhD, and Glenna Bullis, for infant and preschool education; Richard Graham, PhD, in music therapy; Milton Blue, PhD, and William Ambrose, PhD, in language development and hearing.

Perhaps the most significant contributions to the early formulation of what was to become Developmental Therapy can be attributed to Stanley Ainsworth, PhD, Kathryn Blake, PhD, and Frances Scott, PhD, at the University of Georgia, and to Nicholas Long, PhD, at American University, Hillcrest Children's Center and the Rose School in Washington, D.C.

The Technical Assistance Development System (TADS) at the Frank Porter Graham Child Development Center, University of North Carolina, has helped put the entire effort into perspective over a 3-year period. In particular, David Lillie, PhD, Donald Stedman, PhD, Dan Davis, PhD, Patrick Trohanis, PhD, and Richard Surles, PhD, have worked closely with the Rutland Center staff as the model emerged.

Finally, Developmental Therapy, as a transportable model, was tested from 1971 to the present in other centers treating seriously disturbed children. Participating in this effort were several highly effective treatment centers in other locations in Georgia, notably: Carrollton, Georgia, Peggy Pettit, director; Savannah, Georgia, Mignon Lawton, director; Brunswick, Georgia, Virginia Boyle, director; also Ana Alegria in Trujillo, Peru, has translated Developmental Therapy in a Spanish-speaking culture. The contributions of these directors and their staffs have been enormous. Each location has demonstrated that Developmental Therapy can be effective in a variety of locations and can provide a common language among professionals trained in vastly different approaches.

In addition to her contributions as an evaluator to the project, Faye Swindle provided editorial review of this manuscript. Eileen Patrick typed and retyped the many drafts. For their careful work and cheerful encouragement, all of the authors are deeply indebted.

The list of acknowledgments would be incomplete without recognition of the immense talent and effort contributed by every member of the Rutland Center staff during the years of development. The authors recognize that Developmental Therapy is a product of the contributions of each:

Ann Reed Williams Bachrach
James Bachrach
Anthony Beardsley
Mary Beussee
Livija R. Bolster
Nancy Bonney
William Butler
Robert Clarke
Carmie T. Cochrane
Carolyn Combs
Janis Conlin
Cynthia Cook
John Cook
Allan Crimm
Nancy Cudmore
William Cudmore
Allen Curry
John Davis
Steve Davis
Kathleen Deeney
Leroy Dowdy
Bonnie Mailey Eninger
Amy Fendley
Daisy Fleming
Ruby Ann Free
Joyce Garrett
Barbara Brown Geter
Clementine Gigliotti
Barbara Goldberg
Harry Goodwin
Belita Griffith
Andrea Lomax Gunn
Angela Hiley
Patricia McGinnis Hinely
John Humphreys
Linda Javitch
Ola Jennings
Laura Levine
Tucker McClellen
Karen McDonough
Sarah McGinley
Ann McPherson
David Mendenhall
Marilyn Mendoza
Nora Mitchell
Walter Moore
Ada Mosley
Margaret Obremski
Diane Perno
Jennie Purvis
John Quirk
Kathleen Quirk
Steve Reese
JoAnne Rizza
Dixie Lou Rush
Shelley Samet
Ann Seward
Linda Shackleford
Jacqueline Smith
Peggy Smith
Allan Sproles
Patricia Stovall
Carol Stuart
William W. Swan
Faye Swindle
Judi Trebony
Diane Weller
Sally Westerfield
Lesley Whitson
Geraldine Williams
Patricia Willis
Nedra Zisa

Author Index

Subject Index